The Gods Made Flesh

The Gods Made Flesh
Metamorphosis & the
Pursuit of Paganism

LEONARD BARKAN

Yale University Press
New Haven and London

Designed by Susan P. Fillion and set in Caledonia
type by Eastern Graphics. Printed in the United
States of America by Halliday Lithograph, West
Hanover, Mass.

Library of Congress Cataloging-in-Publication Data

Barkan, Leonard.
    The gods made flesh.

Includes bibliographical references and index.
    1. Metamorphosis in art. 2. Arts, European.
I. Title.
NX650.M48B37 1986   700'.94   86–1325
ISBN 0–300–03561–6 (cloth)
       0–300–04742–8 (pbk.)

*The paper in this book meets the guidelines for
permanence and durability of the Committee on
Production Guidelines for Book Longevity of the
Council on Library Resources.*

3   5   7   9   10   8   6   4   2

For David Silverman

Contents

Illustrations

Preface

Once upon a time I wrote a book about the human body, and, all things considered, I found it fairly easy to write. I was concerned with the ways the human body had been seen as an image of the world. Early on I perceived that there were cosmological, political, and aesthetic aspects to the subject and that each of these had its own history from antiquity to the Renaissance. The collective histories fit together reasonably well, and the result was an essay in the history of ideas. When that was done, it seemed plausible to turn next to the question, "what happens to bodies that change?" That is to say, what is the history and meaning of metamorphosis? Surely, I thought, that subject, too, would have its three or four crucial categories that, taken together, would produce a smooth-flowing history. It took many years to learn a simple fact: the human body stands still; metamorphoses do not. A simplistic idea, an evasion, the fallacy of imitative form, you may say. But the truth of the matter is that a subject whose essence is instability and mysterious change does not lend itself to classical orderliness, even in the hands of a historical scholar devoted to exposition and elucidation.[1]

At the same time as my hopes for classical exposition were crumbling, my sense of the subject's scope and significance was burgeoning. I recall at a fledgling point in the career of this book the late Kathleen Williams encouraged me by saying that whoever figured out why the sixteenth century thought metamorphosis was so important would make an important discovery about the Renaissance. Reflecting on her tone years later, I realized she herself probably felt that metamorphosis was rather a queer Renaissance taste, like bear-baiting or Rosicrucianism, so that my discovery about its importance would ultimately be more clinical than celebratory. Whatever she may have meant, I took her remarks as my first sign that it was a Big Subject. Over the years such signs moved me away from encouragement and toward despair as the big subject rapidly seemed to gobble up everything in sight: poetry and paintings, history and philosophy, theology and anthropology.

The book that results from these efforts may enjoy the advantages neither of brevity nor of comprehensiveness; and readers are likely to be surprised equally by omissions and by inclusions. The author himself is a bit surprised by the fact that Apuleius and Ben Jonson make such brief appearances as well as by the space that is required to set metamorphosis in the context of apparently separate questions relating to the survival of Ovid and of paganism in post-classical culture. Even more diverse than the topics that metamorphosis touches upon are the different approaches necessary to do justice to it. Readers may find that among the six chapters there are quite divergent, even perhaps incompatible, critical principles and presuppositions.

Three chapters are studies of individual authors—Ovid, Dante, Shakespeare—which range from close reading to studies of source and historical influence to explorations of intertextuality. Sandwiched with these are chapters whose agenda are yet more divergent. Chapter 1, "Tapestry Figures," tackles the subject in a deliberately synchronic fashion, considering both the aesthetic demands of depicting metamorphosis and the structural significance of the myths, largely divorced from questions of historical evolution. My treatment of "Metamorphosis in the Middle Ages" (Chapter 3) is quite the opposite: a study in the history of an idea, from the time of Augustine, when pagan transformation is anathematized, to the later Middle Ages, when it comes to be celebrated as of the essence in rhetoric and natural philosophy. The fifth chapter, which treats the fortunes of metamorphosis in the Renaissance, is neither quite chronological nor quite structural; it offers a historical account not of ideas but of the imagination.

Such an account does not move with the steady beat of the clock or the calendar, for the artistic imagination evolves with a mysterious genetics. Artists confront their past (especially the work of other artists) partly within the limits of their own historical moment and partly at the level of a personal encounter that is as unique and outside of time as the creative gift itself. Nor are such encounters the province of geniuses (or even artists) alone—even if such cases as Dante meeting Virgil or Titian repainting Bellini or Shakespeare reading the book of Ovid seem especially paradigmatic. For the most essential presupposition underlying the many pages that follow is that a subject like pagan metamorphosis, richly laden with intellectual, sensuous, and aesthetic possibilities, has its own history; indeed its own kind of history—an account of the origins of artistic inspiration. And, like many critics' presuppositions, this stands as a replica, or rather a mirror image, of the author's own intellectual history. For I discovered in my first adult reading of Ovid's *Metamorphoses* the origins of all that most fascinated me in Renaissance literature and art: not the sources of the stories (splendid as they are) but the genesis of a world-view and an aesthetic. I have tried in this volume to trace from that genesis a genealogy and a genetics.

In acknowledging the debts I have—so pleasantly—incurred while working on this volume, I run the same risk that the book itself runs: a brief account will surely not do justice to the subject, and a lengthy account will give the illusion that it is comprehensive. A project which has occupied its author for so many years (I dare not say how many, lest I inflate the reader's expectations) depends on such a variety of help from friends as is quite impossible to enumerate, let alone repay, in a few words. Hospitality has counted for a great deal in the nurturing of the book and the author: of libraries from U.C.L.A. to Northwestern to the Bodleian; of institutions, like the National Endowment for the Humanities, which granted me a fellowship for independent study and research, and St. Catherine's College, Oxford, with special thanks to Eric Barendt, Richard Parish, and Arnold Freedman; of individuals who have welcomed me with invitations to speak on the book's ideas (often still in inchoate form), including John Carey, David Norbrook, Cedric Brown, Mark Rose, José Harris, and Tim Peltason. Colleagues have by their help and by their example all but erased the impression of the interdisciplinary scholar that he is working in the wilderness: Jean Hagstrum, Martin Mueller, and Richard Wendorf have set superb examples for the kind of work that I aspire to; and I have benefited enormously from the expertise of Albert Ascoli, Page duBois, Larry Lipking, Larry Silver, Chip Tucker, and Garry Wills in fields where I was an interloper and they were indulgent guides. I am especially fortunate in friends whose love and intellectual energy have placed me in debts on which there is (luckily) a lifetime mortgage: Albert Braunmuller, Tim Breen, Malcolm Chapman, E. Donald Elliott, Jonathan Freedman, Marjorie Garber, Jon Koslow, Dan Lewis, Ronald Martinez, David Miller, Jerrold Moore. The making of this book has benefited from the indispensable help of my editors Ellen Graham and Stephanie Jones, my students Thomas Troppe and Stephen Heller, my colleagues and friends Michael Warner, Barbara Newman, Barbara Schwom, Douglas Bell, Louise Love, and Mark Richard. Finally there are those whose beneficence transcends the categories of host, colleague, and friend: Robert Durling, Thomas Greene, Robert Hanning, and Stephen Orgel. It is a pleasant impossibility to try to live by their standards of scholarship and humaneness.

A Note on Texts
& Translations

There is a logic here governing the citation of foreign-language texts, though the system involves so many variables that it may require explanation. Except in a few instances where its relevance is a matter of content alone or where the Roman alphabet would not suffice, verse is always cited in the original language. When the verse is itself a principal object of study (as in the cases of Ovid, Dante, and Petrarch), a translation follows directly in the text. Where its relevance is more contextual than literary (e.g., the *Ovide moralisé*), the translation is given in the endnotes. The exception is verse written in modern French (e.g., Ronsard), which is cited without translation. Prose passages are cited in English translation when they are purely expository (e.g., commentators on Ovid or Dante); where their literary qualities are also important (e.g., the *Hypnerotomachia Poliphili*), they are cited in the original language and translated in a note. Foreign-language quotations appearing exclusively in the notes are not translated. Occasional briefly quoted phrases that might lose their pith if rendered into English (e.g., Savonarola's "Ovidio fabuloso, Ovidio pazzo!") are left in their original tongues. Unless otherwise credited, all translations are my own.

CHAPTER ONE

Tapestry Figures

If we approach metamorphosis historically in the narrow sense, that is, chronologically, a single work stands as the clear point of entrance. Ovid's *Metamorphoses*, while not the earliest source nor even the earliest collection of metamorphic tales,[1] is the Bible of a tradition—read, re-read, translated, illustrated, moralized, reborn. Indeed, the *Nachleben* of Ovid's poem is the index to a whole segment in the history of culture, a segment with its own rules that spans centuries, nations, religions, and artistic media. For that very reason we cannot approach the subject "historically in the narrow sense." A history of metamorphosis must be a history of its attractions and meanings, a history of its place in the history of culture. These subjects may not move to the smooth beat of the calendar. Thus the question for this first chapter: what, amid all the transformations of transformation, makes its bewitching power and meaning abide so intensely and so uniformly for two millennia? What glimpses of what visions are poets, painters, theologians, and philosophers summoning up when they trot out the old wives' tales about gods who descend as animals, girls who turn into trees, and heroes who become heavenly bodies?

For all that we plan to eschew pure chronology in this chapter, we must still begin with a locus classicus in Ovid's *Metamorphoses*. At the beginning of Book VI, in a phase of the poem where human beings are beginning to prove themselves by defying the gods, the poet introduces a presumptuous mortal called Arachne. Her story will be a paradigm of metamorphosis. She is, to begin with, a victim of transformation. Her name and identity will be preserved forever as the spider. Arachne's story thus partakes of a mythic paradigm that operates by metamorphosis: the human weaver aspires upward to be the equal of the divine weaver,

Minerva, and she is punished by being plunged downward into the form of the animal weaver. The universe is structured in layers—in this case divine, human, and animal—and metamorphosis is the vehicle whereby individuals are transported among the layers. The girl's pride is, in fact, just as much a metamorphosis as is the opposite movement that punishes the pride. It is for that reason that Ovid describes her crime as ignorance of the limits of humanity:

> scires a Pallade doctam.
> quod tamen ipsa negat tantaque offensa magistra
> "certet" ait "mecum: nihil est, quod victa recusem!"   [6.23–25][2]

(You could know that Pallas had taught her. Yet she denied it, and offended at the suggestion of a teacher ever so great, she said, "Let her but strive with me; and if I lose there is nothing which I would not forfeit.")

Arachne's belief that she is solely responsible for her gifts amounts to an inability to distinguish between mortal and divine qualities: that ignorance prepares her for metamorphosis, and it is fitting that she lose her claim to both realms.

More than her fate, however, it is the substance of Arachne's quarrel with Minerva that defines metamorphosis. In the first place, the combatants confront each other in transformation: Minerva visits the girl in the metamorphosed shape of an old woman; and when she retransforms herself into her divine form, Arachne herself experiences a quite natural set of corporeal changes:

> sed tamen exsiluit, subitusque invita notavit
> ora rubor rursusque evanuit, ut solet aer
> purpureus fieri, cum primum Aurora movetur,
> et breve post tempus candescere solis ab ortu.   [6.46–49]

(Though she did start up and a sudden flush marked her unwilling cheeks and again faded: as when the sky grows crimson when the dawn first appears, and after a little while when the sun is up it pales again.)

These transformations—Minerva's impersonation, Arachne's presumption, her blush, her punishment, even the analogous color changes of the sky—all remind us that metamorphosis is universal in the experience of gods, men, and nature. That fact sets the stage for the main battle, which consists in the tapestry competition between the two great weavers.

Ovid describes the two tapestries in detail. Minerva's central panel is an image of the twelve gods of heaven in all their *augusta gravitate*, among whom Jupiter, Neptune, and Pallas herself are pictured as threatening and invincible. Surrounding this panel, in the four corners of the tapestry, are scenes of presumption against the gods, with each mortal punished by violent transformation. Minerva is offering at once a theology and an aesthetic of metamorphosis: the gods sit all-powerful in the middle (of the universe or of the work of art), whence they deal out punishing metamorphoses to mortals; these mortals are frozen in their nonhuman shape (mountains, crane, stork, temple steps, in these cases) for all eternity. The whole picture is highly moralistic—it is, after all, designed to make a direct point about Arachne's own future—and bound up with that moralism is an aesthetic of sharp definition and finality. In word and picture, the five panels of Minerva's tapestry are perfectly discrete, and metamorphosis is finality rather than process.

Before we turn to Arachne's answer, we must give credit where it is due to Minerva's definition. Punishment, finality, and finite panels of narrative do have their place in metamorphosis—even in Ovid's account, especially in the first third of the poem where the gods rule so powerfully. Human presumption against the gods can be blasphemy, polluting divine forms of beauty with mortal forms whose change tends toward decay rather than perfectibility. Yet on the whole Minerva's work is as much a straw man as it is a woven cloth. As an aesthetic and as an account of metamorphosis, it exists in order that Ovid may shed its sharp moral and aesthetic rules. (And, as we shall see, the metamorphic tradition will be of Arachne's party rather than of the goddess's.) The poet's true partisanship begins to emerge even before either of the tapestries has been described, in his account of the process of art itself. The two women work rapidly and expertly over their weaving and dyeing, producing a subtle range of colors:

> qualis ab imbre solent percussis solibus arcus
> inficere ingenti longum curvamine caelum;
> in quo diversi niteant cum mille colores,
> transitus ipse tamen spectantia lumina fallit:
> usque adeo, quod tangit, idem est; tamen ultima distant.

> [6. 63–67]

(As when after a storm of rain the sun's rays strike through, and a rainbow, with its huge curve, stains the wide sky, though a thousand different colours shine in it, the eye cannot detect the change from each one to the next; so like appear the adjacent colours, but the extremes are plainly different.)

Once again the reference to the metamorphic arts of nature establishes a norm. The art of continuous changes, radiant with multiplicity but confounding clear definition, reflects a reality in the universe that is similarly fluid.

In both subject and method Arachne's tapestry fulfills this aesthetic. Her subject is metamorphosis itself, the transformations of the gods as they love (and victimize) mortal women:

Maeonis elusam designat imagine tauri
Europam. . . .

. . . .

fecit et Asterien aquila luctante teneri,
fecit olorinis Ledam recubare sub alis;
addidit, ut satyri celatus imagine pulchram
Iuppiter inplerit gemino Nycteida fetu,
Amphitryon fuerit, cum te, Tirynthia, cepit,
aureus ut Danaen, Asopida luserit ignis,
Mnemosynen pastor, varius Deoida serpens.   [6.103–14]

(Arachne pictures Europa cheated by the disguise of the bull. . . .
She wrought Asterie, held by the struggling eagle; she wrought
Leda, beneath the swan's wings. She added how, in a satyr's image
hidden, Jove filled lovely Antiope with twin offspring; how he was
Amphitryon when he cheated thee, Alcmena; how in a golden
shower he tricked Danae; Aegina, as a flame; Mnemosyne as a shepherd; Deo's daughter as a spotted snake.)

In contrast to the discrete classicism of Minerva's tapestry, Arachne piles
stories helter-skelter together ("fecit . . . fecit . . . addidit") so that they
flow in a seamless mass, joined not by the logic of cause and effect or of
morality but by the thread of metamorphosis itself. It requires no great
leap of the imagination to see in Arachne's tapestry all the elements of
Ovid's own poetic form in the *Metamorphoses*, which is, after all, a poem
that eschews a clear narrative structure and rather creates a finely woven
fabric of stories related via transformation. Moreover, Arachne responds
to Minerva's morality just as she responds to the goddess's aesthetics, by
representing the complementary form of metamorphosis. Minerva's
corner-figures were mortals transformed by the hatred of the gods;
Arachne depicts gods transformed by their love of mortals. Minerva represents mortals threatening gods, Arachne gods threatening mortals. If
the basis of Arachne's own crime is an inability to distinguish between the
mortal and the divine, she is careful to demonstrate that gods, too—by
their very metamorphoses—commit such a crime.

But is it a crime? Arachne's morality is a great deal more fluid than Minerva's. In one sense the girl speaks for all the victimized mortals of
Ovid's poem, defining metamorphosis as *caelestia crimina*, much as Minerva had defined metamorphosis as the result of human crimes. Yet
while Minerva's definition remains as static as do the objects of metamorphosis that she depicts, Arachne's transformations escape from her own
anger. They take on a life of their own, not as the expression of outraged
mortal victims but as glories of love, magic, and divine beauty. Arachne's
transformations are not fixity but process, as the gods keep changing their
shape while the artistic web in which they are woven keeps changing its

colors. Once again they parallel Ovid's whole poem, and they help define the tradition of metamorphosis, in which morality wars with beauty and is often submerged in it.

Throughout the episode, then, metamorphosis is the key to a series of precarious balances. The vengeance of the gods is just but cruel; the amours of the gods are destructive but beautiful; the talents of the girl are sacrilegious but magnificent; the fate of the girl is degradation but also eternal life as an artist. Metamorphosis is both punishment and reward, morality and beauty. It is a fact of nature, but at the same time it describes a complicated aesthetics, a seamless web of changing narrative and a structure that takes us from crime (mortal presumption) to punishment (animal transformation) via a route that undoes the power of that punishment. For if Arachne's doom is to spin the web, then Ovid in his own person turns that fixity to process by keeping the web-spinning alive as the ultimate mortal expression of art.

Despite the obvious visual interest of Arachne's story, it is not a favorite among artists either in antiquity or in later times. Not only is the drama of girl and goddess rare in the pictorial tradition; even Arachne's tapestry itself seems to exist much more as a verbal construct than as an actual blueprint for artists.[3] Yet one important painting nearly seventeen hundred years after the *Metamorphoses* may illuminate the end of the metamorphic tradition as well as Ovid's account illuminates the beginning. Late in his life Diego Velázquez turned to a self-conscious awareness of art as subject. His great masterpiece of this period, the often analyzed *Las Meninas*, is, by whatever account of it we follow, a complex assertion about art, the artist, and Diego Velázquez in particular.[4] Still later in his career he completed a work which may be as enigmatic and self-conscious as *Las Meninas* but which has had comparatively little attention, a canvas traditionally known as *Las Hilanderas*, or *The Spinners*[5] (figure 1).

Las Hilanderas divides its multiple subject by using different planes at receding distances from the spectator. In the foreground we see five women engaged in tasks appropriate to a tapestry workshop: one winding yarn, one spinning, and the other three less prominent acting as helpers. This whole scene is rendered rather in shadow. But on a higher and more distant plane the painter presents a scene in brilliant light: three courtly ladies, one with a viola da gamba; a helmeted figure with upraised arm; a well-dressed woman making a highly expressive gesture at very nearly the vanishing point of the picture's perspective; and behind this whole scene a finished tapestry.

Some—though not all—of the picture's enigmas are resolved when we give it the name *The Fable of Arachne*, a conclusion partly justified by the appearance of a Velázquez canvas of that name in a Madrid inventory of 1664.[6] Almost certainly the helmeted figure is Minerva, raising her arm to threaten Arachne. But what does this identification tell us about all of the other scenes and the relations among the planes? In the first place, we can say of Velázquez, as of the painters who had inspired him, that his *Arachne* does homage to Arachne's own metamorphic aesthetic. The connections among the seemingly diverse materials of his picture are like those of Arachne's tapestry: the subjects are different but they are bound together by a fine set of progressions from the outermost ring to the tapestry at the center. The foreground scene, which occupies the bulk of the picture, is, in one sense at least, genre painting: the figures are real, contemporary, and authentically observed artisans, who labor hard, surrounded by clutter in semidarkness. As such they figure forth the material or craft basis of the arts; and Velázquez, despite his concern for the nobility of art and artist, does not relegate them to a minor position.[7]

Yet—in true metamorphic fashion—the foreground represents at the same time a quite different scene. The heavily clothed—i.e., disguised—old woman on the left is in reality Minerva in the midst of the weaving contest. The painter alters the Ovidian narrative (in which Minerva reveals herself before the weaving begins) so as to make the goddess's revelation possible in the course of the picture. But we know it is no genuine old woman because her shapely foreleg casts an attractive glow in the middle of the scene. Meanwhile on the right the young Arachne sits winding yarn. So the front layer is at once a genre painting and a very domestic version of classical fable. The next layer of the picture represents a gradual progression. The three ladies in elegant dress face inward toward the finished tapestry in a more or less semicircular position. Like the outer scene, they may have more than one signification: as the Lydian women who so admire Arachne's work or (perhaps) as allegorical representations of the Fine Arts.[8] In their audience-like position they represent the connoisseurs—figures who respond to art much more respectfully than does the goddess.[9] However we read them, the ladies represent an elevation and a distancing from the practical toward the artistic.

The inset Minerva and Arachne take the logical next step of sublimation from the naturalistic spinners in the foreground to the formal ladies in the cubicle: goddess and mortal are placed in the traditional, rather stagy poses so dear to seventeenth-century pictorial aesthetics.[10] They are, in other words, part real story and part self-conscious art. Their relationship—just like that of their lesser emanations in the foreground of the picture—is elaborately complementary. Minerva's upraised arm signifies the power of her godhead,[11] while Arachne's hand on heart signifies the experience of her suffering. As Ovid says of Arachne's tapestry figures, "Omnibus his faciemque suam faciemque locorum / reddidit" (6.121–22: "To all these she gave their own shapes and appropriate surroundings").

All this gradual motion, from the mundane world of artisanship to the mythological source of art, reaches its climax in the tapestry. The subject of the work is the Rape of Europa: not a fanciful new conception of the myth but an accurate rendition of Titian's great canvas, then in the Spanish royal collection.[12] The narrative reason for Velázquez's choice of theme is presumably the straightforward reference to the first and most memorable of Arachne's subjects. But the placement of Europa, and particularly of Titian's Europa, reflects more than narrative necessity. With Titian at the center point we can begin to understand the destination of the picture's motion. The highest point of sublimation—beyond craft, beyond connoisseurship, even beyond the drama of mortal and divine artist—is the work of art itself. Art is defined as a masterpiece inspired by classical antiquity and embodying pagan metamorphosis.

Velázquez dramatizes artistic self-consciousness with his insistent use of framing devices: the outer scene; the inset cubicle, which in the original version[13] itself resembles a picture; the inset audience; the tapestry border on the Titian itself.[14] But within these frames he pays homage to Titian's own methods of metamorphosis and sublimation. Ovid's description of the metamorphic art of tapestries—the *diversi mille colores* that seem all to flow into each other—applies with special aptness to Titian's works and especially to this particular late mythology. In fact, Velázquez quotes just that middle section of Titian's canvas which reveals the most marvelous use of color and light.

Set in the context of the whole *Hilanderas*, that visual quotation demonstrates how the motion from foreground to background of the canvas is made of light: from the spinners with their occasional highlight to the brighter world of the inner stage to the yet brighter mythological figures until we arrive at the Titian itself, whose detail is almost obscured by brightness. More even than Titian, Velázquez uses light as the medium of transition among the planes of his canvas. The brightest figure in the foreground is the spinner Arachne, who is bathed in a diagonal of the same shocking illumination (shocking because its source is obscure, especially in the unextended original picture) that reaches its climax in the Titian.

By the time we get to the work of art itself the illumination is so bright that it seems to engulf even Arachne—so much so that some viewers have felt she is intended to be part of the tapestry. If the work of art is the essence, then Velázquez deliberately inserts the artist herself into that essence. Arachne is not only the centerpoint of *Las Hilanderas* but she is also superimposed on the figure of Europa in Titian's picture. The real essence at the heart of the process is the union of art, artist, and subject made absolute at that point where all light is joined. For Velázquez that identification of Arachne with Europa speaks to a classical aesthetic, which is also an aesthetic of metamorphosis. In uniting the two, the painter not only identifies art and artist; he also identifies both with essence, light, and the great pagan subject of magical transformation, rooted in the encounter of mortals with the divine.

To define metamorphic art self-consciously (as Velázquez did and I am doing) by the complementarity of Arachne and Europa is no mere tangent of a late Renaissance painting. In the first place, the two figures are tightly joined in the literary tradition. Ovid, as we have seen, begins Arachne's tapestry with Europa. When Poliziano adapts that artistic description in *Le Stanze per la giostra*, he gives Europa two stanzas while the others get half a line apiece;[15] and when Spenser translates Ovid in "Muiopotmos," he gives Europa twenty lines and omits all mention of any other subject.[16] Velázquez, heavily influenced, as Madlyn Kahr has shown, by Flemish gallery pictures with all their multiplicity of paintings within paintings,[17] could certainly have offered a tapestry that included many amours of the gods; but he chose Europa alone. The complementarity of Arachne and Europa, of the metamorphic artist with the victim of divine transformation, fixes metamorphosis firmly in the realm of visual image, just as it fixes Europa in a tapestry rather than in real life.

These speculations on the power of Europa as *image* gain in importance when we remind ourselves that she has been at the center of self-conscious reflection about the nature of image. That Europa is at the centerpoint of Velázquez's essay on art is one of a long history of examples. More commonly she appears as the inset work of art within a verbal creation, that is, in ekphrasis. This is not just a function of her prominence in the Arachne story. Achilles Tatius, for example, with no reference to Arachne, introduces his romance of *Leucippe and Clitophon* with a lengthy ekphrasis of a Europa painting and thereby sets up a rhetorical strategy for the whole romance.[18] Those who translate the image of Europa into words tend to describe the scene with minute detail—to such an extent that scholars studying the sources of Titian's painting can argue between Achilles Tatius and Ovid because the Greek writer tells us that Europa is holding the bull's horn in her left hand while in the *Fasti* she is holding it in her right.[19] This exhaustive attention speaks to a talismanic power in the image, almost as though the god were actually contained within it.[20]

The reasons for Europa's power as image may in the end have to do with transformations in both of the icon's personae. The bull is a god; the bull is—even in his beastly identity—an ancient symbol of male power, of fertility, of husbandry, and of divinity.[21] The girl is a victim, but her image speaks as much of mastery over the bull as of victimization. Europa sits above the animal, often sidesaddle or even defying gravity, while the bull underneath seems almost in flight, taking her through the heavens. Furthermore, she is from earliest times often bedecked with a great semicircular veil above her: this decoration sets her in triumphal surroundings and completes the circularity of the image.[22] So Jupiter and Europa—

even as a mute icon—generate strong associations of paradox, of power overcome by beauty, of fertility tamed in agriculture. These doublenesses are part of the enduring appeal of the image and part of its metamorphic nature.

Yet all images, especially when construed in words, are metamorphic. The ekphrastic tradition in antiquity is grounded in a belief that the verbal description of a work of art unfolds into multiplicity and sequential time what the visual work itself captures frozen. The words make the still work of art move, and in the process they remind us that the art of the image is always frozen in multiplicities and changes. The Alexandrian writers of the various *Imagines*[23] are constantly concered with metamorphoses. Sometimes it is just a question of describing the mythological transformation so that the work of art seems to be itself as gradual as the change, as we see here when the Elder Philostratus discusses a representation of Phaethon's sisters becoming amber trees:

> The painting recognizes the story, for it puts roots at the extremities of their toes, while some, over here, are trees to the waist, and branches have supplanted the arms of others. Behold the hair, it is nothing but poplar leaves! Behold the tears, they are golden! [i.e., they have already turned to amber]. [1:11]

The words make us read the figures moving gradually upwards as though the metamorphosis were actually taking place as we read. Another whole set of changes has to do with works of art coming to life—so powerfully authentic are they. It has been argued, in fact, that ekphrasis signifies "speaking out," that is, the bestowing of a voice upon a mute picture.[24] When Callistratus tells us that the statue of a bacchant has become a living bacchant or that a bronze statue of a boy "departed totally from the limitations of its own nature and was transmuted into the true qualities of the subject" (*Descriptions*, 11), artistic power is expressed as metamorphosis from art to life.

Yet another form of change in the meeting of words and pictures comes from a sense of captured conflict. This approach is particularly evident in the romance of Achilles Tatius, which we have already mentioned in connection with the opening description of a Europa picture.[25] Besides Europa, there are numerous other descriptions including pictures of Prometheus, Andromeda, and Philomela. The descriptions carry a remarkable sense of frozen motion and emotion. Conflicting actions and feelings are captured in pictorial stillness. Europa's girlfriends have a look "compounded of joy and fear" (1.1); Andromeda's "face was a mixture of beauty and fear; fear sat upon her cheeks, and beauty shone from her eyes" (3.7); as Hercules is about to slay the vulture tormenting Prometheus, "All seem in motion at once—the bow, the string, the arrow, the hand which holds it; the bow is bent by means of the string, the string is made to run double by means of the hand, the hand is at rest upon the hero's breast. The countenance of Prometheus has a mixed look of hope and fear" (3.8). All these descriptions add up to a strikingly metamorphic notion of graphic art.

In the world of late antiquity, ekphrasis, like metamorphosis, becomes a key to the complex and celebratory rhetoric concerned with the instabilities of matter and the uncertainty of reality. So when Callistratus describes a statue of Narcissus, he tells us,

> For whereas the marble was in every part trying to change the real boy so as to match the one in the water, the spring was struggling to match the skillful effects of art in the marble, reproducing in an incorporeal medium the likeness of the corporeal model and enveloping the reflection which came from the statue with the substance of water as though it were the substance of flesh. And indeed the form in the water was so instinct with life and breath that it seemed to be Narcissus himself. . . . Indeed, words cannot describe [!] how the marble softened into suppleness and provided a body at variance with its own essence. [*Descriptions*, 5]

The relations of image and reflection, of art and reality, of matter and the imagination capture a whole metamorphic aesthetic in the Alexandrian period.

Yet the clearest key to metamorphosis in ekphrasis may well appear in the source of the whole topos: Homer's account of the shield of Achilles in Book XVIII of the *Iliad*. That great locus classicus makes of the work of art a whole universe: cosmos, society, polis, family, nature; and we are so convinced of the authenticity of the artistry that, lost in the middle of the long description, we forget we are on a shield and think instead of the real cosmos itself. At this point Homer inserts a detail to the effect that Pallas Athena was "all in gold"—which amounts to an ekphrastic pun, since the "real" goddess could well appear bedecked in gold just as much as a "forged" goddess could be made out of gold. But then the poet completes the shock by telling us that the men were made of bronze, only to switch back to the fictional world in which a city is at war, and the soldiers are, after all, armed in bronze.[26] A form of art where image automatically lures one to verbal translation and ekphrastic description automatically turns one toward image: this cyclical flow of such ancient myths as we are concerned with here involves the constant transformation from life to art, from picture to words.

Ovid exploits this shifting definition of art in his description of the god-turned-bull as tapestry:

> Maeonis elusam designat imagine tauri
> Europam: verum taurum, freta vera putares. [6.103–04]

(Arachne pictures Europa cheated by the disguise of the bull: a real
bull and real waves you would think them.)

The transformed god is the *imago tauri* that captures (and captivates) Europa. F. J. Miller translates *imago* as "disguise," but the meanings of the word are far more complex in this context. The *imago* is an image of the bull, an imaginary form of the bull, and an alter ego of Jupiter, who created the bull. All of these *imagines* are beautiful and delusive, and all are bound up in the process of metamorphosis. Furthermore Ovid draws an unmistakable parallel between those *imagines* and the images of the tapestry itself. When he tells us "Verum taurum, freta vera putares"—"a real bull and real waves *you would think them*"—the delusion involved is at once our aesthetic response to a visual masterpiece and Europa's response to a fabricated bull. The phrase signals the most ancient of aesthetic principles, going back to those Greek stories about birds who are deceived by painted grapes and artists who are deceived by painted curtains.[27] In the context of the metamorphosed Jupiter, this age-old praise of verisimilitude becomes more powerful and troubling. Once Arachne's metamorphic art has taken us to Jupiter's metamorphic art of verisimilitude, then the act of representation becomes the act of metamorphosis, and both can be seen either as perfect natural authenticity or as deception heavily tinged with libido.

Metamorphosis in the image of the bull not only defines verisimilitude. The *imago tauri* may be dazzlingly true to life, but the very fact that he is not real, that he is a representation, makes him transcend the real at the same time. Ovid tells us (not in the Arachne section but in the direct narrative of Europa's story) of the bull:

quippe color nivis est, quam nec vestigia duri
calcavere pedis nec solvit aquaticus auster.
colla toris exstant, armis palearia pendent,
cornua parva quidem, sed quae contendere possis
facta manu, puraque magis perlucida gemma.   [2.852–56]

(His colour was white as the untrodden snow, which has not yet been melted by the south wind. The muscles stood rounded on his neck, a long dewlap hung down in front; his horns were small, but perfect in shape as if carved by an artist's hand, cleaner and more clear than pearls.)

The *imago tauri* is transcendent at the same time as it is verisimilar, perfect and perfectly authentic at once. What makes the combination possible is the multiform nature of the bull. Consider some of the surprise occasioned by the traveling bull in Nonnos's *Dionysiaca*:

O my eyes, what's this miracle? how comes it that he cuts the waves with his legs, and swims over the barren sea, this land-pasturing

bull? Navigable earth—is that the new creation of Cronides? Shall
the farmer's wain trace a watery rut through the brine-sprent deep?
That's a bastard voyage I descry upon the waves![28]

These reflections on the uniqueness of the bull, his strange form of
travel, his unearthly yet universal powers are always balanced with the
absolute authenticity of the bull. This *imago* is not simply bull, bird, fish,
god, or human lover; he is all these things because he is an image of
metamorphosis.

But Europa is not just an image wrought by Arachne; she is also a
story. And just as the image of Europa encompasses many of the artistic
meanings of metamorphosis, so her story embodies many of the essential
themes in the experience of metamorphosis. To define those essential significances let us begin at the beginning, with the earliest complete version of the story we have, the Alexandrian bucolic poem of Moschus,
which dates from the second century B.C.[29] The poem is useful precisely
because it is not a widely used source for later versions of this or other
metamorphic stories; rather it can stand as a relatively naive—though
fully elaborated—account.

Moschus opens with a dream sent to Europa by Aphrodite. In her
dream Europa is being fought over by two continents who have taken on
the form of women. Asia behaves like the girl's mother and holds on to
her, while the other lady-continent, the stranger who is never named, declares that the girl is destined for her instead. Europa, though frightened,
does not resist; in fact, she experiences a strange longing for the foreign
woman. Upon awakening she declares her hope that the gods prophesy
favorably in her dream, and she rushes off to join her young female companions for a bout of flower-picking. At this point the poet interrupts the
story with a lovely ekphrasis describing the basket in which Europa gathers her flowers: originally a wedding-gift from Hephaistos to Libya and
Poseidon, it depicts Io transformed by Zeus into a heifer and crossing the
sea all the way to the Nile, where she is retransformed.

The flower-picking itself leads to the appearance of Zeus. Overcome by
Aphrodite's power, desirous of avoiding Hera's attention, and eager to
win the beautiful girl, he hides his divine shape and turns himself into a
bull. So beautiful and alluring is the creature that all the maidens experience the desire (ἔρωσ) to approach. Europa in particular touches and
kisses the bull, who responds with sweet musical sounds and kneels at the
girl's feet. She extols his tenderness, his propriety, and his manlike spirit;
she urges everyone to climb aboard. No sooner has Europa herself
mounted than the animal leaps up, arrives at the water, and then crosses
the waves neither exactly flying nor exactly swimming. Instantly the
waters become calm, but they also become the arena for a glorious sea-
triumph, all of which does little to reassure Europa, terrified by the vast

sea and by the mystery of a flying, swimming bull, who is something like a man and something like a god. She is finally reassured, however, when Zeus identifies himself and announces that he is taking her to Crete, his own homeland, where they will be wed and where she will bear him glorious offspring.

At the midpoint of the poem, just before Zeus appears, an obiter dictum places the whole experience in clear light. The maidens are gathering flowers now, but "Not much longer is Europa to take pleasure in flowers, nor long will she keep her maiden girdle undefiled" (ll. 72–73). If the heart of the poem (and of the myth) is the figure of metamorphosis, the multiform creature who himself changes all, then the principal change is sexuality. The encounter of girl and god is in and of itself a metamorphosis: rather like Arachne's presumption, it speaks already to cosmic instability. Insofar as the bull *is* a bull, he images forth powerful sexuality. The sight of the animal inflames all the girls with eros, while the heroine herself is bewitched by his looks and charms. She even kisses him on the mouth.

Yet the bull is more than a sexy farm animal. Erotic attraction via metamorphosis defines sexuality with particular force as the unfamiliar, or even the uncanny. Europa has a glimpse of the mysterious aspect almost at once. She begins the love-making because she is captivated by the unfamiliar. As she says to her playmates, "He does not resemble other bulls; he has the proper spirit of a man but is only lacking speech" (ll. 105–07). Yet it is this same unfamiliarity that nearly scares her to death when the bull abducts her: "Who are you? How can it be that you travel paths so difficult for heavy-footed cattle without fearing the water?" (ll. 135–37), with which she curses her lot and (ironically, for this is another reminder of the multiplicities of metamorphosis) begs for help from the gods. So Europa's rape by the multiform creature defines metamorphosis as an experience that breaks all previously accepted rules. Myths of magical change, again and again, will be stories celebrating the unfamiliar forms of the sexual impulse, with all their terror and allure.

Metamorphosis images forth other forms of the unfamiliar besides sexuality itself. Europa is a pubescent virgin on the threshold of first sexual experience. The multiform creature with whom she is united is a sea-traveling shape-changer who speaks to her in an unfamiliar language and then transports her away from home forever. The issue, in other words, is not merely the threshold of puberty but also the threshold of exogamy, or marriage to a member of another tribe. Anthropologists tell us that there may be no more significant beliefs within a primitive society than those concerning marital unions outside the immediate cricle,[30] and those studying the classical tradition can hardly afford to be any less sensitive to the reverberations of these beliefs in such nonprimitive works as the *Odyssey*, the *Aeneid*, or the *Metamorphoses*.

The terms whereby Europa's story enacts the principle of exogamy should be fairly obvious. Moschus leaves no doubt by introducing the girl's story with the dream in which she is fought over by the motherly figure of Asia and the alien woman who represents the opposite continent. The tension in the dream mirrors the tale of sexual initiation which is to follow: in both cases Europa is at once frightened by and attracted to the alien, and in both cases her destiny is to embrace that figure. Europa's story places great emphasis upon a passage across the water from the known (Phoenicia) to the unknown (Crete), and that passage—again made possible by the metamorphic bull—becomes the expression of many forms of liminality. Metamorphosis is a figure for all the fears and necessities of exogamy, and so stories of metamorphosis are stories of pursuit, of travel, of unfamiliar and alien loves.

Besides the experiences of unfamiliar sexuality and alien travel there is one more threshold crossed as a result of the transformation. To understand this last threshold, we must first remind ourselves that this is a "female" story—not that it is necessarily a true expression of matriarchal myth-making but that it is an attempt to see the sexual experience from the girl's side. The female perspective[31] places the metamorphic myth in a context of powerful inward emotion. Not all myths or metamorphoses concentrate on girls. Yet the whole world of metamorphosis—both Ovid's poem and its tradition—is a world where female emotions, themselves associated with change, are given special prominence. And in just the way that sexuality and exogamy are threshold experiences, so is passionate emotion if it is being discovered for the first time.[32]

Europa experiences these feelings as she faces her mysterious lover. She begins the story in an atmosphere of complete familiarity, picking flowers with her girlfriends, who Moschus reminds us, are just like herself. Then, through her own attraction to the unfamiliar (so that she has no one to blame but herself), she embraces the creature; and on one level, at least, her fate from then on is internal torment. Not only does Moschus give us several tirades in which she agonizes;[33] he has also inserted the ekphrasis of Io, whose story typifies this torment and ties it to the image of metamorphosis. In fact, Europa and Io are perfectly symmetrical. Europa, abducted by Zeus-turned-bull, is taken toward Greece, while Io, herself transformed by Zeus into a heifer, is sent away from Greece. Europa will be accompanied on her travels by a grand sea-triumph; Io on her journey is tormented by furies. Both are tales of metamorphosis; both combine first sexual experience, fearful migration, and psychic agony. The relation between metamorphosis and agonized introspection amounts to more than just the vague common ground of changeability. The experience of metamorphosis, for Europa and Io but also for many others who are not women, raises essential questions about selfhood, typically for the first time. For identity, as soon as metamorphosis divorces it from corporeal shape, suddenly comes to be isolated as a thing in itself.

Time and again, the metamorphic myths revolve around the discovery of that newly isolated identity.

Yet the metamorphic story does not simply rest in chaos and uncertainty. For every signification of metamorphosis that points toward fear and instability, there is a destination that is positive and life-confirming. For the exogamic principle, of travel to unknown frontiers, there is the principle of etiology. When individuals reach the extremes of experience figured forth by metamorphosis (whether as subject or object does not really matter), they are often compensated by giving birth, as it were, to a new species, a new place, or a new society. If, in other words, metamorphosis is sex, it is also new creation. Here the case of Europa is particularly clear. In understanding the migratory significance of her story, we can hardly omit the fact of her name. The linguistic relation between the Phoenician girl and the western land mass has been debated from ancient times. The best current opinion is that the similarity is coincidental, with the girl's name deriving from a word for "beauty visible from afar" and the continental name relating to *erebus*, a term for darkness associated with the West and the sunset.[34] Whatever the truth of the matter, the possibility of identification between the girl and the land mass (originally the mainland of Greece as viewed from Asia Minor) places the myth squarely in the category of etiologies. The fact that the connections were uncertain may even have intensified the power of the geographical and migratory interpretation. So Herodotus in his level-headed way tries to debunk the association of girl and continent, clearly feeling that the tale is far too frivolous to account for the identity of Europe.[35] But when Moschus coyly refrains from naming the "foreign woman" who so mysteriously attracts the girl in her dream, he is deliberately leaving a space in which the girl may ride off into the unfamiliar, while through the figure of metamorphosis she can attain an identity which generates our own familiar world.

If exogamy is balanced by etiology, then fearful first sexual experience is balanced by wedding. We embark here on some paradoxical territory. Despite the fact that Europa seems to be a victim of adulterous abduction, the story develops already in antiquity strong associations with marriage. Moschus's Europa declares in the midst of her suffering, "Oh, what a wretch am I to have left the house of my father and followed this bull; a strange sea-voyage I now undertake and wander off alone" (ll. 147–49). The terms of this complaint put her whole experience in perspective. The fiction concerning the rape of a girl by a god is momentarily laid aside. The girl is rather the fearful newlywed facing mature life afresh, and the sexual voyage points to a different form of metamorphosis: the rite de passage.

What really defines Europa's experience as marriage is the recuperation of the girl's agony into another key of emotion. If exogamy becomes etiology and sexual fear turns to marriage, then psychic turmoil is transformed into triumph. So Moschus: "The sea grew calm under [the god's] steps, sea beasts frolicked around before Zeus's feet, dolphins leapt joyously out of the depths above the water and mounting on the backs of sea beasts all danced in rows" (ll. 115–19). This scene is of paramount interest to many of the Greek authors as well as later artists: the accounts in Lucian and Nonnos are interminable. It is a scene both calm and triumphant, and both these effects result from the alliance of the brothers Zeus and Poseidon, sky and sea. So the abduction of Europa becomes the occasion for a ritual of cosmic harmony. Not only does it turn fear to festivity; it also transforms inward emotion to external expression.

The imagery allows for little doubt about the nature of this ritual. Moschus tells us that with the appearance of Poseidon come the Tritons, "deep-voiced wind instruments of the sea, sounding on their great shell trumpets the wedding music [γάμιον μέλοσ]" (l. 124), and Lucian adds that the Erotes accompany the progress "carrying lighted torches and singing the marriage hymn [ὑμέναιον]" (*Dialogues of the Sea Gods*, 15). Clearly this is a wedding celebration. This cosmic triumph not only confirms natural and personal harmony; it also celebrates the animism of the universe. As sea and sky are anthropomorphically united, the sea itself becomes a playground of living creatures all celebrating love and marriage. The explosive (even orgasmic) scene of animate life is intimately identified with the bull-god-exemplar of sexuality at its center. It is a pageant of metamorphosis as triumph.

All the motifs of threshold sexuality, fear and triumph, rape and marriage form a cluster of associations with other myths related to metamorphosis and Europa. In fact, at the heart of the metamorphic myths we may find that the actual business of magical change has been submerged. If, for example, we consider Moschus's prime sources, the Nausicaa episode in the *Odyssey*, the Homeric "Hymn to Demeter," and the *Suppliant Maidens* of Aeschylus, we can begin to see the clustering of related issues beyond these myths. The "Hymn," for instance, contributes an emphasis on flower-picking, with all its ironic relevance to the soon-to-be-lost virginity.[36] Milton's famous line about the grove "where Proserpin gathering flours / Herself a fairer Floure by gloomie Dis / Was gatherd" (*Paradise Lost* 4.269–71) is no baroque invention. The ironic image, whether applied to Europa or to Persephone, suggests that the maiden is deflowering herself, and that possibility helps mediate between innocence and sexual initiation at the same time as it provides a powerful image of natural and human change.

The Aeschylean tragedy connects Io's experience (captured in Moschus's ekphrasis) with the tale of her descendants, fifty Greek virgins sought in marriage by foreign husbands. The drama is concerned with their rebellion against marriage and their return to the Greek homeland, where they enlist military support. Given such a scenario, the play is charged through with the voice of female militance and of opposition to men and marriage. The chorus speaks continually of all the powerful man-hating figures of myth, e.g., the Bacchae, the Amazons, Artemis.[37] The fable of foreign husbands waging war between Egypt and Greece proves to be a perfect balance to the transforming journey of Io; as the women attempt to avenge their ancestress, their fear embraces both sex and exogamy.

The marvelous scene where Odysseus meets Nausicaa offers perhaps the most illuminating parallels. (Such are the interconnections that it seems to me possible that Homer's vignette was inspired by some earlier, now lost version of the Europa story.) There are many circumstantial similarities: a prophetic dream sends the young girl forth; she goes to the water with her playmates engaging in a charming girlish activity (in this case, laundry); she meets a strange and unfamiliar figure who attracts her; alone of all the girls she addresses him; and (after a fashion) they go off together. Homer's vignette is clearly about marriage: Nausicaa is motivated by an adolescent excitement about her own unknown prospects, and she goes on her laundry expedition with the explicit purpose of preparing her brothers' fancy clothes for courtship, while secretly she is fulfilling the dream in which Athena told her to prepare her own hope chest. In all these cases, metamorphosis is submerged in the male figure(s)—the powerful king of the underworld, the alien Egyptian suitors, the cunning Odysseus rendered beautiful by the patronage of Athena—but it is still at the center of the whole relationship between the man and the woman, of his power and of her attraction and fear.[38]

Finally, the real force of this story and of the image of metamorphosis is as a mystery. Metamorphosis is a question mark, an experience outside the realm of real life that has nonetheless persistently captured the human imagination. When experience is joined to image—for we have seen how the art of metamorphosis is the art of the image—the ensemble demands a caption. But the caption, like the picture, is forever changing. That is why writers as well as artists have been so gripped by metamorphic images like Europa. And that in turn is why artists have taken up the challenge to produce ever more complex and beautiful images in order to explore the mystery. Here we have the ultimate *paragone*, or struggle between the verbal and visual arts. It is owing to the same mystery that Europa herself agonizes so articulately about the strange figure upon whom she rides:

> Neither do sea-dolphins travel on land, nor bulls in the water. But you range fearlessly on land and water. Hooves are your rudders. Perhaps you will suddenly lift yourself into the grey air and fly just like the swift birds. [Moschus, ll. 141–45]

The answer, as the girl herself suspects, is that there is a god inside the bull. And, mutatis mutandis, that is the answer for all metamorphosis. Not all magical transformations amount to animal forms of the Olympian gods—most, in fact, do not. But in the image of magical transformation there is always the mystery of the divine embedded in the real, the natural, the quotidian. Once metamorphosis has been perceived in that way, it emerges as not merely one element in myth but rather at the heart of myth itself. For a mythic view of the universe depends upon seeing the divine in the familiar. Metamorphosis is the moment when the divine enters the familiar.

It is in the very nature of myth that to retell these stories, to celebrate the lore of metamorphosis, is to summon up a cluster of beliefs that underlie these myths. These beliefs join with each other as inevitably as they are joined to the metamorphic myths that embody them. To believe in the lore of Arachne and Europa is to believe that the divine can enter the familiar. It is to believe in the magical power of the image. It is to believe in the superiority of beauty over morality. It is a belief in *das ewig Weibliche*, in an antiheroic upside-down world of flux characterized by a reaction against the masculine-dominated world of stability. It is to believe in an aesthetic that is personal, nonlinear, and fluid. At the same time as metamorphosis embodies this nexus of beliefs in a synchronic sense, it also represents a distinct historical moment—as later chapters in this volume will demonstrate. For post-classical civilization, from St. Augustine to the seventeenth century (at least), metamorphosis is an essential metonym for the classical civilization that gave it birth. Through the repeated reinterpretation and reimagination of metamorphic myths, the cluster of beliefs associated with them comes to define the heritage of antiquity, whether that is viewed through a positive or a negative glass. Looking back through that instrument, we can see how the history of metamorphosis is a key to the career of paganism in the history of the Christian intellect and imagination. Needless to say, few of the sober Christian artists we shall have occasion to discuss in this volume—men like Dante, Correggio, and Spenser—would have recognized themselves under the epithet "pagan." Yet the myths were speaking through the artists as much as the artists were speaking through the myths. The history of metamorphosis, bound up with the great subject of the survival of antiquity, is the history of a two-thousand-year counterreligion of paganism.[39]

CHAPTER TWO

Ovid & Metamorphosis

Ovid's *Metamorphoses* is a book of changes, a great poem explaining the origins of the world, of human personality, and of organized society all through the image of change. Metamorphosis of the kind one usually associates with the poem—magical alteration of physical form from one species to another—stands as the ruling poetic fancy of the poem, designed to capture the imagination through shock and wonderment. But this particular poetic fancy is only the most graphic form of the poem's obsession with changes. Ovid names his poem after what is little more than a mythological absurdity; but no metamorphosis in the poem is ever left entirely in the realm of the magical. Magical change is always closely tied to a transforming spirit in the real world of cosmos, society, and human personality. At the same time, no transformation in the poem is ever allowed to be completely "real," scientific, or logical: all changes in the world, whether natural or mysterious, have an element of magic. The extraordinary fascination that the *Metamorphoses* has exercised over two millennia can be traced in large part to this paradox: it proves the natural world magical and the magical world natural. It ought to come as no surprise, then, that for so many ages this was the poet's poem, because the paradox that Ovid takes as his main expression is at the heart of all poetry.

1. The Book of Changes

We have already discussed the artist Arachne, whose aesthetic of flowing juxtapositions confronts the monumental aesthetic of the stern goddess Minerva; and we have already suggested that Ovid is of the Arachnid party. The metamorphic order of things is revealingly introduced with the opening words of the poem:

> In nova fert animus mutatas dicere formas
> corpora; di, coeptis (nam vos mutastis et illas)
> adspirate meis primaque ab origine mundi
> ad mea perpetuum deducite tempora carmen! [1.1–4]¹

(My mind is bent to tell of bodies changed into new forms. Ye gods, for you yourselves have wrought the changes, breathe on these my undertakings, and bring down my song in unbroken strains from the world's very beginning even unto the present time.)

Nova corpora encloses *mutatas formas*, the gods have changed themselves as well as the world, and the poem is itself one of the creations that the gods will change. The tangle of words already speaks to a multiple, various, and changeable universe. Yet balanced against all those changes is a constant and even heroic endeavor: despite the universal world of change, Ovid declares that he will write a *perpetuum carmen*. That is a claim to which he returns with a deeper, perhaps tragic sense at the end, when the notion of anything *perpetuum* has become so doubtful. Still, these opening lines establish two paths that continue throughout the work: constant change and a unified eternal poem. We have little choice but to follow on those paths. To understand the tradition, we must read the poem deeply. That is to say, we must follow the changes but not forget that it is a *perpetuum carmen*. Without a sense of the poem's wholeness, we shall not grasp the metaphor.²

To begin with, however, let us isolate the act of transformation and follow the *nova corpora* and the *mutatas formas* in a few signal instances. Consider the transformation of Lichas, the unfortunate servant who unwittingly gives Hercules the fatal shirt of Nessus that Deianira has proffered as a love token. The enraged Hercules throws Lichas off a precipice and in midair Lichas becomes a rock that stands to this day in the Euboean sea. This magic change is justified by much logic of cause and effect. The change is, for instance, compared with a familiar process in nature:

> utque ferunt imbres gelidis concrescere ventis,
> inde nives fieri, nivibus quoque molle rotatis
> astringi et spissa glomerari grandine corpus . . . [9.220–22]

(And as drops of rain are said to congeal beneath the chilling blast and change to snow, then whirling snowflakes condense to a soft mass and finally are packed in frozen hail . . .)

Ovid frequently uses similes as protometamorphoses, rhetorically pointing out the direction in which an individual will literally travel when his transformation takes place.[3] Here the simile amounts to a scientific explanation for the change. The emphasis in the lines quoted above is on a gradual process within nature that is set against the violence and suddenness of the apparent action here—both Hercules' throw and Lichas's transformation.[4]

Another form of justification for the metamorphosis is psychological (or even psychosomatic) rather than meteorological. Hercules first spots Lichas "trepidum latitantem rupe cavata" (9.211: "cowering with fear and hiding beneath a hollow rock"), a description that begins the little story with a telling juxtaposition of the servant's mental state with his ultimate physical condition. The stoniness of the rock begins to have a metaphoric relation to Lichas's fear, a relation that the gradual process of transformation will elucidate. Once we are aware of the parallel between emotional state and shape, the terms of description take on the force of puns. Fear makes him *pallidus* (pale) and he *induruit* (becomes stiff), but just as his form is changing, so the implications of these terms are becoming attributes of rock. Finally Ovid finishes the transformation with a description that is true to both anatomy and emotion:

> exsanguemque metu nec quicquam umoris habentem
> in rigidos versum silices prior edidit aetas. [9.224–25]

(bloodless with fear, his vital moisture dried, he changed, old tradition says, to flinty rock.)

Exsanguis metu, a common, rather hyperbolic metaphor suggesting paleness, becomes literally true since the actual definition of rock is based on lightness of color and the absence of vital fluids that sustain animal life.

The final cause of Lichas's transformation is the etiological explanation of a particular rock:

> nunc quoque in Euboico scopulus brevis eminet alto
> gurgite et humanae servat vestigia formae,
> quem, quasi sensurum, nautae calcare verentur,
> appellantque Lichan. [9.226–29]

(Even to this day in the Euboean sea a low rock rises from the waves, keeping the semblance of a human form; this rock, as if it were sentient, the sailors fear to tread on, and they call it Lichas.)

Metamorphosis is as much a beginning as an end. The transformation here is necessary to explain the birth of an object and a legend. But Ovid goes beyond the *aitia* of his predecessors in the field.[5] He takes great pains to maintain the multiplicity of the metamorphosed object. The mystery of that rock in the Euboean sea which so unsettles the sailors is precisely that it contains Lichas's personality and destiny within it, as though still alive. So Ovid has turned magical metamorphosis into natural process and has turned a natural object into a piece of mysterious immanence.

Lichas is defined entirely in the moment of his metamorphosis, but we can observe a different type of transformation in the far greater change that takes place in Hecuba. Once queen of Troy and mother of a large brood, she is reduced to being mother of merely two children; one is sacrificed by the Greeks and when the other is killed by King Polymestor, Hecuba destroys him in a frenzied rage and gradually turns into a vicious, barking dog. In fact, Ovid's description of the change is a good deal less sensationalist than the plot summary sounds:

> clade sui Thracum gens inritata tyranni
> Troada telorum lapidumque incessere iactu
> coepit, at haec missum rauco cum murmure saxum
> morsibus insequitur rictuque in verba parato
> latravit, conata loqui. [13.565–69]

> (The Thracians, incensed by their king's disaster, began to set upon the Trojan with shafts and stones. But she, with hoarse growls, bit at the stones they threw and, though her jaws were set for words, barked when she tried to speak.)

Ovid never goes any further than this to assert that Hecuba became a dog.

There is, then, scarcely anything magical about Hecuba's transformation: rather it follows an emotional logic that runs through the whole of her story. At the opening of the vignette she has lost Troy and lost her penultimate child, but she remains powerful, articulate, and self-possessed, offering a forty-line lamentation full of grace and fine cadence. The murder of the last child accounts for the real beginning of Hecuba's transformation. The first metamorphoses come through simile and literal description of emotional change:

> Troades exclamant, obmutuit illa dolore,
> et pariter vocem lacrimasque introrsus obortas
> devorat ipse dolor, duroque simillima saxo
> torpet. [13.538–41]

> (The Trojan women shrieked at the sight, but she was dumb with grief; her very grief engulfed her powers of speech, her rising tears. Like a hard rock, immovable she stood.)

The repeated *dolor* is the real cause of metamorphosis, and it produces changes that amount to the destruction—literally, consumption—of her personality. Her voice, which has been her essential quality, is now silenced; indeed, Ovid never quotes her again. The comparison to a rock is almost a literal metamorphosis because *torpeo* suggests a stiffening very much like the fate of Lichas. The rock betokens the most extreme possible loss of humanity, and this is not the last we will hear of it.[6] The image of self-consumption in *devorat* begins to convey the futility of Hecuba's condition.

The queen has not lost herself entirely, though, because she must still avenge the crime done against her son. She is compared to a lioness whose cub has been stolen, and she is further reduced to an essential principle of vengeance: "poenaeque in imagine tota est" (13.546: "and was wholly absorbed in the punishment her imagination pictured"). This is a phrase Ovid uses more than once in his poem. Here, as elsewhere, it suggests an aesthetic reduction: her emotional state is on the verge of being so extreme that she is almost nothing but a poetic image of that state. The climax directly preceding the literal metamorphosis (if there is one) is a Bacchic orgy of violence, in which Hecuba and the Trojan women commit extremely gory revenges upon Polymestor. This proves that she is *poenae in imagine tota*. With her reduction to obsessive, animalistic inarticulateness, her transformation to barking dog has been made before the fact. The dog biting at the stones is a sign of complete futility, an individual attacking its own violence and its own metamorphic stoniness. When we consider the parallel case of Niobe and the fact that Hecuba has been *simillima saxo*, it becomes clear that she is both the dog and the stones. The image also stresses the close relation between the organs that speak and those that bite. Violence and inarticulateness have coalesced in the course of Hecuba's human transformations; so it is particularly appropriate that she *latravit* and that her speech be turned into *rauco murmure*. All these oral activities are futile and dehumanized. The story ends, like the Lichas story, with a mysterious transformation of the "modern" landscape. Cynossema ("sign of the dog") is still named after Hecuba, and her howling (*ululavit*) can still be heard there.

Often the business of metamorphosis, then, is to make flesh of metaphors. Between old and new form there may be a variety of logical, pseudo-logical, or illogical connections. The apparently close connections justify the metamorphosis, and these in turn lead the reader to understand the meaning of remoter connections that the poet chooses to postulate. We meet the beautiful red-haired centauress Ocyrhoe just after her father, Chiron, has been given care of the infant Aesculapius by the infant's father, Apollo. The appearance of the child provokes Ocyrhoe into an outburst of prophetic passion. After intricately plotting the futures of both Aesculapius and her father, the girl is suddenly halted, as human speech fails her:

> mallem nescisse futura!
> iam mihi subduci facies humana videtur,
> iam cibus herba placet, iam latis currere campis
> impetus est: in equam cognataque corpora vertor.
> tota tamen quare? pater est mihi nempe biformis.　　　[2.660–64]

(I would that I had never known the future. Now my human shape seems to be passing. Now grass pleases me as food; now I am eager to race around the broad pastures. I am turning into a mare, my kindred shape. But why completely? Surely my father is half human.)

The transformation is from the human to the beastly, but the comic grotesquerie of the situation arises from the apparent interpenetration of the two identities. The physical interpenetration arises from the fact that Ocyrhoe has all along been a centaur, so that she is half beastly to begin with.[7] The spiritual interpenetration results from the continuation of her human consciousness even when all other faculties have turned equine. In this case metamorphosis images forth the incongruity of an organism that has landed absurdly askew in the hierarchies of creation.

When Ovid moves out of the girl's consciousness and actually describes her physical change, he continues to emphasize the combination of congruity and incongruity that characterizes her transformation. Her furious prophetic loquacity and her whinnying are all too similar. The size of her mouth and neck enlarges during her metamorphosis; but anyone who has so insistently paid attention to other people's business and talked about it so much has clearly had a figuratively large mouth and neck all along. Within this comic framework, Ovid creates a tale of dissociation. He begins with a composite creature, the centaur, and uses his narrative to demonstrate the distinct identities of the two components, the human and the beastly. At the moment when Ocyrhoe wants to eat grass but also has the mental awareness to speculate on that desire, she is in effect contrasting the human and the beastly by distinguishing consciousness from form. The beastly component is appetitive, instinctual, uncontrollable, while the human is rational and free. The comedy of Ocyrhoe's little soliloquy arises from just this dissociation: the beastly component satisfies its appetite while the human helplessly speculates upon it. Beyond the human and the beastly, which are so strangely yoked, there is also the visionary, since the girl is not only a centaur but also a prophetess, and the immediate occasion for her transformation is an onrush of prophetic madness. As it turns out, the prophetic voice is more beastly than rational; but all voices are combined in the biform metamorphosed creature.[8]

I close this survey of individual metamorphoses with an episode that demonstrates the great cosmic range that can be covered by a single transformation story: the first metamorphosis in the poem, that of Lycaon. In this story Ovid weaves together a remarkable variety of explanations for and analogues to the magical act. Lycaon commits the greatest conceivable offense at one stroke against both the divine and the human orders of creation by refusing to recognize the divinity of Jupiter and by serving the god half-dead human flesh to eat. Jupiter strikes the whole household with his thunderbolt. The first result, as with Lichas, combines psychology and magical metamorphosis: "territus ipse fugit nactusque silentia ruris / exululat frustraque loqui conatur" (1.232–33: "the king himself flies in terror and, gaining the silent fields, howls aloud, attempting in vain to speak"). The king's reaction makes logical sense as a terrified response to the thunderbolt; but crucial elements in the Ovidian definition of humanity are leaving him even this early in the transformation. The power of speech gives way to *exululare*, a term widely associated with the irrational howling of the Bacchants.[9]

But these early changes are fulfilled in a concrete metamorphosis that goes far beyond the changes in Lichas or Hecuba:

> ab ipso
> colligit os rabiem solitaeque cupidine caedis
> utitur in pecudes et nunc quoque sanguine gaudet.
> in villos abeunt vestes, in crura lacerti:
> fit lupus et veteris servat vestigia formae;
> canities eadem est, eadem violentia vultus,
> idem oculi lucent, eadem feritatis imago est.   [1.233–39]

(His mouth of itself gathers foam, and with his accustomed greed for blood he turns against the sheep, delighting still in slaughter. His garments change to shaggy hair, his arms to legs. He turns into a wolf, and yet retains some traces of his former shape. There is the same grey hair, the same fierce face, the same gleaming eyes, the same picture of beastly savagery.)

The emphasis in these lines is upon the absolute continuity of Lycaon's character as it proceeds through metamorphosis. *Ab ipso* reminds us that Jupiter does not produce the rabid wolf; the god merely hurls his thunderbolt, and Lycaon himself takes care of the rest because his own character is so intrinsically rabid and wolflike from the start. *Solitae* and *quoque* reinforce this sense of continuity, which is spelled out by "veteris servat vestigia formae." The examples of these preserved *vestigia* all testify to the continuity of Lycaon's personality; and the repetition of *idem* and *eadem* leaves us with no doubt.

What happens here, then, is a complex combination of change and continuity. On the personal level of Lycaon's story, we have a metamorphosis that freezes in physical form the spirit that has all along animated an individual of only apparent human shape. If we see the story as both an individual and a generic tale, then we can observe a powerful tension between the flight of Lycaon and the continuity implied by the repeated *idem* and *eadem*. The flight from palace to wilderness represents Lycaon's own wish to escape his civilization, his identity, and his accountability to the gods, but it is paralleled and overwhelmed by the metamorphosis that fixes him in his essential form. Ovid's ruling metaphor enables him to capture at once the enormity of beastly man's distance from his semidivine origins and also the identity between his beastliness and the beastliness of animals. And Ovid is self-conscious about the relation between metaphor and metamorphosis. Early in the story we are told that Lycaon is *notus feritate* (1.198); the last we hear of his metamorphosis is that he is *feritatis imago* (1.239). The artistic effect of metamorphosis is to transform human identities into images.

In delineating Lycaon's fate, Ovid draws upon folk traditions concerning the metamorphic diseases of lycanthropy and hydrophobia. Each of these is allusively woven into the fabric of the story. Many of the traditional beliefs surrounding Lycaon and lycanthropy had quite the opposite thrust from Ovid's, suggesting that Lycaon is the original exemplar of piety but that he went too far in sacrificing an infant to Zeus and so was transformed into a wolf.[10] The traditional reading of this first human sacrifice is powerfully paradoxical; it seems to retain some sanctity even as it becomes an emblem of murder. As a holy act, this sacrifice gives rise to a form of metamorphosis that the Romans tend to associate with the mysteries and miracles of the Hellenistic east. Pliny narrates a fable about which he is pointedly skeptical ("mirum est quo procedat Graeca credulitas!"). It seems that among the clan of the Antaei in Arcadia each year a person chosen by lot is required to swim across a desolate lake; arriving at the other side, he is transformed into a wolf and lives as such for nine years. If (and only if) he refrains from human flesh during that time, he will be retransformed into a man. Pliny also tells of the worship of Zeus Lycaeus during which a priest cannibalized a sacrificial child and was transformed into a wolf for ten years following, after which he could resume his human form and live a normal life.[11] The magical side of the metamorphic tradition is very fully set out here. The story of the Antaei clearly goes back to the Lycaon story: the original bloodguilt must be punished and purified. Transformation accomplishes both of these through a sort of miracle but only works if the metamorphosed wolf purifies himself by not, in his animal identity, tasting any human blood. Pliny's two stories together testify to a magic contagion that unites the sacrificed child, the wolvish form, and the god that is being propitiated. Lycaon's original piety, which induced him to sacrifice the infant, is finally proven not misguided but mysterious. It results immediately in severe punishment, but in the long run it produces purification and magic rebirth—just so long as the wolf abstains from human blood, or, in the other story, the priest fails to taste the human flesh he has sacrificed.

Ovid's story may not be fraught with all the complications of this tradition, but surely the poet is alluding to an ancient story of metamorphosis associated with myths of origin and holy rituals. When Ovid's Lycaon sacrifices the Molossian hostage as part of testing Jupiter's divinity, and when he then serves the body up to the god, he is in fact enacting a parody of propitiation. In the traditional holy act, the celebrant believes in the god and tries to bring about his presence by means of a sacrifice, hoping to arrive at some contagious union between the god and the body of the sacrificed victim. Here the act is physicalized; the priest is a doubter, but the god is literally present, and the priest means actually to serve up the victim to the god, thereby assuring a literal digestive union between the two. The important distinction (as we saw in Pliny's story) between sacrifice and cannibalism is blurred, and Lycaon is by implication defying the gods by imputing cannibalistic motives to the sacrificial act.

All these distinctions are at the heart of Ovid's mystery. He is persistently trying to image forth the mysterious contagions among the elements of creation. Holy acts and beastly acts are dangerously similar. When the individual breaks down the conceptual boundaries between them, order is destroyed. Once he imputes beastliness to the gods, Lycaon brings that charge upon himself. Ovid transforms the figure whom Preller calls "der mythische Urheber des Gottesdienstes"[12] into a Bacchant whose *exululare* is nothing but a case of rabies. That degeneration of prophetic fury not only unites Lycaon with the mad dogs who give rabies,[13] but it also contributes to the human side of the story by suggesting that Lycaon is a hydrophobic, an individual driven to desperate flight and who abhors the very element which he needs to stay alive. The disease recapitulates the relationship we observed between Lycaon's flight from his own identity and the fixity with which Jupiter forces him to be the image of that identity. In fact, it opens out on to a whole universe of human changes.

2. Metamorphosis and the Nature of Things

Had the title not already been used, Ovid might have called his poem *De Rerum Natura*. Ovid always maintains among his primary purposes a concern with how things came to be the way they are and how we are to understand the world that has been given us. The *Metamorphoses* is a grandly cosmological work that attempts to bridge all the orders of creation by understanding heaven and earth, animate and inanimate beings, physical laws, and human emotions through a series of parallel explanations. Ovid's universal explanation is more complex and elusive than that of Lucretius, and Ovid attempts to explain a wider variety of phenomena; but the parallel with the earlier poet points to the great seriousness with which the *Metamorphoses* faces the real world, even amidst its wit and humor. In myths of their origins Ovid finds the nature of things as well as a physical description that can embody this nature in a poetic fable. Such tales of origin via transformation bequeath to all cosmological poetry a metamorphic explanation of the way things are.

The multifaceted process by which Ovid leads us from chaos through the flood and the fire—that is, all those events that define the shape and structure of the world we know—is, in fact, a series of metamorphoses or at least a creation of the preconditions for metamorphosis.[14] Chaos itself is a kind of warring singularity, a state of indifferent flux sharply distinguished from the concreteness of metamorphic change:

> utque erat et tellus illic et pontus et aer,
> sic erat instablis tellus, innabilis unda,
> lucis egens aer; nulli sua forma manebat,
> obstabatque aliis aliud, quia corpore in uno
> frigida pugnabant calidis, umentia siccis,
> mollia cum duris, sine pondere, habentia pondus.　　[1.15–20]

(And, though there was both land and sea and air, no one could tread that land, or swim that sea; and the air was dark. No form of things remained the same; all objects were at odds, for within one body cold things strove with hot, and moist with dry, soft things with hard, things having weight with weightless things.)

More important than chaos itself is the grid or matrix whose absence defines chaos. Ovid describes chaos by negation, reminding us of the firm categories of the cosmos with no fewer than five syntactical series: *mare, terra, caelum* appear (sometimes with synonyms) three times; there is an analogous series in which *caelum* is subdivided into sun and moon; and the section closes with another catalogue of orderly physical qualities. This cosmology of layers is the precondition for a metamorphic universe because it establishes the orders among which the flow of transformations will take place.

History, then, is a series of skewed travels. In the golden age, "nondum caesa suis, peregrinum ut viseret orbem, / montibus in liquidas pinus descenderat undas" (1.94–95: "not yet had the pine-tree, felled on its native mountains, descended hence on the watery plain to visit other lands"). During the iron age, on the other hand, "quaeque prius steterant in montibus altis, / fluctibus ignotis exsultavere carinae" (1.133–34: "and keels of pine, which long had stood upon high mountain-sides, now leaped insolvently over unknown waves"). Wooden boats, we are reminded, are metamorphosed trees; they stand for an unnatural transfer from the land order to the sea order. The traditional criticism of post-golden-age man for wanting to travel is here captured in a metamorphic image.[15] Other disasters are described in the same terms. The flood is an act of metamorphosis because it erases distinctions:

> Occupat hic collem, cumba sedet alter adunca
> et ducit remos illic, ubi nuper arabat.

. . . .

Nereides, silvasque tenent delphines et altis
incursant ramis agitataque robora pulsant.
nat lupus inter oves, fulvos vehit unda leones,
unda vehit tigres.   [1.293–94, 302–05]

(Here one man seeks a hill-top in his flight; another sits in his
curved skiff, plying the oars where lately he has plowed. . . . The
dolphins invade the woods, brushing against the high branches, and
shake the oak-trees as they knock against them in their course. The
wolf swims among the sheep, while tawny lions and tigers are borne
along by the waves.)

The vignette is frivolous and a bit grotesque, but it is precisely the grotesquerie of cosmological metamorphosis. Again land, sea, and air are con-
founded, and species are transformed by being twisted into the wrong
habitat.

Nor is this metamorphic link between chaos and broken categories
merely used as a physical description. Ovid's vision of order and disorder
has direct spiritual implications. Human nature and society recognize categories of order just as does the physical world: to misunderstand or to
skew these categories is to invite moral chaos. We have already discussed
Lycaon, the arch-criminal whose misdeed is to confound murder and propitiatory sacrifice. We might also note Ovid's more general description of
moral collapse in the iron age:

                non hospes ab hospite tutus,
non socer a genero, fratrum quoque gratia rara est;
inminet exitio vir coniugis, illa mariti,
lurida terribiles miscent aconita novercae,
filius ante diem patrios inquirit in annos.   [1.144–48]

(Guest was not safe from host, nor father-in-law from son-in-law;
even among brothers 'twas rare to find affection. The husband
longed for the death of his wife, she of her husband; murderous
stepmothers brewed deadly poisons, and sons inquired into their fathers' years before the time.)

Again, chaos is a breakdown of expectations among rigid categories. As we
shall see more fully in the middle books of the poem, the categories are
very frequently supplied by family relations.

But metamorphosis and movement among the layers of existence are
by no means always destructive. The creation of man offers a different picture of transformation:

natus homo est, sive hunc divino semine fecit
ille opifex rerum mundi melioris origo,
sive recens tellus seductaque nuper ab alto

aethere cognati retinebat semina caeli.
quam satus Iapeto, mixtam pluvialibus undis,
finxit in effigiem moderantum cuncta deorum. [1.78–83]

(Then man was born: whether the god who made all else, designing
a more perfect world, made man of his own divine substance, or
whether the new earth, but lately drawn away from heavenly ether,
retained still some elements of its kindred sky—that earth which
the son of Iapetus mixed with fresh, running water, and moulded
into the form of the all-controlling gods.)

This is the first clear statement of a principle that underlies the whole of
the poem: that matter is flexible and that new forms of life result from this
flexibility. The first product of this metamorphic geochemistry is man
himself; and Ovid's description of this creation proves that man embraces
earth, sea, and air. Only through metamorphic mixtures among the elements can the creator *fingere* a new form—a word that is precisely apposite to so many magical metamorphoses in the poem.[16] And once the different orders have combined in metamorphosis, the product retains
qualities of all its parent constituents.[17] Within a couple of hundred lines,
Ovid has created what will stand for centuries as the translation of Platonic cosmology, with its lore of the elements and parallels between microcosm and macrocosm, into a poetic form whose dynamic, owing precisely to the flux among the elements and to the relation between micro-
and macrocosm, is metamorphosis.

When we consider that the *Metamorphoses* is the great bible of mythological stories, it is all the more surprising that the account here of cosmic
origins is almost entirely free from mythological—that is, narrative—descriptions. Ovid soon turns, however, to a recreation that is situated on
the human plane. Two great fables in the first books of the poem recreate
the universe: Deucalion and Pyrrha, and Phaethon's ride. Both concern
themselves with the issues of chaos and creation that animate the abstract
Platonic myth. The story of Deucalion and Pyrrha, to put it very simply,
begins in chaos and ends in creation. The most obvious form of chaos is
the flood itself, which, as we have seen, is characterized by the loss of all
distinctions. Just as the flood is a reversion to chaos, so the emptiness that
follows it is a reversion to that period before man was created. But times
have changed. Ovid (significantly) repudiates his earlier description of
man's creation, drawn from the more or less biochemical approach of the
Timaeus, and shifts to the Hesiodic tale of Prometheus's breathing life
into human forms.[18] Deucalion, it must be remembered, is Prometheus's
son, and he longs for the creative days of his father: "o utinam possim
populos reparare paternis / artibus atque animas formatae infundere
terrae!" (1.363–64: "Oh, would that by my father's arts I might restore the
nations and breathe, as did he, the breath of life into the moulded clay").
Prometheus's method of creation is fundamentally nonmetamorphic; it is

a single individual's (literal) inspiration and does not derive from the violent confrontation of different types of matter. But once the age of the giants is past, only a materialist—and metamorphic—kind of creation is possible.

The oracle given to Deucalion and Pyrrha threatens them with the breaking of traditional bonds that betokens results as disastrously chaotic as the flood itself: "ossaque post tergum magnae iactate parentis!" (1.383: "throw behind you the bones of your great mother!"). By a strict constructionist interpretation, they are being asked to treat honored ancestors in an unfitting way; and in response they are torn between obedience to the gods and outrage to their families. Where physical chaos consists in distortions among the elements of the cosmos, moral chaos takes the form of conflicts of interest among the demands placed upon an individual by his various roles as child, parent, sibling, spouse, and so on. But the solution is as metamorphic as the problem. When Deucalion realizes that *parens* is to be taken metaphorically—that the bones of his mother are the stones in the earth—he turns the destructive form of confusion among the elements into a creative one. By understanding the proper connections between themselves and the earth, human beings can create new life.

A whole series of parallels is implicit in Deucalion's interpretation: literal mothers and mother earth, bones and stones, stones and the recreated human race. These parallels are the very basis of which Ovid's poem is made, for when we accept—so early in Book I—the metaphoric flow among separate categories of existence, we are prepared to understand how metamorphosis defines the multiple nature of things. In this case it defines the nature of the human species: "inde genus durum sumus experiensque laborum / et documenta damus qua simus origine nati" (1.414–15: "Hence come the hardness of our race and our endurance of toil; and we give proof from what origin we are sprung"), and the transformation itself tells us that we are what we are because of the flow from gods to giants to men to bones to stones.

But it is the process more than the fact of transformation that characterizes human identity. The first stage involves a very beautiful description of the incipient softness that overcomes the stony form:

saxa . . .
ponere duritiem coepere suumque rigorem
mollirique mora molitaque ducere formam.
mox ubi creverunt naturaque mitior illis
contigit, ut quaedam, sic non manifesta videri
forma potest hominis, sed ut de marmore coeptis
non exacta satis rudibusque simillima signis.   [1.400–06]

(The stones . . . began at once to lose their hardness and stiffness, to grow soft slowly, and softened to take on form. Then, when they had grown in size and become milder in their nature, a certain likeness to the human form, indeed, could be seen, still not very clear, but such as statues just begun out of marble have, not sharply defined, and very like roughly blocked-out images.)

Ovid emphasizes beginnings, transitions, and flow. The coming of softness stands before and as a prerequisite to the development of anthropomorphic shape, which is not yet mentioned. The words for softness and the attendant repetition of the letters *m* and *l* seem to lead us toward *ducere formam*, which plays on the two meanings of *forma*, "form" and "beauty." There is here an implicit natural explanation: the stone is not suddenly transformed by divine power into human shape but must be softened, like a piece of clay, if it is to be changed at all.

Ovid is fascinated by this composite instant because it enables him through the juxtaposition (and identification) of two periods of history to break down a complicated identity into its constituent parts. Such is very much the heritage of metamorphosis: it is an image of simultaneous but divisible multiplicity; and throughout its history it maintains associations with the belief that human identity itself is multiple. The simile of the artist tells us that the poem is just such a multiple creation as is the species. The excitement in being present at the creation, conveyed by frequent repetition of *coepio* in its various forms, can be applied both to the ancient act and to the present poem, which here in Book I is just taking shape out of the sculptor's block of stone. After all, the very first reference to the poem within the poem was as *coeptis meis*. There are also in these lines the beginnings of a definition of human nature based on the metamorphic style of birth, a paradoxical definition based on the interplay between hard and soft. The description of how the damp portions turn to flesh, the solid to bone, and the geological veins to human veins develops the physical side of this very equally balanced process. But stone is not our only parent, for there are also the elements of softness, of art, of transformation itself. Finally, there is the place of Deucalion and Pyrrha, foster parents at least to the human race, since they are responsible for the creation and give the newly formed human beings their sexual identity: "missa viri manibus faciem traxere virorum / et de femineo reparata est femina iactu" (1.412–13: "the stones thrown by the man's hand took on the form of men, and women were made from the stones the woman threw").

Together with Deucalion and Pyrrha, the Phaethon story completes Ovid's basic description of our world and the world of the poem. In many respects the two episodes complement each other: the first deals with the formation of human beings, the second with the formation of heaven and earth; the first proceeds from chaos to order, the second (apparently) from order to chaos; the first is a flood, the second a fire; the first treats human values in an abstract and universal way, the second is concerned with human responses in a very specific case. Yet parallels underlie these differences. Both episodes are based upon the inextricability of violence and creation, and both have at their core that peculiarly Ovidian cosmology by which human values are literally infused into the nature of things.

While nothing in the main action of Phaethon's ride can be called literal metamorphosis, the story does concern the stepwise transformation of the world.[19] Ovid opens Book II with the description of a great work of cosmological art as it is found on the doors to the palace of the Sun, and this ekphrasis is by no means gratuitous in a story that will revisit the cosmos with such a disastrous transforming effect. We have already discussed in the introductory chapter the links between metamorphosis and ekphrasis. Here is a case where ekphrasis is rather connected to stasis.[20] Mulciber's work amounts to a highly symmetrical and ordered representation of the universe, balancing sea, earth, and sky, along with their respective inhabitants, including the very regular placement of sea creatures, earthly geography, and heavenly zodiac. As in Arachne's web, Ovid joins aesthetics with cosmic values: a supremely orderly work of art depicts a peacefully layered cosmos. The poet reverts to the triad of land, sea, and sky, populates each one gracefully, and discourages the viewer from any fear of dangerous interpenetration among them.

The next stage in the transformation of the universe moves us from art to life as Phoebus describes a far more disorderly cosmos in an attempt to dissuade his son from assuming control of the chariot. There is no more talk of order and symmetry here:

> ardua prima via est et qua vix mane recentes
> enituntur equi; medio est altissima caelo,
> unde mare et terras ipsi mihi saepe videre
> fit timor et pavida trepidat formidine pectus;
> ultima prona via est et eget moderamine certo.
>
> . . . .
>
> adde, quod adsidua rapitur vertigine caelum
> sideraque alta trahit celerique volumine torquet.
>
> . . . .
>
> per insidias iter est formasque ferarum!   [2.63–78]

(The first part of the road is steep, up which my steeds in all their morning freshness can scarce make their way. In mid-heaven it is exceeding high, whence to look down on sea and land oft-times causes even me to tremble, and my heart to quake with throbbing fear. The last part of the journey is precipitous, and needs an assured control. . . . Furthermore, the vault of heaven spins round in constant motion, drawing along the lofty stars which it whirls at dizzy speed. . . . Nay, the course lies amid lurking dangers and fierce beasts of prey.)

This is a world of active, conflicting extremes. From the symmetry and immobility of the first picture, we have progressed to an irregular and precipitous atmosphere. Again the poet emphasizes the separate layers of creation, but here they begin to threaten each other. Still, this is merely Phoebus's everyday journey. There is nothing chaotic about this description, merely continuous potential for disorder in the cosmos.

The third stage in the transformation is Phaethon's ride itself. Chaos here goes beyond the mere confusion among the categories or layers of the cosmos: Phaethon's ride threatens the very existence of the categories:

> Quae postquam summum tetigere iacentia tergum,
> exspatiantur equi nulloque inhibente per auras
> ignotae regionis eunt, quaque inpetus egit,
> hac sine lege ruunt altoque subaethere fixis
> incursant stellis rapiuntque per avia currum
> et modo summa petunt, modo per declive viasque
> praecipites spatio terrae propiore feruntur.   [2.201–07]

(When the horses feel these [reins] lying on their backs, they break loose from their course, and, with none to check them, they roam through unknown regions of the air. Wherever their impulse leads them, there they rush aimlessly, knocking against the stars set deep in the sky and snatching the chariot along through uncharted ways. Now they climb up to the top of heaven, and now, plunging head-long down, they course along nearer the earth.)

There is a chilling sense through the ride of a complete absence of order, even that offered by *discordia concors*. The horses take no known path but act lawlessly and randomly.

Finally there is the world that results from Phaethon's ride. This is where we live, a world full of irreparable asymmetries of all kinds:

> Sanguine tum credunt in corpora summa vocato
> Aethiopum populos nigrum traxisse colorem;
> tum facta est Libye raptis umoribus aestu
> arida. . . .
>
> . . . .
>
> et mare contrahitur siccaeque est campus harenae,
> quod modo pontus erat, quosque altum texerat aequor,
> exsistunt montes et sparsas Cycladas augent.   [2.235–38; 262–64]

(It was then, as men think, that the peoples of Aethiopia became black-skinned, since the blood was drawn to the surface of their bodies by the heat. Then also Libya became a desert, for the heat

dried up her moisture. . . . Even the sea shrinks up, and what was
but now a great, watery expanse is a dry plain of sand. The mountains, which the deep sea had covered before, spring forth, and in-
crease the numbers of the scattered Cyclades.)

Phaethon's ride concludes in an etiology, a cosmological explanation for
the often malevolent complexity and incongruity of our world. So we have
taken a path from extreme idealization to a state of tension and danger to a
condition of absolute chaos to a quiescent form of irregularity, in which
nonetheless all passion is spent.

Yet these changes in themselves are not, by any but the loosest definition, metamorphosis. Metamorphic cosmology consists in the infusion of
human personality and destiny into the universe. Deucalion and Pyrrha
gave their own piety, their own love, even their gender to the stone-born
individuals whom they created. Yet their responsibility for the cosmos is
in the end only by interpretation; Phaethon's is by action, an action consisting of a tragic rise and fall.[21] The young man is engaged in a search for
his father that also becomes a dangerous attempt to cross the boundary
between men and gods. So Phaethon's quest is from the start problematic, with his very proper desire to know his father set against his prideful
striving to drive his father's chariot. The boy rejects moderation; and this
cosmological fable is perfectly suited to that issue because the proper path
of the Sun's chariot is understood to be absolutely median:

utque ferant aequos et caelum et terra calores,
nec preme nec summum molire per aethera cursum!
altius egressus caelestia tecta cremabis,
inferius terras; medio tutissimus ibis.   [2.134–37]

(And, that the sky and earth may have equal heat, go not too low,
nor yet direct thy course along the top of heaven; for if thou goest
too high thou wilt burn up the skies, if too low the earth. In the middle is the safest path.)

This advice combines cosmology with an orderly philosophy of living.
Phaethon's refusal to listen to reason demonstrates that he has chosen to
seek unattainable glory. As it turns out, mere humans cannot attain the
heroism that Phaethon seeks. The boy goes against the orders of creation
by trying to draw false bridges between them, and he is subjected, quite
literally, to the immense chasms between these orders. What Phaethon
fails to perceive is precisely the metamorphic lesson in cosmology, that
the cosmos is animated by a great variety of intelligences. What he had
viewed as a solitary act establishing his own identity becomes a great animated struggle among anthropomorphized powers. This is typical of
many of Ovid's stories. Metamorphism, as we have seen, involves a special relation between man and his environment; and one of the important

lessons to be learned from this relationship is that we can never act entirely alone.

At Phaethon's most dismal moment, when the cosmos has turned into complete chaos, he switches to an opposite emotional extreme, abjures all striving and even becomes willing to deny his own father, that is, to dissociate himself from any immortal or heroic identity. He is removed by a thunderbolt, and as he dies, his story is reinterpreted:

> At Phaethon rutilos flamma populante capillos
> volvitur in praeceps longoque per aera tractu
> fertur, ut interdum de caelo stella sereno
> etsi non cecidit, potuit cecidisse videri.
>
> . . . .
>
> HIC SITVS EST PHAETHON CVRRVS AVRIGA PATERNI
> QVEM SI NON TENVIT MAGNIS TAMEN EXCIDIT AVSIS.   [2.319–28]

(But Phaethon, fire ravaging his ruddy hair, is hurled headlong and falls with a long trail through the air; as sometimes a star from the clear heavens, although it does not fall, still seems to fall. . . . The Naiads carve this epitaph upon his stone: Here Phaethon lies: In Phoebus' car he fared, and though he greatly failed, more greatly dared.)

What was prideful and destructive in the young man is now seen as glorious. He succeeds in being joined with the heavens and becomes stellified as a mysterious heavenly body that falls but does not fall—or dies but does not die. The disasters to the Earth aside, Phaethon has proved his tragic worth.

But how can we finally reconcile the personal tragedy with those disasters? Phaethon is responsible for a world full of tensions, extremes, inequities, randomnesses. His ride completes the creation of the world we know and the world in which the poem will take place, producing a multiplicity that is a far cry from the beautiful relief carved on the palace doors. But in his tragic glory we can read a glorious cosmology. The world's multiplicity is precisely parallel to Phaethon's striving: dangerously destructive and yet the only source of transcendent triumph. The multiple universe is the precondition for metamorphosis. Deucalion and Pyrrha began to create this multiplicity as they understood the links between the orders of creation and gave of these links and of themselves to their descendants. But human beings are more than mere emblematic creatures mingling hard and soft. Phaethon's story defines us as potential heroes with heavenly parentage and bold striving but characterized by passion, immoderate desires, and human limitation causing us to fall unheroically to earth. So he bestows on our world his own tragic character. That is an essential definition of metamorphosis whether the individual transformation has taken place or not: Phaethon's story unites his personal identity with the physical shape of the world. Ovid has at once reached the full cosmological definition of his ruling metaphor and of the world that it illuminates.

3. Metamorphosis and the Faces of Divine Power

The world of the *Metamorphoses* is ruled by some forces which, however selfish and willful, are fundamentally intelligible, and at the same time other forces which are mystical, remote, and inexplicable. The first group is personified either by the Olympians or by powerful mortals who are essentially identical to the Olympians. The second group is not, strictly speaking, personified at all. These are not so much gods as presences, mysterious forces implanted in particular parts of the universe or occasionally in some mythic creature. They may originate through an etiological story that is explained to us, or they may be simply a given. Often these forces are connected in some vague or partial way with a particular Olympian; yet this connection fails to capture their full power and resonance. Once Ovid has created the world in the first two books, he devotes the next, approximately equal segment to depicting and defining these more powerful and elusive forces.[22]

We have already described the poem's metamorphism as the attempt to build a bridge between individual human personality and the physical nature of the universe. In cosmological etiologies like the Deucalion or Phaethon stories, the travel on that bridge is always from the individual to the universe: metamorphosis is a way of translating personal qualities into the physical world. But we ought to be aware of significant travel in the opposite direction as well. The mysterious holy powers that Ovid begins to define in the sections treating, say, Cadmus and Bacchus are immanent in creation, either by being physically planted in certain loci or by being implicit in a given human situation. When an individual intrudes (literally or figuratively) upon this immanence, he becomes not the perpetrator but the victim of metamorphosis; his mind or body becomes reshaped after the image of that mysterious divinity. So we have the beginnings of a redefinition of the poem's two main concerns, the significance of the physical world and the universality of transformation. The world is seen as something more than a complex of rational and scientific phenomena: it is a kind of holy conundrum. And metamorphosis, for Ovid and for centuries beyond, becomes an image of that conundrum, representing the working of irrational forces which shape and define human personality even more profoundly than do the stories of creation.

Having said that these mysterious divinities are not precisely personified, I must modify that assertion and say that the figure of Bacchus acts as a partial incarnation of this immanent divinity.[23] He is, even more than his Olympian elders, perhaps the quintessentially metamorphic divinity. To begin with, he is associated with largely natural forces like the cultivation of grain or grapes. This latter association points to a significant form of natural metamorphosis: drunkenness. Yet Ovid's Bacchus is far from being merely the patron saint of inebriation.[24] The natural side of the god, his associations with vegetation and wine, are present in Ovid's depiction, but they do not dominate. The poet uses these natural associations as a bridge to much more mysterious ones; here, too, the history of Bacchus is appropriate. The young god was frequently seen as both the creator and the subject of mysterious transformations. There were many stories about his birth, all involving some wondrous form of double parturition; he is frequently associated with bisexuality, a condition Ovid closely connects with metamorphosis; and several non-Ovidian stories concern his transformation into animal form.[25]

Most important, however, are the transformations he effects. Bacchus has a highly significant place in the *Metamorphoses* because he is the deity responsible for a state of half-prophetic, half-destructive madness. This frenzy is a complex and paradoxical condition: it draws upon the god's associations with nature, because it is a form of drunkenness and a return to primitive animal impulses, and yet it has distinctly supernatural implications because the victims of the frenzy seem to be possessed with a god, and specifically with a god of a nonrational and ecstatic sort.

The transformative power of Bacchus tends to exert itself in an atmosphere of sublime confusion. Reason, intellect, and clarity are overcome by an excess that is associated with the senses and that often finds its verbal expression in a series of excessive terms. Ovid invokes the god in just such a series:

> parent matresque nurusque
> telasque calathosque infectaque pensa reponunt
> turaque dant Bacchumque vocant Bromiumque Lyaeumque
> ignigenamque satumque iterum solumque bimatrem;
> additur his Nyseus indetonsusque Thyoneus
> et cum Lenaeo genialis consitor uvae
> Nycteliusque Eleleusque parens et Iacchus et Euhan,
> et quae praeterea per Graias plurima gentes
> nomina, Liber, habes. [4.9–17]

(The matrons and young wives all obey, put by the weaving and work-baskets, leave their tasks unfinished; they burn incense, calling on Bacchus, naming him also Bromius, Lyaeus, son of the thunderbolt, twice born, child of two mothers; they hail him as Nyseus also, Thyoneus of the unshorn locks, Lenaeus, planter of the joy-giving vine, Nyctelius, father Eleleus, Iacchus, and Euhan, and all the many names besides by which thou art known, O Liber, throughout the towns of Greece.)

Never have so many conjunctions appeared in so few lines. The effect is more than just an exposition of all the god's identities, though that is itself significant in establishing Bacchus as a figure of overwhelming multiplicity. The accretion of terms here has the effect of destroying individual categories. Bacchus's names, personal history, effects, and the cries emitted by his followers are all homogenized by the incantatory repetition of terms and conjunctions.[26] The effect is metamorphic because the incantation brings on a condition in which individual categories begin to lose their identity. Ovid not only erases the boundaries between individual aspects of Bacchus; he also obscures the division between the god and his followers.

The series that destroys its own terms is frequently used in connection with Bacchus. The basis of the series is nearly always the senses. Pentheus (3.533–37) disparages the worshippers of Bacchus in another verbal series full of sensuous overload. The Minyades (4.391–93) are punished for their blasphemy by a similar glut of noise and smell. And, most dramatically, the destruction of Orpheus begins with the overwhelming of the singer's music by the noises of the Bacchants:

>   sed ingens
> clamor et infracto Berecyntia tibia cornu
> tympanaque et plausus et Bacchei ululatus
> obstrepuere sono citharae.   [11.15–18]

(But the huge uproar of the Berecynthian flutes, mixed with discordant horns, the drums, and the breast-beatings and howlings of the Bacchanals, drowned the lyre's sound.)

The senses become the means by which metamorphic flexibility can enter the human personality. Once this flexibility has entered, then all clear categories are threatened. Not only do the senses blend into each other, but so do single individuals, moral categories, the two sexes, social classes, and parts of the world. Hence the passions of Bacchism, the ascendancy of the female principle, the bisexuality, the sense of primitive Eastern rites being imposed on the West, and the significant implication that Bacchism unites all sorts and conditions of men and women: "turba ruit, mixtaeque viris matresque nurusque / vulgusque proceresque ignota ad sacra feruntur" (3.529–30: "the people rush out of the city in throngs, men and women, old and young, nobles and commons, all mixed together, and hasten to celebrate the new rites").

Beyond these forces of sense and passion, there is also in Bacchus a supernatural force, often of blinding terror. So the myriad Bacchants throughout the poem may be in part responding to primitive natural impulses, but they are also being driven by powers that are unearthly. The birth of the god himself perfectly typifies this combination of forces. At base there is the natural sexual attraction between Jupiter and Semele. But the poor girl is tricked by Juno into asking her lover that he appear to her in all his Olympian splendor. This blinding flash of ultimate divinity remains a crucial element in the heritage of Bacchus. In one sense it betokens the ultimate in ecstatic pleasure, and in another sense it represents the sacred mystery of godhead that no mortal can look upon if he wants to remain sane or alive.[27]

Sensuality and holy mystery are both powerfully transforming forces in Ovid's world, and in the metamorphoses actually effected by Bacchus they are nearly always combined. The priest Acoetes narrates the god's punishment of the sailors who attempted to act against his will. Suddenly their ship is absolutely stationary: "stetit aequore puppis / haud aliter, quam si siccum navale teneret" (3.660–61: "the ship stands still upon the waters, as if a dry-dock held her"). If this represents a mysterious transfiguration, then the next step in the metamorphosis suggests the triumph of nature: "inpediunt hederae remos nexuque recurvo / serpunt et gravidis distinguunt vela corymbis" (3.664–65: "but ivy twines and clings about the oars, creeps upward with many a back-flung, catching fold, and decks the sails with heavy, hanging clusters"). The transformation of the sailors themselves follows this pattern. They are afflicted with a mysterious madness, but then they are transformed into sporting fishes whose joyous frolics perfectly embody the Bacchic principle in nature. We find exactly the same combination of nature and mystery in the punishment of the blasphemous Minyades. Their artificial tapestry is turned into the fabric of nature herself, with vines, grape leaves, and clusters of fruit. But the spinners themselves are punished by otherworldly apparitions, "saevarum simulacra . . . ferarum" (4.404). Bacchism becomes a powerful, and composite, force, a fusion between the natural world of familiar transformations, like those of vegetation and human sexuality, and an unearthly realm where transformations are terrible and mysterious.

Yet for the very reason that Bacchus—along with the whole otherworldly realm he represents—is a transforming rather than a transformed deity, we cannot speak of this power independently of the mortals who meet it and are transformed. For Bacchus in particular the encounter is most particularly female. Bacchism is associated with passionate love and with extremes of emotion, often quite specifically madness and grief. It nearly always deals in excess and violence. It is inexorable and powerful, highly dangerous, but not entirely negative. In Book III Pentheus is rightfully destroyed because he refuses to recognize its power; in Book XI Orpheus is wrongly destroyed because Bacchic feminine hysteria has gone out of control, so that the harmonious and measured songs of the great singer are literally drowned out by the primitive noise of the Maenads; in this case Bacchus must himself punish the women. Between and beyond these two points, there is a sequence of powerful but deranged women (e.g., Ino, Procne, Medea, Byblis, Myrrha) who are implicitly or explicitly operating under Bacchus's aegis. They translate the god's metamorphic power into the context of human action. Their lives are linked with transformation through the natural and the holy significations of the wine-god.

Mysterious divine power of a transforming kind is not by any means limited to Bacchus. The power is often unnamable, and the focus of Ovid's account is not on the divine cause but on the mortal effect. In Books III and IV he tells a sequence of stories, only a few involving Bacchus, which define divinity as it confronts mortals with the blinding flash of change. Effecting a transition between Bacchus and these Theban mortals is the briefly described figure of Tiresias, harbinger and prophet of Bacchus, who brings the news of the god to Cadmus's grandson Pentheus. The vignette that introduces Tiresias bears in miniature many of the most significant symbols that Ovid associates with divinity:

> Venus huic erat utraque nota.
> nam duo magnorum viridi coeuntia silva
> corpora serpentum baculi violaverat ictu
> deque viro factus (mirabile) femina septem
> egerat autumnos; octavo rursus eosdem
> vidit, et "est vestrae si tanta potentia plagae"
> dixit, "ut auctoris sortem in contraria mutet,
> nunc quoque vos feriam." percussis anguibus isdem
> forma prior rediit, genetivaque venit imago. [3.323–31]

(He knew both sides of love. For once, with a blow of his staff he had outraged two huge serpents mating in the green forest; and, wonderful to relate, from man he was changed into a woman, and in that form spent seven years. In the eighth year he saw the same serpents again and said: "Since in striking you there is such magic power as to change the nature of the giver of the blow, now will I strike you once again." So saying, he struck the serpents and his former state was restored and he became as he had been born.)

Tiresias enters a special landscape where he encounters serpents with mysterious powers whose origins are never explained. Upon these serpents he commits an act of violence, and they turn out to have great metamorphic powers. The serpents were not only sacred but also sexual; and Tiresias' punishment for witnessing their act and violating their sanctified space takes both sexual and sacred form. It is also a mirror metamorphosis. Entwining serpents form a perfect representation of a mirror-image relationship, where gender distinguishes the images on either side of the mirror. Tiresias is turned into his own reflection by the same laws of sexual optics. He becomes himself but also the opposite of himself. Metamorphosis has its origins in an unexplained form of sanctity, its mode is violence, and its result is the expansion of human identity through a mirror image.

It is the special talent of Tiresias to have rather full insight into what has happened to him. Unlike some of the other figures who follow this paradigm, Tiresias comes to control the metamorphic power that has overtaken him. By reconfronting the serpents and effecting the return change himself, he succeeds in coming back from the world of the looking-glass. He becomes the reflection of his own reflection—which is to say, himself again. He is not identical to this pretransformed self because that self has been irrevocably expanded; and the hallmarks of that expansion are his omnisexuality and his capacity to be a holy visionary. So the two final transformations of Tiresias, brought about not by the serpents but by the king and queen of the gods, are part of the whole experience: he is blinded because he has observed (and even violated) a sacred space, and he is given prophetic powers because he has in fact become the equivalent of the holy serpents who set the whole process into motion.

The story of Cadmus, which introduces this theogonic section of the poem, uses many of the same symbols as the Tiresias story. Cadmus, too, sees a mysterious serpent in a sacred setting, he does violence to the serpent, and ultimately he is transformed into his opposite, a serpent who is seen as parallel to the beast that Cadmus destroyed and who will also bear a strong resemblance to the serpents that Tiresias observed.[28] Cadmus is above all a founder, and, as befits a tale of origins, his story casts the issues in a primitivist mode. It begins with numerous images of innocence. Cadmus must found a new land, and Apollo's oracle instructs him to follow a heifer who has never submitted to the yoke. The virginal heifer appears to have a perfectly clear symbolic relationship to the virgin land. But the purity is sullied, or at least complicated, almost immediately. Cadmus very properly elects to make a thankful sacrifice to Jove, and for this purpose he seeks fresh water. What his men come upon is a sacred place:

silva vetus stabat nulla violata securi,
et specus in media virgis ac vimine densus
efficiens humilem lapidum conpagibus arcum
uberibus fecundas aquis.   [3.28–31]

(There was a primeval forest there, scarred by no axe; and in its midst a cave thick set about with shrubs and pliant twigs. With well-fitted stones it fashioned a low arch, whence poured a full-welling spring.)

So far the links seem to be clear: the heavenly oracle has made use of an innocent natural figure to lead the men to a similarly virgin territory that is both natural and holy. Yet in this spot dwells a repulsively ugly and poisonous serpent. The presence of this beast redefines the elements in the story. Holy mystery is no longer equated with virginity and benevolence but with corruption and unmotivated violence.

Virginity and violence are similarly brought together in the sowing of the dragon's teeth, which Cadmus is directed to collect once he has slain the beast. The teeth themselves seem to embody the venom of the monster, and yet they are said to signal the origin of a great nation. They become the agents of a complex form of metamorphosis. Cadmus becomes a farmer: "ut presso sulcum patefecit aratro, / spargit humi iussos, mortalia semina, dentes" (3.104–05: "having opened up the furrows with his deep-sunk plow, he sows in the ground the teeth as he is bid, a man-producing seed"). The virgin land is being violated by the plow and by the teeth of the serpent; yet through this act comes the birth of new individuals. The Thebans are seedlings—so the metamorphic relationship suggests—but we are not allowed to forget the violence of the "blossom" from which these seeds have fallen, for instead of appearing as tender little shoots, they are violent armed men. As they grow out of the ground in complete battle dress, they force us back to the same question raised by the heifer and the serpent: do the transformations of civilization destroy innocence, or is corruption built into the (apparently) virgin land?

The story of origins posits a profound and mysterious confrontation between the civilizing human being and the earth. Cadmus's personal story involves a similar confrontation. He meets the serpent as an absolute antagonist, dressed for battle like a Hercules saving the human race from a predator. But as soon as he finally destroys the beast, their connection is redefined:

> vox subito audita est; neque erat cognoscere promptum,
> unde, sed audita est: "quid, Agenore nate, peremptum
> serpentem spectas? et tu spectabere serpens."
> ille diu pavidus pariter cum mente colorem
> perdiderat, gelidoque comae terrore rigebant.   [3.96–100]

(Suddenly a voice sounds in his ears. He cannot tell whence it comes, but he hears it saying, "Why, O son of Agenor, dost thou gaze on the serpent thou hast slain? Thou too shalt be a serpent for men to gaze on." Long he stands there, with quaking heart and pallid cheeks, and his hair rises up on end with chilling fear.)

The serpent becomes a mirror, since Cadmus is now directed to look upon it as a reflection of himself. The description is primarily visual, and the language even uses chiastic mirroring. If Cadmus is the serpent, then he is partly the holy emissary and partly the bringer of violence and corruption.

Ovid does not explicate the relation between Cadmus's identity and the complexities of the serpent, but he shows us how metamorphosis is, at its deepest level, a transfiguration of the self, a kind of mystic union by which heaven and earth are present in a single individual. When, at the end of his life and after so many misfortunes to his family, Cadmus fulfills the prophecy of his own transformation, the change does not come as a punishment from without but as the result of a prayer by Cadmus himself. The drive toward realizing the serpentine identity has been implanted in Cadmus; but, when it comes, the parallel with the original serpent is incomplete because Cadmus and Harmonia are loving and peaceful serpents. The tormented destiny of Thebes has purged them of the venom that is the origin of their people. Indeed Cadmus's problems with mysterious divinity and sacrilege, with transfigured identity and a mirrorlike self are precisely the heritage of Thebes. Every major figure in this section of the poem, Tiresias, Semele, Actaeon, Pentheus, along with earlier ancestral figures like Lycaon and Callisto and the future (surprisingly) unmentioned figure of Oedipus, experiences a version of the same story. It is Ovid who has focused these traditional stories on the mysterious metamorphoses of divinity and the self.

The story of Cadmus finally concerns the redefinition of human identity as a multiple thing, one that (serpentlike) contains mysterious connections with divinity and that (mirrorlike) reflects back upon itself and upon the world. But only fitfully does Cadmus become aware of his redefined self. The story of Cadmus's grandson Actaeon uses the same elements to bring about great psychological awareness of the metamorphosed (and thus redefined) self.[29] Actaeon's "serpent" is the goddess Diana, who is placed in the center of, once again, a *locus amoenus*:

> Vallis erat piceis et acuta densa cupressu,
> nomine Gargaphie succinctae sacra Dianae,
> cuius in extremo est antrum nemorale recessu
> arte laboratum nulla: simulaverat artem
> ingenio natura suo; nam pumice vivo
> et levibus tofis nativum duxerat arcum;
> fons sonat a dextra tenui perlucidus unda,
> margine gramineo patulos incinctus hiatus.   [3.155–62]

(There was a vale in that region, thick grown with pine and cypress with their sharp needles. 'Twas called Gargaphie, the sacred haunt of high-girt Diana. In its most secret nook there was a well-shaded grotto, wrought by no artist's hand. But Nature by her own cunning had imitated art; for she had shaped a native arch of the living rock and soft tufa. A sparkling spring with its slender stream babbled on one side and widened into a pool girt with grassy banks.)

When we add to this description the fact that Diana's nymphs will surround and protect the goddess, we have a picture not only of a sacred but also of a secret place, fortified against human intrusion. The place must be fortified because the goddess herself is not. By sheer accident, Ovid suggests, Actaeon slips through the fortifications and glimpses the naked goddess. This she takes to be an attack upon her in much the same sense that Cadmus and Tiresias attack their sacred serpents, and from this attack there is no turning back.[30] Actaeon and Diana are both hunters, and so, in perceiving the naked goddess, the young man is looking in a sort of mirror and seeing a transfigured, sacred form of his own identity.

When he looks directly at the unshielded brightness of this numinous version of himself, Actaeon shatters his identity and multiplies it. Part of the metamorphosis is the implicit equation between Actaeon and Diana. This equation—of Actaeon with the holy form of himself as hunter—inexorably brings about the complementary equation, of Actaeon with the beastly form of himself as hunter, the stag whom he has been hunting. Yet the most powerful change is neither on the sublime nor on the beastly level but rather inside Actaeon's psyche. Diana and the stag are both mirror images of the young hunter; but more than these Ovid emphasizes the fact that what Actaeon sees in the mirror after his transformation is for the first time a sense of his own identity:

additus et pavor est: fugit Autonoeius heros
et se tam celerem cursu miratur in ipso.
ut vero vultus et cornua vidit in unda,
"me miserum!" dicturus erat: vox nulla secuta est!
ingemuit: vox illa fuit, lacrimaeque per ora
non sua fluxerunt; mens tantum pristina mansit.

· · · · · · · · · · · · · · · · · · · ·

ille fugit per quae fuerat loca saepe secutus,
heu! famulos fugit ipse suos. clamare libebat:
"Actaeon ego sum: dominum cognoscite vestrum!"
verba animo desunt.   [3.198–203; 228–31]

(And last of all she planted fear within his heart. Away in flight goes Autonoe's heroic son, marvelling to find himself so swift of foot. But when he sees his features and his horns in a clear pool, "Oh, woe is me!" he tries to say; but no words come. He groans—the only speech he has—and tears course down his changeling cheeks. Only his mind remains unchanged. . . . He flees over the very ground where he has oft-times pursued; he flees (the pity of it!) his own faithful hounds. He longs to cry out: "I am Actaeon! Recognize your own master!" But words fail his desire.)

By being metamorphically separated from himself, he discovers himself. The transformation has turned Actaeon into subject and object at once, into victim and human perceiver. His identity has been multiplied and diversified not only by his equivalences with other beings but also by the creation of his consciousness as an entity almost completely separate from any of his physical forms.

The climax of the story comes when his consciousness has been acutely distanced from his shape. He hears his companions calling him and regretting his absence, but, unable to respond, he awaits the onslaught of his own hounds. Actaeon's consciousness exists as a separate entity at this moment in the story, helpless as it oversees his miserable fate. The secret that he witnessed when he saw Diana bathing is the secret of self-consciousness. Metamorphosis becomes a means of creating self-consciousness because it establishes a tension between identity and form, and through this tension the individual is compelled to look in the mirror. Cadmus only began to develop this self-consciousness: he heard the voice telling him that the serpent was a mirror, but he could not grasp the fact. As a result, the whole Theban destiny becomes a working out of that problem of self-awareness. Actaeon experiences the full vision, but he pays with his life.[31]

It is important to point out that the various mirrors in these stories are as much metamorphoses as are the animal forms with which the tales end. In the first place, the mirror image for Tiresias or Cadmus or Actaeon has a metamorphic relation to its subject: both exist simultaneously, just as the different forms of a creature in the midst of metamorphosis exist simultaneously. Yet while the mirror image is an essential (and often savagely debased) metamorphic equivalent of oneself, it also represents a symbolic or actual link with the mysterious powers that rule the universe, for the mirror always has an element of the numinous. This double function of the mirror—and what object could be more appropriate for double functions?—applies by extension to virtually all the poem's metamorphoses. From the werewolfism of Lycaon to the apotheosis of the emperor Augustus, transformation always succeeds in capturing the human essence of the subject and at the same time in filling us with uncomprehending wonder at the immanence and intimacy of otherworldly powers. Perhaps this is why the story of Actaeon is one of the paradigmatic episodes in the *Metamorphoses*: the central figure is perfectly balanced by his two mirror images: Diana, who epitomizes his link to the divine, and the stag, who is his punished, transformed self.

These stories culminate in the tale of an ill-fated youth who, like Cadmus, Tiresias, and Actaeon, has a vision in a holy setting:

fons erat inlimis, nitidis argenteus undis,
quem neque pastores neque pastae monte capellae
contigerant aliudve pecus, quem nulla volucris
nec fera turbarat nec lapsus ab arbore ramus;
gramen erat circa, quod proximus umor alebat,
silvaque sole locum passura tepescere nullo.   [3.407–12]

(There was a clear pool with silvery bright water, to which no shepherds ever came, or she-goats feeding on the mountainside, or any
other cattle; whose smooth surface neither bird nor beast nor falling
bough ever ruffled. Grass grew all around its edge, fed by the water
near, and a coppice that would never suffer the sun to warm the
spot.)

Like the other sacred places, this is absolutely virgin territory, untouched
by humans, animals, birds, and even the sun. That virginity characterizes
both the sacredness of the spot and the identity of the youth who will see
the vision there. The youth is Narcissus, and the vision is directly in the
mirror.[32] Ovid turns the *locus amoenus* into something like the landscape
of the mind, for that unruffled surface of the pool is the *tabula rasa* upon
which the youth's experience will be both literally and figuratively inscribed. Unlike the earlier encounters in sacred places, here no intermediary serpent or godhead reflects a distorted mirror image of the mortal
observer. Here the mirror and the holy serpent are one. Narcissus' own
reflection is the vision that captures his essence and destroys him.

The fact that Narcissus is his own vision makes it clear that this episode is animated almost exclusively by mortal values. It may be the first
such episode in the poem, acting as a pathway from the world of mortals
under the sway of the gods to that world of private persons in which most
of the poem's central section takes place. Yet despite the relative absence
either of Olympians or of more mysterious forms of divinity, this story
makes use of striking parallels to the Theban material. As a consequence,
it translates into mortal terms the issues of innate divinity and the mysteries of human identity. All these individuals touched by mysterious holy
forces are victims of what we might anachronistically call schizophrenia.[33] They experience a split between their rational, daylight self and
another version of themselves characterized by mystery, irrationality,
and, ultimately, metamorphosis. Bacchism is the best shorthand way of
expressing this latter self because it is exotic, ecstatic, and anti-heroic; but
magical metamorphosis is the most powerful expression of this self because it makes the mystery incarnate without removing the mystery. All
the Thebans who are victimized by this "schizophrenia" travel at once into
the mysteries of the gods and the mysteries of the self. The story of Narcissus redefines these terms. There is no god or serpent lurking on the
surface of that unruffled pool: there is nothing but the disembodied re-

flection of the gazer himself. So Narcissus becomes his own god, and from that substitution comes not only his woe but also the emptiness of his experience.

When the mirror world loses its profound meaning, it becomes merely a place of confusion, mistaken definition, and self-absorption without self-understanding. It denies the substantiality of real life without affirming any transcendent realities. Long before seeing his own reflection, Narcissus readies himself to enter the mirror world by being staunchly opposed to love:

> multi illum iuvenes, multae cupiere puellae;
> sed fuit in tenera tam dura superbia forma,
> nulli illum iuvenes, nullae tetigere puellae.   [3.353–55]

(Many youths and many maidens sought his love; but in that slender form was pride so cold that no youth, no maiden touched his heart.)

This little description foreshadows the youth's problem, for it is full of mirroring language. Parallel phrases include the contrast of *iuvenes* and *puellae*, while the mirroring between the first and third lines includes the contrast of *multi* and *nulli*. The middle line uses the oxymoron of *tenera* and *dura*, and the expression "tenera . . . forma" even suggests the mirror reflection to come. Indeed, the equation between the refusal to love and the mirror foreshadows the whole narrative. In declining to go outside of himself through love, Narcissus rejects the world. There is nothing left but himself.

Meanwhile, the story of Echo underlines important aspects of the main action. The poor nymph is the perfect complement of the young man she loves in vain. He has chosen his limitation freely, she is forced into hers. He has too much self, she too little. He will deal with the visual realm, she with the auditory. But underneath these contrasts there are more significant parallels. Echo's metamorphosis from normal, articulate woman to echo imprisons her in herself: she cannot initiate or even experience a fruitful sexual union because she is trapped in imitation and reflection. By setting up the concept of reflection, her character anticipates Narcissus' position as hopeless lover. Even before he has seen his reflection, she must already struggle with the paradox that being identical with your loved one is an obstacle rather than an aid to union with him. Finally, Echo's sad fate also foreshadows that of her beloved, for she wastes away to nothing—that is, to an echo—once she has been spurned in love. If the love of the subject does not reach the object, then love will waste what it feeds upon. When the individual leaves the world of substances, he or she will finish with the loss of bodily substance and become nothing but a reflection.

But Echo's history takes us ahead of the main action. We noted before that Narcissus was refusing to go outside himself when he denied the petitions of all those smitten with his beauty, so that he was being a narcissist before he ever gazed into the mirror. We have already seen that the poem is centrally concerned with the building of bridges between individuals and the world and that the solipsism of Narcissus involves a primary refusal to make such connections. Not to connect, the story tells us, is not to have a self to connect with. Tiresias' prophecy that the youth will live long "si se non noverit" (3.348: "if he ne'er know himself") is, in the manner of oracles, paradoxical. The boy is not being enjoined to ignore the famous Delphic advice; rather, Tiresias recognizes that Narcissus is so full of self that his only hope is to *noscere* someone or something else.

The love scene of Narcissus and his reflection is the central event in the story. In this perhaps overly sober analysis of the whole story we must not overlook the fact that the primary effect of this encounter is comic. Self-absorbed all along, he is now forced by the terms of the fable into acting out his flaw without recognizing the absurdity of his position. The more rapturous his transports of passion, the more he proves he loves himself. The longer he remains in ignorance about his perceptual mistake, the more preposterously immature he comes to seem in his attitude toward the world. But Ovid is not simply making fun of people who fall in love with themselves. His language makes it clear that the situation has broader application:

> spectat humi positus geminum, sua lumina, sidus
> et dignos Baccho, dignos et Apolline crines
> inpubesque genas et eburnea colla decusque
> oris et in niveo mixtum candore ruborem.　　　[3.420–23]

> (Prone on the ground, he gazes at his eyes, twin stars, and his locks, worthy of Bacchus, worthy of Apollo; on his smooth cheeks, his ivory neck, the glorious beauty of his face, the blush mingled with snowy white.)

This is, of course, the language of all romantic love. Such hyperbolic analogies are always narcissistic. They remind us that this love is not only self-directed but also (by definition) purely visual; in a situation where physical beauty is the only communication between a "pair" of lovers, then hyperbole and self-love are nearly inevitable.

The flaw that Ovid is attacking is not just self-love or just hyperbole or just immaturity. He is, for one thing, enunciating an exogamic principle that will become vital in virtually all the poem's love stories. Self-love, homosexuality, and incest account for much of the depiction of human love in the *Metamorphoses*. All these deviations arise from a metamorphic view of human categories, and all represent a refusal to affirm the world outside the self and to build connections with it. In addition, Narcissus is so far from affirming the world that he completely fails to understand it. The crime for which he is proverbial is self-love, but Ovid makes him equally culpable for the feebleness of his perception and intelligence:

> quid videat, nescit; sed quod videt, uritur illo,
> atque oculos idem, qui decipit, incitat error.
> credule, quid frustra simulacra fugacia captas?
> quod petis, est nusquam; quod amas, avertere, perdes!
> ista repercussae, quam cernis, imaginis umbra est:
> nil habet ista sui.   [3.430–35]

(What he sees he knows not; but that which he sees he burns for, and the same delusion mocks and allures his eyes. O fondly foolish boy, why vainly seek to grasp a fleeting image? What you seek is nowhere; but turn yourself away, and the object of your love will be no more. That which you behold is but the shadow of a reflected form and has no substance of its own.)

To be sure, the world is difficult to grasp, in particular because the relationship between shadow and substance is so complex (a relationship made more complex by each case of metamorphosis), but the successful individual masters this relationship and even uses it for his own ends. Narcissus, however, is hopelessly impercipient. Love may hold out great hope of bridging the gap between individuals and the world; but love may also have the effect of blinding its victims. In that case they are caught in the traps of shadow and substance that the world lays; and, once caught, they become the victims of shadow and substance through metamorphosis.

When Narcissus' blindness is lifted, all that he is left with is a sense that he is trapped in paradox:

> uror amore mei: flammas moveoque feroque.
> quid faciam? roger anne rogem? quid deinde rogabo?
> quod cupio mecum est: inopem me copia fecit.
> o utinam a nostro secedere corpore possem!
> votum in amante novum, vellem, quod amamus, abesset.
>
> [3.464–68]

(I burn with the love of my own self; I both kindle the flames and suffer them. What shall I do? Shall I be wooed or woo? Why woo at all? What I desire, I have; the very abundance of my riches beggars me. Oh, that I might be parted from my own body! and, strange prayer for a lover, I would that what I love were absent from me!)

Paradox is to language as the world of mirror reflection is to the world of real objects. Narcissus and his reflection make up a complete and, theoretically, satisfying system ("quod cupio mecum est"); yet in its completeness there is no real satisfaction, since Narcissus cannot unite, cannot have sexual relations, and cannot produce offspring with his love object. The language of paradox is similarly complete and yet unsatisfying: it seems to affirm all things at once, but it affirms nothing. When a linguistic action meets an equal and opposite linguistic reaction, no effective statement is made.

The result of all these paradoxes about form and the self is the loss of form and the destruction of the self. Echo's story, as we have already seen, looms as a threat over the main plot: her transformation into bodilessness threatens the hero from the moment that he gives evidence of rejecting the world. If Narcissus' two crimes are self-love and impercipience about form and substance, then his punishment is the simultaneous loss of that love object and the metamorphosis into a realm where "both" lovers have lost their substance. Like Echo earlier, Narcissus wastes away; he perishes by his eyes. Ovid's description draws a close connection between the literal alimentary undernourishment that diminishes and destroys the boy's flesh and the spiritual undernourishment implicit in imaginary love. He tries to eat with his eyes and finding no food there, he neglects the feeding of his stomach. If this destruction of the body is the boy's punishment, then it is fundamentally identical to his crime.

Metamorphosis, then, is a force that underlies all the motions in the story, and the overriding motion is the transformation of real substance into empty, fleeting images. The imagery of dissolution is unmistakable:

> et lacrimis turbavit aquas, obscuraque moto
> reddita forma lacu est; quam cum vidisset abire,
> "quo refugis? remane nec me, crudelis, amantem
> desere!" clamavit. . . .
>
> . . . .
>
> quae simul adspexit liquefacta rursus in unda,
> non tulit ulterius, sed ut intabescere flavae
> igne levi cerae matutinaeque pruinae
> sole tepente solent, sic attenuatus amore
> liquitur et tecto paullatim carpitur igni.   [3.475–78, 486–90]

(His tears ruffled the water, and dimly the image came back from the troubled pool. As he saw it thus depart, he cried: "Oh, whither do you flee? Stay here, and desert not him who loves thee, cruel one!" . . . As soon as he sees this, when the water has become clear again, he can bear no more; but, as the yellow wax melts before a gentle heat, as hoar frost melts before the warm morning sun, so does he, wasted with love, pine away, and is slowly consumed by its hidden fire.)

The loss of form through the boy's tears on the water, the melting wax, and the melting frost remind us of Narcissus' error at the same time as they stand for an important metamorphic truth in Ovid's world: the mutability of matter.[34] All these types of dissolution finally suggest that the real transformation in the story is that of Narcissus into his reflection. Even if, in one sense, the two figures are identical, in another way the "real" Narcissus through his love drains all the life out of himself and into his unsubstantial mirror image. When Echo repeats his *Eheu* and his *vale*, she is paralleling his reflection in the water. What was a full-blooded young man has now become a reflected image and an echoed sound.

When even the body of Narcissus disappears ("nusquam corpus erat"; 3.509), the boy has entered completely into the mirror realm. Through a kind of metamorphic contagion with his love object, he became a shadow; and once the body that produced the shadow is destroyed, then so is the shadow. Narcissus has entered into that Theban world of the transfigured self, but, being his own god, he has destroyed himself without achieving any perception. His story stands at once as the reduction to absurdity of the religious trope in the poem and the introduction to the bewildering world of human passions. In the process whereby the forces of Bacchus directly or indirectly wreak their influence upon the heritage of Cadmus, Narcissus stands as a kind of ultimate negative example. Through his own failings he becomes the victim of the realm where divinity, mirror images, and selfhood merge; and in that failure he also introduces the poem's readers to a world ruled exclusively by human powers. His story, then, stands as the climax of one trend in the poem and the beginning of another. But it is not the only transitional story dealing with precisely these issues. One of the traits that makes Ovid's work a *perpetuum carmen* is that every major episode, however resolved it may seem, has important links with and depends for its meaning upon the episodes that follow. Hence the impossibility of satisfactorily dividing the poem into discrete chunks. The Narcissus story amounts to only one resolution of the tensions among divinity, violence, and selfhood. If he culminates the Theban failures to tackle the serpent or understand the mirror, then in Perseus at last we have a figure who is master of both serpent and mirror.[35]

Perseus is no ordinary hero of brute force; in fact, there is a clear and parallel stage in each of his three battles (with Atlas, with the monster guarding Andromeda, and with Phineus's men) when he is on the verge of collapse. Rather, his exceptional qualities are versatility, mobility, and canniness, making him precisely apt to wield the powers of metamorphosis.[36] It is no accident that Ovid introduces him as a flier ("aera carpebat tenerum stridentibus alis"; 4.616: "taking his way through the thin air on whirring wings") without pausing to explain how Perseus acquired wings. He is, under his own power, a master of motion, as we see in each of his battles, and his nature makes him immune to the dangers suffered by others who have been the victims of motion—notably Phaethon, whom he parallels at 4.625–30. This mastery of motion, which enables him to elude Atlas, to escape the dragon, and to be everywhere at once in the battle with Phineus's men, is, in a sense, the first prerequisite for the magical powers of metamorphosis that he is granted.

Nowhere is Perseus's ability with motion clearer than in his response to the first sight of Andromeda:

> quam simul ad duras religatam bracchia cautes
> vidit Abantiades, nisi quod levis aura capillos
> moverat et tepido manabant lumina fletu,
> marmoreum ratus esset opus; trahit inscius ignes
> et stupet.   [4.672–76]

(As soon as Perseus saw her there bound by the arms to a rough cliff—save that her hair gently stirred in the breeze, and the warm tears were trickling down her cheeks, he would have thought her a marble statue—he took fire unwitting and stood dumb.[37])

This is one of those great Ovidian images of fixity: Andromeda bound to the stone is, in effect, transformed into stone. The transformation is in part deathly and in part beautiful; deathly because she is helplessly frozen, and beautiful because as stone she is a work of art and quite distinct from the *duras cautes* to which she is bound. To complete the picture, Ovid shows us that life, equated with motion, still flickers within the girl. The motion of her hair and tears contrasts with the maiden's stoniness, but that stoniness is clearly taking over her personality as well as her body because at first Perseus is able to pry no response from her. Eventually Perseus succeeds, however, in bringing her to speech and motion; and it is this coaxing into life that reveals the hero's worthiness to free her from her stony condition and to wed her.

More important than his good moves, though, is Perseus's special ability with shadow and reflection. His capacities with both motion and shadow emerge in his fight with the dragon guarding Andromeda:

> cum subito iuvenis pedibus tellure repulsa
> arduus in nubes abiit: ut in aequore summo
> umbra viri visa est, visa fera saevit in umbra,
> utque Iovis praepes, vacuo cum vidit in arvo
> praebentem Phoebo liventia terga draconem,
> occupat aversum, neu saeva retorqueat ora,
> squamigeris avidos figit cervicibus ungues,

sic celeri missus praeceps per inane volatu
terga ferae pressit dextroque frementis in armo
Inachides ferrum curvo tenus abdidit hamo.   [4.711–20]

(. . . when suddenly the youth, springing up from the earth,
mounted high into the clouds. When the monster saw the hero's
shadow on the surface of the sea, he savagely attacked the shadow.
And as the bird of Jove, when it has seen in an open field a serpent
sunning its mottled body, swoops down upon him from behind; and,
lest the serpent twist back his deadly fangs, the bird buries deep his
sharp claws in the creature's scaly neck; so did Perseus, plunging
headlong in a swift swoop through the empty air, attack the roaring
monster from above, and in his right shoulder buried his sword
clear down to the curved hook.)

Momentarily turning himself into a bird, Perseus bests his opponent not
just by developing a new angle of attack but rather by creating a reflection
of himself upon the water. This reflection—a kind of collaboration between himself and Phoebus, as the translation does not make clear—becomes a more ominous version of himself as it produces an attack that puts
the monster off guard. At that point Perseus can use his actual birdlike position to come in for the kill. So his triumph at this point involves a very
particular manipulation of shadow and substance. The hero undergoes
a kind of simultaneous double metamorphosis, transformations of his
substance into two forms of insubstantiality: the shadow and the bird.
Through insubstantiality the very substantial serpent is destroyed.

Indeed, Perseus's capacity to deal with shadow is precisely what enables him to win the Gorgon's head. When he approaches the Gorgons,
he sees the images (*simulacra*) of the men and beasts who have been
turned into stone by one look into Medusa's face. From this he learns a
lesson: to look at the Gorgon's face only via its reflected image on his
shield. In this way Perseus outwits the monster by using the power of reflection against her. That Perseus's shield becomes a mirror is particularly
significant: here is a warrior who can use mirror reflection as his own pro-
tection. Gazing into the mirror is still, at least by implication, a dangerous
act—it is in a sense Medusa's weapon, since she freezes the image of
every beholder—but the hero never gazes into his own reflection, instead wielding the mirror and turning it against others. So the fate of Narcissus has been overturned.

The Gorgon's head is, of course, the real figure of metamorphosis in
this tale, the union of mirror and serpent. Like many another such Ovidian image, it has a kind of holy beauty. When Perseus decapitates Medusa, he receives the head and treats it to a ritual as a sacred object by
placing it on a pile of soft leaves and twigs. As if in response to this treatment, the head effects a magical transformation of the soft twigs into

coral, petrifying at the same time as it creates. The description is exceptionally beautiful as the sea-nymphs marvel at the new substance and
transmit it throughout the oceans.

Yet Ovid spends more time on the terrors than on the beauties engen-
dered by Medusa. The essential terror of the Gorgon's head is perfectly in
keeping with the whole destiny of Thebes: any individual who gazes into
the face of this holy object is violently transformed not into some new individual or species but into an eternally frigid and unchanging version of
himself. That transformation amounts to death, of course, but also to a
clear, and usually unflattering definition of the individual's essence in
eternity. In the lengthy struggle with Phineus, Perseus petrifies each of
his rival's men in a posture that is quintessentially characteristic: Theselus
scoffing at the *miracula* promised by Perseus, Nileus preening at his false
glorious ancestry, Eryx in a headstrong forward rush, Astyages disbeliev-
ing the sight of his own eyes. But the clearest case is Phineus himself. It
has already been suggested earlier in the fight that Phineus is a cowardly
figure, and now the Gorgon's head fixes that quality in perpetuity:

> in partem Phorcynida transtulit illam,
> ad quam se trepido Phineus obverterat ore,
> tum quoque conanti sua vertere lumina cervix
> diriguit, saxoque oculorum induruit umor,
> sed tamen os timidum vultusque in marmore supplex
> submissaeque manus faciesque obnoxia mansit.   [5.230–35]

(He bore the Gorgon-head where Phineus had turned his fear-
struck face. Then, even as he strove to avert his eyes, his neck grew
hard and the very tears upon his cheeks were changed to stone. And
now in marble was fixed the cowardly face, the suppliant look, the
pleading hands, the whole cringing attitude.)

The repetitive details fix in the poem what the Gorgon's head has fixed in
stone. Perseus makes his rival into a statue that will forever decorate the
house where his crime of presumption was committed. The hapless
Phineus is rendered manifestly impotent without being granted the so-
lace of removal from the scene of his defeat. To extend his life as a piece of
decoration is the worst possible insult.

As we enter the middle books of the poem, shedding the imminent
presence of the Olympians, metamorphosis is gradually being distanced
from these nonhuman powers. Medusa may be strange and holy, but
the particular nature of her effect is such that—at least in an immediate
sense—her victims destroy themselves. It is in the very nature of a
mirror-weapon that its victims are destroyed by their own reflections.
And the wielder of the weapon is also a mortal on his own, who becomes
worthy of magical aid by attaining similar qualities all by himself. This

transition can perhaps best be illustrated by the contrast drawn between Atlas and Andromeda, who are closely juxtaposed in the early part of the Perseus story. First Perseus uses the Gorgon's head to freeze his enemy Atlas, who thereby becomes the giant mountain upholding the heavens: it is a throwback to divine metamorphoses, to etiology, to the creation of the world, and it is a transformation as frigid as the stony form of Atlas itself. Then Perseus uses his power to effect precisely the opposite process, the depetrification of Andromeda. All the emphasis here is upon human motions and emotions being freed from the elemental rocks to which they are chained. These freedoms are closely connected with metamorphosis, whether they are beneficient changes associated with love or dangerous changes brought about by passion and self-destructiveness. These changes now become the subject of the poem.

4. Metamorphosis and the Ties that Bind

Once men and women are truly on their own in Ovid's poem—a phase which begins around the sixth book—the world changes in important ways and the subject of metamorphosis changes with it. Magical transformation, whether in Ovid's work or later, is bound up with literary or religious implications that extrahuman powers are vividly alive in the universe. It is not surprising, then, that such transformations are frequent and significant when Ovid tells stories of the creation or of divine forces. Yet it would be a mistake to conclude that metamorphosis loses its importance in the middle of the poem, or that it degenerates into a mere device intended to hold the work together. In fact, Ovid spends the first third of his poem establishing the methods and meanings of metamorphosis so that in the next third he can apply its lessons to the lives and worlds of private human beings.

To understand these lessons of metamorphosis, we need only remind ourselves how the lives of the Cadmians, of Narcissus, and of Perseus bridge the gap between the god-centered and man-centered worlds of the poem. By Book VI the serpent is largely gone—at least insofar as that figure is defined in terms of divine external forces. But the metamorphic mirror remains. There is the mirror of self-absorption and of introspection: so many agonized figures examining their own motives. There is the mirror reminding us of the complex relations between shadows and substances: so many individuals in the heritage of Narcissus unable to make the distinction. Finally, there is the looking-glass world, where entities turn into their opposites while still seeming identical to their original form. Metamorphosis has taught us that the world is unsettled, and that unsettled world is the scene for most of the great personal stories that Ovid chronicles in the middle books of his poem.

The link between the mirror of Narcissus and those of the passionate lovers in the middle books of the poem is the group of stories told by the Minyades early in Book IV. Like Arachne, these ladies are both weavers and story-tellers; also like Arachne they defy a god and pay for it with their own metamorphosis. In this case, however, the god is not the stern Minerva but the ecstatic Bacchus. As holdouts against the power of Bacchus, the Minyades tell stories about the dangers of all those forces which he represents: love, sensuality, transformation. But the keynote is the perilous uncertainty of the world of love. So they tell the story of Pyramus and Thisbe, who disobey their parents and are thrown into a world of perceptual confusion, barely seeing each other through the chink in the wall, then scarcely seeing any more clearly in the dark once they escape to Ninny's tomb, and finally making fatal perceptual mistakes concerning the question of who is alive and who dead. And, lest we imagine that love leads to confusion of the senses only in the dark, the Minyades then turn to the brilliant light of the Sun, whose brightness is of no avail as he first becomes pale for the love of Leucothoe and then is unable to light his way through the earth where her father has buried her.

These are, however, but introductions to the story that truly translates Narcissus' experience into our world, the tale of Salmacis and Hermaphroditus. Every step in this story is concerned with mirrorings and confusions. Like so many Theban tales, it takes place in a *locus amoenus* specifically parallel to that of Narcissus. But this pool turns out to be as much a mirror of Tiresias as it is of Narcissus, since it turns men into a mirror image of themselves. Hermaphroditus's very name, which Ovid properly etymologizes as coming from his parents Hermes and Aphrodite, suggests another confusion: he is both sexes in one. And Salmacis's relentless pursuit of him, in the face of his very maidenly shame, again makes mirror images of the sexual roles.

Above all, the act of love itself, as Platonists from Plato to Spenser have understood, blurs distinctions by transforming the lovers into a hermaphrodite. Salmacis begs, "ita di iubeatis, et istum / nulla dies a me nec me deducat ab isto" (4.371–72: "Grant me this, ye gods, and may no day ever come that shall separate him from me or me from him"). The poor Naiad has not read the story of Narcissus. Ovid plays on Narcissus' hopeless inseparability from his beloved; here he creates of two people a single mirror image. The result is not only emasculation but, as in the case of Narcissus, a metamorphic—and pejorative—description of the act of love itself:

sic ubi conplexu coierunt membra tenaci,
nec duo sunt et forma duplex, nec femina dici
nec puer ut possit, neutrumque et utrumque videntur.

[4.377–79]

(So were these two bodies knit in close embrace: they were no
longer two, nor such as to be called, one, woman, and one, man.
They seemed neither, and yet both.)

The rhyming *neutrumque et utrumque* reinforces the sense that this
"metamorphosis" is the sexual act itself. From that blend all other confusions follow: Hermaphroditus is both Hermes and Aphrodite, boy and
maiden; Salmacis is female but pursuer; the pool is clear but its results are
cloudy. The final etiology, which also begins the story—"quisquis in hos
fontes vir venerit, exeat inde / semivir" (4.385–86: "whoever comes into
this pool as man, may he go forth half-man")—has been redefined in
rather particular sexual terms. This resolution suggests retrospectively
that Narcissus' experience was not only self-love but also autoeroticism;
and the parallel stories of others who underwent sacred, sometime pool-
side, experiences—Tiresias, Actaeon, Semele, Pentheus—now seem to
involve erotic as well as visionary forces. Prospectively, Salmacis and
Hermaphroditus introduce a world of romantic confusions, where sexual desire transforms those who experience it. The mirror of passion,
whether it is a clear pool of water, a complicated introspective rhetoric, or
a set of parallels among human and family relations, distorts the clarities
of gender, of identity, and of reason.

Yet, for Ovidian characters, Salmacis and Hermaphroditus are exceptionally free; that is, they have almost nothing to struggle against but their
own desire and gender. Most of Ovid's heroes (or, more especially, heroines) are less on their own: they operate within grids of rigid categories
imposed by nature and society. As we have already seen, metamorphosis
simultaneously justifies belief in rigid categories of experience and demonstrates the sometimes glorious, sometimes terrifying occasions when
the categories dissolve. Metamorphosis depends on our prior assumption
that human beings, animals, and plants, or land, sea, and air are rigid distinctions. Ovid assumes we believe in those distinctions, and he reinforces that belief. When he comes to stories of individuals, he adds to
these the categories inspired by family and society; but his treatment is
fundamentally identical to his treatment of literal metamorphosis. The
categories exist in all their clarity so that fictions can be made about spectacular transformations among them.

Once familial and social categories are added to those of the natural
world, the essential structure of an Ovidian story emerges. It takes place
in a context where individuals are assigned clear roles, so clear that they
may be oppressive. The central figure in the story rebels, specifically attacking the clarity and discreteness of the surrounding categories. The essential metamorphosis comes as a direct result of this rebellion: it is not
the hero's or heroine's change of physical shape (that will come too, but it
is later and less important) but rather the discovery that what seemed like

such rigid categories of family and society can dissolve, just as physical categories dissolve in metamorphosis. Once the categories are attacked, similar things are diversified into opposites and opposites are made identical. The central figure reaches a condition that transcends and contradicts all these categories. From that point it is a short step to literal metamorphosis, a condition that merely serves as the final punctuation mark for a narrative experience whose crucial metamorphosis has amounted to the dissolution of assumptions we live by.

The tale of Tereus and the daughters of Pandion[38] is based upon a tension between the order posited by a rigid system of familial and social ties and the disorder wrought by the passions of the individual. The order is extremely fragile and highly susceptible to mutability. Once it is in any way breached, even if the breach amounts merely to an excess of a good thing, then the whole structure of family and society must be systematically transformed and thereby destroyed. The first breach appears in the wedding of Tereus and Procne. By juxtaposing *conubio Procnes iunxit* with *non pronuba Iuno* (6.438), two phrases that are almost anagrams of each other, Ovid emphasizes the tension between the human force trying to cement the union and the withholding of the gods' blessing— with the parallel language reminding us how opposites come together. Rituals act as significant indicators: the fact that the bridal torches had been stolen from a funeral by the Furies is the first of many suggestions in the story that rituals are becoming conflated, that the ties that bind are becoming dangerously tangled up with each other. The presence of the *profanus bubo* at both the wedding and the conception of Itys also associates festivals with funerals, as we can see from Myrrha's experience with the same evil presage: "ter omen / funereus bubo letali carmine fecit" (10.452–53: "thrice did the funereal screech-owl warn her by his uncanny cry").[39] The description of the ceremony ends with an Ovidian comment even more ominous than the screech-owl: "usque adeo latet utilitas" (6.438: "even so is our true advantage hidden"). That hiddenness is a clear sign that we are in a metamorphic world.

The story moves forward through an intense tangle of family ties, which will form the basis of the transformation. Procne begs to be united with her sister, and Tereus goes off to fetch Philomela from her father. Tereus's first sight of the girl instantly produces the transforming violence of lust. Ovid's image is of fire, the spontaneous combustion of dry grain, leaves, or hay, and this picture of sudden fire consuming extremely flammable materials is highly appropriate, for all the familial and social ties in which the characters are enmeshed, far from retarding the spread of Tereus's passion, as they are presumably meant to do, become its fuel. On his side *innata libido* is jointed with a racial history of sexual hotbloodedness: "flagrat vitio gentisque suoque" (6.460: "his own fire and his nation's burnt in him"). On the side of Philomela, who inspires the flames, Tereus's *innata libido* is compounded in a perverse way by the evidences of the girl's passionate devotion to her father:

> spectat eam Tereus praecontrectatque videndo
> osculaque et collo circumdata bracchia cernens
> omnia pro stimulis facibusque ciboque furoris
> accipit, et quotiens amplectitur illa parentem,
> esse parens vellet: neque enim minus inpius esset.   [6.478–82]

(Tereus gazes at her, and as he looks feels her already in his arms; as he sees her kisses and her arms about her father's neck, all this goads him on, food and fuel for his passion; and whenever she embraces her father he wishes that he were in the father's place— indeed, if he were, his intent would be no less impious.)

The whole description is based upon the forcible union of things which ought to be kept separate: the girl's filial piety, her sexuality, Tereus's role as brother-in-law, his *innata libido*. As time planes become confused (Tereus, seeing Philomela in her father's arms, already feels her in his own), so too do the realms of imagination and action, for Tereus becomes incapable of separating his fantasies from his acts.

Pandion's consent to the departure of Philomela intensifies the sense of transformation fueled by intertwining family relationships. His parting words combine the social ties and the ties of love in a way that drenches them in irony:

> hanc ego, care gener, quoniam pia causa coegit,
> et voluere ambae (voluisti tu quoque, Tereu)
> do tibi perque fidem cognataque pectora supplex
> per superos oro patrio ut tuearis amore.   [6.496–99]

(Dear son, since a natural plea has won me, and both my daughters have wished it, and you also have wished it, my Tereus, I give her to your keeping: and by your honour and the ties that bind us, by the gods, I pray you guard her with a father's love.)

Pandion innocently conflates all the loves that Tereus is viciously combining. *Coegit* implies a bringing together of strands, in this case the wishes of the two sisters and the parenthetical wish of Tereus; but as we have seen, these ought to be kept strictly separate.

Tereus's rape of Philomela takes the idea of these conflations and makes it real in flesh and blood. Philomela grasps this perfectly in the lament to her ravisher:

>   nec te mandata parentis
> cum lacrimis movere piis nec cura sororis
> nec mea virginitas nec coniugalia iura?

omnia turbasti; paelex ego facta sororis,
tu geminus coniunx, hostis mihi debita Procne!   [6.534–38]

(Do you care nothing for my father's injunctions, his affectionate
tears, my sister's love, my own virginity, the bonds of wedlock? You
have confused all natural relations: I have become a concubine, my
sister's rival; you, a husband to both.)

The serial language combined with Philomela's *omnia turbasti* amounts to
a total disordering. Tereus has changed into meaninglessness all those
covenants and indicators of value that she lists in her first series above:
commands, tears, loving kindness, virginity, conjugal rights. But the second half of Philomela's plaint is even more significant because it demonstrates how the supportive grid of normal human relations has been disastrously changed. *Paelex sororis* and *geminus coniunx* are, in the context of
the story, living oxymorons, self-contradictions which began when Tereus
started to confuse familial roles in the scene with Pandion and Philomela
and which will culminate in the moment when Procne faces an intolerable
conflict amongst roles of sister, wife, and mother.

Tereus, too, is a victim of transformations. Once he has committed his
crime, he tries to stop all further change. He attempts to confine his victim, but the very construction of the lines describing this confinement
suggests how explosive is the situation that he is trying to bottle up:
"includit fassusque nefas et virginem et unam" (6.524: "He shut her up.
Then openly confessing his horrid purpose, [he violated her,] just a weak
girl and all alone"). *Fassusque nefas* will be strikingly echoed fifty lines
later in the description of Procne's simultaneously moral and immoral revenge ("fasque nefasque / confusura"), and here, too, the language helps
demonstrate the confusion. Tereus's confession is made linguistically parallel with his blasphemy, and the implied oxymoron only begins to demonstrate that the malefactor will be unable to keep order and partition if
such concepts as *fas* and *nefas* are being confused. Tereus's attempt to
"shut up" Philomela becomes a paradigmatic opposition to the very process of change he has set in motion. The mutilation that he inflicts upon
her, the cutting out of her tongue, is an attempt to cancel the consequences of his acts. She is thus shut up in two senses, which Ovid makes
directly parallel: "fugam custodia claudit, / structa rigent solido stabu-
lorum moenia saxo, / os mutum facti caret indice" (6.572–74: "A guard
prevents her flight; stout walls of solid stone fence in the hut; speechless
lips can give no token of her wrongs").

The experience cannot be shut away from Procne, who soon takes
over. Confusion amongst discrete values and family relationships, the
sudden spread of passion's fires, the attempt to freeze into eternal stasis a
constantly altering state of affairs: these are the crucial forces in the last
part of the story. Procne begins, as we have seen, with a vital confusion—

"fasque nefasque / confusura," and so she is herself transformed into an image of punishment ("poenaeque in imagine tota est," 6.586).[40] Again, evils arise from the breakdown of categories, not only *fas* and *nefas* but also individual identities. Procne becomes (dare one say it?) as tongue-tied as her sister. She burns with Tereus's fire and plans a punishment that not only fits but also mirrors the crime, suggesting "aut linguam atque oculos et quae tibi membra pudorem / abstulerunt ferro rapiam" (6.616–17: "Or to cut out his tongue and his eyes, to cut off the parts which brought shame to you.")

Procne's vengeance represents the nadir in the drama of conflation and confusion. Her plan is born when she observes the physical similarity between her son and her husband: "a! quam / es similis patri"; 6.621–22: "Ah, how like your father you are"). A sympathetic magic operates between these individuals of similar appearance, and the avenging Procne wants to strike her husband in the heart of his sexual identity. If Itys is partly a parallel to Tereus, he is also seen by Procne as a parallel to Philomela. Her motherly love leads her to waver, but she strengthens her resolve by comparing her sister and her son:

> inque vicem spectans ambos "cur admovet" inquit
> "alter blanditias, rapta silet altera lingua?
> quam vocat hic matrem, cur non vocat illa sororem?" [6.631–33]

(And gazing at both in turn, she said: "Why is one able to make soft, pretty speeches, while her ravished tongue dooms the other to silence? Since he calls me mother, why does she not call me sister?")

This is precisely the sort of confusion about family roles and obligations that inflamed Tereus's lust when he saw Pandion and Philomela. The parallel of Itys and Philomela is apt, just as were the parallels amongst different sorts of love in the earlier scene; but like her husband, Procne is unable to keep important distinctions clear.

The banquet that concludes the tale climaxes the confusions among discrete categories and identities. Procne claims to be following a holy ritual—again a blasphemous piece of hypocrisy—that requires husband and wife to be alone. But Tereus does not want to be alone, and so he calls for his son. Procne is able to say "intus habes, quem poscis" (6.655: "You have, within, him whom you want"), an expression so cryptic and so inconceivable if meant to be taken literally that Tereus fails to understand. It is not his son who then appears but rather the poor mutilated object of his lust, joined by her fate with the son and tormenting the father by hurling Itys's decapitated head in his face. Now he grasps what it means to have overstepped and destroyed the bounds between individuals: "seque vocat bustum miserabile nati" (6.665: "[he] calls himself his son's most wretched tomb"). Just as he cannot remove the flesh of his son from his own flesh, he cannot extricate his fate from that of his two fellow perpetrators and victims. Cannibalism is the most dreadful physical image of identities that have been confused. All three characters have gone beyond the extremes of human experience; they have reached the endpoint of transformations, where all the distinctions that protect society, identity, and life itself have been destroyed.

The tale of Myrrha, who falls in love with her father and achieves her sexual desire, has much in common with that of Tereus. Categories of human experience are blurred and as a result the individual is left completely unprotected. The familial roles of daughter, father, and nurse, along with the love that is meant to nurture those roles, are all submitted to agonizing tests of redefinition. But, instead of twists of narrative, we have here twists of human emotion and reasoning, and, above all, twists of language. Words develop multiple, changing significances, and rhetoric turns easily to sophistry. *Amor* gets the fullest metamorphic treatment, when, for instance, Ovid coyly unveils the identity of Myrrha's love: "scelus est odisse parentem, / hic amor est odio maius scelus" (10.314–15: "'Tis a crime to hate one's father, but such love as this is a greater crime than hate"). Both filial affection and sexual desire can be called *amor*, and both are clearly opposed to *odium*; yet they are far from identical to each other. The extremely chiastic syntax of this revelation (*amor* framed on each side by *scelus* and *odium*) images forth the convolution—indeed, the mirroring nature—of Myrrha's predicament and the difficulties of definition inherent in her experience.

The multiple redefinitions of *amor* find their parallel in multiple definition of *pietas*. This concept, so closely keyed to Roman racial identity, initiates yet another diversification of moral definitions, for, playing upon the word *pietas*, Myrrha is able to invoke a kind of anthropological and sociological relativism. First *pietas* refuses to condemn this love because it is legal among the animals (10.323–38); then she adds that certain societies think *pietas* is strengthened by combining sexual and filial bonds in an incestuous relationship. Myrrha longs for a more primitive value system, whether in different societies or different species, where individuals are too unsophisticated to understand the crucial distinctions amongst kinds of *amor* or *pietas*. And her desire to be governed by the law of the animals is only a step away from an Ovidian animal metamorphosis, in which the gods punish beastly human behavior by awarding the perpetrators the animal identities they deserve.

But Myrrha is not a primitive or an animal. Blessed (or cursed) with a sense of subtle distinctions among human duties and values, she is forced to agonize over them in wandering mazes of uncertainty. Myrrha's attempts to justify her desire exploit the shifting qualities of verbal rhetoric: "si filia magni / non essem Cinyrae, Cinyrae concumbere possem" (10.337–38: "if I were not the daughter of great Cinyras, to Cinyras I could be joined"). But her very language defeats her. The Cinyras who is her father cannot be separated from the Cinyras whom she would have as lover. Once this crucial distinction becomes difficult, then all systems of order, at least with respect to family relations, break down in an almost comical catalogue:

> et quot confundas, et iura et nomina, sentis!
> tune eris et matris paelex et adultera patris?
> tune soror nati genetrixque vocabere fratris?   [10.346–48]

(Think how many ties, how many names you are confusing! Will you be the rival of your mother, the mistress of your father? Will you be called the sister of your son, the mother of your brother?").

Like Philomela's enraged response to Tereus, Myrrha's speech embroils her in the grid of family relations, with all their confusable names.

Iura et nomina: the story makes it clear that the names are a key to the essences. In Myrrha's confusion those names are subject to metamorphic double meanings. Myrrha tells her father that she wishes a husband *similem tibi*. Cinyras misjudges the extent of the similarity, and he praises her answer as *pia*. Her double entendre was intentional, while his is accidental; but Myrrha instantly recognizes the confusion of meaning behind identical names by guiltily turning away from her father at his mention of *pietas*. With similar bashfulness she dares not use the word *pater* when revealing to the nurse the object of her desire. She merely declares, "felicem coniuge matrem" (10.422: "Mother, blessed in your husband"). Yet in the act of incest names are named. "Forsitan aetatis quoque nomine 'filia' dixit, / dixit et illa 'pater,' sceleri ne nomina desint" (10.467–68: "It chanced, by a name appropriate to her age, he called her 'daughter,' and she called him 'father,' that names might not be lacking in their guilt"). When the terms are used casually in an apparently trivial affair between parties of ill-matched age, the *iura* behind the *nomina* are further violated because the misuse of the names exercises a contagious magic upon the relationships signified. Incest is not only a perversion of these relationships: it is the quintessential confusion or inability to make moral definitions.

In stories like these from the central books of the poem, the literal metamorphosis acts as a footnote to the great transformations of the individual psyche. In Myrrha's case, the dissolution of clear categories puts the heroine in an extreme state beyond the reach of that most basic pair of categories: life and death. Her own longing for metamorphosis confirms that she is beyond the point where mere death is a fitting conclusion. "Mutataeque mihi vitamque necemque negate" (10.487: "Change me and refuse me both life and death"), she herself declares. Metamorphosis, then, serves as a special condition, a cosmic *tertium quid* resolving the unresolvable dilemma of the narrative and at the same time forcibly yoking together life and death. This explains why in Myrrha's case, and in those of several other grave criminals against the natural order (e.g., Tereus, Scylla, Byblis) the final transformation does not really equal the crime. For such characters metamorphosis is not a punishment but rather a definition of the extreme state into which they have brought themselves and a relief from the agony of those extremes.

The transformations at the end of these tales of passion also define the disordering drives that lead to the metamorphic punishment. Such is especially the case with Scylla, who betrays her father and his city in the hopes of winning the heart of Minos only to be repelled by him because of her lack of *pietas*. As Minos sails off, Scylla and her father, with an undying enmity and on the verge of destroying each other, are transformed into different species of birds who will keep their enmity alive but freeze that hostility into an emblematic opposition rather than engage in a bloody squabble. The daughter who has betrayed her father is perched upon her departing lover's ship. The father, his destruction forestalled by metamorphosis into a sea-eagle, is about to pick her off and destroy her, but this destruction too is forestalled.[41] She is transformed into Ciris, a half-mythical bird variously identified as heron, egret, or tern.[42]

That final image of flight reflects back on Scylla's whole problem. The ending is foreshadowed very early in the story, when she is agonizing over her desire for Minos:

o ego ter felix, si pennis lapsa per auras
Gnosiaci possem castris insistere regis
fassaque me flammasque meas, qua dote, rogarem,
vellet emi, tantum patrias ne posceret arces! [8.51–54]

(Oh, thrice happy should I be, if only I might fly through the air and stand within the camp of the Cretan king, and confess my love, and ask what dower he would wish to be paid for me. Only let him not ask my country's citadel.)

This desire to transcend her proper element demonstrates the close ties between metamorphosis and the disordering drives that lead to metamorphosis. The girl's desire to fly is in direct opposition to the evidences of natural order that she is faced with and that she chooses to ignore. She is a human being and therefore cannot fly, she is a woman and therefore ought not to be the pursuer in an amorous adventure, she is living in a city at war and therefore ought not to fall in love with her enemy. The victim of metamorphosis is a victim of illusions about all forms of order.[43]

Minos perceives Scylla's alienation from order, and his curse essentially creates the transformation: "di te summoveant, o nostri infamia saecli, / orbe suo, tellusque tibi pontusque negetur!" (8.97–98: "May the gods banish you from their world, O foul disgrace of our age! May both land and sea be denied to you!"). Denied land and sea, she must become a bird.[44] Such a banishment is typical of the experience of all of Ovid's great wicked women (and some of his men). The denials of order conceived of and acted out by these individuals cause them to be banished from all of the world's categories. For the physical world of Ovid's poem, as we saw earlier, land, sea, and air are the basic categories; and each normal organism has a place in one of these. When human beings break rules of family or society, they banish themselves. This explains why Ovid's characters are so often viewed in terms of the elements: those they belong to, those they are banished from, those they falsely aspire to, and those they are relegated to by animal transformation.

Metamorphosis is an outward sign that the ties that bind have been loosed. As such it proves that the moral freak is a physical freak, for a human being who has become a bird is still a figure outside all clear categories. Yet at the same time it is a kind of triumph. Scylla in fact outwits Minos's curse and in her transformation gives rise to a marvelous and exotic species. The mutilated Philomela sings, Byblis becomes a fountain, Myrrha a tree with comforting ooze. While metamorphosis typifies the crime and reflects the terrible extremes to which the victim is driven, it also provides an escape from entrapment into a higher condition where the blurred categories are no longer meaningful. In either event, metamorphosis is the destination for those who live by the passions.

5. Destinies Manifest and Reshaped

For all its emphasis upon the blurring of clear categories, metamorphosis is as much concerned with reduction and fixity as with variability or complexity. We saw in the story of Lycaon, the first victim of metamorphosis in the poem, subtle reverberations surrounding questions of blasphemy, divine service, and cannibalism. But we also observed that in his transformation he became fixed in his essential identity. So far as that final form is concerned, metamorphosis is a savage reduction of the individual, compelling him to live out in eternity the narrowest possible definition of his nature.

It is significant that the Lycaon story occurs at the beginning of history when the gods have the power to impose this metamorphic fixity. Similar forces are evident in the early stories of divine amours, such as Io, whose various metamorphic shapes—heifer, fury, goddess—become part of a tug-of-war between Jupiter and Juno as well as an attempt to define the girl's own beauty, humanity, and suffering. In fact, throughout the poem, individuals struggle with themselves or with the gods to escape the fixity which their own nature or destiny has determined for them and which metamorphosis realizes in the flesh. Many individuals look into a mirror which turns out to be their own Gorgon's head. We have already discussed the case of Hecuba, who forms a nice example of this reductive metamorphosis. No god presides over the stripping away of her personality but herself; yet such is her personality and the world of the poem that she moves from a human mother to an image of punishment (*poenae in imagine tota*) to an image of futility to the literal shape of a futilely punishing animal.

That *imago* which Hecuba becomes should remind us that metamorphosis by reduction is as much an aesthetic development as it is a psychological one. In this respect the gods often function as divine poets, turning their victims into frozen poetic images. An example of a metamorphosis in which the creation of an *imago* takes primary place is the story of Galanthis, the serving woman of Alcmena, who thwarts Juno's efforts to impede the birth of Hercules. The goddess is making Alcmena's delivery impossible by the voodoo-like act of closing up her own loins. The serving woman notices this posture, cries out that the birth has taken place, and so surprises the goddess that she lets up for a moment, allowing the actual parturition to take place. While Galanthis laughs at her own joke on the goddess, she begins to be transformed into a weasel (*galen* in Greek):

strenuitas antiqua manet; nec terga colorem
amisere suum: forma est diversa priori.
quae quia mendaci parientem iuverat ore,
ore parit nostrasque domos, ut et ante, frequentat.   [9.320–23]

(Her old activity remained and her hair kept its former hue; but her former shape was changed. And because she had helped her labouring mistress with her deceitful lips, through her mouth must she bring forth her young. And still, as of yore, she makes our dwelling place her home.)

With this transformation, Juno creates a poetic image synthesizing the traits that gave rise to the girl's offensive act. Galanthis's crimes, as Juno sees them, are (1) verbal deceit, (2) allowing a hated birth to occur, and (3) laughing at the thwarted godhead. The invention of the weasel's freakish habit, perpetuated through an eternity of weasels, captures all these crimes at once by uniting the organs of speech and parturition and through that union by producing what is in some respects a ludicrous freakish creature. The girl is reduced not only to the direct consequences of an act that defied the gods but also to an eternal caricature of that act and its implications.[45]

Galanthis, of course, has no independent personality; she is a victim of Juno and the poet. The powerful stories of metamorphic reduction are those in which the psychological struggle is as strong as the aesthetic image-making. Niobe boldly claims that her copious brood of seven sons and seven daughters makes her a fitter object of worship than the goddess Latona, who has only two children, Apollo and Diana.[46] Once Latona and her children begin to punish Niobe for her blasphemy, the world of metamorphosis becomes literally reductive. Apollo and Diana can outdo all of Niobe's *copia* and use them against her. To begin with there is perfect symmetry: a goddess with one son and one daughter, a mortal woman with seven sons and seven daughters. With Niobe's defiance of Latona, she reveals a destiny that can take one form only: the reduction of her copious brood to nothingness and her own complete reduction to inhumanity. Throughout the tale metamorphosis amounts to the working out of this destiny, and the literal transformation culminates this process:

> ultima [filia] restabat, quam toto corpore mater,
> tota veste tegens "unam minimam relinque!
> de multis minimam posco" clamavit "et unam."
> dumque rogat, pro qua rogat, occidit: orba resedit
> exanimes inter natos natasque virumque
> deriguit malis: nullos movet aura capillos,
> in vultu color est sine sanguine, lumina maestis
> stant inmota genis, nihil est in imagine vivum.
> ipsa quoque interius cum duro lingua palato
> congelat, et venae desistunt posse moveri;
> nec flecti cervix nec bracchia reddere motus
> nec pes ire potest; intra quoque viscera saxum est.   [6.298–309]

(The last [daughter] remained. The mother, covering her with her crouching body, and her sheltering robes, cried out: "Oh, leave me one, the littlest! Of all my many children, the littlest I beg you spare—just one!" And even while she prayed, she for whom she prayed fell dead. Now does the childless mother sit down amid the lifeless bodies of her sons, her daughters, and her husband, in stony grief. Her hair stirs not in the breeze; her face is pale and bloodless, and her eyes are fixed and staring in her sad face. There is nothing alive in the picture. Her very tongue is silent, frozen to her mouth's roof, and her veins can move no longer; her neck cannot bend nor her arms move nor her feet go. Within also her vitals are stone.)

For the first time Niobe tries to protect one of her children from the disastrous effects of her own blasphemy. The fact that she uses her own body as a cover to shield the girl from heaven's blows is ultimately ironic because the act depends upon a kind of loving flexibility of which Niobe will soon find herself physically deprived. In addition, the connection implied between motherly care and the movements of her body helps to define the moral meaning of the stony condition in which she ends her story.

The flexibility avails her nothing as her own language and the language of the poet's description remind us of Niobe's mistakes and demonstrate the reduction of her quantities. The repetition of *tot* and *tota*, particularly as they are applied to her soon-to-be transformed body and clothing, refer back to her prideful belief in quantity, while the repeated *unam* and *minimam* provide the necessary contrast by referring not only to the last daughter but also to Niobe herself, who is now reduced to *una minima*. The various children, who had seemed to meet their doom at separated intervals and localities, suddenly form a pile of lifeless hulks, mirrored by the pile-up of words for family relations: *natos natasque virumque*. The mother begins to experience a kind of contagion from their lifelessness. *Deriguit* is the first indication we get of an actual metamorphosis in Niobe, and from the start Ovid plays with great care on the question of whether this is merely an emotional or both a physical and emotional change. He generally uses the word to mean a literal hardening; but the accompanying *malis* and the sense that Niobe's horror must have reached the limits of experience allow us still to feel that Ovid is describing her emotional state. The same duality applies to the description of various parts of her face, the hair standing absolutely still (perhaps on end), the pale, bloodless complexion, the eyes frozen in her cheeks. This numbness again acts as a moralized redefinition of the woman's flaw: she has prided herself so on fullness that she must be punished by ending up without motion, without color, and so on.

But we are only beginning to get a sense that this condition is a punishment, rather than merely an emotional reaction; and this change becomes clearer when Ovid steps back from his inward, psychological frame of reference for a moment and tells us "nihil est in imagine vivum." It is the same shift that he makes later in the poem when he describes Hecuba as "poenae in imagine tota." Niobe is reduced in two ways here: her body is becoming a stone, and her story is becoming an emblem. There is little left in her transformation at this point except to tip the balance away from metaphoric stoniness and to the real thing. The transformation becomes real not by physical description but by this final reduction to a picture. The weeping rock gains its identity from its existence as a moralized object in the real world.

Stories like those of Niobe, Hecuba, or Galanthis suggest that the manifest destiny in human personality which reveals itself in transformation invariably involves a reduction to the subhuman; and indeed any animal (or mineral) metamorphosis is liable to capture a particularly base element in the formerly human personality. Yet there is a shift in the later books, with respect to a few stories at least, toward a more liberated, independent, creative role for human beings. As the poem begins to turn toward the foundation of Rome, some of the individual stories suggest that in metamorphosis human beings can shape their own lives. Iphis, a girl born under the threat of death because her father has refused to allow a female child to live, is brought up as a boy through the contrivance of her mother and the goddess Isis. She falls in love with a girl (Ianthe) but is saved at the eleventh hour from abnormality when she is transformed into a man on the eve of her wedding. The girl herself, very much along the lines of Myrrha or Scylla, sees the world in terms of clear categories and recognizes that she represents a break in their clarity:

> nec vaccam vaccae, nec equas amor urit equarum:
> urit oves aries, sequitur sua femina cervum.
> sic et aves coeunt, interque animalia cuncta
> femina femineo conrepta cupidine nulla est.
> vellem nulla forem! [9.731–35]

(Cows do not love cows, nor mares mares; but the ram desires the sheep, and his own doe follows the stag. So also birds mate, and in the whole animal world there is no female smitten with love for female. I would I were no female!)

The argument against homosexuality is of a piece with arguments against incest or self-love. Among all these personal stories of love in the poem, Ovid is creating a kind of metamorphic ethic: to avoid becoming victims of destructive and transforming powers, pairs of lovers must be at the proper distance from each other. Iphis is herself aware of this obligation: by repeating pairs of words like *vaccam vaccae, equas equarum*, and *femina femineo*, she illustrates the meaninglessness of union between identicals.

Similar repetitions characterize the love of Iphis and Ianthe:

> par aetas, par forma fuit, primasque magistris
> accepere artes, elementa aetatis, ab isdem.
> hinc amor ambarum tetigit rude pectus, et aequum
> vulnus utrique dedit, sed erat fiducia dispar. [9.718–21]

(The two were of equal age and equal loveliness, and from the same teachers had they received their first instruction in childish rudiments. Hence love came to both their hearts all unsuspected and filled them both with equal longing. But they did not love with equal hope.)

The conventional descriptions of harmony and equality uniting a pair of lovers bear a different burden when it turns out that their sexes are identical. The repetition of uniting words like *par, isdem, ambarum*, and *aequum* finally produces *dispar*, because the couple cannot be joined if they are already identical. Ovid's often repeated pun on *forma*, meaning both "form" and "beauty," captures the whole problem: he ostensibly means to say they are equal in beauty, but reminds us that they are identical in form. So Iphis at least believes, and Ovid in some respects seconds her belief, that she is a malefactor in just the way that Myrrha and Scylla turn out to be in fact.

Yet there is a manifest destiny of masculinity within Iphis. Her father has by chance bestowed on his child a name applicable to either sex. Her looks are also remarkably adaptable: "facies, quam sive puellae, / sive dares puero, fuerat formosus uterque" (9.712–13: "its face would have been counted lovely whether you assigned it to a girl or boy"). Then there is the quite masculine love for Ianthe. All these signs of masculinity bespeak a deeper accuracy about Iphis's identity than the fact of her sexual anatomy, suggesting that one can earn the right to a transformation that makes one's physical identity accord with the spiritual. The piety of Iphis's mother and the moral rigor of the girl herself form part of this worthiness; at the same time Ovid suggests that experience can itself create metamorphoses that ultimately give physical expression to the values upon which that experience was based.[47] Byblis, desperately in love with her brother in the story immediately preceding, cannot be released from her obstacles to love because there is no manifest destiny toward incest within her. But an individual who has truly loved as a man and been treated as a man need not suffer the torments of those whose desires destroy social and familial ties. Here metamorphosis validates the deepest identity; in fact, to believe in the inevitable rule of sexual anatomy is to be insufficiently aware that one is living in a metamorphic universe.

The story of Iphis, who manifests her/his own destiny, brings us, in the latter part of the poem, to those individuals who shape their lives for themselves. One uses the word "shape" advisedly, for we must keep in mind that in Ovid's poem human destiny is literally shaped through metamorphosis. To "shape" one's destiny, then, is to be a figure of self-transformation, a kind of Proteus.[48] What kinds of powers do real people— not just heroes of magical stories from the past—have to transform themselves and their world, and what sorts of moral values are to be associated with these powers? Those are our present questions. The two great transforming mortals of the poem are Daedalus and Pygmalion. To understand them, we must first review some of those literal examples of self-metamorphosis that form so central a part of Ovid's heritage for later creative artists.

We have already discussed Jupiter's self-transformations at length in the introductory chapter. In the segment of the poem surrounding Europa, he is ringed with bovine shapes, some glorious and some bathetic. Jove abandons his dignity, disguises his true divine identity, and takes advantage of helpless young women; yet, when he commits these breaches, he creates a perfect form by infusing his own divinity into the humble object that he chooses to imitate. So while we are told that "non bene conveniunt nec in una sede morantur / maiestas et amor" (2.846–47: "Majesty and love do not go well together, nor tarry long in the same dwelling place"), we are also presented with a divinely perfect metamorphic bull who has transfigured all of nature. This extraordinary bull is the work of Jove as artist idealizing the forms to be found in nature. The parallel to Ovid the artist is unmistakable. In the poet's case, too, creation by metamorphosis amounts to an idealization of natural forms and to a reawakening of our awareness of them. Metamorphosis thus becomes the marriage of nature and art. The retelling of the Europa story in the context of Arachne's tapestry reminds us that art and self-metamorphosis are close parallels and that both are beautiful but delusive. If Europa is *elusa*, so are we, for in both cases the work is an *imago*, a multifaceted word that Ovid uses quite deliberately for its complex reverberations, ranging from artistic image to mere shadow, or, as we saw in our discussions of Hecuba and Niobe, to the reductive result of metamorphosis.

Without the special glories of Jupiter's power, multiple forms are liable to be false forms. The physical struggle between Hercules and the river god Achelous depends upon a confrontation between the magnificent bodily strength of the great hero and the self-transforming powers of his adversary. As the two strive for the hand of Deianira, they begin with words. Hercules reminds the girl's father of his famous labors, but Achelous is much more verbose, as if rhetoric itself is a protean talent, a shifting quality that acts as a counterbalance to Hercules' fortitude and constancy, expressed in his successful completion of the labors. Hercules insists that they shift from words to blows, but that stage of the combat hinges upon the same contrast between constancy and shifting multiplicity. "Inferior virtute, meas divertor ad artes, / elaborque viro longum formatus in anguem" (9.62–63: "Finding myself no match for him in strength, I had recourse to my arts, and glided out of his grasp in the form of a long snake"), confesses Achelous, implicitly contrasting his *elabor* with his opponent's famous *labor*. The snake is the most protean of animals. With Hercules, however, this transformation does no good, since Achelous is soon reminded of his opponent's power over the Lernaean Hydra, a far more terrifying serpent than the present one; and the succeeding transformation into a wild bull—which also recalls certain labors of Hercules—is similarly ineffectual. Hercules himself gives the best gloss upon these slippery talents when he attacks Achelous for assuming the serpentine form: "quid fore te credas, falsum qui versus in anguem / arma aliena moves, quem forma precaria celat" (9.75–76: "And what do you think will become of you, who, having assumed but a lying serpent form, make use of borrowed arms, who are masked in a shifting form"). Self-transformation is *falsum, aliena, precaria*, and ultimately ineffectual.[49]

Yet Ovid's meanings are never quite straightforward. Hercules is, of course, the arch-opponent of proteanism and all its works. A poet who is, on the other hand, celebrating metamorphosis may see the wonder and glory of this power even as he cultivates moral suspicions about it. The stories of Daedalus and Pygmalion develop these ambiguities concerning the human power of transformation. Neither is literally a protean figure, but each achieves a power that is directly parallel to metamorphosis. The basic principle in Ovid's narration of the Daedalus story is in the relation between nature's creations and those of the clever artificer.[50] That relation embodies both the idea of metamorphosis—for Daedalus transforms human beings through his art—and the kind of negative judgment we have already seen in Ovid's view of self-transformation. Daedalus, after all, designed the equipment that enabled Pasiphae to couple with the bull and hence conceive the Minotaur. Once responsible for that piece of animal transformation, he must deal with the consequences by a further form of artifice, the labyrinth in which the Minotaur is hidden. Ovid's serpentine definition of Daedalus's art suits the connections between proteanism and snakes:

> turbatque notas et lumina flexu
> ducit in errorem variarum ambage viarum.
> non secus ac liquidus Phrygiis Maeandrus in arvis
> ludit et ambiguo lapsu refluitque fluitque
> occurrensque sibi venturas aspicit undas
> et nunc ad fontes, nunc ad mare versus apertum
> incertas exercet aquas . . . [8.160–66]

(He confused the usual passages and deceived the eye by a conflicting maze of divers winding paths. Just as the watery Maeander plays in the Phrygian fields, flows back and forth in doubtful course and, turning back on itself, beholds its own waves coming on their way, and sends its uncertain waters now towards their source and now towards the open sea . . .)

Arachne made use of a realistic aesthetic to depict a realistic transformation, while Daedalus uses an aesthetic of trompe l'oeil, defeating scrutiny, discovery, and eyesight (hence *removere, caecis, includere, turbat, errorem, ambage*) in imitation of a shifting and doubtful world of transformation. There is virtually nothing of the physical obstacle to this labyrinth as Ovid describes it; rather it is a piece of delightful and deceptive architecture. In Ovid's account it claims only one victim: "ita Daedalus implet / innumeras errore vias vixque ipse reverti / ad limen potuit: tanta est fallacia tecti" (8.166–68: "so Daedalus made those innumerable winding passages, and was himself scarce able to find his way back to the place of entry, so deceptive was the enclosure he had built"). Literally and figuratively Daedalus is the prisoner of his own creation. He is set against his own artificial obstacles and the obstacles that nature puts in his path, since Crete is an island from which there is no easy escape.

The great piece of artifice in the story, then, must be seen in terms of that familiar Ovidian structuring by land, sea, and air. Daedalus is cut off from his proper elements of land and sea; so he must undergo protean transformation to become master of the air. As in the case of his earlier achievements, Daedalus maintains a special peer-relation to nature:

> ignotas animum dimittit in artes
> naturamque novat. nam ponit in ordine pennas
> a minima coeptas, longam breviore sequenti,
> ut clivo crevisse putes: sic rustica quondam
> fistula disparibus paulatim surgit avenis;
> tum lino medias et ceris alligat imas
> atque ita conpositas parvo curvamine flectit,
> ut veras imitetur aves.   [8.188–95]

(He sets his mind at work upon unknown arts, and changes the laws of nature. For he lays feathers in order, beginning at the smallest, short next to long, so that you would think they had grown upon a slope. Just so the old-fashioned rustic pan-pipes, with their unequal reeds rise one above another. Then he fastened the feathers together with twine and wax at the middle and bottom; and, thus arranged, he bent them with a gentle curve, so that they looked like real birds' wings.)

Daedalus's act is metamorphic in that it appears to copy the orderliness of nature. The artificer further aligns himself with order in giving advice to his son:

> "medio" que "ut limite curras,
> Icare," ait "moneo, ne, si demissior ibis,
> unda gravet pennas, si celsior, ignis adurat:
> inter utrumque vola."   [8.203–06]

("I warn you, Icarus, to fly in a middle course, lest, if you go too low, the water may weight your wings; if you go too high, the fire may burn them. Fly between the two.")

The order of feathers, the harmony of the pan-pipes, the shape of a bird's wing, the symmetrical dangers of fire and water as one flies through the air: these basic structures of nature Daedalus perceives, imitates, and takes advantage of.

Yet Daedalus defies the order he would imitate by the act of imitation itself. Human metamorphoses, given such motives as these, can never rise from imitation to the real thing. Once Daedalus determines that he and his son shall fly, he has stepped outside order. The flight itself is a genuine metamorphosis (or would-be metamorphosis), as we see from two rather telling descriptions, first from Ovid directly: "pennisque levatus / ante volat comitique timet, velut ales, ab alto, / quae teneram prolem produxit in aera nido" (8.212–14: "rising on his wings, he flew on ahead, fearing for his companion, just like a bird which has led forth her fledglings from the high nest into the unsubstantial air"), and then from the points of view of some lowly human observers: "vidit et obstipuit, quique aethera carpere possent, / credidit esse deos" (8.219–20: "spies them and stands stupefied, and believes them to be gods that they could fly through the air"). The two comparisons remind us how close metaphor is to metamorphosis. Daedalus has transformed himself and his son simultaneously into birds and gods—*in a sense*. In doing so, however, he has violated yet another form of order through categories, those lines that separate men from gods on the one hand and from beasts on the other. Here, as so often in the poem, human beings cannot seek transformation to higher orders without being simultaneously (or finally) relegated to the symmetrical equivalent in the lower realm.[51]

In spite of later Daedaluses, there is little glory in Ovid's account of the artificer's experience and even less a feeling of the creative artist. The one glorious moment belongs not to the father but to the son: "cum puer audaci coepit gaudere volatu / deseruitque ducem caelique cupidine tractus / altius egit iter" (8.223–25: "when the boy began to rejoice in his bold flight and, deserting his leader, led by a desire for the open sky, directed his course to a greater height"). Ovid denies Daedalus the love of the natural element and the sense of limitless soaring because he does not choose to show the artificer in such an ecstatic relation to nature. Nor does he wish to show Daedalus as an artist, for his creations tend to embrace all the flaws of proteanism without achieving its glories. If we continue to think of Jove in bovine disguise as the archetypal protean work of art, we see readily that Daedalus shares with that creation the deceptiveness of transitory forms, but he attains neither the accurate imitation of nature nor the artistic transcendence of nature.

Where Daedalus fails, Pygmalion succeeds, in one of the pivotal episodes of the *Metamorphoses*, uniting art and nature with a positive sense of human affirmation.[52] The affirmations are challenged in the final third of the poem; but they begin to suggest that human beings can effect and undergo metamorphosis in a positive way that celebrates art and nature at once. The story begins, however, with a significant turning away from nature. Pygmalion has observed the immoral Propoetides, history's first prostitutes and the subjects of Ovid's directly preceding story, and he generalizes from their case, remaining unmarried because of the vices which "menti femineae natura dedit." From the start, the issue is joined between art and nature because Pygmalion revolts here not only against women but against the whole rule of nature. Significantly, the punishment of the Propoetides is that they turn to stone.

Ovid introduces the creation of the statue with an ingenuous *interea* as though there were no causal connection between Pygmalion's moral position and his sculpture, but the implication is clear: the young man has turned away from nature and toward art. "Interea niveum mira feliciter arte / sculpsit ebur formamque dedit, qua femina nasci / nulla potest" (10.247–49: "Meanwhile with wondrous art he successfully carves a figure out of snowy ivory, giving it a beauty more perfect than that of any woman ever born"). At this early stage, Pygmalion is still an artificer, but, like Jove in the Europa story, he is a kind of transforming god who can give form (or give beauty), and his creation is both beautiful and accurate. In addition, the creation represents a direct expression of the creator's attitude: he has rejected nature and therefore fabricates a statue-woman beyond any that could actually be born. Ovid's formula of praise for the statue reminds us that birth is the greatest of transformations. For the moment, that is a metamorphosis which the statue cannot convey accurately because for all its beauty and accuracy it originates in an attack upon nature.

The terms change when Pygmalion falls in love with the statue. Though this love may continue to signify that Pygmalion has turned away from real women, it equally signifies that the statue is a true work of art that has actually captured the spark of beauty within itself. Pygmalion proceeds to caress the statue (fearing that he will bruise its flesh), and he brings it love tokens. Such amatory service is a bit comical and bizarre, for there are certainly echoes of Narcissus in a passionate devotion that refuses to know the identity of its object and cannot distinguish between shadow and substance. Yet the love leads to a serious kind of implantation. Pygmalion begins to bestow life upon the statue by believing in her life.

The appearance of Venus is merely a grace note to this story of metamorphosis. She achieves no magic transformations on her own but rather she sends her worshiper back to continue the life-giving process that he has already begun. Armed with confidence from the goddess of love, Pygmalion returns to his creation without any bashfulness. He is transformed into a very different kind of lover from the young man who earlier proffered courtly service and presents but hesitated to touch: "incumbensque toro dedit oscula: visa tepere est; / admovet os iterum, manibus quoque pectora temptat" (10.281–82: "bending over the couch he kissed her. She seemed warm to his touch. Again he kissed her, and with his hands also he touched her breast"). In fact, it is not only the statue that softens under the pressure of love but also the creator himself. Nature as a general force, and Pygmalion's own nature in particular, are seconding the artistic creation and softening the hardness of both individuals. The fate and the texture, as well as the moral position, of the Propoetides have been reversed in a successful metamorphosis that reconfirms the favorable definition of human nature which arose in the very same image of softening stones back in the Deucalion and Pyrrha story of the first book.

That process of softening is one of Ovid's favorite images of transformation. Here, as elsewhere, it is partly a scientific description—the statue softens because Pygmalion's rubbing naturally produces warmth that melts stoniness—but that rubbing is also the act of love-making itself. Ovid's simile for this softening is significant:

> ut Hymettia sole
> cera remollescit tractataque pollice multas
> flectitur in facies ipsoque fit utilis usu.   [10.284–86]

(As Hymettian wax grows soft under the sun and, moulded by the thumb, is easily shaped to many forms and becomes usable through use itself . . .)

The wax stands as an emblem for all matter in this metamorphic poem, staying the same and ever changing, as Pythagoras will quite specifically point out:

> utque novis facilis signatur cera figuris
> nec manet ut fuerat nec formas servat easdem,
> sed tamen ipsa eadem est . . .   [15.169–71]

(And, as the pliant wax is stamped with new designs, does not remain as it was before nor keep the same form long, but is still the self-same wax . . .)

The Pygmalion story illustrates certain ways in which the wax does change. The softening that enables it to take different forms is either *sole* or *pollice*: metamorphosis is related either to nature or to the hand of the artist. Either way, the change in forms is radical and yet valid; ideally, the two ways combine.

In this respect the contrast with Daedalus's story is striking. Early in that episode Icarus casually poked his finger about in the soft wax ("flavam modo pollice ceram / mollibat"; 8.198–99: "[Icarus would] now mould the yellow wax with his thumb"), reminding us of the flexibility of that generative substance, emblem at once of the unity and changeability of all matter. Again the wax can be shaped *pollice* or *sole*. But, unlike Pygmalion, Daedalus works entirely by his own hand; and the results when confronted with the sun are disastrous. The melting of Icarus's wings testifies to the power of the sun and to his father's opposition to nature. In opposition to the sun, no new forms are created by the softening of wax but only the dissolution of form and life.

Whatever the combination of sun and human hands, such transformations as that of Pygmalion's statue are meant to prove that *ipso fit utilis usu*. This statement is part of a credo that develops in the poem, a credo as apposite to Iphis as to Pygmalion. If metamorphosis comes to be associated with a self generating its own benefit, service, beauty, as well as its own form, then the poem can be said to attack all rigid plans of finding out abiding truths. Metamorphosis can be the key to a much more shifting vision of the truth, one in which subject very much affects object. As the Pygmalion story draws to a close, the hero's rather comical imaginings have become flesh, as it were, through his imagination, his artistry, his piety, and his love. And, once the wax has softened and changed its form, it does not stay in the shadowy realm but rather becomes real. Once again, as in the case of Perseus, the damage of the Narcissus story is being repaired. Pygmalion is potentially narcissistic since he falls in love with his own creation, but metamorphosis through his art and his belief in his art makes of shadow a very real substance.

Finally, though, it must be said that Ovid does not leave everything in such an affirmative condition as we have been suggesting. Pygmalion's story leads directly to the tale of Myrrha, the great-granddaughter of Pygmalion and his statue. Myrrha falls in love with *her* creator, and that experience leads to an undoing of all the certainties celebrated by the story of Pygmalion. Still, the Pygmalion story stands not only as a statement about art and not only a vindication of human transformation but also an affirmation of metamorphosis as a force leading individuals to find and define their own nature. The statue coming to life repairs the damages not only of narcissism but also of proteanism, whose metamorphoses are so random and external that they neither seek nor conform to a nature of their own.

6. Changes to End Change

Achelous, as we observed in his protean struggle with Hercules, moves from river to snake to bull and might have gone on until the end of time. But poems and histories and even *carmina perpetua* do come to an end; and in that series of transformations there is a sign of one sort of resolution, at least. Hercules has broken off the bull's horn. It is seized by the naiads, filled with fruits and flowers, and made sacred as the Horn of Plenty. This appears to be a complete invention on Ovid's part, a striking departure from the traditional etiology of the Cornucopia, which Ovid himself offers in the *Fasti*.[53] When he breaks off the horn of Achelous-as-bull, Hercules is in a sense making a solid substance of what was a shifting, protean form—rather as if one were to wake up in possession of a piece of real property from the world of one's dream. This bull's horn, once retrieved from the protean world, embodies a transforming power in the real world—the power of nature's abundance. The natural world is one endpoint of transformation. Ultimately metamorphoses dissolve into metamorphic nature.

So it is with a whole series of human figures whose vitality passes away into the fertility of nature. In each case, Ovid uses the image of transformed or transfigured blood to depict the birth of the immortal organism generating itself from a literal flowing of the dying man's blood. Marsyas, the flute player who strives with Apollo and loses, is the first. Ovid glosses over the crime and concentrates upon punishment by flaying. The description is of blood and motion, with the exposed entrails flowing, throbbing, and palpitating. Soon the flow of blood gives way to the equally organic flow of tears, as country people, forest gods, fauns, nymphs, and shepherds all lament his demise. The series of weepers here ("et . . . et . . . et . . . et . . .") acts as a response to the series of palpitating organs earlier, suggesting that the vengeance of the god has been transformed into the pity of nature and all nature's immanent deities.

The movement from blood to tears then gives way to a process of flow and transformation that is literal and scientific:

fertilis inmaduit madefactaque terra caducas
concepit lacrimas ac venis perbibit imis;
quas ubi fecit aquam, vacuas emisit in auras.   [6.396–98]

(The fruitful earth was soaked, and soaking caught those tears and drank them deep into her veins. Changing these then to water, she sent them forth into the free air.)

The poet here completely eschews magic in favor of a natural process of flow that also amounts to an anthropomorphization of the earth itself, as if she were being metamorphosed into a human organism in response to the human who is turning to earth. Blood has become tears and now tears become water. The final (and proper) metamorphosis orders the whole process: "inde petens rapidus ripis declivibus aequor / Marsya nomen habet, Phrygiae liquidissimus amnis" (6.399–400: "Thence the stream with its sloping banks ran down quickly to the sea, and had the name of Marsyas, the clearest river in all Phrygia"). Flow is here given its proper, natural form, that of the eternally moving river. Marsyas' blood has been almost scientifically transformed from an image of death to one of immortality. In the process his story and his person have been purified. Hence the multiple weight of the adjective *liquidissimus*, suggesting at once the flow of all the liquids associated with the story and also the purity and clarity of this last form that Marsyas takes.

When the beautiful young Hyacinthus is accidentally killed by a discus that his beloved Apollo has thrown, his death not only stains the earth but also signs it:

ecce cruor, qui fusus humo signaverat herbas
desinit esse cruor, Tyrioque nitentior ostro
flos oritur . . .   [10.210–12]

(Behold, the blood, which had poured out on the ground and
stained the grass, ceased to be blood, and in its place there sprang a
flower brighter than Tyrian dye.)

Signaverat, which has the primary meaning of "staining" the earth, also
suggests an imprint, as if Hyacinthus's blood has taken a piece of random
earth and made it distinguished. The flower to which he gives his name is
a sign both of his immortality and of this distinction, as his suffering is literally imprinted on the flower in the *aiai* (or "alas") that shows on the
petals.

Adonis, whose story follows soon after Hyacinthus's, has even more direct associations with immortality. When the boy dies, Venus decrees the
immortality and flowering of his blood to be celebrated by an annual ritual
of lamentation. The reference is to the *Adonia*, the yearly period of
mourning for the dead Adonis.[54] As a preclassical deity of vegetation,
Adonis was closely linked with this order, and in classical times the link
was strengthened by connecting the boy-god with Persephone, whose
half-yearly sojourn with her husband Dis accounts etiologically for the
seasons. Here we can begin to see Adonis as personifying a principle by
which human death can turn through metamorphosis into vegetable
immortality.

There exists a kind of balancing relationship between the self-transforming figure and the figure whose life passes into the metamorphic fertility of nature. The meaning of both figures changes toward the end of
the poem. The story of Acis has a great deal in common with those of
Marsyas, Hyacinthus, and Adonis. Images of flow permeate the narration,
as the hero is the son of a river-nymph while his beloved Galatea is herself
a sea-nymph. The antagonist Polyphemus, on the other hand, personifies
solidity and mass, and, true to his nature, he buries Acis under a mountain. The young man is killed, but the flow of waters is not stopped. Indeed, it is purified, as his metamorphosis produces a whole yearly cycle of
natural flow. But that purification goes several steps further. From the
mass that Polyphemus had thrown, a reed springs up and waters flow, and
then

miraque res, subito media tenus exstitit alvo
incinctus iuvenis flexis nova cornua cannis,
qui, nisi quod maior, quod toto caerulus ore,
Acis erat, sed sic quoque erat tamen Acis, in amnem
versus.   [13.893–97]

(Wonderful! suddenly a youth stood forth waist-deep from the water, his new-sprung horns wreathed with bending rushes. The youth, save that he was larger and his face of dark sea-blue, was Acis. But even so he still was Acis, changed to a river-god.)

Without losing sight of natural fertility, Ovid suddenly takes the metamorphosis in two quite different directions. Acis is reborn as a divinity, and at the same time he is reborn in his own person. The passage is intentionally vague about the identity of this figure, whether it is or is not Acis, whether *amnis* is the river itself or the divine spirit of the river. However we resolve these ambiguities, it is clear that metamorphosis leads to apotheosis and to a transfigured version of the original self. We are witnessing at once the birth of a divinity and the turning away from fluidity toward a stable identity. It is, in short, a change from which there is no further change.

The change from which there is no further change is a new doctrine of metamorphosis, and it is closely tied to Ovid's account of the birth and flowering of Rome. In this poem of great transformations, none is more crucial than the movement of history from east to west, the change, both political and cultural, from the Aegean world to Italy. The assertion that all things have an eternally shifting nature accords perfectly with this "progressive" attitude toward history; but if Ovid is to maintain an orthodox stance—and he surely does at least in part—then his terms must shift somewhat once he has arrived at the supposed culmination of the progress.[55] In keeping with this shift, the story of Acis represents not a rejection of metamorphosis but a turning away from the idea of eternal flow and the beginnings of a more stable affirmation in regard to human identity.

The poem's final example of proteanism, the story of Vertumnus and Pomona, most clearly establishes the change. This is a specifically Roman story, apparently invented by Ovid.[56] Like the other stories of proteanism and immortality, it is couched in images of fertility. Pomona, a goddess associated with fruit trees, typifies the practical, hard-working, agricultural side of fertility, but her concern for fertility is too narrow, since she rejects any possibility of fruit-bearing herself. Vertumnus, too, is a great Roman figure of fertility, celebrated notably by Propertius.[57] His name was thought to derive from *verto*, and this "turning" was associated by the Romans both with shape-changing and with the movements of the seasons and of vegetation toward ripeness. The scenes of Vertumnus's wooing have a great deal in common with the amatory self-transformations of earlier figures in the poem. The signs of dubiety are still there: *imago*, *videri*, many subjunctives and infinitives. But there are important differences. His guises as reaper, mower, cattle herd, leaf-gatherer, vinepruner, and so on are humble and honest. They also fulfill important truths about Vertumnus's own identity and that of the woman he is wooing. In fact, they are more costume changes than bodily transformations, and it is significant that the man underneath remains constant, both in his love and in his identity.

Fittingly, the final triumph of love comes through a completely different sort of metamorphosis, a piece of proteanism that celebrates his essential constancy. He becomes, in a word, himself:

> Haec ubi nequiquam formae deus aptus anili
> edidit, in iuvenem rediit at anilia demit
> instrumenta sibi talisque apparuit illi,
> qualis ubi oppositas nitidissima solis imago
> evicit nubes nullaque obstante reluxit,
> vimque parat: sed vi non est opus, inque figura
> capta dei nympha est et mutua vulnera sensit.   [14.765–71]

(When the god in the form of age had thus pleaded his cause in vain, he returned to his youthful form, put off the old woman's trappings, and stood revealed to the maiden as when the sun's most beaming face has conquered the opposing clouds and shines out with nothing to dim his radiance. He was all ready to force her will, but no force was necessary; and the nymph, smitten by the beauty of the god, felt an answering passion.)

The ultimate protean transformation, as in the case of Acis, is a transfigured form of the original self, but freed of all the metamorphic associations with constant change. Like the Rome for which, in some respects, he stands, he is the product of metamorphoses, but he is now real, unchanging, and eternal.

These final changes in Acis and Vertumnus, with their Roman associations, point to that most particularly Roman form of metamorphosis in the poem: apotheosis. Like the final change of Vertumnus, apotheosis is a metamorphosis that denies metamorphosis, producing a transfigured form of the individual that is and is not the human self. Each of the four times that apotheosis occurs in the last half of the poem it takes the quasi-chemical form that so many Ovidian transformation stories take, but the destination in each case is the removal of all the physicality and particularity that makes metamorphosis possible. So Hercules, Aeneas, Romulus, and Julius Caesar all become their own distilled essence when they enter the realm of the gods just as Vertumnus becomes himself to woo Pomona.[58]

The progression is very steady from the concretely physical to the abstract. The death of Hercules, the first to be deified, is treated in naturalistic fashion. Ovid describes the entrance and progress of the poison from the Lernaean Hydra in almost technical terms. The poison begins to take effect, we are told, when it is melted by the flames at which Hercules is burning propitiatory incense. These deleterious effects are described in graphic physical language. But suddenly the violence is over. It is as though the poison has shifted from an active phase to a passive one, and that change characterizes the whole movement from human to divine. Hercules constructs his own funeral pyre: from uprooting trees in frenzy he moves to felling trees as part of a holy ritual. All this is only a prelude to the real loss of concreteness and humanity. Like the Lernaean poison, the flames have a precise, chemical effect. They destroy the mortal body but also purify some sort of nonphysical essence that makes a decorporealized Hercules ready to enter the company of the gods. The description of the newly regenerated hero is decisively anti-physical:

sic ubi mortales Tirynthius exuit artus,
parte sui meliore viget, maiorque videri
coepit et augusta fieri gravitate verendus.   [9.268–70]

(So when the Tirynthian put off his mortal frame, he gained new vigour in his better part, began to seem of more heroic size, and to become awful in his godlike dignity.)

The language is that of proteanism, but the results turn decisively away from the physicality of protean transformations.

The apotheosis of Hercules in Book IX prefigures a sequence of similar events in Books XIV and XV, the apotheoses of Aeneas, Romulus, and Julius Caesar, who were often identified with Hercules. The culminating figure is Augustus, whose apotheosis ("orbe relicto / accedat caelo"; 15.869–70) is inevitable but outside the poem's time span. The three Roman apotheoses closely follow the pattern in the Hercules story, but they are increasingly abstract. Aeneas goes through a purification when, acting on Venus's orders, the Numician river god "quicquid in Aenea fuerat mortale, repurgat / et respersit aquis; pars optima restitit illi" (14.603–04: "in his waters cleansed and washed quite away whatever was mortal in Aeneas. His best part remained to him.") This almost perfectly complements Hercules' end, even to the point where the earlier hero experiences purification by fire, while Aeneas's is by water. But the beginning and ending states of transformation have become more nebulous. *Quaecumque*, *quicquid*, and *pars optima* (cf. Hercules' *pars melior*) all amount to little more than obfuscations. The apotheosis of Romulus takes abstraction one step further:

corpus mortale per auras
dilapsum tenues, ceu lata plumbea funda

missa solet medio glans intabescere caelo;
pulchra subit facies et pulvinaribus altis
dignior, est qualis trabeati forma Quirini.   [14.824–28]

(His mortal part dissolved into thin air, as a leaden bullet hurled by
a broad sling is wont to melt away in the mid-heavens. And now a
fair form clothes him, worthier of the high couches of the gods, such
form as has Quirinus, clad in the sacred robe.)

The physical change is glossed over even more quickly (note that Ovid has
now used the third of the four elements in describing apotheosis), and the
simile hinges upon a word, *intabescere*, that suggests the complete dissolution of the physical. Again, there is considerable vagueness about the
post-metamorphic form of Romulus: *pulchra facies* does not communicate
very much, and Ovid is deliberately evasive as to whether Romulus is
Quirinus or is like Quirinus.[59] Finally, the apotheosis of Julius Caesar is
purely abstract:

medi cum sede senatus
constitit alma Venus nulli cernenda suique
Caesaris eripuit membris nec in aera solvi
passa recentem animam caelestibus intulit astris.   [15.843–46]

(. . . when fostering Venus took her place within the senate-house,
unseen of all, caught up the passing soul of her Caesar from his
body, and not suffering it to vanish into air, she bore it towards the
stars of heaven.)

There is no metamorphosis here at all, no before and after, no mortal and
immortal bodies. Apotheosis has finally left the ruling image of the poem
completely behind.

Once again, this movement away from metamorphosis reflects the
problem of ending the poem with Rome (or indeed at all). If the poem is
about the endless changes in all things, how can it conclude by celebrating a Roman empire that is meant to be eternal? By inserting this sequence of Roman apotheoses near the close of the poem, Ovid was attempting to shift from a world of constant change to a world purified of all
those questionable and passionate drives that lead, in most parts of the
work, to metamorphosis. It is for this reason that the scenes surrounding
the deaths of these great Romans are all so drenched in *pietas* and the virtues of what we could call progress and proper succession. Aeneas dies
fresh from his military victories and only when his son Iulus is ready to
take over. Romulus may be removed from mortal life, but he is carried off
while on the job, giving forth benevolent judgments to his fellow citizens.
Julius Caesar's death is of course premature and unnatural, but he too
dies on the job and only once an extremely desirable succession is clearly

to follow. Individual Roman leaders perfecting their world and Roman history leading progressively to the Augustan empire are emblems of human change suggesting earthly perfectibility even as the particular characters are undergoing heavenly perfectibility.

Yet, however much Roman orthodoxy may have led Ovid toward terminating metamorphosis in the monumental foundations of Rome, he speaks as well with another voice running counter to the construction of an empire, the perfecting of a people, and deification of its heroes. It has already been suggested that to postulate an order of continuing change beyond human control is to cast doubt upon the substantiality of any great human structure, whether personal or social. But there is an even more basic anti-heroic thrust to metamorphosis. We have seen that this is a poem about the causes of things—these things including the created world itself, the gods and their power, the organisms of nature, the rules and shapes of society. Insofar as Ovid really does explain the causes, he dissolves great public facts into private stories. One of the earliest examples is perhaps the best: the laurel tree. From the heroic slayer of the Python, Apollo is reduced to the lover, and as lover he is altogether unsuccessful. The ultimate product of this hopeless love is the crown worn by emperors and triumphant generals. A quintessential prop of public Rome is infused through the link of metamorphosis with a private story of unrealized love. The sheer quantity and variety of Ovid's explanations reminds us that we live in a world surrounded by the metamorphic results of private stories. Such an impression cannot fail to represent a poetic attack on the primacy of Rome.

The ending of the Apollo and Daphne story only hints at the confrontation between Rome and metamorphosis, and it comes much too early in the poem for those issues yet to be clear. But near the opposite end of the poem, during his rather irreverent retelling of episodes from the *Aeneid*,[60] Ovid joins the tale of a Roman victory with the dissolution of power in the story of Trojan ships that become sea-nymphs. From the start of the vignette, Ovid underplays the issue of Roman might. The ships are not signs of armed force nearly so much as they are animate vegetable matter participating in a kind of Empedoclean tension among the elements of creation, expressed in this case as fire, water, wood, and resin. In this light it is not surprising that he allows his story to turn on the ships' past, rather than their present, identity. The mother of the gods, remembering the original pine trees, declares, "nec me patiente cremabit / ignis edax nemorum partes et membra meorum" (14.540–41: "nor with my consent shall the greedy flames devour what was once part and parcel of my sacred woods.") This is a metamorphosis before the fact. It reminds us that we live in the iron age when trees are felled that restless men may travel.[61] Ovid changes the ships' form here by reducing them to their original constituent vegetable matter; and by identifying the precise source of that matter he bestows a moral and historical value upon the ships quite apart from their current use. The actual metamorphosis of the ships passes smoothly to a vivification which merely confirms their liveliness throughout. They soften even further, and as sea-nymphs they are removed still more from an imperial or military identity. In their final state they disport themselves joyfully in the water, careless of their past. The pleasure, freedom, oblivion of these figures amounts to a return to their "element" and a dissolution of that awkward phase of their lives when they took part in the wars so much more interesting to Virgil than to Ovid.

Military ships which become sea-nymphs, beautiful young men like Acis or Adonis who pass away into flowers or rivers, Roman heroes who become gods: all experience metamorphosis into immortality. Indeed, the foundation of Rome itself is at least a would-be metamorphosis into immortality. The end of the poem affords us a glimpse into a set of principles for metamorphic immortality, which may confirm or contradict these examples. The four-hundred-line speech of the visionary philosopher Pythagoras summarizes, develops, and counterpoints many issues in the whole poem.[62] "Omnia mutantur, nihil interit": Pythagoras' principal message scarcely needs clarification in itself or in its relevance to the poem as we have considered it here.

Yet Pythagoras cannot simply be equated with the poet. Ovid introduces him because he is (among other things) famous for a belief in the transmigration of the soul, and, while there is an obvious connection between that doctrine and metamorphosis, Ovid's poem concerns itself more with the transmigration of the body than with that of the soul. Nor is the philosopher precisely Ovidian in his understanding of metamorphosis as mutability: "tempus edax rerum, tuque, invidiosa vetustas, / omnia destruitis vitiataque dentibus aevi / paulatim lenta consumitis omnia morte!" (15.234–36: "O time, thou grand devourer, and thou, envious Age, together you destroy all things; and slowly gnawing with your teeth, you finally consume all things in lingering death!"). Contradictory as such pessimism is to a belief in metempsychosis, it is equally opposed to Ovidian metamorphosis, in which living energy is not dissipated but rather saved and put to new uses.

Mutability and metempsychosis are, in fact, extreme points that help to define Ovidian metamorphosis. One is altogether concrete, the other altogether abstract. Pythagoras speaks of both, but his most powerful assertions are those that combine the continuity of transmigration with the concreteness of physical change. Side by side with his assertions that individuals and the world as a whole are deteriorating and dying come other suggestions that all is part of a great cycle: "nam quod fuit ante, relictum est, / fitque, quod haut fuerat, momentaque cuncta novantur" (15.184–85: "For that which once existed is no more, and that which was not has come to be; and so the whole round of motion is gone through again"). At every turn, the philosopher makes this process as physical and concrete as Ovidian metamorphosis itself. The cycle exists because nature creates organisms from other organisms. Thus, when Pythagoras speaks in Empedoclean terms about the elements,[63] he does not simply place them in a circle but he rather suggests how they transform themselves into each other: "ignis enim densum spissatus in aera transit, / hic in aquas, tellus glomerata cogitur unda" (15.250–51: "for fire, condensed, passes into thick air, thence into water; and water, packed together, solidifies into earth"). In fact, Pythagoras sees that all forms come from other forms; and his climactic demonstration of this fact is the doctrine we know as spontaneous generation. If insects are bred out of a dead animal carcass, then Ovidian metamorphosis affirms the continuity of vital energy while negating the effects of destructive mutability.

The fact that Pythagoras approaches his argument with a bias toward empirical demonstration is surely as important as the argument itself. Why are animals sacrificed as part of a fertility ritual? "Prima putatur / hostia sus meruisse mori, quia semina pando / eruerit rostro spemque interceperit anni" (15.111–13: "it is thought that the sow was first condemned to death as a sacrificial victim because with her broad snout she had rooted up the planted seeds and cut off the season's promised crop"). A similar directness governs the histories of rivers and the natural history of animals. Frogs, for instance, need legs for swimming; but they also need uneven legs for jumping, and hence their precise shape. Pythagoras' etiologies depend upon internal logic. A ritual, an organism, or a geographical locality develops because of its own peculiar needs. Such an approach fulfills the last phase of Ovidian transformation, the sense, as we saw in connection with Pygmalion and his statue, that *ipso fit utilis usu*. Individual organisms determine their own shape.

Perhaps the greatest force of the speech is the contrast with the Roman direction of the poem, for it forms a kind of alternative ending to the work. Whether we see the subject of the speech as mutability, dissolution, metempsychosis, or endless cyclical change, we must recognize that Pythagoras is no celebrant of the eternal *pax Romana*. He speaks, in fact, of history as an arena of unending change; and though his example is of the passing from Troy to Rome, we can hardly avoid the implication that the present form will also dissolve. Indeed the empirical bias of the speech is also irreverent because it suggests that the primacy of a form— say, Augustan Rome—is not only temporary but also dependent upon its usefulness rather than upon any divine external sanction. So Pythagoras and his speech are tightly bound up with the spirit of Ovid's whole poem and rather strikingly at odds with the Augustan empire. Ovid ends with an uneasy balance between Rome and Pythagoras: apotheosis is balanced against metamorphosis, perfectibility against constant change, social and political improvement against magical transformation. Two differing definitions of immortality coexist. They represent different immortalities and different endings to change and to the poem of change.

Neither Augustus nor Pythagoras actually ends the poem, however. If the Pythagorean world fails to attain substantiality and the Augustan world fails to attain permanence, there is one entity that can attain both:

Iamque opus exegi, quid nec Iovis ira nec ignis
nec poterit ferrum nec edax abolere vetustas.
cum volet, illa dies, quae nil nisi corporis huius
ius habet, incerti spatium mihi finiat aevi:
parte tamen meliore mei super alta perennis
astra ferar, nomenque erit indelebile nostrum.   [15.871–76]

(And now my work is done, which neither the wrath of Jove, nor fire, nor sword, nor the gnawing tooth of time shall ever be able to undo. When it will, let that day come which has no power save over this mortal frame, and end the span of my uncertain years. Still in my better part I shall be borne immortal far beyond the lofty stars and I shall have an undying name.)

The motifs from the speech of Pythagoras (*edax, vetustas, incerti aevi*) are united here with a reality of apotheosis, for the *pars melior*, whose definition was increasingly vague in the Roman apotheoses, is now defined very specifically as the poem itself. Hercules and the others may have become gods in eternity, but Ovid will become his poem.

I have deliberately avoided reducing the *Metamorphoses* to a few central principles, lest the tradition which arises from it be reduced to a few central principles. Yet it may be worthwhile to suggest some ways in which the diversity of the poem combines to produce a heritage of metamorphic thinking, ranging in some cases quite far from the image of magical transformation itself. Above all, the heritage of the *Metamorphoses* is a vision of the universe under the metaphor of *things*. Metamorphosis becomes the quintessential corporeal metaphor, the belief that the nature of a thing can be read in its shape. That may explain why Ovid's poem was such a magnet for visual artists. When one looks at, say, the mid-sixteenth-century Bernard Salomon woodcuts, over two hundred in number, which turn the *Metamorphoses* into an emblem book,[64] one comes to understand that Ovid's stories are visual or "photogenic" because the power and drama are expressed in the objects themselves, in their physical shape. This holds true not only for persons undergoing metamorphosis—it is hardly surprising that a man with a stag's head would be visually arresting—but for the whole range of Ovidian concerns. We have spoken in an earlier chapter of the attractions of a girl riding a bull. A boy falling from the heavens as his chariot and the heavenly bodies collapse around him, another boy gazing at his reflection in a pool, a grisly scene in which a man cuts out a young woman's tongue: these are not metamorphoses, but they still capture human experience in terms of object, body, and shape.

Certain things follow from this metaphor of physicality. First it follows that the world is numinous. The objects of this universe contain some spark of life, of divinity, of poetic meaning, however inanimate and trivial they may seem on first glance. Every thing, whether a wet rock, a plucked flower, or a well-formed javelin, has a story. Every story is necessarily a metaphor, the forcible yoking of the objective present identity of the thing with a set of human values embodied in its story. And most of the metaphors behind things are metaphors of the passions, whether of illicit love or family relations or personal desires. This metaphorizing undermines the objective world, even dissolves it, into a diversity of personal stories as numerous and encyclopedic as Bernard Salomon's two hundred woodcuts. And since the poem aspires to grand cosmological scope, it conveys the same message about the universe as about the topography of the Mediterranean basin: the cosmos is alive, anthropomorphic, passionate, and grounded in human experience. The same metaphorizing and physicalizing applies to divine power. It is no coincidence that such a long sequence of figures, including Cadmus, Actaeon, Tiresias, Narcissus, and Hermaphroditus enter various versions of the *locus amoenus*, which Ovid describes in parallel terms. The sacred place embodies divinity as physical objects embody spirit.

Yet after all it is not things but people that are at the center of the corporeal metaphor. Human nature in the metamorphic universe is inextricable from the human body. The body as we know it—alive, flexible, untransformed—is the measure of all things. That is why the final dissolution of Narcissus, *nusquam corpus erat* (3.509), is balanced against the joyous *corpus erat* (10.289) of Pygmalion. In that metaphor of the body is contained the whole contrast between one story of illusory self-love and another of artistic and amorous outward creation. That is also why we hear more than once about the problems of *copia* and *inops*, as when Niobe declares that plenty makes her safe or when Narcissus realizes that, in Spenser's translation, "plenty makes me poore." In a transforming world the all-important *corpus* or *copia* is under constant threat. All those who defy the gods—Niobe, Arachne, the various disbelievers in Bacchus—think that plenty makes them safe, when plenty, that is, their *quidditas*, is their undoing because plenty dissolves.

This dissolution explains the remarkable persistence of the phrase "tanta est fiducia formae." *Fiducia formae* is faith in one's own beauty. For mortals it turns out to represent a dangerous trust in a particularly unstable form of *copia*. Semele has *fiducia formae* (3.270), but she will be incinerated. Atalanta has it (8.434), but she will ultimately be punished by an angry Venus. Cassiopeia has faith in her daughter Andromeda's *forma*, but that motherly boast leads to a great deal of trouble. *Fiducia formae* is, of course, faith in form as well as faith in beauty. Only the gods can truly possess such faith: so the first *fiducia formae* refers to Mercury appearing, after various metamorphoses, in his own divine form to Herse. The girl does not survive that appearance, any more than Semele survives Jupiter's ultimate *forma*. Mortal *forma*, however it is defined, cannot be trusted in the world of metamorphosis. To boast of beauty is to lose one's form.

One essential metaphor for the body's undoing by metamorphosis is that of turning to stone. Many literally turn to stone, like Niobe and the Propoetides, while others define their life, that is, their body, by turning from stone, including Pygmalion's statue and the figures created by Deucalion and Pyrrha as well as (metaphorically) Andromeda released from the clutches of the dragon. In addition, many transformations into animate (especially vegetable) forms approach the rigidity of petrification because they freeze life and corporeality in eternity. In the opposite direction from stone is the transformation to *imago*. Hecuba, Lycaon, Procne, and many others are, at some point, whether or not as part of literal metamorphosis, reduced by transformation to an image of themselves. Narcissus is literally reduced to an image of himself. And the artists of the poem—Arachne, the self-transforming Jupiter, Pygmalion—create images of themselves. These are not random parallels. All *imagines* are metamorphic reductions; all (unless inspired by true love and life) are frozen into bodilessness. And all metamorphoses are in a sense transformations to *imago*, since all the results of transformation stand eternally as *imagines* in our numinous universe. The turn to *imago* seems to be the opposite but is in fact identical to the stony transformation. Niobe loses her lifelessness to being an image and a rock; Pygmalion's beloved is born out of ivory and art.

It follows from this corporeal metaphor of the human condition that human identity in the world of metamorphosis be also physicalized. The great stories of discovery, the figures of *nosce te ipsum* in the poem, are figures of the mirror. Narcissus—if he may be mentioned one more time—discovers himself in the externalized, numinous *locus amoenus* of a virgin pool. But he is only the most obvious case. To discover oneself in the metamorphic world is to see one's identity reflected in transformation. That is what happens to Io, to Tiresias, to Actaeon, to Ocyrhoe, in more figurative ways to Phaethon, to Hercules, to Myrrha. For many of these the *locus amoenus* is not only a sacred place but also a mirror region. While some unwillingly confront their identities, others search for them desperately. Phaethon is driven partly because definitions of self are so unstable in his world. And, for those characters who do not discover their own identity, metamorphosis still enables the readers to discover it. That is why the Gorgon's head is such a powerful symbol in the poem, the quintessential metamorphic weapon, which mirrors, petrifies, and freezes an *imago*.

Finally, it follows from the metaphor of transformations that human experience is a series of contagions. If things turn into other things, then so do individuals, concepts, rules, emotions. Philomela's terrible *omnia turbasti*, with which she accuses Tereus of confounding all relations, is itself a metamorphic assertion. But the metamorphic world is one of confusions and contagions even without extreme acts of immoral violence. If objects and persons contain secret histories, then they have secret relations to each other. The log that is identified with Meleager's life, the fatal resemblance between Itys and his father Tereus, the pool that is Salmacis's favorite haunt but also is the girl herself, the contagious magic that enables Juno to prevent Hercules' birth by shutting up her own loins, the destructive love affairs of Cephalus with Aura and Aurora, whose names are suspiciously similar and who both represent impalpable forces in nature: all involve the secret intimacies of different things.

These confusions explain the prevalence in the metamorphic world of incest, homosexuality, and self-love. We saw in chapter 1 how the Europa myth relates metamorphosis to exogamy. In fact, the whole career of love in the middle books of Ovid's poem revolves around versions of endogamy. To love oneself, one's close family relations, one's own sex, one's own creation: these are the themes that Ovid concentrates on, and he balances them against such examples of exogamy as Scylla and Medea. Endogamy, like metamorphosis itself, is a form of intimate contagion, and love—the great subject of the poem if the subject is not metamorphosis—is contagion, catching fire easily, uniting individuals dangerously, whether they be Narcissus and his beloved, Salmacis and Hermaphroditus, or Atalanta, who is told by an oracle that in the married state "teque ipsa viva carebis" (10.566: "though living, you will lose yourself"). The occasional happy loves are also tangles: Cadmus and Harmonia as entwining serpents, or Philemon and Baucis as entwining trees. Even the language of the poem fulfills this tangle. The poetic style of metamorphosis consists again and again of similar words forcibly juxtaposed, like all of Bacchus's enclitics, or the *Cinyrae, Cinyrae* whom Myrrha would like to divide between father and lover, or the *viscera viscera, corpore corpus, animantem animantis* which Pythagoras uses to describe meat-eating. And the modes of simile and pun, of the confusion between words and things, of oxymoron and paradox are the precise equivalent in rhetoric of metamorphic language.

Many words and phrases echo through the poem and, by extension, through the metamorphic tradition. We have spoken of *imago*, of *inopem me copia fecit*, of *fiducia formae*, of *usque adeo latet utilitas*. Yet perhaps the essential phrase is *intus habes quem poscis*, "he whom you seek is within you." It stands as a sort of credo for human experience in the world of metamorphosis. We contain our own identity, and we find it in the mirror of transformation. We contain our destinies within us, petrifications of ourselves into stone and image. Narcissus-like, we often seek in love what is within us, and it is revealed through transformation. In the occasional stories with happy endings we are told *ipso fit utilis usu*, which is really another way of saying that what we seek is within us, since it suggests that we make our own lives fruitful in the act of living them.

These are all metaphoric extensions of *intus habes quem poscis*; the actual occasion at which it is spoken is the moment when Tereus, midway through his meal, asks for the presence of his son Itys. *He whom you seek is within you*. Cannibalism is the ultimate extension of metamorphosis and its ultimate crime. If transformation bridges organisms and the universe via a corporeal metaphor, then it can all be reduced to a terrible kind of eating. The poem is full of cannibals: Lycaon and Tereus, Narcissus (again!), who cannibalizes himself, the Cyclops and the Lestrygonians, who eat wayfaring sailors. Pythagoras accuses meat-eaters of being cannibals and characterizes all of us as victims of cannibalism: *tempus edax rerum*. Let us conclude with Erysichthon, the blasphemer against fertility whose punishment is eternal hunger. In describing his plight, Ovid creates a great cosmological epitome not unlike those that confront Phaethon:

> nec mora; quod pontus, quod terra, quod educat aer,
> poscit et adpositis queritur ieiunia mensis
> inque epulis epulas quaerit; quodque urbibus esse,
> quodque satis poterat populo, non sufficit uni,
> plusque cupit, quod plura suam demittit in alvum.
> utque fretum recipit de tota flumina terra
> nec satiatur aquis peregrinosque ebibit amnes,
> utque rapax ignis non umquam alimenta recusat
> innumerasque faces cremat et, quo copia maior
> est data, plura petit turbaque voracior ipsa est:
> sic epulas omnes Erysichthonis ora profani
> accipiunt poscuntque simul. cibus omnis in illo
> causa cibi est, semperque locus fit inanis edendo.   [8.830–42]

(Straightway he calls for all that sea and land and air can furnish; with loaded tables before him, he complains still of hunger; in the midst of feasts seeks other feasts. What would be enough for whole cities, enough for a whole nation, is not enough for one. The more he sends down into his maw the more he wants. And as the ocean receives the streams from a whole land and is not filled with his waters, but swallows up the streams that come to it from afar; and as the all-devouring fire never refuses fuel, but burns countless logs, seeks ever more as more is given it, and is more greedy by reason of the quantity; so do the lips of impious Erysichthon receive all those banquets, and ask for more. All food in him is but the cause of food, and ever does he become empty by eating.)

It is almost a precis of the poem's cosmos, a living organism constructed of the elements. In a gruesome parody of the metamorphic links within the universe, Erysichthon consumes the world. Like Erysichthon himself, the poem oscillates between *natura rerum* and *edax rerum*. Those are the outer limits of metamorphosis.[65]

CHAPTER THREE

Metamorphosis in the Middle Ages: *Figura & Cosmos*

For the first five hundred years of the Christian era there is, in fact, no "Christian era" in any consistent sense. The genius responsible for the fifth-century mosaics at Santa Pudenziana in Rome, in which Christ and the Apostles appear to be vividly alive Roman citizens, did not know that he was supposed to be inventing a new "Christian" (as it turned out, Byzantine) art. Nor did his contemporary Boethius seem to realize that he would be the last Christian ever to write a work of grand cosmic scope that does not mention the Incarnation, grace, or the revealed word. Had civilization proceeded in that course, there would be no such thing as "classical antiquity" and no such thing as the "Middle Ages." Why it did not is difficult to say. To judge from the key figures of the period, it appears that Christians of the empire were a different breed from Christian Romans and that the larger empire was even more difficult to keep centralized than it had been in pagan times.[1] Whatever the causes may have been, the great intellectuals of those centuries—Jerome, Eusebius, Lactantius, Macrobius, Tertullian, above all Augustine—were engaged in creating an order that defined itself as distinctly alien from ancient Rome. In the process they invented the idea that this alien order had a composite unity, a body with its own laws and consistent identity. No such widely agreed upon periodization—that is, historical rewriting—of the past had ever been attempted. Without such an attempt the parallel but complementary rewrite of a thousand years later would not have been possible. And the period between (how appropriate is its name!) these two historical inventions is defined by having invented the historical period.

For our purposes the significance of that invention is the development of a coherent (though not uniform—we are, after all, dealing with a thousand years) set of attitudes toward paganism. However negative (or positive) these attitudes may be, however voluntarily or involuntarily misinformed, they represent a great body of commentary. I use the word *commentary* in its broadest sense: from glosses and marginalia to great poems and cathedrals, medieval culture is a commentary on a past defined by it as either Christian or pagan. The result is that pagan culture from the time of Augustine onward can never again be a thing in itself, viewed "accurately" and directly; rather, it becomes inseparable from its mediating—and alienating—commentary. The history of paganism in the Middle Ages, of which we are concerned with a small but key piece, consists in the development of this communal commentary and its fusion with the materials of antiquity themselves.[2]

1. Hermeneutic Wars

Before we can speak of fusion we must realize the extent of the outrage that pagan culture, and especially the lore of metamorphosis, represented to the anxious patristic writers. The first of these anxieties we have already observed at the heart of Ovid's treatment of pagan myth: the gods are sometimes the mysterious force that rules the universe, like Plato's demiurge, and at other times they are the subjects of frivolous or even immoral fables—in short, there is an enormous gulf between dogma and mythology. Christians were not the first to notice this, but the problem takes on particular force in the context of Catholic theology, in which dogma and mythology are relatively spare and easy to reconcile. It is in these terms that Augustine attacks the religion of the Romans:

> If it is this God—the God who controls all the causes of events, and of all substances, and of all things in nature—whom the people call Jupiter and whom they worship with all those insults and outrageous slanders, they are guilty of greater blasphemy than if they believed in no god at all. Hence it would have been much better for them to have given the name of Jupiter to some other person, someone deserving those degraded and scandalous honours, substituting an idle fiction to be the object of their blasphemies (as a stone, so it is said, was substituted as an offering to Saturn, for him to devour instead of his son). This would have been far better than to represent Jupiter as both the thunderer and an adulterer, the ruler of the universe and an abandoned debauchee, controlling the highest causes of all substances and all things in nature, but not having good motives for his own actions.[3]

Augustine doubtless recalls here the problem Ovid had raised on the occasion of Jupiter's transformation into a bull: "Non bene conveniunt nec in una sede morantur / maiestas et amor" (2.846–47: "Majesty and love do not go well together, nor tarry long in the same dwelling place"). In fact, Ovid uses the act of divine self-transformation as an attempt to reconcile *maiestas* and *amor*, since the king of the gods in that act demonstrates his power while he achieves his love. But Augustine does not choose to believe in such a reconciliation—not for this particular god of love, at any rate.

Yet immorality is a minor matter in paganism compared to the more theologically anathematized matter of divine multiplicity:

> But how can I give a list, in one passage of this book, of all the names of their gods and goddesses? The Romans had difficulty in getting them into the massive volumes in which they assigned particular functions and special responsibilities to the various divine powers. They decided that responsibility for the land should not be entrusted to any one god; they put the goddess Rusina in charge of the rural countryside; they consigned the mountain ranges to the care of the god Jugatinus; the hills (*colles*) to the goddess Collatina, the valleys to Vallonia. They could not even find the goddess called Segetia adequate on her own, to the responsibilities for the crops (*segetes*) from start to finish. Instead, they decided that the corn when sown (*sata*) should have the goddess Seia to watch over it as long as the seeds were under ground; as soon as the shoots came above the ground and began to form the grain (*seges*), they were under the charge of the goddess Segetia; but when the corn had been reaped and stored the goddess Tutilina was set over them to keep them safe (*tuto*). Would not anyone think that Segetia should have been competent to supervise the whole process from the first green shoots to the dry ears of corn? But that was not enough for men who loved a multitude of gods—and so much so that their miserable soul disdained the pure embrace of the one true God and prostituted itself to a mob of demons.   [4:8; p. 144]

A multiplicity of gods, from Augustine's time through the Renaissance, is connected with gods who have the power to transform themselves for immoral purposes. By artfully conflating all sorts of categories within Roman religion, Augustine creates a hilarious picture of a crowded pantheon of helpless demigods further degraded by the specificity and practicality of their functions. Divinity is trivialized by myriad connections with the physical universe. God is turned into a kind of Olympian bureaucracy through a combination of concreteness and multiplicity—the very qualities at the heart of a metamorphic view of the world. By contrast, Augustine makes it clear that sacredness consists in singleness and that multiplicity is proof of demonic power.

Finally, not only is metamorphosis associated with immorality and multiplicity; it flies in direct contradiction to one of the principal Judeo-Christian beliefs: that man is created in the image of God. If human beings, animals, and gods can all exchange shapes, then the definition of man's shape, and indeed the whole hierarchy ranging from the natural world to God, is thrown into confusion. So St. Ambrose in a funeral oration for his brother lumps metamorphosis with metempsychosis; and he attacks metamorphosis for its incompatability with Genesis 22: "those made after the likeness and image of God cannot be changed into the forms of beasts!"[4] Despite the terms of *imago dei*, the problem is not physical. He defines the image of God not as *corpus* but as *ratio*, and so to declare man capable of metamorphosis is to lump man with the irrational animals.[5] That man is at heart multiple, irrational, and immoral: this is the lore of metamorphosis that the early church fathers wish to deny.

The history of metamorphosis from Augustine's time to the fourteenth century will be the record of a radical change in this evaluation of the pagan image. But it does not take a thousand years for that change to come about. Well within the early patristic period, even in Augustine's own formulations, the groundwork is laid for the powerful hold that metamorphosis will exert upon Christian thinkers and artists. To begin with, we must understand what sort of process is implied by the very fact that church fathers were confronting pagan materials at all. The impulse to dismiss the whole mass of pre-Christian civilization is surprisingly rare, even among early zealots. Early Christians, citizens of the empire, presumably had little choice but to follow the language and institutions of Rome. Some were more negative than others, but it was Augustine's own formulation in *De Doctrina Christiana* that carried the day: just as the Hebrews in their flight from bondage carried with them the precious Egyptian vases to use in worshipping the true God, so Christians should not hesitate to take advantage of the great pagan philosophers for the help they can give in preaching the gospels.[6] Needless to say, the patristic writers envisaged a very narrow selection in Egyptian vases—Plato, Cicero, the Stoics, conceivably Virgil, and even these canonized few needed to have the doctrinal wheat separated from the pagan chaff. But, as so often, Augustine's mode of thought is as interesting as his doctrine. He alludes to the other great adventure of assuming an alien past—i.e., the confrontation with the Hebrew tradition—in the service of the present conflict, and he chooses an example showing how that once alien culture had taken advantage of a culture alien to itself. In fact, Augustine was almost certainly referring to a passage in Varro—a pagan author he cites frequently—in which the new appearance of Greek words in Latin is compared to the adaptation of Greek vessels in current Roman use.[7] Augustine's image, then, reminds us of the whole business of cultural translation.

Behind the allusion lies perhaps the real reason why an attempt was made to integrate pagan culture: as I suggested of the whole Middle Ages, Christianity was engaged in the complicated business of defining itself by reference to other traditions. The fathers of the church had taken on responsibility for the Hebrew tradition in toto. That produced a gigantic industry of translation and interpretation, since the Old Testament is only slightly more amenable to automatic Christianization than, say, Ovid's *Metamorphoses*. This is not the place to rehearse Auerbach's great essay "Figura" or D. C. Allen's chapter on "Pagan Myth and Christian Apologetics";[8] suffice it to say, however, that the intellectuals of the early church lived in a highly charged hermeneutic atmosphere, where questions of interpretation, interpretability, and worthiness to be interpreted were constantly being applied to both Judaic and Graeco-Roman "truths." The carrying, the *transfer* of sacred materials across the Red Sea (with its Varronian analogies to the trip of cultural evolution across the Adriatic) represents the relation between pagan image and Christian truth. The Greek for *transfer* is *metaphor*: as the Christians *carry* ancient materials *across* the gulf that separates them from paganism, they perforce create a figurative language of translation.

The first prerequisite that places metamorphosis in line for metaphoric analysis is the complicated question of its truth or falsehood. As Auerbach demonstrates, the essential fact about the development of Old Testament typology in the early Middle Ages was the determination to take the events of the Jewish Bible as true history. Since these events are often fantastic and seemingly immoral, they must also be submitted to some kind of taming interpretation. So they immediately exist on at least two levels. Pagan stories, and especially fantastic metamorphoses, are subject to no such requirements of veracity. Yet among most of the church fathers there is haunting uncertainty about their authenticity. Augustine in particular tends to worry the question. So after retelling (and debunking) the stories of Ganymede and Danae, he says, "Whoever were the inventors of such tales, whether fact or fiction, or facts concerning others and fictitiously attributed to Jove, words fail to express what a low opinion these fable-mongers must have formed of human nature to assume that men could endure such lies with patience" (18:13; p. 777). And after recounting metamorphoses of a more occult kind, he plays with the same terms again: "Stories of this kind are either untrue or at least so extraordinary that we are justified in withholding credence" (18:18; p. 782).

From a theological point of view, the question of veracity is no idle matter. Augustine expounds a religion not only filled with stories of magic but also having an act of transformation at its very center;[9] furthermore, his religion postulates an omnipotent god whose power extends eternally in both past and future directions. Is it, therefore, quite safe to rule out the possibility of metamorphosis, even as understood by the pagans? Just after declaring that we are justified in doubting the metamorphic stories, he adds: "And in spite of them we must believe with complete conviction that omnipotent God can do anything he pleases, by way of either punishing or helping" (18:18; p. 782). In fact, he hedges constantly and even says of some magical transformations that "these stories were told us not by inconsiderable informants . . . but by persons we could not imagine telling lies to us" (18:18; p. 784). Augustine is willing to accept stories of metamorphosis so that he can turn these remarkable images into evidences of God's power. To say, as Ambrose had, "For what is closer to the marvelous than to believe that men could possibly be changed into the forms of beasts?"[10] is essentially to declare such a proceeding beyond the power of God. Rather than that, Augustine attempts to understand how God's power could produce such results, improbable both in terms of ordinary verisimilitude and of Christian teaching.

Augustine's answer comes through the operation of demons. These act with the permission of God, but they act in an extremely complex way:

> Demons do not, of course, create real entities. . . . It is merely in respect of appearance that they transform beings created by the true God, to make them seem to be what they are not. And so I should not believe, on any consideration, that the body—to say nothing of the soul—can be converted into the limbs and features of animals by the craft or power of demons. Instead, I believe that a person has a phantom which in his imagination or in his dreams takes on various forms through the influence of circumstances of innumerable kinds. This phantom is not a material body, and yet with amazing speed it takes on shapes like material bodies; and it is this phantom, I hold, that can in some inexplicable fashion be presented in bodily form to the apprehension of other people, when their physical senses are asleep or in abeyance. Meanwhile the phantom may appear to the senses of others as embodied in the likeness of some animal; and a man may seem even to himself to be in such a state.
>
> [18:18; p. 783]

The demonic explanation of metamorphosis is both satisfying and significant. It locates metamorphosis in that special realm where the pagan and Christian traditions intersect, that of the ancient gods who were permitted to survive as demons or fallen angels. The source usually cited is Psalm 96, where the God of Israel is distinguished from the "gods of the nations," who are described as "idols" or "demons." The parallel between these multifarious and immoral gods and the Graeco-Roman pantheon produces a most attractive setting for classical religion within the Judeo-Christian structure.[11]

That metamorphic deities had a *laisser-passer* within patristic theology accounts for their survival only in part. More important to us than the theology is the epistemology. To characterize the pagan gods as demons is to place them in a realm of phantom, imagination, sleep, dream, and immateriality—and to sanction the existence of such a realm within God's purview. Consider one of Augustine's earlier attacks on pagan religion:

> The one true religion had the power to prove that the gods of the nations are unclean demons. Those demons seized the chance offered by the souls of the dead, or disguised themselves as creatures of this world, in their desire to be reputed gods; in their arrogance and impurity they took delight in supposed divine honours, a medley of infamy and obscenity, and were full of resentment when human souls were converted to the true God. [7:33; p. 294]

Having echoed that influential line in Psalm 96, Augustine goes on to understand the equivalence of pagan gods and demons as being a matter of subtle exchanges. It is in the nature of demons to be intermediaries between men and gods, a fact that Augustine considers at length in reviewing the *De Deo Socratis* of Apuleius. While the Christian thinker rejects any implication that demons are superior to men or capable of acting as messengers to the divine, he denies neither their existence nor their specially protean nature.

As we can see from the account above, demons are intrinsically metamorphic. They gained power through disguise and transformation, and they form the basis for a religion which continues those practices. Augustine further complicates this account with another etiology of the pagan gods, suggesting that they "were once human beings who received adulation from men who wished to have them as gods" (7:18; p. 276). This so-called euhemeristic hypothesis (of which more below) would seem incompatible with demonology. But, as Augustine sees them, the pagan gods were capable of being both demons and human beings because they were from the start shape-changers with indefinite identity. Their very existence as human beings in the first place was a disguise, a kind of changeling relationship. All the transitions from demon to pretended human being to false deification are at base metamorphic.

These assumptions remain implicit in *The City of God*, but in the anonymous and more or less contemporary *Clementine Homilies*, the connection between the demonic and the metamorphic is rendered quite clear: "What is most probable is that the gods depicted by the poets were wicked magicians, who, being perverse men, transformed themselves with the aid of magic in order to destroy legitimate marriages, disrupt lives, and with their fame to pass for gods in the eyes of ancient men who were completely ignorant of magic."[12] The self-metamorphosis of these wicked magicians covers a variety of instances. The notorious power of pagan gods to change their shape—for surely the author is thinking of the Amphitryon story when he speaks of severing marriage ties—is used to reflect unfavorably on the very divine identity of these presumed gods, so that Jupiter's role as cosmic ruler becomes as false and metamorphic as his identity as Amphitryon.

If we now turn back to Augustine's complicated explanation of metamorphosis in terms of phantoms, we can see the significance of metamorphosis in the demonic realm. It is the typically false product of false gods opposed to the true God. Even the already corrupted realm of the body is too sacred and real to submit to genuine transformation. Rather, metamorphosis depends upon a phantom, which has a material existence only in the immaterial world of dreams or the imagination. The gods live on (if they live on at all) in the capacity of weak men to be deluded by figments, just as the pagans were deluded by the figments that they called gods. Augustine attacks these figments but does not deny them. By situating them in the realm of the imagination, he means to emphasize their dangerous power. That power Augustine never denies. In fact, he cites a passage in Terence's *Eunuch* in which the lusty hero sees a painting of Jupiter as a golden shower making love to Danae, and "this suggests an authoritative precedent for his own shameful conduct, so that he can boast that he is following a god's example" (2:7; p. 55). Augustine is not interested in the immoralities that the young man proceeds to commit; rather, he is interested in the inspiration. *Corruptio optimi pessima est*: there is no worse immorality than that urged on us by supposed gods, and metamorphosis has a uniquely divine power to inspire us in that direction.

Yet that very attempt to underline the power of these metamorphic figments can become the basis for a celebration of metamorphosis by those who wish to demonstrate the triumphs of the imagination. If we cast our minds back to the lore of metamorphosis with which this book opened, we can recall how the subject has from the earliest times been tied to immateriality, to love, to nature, to image. Augustine is responding to those ancient associations and filtering them through his own dogma and incredulity. His own powerful figural fancy creates a place for metamorphosis within the imagination. Such a development was uniquely possible for a great thinker—and imaginer—who did not believe in the literal, and more especially the divine, truth of the metamorphic stories. In the earliest times—even before Moschus—the stories may have been taken as simple truth. Ovid is already a threshold figure, who believes in the gods, perhaps in the fanciful tales, but approaches with some irony and distance. It is the "Christian era" that must confirm and solidify that distance by uniting metamorphosis with the imagination. From Augustine's demonic realm, it is a short step to Dante's account of Fra Alberigo and Branca d'Oria, whose souls are changelings taken off to hell though they are not yet dead; and it is a short step to Theseus' "lunatics, lovers, and poets"—as well as the fairies—of *A Midsummer Night's Dream*, who inhabit a shadow world of imagination and metamorphosis; it is not even so long a step to the slippery spirits of Belinda's dressing table in Pope's *Rape of the Lock*. Once metamorphosis must be metaphor, it becomes the definitive metaphor.

We need not skip ahead fifteen hundred years, however. It is the medieval Christian writers who, because of their disbelief and because they were propounding a universal god, not only forged the link between metamorphosis and the imagination but also proposed that the pagan stories had to mean something, since they could not be what they seemed on the surface. This proposition leads to a great thousand-year hermeneutic war in which metamorphosis is a central event. The first battle in this war is over the question whether the fables mean anything at all, whether there were important principles below their distasteful surface. To argue against their meaning is to engage in some theoretical thinking about fictions that is of a highly sophisticated order. So Arnobius in the *Adversus Nationes* goes much further than Augustine in perceiving a gap between the idea of divinity and the fables of the pagan gods: "Either they are in truth gods, and they did not do those things which you memorialize; or else if they did those things you say, without any doubt they are no gods."[13] For Arnobius the tradition of searching for deeper meanings— which of course long predates Christianity but was being kept alive by Christian writers like Fulgentius—attempts to draw connections between divinity and immorality, thus producing a kind of blasphemous apologia.

Arnobius sees the stories of the gods' transformations not as fictions designed to contain secret truths; rather, these immoral escapades are historically true (hence the more to be deplored), and any attempt to sugarcoat them with ethical, natural, or religious interpretation produces an empty figment. In pursuing his argument, Arnobius raises familiar modern arguments against interpretation: uncertainty of the author's intention, the probability of the interpreter "reading in" his own concerns, the impossibility of simultaneous different meanings. The paradox of such an approach is that the more these tales are declared to be true, the less significant they are. To declare them historically genuine is to relegate them to the rather insignificant realm of long-past acts of immorality. Isidore of Seville makes this point with special clarity. Having gone through the usual catalogue of Jupiter's transformations with euhemeristic explanations, he concludes: "And for that reason these are not *figurae* but in simple truth crimes; hence it was shameful that such individuals be believed gods when they ought not even be considered human beings."[14] They are not metaphors but real crimes; those who committed them are not gods but scarcely men. By rejecting *figura* these hard-liners in fact confirm that the place of metamorphosis is either in the world of the imagination or in the world of history: it cannot be both.

And the votes were coming in by greater numbers and influence for the world of the imagination. It is Lactantius, even before Augustine's time, who makes this point most forcefully. After recounting the metamorphoses of the gods, he places the fantastical materials squarely in the realm of poetry:

> The poets, then, have not fabricated the exploits—if they did they were most foolish—but they added a certain color of poetic fancy to the deeds. They said these things not to detract but because they desired to embellish their heroes. In this way men are deceived, especially because, while they think that all these things are feigned by the poets, they reverence that of which they are ignorant. They do not know what the measure of poetic license is, to what extent it is permissible to proceed in fictionizing, since the poet's function consists in this, that those things which were actually performed he may transfer with some graceful converse into other appearances by means of figurative language.[15]

It is a complicated and cautious aesthetic, giving with one hand and taking with the other. The most important thing for our purposes—and this idea will echo, sometimes verbatim, through the centuries of medieval mythography—is that metamorphosis is taken to be the equivalent of poetic imagination; in fact it equals the transfer of historical truth into figura. Within that realm Lactantius sanctions metamorphosis; yet at the same time he is fully, and nervously, aware that poetic imagination and religious reverence exist in uneasy proximity.

2. Demystification, Allegory, Integumentum

In the first six centuries of the Christian era, pagan stories—whatever value they may be assigned—maintain a real currency in the world of Catholic letters. Not only do great theologians such as Augustine and Ambrose retell and interpret them but a Christian mythographer like Fulgentius (sixth century) is able to write analyses of myths as a general part of unearthing the wisdom of the ancients and separating the wheat from the chaff.[16] As I have already suggested, the great issue for the early Christian writers is rhetorical or hermeneutic: what sort of skewed relationship is there, they keep asking, between these fantastic immoral stories and the truth that is meant to attach itself to divinity? What, in other words, are the terms of the separation agreement between fictions and theology—that separation that made Lactantius so nervous? By the seventh or eighth century the question seems to lose its savor: the separation is so complete that pagan fictions no longer figure in common learned discourse at all.

When the materials of paganism resurface, around the twelfth century, they have ceased to be theological. Rather, they are the domain of professionals: scholars, expositors, natural philosophers. Between Isidore's time and the High Middle Ages there is born the professional discipline of Christian mythography, so that the hermeneutical line from the patristic writers forward leads directly to a group of writers who were themselves professional rhetoricians expounding Ovid's *Metamorphoses*. This is more than a professional change. In the process of intellectual development between the Early and High Middle Ages, much of the Augustinian imagination, the sense of dream and demonology, is lost in the confrontation with pagan marvels. Augustine and Lactantius (in very different ways) had placed metamorphosis in a shadow world of the imagination whence it would reemerge only very selectively in the course of the next millennium. In place of the transforming imagination, the mythographers submitted pagan tales to the transformations of rhetoric. That distinction between rhetoric and imagination—which is also a parallel—may well signal the difference between the mundane commentator and the genius.

We shall not be following the whole history of Ovidian commentary in these pages, but it should be noted that there is a considerable manuscript tradition, from the twelfth to the fourteenth century, of rhetorical analyses devoted to Ovid's accounts of the ancient myths, revealing an almost consistent progress toward freer, subtler, and more elaborate interpretations. An early medieval "commentary" by Lactantius Placidus, frequently reprinted in Renaissance editions of the poem, is nothing but a series of summaries, and the rather less specifically Ovidian work of the so-called First Vatican Mythographer (eighth century) is in much the same form. The twelfth century produced in the work of Arnulf of Orleans the first major allegorical commentary on the poem: *Allegoriae super Ovidii metamorphosin*. The Platonism of this work and of its influential successor and partner in many manuscripts, John of Garland's *Integumenta Ovidii*, sets the tone for commentary, both in method and content. Later, in the thirteenth century, with the commentary of Giovanni del Virgilio and the myth interpretations of Alexander Neckam, we find a slight shift away from Platonic cosmology and toward specific moral allegory. Finally, in the fourteenth century in the anonymous *Ovide moralisé* and in the work of Pierre Bersuire, the emphasis moves as far as it can toward specifically Christian, often intricately theological, analyses.[17]

What concerns us in this history is not only the *Nachleben* of Ovid but also the tradition of rhetoric and metaphorics that is born in Ovid, filtered through the patristic writers, and fulfilled in the High Middle Ages. If I seem to slight the evolutionary history of mythography from Fulgentius to Bersuire, that is because I feel that the differences among these approaches to *fabula*, so illuminatingly discussed by several scholars of the

Middle Ages, are balanced by similarities that have not received as much attention.[18] In the tradition of metaphorics over this millennium, the desire to tame the fantastic and immoral tales of ancient metamorphoses in order to grant them admittance into the Catholic cosmos expresses itself in three different modes. All three attempt to shackle the imagination with rhetoric; in most cases there is a loophole through which the imagination escapes. The three are neither completely independent, nor do they follow a clear chronological pattern, though the balance among them may be quite different in the sixth century from what it is in the fourteenth. Let us name them and treat them in what is (very vaguely) the chronological order of their prominence: demystification, allegory, integumentum.

I name demystification first because its history long predates Christianity. The ancients had no obligatory theological objections to the stories of metamorphosis, and they need not necessarily have had any moral objections. Objections on the grounds of verisimilitude, on the other hand, were always possible. Palaephatus's work, the first surviving exposition of the stories of the gods, is called *Peri apiston*, or *On the Unbelievable*.[19] The more famous, though lost, work of Euhemerus is well known for having postulated that the gods were originally human beings raised to the status of the divine owing to the gratitude of their peoples for the good deeds they had done.[20] Pagan euhemerists need not, of course, have been doubting the divinity of their gods by offering this explanation of their origins. There was, after all, no question that certain deifications of mortals had taken place: Hercules was thought from earliest times to have attained godhead via suffering, and by the time Cicero plays with (and rejects) euhemerism in *De Natura Deorum*, the Romans have deified a host of local heroes.[21] Even among the pagans euhemerism is demystification, if not of the gods themselves, then of the fantastic stories surrounding them. Yet it takes the hostile attitude of early Christian commentators to bring out the full demystifying impulse behind Euhemerus's theories. In the first place, they grounded their euhemerism in the Old Testament by associating deified mortals with the idolators of the *Book of Wisdom* (14:15–21), who invent gods by creating statues of their most lamented dead and gradually instituting worship of the statues.[22] Furthermore, the Christian writers are able to list all the mortals that Romans deified and to declare that the earlier members of the Olympian pantheon have as slender a claim to divinity as does Romulus or Augustus.

The translation of, say, Jupiter into an amorous king of Crete is in itself more a theological than a rhetorical matter. But the results of this translation are rhetorically significant. Once the gods are made mortal, then their fantastic transformations come to be denied, explained away, or given a philosophical meaning that at least mitigates their fancifulness or frivolity. So Fulgentius, dismissing as impossible the myth of the hundred-eyed Argus, turns naturally to the improbabilities surrounding Jupiter:

> This is the usual fashion in which Greece and its poetic gossiping, always decked in falsehood and yet lying with good intent, refers to such fabrications as when Danae was seduced by a golden shower, not rain but coins, and Ganymede was seized by an eagle, not a real bird but the spoils of war. For Jove, as the ancient author Anacreon has written, when he had started a war against the Titans . . . he saw close at hand the auspicious flight of an eagle. For so happy an omen, especially since victory did ensue, he made a golden eagle for his war standards and consecrated it to the might of his protection. . . . He seized Ganymede in battle as these standards went before him, just as Europa is said to have been carried off on a bull, that is, onto a ship carrying the picture of a bull.[23]

Fulgentius we might call a "liberal": in the tradition of Lactantius he demystifies, but he reminds us that the lies are poetic license—this I take to be the "good intent" with which the Greeks lie (and they are, of course, the proverbial liars).

The motives behind the demystification become more hostile in the High Middle Ages. Consider Arnulf of Orleans approaching the same group of metamorphoses:

> Jupiter in the form of a satyr seduced Antiopa, daughter of Nicteus. "Satirus" was actually the proper name of some go-between. Likewise in the form of Amphitryon he seduced Alcmena; that is, he used her husband Amphitryon as a procurer. . . . He had Aegina, daughter of Asopus, through the offices of a cook and hence he is said to have been changed into a flame. Also Mnemosyne [for whom he turned himself into a shepherd] he deceived by means of a shepherd of her father's. Proserpina he had as a serpent, that is, through the help of a certain nurse who was compared with a serpent on account of her cunning.[24]

Not only do these revisions deny the divinity of pagan gods; more important, they attempt to debunk the magical glory of antiquity, to make its triumphs seem as paltry as its morals.

The impulse to demystify takes many forms, and in a sense it underlies all the tamings of pagan myth, including allegory. It need not attack the morals of the ancients, but only their credulity. Fulgentius creates a whole science of etymology on the theory that *nomen est omen*; as a result pagan gods and heroes are reduced to the meaning of their names, and the meanings essentially engage in allegorical dramas.[25] The original impulse, however, as in euhemerism, is reductive and demystifying. At the other end of the Middle Ages, Boccaccio invokes natural science in an attempt to explain divine transformations: Semele's disastrous death is the result of the meteorological mixture of fire, symbolized by Jupiter, and air, symbolized by Juno; and in the same breath he repeats the Fulgentian stories about Jupiter as lustful king of Crete. Whether Boccaccio interprets the myths euhemeristically or scientifically, his purpose is still to explain them away.[26]

Yet all this demystification will have a paradoxical effect. The approach is rationalist, but the materials of metamorphosis are highly fanciful. By finding ways to reduce the incredible to the quotidian, the mythographers end up by building a bridge between fanciful fictions and real-life meaning. And it is an extremely imaginative bridge. To "explain," as Arnulf does, Jupiter's metamorphosis into a flame as a way of asserting that he used a cook as a go-between may seem to us ridiculous; yet the absurdity is not owing to its literal-mindedness but to the reverse, an overenthusiasm about metaphor. Consider in a similar vein Giovanni del Virgilio's attempt to explain away the transformations wrought by Circe: "And such a change of bodies is quite possible both in literal fact and in appearance. In literal fact it is possible by the power of herbs that such witches use to make the limbs contract. As did Circe. In appearance it is possible that with magic arts they can often make men appear to be goats or some other dumb animal."[27] In the process of demystifying Circe's transformations, Giovanni, with the sanction of Augustine, grants the existence of powerful realms of magic and the imagination in which, as he presents it, metamorphosis is a plausible event. Indeed the whole euhemeristic tradition brings with it its own backlash. Once Christians accepted with Lactantius and Fulgentius that the Greeks lied "with good intent," then the lies necessarily became fair game for metaphorical unraveling. To ravel or unravel the lies is essentially the same activity.

In fact, the theoretical grounding for euhemerism is itself bathed in metamorphic lore. The development of idolatry out of statue worship has close ties with legends of metamorphosis. The deification of mortals, whether one believes in it or not, is a metamorphic principle; and mythographers so firmly identified it with the *Metamorphoses* that several ascribed the whole subject of the poem to Ovid's sycophantic desire to make the deification of Augustus seem plausible, as in the *Ovide moralisé*:

> li poëte le faignoient,
> Que Cesar fu deïfiez
> Et qu'ensi fu stellifiez;
> Et Ovides meïsement,
> Qui voloit prouver faintement,
> Par fables et par fictions,
> De diverses mutacions,
> Qui sont touchies en cest livre,

Quar par ce cuidoit à delivre
La grace d'Augustus aquerre. [15.7144–53][28]

Again, however harsh the demystification, the rhetorical bridge is built between argument on the one hand and "fables et . . . fictions" on the other. We must also remember that this demystification comes at the end of nearly one hundred thousand lines of remarkable metaphorical fancy.

Allegory is a much broader and more complex concept in the Middle Ages than demystification. Volumes have been written on the principles of allegorical thinking and their literary adornments.[29] While the technique of allegorizing predates Christian writers—indeed, it can be found in Ovid's own poem—it comes to be the mainstream, almost the cliché, of medieval metamorphosis. When Ovid says of the regenerative stones thrown by Deucalion and Pyrrha "inde genus durum sumus experiensque laborum / et documenta damus qua simus origine nati" (1.414–15: "Hence come the hardness of our race and our endurance of toil; and we give proof from what origin we are sprung"), he is not demystifying the magical change of stones into human beings; nor is he denying that it took place. He is, however, making a metaphor out of an ancient myth that he did not invent. For Ovid metaphorizing is optional: that is, he is free to take the story literally or figuratively or both. Christian writers are not so free; and, once metaphor is compulsory, then the very nature of metaphor is different. Here again the experience of Old Testament typology is relevant. The events of the Jewish Bible (somewhat like the pagan myths to Ovid) were both literal and figurative. As such they inspired the creation of great systems of parallels and correspondences. Ovid's *Metamorphoses*, the Bible of the gentiles, denied a literal level, must be metaphorized not casually and occasionally but in a grand and complex system. The turning of individual metaphors into systems produces allegory.

The real point of origin for this allegorical approach to metamorphosis is *The Consolation of Philosophy*, at a moment in the fourth book when Boethius is asserting that vice is its own punishment, just as virtue is its own reward. That metamorphosis, with all its complexities of physical versus mental change, should arise in this discussion is significant. Boethius is wrestling with the ancient (i.e., Platonic) problem of appearances: how can we believe in cosmic goodness and justice if malefactors do not always appear to be changed for the worse by their crimes? The question demands some more figurative approaches to change, and in ancient accounts of metamorphosis Boethius found the perfect system. The poem retells the story of Circe and Ulysses' transformed men:

[Ulysses'] sailors greedily drank the evil cups; they were changed into swine and turned from food to husks and acorns. No part of them remained unchanged—they lost both voice and body; only the mind remained to mourn the monstrous change they had suffered.[30]

The story is by origin Homeric, of course, but the terms are decidedly Ovidian: *mens antiqua manet*, as Ovid so often says in one form or another. What had enabled the pagan poet to separate consciousness from shape makes it possible for Boethius to separate moral reality from worldly appearance.

The poem does not itself take us all the way to allegory, but it is surrounded by prose commentaries that do. In the subsequent prose Boethius understands that "although vicious men keep the appearance of their human bodies, they are nevertheless changed into beasts as far as the character of their souls is concerned" (4.4). That statement—with ancient reverberations in interpretations of Circe—gives the grounding for a whole allegorical approach to metamorphosis: the physical changes narrated by the pagan poets may be magic, delusion, metaphor, lies "with good intent"; but the truth behind them is the deterioration of the human soul when corrupted by sin. That is the first step of allegory, but it is only a partial one because its blanket denial of the figurative level scarcely allows for much allegorical fiction.

In the previous prose, however, Lady Philosophy rides the metaphoric vehicle in considerable splendor:

> You will say that the man who is driven by avarice to seize what belongs to others is like a wolf; the restless, angry man who spends his life in quarrels you will compare to a dog. The treacherous conspirator who steals by fraud may be likened to a fox; the man who is ruled by intemperate anger is thought to have the soul of a lion. The fearful and timid man who trembles without reason is like a deer; the lazy, stupid fellow is like an ass. The volatile, inconstant man who continually changes direction is like a bird; the man who is sunk in foul lust is trapped in the pleasures of a filthy sow.   [4. Prose 3]

In one stroke Boethius transforms metaphor to allegory by means of a barnyard of moralized animals. With this passage he connects the whole Aesopic tradition of the beast fable with the Ovidian tradition, and he rescues both for Christian moral discourse.[31]

Of course the above passage does not mention metamorphosis. Boethius's own strategy mirrors the complexity of appearances that he is discussing. He has already asserted that to fall from the good is to change internally to a beast, while "the appearance of [evil men's] human bodies, which they keep, shows they were once men" (ibid.). Now he creates an animal allegory via simile, and then in the poem that follows he tells the story of Circe's magic transformations. The relations between the concrete object of transformation and the spiritual meaning are very delicate. It is precisely those relations that make the allegorizing of pagan materials a complex business. From real transformation—an avaricious man becomes a wolf—to metaphor—an avaricious man "is" a wolf—to simile—an avaricious man is like a wolf—these are crucial distinctions in rhetoric.[32] Ovidian metamorphosis is clearly the most absolute of these systems, and that absoluteness is theologically dangerous. Thus at the beginning of the Christian era Lactantius in the *Divine Institutes* attempts to demolish all the tangible fancies of pagan myths—in this case speaking not of metamorphosis but of the similar wonders in the life of Hercules:

> Surely he who subdues a lion is not to be considered stronger than he who subdues anger, the wild beast shut up within himself; nor is he who has felled the most rapacious birds stronger than he who curbs the most avid desires; nor he who conquers the warrior-Amazon than he who conquers lust which vanquishes shame and fame; nor he who has cleaned the filth from a stable than he who has driven vices out of his heart, which are the more pernicious because they are one's own peculiar evils, rather than those which could have been escaped from or avoided.[33]

This very interesting passage is in many ways a stern answer to the whole project of allegorizing pagan stories. Lactantius purports to trivialize the vehicles of all these familiar comparisons, indeed to disable the comparison entirely, since he characterizes pagan heroism as exclusively physical —just as its images are purely concrete—and therefore incomparable to spiritual conditions. Yet the very discourse in which he attacks the comparisons turns itself into allegory, as anger becomes the lion, desires the wild birds, lust the Amazon, and internal evils the filth of the Augean stables. As we saw with the demystification of pagan stories, the attempt to deallegorize, that is, to prefer the essential spiritual tenor to the physicalized, frivolous pagan vehicle, merely results in affirming the tie between tenor and vehicle.

By the High Middle Ages these allegorical ties bind very firmly indeed. Whether they mystify or demystify, the allegorizers of the later period never doubt the absolute rhetorical relation between metamorphosis and moral allegory. John of Garland puts the matter (as he puts many other matters) most succinctly:

> Si lupus est arcas [Lycaon], lupus est feritate lupina,
> Nam lupus esse potes proprietate lupi.[34]

There is no hedge or apology in *lupus esse potes*: we may surmise that John does not believe literally that wolvish people turn into wolves, but he asserts the allegorical equivalence without mediation, and his use of the second person verb only serves to intensify the immediacy of moral metamorphosis.

By the end of the Middle Ages the concrete vehicles of metamorphosis are almost completely revalidated as suitable inspirations for allegorical thinking. Consider in this regard Bersuire's commentary on the metamorphic fables in Arachne's web:

> These are they who plot against young women—that is, against the soul—in order to deceive them in different ways and draw them to sin. They lurk under different shapes and fornicate with them spiritually. Under the appearance of a horse the devil corrupts a soul when he gives it the desire for some worldly pride; under the appearance of gold when he makes it desire gold and riches; and, in short, under different appearances tempt souls in order to deceive and corrupt them. They appear in the shape of a serpent when they tempt about malice; in the shape of a horse when they tempt about sins of the flesh; in the shape of a bull when they tempt about pride; in the shape of a vine when they tempt about drunkenness; in the shape of a dolphin when they tempt about the savory pleasure of fish; in the shape of a father or husband when they pretend friendship; in the shape of a ram when they tempt about stubbornness.[35]

This is allegory in the fullest sense: a cosmic image of equivalences built out of Arachne's web. Ovidian metamorphosis is anathematized as sexual immorality, and yet through the metaphor of magical self-transformation erotic experience is identified with deception. So on the basis of that pagan metamorphosis Bersuire builds his whole allegory. In his complete recuperation of these pagan materials, the expositor has translated metamorphosis into that most orthodox of medieval scenarios: the morality play or psychomachia. Pagan forms of change, instability, and multiplicity became via the medium of allegory all the waverings in the mind of a sinner. Spenser is not at all far behind.

Our third impulse I referred to by the technical rhetorical term *integumentum*, whose literal meaning is "covering" or "shell."[36] The origins of the concept are classical, but the term reaches its apogee in the High Middle Ages, when many thinkers approach myths, whether authentically pagan or newly invented, with the assumption that the fables exist as a covering on some essential truth. Integumentum may seem to be the opposite of demystification where in reality they are opposite sides of the same coin, both concerned to demonstrate the bridge between reality and fanciful narrative. Integumentum finds its origins in early antiquity, and its associations from that period remain important in the Middle Ages. The Greek commentators on Homer did not merely allegorize the implausibilities of the stories; they declared them to be secret repositories of truth, especially the truths of natural philosophy or cosmology.[37] Through that particular Homerolatry is born the notion of the poet-philosopher—specifically, natural philosopher—that will remain central to Ovid's account of himself and to later accounts of him.

These exalting notions of the poet's fictions come to be rather strange bedfellows with Plato and Platonism. The poets are excluded from the Republic because of their dangerous lies, which in this context Plato does not choose to see as coverings of the truth. The Platonic tradition moves in quite the opposite direction, however, and indeed Plato himself repeatedly uses myths to hide the truths that he asserts.[38] In the Neoplatonic tradition that process of hiding becomes an imperative. This change completes the preparation for the idea of integumentum: poets do not create myths simply for ornament (as Lactantius would have it) or just to hide the truth for the fun of it; rather they invent fanciful episodes because the deepest truths must remain hidden from those unworthy to perceive them. This idea—which flowers less in the Middle Ages than in the Renaissance—introduces a whole upside-down element in the reception and recuperation of paganism. That is, the more bizarre or repellent or "poetical" the mythic covering, the deeper the truth it hides. Metamorphosis, as we have already seen, can be notably bizarre, repellent, and "poetical." So once again the rhetorical tradition, whether it wishes to or not, legitimizes those very remains of paganism that were in their literal form most anathematized.

In fact, the occult, Platonic tradition is not heard from often in the Middle Ages. To be sure, its voice is very resonant when it is heard; and it is precisely the metamorphoses and other fabulous pagan monstrosities that seem to inspire this kind of speculation. So Dionysius the Areopagite (sixth century) treats the precisely metamorphic subject of angels symbolized by animals:

> Yet perhaps people will think the supercelestial regions are filled with leonine and equine hosts, or with a mooing prayer of praise. . . . But as I see it an enquiry into the truth will show . . . that such symbolism neither wrongs the divine powers (as someone might object) nor bogs us down passively in the base lowliness of images. . . . Rather it is used because it is most seemly for mystic discourse to hide holy truth by means of incomprehensible and divine enigmas and make the deep truth of supernatural understanding inaccessible to the masses.[39]

This is a very extreme position, which will find little agreement in the subsequent millennium. The author absolves animal symbolism of blasphemy, but at the same time he denies its attractiveness as sugar-coating. The "base lowliness of images" is the very goal of many who would cover truths with an integumentum of myth.

To believe in mystic meanings is to reject the notion of pleasing fictions and on the contrary to believe in repellent fictions which will induce the masses to turn away in disgust. But rarely in the High Middle Ages are the secrets covered by the integumentum too mystical to be named. In William of Conches' commentary on Macrobius we do hear about hidden truths that turn out to be *Timaeus*-like cosmology (see below); and Bernard Silvestris refers to Orpheus and "verum claudens," which he promises to discuss elsewhere, but he never arrives at that spot in that extant manuscript.[40] When the hidden truths are not mystical, then the whole integumentum has a different theoretical grounding. Then the fiction is superficially attractive (not repellent) and it "hides" the truth only in the sense that it requires a commentator's ingenuity. Most of the time the truths are allegories of nature. So when William of Conches confronts Jupiter's sexual escapades, he treats them in terms of upper and lower air, earth, and so on.[41] In effect, then, we have two interlocking traditions, both very ancient: one, the Platonic tradition, of hidden mystic meanings approving of the monstrosity of ancient fables but keeping their real meanings a secret; the other, going back to Homeric allegorizations, a "scientific" tradition of entertaining the attractive frivolities of fables and researching in them the truths of nature and the cosmos.

Within the Ovidian tradition itself the notion of integumentum is remarkably ancient. It is implicit in Fulgentius, where the hidden meanings are rational and allegorical; but we have a strikingly explicit assertion of this kind in the writings of the eighth-century Theodulf, Bishop of Orleans. He is discussing his reading habits:

> legebam
> Et modo Virgilium, te modo, Naso loquax.
> In quorum dictis quanquam sint frivola multa,
> Plurima sub falso tegmine vera latent.
> Falsa poetarum stylus affert, vera sophorum,
> Falsa horum in verum vertere saepe solent.
> Sic Proteus verum, sic justum Virgo repingit,
> Virtutem Alcides, furtaque Cacus inops.
> Verum ut fallatur, mendacia mille patescunt,
> Firmiter hoc stricto pristina forma redit.[42]

The good bishop has understood both Ovid and the tradition with extraordinary insight and prescience. Within the orthodox framework of the thousand lies of the poets and the *falsum tegmen* of myth, he has not only seen that philosophical truth lies underneath; but, more importantly, he has adopted an Ovidian, and specifically metamorphic, scenario for the conversion of lies to truth. So the *vertere*, or turning, of *falsa* to *verum* is strikingly juxtaposed with a remarkable allegorical equivalence: "Sic Proteus verum." Even Ovid—and he had no Christian scruples—would hardly claim such an equivalence. To claim it is to assert that the whole rhetorical mode that translates metamorphosis is itself a transformation; and the return of *pristina forma*—a verbatim feature of some of Ovid's more optimistic transformations—confirms that the uncovering of truth in metamorphosis is itself metamorphosis.

That equation is never again as explicit, but it underlies the whole application of the integumentum doctrine to Ovid. We shall see below how commentators on the *Metamorphoses* from Lactantius Placidus to Arnulf and Giovanni turned the poem into a series of *mutationes*, not only interpreting hidden meanings but also making every story a metamorphosis, even where Ovid scarcely included any magical change: the link between *mutatio* and *integumentum* is the permission given by Ovidian metamorphosis itself. That is why it is Ovid—rather than, say, Virgil—who inspires the extraordinary multiplicities of Bersuire's commentary or of the *Ovide moralisé*. These grand works offer sometimes dozens of different, and incompatible, interpretations of a single Ovidian episode. It has been wisely argued by experts that these are not "interpretations" in the traditional sense, or even in the sense that Arnulf or Giovanni interprets.[43] That is, the two fourteenth-century writers do not believe in the authority of the original text and are not seeking hidden meanings in it but are deliberately replacing it with Christian meanings which they refuse to ascribe, even as through a glass darkly, to the pagan Ovid.

Most probably this is true and stands as an important distinction in the theory and history of allegory. But it should not be overstated. Bersuire and the poet of the *Ovide moralisé* rear a gigantic rhetorical structure upon this putatively worthless pagan poem. If they are not discovering hidden meanings under its integumentum, they are nonetheless turning *falsa* to *verum*. They make that turning by a constantly shifting rhetoric including every incompatible form of interpretation within each story. Where did they learn such a multiple vision of hidden truths? In the very metamorphoses of the poem which lies under their integumentum. The metamorphoses are the ultimate *transfer*. So, according to Bersuire, Daphne in transformation can be the Christian soul, or a religious person "virtuous and perfect—by attaching the feet of a good course as roots, by putting on the bark of penitence, by acquiring the branches of good desires, and by never putting off the greenness of an honest life."[44] Yet his Daphne is also (literally) a laurel tree, and the laurel tree is also the cross.

The rhetorical permission given by metamorphosis extends even more significantly to freedom of interpretation than to variety. Once it is accepted that secret truths repose under fables that belie them, then, the greater the distance between surface and truth, the more powerful the truth. Metamorphosis itself becomes a principal object of this transforming rhetoric. In the *Ovide moralisé* the poet consistently draws the parallel between the pagan gods' descent to the bestial and Christ's assumption of human flesh. After all, Ovid's own Jupiter in the Europa story, as we have seen, is at once an authentic creature from the natural realm and also a creature of divine perfection, so that his transformation enables the divine to enter the realm of nature. The parallel to the Incarnation may seem obvious to our syncretistic age; but without the doctrine of the integumentum and consequently metamorphic freedom of interpretation, the analogy would be shocking. Once it is found and believed, however, the details mesh and redefine pagan transformation. God is equated with Leda's swan:

> Qui voire humilité designe,
> Tant fu douz, tant fu piteables,
> Tant fu humbles et charitables,
> Et pour humaine creature
> Vault recevoir honte et laidure
> Et son cors livrer a torment,
> Si s'apresta ioieusement
> De venir a sa mortel paine,
> Si com li cignes, qui demaine
> Grant ioie et trop s'envoise et chante,
> Quant sa mort voit venir presante. [6.834–44][45]

Ovid had criticized Jupiter for betraying his *maiestas*, but Christian theology celebrates the paradox of a God who is at once the highest and lowest of beings. So in moralizing the Europa story the poet tells us that God

> Se vault descendre et abessier,
> Sans sa divinité lessier,
> Si s'en vint vers Sidoine en Tyr,
> C'est: en ce monde, sans mentir,
> Pour raiembre l'umain lignage
> Et giter d'infernal servage.
> D'umaine forme se couvri. [2.5115–20][46]

With the freedom for extreme *translatio*, the poet can turn one man's metamorphosis into another man's Incarnation.

In turn, these sweeping transformations by rhetoric confirm the argument that Christian theology is itself covered by integumentum. Asterie's eagle, which comes to be conflated with Ganymede's, signifies St. John the Evangelist, and the metamorphosis figures forth Christ's election of St. John as his messenger. This process—both the metamorphosis and the privileged position of St. John—the poet sees in terms of divine knowledge and secret vision. St. John

> but en la Sainte Fontaine
> L'iaue de vive sapience;

Qui tant ot haute cognoissance
Et tant fu sages et discrez,
Qu'il connut les devins secrez,
Si com Diex li vault reveler.   [6.788–93][47]

The conjunction of pagan myth and Christian divinity produces a theology that contains divine secrets, if only for the reason that Jupiter's
amours, once transferred to Christ, must be viewed via the doctrine of
the integumentum:

Li filz Dieu fu pluie doree,
Quant il en la vierge honoree
S'aumbra sans lui violer,
Et pour cest mistere celer,
Qu'anemis ne la perceüst,
Vault que la vierge espous eüst.   [6.867–72][48]

The equation of Danae's sexual experience with the Annunciation is inevitable and widespread. Explored so closely, it suggests that the conception
of Christ by the Holy Spirit is itself the highest form of metamorphosis;
and it joins incarnation with metamorphosis as sacred mysteries to be hidden from the unworthy.

Before we leave the rhetorical path, it is important to remind ourselves
how our three impulses combine and add up, especially given the future
traditions of interpretation. Demystification, allegory, and integumentum
will remain the combination not only for the Middle Ages but also for the
Renaissance. The demystifying impulse forges a bond between metamorphosis and tales of daily life, the world of the fabliau, of domestic life, and
of the novella. In the *Decameron*, in Volpone's lusty promise to Celia that
they will "act out Ovid's tales," in Rembrandt's chubby little Dutch girl of
a Danae, that pulling down to earth, and to the baser human impulses, of
pagan metamorphosis remains visible. The allegorical impulse not only
produces a series of equations with the abstract; but, more specific to
metamorphosis itself, it speaks for a very particular view of human nature.
Once we follow the Boethian allegory for the barnyard qualities of Circe's
victims, we come to adopt a multiple, shifting, and animal-like vision of
human personality. That is why St. Ambrose could not accept metamorphosis at all. How could anyone believe, he says in the funeral remarks for
his brother,

that the same soul, which was wont to control anger by a meek and
humble resolve, to be patient, and to abstain from bloodshed, can
now be inflamed with the mad violence of a lion, and, with ungov-
ernable anger and unbridled rage, can thirst for blood and seek for
slaughter; or that the same soul, which by kinglike counsel, used to
restrain the varied storms of popular outbreaks and to calm them

with the voice of reason, can now endure to howl in pathless and desert places in the manner of wolves; or that the soul, which, groaning under an excessive burden, used to low in wretched complaint over the harsh labors of the plow, can now, being changed into human form, look for horns on her smooth brow.[49]

The answer is that many will believe in this corrupted multiplicity and that metamorphosis is its great image. Finally the heritage of the integumentum is that of the search for truths that are within or beyond the secrets of the cosmos. Through the late mythographers it is also the radical tradition of reinterpretation, and of simultaneous multiple interpretation. Above all, it is the tradition of seeing in the hermeneutic act itself the most potent form of metamorphosis. *Sic Proteus verum*.

3. Natura *and* Fabula

By the High Middle Ages, then, the pagan imagination has come to be recuperated through the protean operations of rhetoric, and the materials of antiquity themselves are fused with a body of post-antique meanings. Yet, for all its vigor and ingenuity, the purely rhetorical commentary of the period is something of a closed system. If all we learn from the persistence of metamorphic stories in the Middle Ages is that the stories could themselves be transformed and tamed by rhetoric, are not the pagan tales merely fuel for a Christian impulse that might better be studied, as by Auerbach, in connection with typology? The answer, the force that opens up the closed system, is the study of the natural world. The humanist arts of rhetoric and language comprised that half of the medieval curriculum known as the trivium. The other half, or quadrivium, loosely corresponding to the sciences in our modern "arts and sciences," was concerned with the study of the universe. Pagan stories, and especially tales of metamorphosis, stand squarely between the two: their method of interpretation is rhetorical, but their field of reference is nature. As nature itself comes to be seen as full of transformation, so nature becomes a pagan metaphor. That is the process we shall now follow.

As a bridge let us consider one of the great rhetorical mythographers. What happens when metamorphosis turns into universal metaphor may become clear in the commentary of Arnulf of Orleans. Following and considerably embellishing an old tradition, Arnulf prefaces each book of his commentary on Ovid with a kind of plot summary. Here is the heading for the first book:

The transformations in the first book are as follows: 1. Chaos is transformed into kinds [*species*]. 2. Earth into human beings either by God or by Prometheus. 3. The world into four states or ages named after metals. 4. The year into four seasons. 5. The Giants into

mountains. The blood of the Giants into human beings. 6. Lycaon
into a wolf. Earth into sea on account of the deluge. 7. The stones
thrown by Deucalion into men and by Pyrrha into women. 8. The
earth once again into the serpent Python. Phoebus into a lover. 9.
Daphne into a laurel. 10. Io from a chaste girl into an adulteress, and
from an adulteress into a cow. From a cow once again into a goddess.
11. Mercury into a shepherd. 12. Syrinx into a reed, from a reed
into a pipe. 13. Argus into a peacock.[50]

Arnulf turns every myth into a metamorphosis, and in the process he
turns almost every metamorphosis into a metaphor. To be sure, the Giants, Lycaon, Daphne, Syrinx, and a few others are literal transformations. But in many cases the concept is being reinterpreted. Human emotion is metamorphosis: "Phebus in amantem"; moral decay, physical
change, and apotheosis are smoothly paralleled in summarizing the story
of Io.

But the ruling metaphor that opens this universal catalogue of metamorphoses is the story of natural creation itself: "Cahos mutatur in species." When medieval humanists universalized Ovidian transformation,
they looked not to their own equivalent of the pagan pantheon—the
figures of the Bible and the saints' lives—but to nature. As we follow
Arnulf's catalogue, we see that all the detail of the natural world—human
beings, the four ages, the seasons—is the creation of metamorphosis. So
when Arnulf, earlier in his commentary, glosses types of metamorphosis,
he includes magical change and spiritual change, but he begins with and
gives the most space to "Naturalis":

> The natural type is that which takes place by the joining or dis-
> joining of the elements. By the joining when the elements unite as
> for example when a child is made from sperm and a chicken from an
> egg. By the disjoining of elements when the elements dissolve and
> decompose in whatever body, be it by fire or other means, and re-
> duce themselves into a powder.   [p. 181]

Unlike the other categories of metamorphosis, this makes no reference to
stories in Ovid's poem but rather outlines a whole cycle of nature, including movements among the four elements, sexual generation, growth, and
decay. So, from the rhetorical world of the imagination, the moralized
concept of metamorphosis turns the attention of humanists to the "real"
world of nature. Yet within the realm of natural philosophy metamorphosis does not really need to make a comeback in the High Middle Ages, for
the same thinkers who had earlier tried to undo the myths of transformation had sanctioned metamorphosis as a natural phenomenon. We have
already seen how Isidore of Seville contemptuously dismisses the stories
of divine transformations as being neither images nor metaphors but sim-

ply crimes. It is all the more remarkable, then, that Isidore concludes his section on human beings with a brief chapter entitled "De Transformatis":

> Moreover certain monstrous transformations and alterations into beasts are written about, such as of that most notorious magician Circe, who is said to have transformed Ulysses' companions into animals; also of the Arcadians, who, chosen by lot, swam across a certain pool and were there turned into wolves. Indeed that the companions of Diomedes were transformed into birds they confirm not as a mythical falsehood but as a truth of history. And some claim that witches can be made out of men. After many robberies the faces of criminals are changed, and either by magic incantations or by poisonous herbs their whole bodies turn into beasts. Whether through nature or for whatever other purpose many things experience mutations and change in corrupted form into various other kinds [*species*]. So bees spring from the putrid flesh of cattle, beetles from horses, locusts from mules, and scorpions from crabs.[51]

When Isidore turns from the pagan gods to the world around him, he affirms the existence of metamorphoses. Though he borrows his list of miraculous transformations partly from Augustine,[52] he is more emphatic than his predecessor in asserting the absolute historical accuracy of such events: "non fabuloso mendacio, sed historica adfirmatione"—an almost precise negation of the rhetorical arguments against pagan tales of metamorphosis, already an important indication that the world of nature is different from the world of divinity.

Isidore's remarks, though they come as early as the seventh century, already tell us much about the medieval view of metamorphosis in the natural world. The point of entry for metamorphosis is *monstruosae transformationes*, the bizarre tales that go back to the *mirabilia* of authorities like Pliny or, for that matter, Ovid's Pythagoras. From freakish cases like the Arcadians-become-wolves, however, the principle of metamorphosis generalizes itself to magic and thence to standard natural changes like spontaneous generation. In the process, natural metamorphosis comes to include (in the persons of Circe's victims and the companions of Diomedes) precisely that realm of mythology that in itself could not be taken literally. Isidore's concluding category is the furthest point of domestication, a translation of metamorphosis into the corruption of organisms into lower species. This represents an early suggestion of a great medieval fable joining metamorphosis to moralized cycles of natural change. So even in patristic times the world of nature is understood as susceptible to instabilities that would be intolerable *sub specie aeternitatis*.

There is, however, a considerable distance between admitting metamorphosis via a catalogue of well-known monstrosities and seeing it in myth and nature together as a basic principle of the cosmos. The change comes about in the twelfth century as part of a revolution in conceptions of man and nature. The causes of that Renaissance are beyond our scope here: historians from C. H. Haskins onwards have cited the growth and "modernization" of both ecclesiastical and feudal systems as well as the spread of Western European civilization toward the classical roots offered variously by Sicily and Spain.[53] The effect is the development of humanism, an organized set of intellectual disciplines based, at least in part, on a recognition that the proper study of mankind is man's visible world. In the work of the two great poets associated with the School of Chartres, Bernard Silvestris and Alain de Lille, the goddess Natura herself is reborn from antiquity. With sources in ancient conceptions of *physis* and the Platonic world-view, these poets recreate Nature as a universal force, and they struggle to define her place in the hierarchy that includes God, matter, and the generative impulse. At the same time they personify her—the poetic tradition goes back to Boethius and to the Lucretian Venus—so as to create a figure who represents all the vitality, mutability, and sexuality of the created universe. The classical origins of such a vision are in the Platonized Venus and in the universal *ewig Weibliche* of Apuleius's Isis. And while the twelfth-century poets struggle to separate their *in bono* vision of generative nature from the *in malo* Venus of corrupt sexuality, there is still much contagion between the two conceptions of nature.[54]

That Natura should be a goddess more than a force or an aggregate of raw data demonstrates a crucial proposition of this particular humanist revival: Nature enters the world of discourse as Myth. Plato was a supreme authority, and the nearest approach to a real text of Plato was the Latin *Timaeus*, along with the commentary of Chalcidius. That package of classical learning was understood as a great myth celebrating the cosmic order.[55] With the inspiration of the *Timaeus*, Bernard Silvestris in his *Cosmographia* can render the creation poetical as a Platonic myth.

There are, of course, myths and myths. Those of Bernard, or of Plato in the *Timaeus*, are not to be equated simply with tales in which gods abduct mortal girls or sculptors make love to statues. Rather, they are grandly abstract allegories almost entirely free of human passion or even of human identification. But, as the whole history of our subject demonstrates, it is not so easy to keep noble Platonic myths separated from lusty pagan tales. Medieval humanists (as well as modern scholars) tried, of course. Macrobius, early in his *Commentary on the Dream of Scipio*, makes a detailed series of distinctions among myths. The lowest form are those in which "the presentation of the plot involves matters that are base and unworthy of divinities and are monstrosities of some sort (as, for example, gods caught in adultery, Saturn cutting off the privy parts of his father Caelus and himself thrown into chains by his son and successor), a type which philosophers prefer to disregard altogether."[56] Macrobius was a good commentator but a bad prophet. We have already seen how Arnulf in the twelfth century saw Ovid in nature and, more shockingly, how the four-teenth-century *Ovide moralisé* parallels Jupiter's lusting metamorphoses with God's loving Incarnation. The Chartrain philosopher William of Conches, commenting upon the Macrobian commentary, does not prefer to disregard such unseemly myths: "Sometimes this kind of narrative uses base and dishonourable elements, sometimes beautiful and honourable. 'Such as gods who are adulterers'—the words are base, and yet by that adultery something honourable and beautiful must indeed be meant: as can be read in the case of Jupiter's adulteries with Cybele, and Semele." And William proceeds to find the beautiful in allegories of natural cre-ation: the sexual intercourse of Jupiter and Semele, for instance, signifies the impregnation of the earth by the air, "and thus Bacchus is born, for from this union come the vines."[57] What is significant here is not only the recuperation of lusty pagan tales into the realm of Platonic cosmology, but also the particular role that such a myth plays as an etiology for the appeti-tive forces in nature, associated with love, with generation, and with the vine.

At the same time as some humanists are producing grand myths of Natura, others are collecting the data of creation, writing encyclopedias of natural history devoted to the description and interpretation of the visible cosmos.[58] If the lustier world of pagan myth peers in at the corners of ab-stract Platonic allegory, it fairly overwhelms the encyclopedias, even to the point where it was recognized as remarkable at the time. The same William of Conches who worked to recuperate Jupiter's adulteries into nature lore is discussing the phenomenon of the echo: "'There is one thing that has always amazed me in regard to the sense of hearing. If in a cave or in a deep forest I project my voice, I do not know who repeats it and sends it back to me.' 'Now don't you know that it is Echo the nymph who does that?' 'I am not Narcissus whom she pursued. I seek the physical cause of the thing, not a fable.'"[59] The distinction between *physica ratio* and *fabula* becomes crucial to William because it was so rarely made. Medi-eval naturalists (William included) used pagan myths as essential data in the mapping of the cosmos. Since so many of the myths were from their classical beginnings grounded in descriptions of nature, the corpus of myths was for medieval humanists a ready-made poeticization of the cos-mos that they wished to scrutinize. So *fabula* is generally inseparable from *physica ratio*, not only because the fables are grounded in etiologies and interpreted as nature allegories but also because they exist in the newly rediscovered pagan world of the Goddess Natura.

In the union of *fabula* and *physica ratio* there is an authority even more powerful than Plato, whose work (unlike Plato's) was fully known and in its original language, a work in large part devoted to the junction of fables and physical causes. Ovid's *carmen perpetuum* offered a detailed catalogue of cosmic and natural phenomena. The outside parts of the poem—from the creation through Phaethon's ride at the beginning and Pythagoras's overview at the end—give a system to the whole history of the created universe, while countless stories in the middle of the poem revolve around etiologies that suggest specific pieces of nature lore.[60]

Not only the vogue of Ovid but this whole account of medieval natural philosophy—the importance of the *Timaeus*, the Chartrain fashion for pagan-style poetic cosmologies, the interpenetration of Platonic myths with pagan stories of love and lust, the frequent appearance of these latter myths in encyclopedias—all these circumstances point to the powerful presence of metamorphosis in the medieval mapping of the cosmos. Thus throughout the works of medieval Platonists both direct allusions to Ovid and shared metamorphic ideas abound. Often they consist of retold stories of metamorphosis with an emphasis on their creative or cosmological effect. Baudri de Bourgueil repeats Ovid's description of elemental confusion in the Flood. Alain, describing the stars in the *Anticlaudianus*, accepts the stellification of Castor and Pollux. Albertus Magnus considers seriously the cosmological implications of Ovid's myths concerning Deucalion and Phaethon. And there is very widespread reference in medieval literature to the metamorphic credo offered by Ovid's Pythagoras, both for its principles and for its specific examples.[61]

Most of all, the Chartrains borrow and develop the lore of the four elements, which, as we saw in Ovid's poem, forms a matrix within which the multiplicities of creation can be displayed and the flow among the categories can be structured. Bernard, for instance, orders his description of the world via the elements as habitats, and other authorities like Gervasius of Tilbury and William of Conches explain the real-life transformations of birth and growth as an Ovidian *metamorphoseos* (William uses the word) among the elements.[62] Metamorphosis, then, is joined with a guiding principle of twelfth-century Platonic cosmology: that the cosmic order consists in a *concordia discors*. Such a delicate balance is related to a metamorphic picture of the universe because transformation can either be a sign of peaceful flow, like the Pythagorean description of an elemental cycle (*Metamorphoses*, 15.244–51), or it can be a sign of the collapse of harmony in favor of discord, like the disastrous results of the Flood or Phaethon's ride. A strong interest in the elements, a belief in *concordia discors*, the powerful influence of the *Timaeus*—all connect with the idea of man the microcosm. And in that little world of man there is the potential for the same metamorphic flow that natural philosophers observed in the macrocosm.

In the particulars of nature, as well as in the expression of larger principles, myths of metamorphosis abound, sometimes as decorative references or mere name-dropping but often as an integral part of some demonstration. Etiological tales of transformation, like those of Arachne or Echo, help to clarify the identity and meaning of natural phenomena, even when the author treats the story as fictional and even when he disputes the empirical details. In effect these authors share Ovid's notion that metamorphosis bridges man and nature. So the myths demonstrate that nature is meaningful to human experience because of its metamorphic (i.e., anthropomorphic) origins, while metamorphic myths are made explicable through parallels to transformations in nature which are familiar to us from real experience. *Fabula* is *physica ratio*.

In fact, the encyclopedists' interest in metamorphosis goes far beyond myth to what is almost an obsession with natural transformations. Self-transforming (or reputedly self-transforming) species were of very widespread interest from at least Isidore's time onward. Simone Viarre points out that the color transformations of the *stellio*, or newt, amount to "une métamorphose naturelle à laquelle s'intéressent précisément le pseudo-Hugues de Saint-Victor, Barthélémy de Glanville, Vincent de Beauvais et une foule d'autres auteurs . . . comme Thomas de Cantimpré et Albert le Grand" (p. 145)—to which we could add Isidore and Alexander Neckam. Changes during the life cycles of animals, such as reproduction, molting, and growth, including relevant references to Ovidian mythology, are frequently discussed. More mysterious forms of transformation, often including references to Ovid's Pythagoras, come in for considerable attention: Albertus Magnus speaks of the mystery of fossils in metamorphic terms, seeing them as a joining of the animal with the mineral order, and many others describe spontaneous generation.[63]

Ovidianism and metamorphism demonstrate more than the lure of old fables or the power of ancient authority. In fact, Ovid's vision of the creation, as we have seen, is informed by metamorphosis, and the Chartrains shared this vision in its deepest spirit as well as in its Ovidian ornamentation. Indeed, the whole tradition of what we might call Natura poetry, from Bernard to Spenser (nor would I exclude Botticelli) is based on Ovidian metamorphic principles: nature is an anthropomorphic force, ever-changing, maturing and decaying, and nature is generated by love. So the Ovidian *fabula* of human passion that results in the creation of a new species produces via metamorphosis a bridge between love and Nature as we know her. Not literally in person but figuratively in passion, the Nymph Echo is the *physica ratio*.

With William's cry for causes rather than fables we have strayed toward the very unmedieval path of empiricism. Yet all the details about echoes or newts, and still less all the accounts of creation, should not fool us into thinking that medieval humanists studied nature as an end in itself. If we compare twelfth-century natural philosophy with, say, the world-view of Isidore of Seville, we are struck by the freedom, the directness, the anthropocentrism of the later thinkers. Yet, if they are more independent from an absolute Christian eschatology than the early patristic writers, they are on the other hand more bound up in grand symbolic systems. What truly distinguishes twelfth-century "science" is its simultaneous capacity for empirical detail and abstract symbolism. The Platonism of the School of Chartres and the obsessive concern with the parallels between macrocosm and microcosm invest all the natural *visibilia* with meaning. Whether the visibilia are plant and animal lore, anatomy, astronomy, poetry, erotic feeling, or any other aspect of the human psyche, the twelfth-century thinkers were capable of intense concentration on the visible detail and at the same time on larger systems of meaning that dissolve the visible detail.

To search for a meaning in nature is to produce a rhetoric of interpretation of plants, animals, minerals, and so on. Such a rhetoric is like that applied to the word, whether the word is the New Testament, the molting of snakes, or even the recuperated text of pagan myth. The Book of Nature is very like the book of pagan myth, both in its principles and in its form.[64] As a result, the realms of rhetoric and natural philosophy come together. Medieval study of nature is rhetorical, involving the same demystification, allegorization, and search for secret meanings that pagan myths required. In nature as in myth, metamorphosis becomes the vehicle for metaphor, and in studying the cosmos as a metamorphic metaphor, the medieval humanists find paganism in the nature that surrounds them. Paganism is the meeting place of figura and cosmos.

One particular natural history, Alexander Neckam's *De Naturis Rerum*, demonstrates the remarkable interrelations of nature and myth, of rhetoric and natural philosophy. Neckam was an English friar educated in Dunstable and Paris who also produced a devotional verse natural history and some treatises on practical matters; he may in addition have been the so-called Third Vatican Mythographer. The range of interest throughout his work includes the by now familiar elements of encyclopedic natural history, Chartres-influenced cosmology, mythography, and wide-ranging concern with metamorphosis.[65]

The *De Naturis Rerum* is divided roughly into a book of cosmology and a book of natural history. The cosmology reveals that he believes in the transmutation of the elements, which exist in a state of *concordia discors*. His explanation of the "mutuam elementorum reciprocitatem" owes much to the *Timaeus*, and an even deeper Platonic debt is evidenced in his sense that things exist in their pure forms only in remote or heavenly realms. Thus, when he turns to a description of our world, it is clear that he has understood it as a place of impure, multifarious, and changing things whose very shadowiness demands rhetorical analysis.

Metamorphosis is especially significant as the essential image of this earthly condition. He returns to it frequently as subject, sometimes simply as a way to understand the behavior of animals. Even in the case of "pure" nature lore, Neckam's language seems automatically to metaphorize and moralize. Of the chameleon, he tells us,

Its color is mottled and quickly changeable, so that whatever thing it is joined to, it makes itself the same color. There are two colors that it cannot succeed in fashioning [*fingere*], red and white; it feigns [*mentitur*] the others easily. . . . The chameleon should signify to you the flatterer, who adapts himself to most people yet cannot to the innocent and the just. The white signifies the innocent, and red signifies the fire of *caritas*. [chap. 21; p. 69]

Transformation is described first as *fingere*, which has a basic meaning of "fashion" or "form" but a connotation of false form. Then the same action is designated as *mentiri*, which leaves no doubt that it is a false form. To allegorize chameleons as flatterers is to interpret metamorphic nature as though it were metamorphic myth, and Neckam goes yet further by allegorizing the chemistry of those colors that the chameleon cannot *fingere*.

The world of allusion to antiquity allows Neckam to spread the metaphor wider. In one chapter ostensibly explaining the phenomenon of the echo, he uses the metamorphosis of Narcissus into a flower to draw the rather unconventional moral of *sic transit gloria mundi*. Having given metamorphosis that sort of moral signification, he turns to some other examples of the *ubi sunt* topos, leading him to Sardanapalus, who wore women's clothes, and thence to the effeminizing metamorphosis of Tiresias:

What a pity! Forgetful of the dignity of his own sex, Tiresias still had longings. The masculine is preferred by nature, but he chose to degenerate wickedly into the feminine. What has become of Orpheus of the wretched pleasures inimical to nature, who, changing the exercise of his sexual pleasures on to tender youths, dared to snatch that brief spring and those first flowers? [chap. 20; p. 67]

Through the case of Tiresias, sexual diversity is joined with metamorphosis, which in turn becomes *turpiter degenerare*. The reference to Orpheus's homosexuality—with a direct quotation from the *Metamorphoses* (10.84–85)—confirms the connections among metamorphosis, sexual polymorphousness, and figures of pagan myth. So Neckam has progressed from natural metamorphoses (echoes and flowers) to mythic transformations that are unnatural but also vatic. Thence he passes to an aesthetic celebration, along with a moral critique, of the effeminization produced by the beautiful singing of high male voices—again, a Tiresias-like image of sexual transformation. From there he effects a rather arbitrary transition to a discussion of the chameleon, the prototype of natural transformation. He has made a great circle from transformations in nature through pagan myth to allegory to celebration and back to nature.[66]

4. Metamorphic Dramas, Cosmic and Microcosmic

We have seen myth interpreted as nature and nature interpreted as myth; both are, to use a phrase applied by one scholar to twelfth-century man, "lieux de métamorphose,"[67] and both are subject to transforming rhetoric. We can best understand the way the Middle Ages made metamorphosis its own if we finally turn away from individual myths and individual pieces of natural history toward a kind of composite picture of the universe. There is a grand medieval drama, a vision of human destiny, never perhaps rendered complete in any one literary example, that emerges in the survival of metamorphosis. The first element in this drama is the equivalence of metamorphosis with mutability, decay, and death. Countless commentators glossing the word "metamorphosis" repeat an epitaph, sometimes said to belong to Matthew of Vendome: "Sum quod eris, fueram quod es. Vel quod es ante fui. Methamorphosis ita [sometimes *ista*] humanis rebus subdere colla vetat."[68] Death is the great metamorphosis: all other magical changes remind us of death; and the instability of matter implicit in metamorphic stories acts to free us from matter. Arnulf ascribes such an intention to Ovid:

> Or his intention is to bring us back from the immoderate love of temporal things and to urge us to the sole worship of our creator, by showing us the stability of heavenly things and the variability of the temporal. So, ethically, it can be added that he teaches us to despise those temporal things, which are transitory and changeable—a teaching which concerns morality.[69]

It is a perfect blend of Plato, Ovid, and Christian *contemptus mundi*.

But the discovery that man is mortal can hardly depend on pagan metamorphosis. The next element in the drama involves not physical destruction but moral decay. We saw the beginnings of this idea in Boethius, where the failure of human virtue and rationality is expressed by beast similes, which in turn are closely related to animal transformations. Medieval literature of metamorphosis is filled with this melancholy vision of human personality. So Thomas Walsingham on Io's metamorphosis into a cow: "For neither men nor women are in fact changed into beasts, even if they seem to be. If we read, for instance, of Io that she bellowed like cattle while her shape remained with human consciousness; in such a way many lose their human aspect through the snaring tricks of evil, and hence this is said of Io."[70] And, yet more directly, the reflections of the Third Vatican Mythographer, referring back to Servius, in explaining the changes of Proteus: "For [Servius] says that man has within him sexual desire, foolishness, savagery, and cunning. When that part in which he is closest to the divine does not appear—that is, prudence, which can hold him in check, then to that extent those things are banished which are free from all vices."⁷¹ Metamorphosis, in other words, is a reminder of the fragility of human virtue and reason.

The actual narratives of transformation become in medieval hands beast fables or psychomachias. Not only Boethius but also Arnulf lists a variety of Circean victims, each of whose punishments represents the symbolic value of that animal, "the wrathful becoming lions; the unclean becoming swine; the envious becoming stags."⁷² It is easy for medieval thinkers to turn to this sort of psychomachia because there exists concurrent with these pagan images of metamorphosis a whole tradition of purely Christian metamorphosis. Implicit in Boethius's account of evil, and explicit in some contemporary patristic writers, is the fact that sin turns men into beasts. By the twelfth century the position of man between beasts and angels can account for a cosmic drama of what is sometimes explicitly known as metamorphosis. If man is in the image of God, then his transformation to beast is the more spectacular.⁷³ Thus John of Salisbury: "As the rational creature becomes brutish, so the image of the Creator by analogy is deformed into the beastly"; and Thomas of Citeaux speaks of metamorphosis as the descent into brutish hell inscribed on man's heart by the devil.⁷⁴

But the drama of metamorphic change and human destiny is rather less static (or unidirectional) than these examples may suggest. Returning to the Third Vatican Mythographer on Proteus, we remember that man was not left simply to decay physically and morally because he possesses "libidinem, stultitiam, ferocitatem, et dolum." Rather, man exists eternally at odds between those qualities and "pars illa, qua vicinus est divinitati." The real drama of metamorphosis is the freedom of the will to flow in either direction; and the great pagan fable offers a set of imagery and a natural cosmology for this drama. Consider one of Arnulf's definitions of metamorphosis:

> There are two motions in the soul, one rational and the other irrational. The rational is that which copies the motion of the firmament, going from the east to the west; and contrariwise, the irrational is that which imitates the motion of the planets, which move against the firmament. For as God gives reason to the soul by which he curbs sensuality, so the irrational movement of the seven planets is curbed by the movement of the firmament. Ovid, perceiving all of this, wishes to show us by a mythical fable that motion of the soul which is within us.⁷⁵

This statement represents one of the most sweeping definitions of metamorphism ever. It goes back to an often cited passage in the *Timaeus*, in which Plato, having already described the origin and motion of the world-soul, proceeds to offer an analogous description of human souls:

He who lived well during his appointed time was to return and dwell in his native star, and there he would have a blessed and congenial existence. But if he failed in attaining this, at the second birth he would pass into a woman, and if, when in that state of being, he did not desist from evil, he would continually be changed into some brute who resembled him in the evil nature which he had acquired, and would not cease from his toils and transformations until he helped the revolution of the same and the like within him to draw in its train the turbulent mob of later accretions made up of fire and air and water and earth, and by this victory of reason over the irrational returned to the form of his first and better state.[76]

The bridge from cosmic order to the irrational self-destructiveness of human personalities is complete in this Platonic tradition. Human beings attempt to remain in the realm of the spirit but, through passion and irrationality, they transform themselves and fall into the realm of the flesh until some decision of reason turns the cycle again upward toward heaven.

Such cycles represent, in true twelfth-century fashion, a microcosmic vision: as man contains the elements of the metamorphic cosmos within him, so his fate consists of elemental changes as he embraces one form or another of those identities he carries inside. In a new Ovidian form, the *libido*, *stultitio*, *ferocitas*, and *dolus* of man's character account for a metamorphic drama that unites the individual and the cosmos. And the pious hope of St. Ambrose that man could not be so multiple as to degenerate into beastly form has been dashed. In addition, the purely Christian tradition of metamorphosis confirms this medieval vision. Alain equates *metamorphosis* with *exstasis*: he speaks of two kinds, one of which is the familiar Circean degeneration, while the other is apotheosis or union with God, equivalent to St. Paul's seeing face to face.[77] So the dual directions of metamorphosis toward the image of God or away from it place the Christian transformation at the heart of man's free will.[78]

Ovidian metamorphosis dramatizes this transformation because it takes place in a world of irrational passion and because it captures the spirit imprisoned in bestial flesh. So medieval exegeses of Ovidian transformations tend to draw close connections—much closer than Ovid's—between the passions and grand cycles of decay. Tiresias descends from perfection to imperfection when he is transformed into a woman, while Myrrha is given over to diabolical *amaritudo* with her final change into a myrrh tree. Jupiter-as-swan descends in his lust for Leda from divine glory to the level of a bird associated with vicious insult, and the victims of Medusa's petrification are hardened by being weighted down with too much worldliness.[79] The cycle is even clearer when the Ovidian story is itself cyclical. So Io ("de casta in adulteram, et de adultera in bovem. De bove iterum in deam") brings forth a whole psychomachia, a movement which begins with her being beloved of God, then losing her virginity and descending to the beastly level, where she is trapped in the travail and animality of the world so that she can no longer recognize God. Either through independent moral determination or through the intervention of the eloquent teacher Mercury, she returns to virtue. Her final metamorphosis into a goddess signifies her personal redemption.[80] We shall have to turn to Dante to see the depth and scope of this metamorphic drama, which is at once personal and cosmic, rhetorical and cosmological.

But in that composite drama of individual passion and cosmic revolution much is left out that bears heavily on medieval definitions of metamorphosis. If the vision of cosmic cycles can count as the otherworldly medieval drama of metamorphosis, there is also a this-worldly drama. As in earliest antiquity, so in the Middle Ages an interest in metamorphosis is associated with the cultivation of the here-and-now in all its beauty and instability. The rhetorical tradition, as we have implied, dramatizes this world in spite of itself: that is, by trying to turn our attention away from the "superficial" attractions of pagan stories and toward divine deeper meanings, the commentators build permanent bridges between this-worldly paganism and truth. The tradition of natural philosophy is, of course, more directly bound up with this world, as metamorphosis comes to be associated with the liveliness, the variety, and the exuberance of human life *sub specie naturae*.

What we see here is the familiar contrast between two different survivals of antiquity. The mainstream tradition, especially in the Middle Ages, is the serious, scientific, cosmological survival of antiquity: the names of the planets, the system of cosmic cycles, the concept of nature and the figure of Natura. The Chartrain poets and philosophers, Bernard Silvestris, William of Conches, Alain de Lille, and the rest are "humanists" or students of antiquity in that they seek to revive ancient learning and to cast it in an appropriate classical imagery. This form of medieval classicism has received most of the scholarly attention, as, for example, in the work of Panofsky and Saxl on "Classical Mythology in Medieval Art" (see note 2), or in Jean Seznec's division of the mythological heritage into historical, physical, moral, and encyclopedic traditions. Yet there is another voice, which Seznec describes (perhaps somewhat slightingly) as "the kingdom of Aphrodite and Bacchus, peopled by nymphs and satyrs."[81] In the long run of classical survival, especially in the Renaissance and after, it is this kingdom more than the other which counts Ovidian metamorphosis as its subject. During the Middle Ages "the kingdom of Aphrodite and Bacchus" is little in evidence—so little that Seznec can claim it is unseen between the end of antiquity and the Renaissance. But that is not quite the case. Through the image of metamorphosis it raises a still small poetic voice against the prevailing orthodoxies of medieval imaginative thought.

The small voice does not speak often. When it does, it is generally with a deliberate irreverence, highly conscious of the more orthodox position and metamorphic itself in its shifts from orthodoxy to a kind of secret subversiveness. Not surprisingly, the Goliardic poets make many references to Ovid and often speak in this voice. Two apparently related lyrics from the *Carmina Burana* approach metamorphosis directly through the image of remade clothing.[82] The earlier of the two begins by citing the opening lines of the *Metamorphoses* verbatim; it proceeds then to describe the life cycle of the *cappa*, which, as it grows older, can become a *mantellus*:

> Sic in modum protheos
> Transformantur vestimenta,
> nec recentis est inventa
> lex methamorphoseos.
> Cum figura sexum mutant,
> rupta prius clam recutant
> primates ecclesiae.
> Nec donantur, res est certa,
> nisi prius est experta
> fortunam tyresie.
> Cappam quidem femini,
> sed mantellum masculini
> constat esse generis.
> Cappa fit mantelli deus,
> ergo potest esse reus
> utriusque veneris.[83]

The conceit proceeds at length. It is explicitly linked with the conversion of non-Christians, and once tied to that subject it gives way to even more elaborate conceits relating bigamous second marriages to new cloaks and new religions. It may be inappropriate to analyze the symbol of the *cappa* too solemnly. What we can say for certain is that the poet is well steeped in Ovid and that while he pretends to scorn the reforming of cloaks (ostensibly because the practice deprives beggars of hand-me-downs), he is nonetheless fascinated by the linguistic and symbolic possibilities of all this transformation. The various tenors of the metaphor—bisexuality, multiple marriage, sudden religious conversion—place the poem precisely in the goliardic world itself; and that world is being characterized via metamorphosis as passionate and unstable—in short, Ovidian. To celebrate transformation is to mock the most serious continuities of the established world. The ancient *lex methamorphoseos* ("nec recentis est inventa") may be a worthy match for other ancient laws.

The later lyric, "Nullus ita parcus est," becomes even more enthusiastic about transformation itself, despite (again) an ostensibly stern disapproval of the refashioning of clothing. Metamorphosis is the occasion for an exuberant explosion of energy, particularly in the language:

Cum hoc tritum sepius   sepius refecit
et refectum sepius   sepius defecit,
noluit abicere   statim, nec abiecit,
sed parcentem tunice   iuppam sibi fecit.

Sic in modum Gorgonis   formam transformavit,
immo mirus artifex   hermaphroditavit;
masculavit feminam,   marem feminavit,
Et vincens Tiresiam   sexum tertiavit.

Parum sibi fuerat   pallium cappare,
e converso deinceps   cappam palliare,
recappatum pallium   in iuppam mutare,
si non tandem faceret   iuppam caligare.[84]

Through the repeated words, the slightly altered words, and the properly transformed words, the poet achieves a remarkable metamorphosis in language. Yet the incantatory power of such phrases as "pallium cappare . . . cappam palliare" reminds us of that characteristically Ovidian message: *plus ça change. . . .* The words change but stay the same in just the way that the cloak retains its identity as it submits to new forms.

But what is the cloak's identity? Symbols in the world of metamorphosis are meant to be slippery; still I think we can hazard some guesses. The new cloak was meant for Christmas, but it gets to be so old that it might have been worn by the homecoming Ulysses. Its colors keep changing according to a decidedly Ovidian pattern:

Forma, cum in varias   formas sint formata
vestimenta divitum   vice variata
"in nova fert animus"   dicere mutata
vetera, vel potius   in reveterata.[85]

It transforms us like the Gorgon's head; and it transforms gender like Tiresias. A certain *clericum* knew just how to turn it inside out for every season; another sterner cleric has decreed that such changes be forbidden, but nobody pays any attention. Surely we are dealing with the fabric (if the inevitable pun may be excused) of culture itself. And the fabric will not hold still: a Christmas cloak is also the garment of a (rather disreputable) pagan hero; Ovidian quotations develop Christian meaning; the pleasures of love and sexuality shift; doctrine itself may decline into a new fashion for every season, while the opposite attempt to fix it absolutely is hopeless. The combination of exuberant change in thought, word, and deed, along with an Ovidian recognition of the passions ends up by defining this vision of the world as neopagan.

The voice of the Goliard poet or poets is deliberately un-, even antisystematic: metamorphosis in those lyrics, almost as if in response to the great Platonic cycles, forms no part of a consistent picture of the universe. Yet there is a this-worldly voice surviving from antiquity that does make of metamorphosis a system for this world. Consider some of the exegeses of myths that we cited earlier as visions of decay via the passions. Fulgentius and a host of later commentators speak not only of Tiresias' degeneration into the feminine, but they also allegorize him as representing the cycle of the seasons. Myrrha, despite her *amaritudo*, produces a rich medicinal gum in the allegorized version of her sexual union with her father, the father of all things, i.e., the sun. Medusa is allegorized by Fulgentius and Giovanni del Virgilio as agriculture (with *gorgo* equalling *georgos*).[86] In the same vein we saw earlier how William of Conches turned the adultery of Jupiter and Semele into an integumentum covering the passionate origins and definition of the vine. This response represents not only the "scientific" impulse applied to myth; it is also a direct set of associations between metamorphosis and the generative impulses of nature and love. The poetic cosmologies of Natura among the Chartrain poets provided a system whereby it could be asserted without loss of orthodoxy that *amor vincit omnia* since Natura, often a thinly disguised classical Venus, was given a fixed position between God and man, from which she could legitimize properly ordered natural impulses. So an Ovidian (with which we should include "Pythagorean") system of nature and man transformed by love could combine with Chartrain Platonism, according to which Love rules the spheres of the universe.[87]

By the later Middle Ages the mythographers have in part admitted this vision to their cosmology. John Ridewall, discussing the king of the gods in his *Fulgentius metaforalis*, does not mention amorous metamorphoses in themselves, but they are implicit in Jupiter's role as the personification of *benevolencia*:

> By Jupiter, therefore, is meant poetically the virtue of love and good will. Hence according to Fulgentius, Jupiter is known in the Greek language as Zeus, which in our Latin language means the same thing as heat or life. Love, moreover, is fire; and love well governed is life itself. . . . Wise and holy philosophers in fact teach us that love is fire, as one can find in the book of Dionysius [the Areopagite] on the angelic hierarchy. It is evident as well in the poetical picture in which Amor is customarily painted with a quiver containing lighted

arrows. And it is to be noted, as Fulgentius tells us, that Heraclitus was of the opinion that vital heat in living things is the very principle of life itself. And so, speaking on the moral level, proper love, that is, the virtue *caritas*, is the principle of the devout life.[88]

The range of this little passage is extraordinary. To the equivalence of heat and life is added the poetic equation of love and fire—an equation made the more possible by Jupiter's well-known propensity for love. Upon that scientific and linguistic foundation, Ridewall builds a cosmogony ("amor eciam ordinatus vita est"). When he comes to moralize this world-order, he rederives the Christian concept of *caritas*. The operation of *caritas* in the world is as basic and essential as heat is to life. To turn Jupiter into such a god of love is to identify the chief pagan deity, in one of his most pagan aspects, with the ruling principle of a Christian universe.

It is not so surprising, therefore, that the more or less contemporary *Ovide moralisé* is able to take the principle of pagan metamorphic love higher than merely the realm of nature. When the poet equates Jupiter's amorous transformations with Christ's metamorphosis into flesh, he places striking, almost shocking weight upon God's love as the cause of the Incarnation. More than once in moralizing these stories the poet speaks of "l'amour d'umaine nature," which in joining Christ and Jupiter yokes together quite different forms of love. Such an equation gives rise to a remarkably passionate, almost pagan theology. If God is love in the Jovian sense, then the human objects of God's love must be experiencing something like ecstatic transports. Europa's flight over the water becomes a figure for the soul's ascent to heaven; and Semele's violent sexual death demonstrates that she signifies "ame yvre / Et plaine de devine amour" (3.906–07).

A single poem, not particularly famous or (so far as we know) influential or even obviously connected to a widespread school or genre, offers such an incisive reading of all these dramas of transformation that it must stand as the capstone of these reflections on medieval metamorphosis, even though the greater and more deeply rooted works of Dante and Petrarch (whom we shall consider later) swim in the mainstream of the Ovidian tradition. The twelfth-century lyric "Profuit ignaris" is a poem of sexual invitation written by a churchman to some young women who are behind the walls of a cloister.[89] The speaker turns his simple request into an elaborate argument considering the purposes of love as the guiding principle of nature and the cosmos, and he uses Ovid's poem and the subject of metamorphosis as the central evidence in his argument.

The poet begins with a lengthy formula to conceal his own identity. His references are broadly typological: Job approved of silence, St. Paul concealed his own name; and so it follows implicitly that the present apostle of the third creed should do likewise. The prologue puts us immediately in mind of the whole figural tradition: of commentaries, of parallels, of secret meanings. Having professed his own secret wisdom, he proceeds directly to exactly those most repellent pagan fictions to which commentators had assigned occult meaning:

> Cum Iove Iunonem,   cum fratre coisse sororem,
> Fertur amasse thorum   primus de gente deorum,
> In dampnum matris   truncasse virilia patris.   [ll.35–37][90]

The examples are familiar, and they point directly to the doctrine of the integumentum.

Indeed, the poem that follows is enigmatic enough to suggest that its truth is being concealed from the uninitiated—presumably the more narrowly orthodox. Yet at heart it is a question-and-answer poem. The question is the same that Christians had been asking from the time of St. Augustine: "Quis lascivire,   scortari sive coire / Numina concedat?" (ll. 41–42: "Who would admit that gods can wanton loosely, or make love?"). Yet how different the answer is from that of the patristic writers! The very description of the problem has changed radically. Jupiter's amorous metamorphoses are grand descents from heaven to earth with glorious effects; and, when the poet points the weapons of medieval interpretation at such a vision, he turns the conventional approach to the *mystica fabula* upside down. The gods are not made to conform to or to signify Christian life; rather the clerics signify the lives of the gods. Since passionate love is a union of heaven and earth, it follows that to be nearer to god is to be a lover: "Cum deliramus,   ea numina significamus" (l. 72: "It is when we run riot that we signify the gods").

At the heart of this union of heaven and earth is that familiar subject which has joined the two in love so often:

> Iuno, Venus,   Amor—hic mutare videmus
> Iupiter in taurum   fertur mutatus, et aurum.
> Ut mutaretur   Amor hoc fecisse docetur
>
> . . . .
>
> Cum de mutatis   formis metaphora vatis
> Hec commentatur,   opus et res magna paratur.   [ll. 95–103][91]

Ovid stands explicitly at the center of the poem, just as though this were a conventional work of mythography. Metamorphosis is not merely a divine tactic or a poetic embellishment or an accidental by-product of paganism. It is the essential fact, perhaps even the final cause, of a cosmology ruled by love. For this reason the central section of the lyric retells Ovid's metamorphic tales of the foundation of the universe: the creation, Deucalion and Pyrrha, Phaethon's ride.

Once the universe is established as metamorphic, the poet can interpret it in two different ways, quite parallel to the two significations we have discussed at the end of this chapter. The first is the great Platonic cycle, guided by the interplay of passion and reason:

Miror cur vates   tot feda, tot improbabitates
Dicturus demum,   voluit primordia rerum,
Celi vel terre,   subtiliter ante referre.
Iuxta Platonem   Nature condicionem,
Post res mutatas,   rerum species variatas,
Et mutatorum   scelus, impia stupra deorum
Explicat—et quare?   Vult nobis significare
Quantum Natura,   quondam sine crimine pura
Nunc degravata,   corrupta sit et viciata.
Cum perscrutamur   celum, cum philosophamur
De planetarum   cursu, sedes animarum
In stellis esse,   nascentibus inde necesse
Rebus prodire,   sic debita *fata* subire,
Huc se migrantes   in corpus et hic habitantes,
Felice[s] anime   qua lege cubilia prime
Nunc repetant sedis,   vel, cum moriendo recedis,
Suppliciis dignis   commissa quis expiet ignis,
Quo redeas purus,   perpes celo fruiturus—
Hec de virtute,   de vera verba salute
Quando tractamus,   ad sidera mente volamus:
Sic celum petimus,   non ut ferat ossan Olimpus.
Hunc habitum mentis   tum rursus ad impia sentis
Prave mutari,   scortari, luxuriari.
Mortales actus   Iovis implet ad infima tractus,
Mens vitio victa   pecca[t] virtute relicta.   [ll. 137–61][92]

This is one of the essential metamorphic dramas. In recapitulating it the poet uses his most negative terms for pagan love; on the other hand, he proposes the highest flights for those wise enough to read the fable Platonically.

But as soon as he has relegated pagan transformation to the realm of sin, he turns to the other great fable of metamorphosis:

Est quod in illorum   discas deitate deorum,
Nec sine doctrina   migrare feruntur ad ima.

. . . .

Quidquid in hoc mundo   crudeli sive secundo
Sidere versantur,   et quicquid in hec operantur,
Ex quibus omne genus   rerum constare videmus,
Quod sapis et sentis,   quod an his fit et est elementis—
Hoc opus istorum   coitum dixere deorum.   [ll. 162–77][93]

That the visible world is created of metamorphosis proceeding from divine passions is just as much a *doctrina* in this theologically sophisticated jeu d'esprit as is the lore of the *Timaeus*. Clearly the poet is echoing the invocation to Venus in the great classical work whose very title typifies this tradition: *De Rerum Natura*.[94] So the answers to Augustine's question, filtered through nearly a millennium of rhetorical interpretation, are that pagan metamorphosis can describe the cosmic cycle built on the image of human free will; or it can celebrate the generative vitality of nature.

CHAPTER FOUR

Taccia Ovidio:
Metamorphosis, Poetics, &
Meaning in Dante's Inferno

How was the *Commedia* possible?" asks Ernst Robert Curtius in a culminating chapter of what remains the great overview of medieval literature.[1] His answer is essentially the whole thesis of *European Literature and the Latin Middle Ages:* Romania, the pan-European redaction of classical culture with its roots in late antiquity, its blossoms in the twelfth and thirteenth centuries, and its fruit as late as the Spain of Cervantes and Gongora. Such an argument sees *The Divine Comedy* as deeply imbedded in the intellectual and aesthetic currents of its time, ranging from twelfth-century nature poetry to Aquinas and the revival of Aristotle to the rhetorical theories and linguistic experiments of such figures as Arnaut Daniel and Dante himself. There can, of course, be no doubt that the *Commedia* belongs to the Middle Ages. The cosmic journey made by Dante the poet and Dante the pilgrim comes as the summation and climax of medieval Christianity and medieval humanism. In its conception the poem is a monument to all the systems of order celebrated in the Middle Ages, and especially to the typological vision that saw both real and metaphorical parallels amongst the sets of categories that structure the universe: past, present, future; individual, society, cosmos; pagan, Hebrew, Christian; this world, the next world; hell, purgatory, heaven.

When it is placed in the context of Curtius's version of the *Commedia*, the heritage of paganism, so powerful in the poem, emerges as *medievalized*, that is, heavily mediated by such topoi as dream vision, allegory, typology, and *exempla*. In effect, this is the medieval humanism we have just considered—respectful and learned but constrained by distance, abstraction, and rhetoric. Yet there is something entirely new here as well. The poem's monumental typology, with all its orthodox symbolism, starts to transcend its own system in part because of the sheer size of the project. More important than the size, however, is the fact that Dante—as both author and character—confronts the symbolic ordered universe with an intimacy and directness that begin to dissolve symbol and metaphor into the thing itself. As Dante sees everything through his own eyes, so do we. In the process, the poem works to break down the mediations of similitude and turns them into direct confrontation and identity.

This mode of face-to-face meeting, so different from the rhetorical distancing of medieval humanism, colors all the worlds of *The Divine Comedy*, Christian and classical. But it is initiated by the most startling meeting of all. Many Christians from St. John onwards had had visions of heaven. None had met the greatest pagan poet face to face. At the opening of the poem, Dante is as yet no cosmic voyager but merely a man lost in the journey of *nostra vita*. From this deathly despair he is rescued by Virgil, who, before he is identifiable, appears in the dimness as "chi per lungo silenzio parea fioco" (1.63: "one who seemed faint through long silence").[2] There is, of course, an allegorical significance to the Latin poet's appearance at this moment: the return of *ratio* to a life lately given over to self-wasting passion.[3] But that *lungo silenzio* is more than an allegory of Dante's personal psychomachia. It is also a direct reference to the intellectual history of Europe, Dante's first defiance of the limitations of his own age. He introduces himself as a character and then Virgil as a character so that, for the first time in nearly a thousand years, a Christian can see pagan civilization not just through a glass darkly, but face to face.[4] That is why the younger poet addresses the elder as "lo mio maestro e 'l mio autore" (1.85: "my master and my author"), not only his *writer* but also his *originator*. This may be the first great sign since the time of Augustine that a pagan torch could be handed on to a Christian, that pagan and Christian culture could exist in continuity as well as in rhetorical parallel.[5]

The promise of a face-to-face relationship with Virgil is in many ways fulfilled in Dante's poem. *The Divine Comedy* neither copies nor scorns nor allegorizes the *Aeneid* but exists as an independent response, building upon its vision of the cosmos and of history but also adding the truths of Christian eschatology which Virgil himself could only glimpse dimly.[6] In this respect Dante's achievement foreshadows (and influences) the humanism of the next generation. Petrarch would attempt to distill the greatness of antiquity and turn it into the basis of a new creation; and he expressed this desire in personal letters to the great (dead) authors of antiquity.[7] Dante does not need to write letters: he becomes Virgil's intimate friend, his competitor, his child, even his salvation.[8]

Dante's confrontation with the pagan past is crystallized in his encounter with the great pagan poets and the virtuous heathen early in the *Inferno*.[9] To begin with, there is no doubt that Dante honors these pagans as much as he possibly could without running very much afoul of Catholic orthodoxy. He places them in limbo, that is, outside of hell proper; they exist in a kind of gloomy calm to be found nowhere else in the *Inferno*; they suffer "duol sanza martiri" (4.28: "sadness, without torments"). Dante has done more, however, than spare the pagans the full force of damnation. He has also created his own classical Parnassus set apart in the surroundings of hell: first a quartet of great pagan poets (Homer, Horace, Ovid, Lucan) and then, in a separate place, larger groups of noble warriors, great philosophers, and learned scientists. Dante's Parnassus is itself a Virgilian inspiration, from the underworld journey in Book VI of the *Aeneid*. The Latin poet distinguishes the shadowy realm of unsatisfied lovers and unburied warriors from the Elysian Fields, where great poets and noble heroes live out happy lives in eternally peaceful togetherness. Dante amalgamates the two, balancing the pagans' sadness at the loss of salvation with a sense that they continue to possess and enjoy their nobility and their genius.

Not surprisingly, it is the poets and philosophers who fare best, each group recreating a kind of academy. Homer and the others (including Virgil, who has left them temporarily to guide Dante) take part in a *bella scola* of mutual poetic admiration, while Aristotle acts as the leader of a *filosofica famiglia* which includes Socrates, Plato, and the pre-Socratics. Such a vision of a worthy pagan universe is very new in the early fourteenth century. (Indeed it has not changed all that much by 1500 when Raphael paints his *School of Athens* and his *Parnassus* in the Vatican.) More striking yet, however, is the entry of the Christian pilgrim Dante into that universe:

> volsersi a me con salutevol cenno,
>   e 'l mio maestro sorrise di tanto;
> e più d'onore ancora assai mi fenno,
>   ch'e' sì mi fecer de la loro schiera,
>   sì ch'io fui sesto tra cotanto senno.   [4.98–102]

(They turned to me with sign of salutation, at which my Master smiled; and far more honor still they showed me, for they made me one of their company, so that I was sixth amid so much wisdom.)

This is another of those face-to-face meetings with the pagan past that derive from the original meeting with Virgil. The event is not just an egoistic self-tribute; it is the conscious creation of a line of ancestry from the pagan onwards.

In fact, this meeting with the classical Parnassus or the Elysian Fields becomes the keystone for the poetic world of the *Inferno*. For it is not only Dante the virtuous Christian who can meet on equal terms with virtuous pagans, but all the sinning Christians who live side-by-side with sinning pagans (Paris with Tristan, Eurypylus with Michael Scot, Myrrha with Gianni Schicchi, and so on), divided not by their creed but by the terms of their sin. And these scenes of the *Inferno*, crowded with the lives of so many disparate figures—what Curtius referred to as the poem's *Comédie Humaine*—bristle with the full-blooded life of the pagan universe.[10] To be sure, in all these "proto-Renaissance" gestures toward humanism there are strikingly medieval elements: Dante's Virgil is a magus, a rhetorician, a harbinger of Christ,[11] the Elysian Fields are also an allegorical *castello* with the mystic seven walls and seven gateways, while the mixture of pagans and Christians may be due as much to the medieval lack of historical perspective as to any humanistic desire to equate the groups. Still, for posterity, whether it be characterized as Petrarch's letters to dead authors or Michelangelo's *Last Judgment*, the *Inferno* is the starting point of a direct, unmediated line, *in bono* and *in malo*, joining paganism to the present moment in history. For us, this direct line signals a new immediacy in the inspiration offered by pagan poetics. It is not the Virgilian, of course, that primarily concerns us here. Dante merely meets Ovid in a crowd in the fourth canto and defies him boldly in a few lines in the twenty-fifth canto. Yet Ovid provides him with a powerful example in a way similar to Virgil: the great pagan vision of metamorphosis is to be respected, confronted, saved, and recast in an original form.

1. Contrapasso *and Mirror*

Dante's hell is a vast and complex metaphor. The whole construction—geography, history, narrative action—is an objectification of spiritual conditions. For in a very real sense Dante has built something out of nothing; that is, faced with the orthodox doctrine according to which evil is not a thing in itself but rather the absence of good,[12] Dante had still to construct a model of evil whose concreteness would grasp the imagination. Nor did he compromise with notions of evil-as-absence, for the *Inferno* is in fact crammed with substance, with structure, rules, personages, fauna, flora, the past, the future—indeed all the concreteness of the sublunary universe reduced to a very strong essence. The fundamental aesthetic problem of hell, then, is the imaginative objectification of forces that are internal, moral, and spiritual. That solution was provided by the phenomenon of Ovidian metamorphosis, as born in a poem that was clearly one of Dante's favorites, as richly adumbrated by medieval interpreters, and as reinvented for his own new purposes by Dante himself. Metamorphosis, I believe, is more than an occasional instrument whereby certain sinners receive their poetic justice; rather, it is the basic principle, or set of principles, upon which Dante builds hell, both as a poetic creation and as a statement about man in the universe.[13]

For all the directness of Dante's confrontation with the pagan world, the transformations of the *Inferno* still find their roots in the medieval understanding of metamorphosis which we have just discussed. Two aspects of this metamorphic vision are particularly relevant. From the time of Boethius and Origen to that of Dante's near-contemporaries John of Salisbury and St. Bernard, sin had frequently been described as a descent of man into beast. That is in itself an abstract truism by no means invented by Christian theologians. What begins to make this abstract idea concrete is the sense that this degradation is a literal metamorphosis of the *imago dei*.[14] So, two authorities from opposite ends of the Middle Ages:

> So if I have allowed the image of the image [of God], that is, my soul, to become greater and if I have magnified it by my thoughts, words, and deeds, so the image of God will have become greater, and the Lord himself, of whom our soul is the image, will be magnified. And just as the Lord allows that image of himself which is within us to grow great, so if we are sinners, he diminishes and decreases it. Or rather the Lord neither diminishes nor decreases it but we ourselves, instead of the image of the Lord, clothe ourselves in other images. . . . Indeed we clothe ourselves in the *persona* of the lion, the dragon, or the wolf when we are venemous, cruel, or cunning; in the image of the goat when we are more driven to sexual pleasure.[15]

> There are four levels of wisdom. The lowest is called "metamorphosis." . . . It pushes us downward. . . . It is unstable and weakens us, sometimes by deforming and sometimes by conforming. . . . For man deforms the image of God, in which he is made, by pursuing physical pleasures, behaving "as the horse or mule which have no understanding" [Psalm 32].[16]

That picture of a moral transformation involving both the figurative and the literal *imago* joins in the late Middle Ages, as we have seen, with a Platonic vision of cosmic cycles of change based upon the degradation of man's free will and the contrasting power of God's redemption.[17]

Such a vision of human and cosmic change is one medieval source for the metamorphic conception of Dante's poem. The other is rhetorical. In the various medieval responses to classical mythology we observed a process of translation, from the concrete details of the Ovidian stories to a whole range of moral abstractions. That persistent hermeneutic impulse produced a system of metaphor by which physical conditions were yoked to spiritual meaning. Dante is the first to cross the bridge in the other direction: that is, to begin with the moral condition of man, degraded from *imago dei*, and to translate that abstraction back into a myth of metamorphosis, at once Ovidian and yet indubitably Christian.

The most basic principle of metamorphosis in the *Inferno*, then, we might call physicalization. The living sinner, through his death but more particularly through the fate of his special damnation, is transformed into an eternal objectification of his sin. Ultimately the inspiration is Ovidian. Just as the significances of the laurel tree define Daphne's nature, as the cringing statue does for Phineus, as the weeping rock for Niobe, as countless animal species eternally bear witness to the spiritual condition of their progenitors, so Dante's infernal world is an outward and visible sign of the many varieties of sin transformed and defined through their physical damnation. Yet medieval rhetoric and the Christian notion of a metamorphic *imago* transform this paradigm into Dante's *contrapasso*, which we might translate as retaliation, reciprocation, or retribution.

The abstract idea, which is crucial to the notion of a just hell, Dante derived ultimately from Old Testament concepts of justice and from the *Nichomachean Ethics* as interpreted by Aquinas.[18] The fact that Christ sought to overturn the Mosaic law and replace it with a nonretaliatory code only serves to confirm its appropriateness in hell, where Christ is never mentioned and his law too remote to be relevant. Still, it is a long way from the idea of retaliatory justice to the concreteness of the Dantesque *contrapasso*. Dante took particular inspiration from the equation implicit in "an eye for an eye," for sinners in the *Inferno* are punished in such a way that they act out, or embody, or become the victims (or all three) of the sins that they practiced in their lives. It is not always a perfect equation, as we shall see: misers do not simply act miserly in hell, nor do alchemists merely continue their irreligious practices. Rather sinners are rewarded with a condition that is simultaneously the sin itself and a fitting punishment for the sin.

Dante builds his metaphor gradually. Early in the *Inferno*, amongst the least culpable of the sinners, retaliatory justice is not entirely physical and certainly not yet metamorphic; that is, it merely begins to touch the persons of the sinners. The very first punishments we hear of are simply, in a quite general sense, appropriate. The morally equivocal and the neutral angels appear in an almost random series of sufferings whose rather chaotic and obscure description captures the victims' spiritual condition. The punishment of the lustful fits their crimes in a more direct way: they suffer turbulent storms that appear to be a transformed type of sexual desire. The gluttonous, in a fitting image of excess, suffer eternal rain, while the hoarders and prodigals endure a Sisyphean punishment under the weight of great masses. The wrathful and sullen dwell in an environment characterized by gloom, murkiness, and malignity; and the violent are punished in a river of blood. These are physical metaphors but not metamorphoses. Indeed Dante shows a striking tendency to conceive the punishments of the least culpable sinners as precisely anti-physical, though still characterized by the familiar poetic justice of the *contrapasso*. The gluttonous are rewarded for their massive intake by emptiness (*vanità* is the word the poet uses); Plutus, for all his control of wealth, gets punctured like a balloon; and numerous figures in the early cantos are said to lose their corporeality and hence their individuality.[19]

The physicality of this poetic justice intensifies after the point when Virgil offers a concrete plan for hell and when explicit metamorphoses begin to take place (i.e., Cantos XI–XIII). The process begins when the sinners in the lower depths are surrounded (if still not transformed) by a physical form of their sins. The flatterers are swimming in *sterco*, a fate which suggests that their empty sweet words have been morally transformed into an opposite but fitting condition and turned against them. The hypocrites, for their part, are dressed in cloaks which look beautifully golden on the outside but torment the wearers on the inside with heavy lead.

The deeper levels of sin are more directly metamorphic. The diviners are physically twisted in recognition of their crime:

> mirabilmente apparve esser travolto
> ciascun tra 'l mento e 'l principio del casso,
> ché da le reni era tornato 'l volto,
> e in dietro venir li convenia,
> perché 'l veder dinanzi era lor tolto.   [20.11–15]

(Each seemed to be strangely distorted between the chin and the beginning of the chest, for the face was turned toward the loins, and they had to come backwards, since seeing forward was denied them.)

The implication in the last line of a controlling moral justice is rendered explicit by Virgil's comments on Amphiaraus:

> Mira c'ha fatto petto de le spalle;
> perché volse veder troppo davante,
> di retro guarda e fa retroso calle.   [20.37–39]

(See how he has made a breast of his shoulders: because he wished to see too far before him, he looks behind and makes his way backwards.)

Here we have the simplest and most direct form of metamorphic *contrapasso*, parallel to the familiar Ovidian punishments where those who aspire high are plunged low, and in a precisely complementary direction.

An equally explicit example of the transforming punishment appears in the canto where the word *contrapasso* itself is used. The sowers of discord are par excellence enemies of harmony; so it is fitting that their own bodies are in a ceaseless state of mutilation. Mahomet's entrails are ripped open, as is his son-in-law Ali's head, Piero da Medecina is mutilated about the face and throat, and Curio (Caesar's fatal advisor) has his tongue slit. Bertran de Born, whose crime was to have brought about war between Henry II of England and the king's own son, is punished by having his head severed from the trunk and being forced to carry the head like a lantern before him. The appropriateness of such corporeal schism is obvious, as the victim himself informs us:

Perch'io parti' così giunte persone,
  partito porto il mio cerebro, lasso!,
  dal suo principio ch'é in questo troncone.
Così s'osserva in me lo contrapasso   [28.139–42]

(Because I parted persons thus united, I carry my brain parted from its source, alas! which is in this trunk. Thus is the retribution observed in me.)

The falsifiers of Canto XXX receive similar treatment: the impersonators are punished with madness—explicitly metamorphic, since analogies are drawn to Ovid's Athamas and Hecuba—which fits sinners whose crime was to be, quite intentionally, beside themselves. In the same canto the counterfeiter Master Adam is turned into a grossly disproportionate body in memory of his similarly insufficient coinage.

Ultimately, the poetics of the pure *contrapasso* are limited by the very exactness of the metaphoric equations. Punishments like the mutilation of the schismatics and the disproportioning diseases of the falsifiers are by their very nature simple and moralistic—in short, as straightforwardly righteous as the Mosaic law and the medieval system of Ovidian interpretation from which they are derived. Bertran de Born may be radically transformed in body, but a perfect and simple continuity is expressed in the equation between his sin and his punishment. There is, however, another transformative principle underlying the *Inferno*, which takes Dante further from the medieval heritage and toward a new metamorphic aesthetic of his own. Let us call it the principle of the mirror. Once Dante conceived of his hell in physical terms, he proceeded to generate its objective variety through the juxtaposition of complementary, but not identical, entities. To begin to understand how this mirror principle is metamorphic, we must again return to Ovid. The example of Narcissus, suggesting that the mirror image is a metamorphic version of the boy, tells only part of the story. All metamorphoses are skewed mirrors of the original form. In addition, the mirror relations in Ovid's world and Dante's suggest a constantly shifting relationship of matter and of morals. Dante learned a great deal from the middle books of Ovid's poem, where mortals are forced to make subtle choices—most typically among different types of love—which turn into moral oppositions of the most powerful kind.[20] That is an essentially metamorphic vision of the world, and, in sharing that with Ovid, Dante reveals at once a more direct understanding of Ovid and a more original metamorphic poetics than any of his contemporaries.

Dante skews his mirror: sins are juxtaposed with other sins such that their interconnections only become apparent through a subtle reading of their complementary punishments. Within the world of the damned, Dante keeps bringing together groups that are at once similar and different. Consider the climactic (if rather obscure) final line of Canto XIII, which depicts the suicides and the squanderers. The last victim in the canto, an anonymous Florentine, utters only one sentence in regard to his own sins: "Io fei gibetto a me de le mie case" (13.151: "I made me a gibbet of my own house[s]"). Now we know from the fact that the speaker has been transformed into a bush that he must be a suicide, and his comment suggests clearly enough that he must have hanged himself on his own property. But this bush first speaks because it has been mutilated by the canto's other principal action, the violent hunt of the spendthrifts. The Florentine is as much a party to that acted out punishment as he is to the metamorphosis of the suicides, and if we read his final line again, we can clearly see that it contains a double meaning. The Florentine is not only a suicide but also a spendthrift, whose houses (hence the significance of the plural) have destroyed him.[21]

This conflation among the damned we could multiply with many examples. The hoarders and prodigals punish each other in an elaborate mutual dance. The flatterers and prostitutes belong together logically enough since flatterers have prostituted themselves; to that abstract equivalence Dante adds the punishment of swimming in *sterco*, such that the substance which so perfectly characterizes flattery comes also to objectify the degradation of the courtesans' physical beauty. Between the damned and the devils who guard and torment them Dante is particularly fond of introducing these mirrorings. The dog Cerberus watches over gluttons who howl and keep turning from side to side in an effort to lie down comfortably. Phlegyas is a notably angry guardian of the wrathful, and the centaurs most violently govern the violent. Indeed the whole farcical scene of struggle within the lake of pitch between devils and barrators that closes Canto XXII suggests that all are (so to speak) tarred with the same brush. The very categories of crime, though designed to appear theologically rigid, often coalesce, as one sinner turns into another kind of sinner. Many of the schismatics are also evil counselors; simonists in hell are treated like murderers on earth; and certain figures like Vanni Fucci and Ugolino are master criminals in several areas.

This imaginative habit of Dante's not only contrasts with but also helps fulfill the rigid scholastic outlines of the poem's moral universe. Discussions of the categories of sin (such as in Canto XI) frequently attempt to offer a logical structure in which seemingly divergent misdeeds can be understood as deriving from like defects of morality and will. So in the cases we have mentioned there are important connections between squandering one's life and soul, or between prostituting one's body and prostituting one's judgment. (At the same time, similar evil actions may belong in quite remote categories of sin since they proceed from different underlying causes.) The effect of these shifting relations is crucial to Dante's definition of sin. If we cannot decide whether the anonymous Florentine is a suicide or a spendthrift, if flatterers and prostitutes are swimming in the same bilge, what does it matter, since the damned have by definition lost their definition? And just as there is an aesthetic tension between the simple clarity of poetic justice and the shifting relationships of the mirror principle, so the firm God-given structure of the universe —such as set forth in the eleventh canto—is continually subjected by the force of evil to dissolution and transformation. Clarity of form, clarity of body, clarity of spiritual condition may be properties of God's cosmos, but they are denied to the sinners by Dante, even if with other strokes of his brush he portrays them with brilliant clarity.[22] That peculiar combination of poetic vividness with loss of form is, again, the heritage of Ovidian metamorphosis.

Beyond the world of the damned, there are other mirrors. The figure of Dante, with his own chequered past, is partly in a mirror-relationship to the sinners he scrutinizes. Dante and Virgil exist in another such relationship. And what is the whole world of Dante's hell if not a severely skewed mirror of paradise and a more moderately skewed mirror of earth itself? Perhaps the clearest example of this mirroring is the canto of the simonists. Since their crime amounts to an overturning of the secular order with corrupt temporality, they are doomed to the fitting *contrapasso* of being planted upside down in rock. They are thus turned into a mirror image of the upright righteous, especially as the fire that radiates from their feet is a parody of the flame that plays on the heads of the Apostles in heaven.[23] But it is the association of this upside-down burial with events beyond the *Inferno* that provides the farthest ranging mirror:

> Non mi parean men ampi né maggiori
> > che que' che son nel mio bel San Giovanni,
> > fatti per loco d'i battezzatori;
> l'un de li quali, ancor non è molt' anni,
> > rupp'io per un che dentro v'annegava:
> > e questo sia suggel ch'ogn' omo sganni.   [19.16–21]

(They seemed to me not less wide or larger than those that are made for the baptizings in my beautiful San Giovanni; one of which, not many years ago, I broke to save one who was drowning in it—and let this be the seal to undeceive all men.)

The passage contains many surprises. The time and place of the *Inferno* are left behind; and a comparison is made between unholy punishment and sacramental baptism. Above all the skewed mirror is Dante himself, who juxtaposes the crime of the simonists with his own actions, which had been characterized (unjustly, to be sure) as blasphemy. The interrelations are complex: the simonists are truly corrupting the sacraments and are punished with a notorious form of execution for murder; Dante's action merely seemed to blaspheme against the sacrament, while in fact it was life-giving, just as baptism itself is meant to be. Yet however conceptually clear the opposition, the mirroring itself suggests unavoidably that crimes against the church or religion can somehow spread to the (presumably) guiltless figure of the devout Christian Dante.[24]

Whether the poet is trying to suggest in himself an internal capacity for blasphemy or (as is more probable) merely a susceptibility to false accusations and to the effects of others' blasphemies, we cannot say from this canto. What is clear is that the voyager Dante cannot shake himself loose from contagion. Having himself made the comparison to his behavior in San Giovanni, he is then confronted by Pope Nicholas, who identifies him as the egregious Boniface VIII. In effect, as Dante is turned into Boniface, Nicholas is turned into Dante, for the pope is usurping the poet's role as savage critic of Boniface. In a further loss of self, Dante needs to be instructed by Virgil to say "Non son colui, non son colui che credi" (19.62: "I am not he, I am not he whom you think"), but it is the Roman poet who actually utters that attempted self-clarification. The canto reaches its climax in a twenty-eight-line tirade by Dante against simony and the secularization of the church. This outburst is unparalleled in the *Inferno*, and it tends to confirm the especially tense relationship (or anti-relationship) between Dante and the sins of this canto.[25] The effect of this skewed mirroring is to create a world that bridges earth and hell and in which moral categories are dangerously shifting and contagious.

This sense of metamorphic contagion is not merely a metaphor; in fact, it is crucial to Dante's definition of evil in *The Divine Comedy*. Thus it is not surprising that the last fully developed human figure in the *Inferno*, at all but the deepest pit of hell, forms the climactic case of mirroring and moral contagion. Dante understands betrayal (much as Ovid did) as the most extreme example of an attack on the clarity of the categories by which human life is ordered. The collapse of order brought about by Tereus or Myrrha was conceived much as Dante conceives the final groups of his sinners who betrayed kin, country, party, and those for whom they were responsible. Ugolino is unique among Dante's sinners (so far as I can see) in being to an equal extent perpetrator and victim of the same sin. He was a Guelph who betrayed the interests of his party and a Pisan who betrayed the interests of his city; yet Dante is even more interested in the

fact that he was betrayed by his (temporary) ally and host Archbishop
Ruggieri. The intimate connection within Ugolino between betrayer and
victim of betrayal is the basis for the mirroring quality of the episode.

The two betrayers betrayed by each other are subjected to a *contrapasso* in which they form a terrible mirror:

> . . . due ghiacciati in una buca,
>   sì che l'un capo a l'altro era cappello;
> e come 'l pan per fame si manduca,
>   così 'l sovran li denti a l'altro pose
>   là 've 'l cervel s'aggiugne con la nuca.   [32.125–29]

(. . . two frozen in one hole so close that the head of the one was a
hood for the other; and as bread is devoured for hunger, so the upper one set his teeth upon the other where the brain joins with the
nape.)

The two figures who ought to have been allied are now at one; indeed via
mirror reflection they are virtually transformed into a single organism.
But this oneness is entirely perverse. It is a physical monstrosity, and it
operates by the dreadful means of anthropophagy which is also self-consumption, in an act which takes place at the point where the head joins
the body. The result is a viciously skewed mirror of all the ties of order
that bind one human being to another; and when Ugolino offers to explain
his relationship to Ruggieri and "perché i son tal vicino" (33.15: "why I am
such a neighbor to him"), he encapsulates in that *vicino* all the spiritual
connections that have such grotesque physical expression in the fate of
the characters.

The punishment itself skewedly mirrors the crime. Ugolino narrates
the scene of his and his sons' starvation in prison, perhaps the only instance in the *Inferno* where the crime is more grotesque than the hellish
punishment. That Ugolino should be eternally gnawing on his sometime
ally, sometime enemy Ruggieri is a pale reflection of the more immediate and terrible mirroring in the death scene, once father and sons have
realized that they are shut up in the tower:

> Come un poco di raggio si fu messo
>   nel doloroso carcere, e io scorsi
>   per quattro visi il mio aspetto stesso,
> ambo le man per lo dolor mi morsi;
>   ed ei, pensando ch'io 'l fessi per voglia
>   di manicar, di sùbito levorsi
> e disser: "Padre, assai ci fia men doglia
>   se tu mangi di noi: tu ne vestisti
>   queste misere carni, e tu le spoglia."   [33.55-63]

(As soon as a little ray made its way into the woeful prison, and I discerned by their four faces the aspect of my own, I bit both hands for grief. And they, thinking I did it for hunger, suddenly rose up and said, "Father, it will be far less painful to us if you eat of us; you did clothe us with this wretched flesh, and do you strip us of it.")

Ugolino sees himself in his sons: their origin, as Anselmuccio reminds him, but also their terrible hunger. The grieving gesture of biting his hands, which his son reads literally as self-cannibalism, gives rise to a notion of sacrifice which appears abominable at the same time as it offers a reminder of the ties that bind father and child.[26] The result is a ghastly inversion of the developmental relationship between them, an undoing of creation, like the anthropophagy of Ovid's Tereus; and similarly the act is a grotesque form of metamorphosis among the ties that bind the family.[27] In addition there are echoes of Lycaon's cannibalism in a parody of the relation between man and god: just as Ovid's arch-criminal literalizes the propitiatory act by giving Jupiter human flesh,[28] so here Ugolino enacts a grotesque version of God liberating suffering humanity from the "doloroso carcere" of "queste misere carni." Whether the horrible act takes place or is merely contemplated[29] matters less than the idea of a metamorphic union between sinner and victim which is in turn mirrored by the composite self-consuming figure of betrayer and betrayed in hell.

2. Mutare e trasmutare

The translation of the spiritual into the fleshly and the contagion of forms and natures: these are the essential traits that underlie Ovidian transformation, and in the *Inferno* as well they form the context for literal metamorphosis. The appropriate punishments of the sins in upper hell are, as we have seen, proto-metamorphic: the lustful, the wrathful, the gluttonous are rewarded with an appropriately transformed milieu that stands at least as a metaphor for their sins. The transition from metaphor to metamorphosis appears after the eleventh canto, when Dante and the reader are initiated into the physical and spiritual plan of hell. The circle of the violent, in Canto XII, is first personified (if that is the right term) by "l'infamïa di Creti . . . / che fu concetta ne la falsa vacca" (12.12–13: "the infamy of Crete that was conceived in the false cow"). The Minotaur is a figure of violence; it is also the product of a false metamorphosis, and it is itself a composite creature, captured in the midst of transformation. On earth, it was famous for its violence against others, but in hell "sé stesso morse, / sì come quei cui l'ira dentro fiacca" (12.14–15: "he bit himself, like one whom wrath rends inwardly"). This self-violence is in fact the war between the human and the animal natures of the half-transformed creature, and it introduces us to a metamorphic concept of the two natures.[30]

Dante defines violence as the war of the human and the beastly natures, and he embodies this image not only in the Minotaur but, more significantly, in the centaurs, who torment the violent. Dante reads them according to the orthodox medieval view of metamorphosis, as beastly degradations of the human. In a brilliantly original physical allegory, he measures space in relation to Chiron's chest, where "le due nature son consorti" (12.84: "the two natures are consorted"). That image turns the composite beast-human into a corporeal map of the Platonic levels of the soul.[31] The conjunction of "le due nature" is specifically moralized when Dante applies a similar system of corporeal measurement to the violent, over whom the centaurs are watching. Like those of the centaurs, the natures of the violent are divided; but in this case it is the lake of blood that objectifies their moral condition in dividing them. Chiron's two natures are joined at the chest; among the violent, some are sunk in blood to the eyebrows, some to the throat, some to the waist, and some only to the ankles. The corporeal measuring system of the centaurs provides a matrix by which to gauge the sinners, who are in turn measured by blood—their own and that which they have violently spilled.

A different set of composite creatures introduces us to the suicides in the thirteenth canto: the Harpies, who "Ali hanno late, e colli e visi umani" (13.13: "have broad wings, and human necks and faces"). The Harpies live in trees ("alberi strani," says the poet); and at first the setting appears, both to us and to Dante, simply as another in the series of infernal milieux. Here, however, it does not constitute surroundings for the damned. The setting *is* the damned, the suicides who have been metamorphosed into leafless, gnarled, and thorny trees. That metamorphic doubleness introduces a set of perplexing questions:

> Io sentia d'ogne parte trarre guai
>   e non vedea persona che 'l facesse;
>   per ch'io tutto smarrito m'arrestai.
> Cred'ïo ch'ei credette ch'io credesse
>   che tante voci uscisser, tra quei bronchi,
>   da gente che per noi si nascondesse.   [13.22–27]

(I heard wailings uttered on every side, and saw no one who made them; wherefore, all bewildered, I stopped. I believe that he believed that I believed that all these voices from amid the trunks came from people who were hidden from us.)

Dante introduces metamorphosis as a surprise because from the start he associates it with the deepest mysteries of God's justice and of the lessons to be learned about the divine plan. Metamorphosis is a tremendous challenge to belief, and here the poet's increasingly subjunctive play on *credere* at once sets off the strangeness of human beings turned to trees and forces us on to the most challenging questions about believing. Indeed the humans are *hidden* in the trees just as the most difficult truths are hidden under the integumentum (itself a vegetable metaphor) of transformation.[32]

Such was the dark implication several cantos earlier at the very first mention of metamorphic material. The Gorgons had threatened Dante with petrification from the head of Medusa, but Virgil protected Dante by using his own hands to cover the younger poet's face.[33] The narrative is suddenly broken with a warning:

> O voi ch'avete li 'ntelletti sani,
>   mirate la dottrina che s'asconde
>   sotto 'l velame de li versi strani.   [9.61–63]

(O you who have sound understanding, mark the doctrine that is hidden under the veil of the strange verses.)

As befits the deliberately mysterious references, we never learn the nature of this *dottrina*, but the language of strangeness and hidden truth appears almost every time that metamorphosis takes place. Thus the suicides of Canto XIII are partly "hidden" in their trees by literary traditions of transformation. Barren trees become a physical metaphor for the spiritual conditions of suicide because they are an Ovidian and Virgilian emblem of life frozen in a deathlike state. Virgil's Polydorus (the primary source here) and some of Ovid's plant-metamorphosed figures like Daphne and Myrrha are in a pagan sense unquiet souls whose transformation demonstrates their marginality between life and death.[34] Viewed in Christian terms, suicide is the perfect equivalent of this inquietude. Myrrha, we recall from the *Metamorphoses*, had demanded to be punished with neither life nor death; so the Christian who commits suicide cannot be rewarded with life, of which he is unworthy, nor with death, which is no punishment since it is the end he has himself sought. To physicalize this doctrine, Dante creates a myth of transformation in which suicides are an exception to the rule that the damned will reassume their bodies on the occasion of the Last Judgment:

> Come l'altre verrem per nostre spoglie,
>   ma non però ch'alcuna sen rivesta,
>   ché non è giusto aver ciò ch'om si toglie.
> Qui le strascineremo, e per la mesta
>   selva saranno i nostri corpi appesi,
>   ciascuno al prun de l'ombra sua molesta.   [13.103–08]

(Like the rest we shall come, each for his cast-off body, but not, however, that any may inhabit it again; for it is not just that a man have what he robs himself of. Hither shall we drag them, and

through the mournful wood our bodies will be hung, each on the
thornbush of its nocuous shade.)

As we pass from pagan to Christian transformation, the secrets become
more deeply hidden. The metamorphic connection between the persons
of the damned and the barren trees, which may have seemed no more
than a piece of infernal poetic justice, is now redefined as the relation between body and soul. The trees may have appeared at first to be the physical punishment of the damned. Yet neither are they the bodies of the
damned nor are they the souls. Rather they are the *nocchi*, or knots, in
which "l'anima si lega" (13.88: "the soul is bound"). That metamorphic
knot is as much a crux as it is a body or a tree.

This crux conceals more mysteries than the theological. The play on
credere introduces a visionary experience within the larger vision of the
poem. Dante cannot decide what he believes; on top of that, Virgil, who
seems to know what Dante thinks better than Dante himself, urges him,
"Se tu tronchi / qualche fraschetta d'una d'este piante, / li pensier c'hai si
faran tutti monchi" (13.28–30: "If you break off a little branch from one of
these plants, the thoughts you have will all be cut short"). The breaking of
the branch puts Dante in direct physical touch with the transformed Pier
della Vigna, and thus the poet introduces an imitation of Virgil's own
Polydorus episode. But another Virgilian branch may be even more relevant here: that is, the golden bough that Aeneas must pluck in order to
descend and experience the underworld.[35] Dante's broken branch is his
own entry to visionary thoughts that are not *monchi*, that is, broken. The
sin of suicide has special relevance because it is the ultimate *in malo* loss
of self; as such it is contrasted with the *in bono* loss of self offered by such
a visionary experience as Dante's whole project. Indeed, recollecting
Dante's miserable condition at the beginning of the poem, we may conclude that the visionary stands as his rescue from the suicidal—which
may explain the close mirroring between the poet and the sufferers of this
canto. The metamorphic image of suicides-become-trees from which
Dante breaks off a branch combines the deadly, the fragmented, and the
visionary in a single knot.

That conjunction is intensified by the complementarity of the sinners
who suffer together with the suicides. The spendthrifts are also self-
fragmenters. But Dante does not have to break off their branches, for
their punishment is an image of the most famous of all metamorphic
myths of dismemberment and fragmentation. They appear as the objects
of a savage hunt:

> Di rietro a loro era la selva piena
> > di nere cagne, bramose e correnti
> > come veltri ch'uscisser di catena.
> In quel che s'appiattò miser li denti,

e quel dilaceraro a brano a brano;
poi sen portar quelle membra dolenti.   [13.124–29]

(Behind them the wood was full of black bitches, eager and fleet, like greyhounds loosed from the leash. On him who had squatted they set their teeth and tore him piecemeal, then carried off those woeful limbs.)

Ovid's story of Actaeon has initial relevance here because of a medieval demystification according to which it is a tale about a man who lost his property by spending too much on hunting dogs. But Dante's context reverberates with all the more powerful associations of the myth: the visionary experience and its intimate associations with discovery of identity and fragmentation of that identity.[36] As Dante breaks the branch which mutilates the suicide but inspires his own vision, so he watches the dissolution of the Actaeons and translates their experience into a mirroring recognition of himself. The metamorphoses of Canto XIII, then, reveal a kind of progression from the *contrapasso* to the skewed mirror, from the physical metaphor for a spiritual fault to the complete sense of contagion among forms, sins, and sinners, as well as within the self of the living and the damned.

In the climactic episode of metamorphosis in the *Inferno*, the damnation of the thieves in Cantos XXIV and XXV, the balance has shifted yet further from *contrapasso* to the skewed mirror. At first the thieves are merely decorated with coiling serpents, but the punishment intensifies to the point where the humans dissolve, metamorphose into serpents, or interchange identities with serpents. The punishment does, of course, fit the crime. Thieves are slippery figures of deceit, like serpents. They are in their nature shape-changers, thus justifying the transformation to serpent, and they alienate property, thus justifying the condition of constant and exchanging metamorphosis.[37] In addition, for the principal thief, church robber Vanni Fucci, the transformation to beast is especially appropriate since by his own admission he lived his human life as a beast—in fact, we learn that his nickname was "Bestia":

Vita bestial mi piacque e non umana,
  sì come a mul ch'i' fui; son Vanni Fucci
  bestia, e Pistoia mi fu degna tana.   [24.124–26]

(A bestial life, not human, pleased me, mule that I was. I am Vanni Fucci, beast, and Pistoia was my fitting den.)

A deeper poetic justice operates here than even the victim knows. Fucci escaped detection on earth in his own lifetime (according to tradition an innocent man was hanged in his stead)[38] and so he becomes a particularly fitting candidate for poetic justice in the next world. Thus, in addition to being tormented by serpents, he is expressly enjoined to reveal his guilt ("Io non posso negar quel che tu chiedi"; 24.136: "I cannot refuse you what you ask"). And even the bold self-declaration of bestiality is part of his own punishment, a recompense for escaping earthly justice and a rhetorical form of animal transformation.

But *contrapasso* itself does not go very far to explain the power and meaning of the events in these two cantos. The equation of thieves and serpents is a bit strained; and the lives of the thieves who experience the truly grotesque transformations are barely sketched out in the poem. In fact, the movement of the *Inferno* is away from simple poetic justice equating crimes on earth with punishment in hell. The first metamorphic motif, men becoming beasts—which we associated with the *contrapasso*—begins to coalesce with the second, the fragmentation and loss of form. In the early stages of the thieves' punishment, the serpents decorate the bodies of their victims so thoroughly that the two species seem almost to become one before any metamorphosis takes place:

> quelle [serpi] ficcavan per le ren la coda
> e 'l capo, ed eran dinanzi aggroppate.
> Ed ecco a un ch'era da nostra proda,
> s'avventò un serpente che 'l trafisse
> là dove 'l collo a le spalle s'annoda.   [24.95–99]

(These [serpents] thrust through their loins the head and tail, which were knotted in front. And lo! at one who was near our bank darted a serpent that transfixed him there where the neck is joined to the shoulders.)

The serpents define the bodies they surround. The conjunction of man and beast in the midst of transformation defines two realms of human beastliness. Not only do the snakes mark out the boundary between head and neck, i.e., between the divine and the appetitive; they also define the lowest human impulse by transforming themselves into the shape of the man's sexual organs—indeed they almost seem to be engaged in a sexual act with their victims. Once again Dante physicalizes the levels of the soul. Chiron was a composite of "due nature," joined where the head meets the body. The thief Cacus will appear as a centaur whose neck is described as the place "ove comincia nostra labbia" (25.21: "where our form begins"). It is generally asserted that the mythologically inaccurate rendition of Cacus as a centaur was due to Dante's misreading of Virgil's *semihomo*, originally intended to describe not his physical form but his monstrous moral condition.[39] More likely, however, Dante deliberately metamorphosed the spiritual description into a physical form.

The fragmentation of animal transformation soon gives way to complete dissolution. The serpent-encrusted figure, who turns out to be

Vanni Fucci, burns up in an instant, is reduced to ashes, and then reforms itself into its original shape. In itself the activity is quite mysterious. Dissolution is no sort of obvious punishment for thievery, and the language Dante uses intensifies the obscurity of the events themselves. It takes place faster than you can write *o* or *i*, the poet tells us ("Né o sì tosto mai né i si scrisse," 24.100), in an enigma which seems to point to secret writing, possibly suggesting the metamorphic figure of Ovid's Io, or possibly the pronoun of personal identity, *io*.[40] Dante then compares the hellish conflagration and reforming to the activity of the Phoenix. Not only is that bird an ancient image of the resurrection and therefore shockingly inappropriate to this hellish metamorphosis, but it is also described with pointed reference to the mystic rites of the East, in just the way Ovid's Pythagoras characterizes the bird amongst his miraculous examples of transformation.[41] The enigma receives some clarification when we think back to the dissolutions of the metamorphic suicides and spendthrifts: there, too, transformation was fragmentation, and there, too, the Actaeon-like punishment consisted in eternal dissolving and (presumably) reforming. But the meaning of these metamorphic enigmas can only emerge fully with the events of the following canto, which perfectly fuse the beastly transformation with the dissolution of form.

The process is quite logical. Vanni Fucci, with serpents coiled around him, had dissolved into ashes and been reformed. Agnello Brunelleschi is assaulted by a serpent and becomes united with it as a single organism. Then Buoso Donati, also attacked by a serpent, unites with the beast but suddenly starts exchanging form with it, and the two escape in opposite directions with opposite identities. The first of these two metamorphoses concentrates on the fearful loss of individual form. As Agnello and the serpent unite, "né l'un né l'altro già parea quel ch'era" (25.63: "neither the one nor the other now seemed what it was at first"), and his former fellows cry out, "Vedi che già non se' nè due nè uno" (25.69: "Lo, thou art now neither two nor one!"). The allusions are notably Ovidian, with much of the language taken from the episode of Salmacis and Hermaphroditus, which, as we have seen, is a paradigm of the mirror and the dangerous loss of selfhood.[42] Like the closely related myth of Narcissus, it is also a perverse love story. That association is quite apposite to Agnello's transformation, which appears as a kind of hellish sexual act that follows quite logically from the genital implications of Vanni Fucci's serpents.[43]

Buoso's metamorphosis, or complete interchange, fuses the dissolution of forms with the beastly. Buried in the lengthy and intricate description of exactly how each member of man and serpent gradually switches form are numerous references to those moralized categories that had always provided the metaphoric vehicles to distinguish man from brute. Man is *molle*, serpent *dura*; "lo membro che l'uom cela" is not hidden by beasts; "quel ch' era dritto" contrasts with "quel che giacëa"; the tongue, which had been "presta / prima a parlar" now becomes forked and serpentine. Softness, shame, uprightness, speech: these are definitions of the human which are built into Ovidian metamorphosis, especially as it was understood in the medieval Platonic tradition that goes back to Chalcidius's version of the *Timaeus* and the nature poetry of the twelfth century.[44] Such a degradation of the human we have seen elsewhere in Dante and throughout medieval Ovidian lore. But the mode of metamorphosis as complete interchange suggests not so much the opposition of the beastly and the human as their interchangeability.

The mythological allusions here—notably to Ovid's Cadmus—confirm this sense of immediate interchange between man and beast. We have seen how the whole Theban race was plagued by serpents and mirrors.[45] Cadmus's own end in the *Metamorphoses* not only involves his transformation; it also mirrors his killing of a sacred serpent, and it is foreshadowed by the voice that tells him, "quid, Agenore nate, peremptum / serpentem spectas? et tu spectabere serpens" (*Metamorphoses* 3.97–98: "Why, O son of Agenor, dost thou gaze on the serpent thou hast slain? Thou too shalt be a serpent for men to gaze on"). Dante builds here upon the visionary qualities of Ovid's scene, for the twenty-fifth canto and the whole transformation are shrouded in mystic smoke. But he also alludes to all those Ovidian metamorphoses in which there is small change between the criminal and the animal form in which he eventually finds himself. That combination in a sense underlies the whole Dantesque technique of the mirror, for the mirroring relations between crime and punishment, or between one group of sinners and another, or even between good and evil, may suggest a mystic relationship of opposites or else a dangerously easy shift of like to like—or even a dangerously easy shift of like to unlike, as in the comparison of baptismal font to tortured burial or of Vanni Fucci to the Phoenix. It is the interchanges of the seventh *bolgia* that bring these opposites together.

Yet if Dante's origins and meanings are so clearly Ovidian, we must further ponder the meaning of his famous challenge:

> Taccia di Cadmo e d'Aretusa Ovidio;
>   ché se quello in serpente e quella in fonte
>   converte poetando, io non lo 'nvidio;
> ché due nature mai a fronte a fronte
>   non trasmutò si ch'amendue le forme
>   a cambiar lor matera fosser pronte.   [25.97–102]

(Concerning Cadmus and Arethusa let Ovid be silent, for if he, poetizing, converts the one into a serpent and the other into a fountain, I envy him not; for two natures front to front he never so transmuted that both forms were prompt to exchange their substance.)

Perhaps the ultimate expression of Dante's face-to-face meeting with the great pagans is his willingness to defy them. But what exactly makes Dante feel so superior here? Is this simply a piece of aesthetic egoism, or a slur such as offered by medieval mythographers on the morals or credulity of the pagans? Or is it a new kind of challenge? Dante is, as ever, enigmatic. At one level he seems to feel that Ovid's metamorphoses are merely poetical, rather as Lactantius suggested by justifying Jupiter's transformations as figures of speech.[46] The word *poetando* seems to damn Ovid with faint praise; it is opposed to *nature*, for Dante intends to deal with essences and not just shapes.

These *nature*, as we have seen almost every time Dante introduces a composite creature, are also the natures of man and beast, and it is clear that Dante's claim to originality has to do with the interchange of those natures. Yet it is hardly news in 1300 (or even at the beginning of the Christian era, when Ovid was writing the *Metamorphoses*) that man can descend to the beastly level. Even Dante's Ulysses, hardly a paragon of wisdom, urges his men, "fatti non foste a viver come bruti, / ma per seguir virtute a canoscenza" (26.119–20: "You were not made to live as brutes, but to pursue virtue and knowledge"). What Ulysses cannot see and what neither Ovid nor even Plato (at least in Dante's opinion) could see was the third term in this typology of likenesses. The ancients could see the intimate connections between the image of man and the image of the beast; they could not see that man was in the image of God.[47]

Imago dei is a term that cannot be spoken in hell, but it is the mystery that lies beyond all the transformations. Once we have added this term, we can see how all the metamorphoses are desecrations of the divine as well as of the human. Fittingly, the plot of changes climaxes in the metamorphosis to serpent, since the serpent is God's ultimate enemy. The process of the changes in Canto XXV, then, is the complete undoing of man's divinity. When we are told of Agnello in the midst of transformation, "Ogne primaio aspetto ivi era casso" (25.76: "each former feature was blotted out"), we realize that it is not only the human form that is undone but also the unfallen likeness of God. Metamorphosis also becomes an inversion of human growth. That is why Buoso's interchange with the serpent begins at the navel ("quella parte onde prima è preso / nostro alimento"; 25.85–86: "that part by which we first receive our nourishment"), just as the previous metamorphosis began with an image of the procreative act. That also explains the inversions of other directly or indirectly sacred images of transformation, including the comparison of Vanni Fucci's dissolution to the Phoenix, emblem of the resurrection, and, later, the terrible undoing of procreation and growth in the family relations of Ugolino and his children.

Dante's term for this special kind of metamorphosis that goes beyond the pagan is *mutare e trasmutare*, the condition in which he leaves all the individuals as he and Virgil depart from the seventh *bolgia*. The phrase is enigmatic since it seems to have a different meaning for each of the transformations he has witnessed there. Vanni Fucci goes back and forth from serpent-covered man to burnt cinders to man. Agnello and the serpent unite, crawl off, and (presumably, since activities in hell are repeated eternally) separate so that they can repeat the procedure. But these are stages toward the climactic *mutare e trasmutare*. It is the *exchange* of identities between a man and a beast that Dante vaunts as his special break with the pagan past. Buoso and his "partner" *mutano e trasmutano* in the sense that human turns to serpent and serpent to human, and throughout that transformation Dante emphasizes its unique and unearthly mystery.

The poet adds to the mystery by burying in obscure references the fact that both serpents, the first with whom Agnello unites and the second with whom Buoso exchanges shapes, are themselves former human beings. Cianfa (Agnello's "partner") is present, as it were, by absence: Dante, curious about the names of the humans he sees, hears one of them ask "Cianfa dove fia rimaso?" (25.43: "Where can Cianfa be?"); we never hear about him again. Francesco Cavalcanti is yet more remotely identified and without direct reference to his serpentine form as "quel che tu, Gaville, piagni" (25.151: "he whom you, Gaville, lament"). It is a complete world of interchangeability among forms and identities, back and forth between individuals and between species. Eternal change and, especially, *exchange* (as Dante sees them) contrast with Ovid's unidirectional metamorphoses, which, like the punishments of the *contrapasso*, seem to be simple pieces of earthly justice. The eternally re-enacted crime and punishment points to an ultimate principle of justice in the universe, while the exchange metamorphosis, with its union and recreation of serpent and man, stands as the essential desecration of the image and likeness of God, since it not only suggests the degradation of man but, more horribly, the elevation of the serpent to the image of God.

If metamorphosis is the link between the damned and the image of God, then the hellish transformations become coverings, or *integumenta*, for all the sacred truths about God and man that cannot be approached directly in the *Inferno*. These truths are, in fact, the whole analogical system that unites the elements of creation. At one level, roughly corresponding to the "anagogical" in the language of scriptural interpretation,[48] the distorted sinners are metamorphic images of the divine, and at the allegorical level they are metamorphic images of the body of the universe, just as at the moral level they represent images of sin itself. This set of parallels explains the special weight that both Dante the poet and Dante the character give to the distortions of the human body.[49] The motif intensifies throughout the last third of the *Inferno*, beginning with the moment when Dante sees the warped bodies of the diviners. He ad-

dresses the reader, always his device to single out an especially important
issue:

> or pensa per te stesso
> com'io potea tener lo viso asciutto,
> quando la nostra imagine di presso
> vidi sì torta, che 'l pianto de li occhi
> le natiche bagnava per lo fesso. [20.20–24]

(Think now for yourself how I could keep my cheeks dry when near
at hand I saw our image so contorted that the tears from the eyes
bathed the buttocks at the cleft.)

The partial transformation of the diviners is a distortion of *la nostra imagine*, and *la nostra imagine* is as close as one can come in the language of
hell to speaking of the image of God.

In this same connection Dante introduces Ovid's Tiresias in explicitly
metamorphic terms:

> Vedi Tiresia, che mutò sembiante
> quando di maschio femmina divenne,
> cangiandosi le membra tutte quante. [20.40–42]

(See Tiresias, who changed semblance when from male he became
female, transforming all his members.)

The distortion of sexual clarity in the seer's own history is an image of the
distortions wrought by magic; both threaten the order implicit in *la nostra imagine*.[50] The canto of the thieves' metamorphosis is the real turning
point where our form and its stability become so vitally important in defining the universe, man, and God. Beyond it we have figures like the
schismatics and falsifiers whose crimes explicitly involve the destruction
of the world's harmonious fabric and whose punishment is accordingly organic. Many of these characters have sinned in such a way that they were,
like Tiresias, guilty of a kind of metamorphosis in their lives. Impersonators tried to transform themselves, and alchemists dabbled in dangerous
powers of transformation within nature. Dante surrounds these individuals with references to figures of Ovidian transformation, whether to the
insane, like Ino and Athamas, or to prideful shape-changers, like Daedalus or Myrrha.

Master Adam, who produced false coinage, is transformed into an orthodox medieval image of disordered corporeal humors.[51] He suffers

> La grave idropesì, che sì dispaia
> le membra con l'omor che mal converte,
> che 'l viso non risponde alla ventraia. [30.52–54]

(The heavy dropsy which with its ill-digested humor, so unmates the members that the face does not answer to the paunch.)

It is a disease described explicitly in terms of distorted corporeal harmony. His explicit reference to "lo specchio di Narciso" (30.128) suggests all the familiar Ovidian play on *imago*. His false coins are false images and they have turned him into an empty image of his living self.[52] When Capocchio the alchemist boasts, "com' io fui di natura buona scimia" (29.139: "How good an ape of nature I was"), he is intentionally vaunting his transforming powers and without realizing it describing his degrading metamorphosis into that animal which always stands as a poor imitation of the human. These corporeal metamorphoses are more than a *contrapasso* for metamorphic sins; the transformations also point negatively to the wholeness of cosmic order that they have breached. So Bertran de Born, having created schism between father and son, must carry his brain "partito . . . dal suo principio," an emblem par excellence of the destruction of the organic order of the body and hence of family, state, and world. That *principio* is not only his own head but allegorically the fabric of order and anagogically the divine source from which all order emanates.

In effect, Dante was right to vaunt his metamorphoses above those of his master Ovid. For only a great Christian poet could use the doctrine of man conceived in the image of God to join the lore of metamorphoses with the whole analogical world-view, that is, all the parallel systems of body natural, body politic, body of the world, and image of God. That link is Dante's greatest of all contributions to the history of metamorphosis. Dante saw that in the infinite regress of parallel worlds which constitutes his universe the principles of metamorphosis offer a key both *in bono* and *in malo*.[53] Just before the appearance of the self-transforming thieves, a grand epic simile explores the seemingly minor issue of Virgil's various moods, which the poet compares with a scene in January:

> quando la brina in su la terra assempra
>   l'imagine di sua sorella bianca,
>   ma poco dura a la sua penna tempra,
> lo villanello a cui la roba manca,
>   si leva, e guarda, e vede la campagna
>   biancheggiar tutta; ond' ei si batte l'anca,
> ritorna in casa, e qua e là si lagna,
>   come 'l tapin che non sa che si faccia;
>   poi riede, e la speranza ringavagna,
> veggendo 'l mondo aver cangiata faccia
>   in poco d'ora. . . .   [24.4–14]

(When the hoarfrost copies on the ground the image of his white sister, but the temper of his pen lasts but short while—the peasant,

whose fodder fails, rises and looks out and sees the fields all white;
at which he smites his thigh, returns indoors and grumbles to and
fro, like the poor wretch who knows not what to do; then comes out
again and recovers hope when he sees how in but little time the
world has changed its face.)

The vehicle may be more important than the tenor. It is a beautiful medieval image of the orderly world, with motions of the cosmos and of the individual in happy harmony.[54] Yet more important is the fact that it is a
world in transformation: the days are getting longer, the weather changing, the rime-frost melting, the shepherd returning to the land. Placed at
the introduction to the hellish metamorphoses the simile stands as an organic picture of orderly change against which we can measure the grotesque changes of man and beast in hell.[55]

The effect of placing metamorphosis in the mirror of analogies is to define it as a universal principle, not just limited to hell or (still less) to the
poetics of depicting hell. In countless ways the images of the depths of
hell tend to spread to our own world, and metamorphosis, as we have already seen, is notable among these. In the very last cantos Dante uses
metamorphosis to blur the distinction between the living and the dead, or
more specifically, the living and the damned. Fra Alberigo and Branca
d'Oria, the last characters we meet before we reach the absolute floor of
hell, are damned but not yet dead. To Dante's surprise at such a possibility, the friar responds that he knows nothing about the current fate of his
body in the world of the living but that his soul is already damned:

> sappie che, tosto che l'anima trade
> come fec'ïo, il corpo suo l'è tolto
>   da un demonio, che poscia il governa
>   mentre che 'l tempo suo tutto sia vòlto.   [33.129–32]

(Know that as soon as the soul betrays as I did, its body is taken from
it by a devil who thereafter rules it until its time has all revolved.)

With this stroke not only does the poet suggest a contagious interchange
(not unlike the metamorphoses of Canto XXV) between our world and
hell; he also postulates a highly metamorphic vision of our world, in which
evildoers are in fact changelings, demons in disguised shape. The source,
as we have seen, is the demonological lore that Augustine advanced in order to give credence to pagan marvels.[56] For Dante, however, it is the final metamorphic stroke of the *Inferno* in which all hell breaks loose.[57]

Beyond hell there are yet greater principles of change. One that hangs
heavy over the whole of the *Inferno* is the Last Judgment, the change beyond which there is no more change. Early in Virgil's education of Dante
he annunciates a developmental principle that covers both the changes of
hell and those beyond. Dante asks his guide what will happen to the pun-

ishments of the damned after the Last Judgment, whether they will in-
crease or decrease in intensity:

> Ed elli a me: "Ritorna a tua scïenza,
>   che vuol, quanto la cosa è più perfetta,
>   più senta il bene, e così la doglienza.
> Tutto che questa gente maladetta
>   in vera perfezion già mai non vada,
>   di là più che di qua essere aspetta." [6.106–11]

(And he to me: "Return to your science, which has it that the more a
thing is perfect, the more it feels the good, and so the pain. Although this accursed folk can never come to true perfection, yet
they look to be nearer it then than now.")

Just as hell can come to equal paradise or the world upside down, so this
doctrine of change unifies the struggles of transformation of the evil and
the good. The metamorphoses of the sinners in hell are, in these Aristotelean terms, labors to achieve their own inverted form of *perfezion*.
Hence the cry of Cacus as he applies his torments to Vanni Fucci, "Ov' è,
ov' è, l'acerbo?" (25.18: "Where is he, where is the unripe one?"): the
sinner is still sour and has yet to ripen in the hellish heat.[58] Meanwhile,
in the life of Dante himself or in the struggles of our world the sequences
of changes—whose personal history goes back to Ovid and whose natural
history goes back to Ovid's Pythagoras and his medieval followers—are in
Dante's Christian and Aristotelean framework movements toward perfection. Not that it is all such a happy gospel: "questa gente maladetta" who
will never arrive at perfection may just as well include Dante's own real-
life countrymen as the damned in hell, the groups being, after all, closely
connected. Still, in the great scheme of analogies Dante has fused Ovidian metamorphosis with a multiple process whereby sinners achieve their
inverse perfection, the world fulfills itself in the image of God, and the
voyager finds his own psyche drawn through perplexities upward.

Beyond the *Inferno*, the lore of metamorphosis is not abandoned. The
thieves' exchange with the serpents is perfectly balanced by the canto of
the same number in the *Purgatorio*. There, instead of a perverse procreative act between the *imago dei* and the enemy of God, Dante witnesses
the purgation of lust. As the suffering souls are cleansed, the poet is instructed in a complete history of human generation and of the generation of the soul. Statius offers first a physical embryology, detailing the
changes that begin with the *sangue perfetto* (the semen) through the procreative act and then through natural growth.[59] From the physical evolution Statius passes without break to the evolution of the soul. It is not a
layered multiplicity, like the Platonic and Averroistic soul in which the
composite creatures of hell were imprisoned, but a single entity uniting

body and spirit. What Dante celebrates here is precisely the medieval metamorphic lore of nature. The abstract growth of body and soul is rendered concrete through an image of metamorphic natural vitality:

> E perché meno ammiri la parola,
>   guarda il calor del sol che si fa vino,
>   giunto a l'omor che de la vite cola.   [25.76–78]

(And, that you may marvel less at my words, look at the sun's heat, which is made wine when combined with the juice that flows from the vine.)

The familiar metamorphic image from medieval science is bound up with the pagan associations of transforming nature. It is one element of the Ovidian heritage that had to be excluded from hell.

This vitality also points to elements beyond pagan nature, for Dante here creates a metamorphic myth of the growth of the soul after death:

> E come l'aere, quand'è ben pïorno,
>   per l'altrui raggio che 'n sé si reflette,
>   di diversi color diventa addorno;
> così l'aere vicin quivi si mette
>   e in quella forma ch'è in lui suggella
>   virtüalmente l'alma che ristette.   [25.91–96]

(And as the air, when it is full of moisture, becomes adorned with various colors by another's rays which are reflected in it, so here the neighboring air shapes itself in that form which is virtually imprinted on it by the soul that stopped there.)

The natural miracle of the rainbow points toward the evolution of a spiritual body after death just as the miracle of wine pointed to the evolution of a physical body in life. The moment when these truths are vouchsafed to Dante, poised near the top of the mountain of Purgatory, is as far as the lore of pagan metamorphosis can take him: the visions of change in, for instance, the same canto of the *Paradiso* are those of personal hope and the blindness of the imminence of God. Here, near the end of the *Purgatorio*, Virgil is about to speak for the last time, and Ovid must now be silent too.[60] Yet Dante has taken him further than any Christian had before, fusing pagan metamorphosis with Christian teleology.

3. Rhetoric and Images

Two extratextual traditions deriving from the *Commedia* merit some brief attention as we conclude our consideration of Dante and turn toward the Renaissance. Within a very few years of its appearance, the poem gave rise to one industry of commentary and another of manuscript illumination. Commentary begins with Dante's son Jacopo around 1322 and proceeds through later contemporaries, then into the high humanist period of Boccaccio and Petrarch, and finally to the Neoplatonic version of Cristoforo Landino near the end of the fifteenth century.[61] The earliest illustrated manuscripts date from the 1330s, and the tradition is alive and well for a hundred and fifty years, when printed books begin to diminish the quantity and quality of illuminations.[62] Both practices, despite their longevity, have a unique significance in Dante's own century, when they are still closely tied to the milieu of the poem itself and to the challenges of its newness. As commentary and illustration attempt together to interpret and frame a medium for the *Commedia*, so they will interpret and frame metamorphosis as well as those revivals of paganism which Dante helped bring into being.

The allegorizing of myth, as we have seen, dates back to antiquity and the early patristic period; the fourteenth century was the height of its Christianization and the beginnings of a turn toward the inclusion of pagan values within a Christian scheme. Dante was himself inspired by this tradition just as he in turn provided inspiration for it.[63] I have already suggested how his transformations represented a kind of reverse travel on the bridge erected by so many mythographers between physical metamorphosis and spiritual meaning. But Dante travels the bridge in both directions. When he interprets his own *contrapassi*, as in the case of the diviners whose heads are twisted backward as punishment for their wish to see forward, or when he uses traditional mythological figures like the Minotaur in a moralized sense, he translates allegory back into imaginative expression. When he invents his own transformations, as with the suicides or the thieves, he builds in part upon earlier mythographic speculations concerning the varieties and meanings of metamorphosis.[64]

In turn, the commentary on Dante in the fourteenth century continues to raise the same questions that mythographers had raised in regard to classical texts. Dante's face-to-face meeting with pagan antiquity, of which we have already spoken, has the effect of transferring many elements of ancient myth and history into the mainstream of the Christian tradition. Most of the commentaries respond as they did to Ovid. Guido da Pisa (ca. 1330), for instance, gives two significations to the Minotaur.[65] The first debunks the story historically by explaining that, instead of having intercourse with a bull, Pasiphae had an affair with the king's secretary named Taurus, consummated it in Daedalus's house (equivalent to the creation of a false bull in the original myth), and gave birth to a son called Minotaurus, who turned out to be inhumanly cruel and therefore needed to be shut up in a labyrinth. The commentator then turns around and moralizes the story by seeing the Minotaur as the devil and Theseus as a Christ figure who slays the devil and brings about the resurrection.

Yet for all the familiarity of such Ovidian allegorizations—and there are many more—Dante's Cretan monster is not the same as the creature of the pagan imagination. It is one thing for the poet of the *Ovide moralisé* to dissolve and rebuild an Ovidian myth so as to force it into the mold of a Christian truth; it is quite another for a character from the *Metamorphoses* to appear as a denizen of hell in a canonical Christian text. And that status is the first lesson we learn in reading the early commentaries: from the start, the *Commedia* is being read as an authentic visionary experience. When confronted, then, with the dozens of figures from antiquity who populate the *Inferno* (and the *Purgatorio* as well), the commentators must authenticate and recuperate as much as they can within Christian theology. So, according to Jacopo della Lana (ca. 1325), the Medusa's power of petrification signifies that "heresy turns men to stone because the heretic would rather believe in the sensualities that are based on bodily experience than in the sacred scripture as revealed by the Holy Spirit."[66] The allegory itself is no different from those of the mythographers, but its context has changed. Dante's Medusa appears in the canto of the heretics, themselves frozen in death and trapped within "le tombe carche" (9.129). Jacopo's analysis, joining heresy with the distinction between body and spirit, demonstrates how reader and poet exist in a shared context that authenticates the allegorical relevance of the pagan transformation as Ovid could never have been authenticated. Guido da Pisa, after conventionally allegorizing the Medusa as terror and oblivion, glosses the *dottrina* in the poet's address to the reader ("mirate la dottrina che s'asconde"; 9.62: "mark the doctrine that is hidden") as referring to his own allegory. Dante and the commentators together have made it possible for the allegorized Medusa to become *dottrina*.

It is Dante's own metamorphic inventions, by the very nature of their syncretic origins, that point most clearly towards a new partnership of classical and Christian traditions. Nearly all the early commentators understand the tree-metamorphosis of the suicides as referring allegorically to the tripartite division of man into rational, sensitive, and vegetative; when a man kills himself, he destroys the rational and the sensitive soul, and he is left only with the vegetative, aptly metaphorized in his transformation to tree.[67] Such an approach, whether or not literally part of Dante's intention, is very much in keeping with his vision, and it builds a bridge between pagan traditions of metamorphosis and a Christian theology heavily influenced by medieval Platonism.[68]

The transformations of the thieves offer the commentators the greatest field for the discussion of metamorphosis precisely because Dante himself has in these cantos pondered the varieties of transformation. The commentators fix upon the sequence of different metamorphoses as signifying different types of change. Guido da Pisa, for instance (p. 470), repeats almost verbatim Arnulf's list compiled for Ovidian allegoresis, while the Anonimo Fiorentino takes the occasion for a division that speaks to a whole history of changes:

> There are three ways in which one thing transforms itself into another. Either it transforms itself in reality, like a grain seed, which when sown changes and transforms itself into grass and thence into straw, and the same for any other seed; or it transmutes and changes itself in potential, that is, a fall of fortune, like a rich man who becomes poor or a great lord who loses his power; or it transmutes itself morally, like a stupid man who becomes wise, or a man who becomes like a beast.   [pp. 511–12]

This continuum of metamorphoses legitimizes and unifies the changes of nature, of fortune, and of morality. It also places them in the context of orthodoxy. But the commentators recognize as well that Dante, especially in the final reciprocal metamorphosis of Buoso, seeks to go beyond this history. So Guido adds to Arnulf's list a "transformatio . . . miraculosa sive supernaturalis" (p. 472), whose history includes the pillar of salt, the rod of Moses, and, most notably, the sacramental transformation of baptismal water and the transsubstantiation of bread and wine in the eucharist. Guido does not, to be sure, connect this type of metamorphosis with any particular event in Canto XXIV or XXV—and he would not have an easy time of it if he tried. What counts, though, is the giant step he takes in joining Christian with classical allegory. Because the *Commedia* is at once a Christian vision and a re-vision of pagan antiquity, it can bring about a new syncretic vision of metamorphosis.

The tradition of manuscript illumination has a great deal in common with that of commentary. Both attempt to mediate between the text and the audience, to simplify and domesticate Dante's conception. Both traditions inspired Dante and were in turn inspired by his work. Both are important to us because they exist as part of a heritage which translates antiquity into new languages and contexts. And, in regard to *The Divine Comedy* in particular, they grow up together, following a similar conceptual pattern in the century after Dante's death, emphasizing the devotional, then the personal, then the cosmic aspects of the poem's journey.[69] Yet historically, and especially from the point of view of the persistence of paganism, there are crucial differences between the two traditions. When commentators begin to interpret Dante's metamorphoses and other classical references in the 1320s, allegorical mythography has been thriving for almost a millennium. When the first illuminated manuscripts appear (about fifteen years later), artists are faced with countless subjects for which no visual models are in existence. These include not only Dante's inventions but indeed the whole corpus of classical mythology for which there were so many words and so few pictures in the High Middle Ages.

Very little has been said so far about visual representations of pagan subjects in the Middle Ages.[70] Before Dante's century it is a very sparse history indeed. There are no extant illuminated Ovid manuscripts from the medieval period. The iconographic heritage of the pagan pantheon persists only through the equivalence of the planets with the ancient gods in visual representations of astronomy and astrology, but these have little in common with classical images or with the Ovidian heritage. When figures from ancient myth begin to be illustrated at the end of the fourteenth century, they generally follow a slavish reading not of classical authors themselves but of the contemporary mythographers. The results are an inconvenient marriage of word and picture. Artists working without first-hand knowledge of pagan images and possessing only intermittent familiarity with ancient texts can translate into visual form what they have read but cannot grope their way toward an authentic or even an inspired version of classical icons.

Within this context the *Commedia* offers special challenges. The general outlines of heaven and hell had, of course, long been illustrated in manuscript, fresco, and sculpture. It is possible that Dante himself had seen Giotto's *Last Judgment* on the walls of the Scrovegni Chapel in Padua. But the pagan population of the *Commedia* as well as all of the new creatures of Dante's imagination—for these there can have been no precedents. The poem was illuminated for precisely the same reason that it was allegorized: upon its first appearance it was immediately taken as almost the equivalent of scripture. Yet because it stood between scripture and imaginative literature it could, and indeed had to, inspire originality in visual execution. The purely pagan subjects are represented as haphazardly as they will be in the first Ovidian illustrations. There is little consensus and less classical authority for the placement of Cerberus's three heads, or indeed for his identity as a classical dog rather than a Christian demon; nor is there agreement as to whether the Minotaur has the head of a man and the body of a bull or vice versa. Within a hundred years these questions will be answered by means of greater classical learning; what matters here, though, is the freedom to experiment in visual icons with the mutable forms of antique monsters.

Such freedom is even greater with Dante's inventions. Countless instances among the damned offer opportunities to depict forms in the midst of motion and change, indeed to create a new set of icons like those classical ekphrases that we saw so closely related to metamorphosis.[71] The attitude of constant motion in which the three Florentine sodomites of Canto XVI are required to endure the flames offers a particular challenge, and the results range from vague dancelike action to complete *contraposto* to circles that seem to suggest some vestigial awareness of the classical Graces.[72] Other groups in motion demand similar inventiveness. The avaricious and the prodigal, with their mutual dance, receive interestingly mirroring treatment; the panders and seducers moving around as they squat seem almost to have been transformed into animals in one manuscript.[73]

The cantos of the thieves provide perhaps the first important new stimulus for the visual representation of metamorphosis since the *Metamorphoses* themselves.[74] Just as the commentators, faced with the varieties of transformation in XXIV and XXV, responded with theories about the types and meanings of metamorphosis, so the illuminators (with much less tradition behind them) turned the cantos into a series of studies in the varieties of metamorphic representation. The problems of representation are the same as they were in antiquity: how does one capture motion in a frozen image, and how does one depict two simultaneous different forms? The answers in this case are built into Dante's text and its own relationship to a Christian and classical heritage. Snakes and serpentine monsters destabilize the human form in visual terms just as they undo man's *imago dei* in theological terms. So even in pre-metamorphic state, the thieves of canto XXIV with serpentine genitals or Vanni Fucci in XXV coiled around with snakes as he makes his obscene gesture are already mutable forms even in the earliest manuscripts.[75]

Once the actual transformations are underway, the artists must separate forms and stages just as the text does. A southern Italian manuscript, which Professor Brieger dates in the third quarter of the fourteenth century, represents the events of XXV in a long strip that suggests continuous process (figure 2).[76] Dante and Virgil are at the far left; then Vanni Fucci, his arms entangled with snakes so that human and animal organisms are not altogether separable; then we are shown two stages in the metamorphosis of Agnello, the first with man and serpent quite separate, the second with the serpent almost subsuming the man; then two untransformed bystander thieves, their naked humanness strikingly contrasting with the more mutable shapes. In the final panel on the next leaf (figure 3), two unmetamorphosed human forms (presumably Buoso and Cavalcanti before and after respectively) divide the composition symmetrically between the attack of the serpent Cavalcanti upon the human Buoso on the left and the exit of a serpent titled "Buoso" on the right. But the transformed serpent must be labeled to convey his former identity. What has notably not taken place, even with this variety of images, is the simultaneous representation of a double form, the real icon of metamorphosis. That we find in a similarly shaped set of panels in an early fifteenth-century manuscript from Emilia (figure 4), which first shows the Agnello metamorphosis in a sequence of three closely compressed images of man being kissed or eaten or encompassed by the serpent, and then, at a distance, the final product, an extraordinary man-serpent, upright of stature but with monstrous head and webbed feet.[77]

But perhaps the most impressive image of all is the earliest to contain visual metamorphosis, a Pisan manuscript from the mid-fourteenth century, now at the Musée Condé in Chantilly.[78] There are three illuminations for Canto XXV. The first (figure 5), showing Vanni Fucci giving his obscene gesture, presents him as riding or possibly even fused to a fabulous winged dragon, while directly behind them is Cacus the centaur, a powerful human upper body joined to a horse, itself menaced by a dragon hovering above it: the whole ensemble has already turned the clarity of the human form into composite confusion of man and beast. The second panel (figure 6) presents a straightforward version of the beginning of the Agnello metamorphosis, an obscene kiss of man and dragon, with the beast's long tail curved in between Agnello's legs. The reciprocal metamorphosis of Buoso and Cianfa is the masterpiece of the sequence (figure 7). The man is in a semi-upright posture, as befits his closer resemblance to the *imago dei*, while the serpent is recumbent. But they have already begun to exchange natures. The man has a sinuous, snaky, mermaid-like tail curving (fittingly) on the ground; the serpent next to him reclines upon long, graceful human legs. They are in close eye-contact, but the real medium of exchange, emitting from the serpent's jaws and pointing directly at the man's navel, is a curve of black smoke ("fummavan forte, e 'l fummo si scontrava"; 25.93: "[they] smoked violently, and their smoke met"), its shape mirroring the serpentine curves of the snake's belly and the metamorphic lower part of the man's torso. Here, then, we find for the first time in nearly a thousand years the visual language of metamorphosis fully developed in both technique and meaning.

The remarkable images of the Chantilly manuscript, it should be remembered, illustrated not so much the actual text of the *Inferno* as the commentary by Guido da Pisa, whose influence on the iconography is clear.[79] That combination is important in the histories of both Dante and Ovid—as well as of the two together. We have already seen how the *Inferno*, with its countless tales of human changes, is in itself a kind of Christian *Metamorphoses*. In their cultural heritage, the two play parallel roles as well. Born in the context of rhetoric and allegoresis, the *Inferno* offers materials for rhetorical analysis that can apply the techniques of scriptural study with new justification to the world of pagan mythography. At the same time as the moral content of the poem was subject to hermeneutic scrutiny, the sensuous power of the images inspired visual imaginations that were just beginning to be freed from the narrow range of subjects and orthodox treatments possible in the religious iconography of the High Middle Ages. There is a kind of leapfrog history in the antiquity of myth, with its characteristic traditions of interpretation and illustration, declassified as religious expression but inspiring Dante and thus legitimizing new departures in the approach to formerly anathematized pagan materials. In this process, commentary and illustration also leapfrog. One way to see the transition from the Middle Ages to the Renaissance is as the passing of the torch from rhetoric to illumination, from allegory to image. The fullness of Dante's text—his own words and the response of his readers—in part makes that change possible.

CHAPTER FIVE

Metamorphosis, Paganism, & the Renaissance Imagination

To study the Renaissance revival of paganism as one does the Middle Ages, that is, from the point of view of the history of ideas, is to court disappointment. For the ground-breaking intellectual systems in the approach to pagan antiquity of the Middle Ages—developments in hermeneutics, in natural philosophy, in the constructing of cosmic models—there is no equivalent set of innovations in the Renaissance. And for all that the medieval period is associated with anti-humanistic narrow-mindedness, it must be said that the intellectual daring of Arnulf's universal Platonic model for the *Metamorphoses*, or of John Ridewall's syllogism leading from Jupiter to *caritas*, or of the sexual invitation based on Ovidian cosmology in "Profuit ignaris" (among other examples) was never exceeded and rarely equalled in the sixteenth century.[1]

Some of the intellectual achievements in the Renaissance revival of paganism look remarkably like their medieval equivalents: the mythographer Natalis Comes, for instance, is at least as reductive and moralistic as the earlier commentators, and his Platonism seems to be an innovation only until one has read Arnulf and John of Garland. Where the works of Renaissance paganism do not resemble their precursors, they usually represent the fulfillment of intellectual possibilities that were born in the millennium between Augustine and the *Ovide moralisé*. The equation between classical myths and the artistic imagination, the associations of paganism with the world of the senses, the interpretation of ancient myth as containing hidden occult truths, the creation of cosmologies that syncretize pagan and Christian mythic traces: these are crucial to many Renaissance works of art inspired by antiquity. But every one of these aesthetic tropes fulfills an intellectual credo of the Middle Ages.

171

What, then, is contained in this "fulfillment," since that appears to be the real difference between the medieval period and the Renaissance? One answer would be that the Renaissance consists in the bringing to life, that is to say, aesthetic life, of medieval intellectual theories. That "bringing to life," as we shall see, is often figured as a metamorphosis; and, like other metamorphoses, it is no merely mechanical translation. If the Renaissance does not invent new theories about paganism, it does gather in a great deal of new, and newly accurate, data. The greater abundance of the raw materials of antiquity in pictures and words coincides with a greater disposition to see these in their own terms. Among the results is the appearance of a series of geniuses who are great and profound readers of pagan civilization—and especially of Ovid's *Metamorphoses*. The paradox of that reading is that the more profoundly they see into the spirit of Ovid, the more their own originality is enabled. In their Ovid-inspired masterpieces the facts of the original may be grossly distorted; yet the spirit of paganism and metamorphosis is resurrected from the dead and at the same time alive as though there has been no interval of dormancy. So the myth of Daphne is almost unrecognizable in Petrarch's great sestina "Giovene donna sotto un verde lauro"; yet the poem is a brilliant fugue on themes of metamorphosis. Titian and (either by coincidence or by direct influence) Shakespeare introduce a plot of sexual temptation completely absent from the original Venus and Adonis story; yet in the end it appears truer to the spirit of Ovid's work than the narrative he himself handed on. Milton translates Ovid's myth of Narcissus into the birth of Eve's consciousness; yet, while no medieval moralizer could produce a more shocking Christianization, the result in *Paradise Lost* is an extraordinary fulfillment of Ovidian notions of identity that quite transcend scholastic distinctions between pagan and Christian eras.[2] Our investigation of the Renaissance here, then, cannot proceed so much by the logical succession of the history of ideas. Rather, we must investigate the career of Ovid and of paganism via the far less linear history of the imagination.

1. Before the Ovidian Renaissance

By many measurements the second decade of the sixteenth century may be considered well within the High Renaissance, perhaps even the beginning of its decline. The great Florentine humanist circle of Lorenzo the Magnificent, Ficino, Poliziano, and Botticelli has come and gone. The papacy of Julius II, and the commissions of Raphael and Michelangelo for which he is most remembered, are concluded early in the decade. The *Orlando Furioso* is well underway. Giovanni Bellini comes to the end of his long career, and Titian has been fully launched into his (perhaps) longer career.[3] Yet the Ovidian Renaissance—if we may use that term for the revival and transformation of metamorphosis and paganism—has scarcely begun. The materials are, to be sure, available. Besides the continued popularity of medieval commentaries and handbooks, the *editio princeps* of the *Metamorphoses* has appeared. Leonardo has painted a (lost but much copied) Leda, and Michelangelo will soon do the same. A number of Northern Italian artists, including Apollonio di Giovanni and the Pollaiuolo brothers, have started decorating wedding chests with pagan subjects. Artists have been rendering the gods on fresco or stone in private homes, public buildings, and even religious shrines since the mid-fifteenth century.[4]

Three modes dominate in the artistic portrayal of the pagan world during this Ovidian pre-Renaissance. Most important is the strong continuity of medieval cosmology and cosmography. The fourteenth and fifteenth centuries witness a massive interest in the systems of correspondence—microcosm and macrocosm variously interpreted—that link the earth to the heavens.[5] Among the most important of the systems is astrology, which gives prominent place to the planetary gods. This obsession with cosmic correspondences expresses itself in the creation of vast diagrams, sometimes merely verbal, as in Chaucer's *Knight's Tale*, but usually in manuscript illustrations or, as the technology allows, in woodcuts or printed books. The tradition culminates in the *Planetenkinder*, or Children of the Planets, illustrations of a whole society of human beings organized among the appropriate conditions, occupations, classes, and so on, each society depicted underneath its respective planet/god.[6] In the earliest of these representations, including illustrations to Christine de Pisan's *Epître d'Othéa* or the Spanish Chapel of Santa Maria Novella in Florence, this tradition would appear to have nothing to do with pagan antiquity at all, since the figures of gods and men have all been assimilated into medieval Christian tradition. Yet, even if the style is medieval, the departure from angels and saints as presiding figures in the universe is significant, and the whole astrological system does depend upon classical and non-Christian texts. By the time of Baldassare Peruzzi's ceiling in the Villa Farnesina (ca. 1510), astrology has been fairly well recuperated into the world of paganism. The subject is the horoscope of Agostino Chigi, but the ceiling is filled with Ovidian figures, including Perseus, Leda, Venus, Ganymede, and the rarely depicted Tereus, Procne, and Philomela. Yet even here the representation remains firmly rooted in the cosmological tradition. The Ovidian characters, portrayed in a cold, sculptural style, have no narrative life of their own but exist only as tableaux in an astrological diagram.[7]

The second milieu is associated with the traditions of medieval romance. There is what we might call a grand homology between the materials of romance and those of Ovidian mythology, especially as it was understood in the later Middle Ages. They meet at the nexus of Platonic love and Christianized allegory. The *Romance of the Rose* includes Venus, Narcissus, Pygmalion, and others on equal footing with romantic and allegorical figures. When Pygmalion prays to Saint Venus, who in return bestows a soul upon the statue, or when he sees the metamorphosed statue and debates whether it be a devilish temptation or a beautiful dream, it becomes clear that certain pagan stories, at least, adapt very well to the materials of medieval romance.[8] The favor is returned by those manuscript illuminations of Ovidian material in which the ancient gods are placed in the context of hierarchical structures, gardens of love, or other medieval topoi plausibly suited to Ovid.[9] In short, the milieux of romance can comfortably contain amorous pagan gods dressed in four-teenth-century regalia, and by the early Renaissance such syncretism is quite conventional.

It is not surprising, then, to see cosmography mix with romance in the late fifteenth-century cycle of the months painted by Francesco Cozza at the Palazzo Schifanoia in Ferrara.[10] Among the twelve panels (of which only seven survive) the pattern is strictly geometric with three horizontal layers. The middle section, sharply defined against a dark background, shows an anthropomorphized zodiacal rendering of each month. Above is the universe of the pagan gods, March for Minerva, April for Venus, May for Apollo, and so on. Below, at the spectator's eye level, is the "real" world of each of those months, the familiar earthly activities that take place in the round of the year. The designs build a parallel construction among the heavenly bodies, the pagan gods, and the lives of ordinary men; and the ensemble creates a monument that situates paganism within the framework of time and the governance of the universe. Yet the panels of the gods themselves are not painted in the somber style of Peruzzi's horoscope; rather, they exist in a world of romance, including gardens of love, knights with their ladies, and allegorical triumphs.

Compared to cosmology and romance, our third mode, at least in its pre-1500 form, is the most specialized and arcane. The Florentine Neo-platonic circle surrounding Lorenzo de' Medici stretched the fabric of or-thodox Christianity almost to the breaking point. Marsilio Ficino and Pico della Mirandola not only attempted to reconcile pagan and Christian the-ology; they also treated the mythic figures of both religions as exchange-able. The result is a composite mythology that must be read as a sequence of mysteries, with the frivolous elements of pagan lore overturned (as they are in the medieval doctrine of the integumentum) and transformed into the deepest truths. We shall have more to say about this tradition— and others have still more to say about it.[11] For the moment, however, it is important to point out that this philosophical milieu is one of obscure enigmas and deep Platonic significance. How this emerges in an imagina-tive milieu is most clearly evident from the famous canvases of Botticelli. The *Primavera* is certainly cosmological in the sense that it is concerned

with the great motions of time in the universe; its style and setting, moreover, owe much to the world of romance. But there is something apart
from these physical facts that requires the viewer to look beyond the veil
(where different viewers, to be sure, see different messages) at a world in
which the pagan gods represent some natural essence as well as a truth
beyond nature. Neoplatonism, as we shall see, is alive and well for another century at least; but by and large the successors of the Florentine
circle will retreat from this mysticism into a more safely Christian hierarchy of myth and truth.

These three milieux of cosmology, romance, and Platonism must be
understood as a group in the context of the preceding centuries. We saw
how medieval paganism imposed its own Christianized rhetorical systems
on classical materials. That imposition remains alive in these milieux as all
three attempt to assimilate the classical subject into an eternal present;
none of them really recognizes antiquity as an independent past age with
its own characteristic environment. We also saw how medieval paganism
divided itself into the scientific or cosmological survival of antiquity, including disciplines like astronomy or natural philosophy, and the world of
love and sensuality, the amours of the gods, cavorting nymphs and satyrs,
etc. The early Renaissance milieux of the gods fit largely into the first of
those traditions. That is self-evident in regard to the *Planetenkinder*. The
Neoplatonic mode similarly looks beyond the integumentum of carnal
myth toward some serious reality.[12] Even the romance milieu, while it
comes closest to a delight in pagan pleasures for their own sake, is con-
stricted by its own allegorical idealizations.

2. A Renaissance of Images; Correggio and Titian

Two artists, both working around 1520, reveal so sharply the beginnings of an Ovidian Renaissance that it almost seems like a conspiracy.
Yet Correggio and Titian are so different in taste and education that their
part in the freeing of pagan materials from cosmological, allegorical, and
philosophical constraints demonstrates wider symptoms of a change.[13]
Correggio's entire creative life spans some thirty years and scarcely more
than a fifty-mile radius from the eponymous town of his birth; Titian's career lasts for nearly eighty years, while he and his pictures travel and gain
fame throughout Europe. Titian is the keystone in a closely constructed
arch of Venetian art and humanism, including artistic predecessors and
followers (Giorgione, the Bellinis, Veronese, Tintoretto) and writers who
could influence him intellectually and publicize his achievements (Lodovico Dolce, Pietro Aretino). Correggio can be only conjecturally connected with contemporary artistic styles and humanist learning. Their
styles, too, are radically different: Titian, despite enormous range, always

exhibits aggressive and weighty muscularity; Correggio, whose vastly smaller oeuvre is very much all of a piece, reveals his inimitable style in delicate, melting sensuousness.

What concerns us most particularly, however, are the parallels and contrasts between the two as painters of pagan subjects. Correggio's may be the more unusual case. He is not a learned or philosophically subtle painter; he did not (apparently) move in humanist circles. Rather, he seems to have turned to mythological subjects for a reason more characteristic of the eighteenth than the sixteenth century: stylistic affinity. As Vasari well understood, Correggio possessed an exquisite and original technique for the representation of beauty.[14] The Christian subjects that constitute the vast majority of his work exhibit this sensuous loveliness in precisely the same measure as the pagan—indeed that distinction may be more blurred in his work than in that of any other major Renaissance painter. A technique that aims above all to give pleasure to the eye stands quite simply in a natural harmony with pagan materials, whether the artist is schooled in the arcane aspects of the tradition or not. At the same time, Correggio's intellectual naiveté is revealed by the relatively simple and conservative intellectual patterns in his treatments of subjects from antiquity: straightforward dualities rendered in a traditional language of visual allegory but redeemed from frigidity by their liveliness and beauty.

Correggio's painted works on profane subjects number perhaps fewer than ten; Titian's historical and mythological paintings in Harold Wethey's catalogue run to more than five times that. More significant than their quantity, however, is their diversity. Titian's life-long love affair with antiquity spans the entire range of Renaissance possibilities in the representation of pagan subjects—not so much because he was soaking up different influences during his long career as because he was inventing that range of possibilities. His earliest efforts depend upon a mix of qualities not at all unlike Correggio's: a lush delight in the flesh together with a taste for visual emblem and allegory. To be sure, the sensuous beauties of the *Concert champêtre* (Paris) or the *Three Ages of Man* (Edinburgh) are not, as in Correggio's case, an inevitable signature of the artist's style; they are adopted for the specific purpose of defining antiquity as a golden age of the permissible pleasures of the senses. Nor are the allegorical operations of such canvases as the *Three Ages* or *Sacred and Profane Love* conventional and straightforward, as the collective ingenuity of several generations of twentieth-century scholars has demonstrated.[15]

Over the succeeding forty years Titian introduces events into this world of pleasure and calm allegory. Titian did not, of course, invent narrative painting, and yet no artist before him had realized the possibilities of a single image in translating all the energies of narrative myth: action, rhythm, theatricality, psychology—in fact, qualities inspired by a sensitive reading of Ovid. Nor does he leave allegory and sensuous beauty behind in the process; rather, he seeks different balances among these elements. The early Bacchanals (to which we shall turn in a moment) only begin to show the signs of narrative. The emblematic Venus canvases—a whole range of representations with musicians, Cupids, and so on painted in the middle of Titian's career—depend not on narrative per se but on the infusion of pictorial psychology into the allegorical relations of the figures. The Ovidian subjects of the mid-century, to which the artist gave the significant name of *poesie*, represent the real breakthrough in the invention of pictorial drama; they tend to depend less on allegory, and in some cases they are quite deliberately unbeautiful.[16] But they are, as the name he gave them suggests, narrative poems, authentically and yet originally Ovidian, with a complete range of drama and psychological intensity. Very late in his career Titian invented yet another genre in the representation of antiquity, not really pursued again until the time of Poussin. Paintings like the London *Death of Actaeon* and the Vienna *Nymph and Shepherd* are not so much concerned with narrative and certainly not with beauty; rather, they see the values of antiquity as essentially unrecapturable, in a landscape of loss and decay.

The two early projects by Correggio and Titian that characterize what I have called the Ovidian Renaissance of ca. 1520 distinguish themselves precisely as do the two painters. Correggio's is an obscure one-of-a-kind commission from an enlightened nun of local Parmesan gentry; Titian's is the highpoint of a sequence of humanist works ordered by perhaps the most important family of patrons in Northern Italy. Correggio's discovery of a new Ovidianism proceeds from an aesthetic investigation of the styles of his own art; Titian's from a brilliant investigation of the texts and images of antiquity. The Camera di S. Paolo, located in the private apartments of Gioanna da Piacenza, abbess of a Benedictine nunnery in Parma, is a combination of beautiful images and obscure iconography (figures 8–11).[17] Apart from a chimney-piece painting of Diana, who is temperamentally and heraldically related to the formidable abbess who commissioned the room,[18] the fresco-work consists of sixteen segments of vaulting, each of which contains a decoration of trellises and bunches of fruit broken by an oval opening to the "sky" in which *putti* are visible in strenuous occupations. At the bottom of each is a lunette painted to look like a shell in which sculptural figures appear in grisaille. The grisaille subjects include a wide range of figures from classical iconography, only a few of which—the Fates, the Graces, the Homeric Hera punished for her cruelty to Heracles—are clearly identifiable. There seems no doubt that the ensemble was meant to be understood as a whole, even if modern attempts to reconstruct it have shown complete lack of accord even on the identification of individual figures.

What is immediately clear is that we are in the presence of a visual dialectic. The grisaille figures are trompe-l'oeil imitations of ancient sculpture and, especially, ancient coins. Their subjects, so far as we can identify them, are not narratives in anything like the Ovidian sense. Many are solemn religious personifications, while others appear to be rather straightforward emblems of abstract values. In fact, they are allegories: identifications tend to take the form of concepts like Meditazione, Amore Onesto, and Confident Integrity, or of rather simplistically allegorizable classical figures like Fortuna, Pan, or Bellona. As an aggregate, they may represent a warning to wayward nuns, a Platonic program centering on strife, concord, and the four elements, or a depiction of the ages of man coupled with symbolic representations of human history.[19] In any of these cases the pagan element is rooted in cosmic order and purged of moral taint by frequent reference to the most earnest aspects of ancient religion.

The style of the lunettes is their real content, however. Whether they are fictional coins or fictional statues, they are frozen in an unrecapturable past. Though they partake of the cosmological and the Neoplatonic visions of antiquity, they break with earlier Renaissance representations because they recognize—in style, if not in intellectual grounding—the classical past as past and not as part of a seamless fabric of time. They are beautiful, but at the same time they are cold and colorless. The visual style correlates with their status as allegories and, even more, their status as hieroglyphs, for their obscurity is an important part of the intention behind them. This is, in short, a reductio of the ruling strand of medieval paganism: allegory, mysterious integumentum, a cold design of cosmic meaning requiring learned interpretation. In fact, their very frozen nature renders that whole view of antiquity as both figuratively and literally anti-metamorphic.

But the sculptural/numismatic lunettes account for only a small proportion of the vault space. Above the horizontal semicircles of the lunettes are trellis-work and vertical ovals which are also trompe-l'oeil. Here, however, the imitation is of nature rather than of art. The ceiling of the room is a lushly painted thicket of foliage, fruit, and bamboo ribs. Through the ovals we see the (fictive) sky, and in those openings pairs of putti are playing or struggling with weapons, with dogs, or with each other. The contrast with the lunettes could not be greater. In place of abstract personifications we have a set of figures engaged in sheer play of a frankly physical kind, with the supposedly stern emblems of the hunt —horn, stag's head, dogs, bow—defused into a soft and sensual *chasse d'amour*.[20] In place of the artificial rendering of painted statues, each isolated in its own frame, we have a "realistic," indeed almost aleatoric, set of poses quite indifferent to the formal design of the ovals: some of the putti climb out of the assigned decorative hole (one reaches out to pick fruit from higher up on the ceiling), while others relate among themselves from adjacent holes as though there were in the sky a continuous world of putti of whom we merely catch oval glimpses. In place of the "meaning-ful," if obscure, classical emblems that are grey and frozen against their stone-like lunettes, we have colorful figures who exist for the sake of deco-ration itself, engaging in strenuous motion and activity against a back-ground of the open sky and the fruits of nature.

If the style of the vaulting points toward an opposite iconography from that of the lunettes, it is, all the same, another vision of paganism. The very origins of the putti are in classicizing impulses in Michelangelo's and Raphael's work in the Vatican,[21] and Correggio's particular putti are clearly engaged in tasks that relate them to the hunt of Diana, herself the presiding genius of the Camera. In addition, they are exuberant figures basking in nature and their own corporeality with no purposeful activity at all. As such, they offer us an early glimpse at the revival of the tradition that links paganism and the flesh. And, unlike figures in the romance mi-lieu (with which their *chasse d'amour* has some common ground), these give new life to the fleshly tradition because they exist as an original set of mythic representations independent of convention. To contrast with the solemn religious hieroglyph frozen in the past, the painter creates a world of flowing sensuality. The ruling visual metaphor is motion (or the lack of it), and the quintessential motion is that which brings the "statues" of an-tiquity to life as an animate heaven of cavorting putti.

At the same time as Correggio is developing a new medium for pagan expression in the relatively obscure precincts of a nun's private *camera*, Titian is discovering his new language of celebrating antiquity in the con-text of some of the most famous artists and patrons in the earlier sixteenth century. Not that the two artists are working at opposite ends of the earth: Correggio's Parma is some sixty miles from Ferrara, where Titian's can-vases will hang; and the origins of the Ferrarese project are closely bound up with the patronage that will bring Correggio's later pagan works to birth. The Este family—for us especially Isabella d'Este, her brother Alfonso d'Este, and her son Federico Gonzaga—may do as much to ac-count for the origins of what I have called the Ovidian Renaissance as the individual genius of the artists who worked for them. Why the Este family developed its taste in these directions is uncertain; suffice it to say that such small humanist courts as theirs existed in relative isolation and free-dom from the narrower uses of art characteristic of rulers, powerful fami-lies, confraternities, and ecclesiastical patrons in the greater urban cen-ters.[22] Whatever the causes, the results are prodigious: in a sequence of projects from the Grotta of Isabella d'Este (around the turn of the cen-tury) to the Camerino of Alfonso (in the 1510s) to the work of Correggio and Giulio Romano for Federico (in the 1530s) we can observe the whole Renaissance development of representing antiquity from neo-medieval allegory at one end to erotic fantasy at the other. Titian's work will form the turning point; but to appreciate that change we must observe the earlier stages of the process.

Isabella d'Este is the very model of a dictatorial patron, and thanks to excellent documentation of her correspondence with artists and with her humanist advisor Paride da Ceresara we are in a good position to observe the specificity of her intentions and hence the origins of the works she commissioned.[23] The programs which she and her advisor imposed upon the artists (often with specific instructions not to vary anything in the least degree) speak to a taste for learned, philosophical allegory of the kind that is meant to be decipherable only by the initiated. That the pagan materials were not intended to be viewed in the light of frivolity or pleasure is abundantly demonstrated by her choice of the artists: Mantegna, associated with antique subjects but only in the monumental vein; Correggio, only in the emblematic mode (the *Allegories of Virtue and Vice*); the rather old-fashioned sacred painter Perugino; and the elderly Giovanni Bellini, famous for his piety. The completed works fulfill Isabella's pre-Renaissance taste. Perugino closely followed her instructions, which demanded "a battle of Chastity against Lasciviousness, that is, Pallas and Diana struggling manfully against Venus and Cupid,"[24] along with many other Ovidian figures—all relegated statically to a kind of allegorical tug-of-war. Mantegna's far greater contributions, *Parnassus* and *Minerva Expelling the Vices from the Garden of Virtue*, cannot be so easily dismissed as neo-medieval allegories, for they exhibit the painter's archaeological awareness of antiquity and his taste for lush detail. Yet they recall the milieux of Botticelli and of the Schifanoia frescoes, offering emblematic representations whose lively beauties are derived from the visual language not of antiquity but of romance.[25]

The transition begins with Giovanni Bellini, whom Isabella had been importuning as early as 1496. Whether owing to the paganism of the subject or the imperiousness of the patroness, or both, his work seems to languish as Isabella persists in frantic correspondence throughout the first several years of the century. In the mid-1510s Bellini's *Feast of the Gods* turns up in Alfonso d'Este's *camerino* (figure 12). Whether or not this is the same picture which Isabella failed to obtain—and the evidence is very ambiguous[26]—it stands at the midpoint between the two projects. Alfonso's wish list of artists (as in his sister's case, not all the patron's wishes came true) is of a younger generation than Isabella's, including Dosso Dossi, Raphael, and Titian, all of whom possess education and sensibilities more in tune with pagan materials than their predecessors. Testifying even more strongly to new developments in taste is a different kind of content. Alfonso's orders (and, as with his sister, there can be no possibility that the content of the pictures was left to the whim of the artists) move decisively away from allegory. In addition, all the works either contemplated or realized in Alfonso's *camerino* concerned themselves with the revelry of the gods, and especially under the aegis of the two most pleasure-loving Olympians, Bacchus and Venus.

Bellini's subject could hardly be less earnest, consisting of Ovid's account (from the *Fasti*) of Priapus's attempt to rape the nymph Lotis, which is interrupted by the inopportune braying of Silenus's ass.[27] In the context of Isabella's moral allegories, the choice of such a theme is almost inconceivable, except for the fact that, like the subject of the Perugino and both the Mantegnas, the episode in the *Fasti* permits the painter to represent the whole Olympian pantheon in one moment. Whether *in bono* or *in malo*, such an image may well have been a figure for the complete Este court, as it certainly is in Giulio Romano's Cupid and Psyche festivities designed for Federico Gonzaga's Palazzo del Te.[28] If Bellini's painting does have its origins in the plans for Isabella's Grotta, then this lascivious passage may have been chosen to illustrate a negative view of the gods' frivolity and immorality—perhaps even in contrast to the nobler activities of the Olympians in the two Mantegna canvases. It may even be that Bellini's inability to color his subject with moral condemnation accounts for all the difficulties in furnishing the picture *sur commande*. If the subject was chosen by Alfonso rather than by Isabella, then it is the first sign of a great shift in taste between sister and brother. Whatever the beginnings of the work, it is likely that the aged Bellini lagged behind the tastes of the Ferrarese court. As we shall see, the canvas we now possess was not by the hand of Bellini alone; but his original contribution (as best we can consider it) presents a highly equivocal view of the ancient gods. They are certainly brought down to earth, engaged in homely tasks within an unremarkable setting. At the same time, the painting has an authentically classical mood with the figures arrayed horizontally as though sculpted with monumental serenity on a frieze or sarcophagus. The gods, who are barely given iconographic attributes, appear to be neither condemned, nor celebrated, nor allegorized. Some students of the picture find humor and even mock-heroic. I find rather an uncertainty in the search for a classical medium and hence a kind of accidental bathos that does not attain anything like Ovidian light-heartedness.

That the canvas we now have was altered by Titian affords us a specially sharp sense of the new pagan language. Titian's multiple reworkings of the Bellini canvas and the significance of the changes are the subject of a magisterial essay in which John Walker finds by minute X-ray examination of early and later versions the fundamental transition in styles between the quattrocento and the cinquecento.[29] Turning his argument from style to substance, one observes in the changes a powerful rebirth of true Ovidianism—humor, sensuality, worship of natural beauty. Titian repaints the landscape, for example, taking the scene of the gods' pleasures out of a static decorative background and placing it in a context with pagan associations like those of the *Three Ages of Man*. Titian also undrapes several female figures, and he goes so far as to invent an almost indecent gesture by Neptune in Cybele's lap.

Yet there were severe limits in what Titian could do with Bellini's rather lapidary composition. In his own succeeding canvases—*The Worship of Venus, Bacchus and Ariadne, The Bacchanale of the Andrians* (figures 13-15)—all paganism breaks loose. Once again, however, the influence of the patron ought to count with that of the artist. Isabella's inventions we have already characterized as a kind of neo-medieval allegory (though Mantegna may have realized his efforts with some more up-to-date touches). For the Bellini work, which seems to straddle the two courts, the invention is narrative rather than allegorical and a fairly racy narrative at that (even if Bellini is as far behind his orders as Mantegna was ahead of his). Titian's instructions come neither from allegory nor precisely from narrative but rather from classical descriptions of works of art. *Venus* and *The Andrians* are both taken from ancient paintings as described by Philostratus the Elder, while the *Bacchus and Ariadne* has as its principal (though not sole) source Catullus's description of the tapestry covering the marriage bed of Peleus and Thetis.[30] As we saw in chapter 1 and as we shall see throughout our consideration of paganism and metamorphosis in the Renaissance, there is a natural affinity between paganism in its most sensuous aspect and the history of beautiful images. Alfonso chooses a great artist to recreate not the ideas nor the events of pagan antiquity but the lost images of earlier artists. It is an enormously significant symptom (or even cause) in the establishment of ancient art as a theme and an end in itself.

Once Titian is set upon a project of artist-to-artist competition, he operates in a highly self-conscious relationship to his ancient predecessors. These predecessors may be visual artists, whom he transforms into his own language in such figures as the *Laocoön*-like follower of Bacchus in the *Bacchus and Ariadne* or the *Sleeping Ariadne* whom he recreates in *The Andrians*. Or his predecessors may be artists of the word—not only in the direct source of the *Imagines* but also in such touches as the visual interpretation of Bacchus's leap toward Ariadne and her half turn away, both of which are quite specifically signaled in the Ovidian sources.[31] The two Bacchus canvases in particular demonstrate how the competition with antiquity inspires Titian to achieve a new vision of the pagan world, completely freed from the remote, the frozen, and the emblematic. In place of those qualities the scene of antiquity celebrates the beauties of nature and art, of music and dance, of the corporeal and the irrational.

Bacchus and Ariadne is Titian's first great achievement in narrative mythology: the artist fuses in a single moment the past—Ariadne's gesture toward Theseus's ship sailing away—and the future—her bridal crown of stars in the sky—with the present meeting of the two lovers.

The body language of the two principal characters appears to be an exotic, graceful dance; at the same time it is a highly concentrated visual account of complex verbal narratives. The inconclusive efforts of modern scholars to decide exactly which part of what version of the Theseus-Bacchus-Ariadne cycle is being depicted[32] should serve to remind us that Titian has transformed the action out of such cognitive specificity into a visual language that evokes the senses more than the intellect.

The Bacchanale of the Andrians not only translates classical words and images into new life but also remakes Bellini's *Feast of the Gods*. The themes of the two works are closely related; so, too, the compositions, including the horizontal band of figures crowded together and the reclining nude framing the canvas at the lower right. But what were touch-ups in Titian's work on the Bellini landscape become here a newly conceived natural world *all'antica*, in which people and setting become fused via the myth of an island where the rivers flow with wine. And Titian turns Bellini's rather dour and independently composed figures into a joyous orgy of interlocked revelers who relate to each other through a variety of cyclical motions. These include corporeal cycles of drink, urination, and sleep as well as the more complex body rhythms of the dance and the cyclical rhythms of the musical canon, which is being sung in praise of drinking and (as the lyrics have it) of redrinking.[33] That all these new expressions of paganism are achieved by the imitation and transformation of ancient art represents the great paradox of the Renaissance revival of antiquity. It is a paradox that links rebirth with originality via the artist's ability to transform the ancient letter into a new spirit. The same paradox lies behind the dialectic in Correggio's Camera di S. Paolo. It is a new kind of pagan myth-making, at once studiously authentic and yet brashly original, with implicitly godlike claims for the artist who can achieve the transformation. As the artist brings the old, the dead, and the frozen to new life, *metamorphosis* becomes a ruling conceit of *Renaissance*.

The most important aesthetic element in the Camera di S. Paolo and in Titian's Bacchanals is the independence of the images: independence from narrative, from allegory, from moralization, indeed from any reference beyond themselves except for the reference to the world of the senses. The history of such independence is bound up with notions of style, elegance, and *maniera* that are just beginning their conquest over the arts around 1520.[34] Artistic style takes its place in the mannerist aesthetic as a pleasurable end in itself. The classic examples are Michelangelo's *ignudi* on the Sistine Chapel ceiling. In the midst of complex religious iconography narrating and commenting upon the story of the Creation and linking that story typologically to both New Testament and pagan prophecy, the artist creates a set of figures who have no iconographic purpose whatever. To compound the act of uselessness, he places them in a trompe-l'oeil architectural framework where they seem to be required for support, but in fact their effort is out of proportion to the supposed weight that they are bearing. I digress to the *ignudi* because of all the figures on the Sistine Chapel ceiling they are among the most self-consciously classical.[35] That is to say, Michelangelo joins this conception of artistic beauty as an end in itself with the image of antiquity. There are logical reasons for that association, and it will remain powerful throughout the Renaissance. Christian subjects by definition cannot be beautiful merely for the sake of artistry; nor can the modes of cosmography, romance, or Neoplatonism shed their external and idealizing references— even though any art can gain part of its effect through its style. But the visual art of antiquity, from the very circumstances of its emergence in the Renaissance—that is, free of theological, political, or social context and merely as a series of *objets trouvés*—was destined to be seen as deriving from an aesthetic of beauty for its own sake.[36] So the mannerist aesthetic, based in part on these ancient influences, becomes a crucial aspect of the movement in the Renaissance away from the learned or scientific revival of antiquity and toward the sensuous rebirth of pagan images.

Image is the crucial term. We have seen how Christian and cosmological subjects do not lend themselves to the pure and unreferential love of beauty; the art of words, whatever its subject matter, lends itself even less. The sounds of poetry can be abstractly—that is, musically—beautiful, and poems can call up sensuous pictures. Indeed, the style of poems can be mannerist in the way that a pictorial Madonna can emphasize the artist's *maniera* at the same time as she bears a crucial religious meaning. But words cannot (at least within the bounds of Renaissance aesthetics) float free from significations in the way of Michelangelo's *ignudi* or Correggio's *putti*. To understand paganism in the Renaissance, it is necessary to understand that the power of the image in itself, the aesthetic of sensuous beauty, and the survival of antiquity are closely bound together. The vehicle in which antiquity traveled through to the modern world was above all the image; and larger-scale artistic creations of the sixteenth century, whether they come in multiple pictures or multiple words, are built, cell by cell, out of individual images.

Historical as well as theoretical considerations govern the affinity between image and pagan myth. Mythographers throughout the Middle Ages were largely concerned with the interpretation of narratives—that is, with the words of pagan myth. But even Fulgentius shows some interest in the physical attributes of the gods, which he submits to the same kind of analysis as the stories themselves. With the appearance (probably in the early thirteenth century) of Albericus's *Liber imaginum deorum*, the description and interpretation of the images of the gods becomes a study in itself, and by the end of the Middle Ages this form of mythography has almost replaced the purely verbal.[37] The description of these attributes is in itself a far cry from mannerist images for their own sake, since the pictures as rendered, say, by Albericus, exist solely for the sake of moralization. Yet various factors conspire to give the *imagines* a life of their own. In the first place, these manuscripts were illustrated with real pictures which could be viewed and interpreted independently from the text. In addition, the very arbitrariness of the assigned attributes and interpretations encourages independence between words and pictures.

The crucial change comes with Petrarch's *Africa*, in which the poet describes the gods of Olympus in a lengthy ekphrasis. Petrarch's source is Albericus, but he removes most of the narrative and all of the allegorization:

> Next comes Apollo with his flowing locks,
> a beardless boy, a youth, and all at once
> with temples shining white. Before him stands
> his sacred courser, quivering, swift of foot,
> pawing the earth and champing at the bit.
> . . . .
> And from the sacred lyre there portrayed
> one seems to hear the plucked chords yield sweet notes.
> There too are seen the quiver and the bow
> with sharp swift arrows on the shoulder slung;
> and lo, within the Delphic cave in death
> the monstrous Python lies. And there appears
> the sacred laurel, green and gold, the plant
> beloved by the bards of Italy
> and Hellas. Far it casts its fragrant shade,
> cooling the bowers where the Muses nine
> seem with alternate song and sweet refrain
> to charm the stars and halt them in their course.[38]

It is not as though Petrarch has taken the images of the gods out of the realm of words—after all, he is writing a poem. Rather, he has given the pictures an independent existence free from allegory and morality. In this lush description of images alone, the gods become an occasion for feasting all the senses—for here already there is a connection between the pagan gods as images and the pagan gods as representing beauty for its own sake. Petrarch's friend Bersuire follows suit by separating in his volume the images of the gods from the interpretation of Ovid's text.[39]

Only in the Renaissance, then, when words and pictures are independent, can the images develop a life of their own, which is to say, inspire new words. Several sixteenth-century mythographers (e.g., Pictor, Cartari) treat the images of the gods as absolutes and use their words as subordinated explanations.[40] Others, like Valeriano, place the images of the gods in the tradition of Egyptian mystery learning, popularized by the publication of Horapollo's *Hieroglyphica*.[41] Here the words are an attempt to unlock the profound hidden wisdom that appears in the images. Finally, the hieroglyph attains its widest dissemination in the emblem, as made famous by Alciati.[42] The emblem books include many images of pagan antiquity, each joined with a moralizing set of verses. In a sense they complete the circle of word and image, rejoining the two on something like equal footing, with moral allegories returning as suitable words for ancient pictures.

There is another, perhaps more obvious sense in which one can speak of unions between picture and word: the actual practice of illustrating pagan texts. Barring appearances of the planetary gods in astronomical literature, pagan subjects are rarely illuminated until the late Middle Ages. Even then, as Panofsky and Saxl and, later, Jean Seznec have demonstrated, the imperfect transmission of visual materials from antiquity produced a disjunction between the verbal iconography of ancient tales and the conventional pictorial iconography. A tonsured cleric picking leaves off a tree as a version of Apollo embracing Daphne turns out to be more than just anachronistic and incongruous: such an image, severed from literary traditions, is deprived of that element of the marvelous that animates the great metamorphic icons like Europa.[43] Consequently, it is not what Saxl referred to as a "classic image," and it is likely to remain a curiosity.[44] In fact, the failure to create medieval traditions of visual representation for pagan stories demonstrates ultimately the importance of ekphrasis in iconography, that is to say the marriage of great words to great pictures.

Just as the abstract relationship of image and caption was balanced in the High Renaissance, so the actual words and pictures were appropriately reconciled. Two new sources of images, whose importance we have already observed in connection with Titian, are added to the mythographic tradition: the careful reading of ancient descriptions of art (along with the will to realize them in modern times) and the actual excavation of ancient sculpture and even painting. Great words were newly appreciated and great images newly recovered. In this process the *Metamorphoses* is all-important. Ovid's text was widely available in accurate form throughout the Middle Ages, and, as we have seen, it was subject to a tradition of interpretation. But it is also a powerfully pictorial poem; and any humanist searching for authentic images of antiquity can be certain of finding them in those well-known verses.[45] It is therefore no coincidence that the fifteenth and sixteenth centuries, which see the last flowering of illumination and the beginnings of book illustration, also witness a tremendous Ovidian vogue. A great "visual" poet is reread, reilluminated, and reprinted in a period when new resources, historical, artistic, and technological, make it possible to realize those visual elements and help recreate the golden classical past when those illustrations were common language.

It is less than imagery of Ovid's poem, however, than its subject that makes it so important. To explain the centrality of metamorphosis to all our present discussion would be to return over much ground already covered. The links between metamorphosis and image have already been established; we have also observed the power of the metamorphic image independent of narrative. Those associations of pagan transformation, when filtered through the intellectual structures of the Middle Ages, come to suggest that metamorphosis epitomizes the imagination itself, with all its glory and danger, unfettered by the rigors of theological or cosmological systems. When an interest is reborn in images to be viewed for their own sake, then pagan transformations will be among the most powerful and persistent of images. Among the greatest examples of the first half-century of Ovidian book-illustration—and I would single out the *Bible des poètes* of Antoine Vérard (Paris, 1493), the Italian translation by Titian's friend Lodovico Dolce (Venice, 1553), and the emblem-book versions, including woodcuts by Bernard Salomon (Lyons, 1557)—many of the greatest inventions and inspirations arise from the need to depict the act of transformation.[46] Between the fifteenth- and the sixteenth-century examples, there are sharp differences, as though Renaissance familiarity with the visual world of antiquity arrived in the interval; yet even in the naive earlier style metamorphosis receives careful treatment. Arachne as an overturned spider in the midst of a mass of fabric (1484 Bruges edition), or the "offspring" of Deucalion and Pyrrha emerging from the ground fully clothed and sexually differentiated (figure 16), or the torsos of Cadmus and Harmonia beginning to develop into serpents' tails (1493 Paris edition): these suggest not the pursuit and development of visual conventions, but a close reading of the words and a sedulous attempt to represent in logical terms how such a prodigious event as metamorphosis could take place.

Fifty years on, metamorphosis is absolutely the heart of the matter, and the multiple representation of simultaneous differing conditions has become very elaborate art indeed. The Venetian edition includes (just to cite some of the less familiar icons) an extraordinary naked Tiresias in a peculiarly mincing stance that may be intended to suggest bisexuality (figure 17), Haemus and Rhodope at once a king and queen and a pair of mountains, and the Lycian peasants (victims of Latona's anger after they muddy the water she wishes to drink from) in midtransformation, some standing and still relatively human, some crouching and semi-froglike. Bernard Salomon is a master of the multiple body: the stag's head on Actaeon (figure 18) and the wolf's head on Lycaon are at once shocking and graceful. Elsewhere he translates metamorphosis into elements of motion and stillness. The development from ants crawling on a tree downward toward the beginnings of human shapes on the ground (the story of Aegina and the etiology of the Myrmidons) is quite marvelous (figure 19), while the contrast between the lively motion of Perseus and the petrified troops of Phineus almost defies the bounds of the still picture.

It is not only the individual cuts but the whole project and nature of the illustrated Ovid that testifies to the importance of metamorphosis as image. These books, especially by the middle of the sixteenth century, are *Gesamtkunstwerke* in the fullest sense, with words and pictures closely joined as living ekphrases. That might be true of any heavily illustrated book, but the Ovid editions respond tellingly to the nature of the original text and to the traditions of its interpretation. The influential and often reprinted Bernard Salomon volume, for instance, consists of nearly two hundred pages, each of which contains an antique-style border of *grotteschi* (Henkel counts seventeen different examples frequently repeated), a title for each individual story, a woodcut illustration, and an eight-line stanza of unmoralized but somewhat epigrammatic plot summary. The semiotics of this volume speak powerfully of all the impulses behind the persistence of metamorphic myths in the sixteenth century; and its influence will in turn solidify these associations for the later Renaissance.

The convention of illustration owes a great deal to the tradition that goes back to Lactantius Placidus and, more particularly, to Arnulf of Orleans, in which Ovid's poem was categorized as a sequence of numbered *mutationes*.[47] Those metaphorical but ultimately reductive moralizations now become a similar sequence of illustrations, story by story, that metaphorize and reduce in a similar way. Each story is captured in the image of a single moment, and most of those images are metamorphoses. That image of metamorphosis is decorated by subordinated words, and the whole thing is set in a frame celebrating the beauties and mysteries of antiquity. The stories are reduced to their essential form, which is image and metamorphosis at once. But, if the technique of the illustrated Ovid parallels medieval allegorizations, the ultimate significance of the project is very different. By concentrating on metamorphoses rather than allegories, the printers and illustrators of sixteenth-century editions are not moralizing but rather celebrating images for the sake of their own beauty and freed from the orthodoxies of interpretation. They are, in fact, responding to the aesthetic of Arachne's web: metamorphic, fluid, imagistic, and multiple. This we might call the *Ovide imagisé*, the Renaissance answer to the moralization of metamorphosis.

One must be careful, however, not to exaggerate the purity, abstraction, or wordlessness of these images. Arachne (not to mention Ovid) creates a whole tapestry of these images, and such a large design cannot be free of words, of traditions, or of external references. The texts and pictures from Petrarch and his illustrators on to Correggio and Spenser often seem independent but operate in complex interrelation. So the *Ovide imagisé* has as its natural balance what we might call an *Ovide tapisserisé*, which construes these individual images as part of a grand design. Both of these "Arachnid" impulses leave their mark strongly on the pictorial traditions of metamorphosis in the Renaissance. Images of transformation in the sixteenth century often stand as concentrated miniatures speaking their own language and epitomizing whole metamorphic stories; they are also often elements in a multiple design with a complex philosophical play of external referents. Indeed, there is a natural opposition and balance between these two impulses, the one tending toward the individual, the subjective, and the ephemeral, the other toward the great cognitive construction of many subordinated parts. The very oscillation between image and structure is built into the subject of metamorphosis precisely as it is built into the poem that gave birth to the tradition. To see it in full Renaissance operation, we must return to Correggio and Titian.

Let us begin not with a whole tapestry but with a single image. The myth is Jupiter's metamorphosis into a shower of gold for the love of Danae, and the painter is Titian. The story tells of an oracle according to which Acrisius will be killed by his grandson; to forestall this event he causes his daughter to be walled up in a tower. But Danae's great beauty is not so easily immured, and the god transforms himself into a golden shower that penetrates the tower and impregnates the girl. Titian, like the illustrators we have discussed, focuses entirely on the metamorphic moment. Not only is the background narrative omitted; it is contradicted by Titian's image, which sets the events in a partly open space that mingles the elegant interior trappings of Danae's bedroom with a wide landscape and natural vista. The outdoor scene, which denies the very basis of the story, enables the painter to translate Jupiter's metamorphosis into a grand meteorological event. The result is a spectacular drama of metamorphosis itself: a divine *Iuppiter tonans* manifesting himself suddenly in the familiar world of a Venetian boudoir. The implications go back to a familiar duality in understanding the supreme pagan divinity. Ovid spoke of the opposition between *maiestas* and *amor*, and Augustine decried the irreconcilability of Jupiter the thunderer with Jupiter the debauchee.[48] With his metamorphosed god in the sky, Titian fuses them in a single image.

Titian balances the god in the cloud with the image of a reclining nude female, which has its own power and significance. The sources are various: Michelangelo's *Leda* and his closely related statue of *Night* in the Medici Tombs; the Hellenistic *Sleeping Ariadne* which, as we have seen, Titian translated in the reclining figure of his *Andrians*; and the *Sleeping Venus* of Giorgione, which Titian almost certainly completed. Within his own work Titian produced variations on this theme that range from the early *Venus of Urbino* and the nymph and satyr in the *Pardo Venus* through the *Danae* and a whole series of Venuses with musicians, both of which subjects occupied him for some decades. This figure seems to have its own associations. First, it tends to exist in an ambiguously indoor/outdoor space.[49] Second, the history of the figure suggests that it has become (and not only for Titian) an emblem of sensuous beauty in the specifically antique manner. Finally, the arrangement of the body in the dramatic scene within the space of the canvas and in relation to the viewer's space defines classical beauty as sensual, visual, and voyeuristic. All the associations are especially appropriate to the Danae icon: the mixed space dramatizes the intrusion via metamorphosis of pagan nature into familiar domesticity, and the emblem of ancient sensual beauty accounts for the power that can shine through walls and thus capture the desire of the god.

But Danae is more than a wordless image, and Titian's successive versions of the subject point toward the varieties of meaning conveyed by the image. It is not clear just how many *Danae*s Titian produced. Among the contemporary copies, visual records of variants, and partly or wholly workshop pieces, two autograph works stand out. The first, now in Naples, dates from 1545–46 and was executed for the Cardinal Alessandro Farnese during Titian's stay in Rome; the second, now in Madrid, was painted around 1553–54 for Philip of Spain (figures 20, 21).[50]

The 1545 *Danae* was Titian's first mythological narrative in over twenty years—indeed since the time of Alfonso d'Este. It is not surprising that Titian was inspired by his trip to Rome, which placed him in the direct light of antiquity and of its most brilliant student: Michelangelo. Danae, as we shall see, is partly adapted from Michelangelo's *Leda*, whose own origins were in the otherwordly atmosphere of antique funerary monuments. The standing Cupid, whose glance is riveted to the golden shower while his body is turned away, may well owe its inspiration to Michelangelo's *Risen Christ* in S. Maria sopra Minerva, itself conceived in the image of an ancient nude athlete, while apart from that contemporary statue Titian may have drawn inspiration from the *Cupid Bending His Bow* of Lysippus, reproduced in many Roman copies.[51] The girl herself is massive, and the whole scene is simple and abstract, free of particularizing details. The shower consists in a decorous radiance framed by shadowy clouds, and the limited palette of colors adds to the sense of ancient sculptural authenticity.

The Philip II *Danae*, painted some eight or so years later, moves decisively away from the cool, classical, and statuesque. The most obvious change, however, is the replacement of Cupid with a shriveled hag as nursemaid. The hag's appearance contrasts violently with the girl's, and her gesture is another form of contrast: while the bulk of the golden shower directs itself toward Danae's sexual organs, a separate and smaller rain of disks drops into the hag's apron. The large, plainly visible, open apron parodies the concealed and presumably small and *intacta* virginity of the girl. The second Danae herself is clearly more human in scale than her Michelangelesque predecessor, and the setting contains more real-life particulars, even apart from the nursemaid, including the lap-dog and the embroidery on bolsters and drapes. The bedclothes, which were so smooth in the earlier canvas, here find themselves in an almost implausibly uneven mess of ridges and folds. The extraordinary coloration of the picture, which makes it so quintessentially Titianesque, consists of shocking juxtapositions. The golden shower itself, relatively subdued in the Roman *Danae*, here erupts as a blaze of cloud, fire, and gold. If the metamorphosis in the first picture is heavenly light, here it is a tempest; if the approaching god of the first picture is Platonic radiance, here he is a shooting star.

To understand what lies behind these different choices we must look into the pre-Titian background of Danae as both myth and image. The literary tradition for the subject is, by comparison to many other metamorphic myths, meager: barely mentioned by Ovid, Danae was nonetheless subsumed into the mythographic tropes of Jupiter's transformations as those were moralized in the Middle Ages. The metamorphosis of Jupiter into a golden shower is particularly condusive to demystification—it translates readily into money paid for Danae's favors.[52] On the other hand, there is a notable tradition, including references in the *Ovide moralisé* and in Franciscus de Retza's *Defensorium inviolatae virginitatis Mariae*, in which the metamorphic gold figures the Virgin's divine impregnation.[53]

Visual representations are scarcely more numerous than the literary discussions. A set of illustrations in the *Hypnerotomachia Poliphili*; a Primaticcio at Fontainebleau, often reproduced in woodcuts; Correggio's version as part of his *Amori di Giove*, a remarkable 1527 *Danae* of the Flemish artist Jan Gossart, influenced by a stay in Rome but painted in the North: such is the catalogue of pre-Titian examples—in decreasing order of likelihood that Titian knew them.[54] The alternatives of representation—to the extent that we can judge from so few—follow those of the mythographic tradition. In one sense the Danae icon is the most erotic, or even pornographic, of the images of the transformed Jupiter because it all but omits the powerful masculine figure of the god, such as might be rendered by a bull or an eagle. Thus it allows the viewer the fullest opportunity to fantasize himself into the picture. At the same time, a beautiful young girl awaiting the manifestation of a god in a blaze of heavenly light is a twin to the Virgin of the Annunciation. The metamorphic image stands at the nexus of these opposite readings. The golden shower must be an incarnation of love: but is it the Holy Spirit, semen, or a prostitute's pay? Pictures, to be sure, do not demand the use of quite such brutal terms. Yet the Danae iconography does ask questions of precisely that kind.

It is not only the tradition of Danae iconography that testifies to these alternatives and influences Titian's choices. Two of the most famous paintings of the early sixteenth century painted by the two greatest artists, both widely copied (though both lost to us) were images of Leda by Leonardo da Vinci and Michelangelo.[55] Their influence radiates throughout the pagan revival, but the two works tend to inspire artists in opposite directions. In its various copied versions, Leonardo's *Leda* (conceived in the first decade of the century) stands upright in the open expanse of the natural world (figure 22). She is engaged in a serene, almost Madonnalike loving gesture with the swan, but she is surrounded by her progeny (Castor and Pollux; Helen and Clytemnestra), sometimes newly born, sometimes still in the egg. While there is certainly a strong erotic feel to Leda's posture, the overall impression of the canvas—so far as we can judge—is of a blissful maternal figure set in a context of earthly nature and cosmic beauty. Michelangelo's image (created for none other than Alfonso d'Este around 1530) is strikingly opposite (figure 23). For the first time since antiquity (I believe) an artist pictures the metamorphic union as the act of intercourse itself. But this is no moralization of metamorphosis as beastly sexuality. Leda's state of sleep and total self-absorption translates pagan eroticism into an atmosphere of dream and imagination. Michelangelo's sources, as Edgar Wind has shown, were in the mystic funerary art of antiquity.[56] In that context the image evokes the ancient link between death and apotheosis but suggests that both are versions of sexual ecstasy. Images of pagan female sexuality in the Renaissance— Ledas, Danaes, Antiopes, Europas, nameless nymphs—can be traced to the alternatives offered by these famous works, the one open, natural, sublime, maternal, the other dark, carnal, involuted, and secret. Some will choose between the alternatives, and some will attempt to fuse them.

In the face of such oppositions, the Roman *Danae* attempts to introduce serenity and balance. The direct and indirect allusions to classical and classicizing sculpture set the story in a Michelangelesque antiquity associated with noble, heroic, and mystical values. The choice to eliminate the narrative, of which we have already spoken, turns metamorphosis into the most abstract of incarnations. Without the girl's imprisonment in a tower, Jove's self-transformation into gold fulfills no practical purpose, except as a distillation of his love or desire. That distillate appears as pure radiant light, while at the remotest points from its source it is translated into disks of actual gold, as though by a Platonic scheme of descending emanations from the heavenly essence to the earthly material. The infinitely serene glance with which Danae responds to this manifestation and the openness of her body to receive the shower of gold represent a remarkable achievement in the sanctifying of sensual beauty. The response of the Cupid is almost a visual allegory; he becomes (if the pun may be forgiven) a pivotal figure, a representation of that form of erotic love which we expect in the Danae story but which is outclassed, awed, and (literally) wrongfooted by a higher god of love than himself.[57]

To be sure, many a viewer feels that the erotic expectations of the Danae material are plentifully fulfilled in this canvas. It is, after all, a feast of naked and complaisant feminine beauty, arguably almost pornographic in its appeal. That this Danae retains her erotic force is a tribute to the power of the image and to Titian's determination to achieve harmonic balance: sensuality and sacredness, *disegno* and *colore*, Venice and Rome. The result is a serene, even abstract, form of classicism. But a balance among such warring elements is not easy to maintain, nor inevitably desirable. The persistent wish to paint the subject may have derived from Titian's awareness that the conflicting claims of the material were not all being allowed their full force in a canvas where everything seems at rest.

In the second *Danae* nothing is at rest. The violence of colors and brush stroke, the chaotic state of the linen, the tempestuous nature of the metamorphic cloud—all testify to the unresolved dualities between erotic fabliau and divine manifestation, between eros and Platonic god of love. The replacement of Cupid with the nursemaid begins to establish the terms of the oppositions, as it decisively moves the picture away from allegory and toward narrative.[58] Abstract love is out of the question (or at least pushed to one side of the canvas) when the stereotypical figure of the hag confidante-companion is given such a prominent place. Classical love heroines from Phaedra to Juliet, including many of Ovid's amorous ladies, come with a sidekick. Typically, the nursemaid's employer (the girl's father or guardian) expects her to enforce his restrictive will; but just as inevitably the nursemaid turns around and abets her young mistress's romantic inclinations. And that, in shorthand, is precisely the figure we have here. The nursemaid wears a heavy chain with several keys—thus at least implicitly introducing the whole Acrisius narrative of the girl shut up in a tower. Yet, far from being a jailer, she is enthusiastically cooperating in receiving the golden rain which symbolically breaks down the walls of the sexual jail. Indeed, this activity is virtually a parody of the Ovidian myth, since it materializes the golden shower as literal wealth for which the hag can compete with Danae. If the Cupid of the first *Danae* is visual allegory, then the hag with her mercenary gesture is visual demystification—a representation of that debunking attitude toward the amours of Jupiter developed among mythographers from Fulgentius's time well into the Renaissance. Titian's nursemaid fits clearly in this tradition. She is the girl's exchequer; and, as she attempts to collect the gold, she turns the whole scene into a bawdy tale.

Despite these particularities the girl still gazes rapturously upward. Whether we want to go so far as the implication in Panofsky's description of this Danae as "a mortal virgin [who] looks up, in ecstasy, at an approaching god,"[59] we cannot fail to see that there is still an annunciatory aspect to the scene, perhaps all the more strongly because, unlike the Cupid who shares in and balances this depiction of reverence, the nursemaid by her contrasting attitude makes us more aware of Danae's special destiny. This canvas does not resolve the oppositions; it celebrates them.

There is yet a later *Danae*, usually classified as "Titian and Workshop," which was painted in the last half of the 1550s, possibly for Rudolf II; it is now in Vienna (figure 24). Its special interest to us lies in the fact that it seems to resolve the oppositions by a kind of schematic reduction of the conflicting elements we have considered. The girl is still serenely white, and she dominates the canvas more than ever. The hag, on the other hand, is dwarfed by the collection plate that she brings to catch the gold; she must, in other words, have planned ahead to collect her fee. The schematization emerges most sharply in two new details. On the sheet, at the farthest distance from the source of the golden shower, there appears a pile of realistically depicted gold coins. The medieval demystification of the story becomes a literal image on the canvas, leaving us little doubt how we should interpret the "love scene" in progress. At the same time on the opposite side of the canvas from the coins there is the disembodied and sketchy face of Jupiter in the clouds from which the gold emanates.[60] The divine face speaks as conventionally for the sacred version of the story as the coins on the bed sheet speak for the debased version. Perhaps that flow of possibilities, as one reads down the picture from the face of the god to the money on the bed, indicates most clearly the alternatives and the range of giving meaning to the metamorphic image. When this god is made flesh, it may be as a sacred emanation, as a glorious representation of sensuality, or as a bunch of gold coins whose presence acts as a moral judgment upon the delusions of both the sacred and the sensual. The multiple possibilities inevitably turn the pagan image into a dialectic. The history of Titian's *Danae* points to an internal struggle among the alternatives; let us now turn back to Correggio and consider the unfolding of the multiples into a composite work of art.

In the Camera di S. Paolo we saw the pagan image in almost abstract terms. What happens at the other end of Correggio's career, when the images are concrete, narrative, and explicitly metamorphic, we can observe with the series of paintings usually called the *Amori di Giove*.[61] There is some reason to believe that more examples were originally contemplated and a more complex set of relations established among them;[62] but what was actually executed were two pairs of canvases: *Io* and *Ganymede; Leda* and *Danae* (figures 25-28). These late paintings are Correggio's first profane works in a purely narrative mode.[63] They are also his greatest Este commission, created for Federico Gonzaga, of the generation after Alfonso and the *camerino d'alabastro*. The circumstances of the commission and the planned disposition of the works are somewhat shadowy. It is quite possible, however, that this series may have been intended to pay a sexual compliment to Federico's liaison with the commoner Isabella Boschetti—the mortal girl, as it were, to whom he could play amorous Jupiter.[64] If that is so, the *Amori* exist in a yet more bluntly pagan milieu than that of Federico's uncle; and Correggio's own efforts must be seen as an attempt to keep up with modern taste while remaining true to his own emblematic visualization of the pagan gods. That tension between pleasure (visual or erotic) and meaning will be at the heart of the dialectic.

In the *Amori*, then, Correggio takes a middle path between the abstract classical allegory of the Camera lunettes and the lush but "meaningless" paganizing images of the ovals. That is, he embraces the world of Ovidian myth. And myth, in the first place, means metamorphosis. Though the paintings are referred to as the *Amori di Giove*, the real subject is the transformations of Jupiter, as is evident from the remarkable iconography of *Io*, enveloped in a cloud which on closer examination proves to contain the shadowy face and hand of Jupiter. In Ovid's story the transformation belongs to the girl and not to the god. Io is turned into a heifer for purposes of concealment, and the cloud is no metamorphosis but a covering ordered by Jupiter to protect the scene of dalliance from his wife's suspicious eye; or, as in the *Fasti* or the *Ars Amatoria*, it may be Juno who transforms the girl into a cow to prevent Jupiter's amours, only to find herself foiled by his self-transformation into a bull. Transforming Jupiter himself into the amorous cloud is a brilliant, as well as a logical, step in conceptualizing these images as a series, and it is also a celebration of the image of metamorphosis. Correggio was not the first to make this step,[65] though it is possible he was unaware of the rather obscure earlier texts in which this new metamorphosis was to be found. Whether the sources were entirely in his own imagination or not, the painter's choice in the *Io* reflects on the Ovidian inspiration behind the whole series: four metamorphoses in two pairs, each consisting of one bird and one cloud, both supremely ephemeral—which is to say metamorphic—forms.[66]

The metamorphic images in the first pair of paintings are enigmas that turn the pictures into a set of studies in unstable forms. The *Ganymede* is perhaps the simpler case. This strikingly vertical composition is animated by a sequence of strangely shaped upward-pointing triangles that culminate in the great downward-pointing triangle of the metamorphic act itself, the huge menacing eagle—too wide, as it were, to fit on the canvas—and the boy, who in color and position balances the dog on the ground. In fact, the dog is the pivot of the whole canvas, establishing in his odd position and his lack of normal contact with the ground an instability of space that is connected to an instability of matter. Whatever the images may "mean," the shapes force our gaze upward with a kind of increasing mystery until the progression culminates in the dark, threatening eagle who is at the same time licking the arm of the boy he abducts. To add to the mystery, the boy in this presumably terrifying situation stares complacently and serenely (even angelically)[67] at us.

It is not so easy to translate into words the effect of Jupiter as meta-morphic cloud in the *Io*. More than in the *Ganymede*, real space here is annihilated by an undefined shifting form that dominates the canvas. The barely visible face and hand in the cloud represent one of the most ex-traordinary images of metamorphosis ever conceived. Correggio invents a new form within the convention of metamorphic doubles (semihuman laurel trees, semivulpine Lycaons, etc.) based on the shape-changing na-ture of cloud itself,[68] and he plays with our own perceptual processes as we move in and out of seeing the enveloping cloud as anthropomorphic. The result is self-conscious attention to the medium of transformation expressed in a pure language of images. Such a wordless visual idiom is closely related to the similarly noncognitive eroticism of the image. Michelangelo is an important inspiration. We know that Correggio had sketched the *Leda*,[69] and the results show in his *Io* as well as his *Leda*. Correggio's Io experiences metamorphosis and the sexual act simul-taneously; together they engulf her in the (literal) shadow-world of the dream. It is as though his invented metamorphosis has literalized the mystical dream-world of Michelangelo's Leda.

Metamorphosis is not just an arresting image on this pair of canvases, however. It also forms part of a conceptual design. The metamorphic mass of eagle and boy in the *Ganymede* clears the earth in its upward mo-tion like a rocket at the moment of lift-off, while the balancing "real" forms of dog, rock, and tree point in the heavenly direction. Contrariwise, the *Io* has no heaven, for the metamorphic cloud has come down and ob-scured the distinction between earth and sky, while the corresponding "real" forms in this canvas—hillock, bushes, rocks, brook—keep the ac-tion on the ground. Other elements in the pictures stress this opposition: the upward-pointing dog vs. the downward-facing stag slaking its thirst,[70] the serene gaze of the Ganymede vs. the sexual rapture of the Io, the sharp outline of the eagle vs. the amorphousness of the cloud. The meta-morphoses reproduce the distinction between Jupiter's place in heaven and the earthly site of his sexual affairs.

The conceptual opposition works in similar ways in the second pair. The sensuality of Leda obviously enjoying the act of intercourse contrasts with the chaster Danae, who calmly awaits her destiny with neither fear nor pleasure. In that way we can liken Danae to Ganymede and Leda to Io, which reverses the left-right relationship, just as it reverses the rele-vance of birds and clouds. The range of colors in the *Danae* is a good deal cooler and more limited than in the *Leda*; and with the brighter colors comes a more open, crowded, and lively scene than in the strikingly en-closed and spare canvas of the *Danae*. Yet once again, the heart of the pic-tures, as well as of the contrast between them, is the image of metamor-phosis. Both compositions hinge upon a central semicircle: Leda and the swan form an earthbound shape, while the golden cloud of the *Danae* contrasts with it as a heavenly semicircle.

The semicircles are focal points of the pictures, and both are the loci of metamorphosis. In the *Danae*, the shape remains mysterious. It is a curious version of the golden shower, emitting little light or rain—though Correggio does take it literally as gold. The rest of the picture directs us physically or conceptually toward the shower without really explicating that shadowy form. The long lines of the Amor's right side as well as his lofty gaze point us toward the cloud, while the extended apron of the girl, which seems just the right size to hold the cloud if it were to descend bodily, confirms our awareness of the mysterious shape. Meanwhile the pair of putti, whose meaning has intrigued viewers from Giulio Romano's time onwards,[71] enacts some sort of essential opposition that must bear upon the binary design of the whole series. Earthly and heavenly love, Eros and Anteros, the golden vs. the leaden arrows of Cupid: some such antinomy is surely meant by this contrast between a winged and an unwinged figure, one bearing an arrow, the other a stone. The tone, both visual and conceptual, of the *Danae* is established by the metamorphosis itself. Just as the golden cloud seems sacred but indefinable, so the whole picture is a conundrum.

The semicircle of metamorphosis in the *Leda* is no conundrum but once again the image of sexual pleasure itself, and all the images radiate both visually and conceptually from that central metamorphosis. The line starting with the large tree and continuing down the neck of the swan to between Leda's legs almost perfectly divides the composition in half. Such a structure is unusually geometric, and its importance is confirmed by the differences in the material on either side of the line. On our left, Leda and the scene around her are shadowy, and the figures are symbolic; on our right the scene is colorful and brilliant, and the action is plainly narrative. The union of girl and god is at the nexus. The right half of the picture seems to be the daylight realm of amorous intrigue. Whether these are other girls and swans or different stages of Leda's own story, the essentially commonplace (even comic) activity here, of being clothed or unclothed, of protecting oneself from the advances of a swan, of watching with an equivocal look as the bird flies away—these represent the divine amour related as titillation.

The other side speaks in a symbolic language. To balance the opposing putti of the *Danae* we have another such pair, again one with and one without wings. To balance them (and perhaps also the Amor of the *Danae*) we have a large winged Cupid. All three of these figures are making music, and the coarse wind instruments of the putti are probably meant to stand in opposition to the more celestial harp of the large winged Cupid. Because of ancient associations with swans, music is highly appropriate to the Leda story.[72] Quite possibly there is meant to be an allegory of music here that joins the Apollonian figure of the swan with heavenly music. If so, the noble version of the swan implied in the music-making side of the picture stands in contrast to the lascivious swans of the right side; and, in a larger contrast, music itself as one inspiration or signification of love must be contrasted with the opposing arrows from the *Danae*, which inspire and signify love in a different sense. It may even be that the structure of the picture—with its eight human figures—is based on musical principles. Certainly the division of the canvas in the (approximate) center points to a special significance of the amorous and metamorphosed god as the junction of the Apollonian and symbolic with the terrestrial and titillating scene of sexual amusement. The union of oppositions even includes the source images in Leonardo and Michelangelo, for this is one of the few canvases that achieves a perfect balance between the one painter's celebration of sunlit nature and the other's vision of erotic self-absorption.

One may not entirely agree with this explanation of the larger tapestry; what cannot, however, be denied is that the image of metamorphosis takes its place at the center. As in the *Io*, metamorphosis is here made literally inextricable from the sexual act; and both are placed at the meeting point of all the opposites depicted in these works. That was perhaps the goal toward which all the *Amori di Giove* were moving: not merely of distinguishing between the heavenly and earthly but of using the moment of amorous metamorphosis to unite them.

The composite works of Correggio and Titian that have rounded out our discussion of the Renaissance so far have taken us from abstract pagan images to images in the midst of a conceptual design. But are there, in fact, concepts inside the design? Binary oppositions certainly have appeared in all these works, taking an almost purely abstract form in the Camera and edging toward a somewhat more intellectual identification in the *Danae*s and the *Amori di Giove*. Even in the latter set of canvases, however, metamorphosis can hardly be said to build a complex system. Correggio, as a particularly sensual image-maker, may represent an extreme case. Yet it can be said of all Renaissance artists, including intellectuals like Petrarch and Spenser, that they use metamorphosis not so much to epitomize as to stand in place of philosophical systems, embracing but not analyzing conceptual doubles in the multiple image of transformation.

We saw in chapter 1 how the fear and triumph in the Europa story are specific examples in a tradition that situates metamorphosis at the nexus of opposites. In the Renaissance as in antiquity, the yoking of opposites into an inevitable pattern of stimulus and response itself comprises part of the multiplicity of metamorphosis. The Renaissance loves paradox, the tension of opposition and containment such as we have already observed in the Camera di S. Paolo. As a consequence, the essential oppositions in classical myths communicate very directly through the spirit of sixteenth-century artists, whether these tensions are mediated by an intellectual grounding (in the style of medieval classicism) or not. Titian's *Rape of Europa* (figure 29), the last of his Philip II *poesie* and the canvas that Velázquez took to be so prototypical, can stand for us, too, as a paradigm.[73] The structure of the picture is sharply defined. The land is in the left-hand distance, the water occupies the central section, and Europa and the bull dominate the right foreground. We can draw a fairly sharp diagonal from lower left to upper right following from the putto on the dolphin through the line of Europa's body and scarf and up to a dark cloud in the upper right corner. To the left of this line all is soft and familiar; to the right there is sharp terror. Indeed the palette—and even more vividly the brush stroke—change sharply across that line: on the left the paint is soft and muted, while on the right there is an extraordinary variety of thick strokes, including those depicting the water, the fish, and the bull himself. In fact, nothing could demonstrate more forcefully the continuity of those classical associations of the Europa myth with passionate female emotion, fears about first sexual experience, and anxiety in regard to the crossing of unfamiliar thresholds.

Yet Titian expresses these familiar emotions in a new way. The traditional Europa, as we have already seen, is depicted as riding very gracefully atop the bull, her scarf usually forming a perfect semicircle above her to balance the body of the bull below. Here she holds on to the bull very precariously while her limbs are arrayed awkwardly and her long scarf flows jaggedly from the water up to the heavens. Significant feminine features are treated almost grotesquely. Her torso is twisted so much that the exposed breast is hardly identifiable as female; her face is darkened by the threatening shadow of her arm. Covered by this shadow and rolling her eyes dramatically, the girl has absolutely no prettiness of feature. The only still and vivid part of her body is the sharply outlined pubis, emphasized by the arrowlike pointing of her clothes on one side and the bull's overlong tail on the other. In fact, the painter has transferred metamorphosis from the bull to the girl. He translates all the fear and passion in the girl into the corporeal manifestation of her skewed physical position.

The shift from the god to the girl points to an important development: if Titian is not building a conceptual system, he may on the other hand be creating a psychological medium. The change may perhaps best be illustrated by comparison to another transfer of which we spoke earlier: Correggio's shift of transformation in the *Io* from the girl to the god. In fact, the two changes are as opposite as they seem. Throughout the *Amori di Giove*, Correggio exploits the traditional icons of metamorphosis, focusing each picture on them and joining them with further allegorical dualities that mirror the doubleness of form and conception inherent in the self-transforming god. Jupiter in the cloud is an original metamorphic double but very much in the tradition of those double forms like a stag-headed human Actaeon or a laurel-fingered Daphne. With the exception of the simplistic last *Danae* and the very late *Death of Actaeon*, which was created in a wholly different atmosphere,[74] Titian seems to have deliberately eschewed these conventions. The *Europa* shows why: Titian is redefining the physical shape of metamorphosis, determined that it be psychological and humane rather than merely frivolous and Olympian. Velázquez was right to make the Europa the centerpiece of his *Fable of Arachne*: Titian has fulfilled the intention and meaning of Arachne's humanist message to the Olympian gods. Technically, this transfer meant the creation of new iconography that downplayed or omitted the conventional composite image in favor of some other means to express such powers of metamorphosis as we discussed in chapter 1: the divine appearing incarnate in the natural world, with all the unsettlingly erotic and visionary quality of that manifestation. The *contraposto* of the Cupid in the first *Danae* is one such effort to depict a world in transformation; the violence of brush stroke and color in the second is another. In the *Europa*, as we have seen, the transfer of metamorphosis is to be seen in the whole jagged drama of the right side of the picture. But it is more than merely technical; it involves the creation of a visual psychology.

To see this transfer in its most radical form we must momentarily leave *Europa* for another of Titian's Ovidian *poesie*, the *Diana and Actaeon* painted for Philip II in the 1550s (figure 30).[75] What makes this great painting important for the subject of metamorphosis is that it contains no metamorphosis. The convention from Roman times at least was to depict Actaeon at the moment he gazes at Diana bathing while he is simultaneously becoming a stag from the neck up. The juxtaposition of Actaeon's crime and punishment—voyeurism and death in metamorphosed shape—is in the heritage of the *Ovide moralisé* and the *Ovide imagisé*. That is, it uses the image to moralize and allegorize the story of mortal presumption and divine revenge.

So far as I know, Titian's is the first Actaeon ever to take part in the bathing scene without showing any signs of metamorphosis either in himself or in some sequential episode elsewhere in the picture or series of pictures.[76] The effect, as in the case of the *Europa*, is profoundly humanizing. By excluding the composite figure of the transformed Actaeon, Titian transposes the drama into a different key of metamorphosis—in fact, into the original Ovidian drama of a mortal confrontation with unmediated divinity. Without a metamorphic telos illustrated as part of the scene, Titian's Actaeon and Diana become equals. They balance the canvas with a pair of powerful gestures less concerned with the shock of outraged *pudeur* than with the horror of unexpected sight. Titian emphasizes seeing not only by countless forms of eye contact but also by framing the scene with arches and bright red curtains. With Actaeon on the threshhold, the bath almost becomes a picture within a picture. The result is a powerful identification between the viewer and Actaeon as both participate in the visual, the voyeuristic, and the visionary. The idea of Ovidian transformation is contained in the radically unsettling drama of god and mortal, while the technique is transferred to a whole language of visual disorder: diagonals in the landscape, sky, fountain, and flowing water; no level plane anywhere in the foreground; body positions (like Europa's) twisted and ungraceful.

We have been speaking of binary oppositions and of humanized metamorphosis as though they were quite separate, but that is not the case. For Correggio the balancing within and between canvases is fundamentally emblematic: upward vs. downward motion; sublime vs. carnal love, and so on. When Titian thinks in pairs, the relation is rather one of stimulus and response. While Titian may have planned an *Actaeon Torn by His Own Hounds*,[77] the pendant he actually executed for King Philip is the *Diana and Callisto*, another Ovidian episode of Diana's vengeance upon a breach in chastity, but by no means a traditional twin of the Actaeon story (Figure 31). Compositionally, the two pictures are symmetrical, so that Actaeon in the left-hand picture is paired with Diana in the right-hand picture, while the two adjacent sides involve the clothing and unclothing of a female form. The emphasis upon nakedness reminds us that both are stories of the revealed flesh; but the subject of love by eyesight in the Actaeon picture is balanced in the *Callisto* by carnal love fulfilled in pregnancy. In a sense, then, the *Diana and Callisto* pendant becomes the metamorphosis that follows upon Actaeon's crime. The goddess wreaks her (displaced) vengeance by sitting in judgment upon another presumptuous mortal; and she sentences the girl to be denuded in return for her own victimization. In the process metamorphosis has turned toward the extended story of human change, as love by the eyes ultimately leads toward procreation, and toward mutability and decay as the abstract visionary stimulus of the *Actaeon* is translated into its earthly and fleshly result in the *Callisto*.

In the case of the *Europa* we have already observed binary oppositions at the very heart of the myth. But Titian's *Rape* in itself does not contain them. The painter devotes himself exclusively to the terrors of the abduction, with no reference to wedding or triumph to balance the fears associated with transformation and sexuality. In fact, he takes the visual icons of Europa-like triumph, putti and sea-creatures, and puts them to rather equivocal uses. The flying Cupids are more strange and ominous than celebratory, while the putto riding the dolphin seems rather vigilant or awestruck than triumphant. And dimly visible in the water directly under Europa and the bull is the farthest translation of the classical sea-triumph: a big fish consuming a little fish, presumably replaying Europa's victimization.[78]

As in the case of the *Actaeon*, the omissions in the "stimulus" canvas can be explained by the "response." Evidence suggests that the *Europa* was paired (again unconventionally, and even more so this time)[79] with the Wallace Collection *Perseus and Andromeda*, which would probably hang on the right side (figure 32).[80] Given that arrangement, we have, reading from the center outwards, the two damsels in distress, then semi-circular shadowing of a similar kind, then fearful passages of water, then land with helpless observers upon it. The real significance of the pairing is not merely compositional; rather, it goes back to the oppositions inherent in the myth. Having banished marital triumph in his *Europa*, Titian answers with a myth that does include marriage. As so often in Titian's pagan pictures, the conceptual relations are conveyed by body language. The strangely hovering putti in the *Europa*—quite original with Titian—act in connection with the figure of the heroine herself to define the power of passion and displace it from the bull. In their odd position on the left-hand canvas they are perfectly balanced by the even stranger flight pattern of Perseus on the right.[81]

Once we link these iconographically unrelated figures, we can observe the process of the two canvases. The putti in the *Europa* register the first thrust of passion's arrow, which aims for and terrorizes the girl. Reading from left to right, from Europa at the moment of losing her virginity to Andromeda in chains, we witness the intensification of sexual enslavement. As Perseus hovers over Andromeda on his way to slaying the dragon, he is undoing the damage done by the cupids in the Europa picture against whom he is balanced. The dragon is a further metamorphosis of the beastly element that emerges in the bull. In the story of Perseus there will be a marriage with a great (though, to be sure, troubled) wedding celebration. The transformations that begin with love's arrow and move on to defloration and to the prison and dragon of lust are balanced by the savior Perseus who will free his lady and take her to wedding, triumph, and the safe far right-hand shore, where no metamorphic creatures roam. Again, the icons of metamorphosis are transformed into dramas of human change.

So inevitable does the pattern of binary opposites become in the Renaissance that it is not only Titian himself but also other artists who must make a response to the stimulus of a terrorized Europa. Titian's response, as we have seen, is complex and deferred. But his less iconographically adventuresome follower Veronese responds directly in traditional form. When the younger artist, toward the end of his career, produced a *Rape of Europa*, it could hardly fail to be indebted to an important late work of his master on the same subject (Figure 33).[82] In the Veronese canvas the indebtedness emerges largely by negation. Where the first Europa looks up, the second looks down; where the first is nearly nude, the second is (except for one breast) heavily clad; where the first is alone in a great expanse of space, the second is crowded and surrounded.

Compositionally the Veronese is almost a mirror image of the Titian, but all these reversals appear in themselves random until we realize that Veronese is responding to the terrors of the Titian by creating a picture of nuptial triumph. This is no chance alteration between two artists of different sensibilities. Veronese copies Titian's floating putti and (despite the left-right reversal) places them in the same location on his canvas. But, while Titian's cupids are holding arrows and hovering menacingly, Veronese's are balanced precisely over Europa and the bull, where they hold wreaths of flowers that form part of the ceremonial celebration of a wedding. Indeed the very position of Europa on the bull surrounded by her ladies suggests that she is being decked out for nuptials. In response to the end-stopped nature of the Titian, Veronese moves from his closed space into an open distant landscape where the future is proleptically depicted. And it is these same nuptial wreaths that tie together the stages of the story. Some descend from the floating putti toward Europa, others adorn the "bridal" pair, and still others are held in the distant airscape to bless the couple as they proceed on what looks less like a fearful rite of passage than a honeymoon. As he turns fear to triumph, Veronese makes explicit what was implied in the *Perseus*: the earthly patterns of human change and development.

The coincidence of oppositions that surrounds Titian's *Rape of Europa* is no fluke. Antoine de Baif's "L'Enlèvement d'Europe" and Spenser's "Muiopotmos" are extremely faithful to their respective originals, Moschus and Ovid, but in both cases the most intense and original parts of the new material go to emphasize the two opposite poles of the girl's experience: fear and triumph. The Pléiade poet extends ad nauseam all the passages involving Europa's fear of the bull; he also beefs up Moschus's account of the triumph. He characterizes it as a "chant nossal" and speaks of the maiden's nuptial destiny whereby Jupiter's "jeux" will be transformed into "feste"—that is to say, his sexual games will become celebratory festival.[83] In "Muiopotmos" Spenser inserts a translation of Ovid's Arachne-Minerva contest in the midst of a struggle between the spider who is Arachne's descendant and the joyous young butterfly Clarion. For eight lines the translation of Ovid is almost literal, up to the point where Europa seems to be adapting as comfortably as possible to the sea-crossing. Then Spenser adds his own invention:

But (Lord) how she in euerie member shooke,
When as the land she saw no more appeare,
But a wilde wildernes of waters deepe:
Then gan she greatly to lament and weepe.   [ll. 285–88][84]

These marvelously original lines, inspired by meditations on the girl's fear, are followed immediately by a whole original stanza:

Before the Bull she pictur'd winged Loue,
With his yong brother Sport, light fluttering
Vpon the waues, as each had been a Doue;
The one his bowe and shafts, the other Spring
A burning Teade about his head did moue,
As in their Syres new loue both triumphing:
And manie Nymphes about them flocking round,
And manie *Tritons*, which their hornes did sound.　　　[ll.289–96]

The intensity of the fear inevitably produces an intense orgasmic sea-triumph. To put the matter at its most tendentious, in the Renaissance as in antiquity, artists who respond to this myth have no choice but to express the wholeness of the story. Triumph must include fear, and fear inevitably gives way to triumph.

Other myths of metamorphosis, to be sure, consist of different elements in tension. The transformation of Daphne joins the destructive war of Apollo's passion and the girl's frigidity with the triumphant crowning of poets and emperors. Actaeon's experience defines him as a lustful voyeur at the same time as he becomes the prototypical visionary; and what goes for Actaeon as stag holds true for Tiresias as hermaphrodite. Perhaps the most striking example of simultaneous oppositions in metamorphosis, however, is the myth of Ganymede, a story whose very marginal nature, even in antiquity,[85] demanded reinterpretation if it was to be granted canonical status at all. Metamorphosis in this story yokes the unsavory sexual connection of boy and god—the more unsavory given the tinge of bestiality—with the miraculous flight to heaven. So the myth lives on two planes (literally, in this case), with the connection being metamorphosis itself. Dante may have a vision of Ganymede as he begins his ascent to Purgatory; Alciati may contemptuously dismiss the carnal in favor of purity which attracts the soul to God; Claude Mignault, a commentator on Alciati, may even equate Ganymede's assumption into heaven with Christ's "Suffer the little children to come unto me."[86] Still, the carnal basis of the myth never quite drops away. The very intensity of the Renaissance Platonization of the story—another Alciati commentator, Pignorius, virtually rehearses the *Integer vitae* in his summing up—suggests the living presence of a less elevated interpretation. The definitions of heavenly joys in connection with the myth can take on a particularly fleshly tinge. Mignault speaks of "aeternae beatitudinis deliciarum" (p. 61), and Achille Bocchi refers to the boy's assumption into heaven as "summa voluptas."[87] The story becomes the occasion for multiple interpretations and *obiter dicta* about the business of interpreting pagan tales. Natalis Comes, for instance, dismisses the euhemeristic reading (Jupiter stole away the boy while fighting under the sign of an eagle) saying that such interpretations pull "divine things down to our level when it is far preferable to raise human beings up to the divine nature."[88] He praises poets who invent such tales because "they bring us more profitably up to the level of things divine than if they had pulled the divine things down to us." The act of interpretation becomes itself a flight of Ganymede, and the flight of Ganymede a metamorphosis.

The simultaneity of opposites emerges with particular force in a pair of drawings that Michelangelo produced in the 1530s for Tommaso Cavalieri (figures 34, 35).[89] The artist couples the heaven-bound boy with Tityus, eternally damned for having attempted the chastity of Latona and permanently pinned to the floor of hell, where a vulture eats out his liver. The unconventional but brilliantly effective pairing appears to set the two myths and compositions in diametric opposition. Tityus lies manacled on a horizontal plane, probably in response to Virgil's description of him as gigantically stretched out to the length of nine acres.[90] Ganymede, especially if it is true that the original included his dog looking up at him, is on the other hand a vertical composition; and in place of Tityus's tight squeeze between the rock below and the bird above, Ganymede is completely relaxed in the powerful but gentle grip of the bird. That Michelangelo would have a Platonic conception in mind can hardly come as a surprise: the pair clearly expresses a moral opposition between corrupt carnality as punished in hell and sublime love, which transports the lover to heaven.

But Michelangelo's design tends as much to the contagion as to the contrast of the two images. As he did with *Leda*, he construes these myths as erotic: in both images bird and human being are positioned highly suggestively. So if Tityus partly purges the sexuality of Ganymede, he also reminds us of it. And, in reverse, Ganymede's carnal relation with the eagle—which is certainly part of the myth—begins to ascribe a similar liaison to Tityus and his bird—which is not part of the myth. These interconnections make sense once one sees Michelangelo's depiction of love as more psychological than Platonic. The tale told by this pair of images is of the simultaneous ecstasy and torment of passion. His Ganymede is not merely sleeping the visionary sleep of Dante-as-Ganymede in the *Purgatorio*; he is also experiencing a relaxed state of blissful pleasure. Tityus is not merely being punished after committing a sexual crime; he is being punished by the agonies of the libido itself. Thus heaven and hell turn out to be characterizations of the emotional state of the lover as much as Platonic or moral conceptions. (This translation of myth into psychological terms, as we shall shortly see, would scarcely be possible without the example of Petrarch.) Even more fully than on a Platonic ladder, the psychological definition allows the opposites to be fused in a single experience. Hence Michelangelo's conflation of eagle and vulture into a single bird, noble and predatory, carnal and sublime.

Europa, Actaeon, Daphne, Ganymede: the place of metamorphosis in the stories is not identical, nor are the terms of opposition the same; yet in every case magical transformation mediates between some expression of passion (it matters little whether one is the subject or object of passion) and a grandly triumphant or cosmic ritual that not only gives permission for passion but also celebrates it. All of these combinations existed already in antiquity, in the works of Moschus and Apuleius, of Achilles Tatius and Nonnos. Yet artists and thinkers of the Renaissance intensified the simultaneity of oppositions, as Spenser does when he joins "the wilde wildernes of waters deepe" with nymphs and tritons, or as Shakespeare does in making a metamorphic jackass into a visionary, or as Michelangelo does by pairing an ecstatically floating Ganymede with a libidinously enslaved Tityus. So the opposing powers we observed in the Europa myth in antiquity not only speak to the Renaissance, but they also become the coordinates for a drama that confronts passion and order. Pagan images are revived for both coordinates, and both are figured in metamorphosis.

3. Metamorphic Passions: Petrarch and Ronsard

If the essential oppositions remain largely the same between the time of Moschus and that of Michelangelo, then the change is to be seen in the form that the two sides of the opposition take. What separated Titian's *Europa* from its classical prototypes was the concentration upon the heroine and the intensity of her own emotional experience. The painting's most powerful metamorphosis — if we understand the term as referring to physical transformation — was from the beautiful girl of the legend (or of the earlier phases of the story) into a tormented figure of fear. The Renaissance artist has made metamorphosis an explicitly psychological condition, just as those who allegorize Actaeon's dogs as his desires make the beastly element in his story psychological. The performance of metamorphosis in the arena of the psyche is the first of the great Renaissance innovations, and the source for this connection between passion and transformation can be traced directly to the *Rime* of Petrarch.

It could be argued that all of Petrarch's works amount to an extended act of introspection and autobiography. Whether we construe this as the profound search for self-knowledge or the grandest example of literary egoism in history is a matter of personal reaction. Either way (and the *in malo* interpretation has considerable biographical corroboration), Petrarch's works probably represent the first sustained attempt at self-consciousness in Western writing. Among these studies in the self, the vernacular *Rime sparse* stand apart. They were, of course, more widely read and copied than any other of Petrarch's self-explorations. They also codify the psyche in terms that are closely linked with paganism and metamorphosis.[91]

The self of the *Rime* is, in the first place, intensely changeable. Most of the time it is the poet's self which is engaged in constant change. The examples are so famous that one hesitates to cite them: "e temo e spero, et ardo et son un ghiaccio, / et volo sopra 'l cielo et giaccio in terra" (134.2–3: "And I fear and hope, and burn and am of ice; and I fly above the heavens and lie on the ground"); "vegghio, penso, ardo, piango. . . . mille volte il dì moro et mille nasco" (164.5, 13: "I am awake, I think, I burn, I weep. . . . A thousand times a day I die and a thousand am born").[92] On other occasions it is the object of his love who appears emotionally unstable:

l'aura mi volve et son pur quel ch' i' m'era.

Qui tutta umile et qui la vidi altera,
or aspra or piana, or dispietata or pia,
or vestirsi onestate o leggiadria,
or mansueta or disdegnosa et fera.   [112.4–8]

(Here I saw her all humble and there haughty, now harsh, now gentle, now cruel, now merciful; now clothed in virtue, now in gaiety, now tame, now disdainful and fierce.)

So far we are in the world of flux but not of metamorphosis. Petrarch's verbal effects (the repeated *or* and *et*, the play on *ghiaccio/giaccio*) doubtless owe something to the similar emotional storms of Ovid's tormented heroines. Still, oxymoron is not in itself transformation.

The first and last words of the above quotation begin to move us toward metamorphosis. *L'aura* is the breeze; and it is also, of course, the name of the beloved, the apostrophe not being part of fourteenth-century orthography. Laura's identification with the breeze makes her variable in herself and the cause of variation (*mi volve*) in her lover. If that is one metamorphosis, then *fera* is another. Here the term is adjectival, but frequently *fera* is the wild fugitive beast of a beloved whom the poet is hunting even as he is threatened by her violence:

Questa umil fera, un cor di tigre o d'orsa
che 'n vista umana o 'n forma d'angel vene,
in riso e 'n pianto, fra paura et spene
mi rota sì ch' ogni mio stato inforsa.   [152.1–4]

(This humble wild creature, this tiger's or she-bear's heart that comes in human appearance and in the shape of an angel, so wheels me about in laughter and tears between fear and hope, that she makes uncertain my every state.)

These lines reveal close connections between the animal form of the beloved and the changeability of mood in the lover. Laura is not only a breeze but also a beast, a human being, and an angel all in one shape. With this identification, the emotional changes of both characters appear not as random but as intertwined and governed by metamorphic principles.

Such principles emerge most fully, and take us the final step toward our subject, in a sonnet that deserves to be quoted in full:

> Poco era ad appressarsi agli occhi miei
> la luce che da lunge gli abbarbaglia,
> che, come vide lei cangiar Tesaglia,
> così cangiato ogni mia forma avrei.
>
> Et s' io non posso trasformarmi in lei
> più ch' i' mi sia (non ch' a mercé mi vaglia),
> di qual petra più rigida s'intaglia
> pensoso ne la vista oggi sarei,
>
> o di diamante, o d'un bel marmo bianco
> per la paura forse, o d'un diaspro
> pregiato poi dal vulgo avaro et sciocco;
>
> et sarei fuor del grave giogo et aspro
> per cui i' ò invidia di quel vecchio stanco
> che fa co le sue spalle ombra a Marrocco.   [51]

(Had it come any closer to my eyes, the light that dazzles them from afar, then, just as Thessaly saw her change, I would have changed my every form. And, since I cannot take on her form any more than I have already (not that it wins me any mercy), my face marked with care, I would be today whatever stone is hardest to cut, either diamond, or fair marble white for fear perhaps, or a crystal later prized by the greedy and ignorant mob; and I would be free of my heavy, harsh yoke, because of which I envy that tired old man who with his shoulders makes a shade for Morocco.)

Here metamorphosis turns explicit, and it becomes clear that the sympathetic changes within and between the two characters are part of a fantasy of absolute union between them via metamorphosis. *Trasformarsi in lei* is a ruling image of the whole sequence, combining two of the main preoccupations of the speaker, sexual desire and the search for identity. What brings that image alive in this sonnet and throughout the *Rime* is the one final element in the metamorphic tradition: the translation of individual experience to the language of Ovidian myth. One Ovidian myth we have already approached without mentioning it explicitly. The equation of *Laura* and *l'aura* cannot fail to remind us (and such a careful student of Ovid as Petrarch) of Cephalus and Procris, whose story of willful and accidental errors in a forest climaxed in confusions of identity among such essentially metamorphic terms as *Aura* and *Aurora*.[93] Their tale is a tragedy of metamorphosis, with all its emotional and material uncertainty. Its threat surely hangs over the whole story of Laura.

But Poem 51 embraces two of the ruling myths of transformation more explicitly present in the sequence: the tales of Daphne and of the Medusa. Apollo, patron of poets, chases the militantly virginal Daphne through the woods (the setting for the *Rime* is perpetually the *selva*), but, failing to achieve sexual union with her, he ultimately embraces her tree, the laurel, or *lauro*, which, among other significations, is the poet's crown as well as the masculine form of *Laura*. Without close analysis of a score of poems we cannot hope to appreciate the full richness of Petrarch's use of this material. Not only does he build upon the Ovidian associations— Apollo's former scorn for love, the *chasse d'amour*, the helplessness of the god, the sublimation of the story's conclusion, just to name a few—but he also works in the medieval tradition of mythography, which associates Daphne with the Virgin, with permanence, with eternal fame.[94]

The relevance of the Medusa myth may seem less broad; yet it, too, takes a double form. The gaze of the Medusa turns men to stone. Laura is a kind of Medusa whose blinding beauty freezes the poet into impotence (alternatively, his own reactions against love may be characterized as stoniness); at the same time she is herself a stone, a *donna petrosa* related to the heroine of Dante's early love lyrics.[95] In addition, the Medusa, like the Daphne myth in Petrarch's hands, becomes an emblem of poetry. In the canzone immediately preceding the sonnet quoted above, the poet characterizes his first sight of Laura as a time

> quando primier sì fiso
> gli tenni nel bel viso
> per iscolpirlo, imaginando, in parte
> onde mai né per forza né per arte
> mosso sarà . . .   [50.64–68]

(When for the first time I kept them so fixed on her lovely face, to sculpture it for imagination in a place whence it would never be moved by any art or force.)

The lines, enigmatic though they are, establish a strong connection between seeing or imagining on the one hand and sculpting in stone for eternity on the other.[96] So the same paradox that unites the unfulfilled love for Daphne with the eternal (i.e., evergreen) laurel crown reappears in the Medusa myth: the stony transformation betokens both the failure of love (her sternness or his lack of fulfillment) and the eternity of the amorous imagination metamorphosed into artistic stone. If one myth is memoralized in the name of *Laura*, the other finds its expression in the *petra*, who is the poet.

More important even than Petrarch's individual code for the meanings of the various metamorphic myths is the example he sets for the clustering of myths, transformations, and the human experiences that he depicts. From the example of Petrarch, throughout the Renaissance passion comes to be described (or depicted) not only by myths of metamorphosis but also by transformations among the myths. The locus classicus is the so-called *canzone delle metamorfosi*, Poem 23, incidentally the longest poem in the sequence.[97] This apparently early work, much revised, is the first canzone in the *Rime*, and its special place may be accounted for by the fact that it represents a rather complete spiritual autobiography from "la prima etade" in the past to a highly uncertain present tense one hundred and sixty lines later. It may consequently stand as a kind of précis of the whole sequence; and, since its principal mode is that of Ovidian transformations, it affords us an opportunity to study the developments in metamorphosis.

The opening stanza makes it clear, even before the narrative of metamorphoses begins, that the actual experience is mediated by two balanced forces that dominate the whole sequence: the act of remembering and the act of writing. Both will ultimately be seen as transformations, and even now we are told that the memory and the text "ten di me quel d'entro, et io la scorza" (l.20: "it holds what is within me, and I only the shell"): the mediated version is the essence, and *io* is defined in the precise language of medieval mythography, since *scorza* is really a translation of *integumentum*. The first change appears early in the subsequent stanza, but it is not a mythical transformation at all: "molt' anni eran passati, / sì ch' io cangiava il giovenil aspetto" (ll.22–23: "many years had passed, so that I was changing my youthful aspect"). The connection in the *Rime* between the changes of aging and those of metamorphosis is by no means random or adventitious. The poet builds more than one conceit out of the contrast between the evergreen nature of the laurel and the mutability of the speaker who spends such long years (repeatedly counted in the poems) pursuing that unchanging goal.[98]

Yet *trasformare* in the sequence is generally more a tribute to the power of love than to that of mutability;[99] and here Amor and "una possente Donna" give the speaker an identity via transformation:

ei duo mi trasformaro in quel ch' i' sono,
facendomi d'uom vivo un lauro verde
che per fredda stagion foglia non perde.   [ll.38–40]

(Those two transformed me into what I am, making me of a living man a green laurel that loses no leaf for all the cold season.)

A complicated give and take, to be sure: in perfectly authentic Ovidian fashion the metamorphosed human being loses his earthly life for an eternity in transformed shape. This eternity of the speaker as laurel is partly amatory—his unending identification, indeed absolute interchange, with Laura—and partly poetic, since *foglia non perder* means that his manuscripts will survive forever. On both counts metamorphosis seems for the moment quite positive. But when Petrarch completes the equation of speaker with metamorphosed laurel tree ("la trasfigurata mia persona"), the transformation is so absolute—indeed, when he takes root, he is as frozen as any of Medusa's victims—that his own identity is lost in the change. "I capei vidi far di quella fronde / di che sperato avea già lor corona" (ll. 43–44: "[I] saw my hairs turning into those leaves which I had formerly hoped would be my crown") suggests that in the throes of passion he no longer possesses the independent identity that can make him a poet.

The sequence of transformations that follows continues the complicated play on these same issues: a transfigured identity, a poetic voice built out of a suffering that may itself silence the poetic voice, endless change, endless frozenness. The speaker becomes Phaethon ("il mio sperar che tropp' alto montava"; l. 53: "my hope that was mounting too high") and Cygnus, the singer of the swan song lamenting Phaethon's death. The combination is significant: subject and object at once, the hero of a divine tragedy and the poet chronicling that tragedy. As Phaethon he is destroyed, but as Cygnus he is an image of flow and communication. If Phaethon and Cygnus are all too perfect a pair of identities for an autobiographical poet with heroic aspirations, the triumph still does not last. His lady directly silences him. Taking his heart in her hand, she says, "Di ciò non far parola" (l. 74: "Make no word of this"), and the action turns him into a Battus, who was tricked by Mercury into revealing the god's secrets and thus proving himself untrustworthy. In the process, Laura's identity is multiplied just as her lover's has been, for in the story of Battus, Mercury appears in two different guises and goes unrecognized both times. Battus's crime was speech and his punishment was petrification. So the swan song of poetry is silenced, and metamorphic fixity becomes that of a rock.

A similar process emerges in the next pair of transformations. The tears, as in Cygnus's swan song, flow again, and the lover becomes, Byblis-like, a fountain of sorrow, for the power of metamorphosis enables rocks to dissolve through sorrowful suffering. He loses himself in the flow and is ultimately pardoned by his beloved. Then, however, he makes the mistake of renewing his pleas (*ri-pregando* tips us off about the myth that is to follow), and the flow is stopped when the lover becomes Echo, at once rock and voice:

> i nervi et l'ossa
> mi volse in dura selce, et così scossa

voce rimasi de l'antiche some,
chiamando Morte et lei sola per nome. [ll. 137–40]

(She turned my sinews and bones into hard flint, and thus I remained a voice shaken from my former burden, calling Death and only her by name.)

As in Petrarch's version of the Daphne myth, the poet in the person of Echo is again transformed into his beloved, but it is an ironically empty union of identities. He is one with her only in the sense that he can repeat her name, while his physical form is flinty rock.

The Actaeon myth is the suitable climax for all these transformations. Just as we are prepared for Echo by *ripregare*, so we are prepared for Actaeon by the introduction to the final full stanza:

Spirto doglioso errante mi rimembra
per spelunche deserte et pellegrine
piansi molt' anni il mio sfrenato ardire,
et ancor poi trovai di quel mal fine
et ritornai ne le terrene membra,
credo per più dolore ivi sentire. [ll. 141–46]

(A wandering sorrowful spirit, I remember, through desert ravines and strange, I bewailed for many years my unleashed boldness, and still later found release from that ill and returned again to my earthly members, in order, I believe, to feel more pain there.)

It is not only that being unleashed in the wilderness is at the heart of Ovid's Actaeon story; more important is the very telling use of *rimembra* and *membra*. These are terms that resound through the sequence, which in its entirety is an act of *rimembranza*. The positive hope is that through poetic re-memberment, the speaker will save his own life and limb from the dangers of passion and also from the physical depredations of age.[100] The myth of Actaeon, however, is par excellence the tale of *dis*memberment. As such it speaks not only of the failure of the poetic effort but also of the fragmentation of identity. Throughout its history this myth has been connected with shifting and mirror-like identities,[101] and it forms the climax of this canzone because all the identities in the poem have been made uncertain through metamorphosis. "I' non son forse chi tu credi" (l.83: "I am not perhaps who you think I am"), says the beloved, and a few lines later the poet cries, "Non son mio" (l.100: "I am not my own"). Identities have been shifting as with mirrors. The poet and Laura, Phaethon and Cygnus, and the sequence Battus, Byblis, Echo: all suggest mirrored oppositions. Finally, as Actaeon the poet is definitively drawn out of himself:

Io perché d'altra vista non m'appago
stetti a mirarla, ond' ella ebbe vergogna

et per farne vendetta o per celarse
l'acqua nel viso co le man mi sparse.
Vero dirò; forse e' parrà menzogna:
ch' i' senti' trarmi de la propria imago.   [ll. 152–57]

(I, who am not appeased by any other sight, stood to gaze on her,
whence she felt shame and, to take revenge or to hide herself, sprin-
kled water in my face with her hand. I shall speak the truth, perhaps
it will appear a lie, for I felt myself drawn from my own image.)

The separation of objective form and perceiving subject—a very Ovidian
motif well prepared for by the earlier groups of transformations—is complete. The lover's identity is finally split between the helpless victim and
the poetic lamenter. Most of his earlier forms have involved these combinations: Phaethon vs. Cygnus, Battus vs. Byblis, and finally Echo, who
helplessly combined the two roles. Now we have the stag and the hounds,

et in un cervo solitario et vago
di selva in selva ratto mi trasformo,
et ancor de' miei can fuggo lo stormo.   [ll. 158–60]

(And into a solitary wandering stag from wood to wood quickly I am
transformed and still I flee the belling of my hounds.)

The stag is the frightened lonely victim and the hounds are the passionate
forces that may represent his love, his moral instincts, or his capacity to
perceive. The objects of transformation have been steadily devalued.
From poetic and amorous *lauro*, we have moved to swan song to fountain
to the relatively empty Echo; finally the dismembered poet can produce
nothing more than the barking of dogs—at the furthest possible remove
from poetry.

But the poem does not end here; nor does the subject of metamorphosis. The *congedo*, or envoy, amounts to a radical revision:

Canzon, i' non fu' mai quel nuvol d'oro
che poi discese in preziosa pioggia
sì che 'l foco di Giove in parte spense;
ma fui ben fiamma ch' un bel guardo accense,
et fui l'uccel che più per l'aere poggia
alzando lei che ne' miei detti onoro
né per nova figura il primo alloro
seppi lassar, ché pur la sua dolce ombra
ogni men bel piacer del cor mi sgombra.   [ll. 161–69]

(Song, I was never the cloud of gold that once descended in a precious rain so that it partly quenched the fire of Jove; but I have certainly been a flame lit by a lovely glance and I have been the bird
that rises highest in the air raising her whom in my words I honor;

nor for any new shape could I leave the first laurel, for still its sweet
shade turns away from my heart any less beautiful pleasure.)

These metamorphoses of the poet follow logically from all the earlier ones
in that they are unmediated identifications with the mythic objects of
transformation. But, by shifting from stony mortal metamorphoses to the
ecstatic changes of Jupiter the lover-god, the poet not only identifies love
and metamorphosis but also revalues that connection as absolute and joyous. He tells us that he was not Danae's golden shower because his desire, unlike Jupiter's, was not quenched. But he is the flame (of Aegina or
Semele) because of his passion, and he is Ganymede's (or Asterie's) eagle
because of the emotional exaltation he has felt. Through the figure of
these metamorphic loves, he can declare that passion and exaltation are
valuable metamorphoses in spite of the agony that accompanies them.
What makes them worth the trouble is the poetic act itself; and as we saw
in discussing medieval rhetoric, Jupiter's transformations were often used
as emblems of the poetic imagination. So, using two key words in the history of our subject, Petrarch at the nadir point of his experience declares
that he is drawn out of his own *imago*, meaning that he is metamorphosed
and poetically bankrupt; now, in the envoy, he tells us that he would not
leave that original laurel for any *nova figura*. The laurel is the primary
metamorphosis, and that *figura* brings Petrarch's art back to life.

This discussion of Petrarch's art is not meant to suggest that his Renaissance successors learned to practice all his complex nuances in their presentation of pagan metamorphosis. Indeed, in this as in other realms, it is
quite possible to argue that Petrarch was more Renaissance than the Renaissance and that his successors over the next two centuries retreated
rather than advanced from his example. Yet, even if they could not equal
him, they could (and did) certainly read him. The *Rime* in particular existed as a great encyclopedia for the depiction of passionate human emotions expressed in the mythic language of metamorphosis. In a sense they
stand to their posterity as Ovid stands to his. Like the *Metamorphoses*,
the *Rime* not only collect myths of transformation but also transform the
myths. Poems like *Rime* 23 revise myth and make it over into a personal
vehicle for the communication of intense feelings. The poet goes even
further after Laura's death in *Rime* 323 (the number is surely no coincidence) to transform the transformations with the metamorphoses re-
played in jumbled form as apocalyptic visions. A "fera . . . con fronte
umana da far arder Giove, / cacciata da duo veltri . . . / . . . [e] chiusa in
un sasso" (ll.5–6, 10: "a wild creature . . . with a human face such as to en-
amor Jove, pursued by two hounds, one black, one white . . . closed in a
stone") combines Actaeon with the loves of Jupiter and with the myths of
petrification. The laurel seems to be "un delli arbor . . . di paradiso" (l.27:
"one of the trees of Eden"), but it is pulled up by the roots. There are

metamorphoses of a fountain from stone and of a phoenix. The canzone concludes with an almost inevitable myth never cited elsewhere, that of Orpheus and Eurydice, a type of the dead beloved whom the poet-lover finally cannot bring back to life. It may seem a long way from Petrarch's transformed metamorphoses to, say, Titian's highly original Europa. But it is not. Both artists are concerned with passion, and both find in the codes of metamorphosis a language for passion and at the same time a freedom to remake the very myths that form the basis for that language.

Two hundred years after Petrarch's *Rime*, passionate love and mythic metamorphosis remain closely paired, but the changing significances of the pairing help demonstrate the nature of the intervening period—in fact, the Renaissance proper. Pierre Ronsard, especially in the early part of his career, is obsessed with metamorphosis, as many critics have noted; to understand its position in his work is also to observe the history of its connections with Petrarchism in the Renaissance.[102] Among the early *Amours* of the 1550s, the reference to a hundred (or a thousand) *metamorphoses* turns up with sufficient regularity to be termed a cliché by one set of editors.[103] The contexts, for the most part, are familiarly Petrarchan: in one case, the escape to solitary suffering in the wilderness, in another the myths of Jupiter's transformations, in a third a blazon to his lady's face.

Following the example of Petrarch, Ronsard sets the experience of metamorphosis in the lush context of classical mythology reborn:

> Je veulx darder par l'univers ma peine,
>> Plus tost qu'un trait ne volle au descocher:
>> Je veulx de miel mes oreilles boucher
>> Pour n'ouir plus la voix de ma Sereine.
> Je veulx muer mes deux yeulx en fontaine,
>> Mon cuoeur en feu, ma teste en un rocher,
>> Mes piedz en tronc, pour jamais n'aprocher
>> De sa beaulté si fierement humaine.
> Je veulx changer mes pensers en oyseaux,
>> Mes doux souspirs en zephyres nouveaux,
>> Qui par le monde evanteront ma pleinte.
> Et veulx encor de ma palle couleur,
>> Dessus le Loyr enfanter une fleur,
>> Qui de mon nom & de mon mal soit peinte.   [*Amours* 16]

It is a condensed imitation of Petrarch's first canzone. What Ronsard captures in the original (and it is intensified by the condensation) is the relation between myths of transformation and transformations of myths. Homeric, Ovidian, and Petrarchan materials are elided in the flow of the verse and amalgamated in a continuous mode of desire. Some of the mythic materials are clearly identifiable—Odysseus, whose wax is sensuously changed to honey, and the memorializing flower-metamorphosis of Ajax—while others are deliberately vague and allusive, so that we think of the Ovidian universe without being able to assign a precise mythic analogue to the lover's present experience.

In fact, the amatory meaning of metamorphosis, which receives such a complicated definition in the Petrarchan original, is here almost completely undermined. *Je veulx* begins each section of the sonnet in traditional erotic fashion, but what does he want, and why does he seek metamorphosis? The stated objective is generally anesthetic and anaphrodisiac; yet the erotic associations of Cupid's arrow, or of *miel* rather than wax, or of *mon cuoeur en feu*, as well as the repeated verb of desire, contradict that objective. The only consistent objective is the desire for fame and immortality, which opens the poem with reference to the poet's suffering and closes it with a myth of signature, the metamorphosis that memorialized both the name and the suffering of Ajax by including the syllable AI on his flower.[104]

Literary self-consciousness does not distinguish this sonnet from Petrarch's, but its refusal to interpret the myths does. From the retrospect of Ronsard, Petrarch seems to have viewed the pagan materials in fundamentally intellectual and rhetorical terms. Ronsard, on the other hand, dissolves meaning much as metamorphosis dissolves clear shapes. For him myth and change exist in a world of sensuality:

> Soit que son or se crespe lentement
>> Ou soit qu'il vague en deux glissantes ondes,
>> Qui çà qui là par le sein vagabondes,
>> Et sur le col, nagent follastrement:
> Ou soit qu'un noud diapré tortement
>> De maintz rubiz, & maintes perles rondes,
>> Serre les flotz de ses deux tresses blondes,
>> Je me contente en mon contentement.
> Quel plaisir est ce, ainçoys quelle merveille
>> Quand ses cheveux troussez dessus l'oreille
>> D'une Venus imitent la façon?
> Quand d'un bonet son chef elle adonize,
>> Et qu'on ne sçait (tant bien elle desguise
>> Son chef doubteux) s'elle est fille ou garçon?   [*Amours* 90]

Metamorphosis itself is never mentioned here, but the atmosphere is one of constant movement and flow. All exists in the hypothetical mode ("Soit que . . . "), and within that hypothesis there is an easy sense that traditional distinctions are unimportant. The speaker requires no rigidly upright headdress for his mistress, and once that order dissolves, then it matters little just how her hair flows. But flow it does: *vague* plus *ondes* equals *vagabondes*; and the sense of aqueous motion quite naturally introduces the figure of love who rises from the sea. Yet just as the words dissolve, so do the myths. *Une Venus* suggests as much a work of art as a goddess, and *adonize* is a present-tense process rather than a Greek boy. If the ancient myths dissolve into the here-and-now, they also dissolve into each other. The *adonizification* of Venus is a metamorphosis that climaxes the *soit que* mode of the poem. It changes a girl into a boy just as it changes a person into a myth. Petrarch struggled to make distinctions with his reinterpretations of classical myths, while Ronsard enjoys the unclarity of distinctions. His delighted indifference to the various possibilities of his mistress's hair leads to an even more delighted indifference to her (apparent) gender. In the changes comes the erotic pleasure itself.[105]

Metamorphosis, then, becomes something more than pure psychic agony:

> Ha, seigneur Dieu, que de graces écloses
>   Dans le jardin de ce sein verdelet,
>   Enflent le rond de deus gazons de lait,
>   Où des Amours les fléches sont encloses!
> Je me transforme en cent metamorfoses,
>   Quand je te voi, petit mont jumelet,
>   Ains du printans un rosier nouvelet,
>   Qui le matin bienveigne de ses roses.
> S'Europe avoit l'estomac aussi beau
>   De t'estre fait, Jupiter, un toreau,
>   Je te pardonne. Hé, que ne sui-je puce!
> La baisotant, tous les jours je mordroi
>   Ses beau tetins, mais la nuit je voudroi
>   Que rechanger en homme je me pusse.   [*Amours* 41]

At first the poem seems neatly posed between chaste contemplation and active sexual desire. While the object of the lover's gaze is the breast, the images of spring and of blooming hillocks seem distanced from direct sexuality. The hundred metamorphoses, with all their Petrarchan associations, refer apparently to the emotional excitements of love. But the train of the lover's thought is sharply diverted when his own metamorphoses make him think of Jupiter. The *seigneur Dieu* of the first line turns from Christian to pagan in retrospect, and with that love turns to sex. That Ovid's Jupiter changed his form for strategic purposes is irrelevant here; rather, it is the girl's beauty that directly produces animal transformation. Indeed, "De t'estre fait" seems first to be the object of "aussi beau" before it becomes attached to "Je te pardonne," intensifying the sense that Europa's anatomy was directly responsible for Jupiter's metamorphosis.

The purpose of the transformation is further clarified when the poet proposes his own equivalent: he will become a flea so that he can have the pleasure of biting her breasts. This is, of course, a common Renaissance trope[106] but, placed in the context of the metamorphic loves of the gods, it deflates all the pretensions of that tradition and leaves only the animal sexuality. The sharp break of "Je te pardonne" in the flowing melodic line of the poem signals the change from amorous contemplation to amorous action, and the simple, almost colloquial "Hé, que ne sui-je puce!" suggests that it is not so much the speaker who has pardoned Jupiter as the reverse: the god's example offers the lover permission for his explicit sexual fantasies. The last lines solidify the redefinition of metamorphosis. The lover abandons his flea-transformation and *rechange* into a man at night: metamorphosis, in other words, is tumescence. With that definition, all the poem's other changes in turn change their meaning: the "cent metamorfoses" can now be seen as a sexual response to a naked breast, and the story of Jove and Europa consists in an *estomac beau* inspiring animal lust.

The equation of Jupiter's animal shapes with sexual arousal is not merely the isolated notion of a single poet with a lurid imagination. We have already seen how Correggio's *Amori di Giove*—especially the *Io* and the *Leda*—use metamorphosis to depict the sexual act. The image of girl and god in the midst of love-making finds its proximate origins in Michelangelo's *Leda*, of which the (now lost) original went to France and clearly inspired some of the mannerist decoratioms at the court of Fontainebleau, Ronsard's precise milieu.[107] But the equation of metamorphosis and sex is no mere consequence of mannerist libertinism. Given the moralistic traditions surrounding the Ovidian material, sexual arousal could easily be understood as animal transformation. Moreover, a rampant bull, or the long phallic neck of a swan, or a golden spray that points itself toward a girl's womb, especially once they are seen as pictures, possesses strong powers of suggestion.

There is also a special kind of tease in images of metamorphic love not present in, say, pictures of Mars and Venus or Cupid and Psyche. The icons of Jupiter's sexual conquests replace the anthropomorphic male lover with another creature or manifestation. (Indeed, that is what makes it permissible to depict the sexual act.) Quite often the metamorphic substitute for the aroused male almost disappears from the picture. Golden showers are especially ephemeral: Primaticcio's *Danae*, surely well known to Ronsard, is just one example of a figure who spreads her limbs and lifts away the covering garment so that we can see the results. Michelangelo's swan seems to fade away in the embrace of Leda's legs, Titian's bull is on the wrong side to receive any of the pleasures of Europa's open-limbed position, and the satyr in many an *Antiope* watches the naked sleeping girl from behind while we get the full frontal view. The intention of such design is to enable the male viewer to imagine himself entering the scene and replacing the displaced lover; and the great collections of mythological subjects assembled in the sixteenth century by patrons like Philip II, Federico Gonzaga, and François I were in part motivated by this pornographic impulse. It is more than pornography; it is also egoism. Love sonnets like Ronsard's are inspired by these images in part because they, too, are erotic fantasies, frames inside which female beauty is celebrated but in which the reader/viewer (who may also be the poet/painter) can insert his own sexual imagination.

The imagination is all-important. We saw in the *Ledas* of Correggio and Michelangelo that they were not only in sexual ecstasy but also in a state of dream. If one Renaissance redefinition of amorous metamorphosis is as a version of the sexual act, another is that of the dream:

> Quand en songeant ma follastre j'acolle,
>> Laissant mes flancz sus les siens s'allonger,
>> Et que d'un bransle habillement leger,
>> En sa moytié ma moytié je recolle:
> Amour adonq si follement m'affolle,
>> Qu'un tel abus je ne vouldroy changer,
>> Non au butin d'un rivage estranger,
>> Non au sablon qui jaunoye en Pactole.
> Mon dieu, quel heur, & quel contentement,
>> M'a fait sentir ce faux recollement,
>> Changeant ma vie en cent metamorphoses:
> Combien de fois doulcement irrité,
>> Suis-je ore mort, ore resuscité,
>> Parmy l'odeur de mile & mile roses?   [*Amours* 127][108]

The elements in the fantasy world read like a cast of characters of Renaissance metamorphosis: dream; the Platonic myth of the Androgyne given a directly sexual implication; madness; Ovidian mythology. The elision amongst the elements, such as we saw in "Soit que . . . ," itself forms part of the dream-world, and it is expressed by countless words with similar sounds and transformed meanings: *recoller* (stick together) and *recollement* (recollection), or *follastre* (playful), *follement* (madly), and *affoller* (seize with love). The *cent metamorphoses* are the central hinge upon which the poem turns. They sum up the dream-world of the first part with all its changes of mood, subject, and poetic language, and they point toward a different vision of change in the second, as the sweet irritation and the life and death develop an unmistakable primary meaning of carnality.

Unrealized sexual desire ("Je veulx . . . Je veulx . . . Je veulx . . . ") unites itself quite logically with fantasy. For Ronsard, the world of myth is almost literally a golden age—hence his telling reference to the transformations of Midas. It is a world of escape from harsh reality. That reality may be the cruelty of a lady who cannot or will not love him, or it may be the harshness of life in France during the period of the religious wars. The escape from such a reality is itself a metamorphosis, a translation from the quotidian world into the golden, like the *adonizification* of the beloved's hair. Whether the poet longs to be transformed into water so that he can touch the boat on which his lady is sailing away:

> On dit au temps passé que quelques uns changerent
> En riviere leur forme, & eus mesmes nagerent
> En l'eau qui de leur sang & de leurs yeux sailloit,
> Quand leur corps ondoyant peu à peu defailloit:
> Que ne puis-je muer ma resamblance humaine
> En la forme de l'eau qui cette barque emmeine!

> ["Voyage de Tours," ll.229–34]

or whether he is longing to identify himself with the figures of pagan myth ("Je voudrois estre Ixion & Tantale"; *Amours* 45), he is indulging in the fantasy of replacing his world with the golden world of myth,[109] and that fantasy is itself a metamorphosis. In that world, dream becomes reality, base metals become gold, and amorous wishes come true.

The masterpiece of the wish-fulfillment poems is also a poem of metamorphosis:

> Je vouldroy bien richement jaunissant
> > En pluye d'or goute à goute descendre
> > Dans le beau sein de ma belle Cassandre,
> > Lors qu'en ses yeulx le somme va glissant.
> Je vouldroy bien en toreau blandissant
> > Me transformer pour finement la prendre,
> > Quand elle va par l'herbe la plus tendre
> > Seule à l'escart mille fleurs ravissant.
> Je vouldroy bien afin d'aiser ma peine
> > Estre un Narcisse, & elle une fontaine
> > Pour m'y plonger une nuict à sejour:
> Et vouldroy bien que ceste nuict encore
> > Durast tousjours sans que jamais l'Aurore
> > D'un front nouveau nous r'allumast le jour. [*Amours* 20]

What the poet cannot achieve in reality can be wished for in the world of Ovidian transformation. If metamorphosis is dream, it is also sexuality: the drops of the golden shower and the plunging into the beloved as fountain are clearly transformations of carnality. Sex and dream combine here in a metamorphic poetics of constant motion: *jaunissant, glissant, blandissant, ravissant*. The gradual present participle in the first case emphasizes the process of change: the poet has not become a golden shower but is rather in the process of goldening. *Glissant* turns the rather static condition of sleep into a gradual domination of Danae's eyes by the force of *sommeil*. In the context of *jaunissant, blandissant* becomes a pun. The editors gloss the word as "caressant, séducteur," which is accurate, so far as it goes. Yet the parallel to *jaunissant* makes us think of the process of whitening, and we must recall, as Ronsard surely would have recalled, the emphasis Ovid places in his account of the Europa story upon the whiteness of the bull.[110] So the lover "whitens" his way toward the bull just as he "goldens" his way toward the shower. *Ravissant* is the climactic participle of this sequence, ostensibly referring to Europa's flower-picking, but in the context of all the metamorphic progressives that precede, the word obviously takes on its sexual meaning. Thus Ronsard reenacts the relation we observed many pages ago between Europa's activities and the conquest of her innocence.[111]

The participles cease in the sestet because the poet has reached the goal of his metamorphic progression. Narcissus breaks the sequence of Jovian myths but not of metamorphoses since "estre *un* Narcisse" surely suggests a flower-transformation as much as a transformation of the speaker into Narcissus himself. Water, which Ronsard frequently sees as the most metamorphic of elements, suggests in the context of the Narcissus myth the barrier that the speaker must cross so as actually to enter the reality of the pagan dream-world. To plunge into the fountain is to enter that reality and to experience the sexual act at once. The final three lines take place in the world that unifies metamorphosis, dream, and sexuality. Which night, exactly, is *ceste nuit*? It is the night in which the lover is dreaming of his desires. But *ceste nuit* that lasts so long is also an important feature of another of Jupiter's amorous metamorphoses, his impersonation of Amphitryon, in the course of which he arranges a triple-length night in which to enjoy Alcmena's charms. The final vision is one of eternal sensuality. Metamorphosis creates a permanence of sex, dream, and the golden imaginary world of myth. Other Renaissance poets may elide the terms less completely and may subject eros to sterner judgment than does Ronsard, but the associations among passion, paganism, and transformation continue to reflect a Petrarchan heritage not entirely in keeping with Petrarch himself.[112]

4. Triumphs and Ceremonies

Considering Europa's triumphant wedding, Actaeon's visionary confrontation with the divine, Ganymede's heavenly assumption, and Daphne's creative relation to the poet's laurel, it comes as no surprise to a modern reader that metamorphic myths might celebrate order just as well as they celebrate passion. All of these results taken together speak to a belief that passion can produce via metamorphosis some triumphant result that unifies earth and heaven. This belief is not entirely new in the Renaissance. We have seen how from the twelfth century onwards the Ovidian pantheon coexisted with Natura. We have also seen how the tortured *in bono* analyses of late medieval mythography gave Christians permission to look beyond the merely moral level in imagining the connections among pagan religion, love, and metamorphosis. Another factor emerges with the greater secularization of European society at the end of the Middle Ages. Individuals, families, monarchs, and temporal institutions begin to look for sets of images, myths, and rhetorical devices that will give them the kind of grounding that the church has long enjoyed.[113] The recuperated world of pagan mythology offers such a set of images, whose cosmic and natural associations place the individual in a context of universal harmony. So the Renaissance invents or reinvents whole languages and genres to express this harmony.

The most straightforward of these genres takes us back to our touchstone Europa. There was no doubt in antiquity that the triumphant ritual which affirmed the fearful metamorphic experience in her case was the wedding; and, as has often been pointed out, epithalamic conventions were charged with intense significance in the Renaissance.[114] It is no surprise that for Spenser and the others marriage should become an emblem for the individual's link in the great chain uniting love with universal harmony. What is more surprising is the link between pagan myths and Renaissance celebrations of wedding. There are, to be sure, some ancient myths that might be expected to appear in the context of chaste Christian marriages. One thinks of Odysseus and Penelope, Philemon and Baucis, perhaps Lucretia. But in most of the Ovidian heritage there is little tailormade to adorn the marriage bed and much that had best be kept away from bride and groom, lest it set a bad example. In spite of this obvious fact, marriage celebration and pagan myth were joined all over Renaissance Europe.

A concrete set of exhibits demonstrates this conjunction of pagan eroticism and Christian wedding. Beginning in the early fifteenth century it became customary among the wealthy urban families of Northern Italy to provide painted hope chests, or *cassoni*, for their newlywed daughters.[115] As Vasari explains, these were painted on different sides and decorated "for the most part with myths drawn from Ovid and other poets, or else from histories recounted by Greek and Latin historians";[116] he also indicates that the greatest painters of the time strove for these commissions. Among the numerous examples preserved, pagan subjects far outnumber Christian; nor is there any particular emphasis upon the more elevated of pagan tales. There was, to be sure, a Christian backlash against the practice. Even contemporaries were surprised and dismayed that tales of ancient concupiscence should be chosen for wedding celebrations. Savonarola in one of his sermons despairs over the fact that young brides know more about the adultery of Mars and Venus than about biblical examples of chastity. Elsewhere he comments, "Tu direi, Ovidio Metamorphoseos è pure buono. Io ti rispondo: Ovidio fabuloso, Ovidio pazzo!"[117] Despite Savonarola the tradition continued, and as early as

1500 the cassone was already a significant vehicle for the dissemination of pagan iconography and an important medium for major artists.

If we look at the cassone subjects—so many of them involving Jupiter's transformations, the rapes of Helen and Proserpina, forbidden loves between gods and mortals, and so on—and ask what the painter (or the family who commissioned the painter) was trying to tell the newlyweds, we are left rather in confusion, as is Burckhardt when he declares that the Rape of Helen was unsuitable for the didactic purposes of a wedding plate.[118] If, on the other hand, we view the practice in the light of recuperated paganism, then it becomes clear that the occasion of a marriage speaks to all those powerful natural drives that operate so triumphantly in the Ovidian world. Hence the frequency of amatory (even dangerously amatory) subject matter, not only of an Ovidian kind but also including the Judgment of Paris (where Venus *vincit omnia*) and certain tales with a similar burden from the *Decameron*, including those of Alatiel and Nastagio degli Onesti.[119] To reenact pagan tales of all-powerful love, natural growth, and metamorphosis in the safe and sanctioned precincts of a hope chest is to express once again the balance between passion and order. Metamorphosis plays a particularly significant role because it is a miracle of love; it is joined with all sorts of fabulous subjects, Christian as well as pagan, to suggest (as so often) the divine emerging from the natural.

This emergence may be clarified with the example of a very beautiful early sixteenth-century Europa cassone now in the Louvre (figure 36).[120] We see the story proleptically as we read from right to left: the arrival of the girls at the shore; their dance; Europa climbing aboard the bull; Europa and the bull traversing the water while the girls look on; finally Europa and Jupiter on Crete. The visual language of this depiction emphasizes the rite de passage. The painter uses the inevitable cassone shape to dramatize the gradual progress, a long separation from the beginning to the end of the story; he also makes much of the dark expanse of sea that the girl must cross. Nor does the land on the other side seem nearly so secure and supportive as the coast from which she came. Yet if these features suggest the artist's preoccupation with Europa's painful process, in other ways the style seems to convey a sense of propriety and orderliness that befits the wedding celebration for which the piece was destined. The very use of a proleptic narrative without separating the different stages into individual panels stresses the inevitable flow of the story.[121] There is also a particularly graceful quality to this flow, especially given the various pointings to the left (i.e., toward the resolution of the story) which can be observed in the representations of Europa in the beginning of the story and of the bull from the middle onwards. Uniting all the stages in the story is the repeated icon of the metamorphic creature.

The cassone serves for a private ceremony. Of greater importance was the paganizing imagery in public ceremonies. We cannot do full justice to the spectacular public entertainments of the Renaissance here, but their relevance cannot be ignored. From Burckhardt onward scholars of the period have focused upon these events as essential to the spirit of the time.[122] They exist at the junction of art and life, of aesthetics and politics, of the plastic and the dramatic arts, of words and pictures. Whether they take the form of royal entries into cities, banquet-hall ballets, or staged tournaments, they are celebrations of power and harmony, and by the High Renaissance their language is above all that of antiquity. The origins of the form are not in themselves classical. In the later Middle Ages, and continuing into the sixteenth century north of the Alps, the entry of a king into a town was celebrated with a procession of largely liturgical origins, eventually coming to be decorated with the figures of medieval allegory and romance. But, as early as the mid-fifteenth century in Italy, the public outdoor spectacle became a great stage of antique images. A revival of interest in the more imperial aspects of Roman antiquity—precisely those we have paid little attention to here—was not inspired by pure learned humanism but by the pressure of princely families looking for a personal mythology. Mantegna's well-researched *Triumph of Caesar* series, executed for the Gonzaga family, became the basis for three-dimensional pageantry all over Europe.[123] The Roman triumphal procession came to be understood as the model for all such political ceremonies at just the time when Roman imperial values were being revived as (attempted) state ideology. Charles V sought to consolidate an empire and so used Roman architecture and classical myth; Catherine de Medici sought to pacify a tumultuous kingdom with Roman-style bread and circuses and so revived ancient music, poetry, and dance.[124]

Even if the origins of the spectacle are purely imperial, the whole pantheon of antiquity moves into the show. All the verbal and pictorial imagery in which the world of the pagan gods is revived soon becomes three-dimensional in the spectacles. The same Borso d'Este who commissioned the Schifanoia frescoes is celebrated in a classical pageant.[125] Medieval images of the gods like those of Boccaccio, Martianus Capella, and Macrobius are all combined in the *Masque of the Genealogy of the Gods* performed in celebration of the marriage of Francesco de' Medici.[126] The hieroglyphics of Valeriano and the emblems of Alciati are brought to life, inspiring the same complex aesthetics of picture and word associated with two-dimensional images of the gods—that is, a set of tensions between manifest and occult allegory.[127] So, just to choose an example familiar to us, we have in the 1571 entry into Paris of Elizabeth of Austria (the text of which was partly written by Ronsard) a triumphal arch surmounted by what appears to be Europa on the bull until we learn from the text that it is the nymph Asia, whose presence in this "European" context is meant to remind us that the French monarchs are descended from Troy and that they will conquer both Europe and Asia.[128]

Both wedding celebration and political pageant as they are practiced in the antique style emanate from a pre-Renaissance source whose very nature is defined by its own classical origins, the *Trionfi* of Petrarch.[129] The first (particularly influential and important for us) is a Triumph of Love, and each succeeding triumph overwhelms the previous victor: Chastity, Death, Fame, Time, and Eternity. The form is in some ways typically medieval, since these triumphs arise out of a dream vision and essentially take the form of allegorical processions asserting the unstable and fleeting nature of earthly things. Yet the spirit of these poems is classical and humanistic. Inspired by Dante—and no works show more powerfully the influence of the *Divine Comedy*—Petrarch peoples his world with figures of mythology and classical history indiscriminately joined with biblical characters and contemporary Europeans. But it is not just the personages that make the poems classical: it is the form itself. Petrarch makes the Roman triumphal procession of victorious generals, with all their slaves and booty, into a universalizing metaphor that gives love, chastity, death, and so on a history and a mythology. So he takes Dante's dramatic world and gives it his own invented version of a classical Roman structure.

The triumph is not only classical; it is also metamorphic. Petrarch invented a form in constant flux between shadow and substance. Out of the proverbially insubstantial world of the dream, he builds a gigantic structure of materiality, which (especially in the earlier triumphs) is above all the classical world itself.[130] Yet that materiality is ultimately a sham that crumbles to dust before a greater reality. These shifts are at the very heart of metamorphosis. In part this metamorphic flux reminds us of the ancient connections we observed between image and metamorphosis. Petrarch's triumphs are gigantic ekphrases, or verbal descriptions of a visual work of art. When, as so often, they are translated back to the visual in cassone panels, paintings, or staged pageants, they keep alive the vision of antiquity as a glorious but fleeting moment of frozen change.

The Triumph of Love—Petrarch's and the whole tradition—is especially relevant. The very junction of *triumph* and *love* goes back to myths of metamorphosis, especially Ovid's story of Apollo and Daphne, hardly a surprising reference in the mind of a poet so obsessed with Laura and laurels. Ovid began that story with a Triumph of Amor, when Apollo boasts that his own weapons are more powerful than those of the young love-god and is punished by falling hopelessly in love with Daphne. The ultimate effect of that love is the creation of the laurel tree, which Apollo apostrophizes,

> tu ducibus Latiis aderis, cum laeta Triumphum
> vox canet et visent longas Capitolia pompas.   [1.560–61]

(With thee shall Roman generals wreathe their heads, when shouts of joy shall acclaim their triumph, and long processions climb the Capitol.)

It is an etiology not only of laurels but also of triumphs and of the associations between the two. Here, in one of the first and most important stories of his poem, Ovid is concerned to dissolve the military power of the Roman general's triumph by reminding us that its iconography goes back to a passionate love story and that such a hero as the Python-slayer was himself defeated by love. These shifts in power may well be the source of that whole motif in the *Trionfi*; in addition, if Ovid dissolves the military laurel into the laurel of love, then Petrarch can add the laurel of the poet.

If there are metamorphic shifts in power within this form, there are also metamorphic shifts in meaning. What is a *Trionfo d'Amore*? If *Amore* is the abstract noun, as in Europa's various orgasmic sea-crossings, then everyone involved—Venus, Mars, Theseus, Sophonisba, and the rest —is triumphantly celebrating love. If *Amore* is Cupid, as the Latin subtitle *Triumphus Cupidinis* suggests, then all the rest are slaves of their passion. Needless to say, both meanings are suggested; and the whole strategy of the poems points to these shifts in power: world-conquering figures of classical history like Caesar and Alexander appear toward the front (greater rank, or greater slavery?), while Jupiter, as befits his greatest power and greatest sexuality, is chained at the head of all. And of course even the all-powerful Amor will be dethroned in the next triumph, and so on and so on.

Petrarch's form may universalize, and he may (quite provisionally) celebrate a Triumph of Love, but he does not attempt a cosmic justification of sexuality. If he invented a new form in which that was possible, then it was Francesco Colonna, in that remarkable source-book of iconography, allegory, and mystery lore, the *Hypnerotomachia Poliphili*, who created the influential triumphs that achieved this translation.[131] This dream-vision, the great visual masterpiece of early printing, was the first work of nonclassical literature published by the important Venetian printer Aldo Minutio. It is written in a patois of Italian and Latin, decorated with dozens of beautiful woodcuts that are among the most influential pieces of Renaissance iconography, and it finds its sources in all the paganizing literary traditions of the past: Ovid, Apuleius, the Greek Romances (among authentic pagans), along with twelfth-century nature poetry, Petrarch, and the arcane learning of the early Renaissance. The "plot" of the first part of the dream vision concerns the initiation of the lover by his beloved, beginning with the rejection of abstract paths of love and culminating with a vision of the goddess Venus. At approximately the midpoint of this progress, Polifilo is shown a four-part triumph of love. Each of the four focuses on one of the metamorphic loves of Jupiter: Europa, Leda, Danae, and Semele, with all the chariots but the last surmounted by representations of the girls in amorous contact with Jupiter in his transformed shape. (Semele, whose story is not literally metamorphic, differs: her chariot is surmounted by a vase with Bacchic emblems.)

Colonna describes—and his volume illustrates—the front, back, and sides of the four chariots, as well as in each case a long view, including attendants, insignias, and exotic animals drawing the carts. All these surroundings speak to a universalizing of metamorphic love. The sides of the chariots extend the act of love historically. In a few cases they are events prior to the sexual union (Europa placing a garland on the bull's neck, then beginning to cross the water; Danae's father receiving the oracle and enclosing her in a tower). For the most part, however, the emphasis is upon future progeny and result: Leda's *accouchement*, the delivery of the mysterious eggs, one bearing a flame and the other two stars, along with the riddling explanation of this prodigious birth by the oracle of Apollo; the career of Perseus, Danae's child; the birth of Bacchus and his infancy among the nymphs. These are not random pieces of history. In every case they place the sexual union in the context of grandly far-ranging results; for the lives of Perseus, of Bacchus, of Helen and the Dioscuri represent some of the vastest sagas of antiquity.

If the sides of the chariots tell the history of love, then on the front we can read its cosmic power. In a kind of riposte to Petrarch's *Triumphus Cupidinis*, where Jupiter appears on the front, here on the triumphs of Jupiter it is Cupid whose figures on each front panel. In each case, the picture is a tiny cosmology of the amorous universe: on the ground a group of amorous mortals *vulnerata* or *sagittati* by love's arrows, while the heavens above are depicted under the sway of the little love-god himself. As we proceed through the sequence, Cupid's triumph escalates. First he is on the ground, shooting upward toward an indefinite mass of stars, then he is among the heavenly bodies with his arrows. In the third (which corresponds to the Danae story), Cupid is in the heavens, "cum l'area sagitta sua verso li stelliferi caeli tragendo, gutte d'oro amorosamente faceva piovere" (1:160), thus continuing a cycle by bringing the amorous god down to earth. In the last, Cupid is seen at the right hand of a Jupiter who strikingly resembles representations of God the Father (thus appropriate to his thunderous appearance in the Semele story), but appearing, according to the text, not for any sublime purpose but "ad contemplatione d'una mortale fanciulla" (1:164).

All of these representations suggest a universal cosmology of love, occupying the earth and the heavens and proceeding in a ceaseless cycle between them.[132] Metamorphosis is the essential image of this flowing cosmology. If (as seems most likely) Colonna was unfamiliar with the twelfth-century lyric "Profuit ignaris," he was still in deep sympathy with its vision of metamorphic cycles. Metamorphosis is the medium whereby love moves from earth to heaven and from heaven to earth, where ultimately it generates the great events of history as well as created nature itself. When Cupid appears in heaven on the second triumphal chariot (figure 37), the heavenly bodies that surround him are represented in the animal forms taken by the self-transforming gods. But the representation makes the little celestial menagerie look remarkably like a zodiac—thus confirming the cosmology of metamorphosis. It is not only the heavens; the earth is repeatedly seen in metamorphic terms as well. The fourth and climactic triumph, of Semele/Bacchus, turns love very directly into nature. In place of the metamorphic representation of Jupiter and his beloved on the first three chariots, here there is a vase (described in extremely exact detail) which seems to contain the natural world. One face shows putti trimming, harvesting, and sporting around a grape arbor. The other (Figure 38) depicts a scene described (not quite accurately) as

> uno festivante choro de sette nymphe, candide di indumento, religiosamente indicando di cantare, cum venerabondo plauso; le quale poscia se transformavano in verdigiante arbore di smaragdina perspicuitate, conferte di flosculi cyanei praelucenti, et al summo numine se divotamente inclinavano. Non che tutte le nymphe fusseron tramutate in fronde, ma la novissima essendo tutta in arbusculo conversa et gli pedi in radicule, et la vicina gli pedi exclusi, et la tertia dal cingere supra cum lo exordio degli brachii, et subsequente ciascuna poscia. Ma nella summitate del virgineo capo indicavano el metamorphosi che de tutte doveva successivamente sequire.   [1:167–68][133]

At the dawn of the sixteenth century we see here one of the highpoints of Renaissance paganism: a sacred ritual whereby metamorphic love is itself metamorphosed into nature. It is the climax of these triumphs, and it leads directly to yet higher points in Colonna's vision: the triumph of Vertumnus and Pomona, a vision of natural abundance, and ultimately the appearance of Venus Physizoa, a principle of love concerned with the propagation of the whole created universe.

The Renaissance triumph, then, represents both a conventional content and a conventional form. The convention of content, particularly in the Triumph of Love, is of a universe entirely moved by the spirit of love, which generates innumerable forms out of an amorous and metamorphic impulse. The history of that idea goes back to Lucretius and Ovid as well as to the Greek Romances, but it is (relatively) alive and well in the Middle Ages with the fashion for nature poetry and the occasional fleshly lyric like "Profuit ignaris" or those in the *Carmina Burana*. With Petrarch, this idea of love metamorphosing into a whole cosmology of forms begins to be attached to the vehicle of the triumph. That stroke redefines (in specifically Ovidian terms, as we saw from our discussion of the Daphne episode) a genre of imperial might into an expression of universal love. And throughout the Renaissance, when the triumph lives on verbally, pictorially, ceremonially, and dramatically, even when it reverts to its imperial message, it never entirely loses its associations with *amor*.

It is not surprising, then, to see a positively Europa-like triumph of love in the midst of a late Renaissance drama where the issues concern the tensions between the imperium and universal love:

> The barge she sat in, like a burnish'd throne,
> Burn'd on the water: the poop was beaten gold;
> Purple the sails, and so perfumed that
> The winds were love-sick with them; the oars were silver,
> Which to the tune of flutes kept stroke, and made
> The water which they beat to follow faster,
> As amorous of their strokes. For her own person,
> It beggar'd all description: she did lie
> In her pavillion—cloth of gold of tissue—
> O'er-picturing that Venus where we see
> The fancy out-work nature. On each side her,
> Stood pretty dimpled boys, like smiling Cupids,
> With divers-colour'd fans, whose wind did seem
> To glow the delicate cheeks which they did cool,
> And what they undid, did. . . .
> Her gentlewomen, like the Nereides,
> So many mermaids, tended her i' the eyes,
> And made their bends adornings. At the helm
> A seeming mermaid steers: the silken tackle
> Swell with the touches of those flower-soft hands,
> That yarely frame the office. From the barge
> A strange invisible perfume hits the sense
> Of the adjacent wharfs.[134]

Though the supernatural is carefully reduced from metamorphosis to simile (*like* Cupids, *like* Nereides, *seeming* mermaid), this description of Cleopatra's meeting with Antony is clearly a triumph of love in the mythological tradition of Europa, according to which love itself animates the seas. And of course it is placed in a drama where the sea is also the locus for the animated events of imperial ambition, which, for both winner and loser, are the furthest thing from triumphs.

The heritage of the triumph as a *form* is yet more extensive. The royal entry, the pageant, the masque, the magic play, the public ceremony, the staged tournament, and so on arise out of the triumph, and that heritage gives this whole impulse in Renaissance art a base in metamorphosis. Not only do Ovidian myths abound in these works. In their very nature, these entertainments are gigantically elaborate pageants that arise out of nothing, overwhelm the spectator, and then dissolve to nothing again. There is, of course, a meaning implicit in this flux, a properly medieval moral that Petrarch clearly has in mind in his triumphs, i.e., that earthly shows are mutable and delusory. But the great sixteenth- and seventeenth-century shows of imperial power, and the triumphs of secular stagecraft, are hardly designed to inspire contempt for the world or even contempt for illusion. Rather, they dramatize how much can be made out of nothing and how spectacularly it can return to nothing again.

It is not only the beginning and the end of the show that suggests metamorphosis but also the whole progress of the pageant. These great Renaissance ceremonies, whether merely verbal or dependent on elaborate technology, are sequences of metamorphoses, stage pictures changing into other stage pictures, scenes shifting, revelations and disappearances, costume changes, transformations of a familiar individual into a fantastic mythological personage and back into a redefined familiar figure.[135] The masterpieces of Ben Jonson and Inigo Jones are the most famous (but not the only) examples of royal pageantry in which both stagecraft and meaning are grounded in metamorphosis.[136] The spectacular discoveries, the relations of masque and antimasque, the alchemical imagery, the very idealization of the court itself all become exercises in transformation. By the latter part of their collective career, metamorphosis comes to be the subject itself: *Pleasure Reconciled to Virtue* not only operates in the mode of stage transformation, but it also dramatizes the move from Circe to Daedalus as metamorphic geniuses; and *The Gypsies Metamorphosed* is sufficiently self-conscious to arouse our expectations with its title only to report at the end that the transformation was merely

> an ointment
> Made and laid on by Master Wolf's appointment,
> The court *lycanthropos*, yet without spells,
> By a mere barber and no magic else.
> It was fetched off with water and a ball,
> And to our transformation this is all.   [ll. 1387–92][137]

To demythologize the myth is merely to emphasize its power.

I hazard a return to the same authority we considered in regard to the triumph as content. There is one great play and pageant that is, by comparison to others, made out of nothing; a handful of characters, one locale, a brief period of time; but more than any other of his plays it involves a succession of spectacular changes: a storm that appears and disappears, likewise a banquet, harpies, and the goddesses Iris, Juno, and Ceres. In lines as famous as those quoted above, the principal character reminds us that this art of changes is the art of making grand substance out of nothing and returning to that nothing:

> These our actors,
> As I foretold you, were all spirits, and
> Are melted into air, into thin air:
> And, like the baseless fabric of this vision,

The cloud-capp'd towers, the gorgeous palaces,
The solemn temples, the great globe itself,
Yea, all which it inherit, shall dissolve,
And, like this insubstantial pageant faded,
Leave not a rack behind.[138]

It is the same metamorphic paradox that we saw in Pythagoras and that
we shall see Spenser wrestle with in *The Faerie Queene*: to celebrate the
endless vitality of earthly change is to contemplate a change beyond
which there is no more change, whether that final change is nihilism, apotheosis, the Last Judgment, or the end of the play. Through the art of the
triumph, then, metamorphosis stands at the nexus between nothingness
and man's grandest designs, just as it stands between passion and the cosmic celebrations of passion.

5. Fusions: Platonism and Spenser

Considering binary systems in Renaissance myth-making earlier in this
chapter, we documented not only the opposition but also the fusion of opposites. Now we must turn that same awareness back upon the whole Renaissance attitude toward metamorphosis. If the image of magical transformation describes both the passionate fragmentation of the self and the
universal harmony of the cosmos, then the two must take part in a system
which reconciles the opposition; and metamorphosis must count as a central image in that system as well. Such a system is to be found in Renaissance Platonism.[139] From the Florentine Neoplatonic circle of the late
fifteenth century there emerges an antimaterialist philosophy that looks
through and beyond the surfaces of this world toward a realm of essences.
Such an attitude, because of its visionary, even escapist, nature, might
turn its back upon material reality; more often in the Renaissance, however, it chose to accept material reality as the beginning level of a series of
translations into ultimate reality. To see in the immediate here-and-now
some transcendent essence is to operate in a world of occult mysteries,
since most observers see in the immediate little else beyond itself.

For reasons bound up with the medieval tradition of figura and the
doctrine of the integumentum, these mysteries come to be associated
with just those cultural materials that had to be interpreted metaphorically, among which are those of Jewish cabala, pagan myth, and—a new
element in the early Renaissance—the wisdom of the Egyptians and of
the East. We have already discussed the popularity of hieroglyphic images, which seem to be one thing and mean another. In the world of Renaissance occulta, all the familiar images of pagan myth may take on the
status of hieroglyphs, pleasingly beautiful to the uninitiated but bearing
secret messages to those in the know. In art, of course, the messages are

not really secret. Still, the aesthetics of a Platonist like Botticelli, if we read him correctly, do suggest a gap between the sensuous beauty of the canvas and the intellectual rigor of the program.[140]

Metamorphoses are in themselves mystery images, as we have seen throughout this book, since they are naturalistically and theologically impossible and since they combine opposites in a single act. This last is of particular significance in Renaissance Neoplatonism. If material reality and ultimate essence are secretly joined, then opposites are one; or there exists, at least, a mysterious process of thought or action whereby opposites become one. Hence the motion of the Graces, so masterfully studied by Edgar Wind; hence, too, the Renaissance interest in such mythic scenes of choice as Hercules at the Crossroads or the Judgment of Paris, whose seeming oppositions can now be resolved into a higher unity.[141] With that resolution, all the oppositions and multiplicities of pagan myth (whose Augustinian associations with metamorphosis gave it such a bad name) are now assured of contact with ultimate truth. Pico della Mirandola's assertion in *De Hominis Dignitate*[142] that man is a chamaeleon, who discovers the multiplicity of the universe in exploring his own multiplicities, overturns in one stroke much of the moral argument against the self-transforming gods. In fact, a new pantheon of multiple gods like Venus-Diana or Hermeros is invented in the Renaissance in order to contain and enshrine the oppositions among the pagan gods and also between pagan and Christian values.[143]

That this spirit of uniting opposites is closely tied to the image of metamorphosis we have already observed in Renaissance myth-making. Tales like those of Actaeon or Ganymede depend not just upon a logical juxtaposition of the profane and the sacred but a direct relation between them. Ganymede unites the carnal pleasures of pederasty with the sublime knowledge of God. And Giordano Bruno in *Gl'Eroici Furori* begins with an Actaeon consumed by amorous desire but figures forth in his transformation to a deer a complete visionary experience:

> . . . in that divine and universal chase he comes to apprehend that it is himself who necessarily remains captured, absorbed, and united. Therefore, from the vulgar, civil, and ordinary man he was, he becomes as free as a deer, and an inhabitant of the wilderness; he lives like a god under the protection of the woods in the unpretentious rooms of the cavernous mountains, where he contemplates the sources of the great rivers, vigorous as a plant, intact and pure, free of ordinary lusts, and converses most freely with the divinity, to which so many men have aspired.[144]

Metamorphosis itself unites the two extremes, describing at once the beastly condition of the passionate lover and also the transfigured state of an individual who has seen ultimate reality.

But the locus classicus for the metamorphosis in which carnal passion and divine insight come together is the book which its author called the *Metamorphoses* but which we call *The Golden Ass*. The great romance of Apuleius, written in the second century by a celebrated (even notorious) Platonist and magician, chronicles the transformation of the hero from young libertine dabbling irresponsibly in the black arts to jackass who undergoes a year's beastly travail. The nadir of his experience is reached when he is about to perform an act of sexual bestiality on a public stage. Revolted by the prospect, the hero/jackass (who happens to have the same name as the author) escapes and is retransformed—not, however, into the human being he was, but into a priest of the goddess Isis. The last book is an incantatory initiation into the mystic rites of that goddess. In this initiation we see his essential metamorphosis: his curiosity about the occult is redeemed by his new intimacy with divinity, and his sexual appetite is redeemed by his union with a female deity who is characterized as all gods in one. Nor is it coincidental that Isis is the deity for whom Lucius is so prepared. She is, after all, a double of Ovid's Io, who herself moves from being the object of Jupiter's lust to a tormented beast to a victim of furies to an Egyptian goddess.

Apuleius's romance was widely read and translated at least from Boccaccio's time onwards. On its first publication (1469) it was offered as an occult exposition of Platonic doctrine, and its sixteenth-century commentator Phillipus Beroaldus treats metamorphosis as closely connected to other mystic changes, including those of metempsychosis and alchemy.[145] The powerful influence of Apuleius turns up wherever Renaissance writers wish to affirm a mystic union of passion and sacred mysteries (as in the *Hypnerotomachia*) or merely to look at the world upside down in order to provide a deeper truth, as in *The Praise of Folly*.

Actaeon as stag or Lucius as jackass amount to radical Neoplatonic transformations—that is, cases where beastly metamorphosis provides intimate union with the divine. Most Renaissance metamorphoses, however, partake of a sort of poetic Platonism merely by juxtaposing the alternatives of passion and cosmic harmony so as to create the impression that metamorphosis joins the extremes, much as Botticelli juxtaposes, but does not actually join, the metamorphosed Chloris-Flora in the *Primavera* and as Titian juxtaposes his two Venuses in *Sacred and Profane Love*. Petrarch is both fragmented and poetically reborn by the experience that turns *Laura* into *lauro*. Correggio's image of Leda and the Swan is located at the centerline of a canvas where earthly and heavenly visions of love meet, even though they are not literally united there. In the world of art, the Platonic synthesis can best be seen as a multiple *discordia concors* whose individual terms are related by metamorphosis.

The Faerie Queene offers us the chance to observe not only that Platonic synthesis but indeed the complete operation of Renaissance metamorphosis and the revival of paganism.[146] Very near the midpoint of Spenser's poem as we now have it, Britomart, the heroine of chaste love, reaches one of the climactic points of her adventures when she rescues Amoret, a virtuous but somewhat wavering foster-daughter of Venus, from the house of the enchanter Busyrane. Spenser follows Britomart through three rooms of the house: the first contains tapestries modeled after the work of Ovid's Arachne depicting the metamorphic loves of the gods; the second room, decorated with non-narrative pagan images, is the scene for the Masque of Cupid, an allegorical pageant displaying the psychological conditions of unhealthy love; the third room, apparently without decoration of any kind, is the lair of the enchanter himself, whom we see casting spells upon Amoret.

In every way this episode is a locus of metamorphosis. To begin with, the image is all-important here, as becomes evident in the second room:

> Much fairer, then the former, was that roome,
>> And richlier by many partes arayd:
>> For not with arras made in painefull loome,
>> But with pure gold it all was ouerlayd,
>> Wrought with wilde Antickes, which their follies playd,
>> In the rich metall, as they liuing were:
>> A thousand monstrous formes therein were made,
>> Such as false loue doth oft vpon him weare,
> For loue in thousand monstrous formes doth oft appeare.
>
> [3.11.51][147]

Spenser uses the image of gold paintings, in all their varied style, to epitomize the world of changing forms. Then, with a brilliant pun, he identifies the *antic* nature of metamorphic images with the *antique* source of such representations. In fact, Spenser is referring to a quite particular set of antique antics. With the unearthing of Nero's Golden House at the beginning of the sixteenth century, the Renaissance received its first real view of classical painting, a brilliant decorative ensemble consisting of strange forms from nature and myth.[148] Because the Golden House was thought to be a grotto, the paintings came to be known as *grotteschi*. The style was imitated widely throughout the Renaissance, both in painting and in book-illustration. By Spenser's time *grotteschi* exemplify the visual world of paganism. For him as for us, such visions are *grotesque*. But the particular grotesquerie is that of multiple and changing forms. Spenser has in his pun identified antiquity, metamorphosis, and the making of images. Through the whole Busyrane episode, but especially in regard to Arachne's web, the power of seeing is above all stressed. Borrowed from Ovid but much intensified is the praise for the verisimilitude of the artist's work, along with the strongly suggested parallel between metamorphosis and representation. As the poet describes these, he suggests that in the act of seeing beautiful representations there is sheer delight.

If the House of Busyrane is an explosion of visual images, it is also a Triumph of Love. The tapestry and the masque both take the form of Triumphs of Love, while the underlying significance of this allegorical locus suggests a universe ruled by love. Britomart's first response as she contemplates the flame outside is all-important:

> Greatly thereat was *Britomart* dismayd,
>   Ne in that stownd wist, how her selfe to beare;
>   For daunger vaine it were, to haue assayd
>   That cruell element, which all things feare,
>   Ne none can suffer to approchen neare:
>   And turning backe to *Scudamour*, thus sayd;
>   What monstrous enmity prouoke we heare,
>   Foolhardy as th'Earthes children, the which made
> Battell against the Gods? so we a God inuade.   [3.11.22]

The flame, which is as much an emblem of pagan religion as it is of passionate love, images forth at once the *amor* and the *maiestas* of the Ovidian gods, and Britomart is right to perceive that she is entering a holy place, even if both she and the reader will soon realize that it is the holy place of a false religion. The reference to the war of the Titans against the gods reminds us that this entry of Britomart into the House of Busyrane is also an assault against Jupiter and the Olympians.

Finally, this world of love is informed by the metamorphic principles of Petrarchan passion. The mortal girls on the tapestries may be victims of the gods, but even as Jupiter may tyrannize over Europa and the rest, he is himself the loser in "all *Cupids* warres . . . / And cruell battels, which he whilome fought / Gainst all the Gods, to make his empire great" (3.11.29). Other gods, including Phoebus, Neptune, and Mars, are even greater losers because their unlawful love is depressing or self-destructive. To the extent that the gods are themselves the victims, their metamorphoses becomes figures—precisely as they were in *Rime* 23—for the psychic changeability of passionate love. It is in this sense that the metamorphoses in the Masque of Cupid follow directly from those in the tapestries. The personifications of Fancy, Desire, Doubt, Danger, Fear, Hope, Dissemblance, Suspect, and the rest dramatize all the emotions of Petrarchan love.

Within the Busyrane episode, these elements of metamorphosis are decidely *moralisés*. The image is a deceitful image. The poet repeatedly emphasizes visual deception as he retells the stories: Danae's guardian is supposed to look out for the appearance of the god, but "Vaine was the watch, and bootlesse all the ward, / Whenas the God to golden hew him selfe transfard" (3.11.31); Semele is victimized when she "Deceiu'd of gealous *Iuno*, did require / To see him in his soueraigne maiestee" (3.11.33); and of Ganymede we are told,

> Wondrous delight it was, there to behould,
> How the rude Shepheards after him did stare,
> Trembling through feare, least down he fallen should
> And often to him calling, to take surer hould.   [3.11.34]

There is a telling contrast between the "delight" we are supposed to feel in observing the airborne Ganymede and the fearful vision of the shepherds who are less well informed about the real meaning of the flight. The implications of image and seeing are most fully developed in the description of Leda:

> Then was he turnd into a snowy Swan,
> To win faire *Leda* to his louely trade:
> O wondrous skill, and sweet wit of the man,
> That her in daffadillies sleeping made,
> From scorching heat her daintie limbes to shade:
> Whiles the proud Bird ruffing his fethers wyde,
> And brushing his faire brest, did her inuade;
> She slept, yet twixt her eyelids closely spyde,
> How towards her he rusht, and smiled at his pryde.   [3.11.32]

The passive construction in the first line obliterates the distinction between the artist and the divine force behind metamorphosis. Once that has happened, the whole work of art—Leda as well as the swan—comes to be understood as a metamorphosis. It is an almost uncanny description of Correggio's *Leda*, and, as in the metamorphic world of Correggio, all the categories of seeing become unstable. By her act of seeing, Leda is just as much a deceiver as her lover. While we peer voyeuristically at the love scene, she peers back, unwilling to miss the pleasures of seeing and of outdoing Jupiter at his own game of visual deception.

Indeed the whole aesthetic of the tapestry's imagery is deceitful:

> Wouen with gold and silke so close and nere,
> That the rich metall lurked priuily,
> As faining to be hid from enuious eye;
> Yet here, and there, and euery where vnwares
> It shewd it selfe, and shone vnwillingly;
> Like a discolourd Snake, whose hidden snares
> Through the greene gras his long bright burnisht backe declares.
>   [3.11.28]

The gold transforms itself into and out of visibility like a snake, and the double meaning of *fain* (i.e., "wish" and "pretend") makes the whole business of a metamorphic image very uncertain, while the (similarly meta-morphic) difficulties of distinguishing between snake and grass make it dangerous. The insubstantiality of the image resides in the fact that it is *only* an image. Tapestries are of course two-dimensional, but that same sense of tenuousness attaches itself to the whole House of Busyrane. The "thousand monstrous formes" are nothing but forms without content, and the personages in the Masque of Cupid are as phantom-like as the states they allegorize. Busyrane, meanwhile, as the only flesh-and-blood inhab-itant of the place, receives little attention. When Britomart enters, she expects a castle gate but finds only a flame; when she leaves in victory, such castle as there was has collapsed of its own accord. The whole House of Busyrane appears to have been nothing but an image; and metamor-phosis makes images as susceptible to dissolution as to change.

The notion of a metamorphic universe ruled by love, and celebrated in triumphs, sustains a similar moral attack. Spenser's loves of the gods are at this point very much in the world of Petrarch's *Trionfo d'Amore*. Their passion makes them seem strong, but it ultimately proves them weak. Both the strength and the weakness raise painful questions about divine power. Spenser goes Arachne one better by suggesting, in the case of Eu-ropa, that metamorphosis is a fearful misuse of such power:

> Now like a Bull, *Europa* to withdraw:
> Ah, how the fearefull Ladies tender hart
> Did liuely seeme to tremble, when she saw
> The huge seas vnder her t'obay her seruaunts law.   [3.11.30]

Seruaunt becomes a pun that contains the whole paradox directly from the *Trionfi*: Jupiter is the greatest of all masters, as is demonstrated by his power of self-transformation and his power over the tides, but in the same act that frightens Europa with these masterful powers he becomes a "ser-vant" in the sense of a Petrarchan love-suitor.

The problems of the anti-triumph are more severe than the enfeeble-ment of the king of the gods. When Jupiter abandons his *maiestas* for *amor*, there is a great vacuum in the governance of the universe, and the results are chaotic:

> Whiles thus on earth great *Ioue* these pageaunts playd,
> The winged boy did thrust into his throne,
> And scoffing, thus vnto his mother sayd,
> Lo now the heauens obey to me alone,
> And take me for their *Ioue* whiles *Ioue* to earth is gone.   [3.11.35]

This is the *Triumphus Cupidinis* indeed: Jupiter's metamorphic degrada-tion in sexuality leads to a universal instability imaged forth as Cupid's sexual conquest of the Olympian throne. In the resulting disorder both society and religion are overturned as all classes unite and mingle ("Kings

Queenes, . . . with the raskall rablement"; 3.11.46), and before the icon of blindfolded Cupid "oft committed fowle Idolatree" (3.11.49). Finally, the changeful world of Petrarchan love is criticized on the same grounds. Metamorphosis describes a love which is both immoral and barren: just as Jupiter deceives and is deceived, so the qualities in the Masque of Cupid oscillate between those that suffer love and those that inflict the sufferings of love.

Underlying all these moralizations are medieval and neo-medieval traditions of intellectual history. We have already had occasion to mention that the amorous metamorphoses of Jupiter in Bersuire's commentary on Ovid become not only a paradigm of beastliness but also a kind of psychomachia detailing the various temptations of the soul. Renaissance mythography does not retreat at all from this moralism. So Natalis Comes, characterizing Jupiter's transformations as signs of false appearances, arrives at a climax defining metamorphosis as a basic principle of hypocrisy: "For love makes those things which are most filthy, deformed, disagreeable, and dangerous to appear righteous, beautiful, pleasant, and profitable" (2.2). Such an account of false appearances underlies the whole presentation of appearances in *The Faerie Queene*. In this way, some strands of Renaissance Platonism run precisely counter to the Florentine celebration of multiplicity, suggesting that it bespeaks an unbridgeable gap from essences. Spenser is influenced by the revival of an ancient and Augustinian attack on the metamorphic god. When Plato in the *Timaeus* defines the principle of a perfectly created cosmos arising from a perfect creator, he suggests that perfection consists partly in the absence of locomotion. The spherical cosmos, Plato tells us, "was made to move in the same [orbital] manner and on the same spot, within his own limits revolving in a circle. All the other six motions were taken away from him, and he was made not to partake of their deviations" (34a).[149]

If perfection is the absence of deviant motion, then the monarch of Olympus—himself often equated by the ancients with the cosmos—is a more immoral ruling principle for his extremely deviant habit of self-metamorphosis. Hence Augustine's innumerable names for the pagan gods, and hence Comes' climactic description of the metamorphic Jupiter: "For now he is in heaven, now in the air; now he is the air itself, now he is destiny. Now he is under water, now under the earth. Now he transforms himself into rain, now into various types of animals. Can one imagine a more miserable condition than this?" (2.2). Jupiter's condition is miserable not because he is evil but because as a figure of metamorphosis he is, like Spenser's Jupiter, the victim of insubstantiality.[150] But, to the moralist, distinctions between what is evil and what is unsubstantial are ultimately pointless. St. Augustine had long since equated the two in his attempt to explain the presence of evil in a universe ruled by an all-powerful and perfect deity.[151] Metamorphosis unites the two terms.

Yet the House of Busyrane is set in a context where its moralism represents one rung on a greater ladder. The larger construction is postulated in a definition of love offered earlier in Book III:

> Wonder it is to see, in diuerse minds,
>   How diuersely loue doth his pageants play,
>   And shewes his powre in variable kinds:
>   The baser wit, whose idle thoughts alway
>   Are wont to cleaue vnto the lowly clay,
>   It stirreth vp to sensuall desire,
>   And in lewd slouth to wast his carelesse day:
>   But in braue sprite it kindles goodly fire,
> That to all high desert and honour doth aspire.   [3.5.1]

With this introductory stanza, the poet builds the Platonic ladder of love and animates the structure with the spirit of metamorphosis. The diversity of types of love is joined with the variable nature of love itself; and the medium in which love (or Love, i.e., Cupid) operates is the *pageant*, the quintessential term for metamorphic drama such as Spenser stages in the Busyrane tapestries or the Masque of Cupid. Thus the variety of types of love put before us in Book III can be traced back to the metamorphoses of the single principle of Amor. Near the center of the book, when the goddess of love is searching for her wayward son, we are told,

>   she left her heauenly hous,
>   The house of goodly formes and faire aspects,
>   Whence all the world deriues the glorious
>   Features of beauties, and all shapes select,
>   With which high God his workmanship hath deckt.   [3.6.12]

The descent from that perfect haven of divine love—presumably the Garden of Adonis, which Spenser is about to describe—defines love on earth, where Cupid "wandred in the world in strange aray, / Disguiz'd in thousand shapes, that none might him bewray" (3.6.11). The tapestries, the "antickes," the transformations of amorous gods, even the sufferings of Britomart and Artegall: all these are the metamorphic disguises of Cupid.

Consequently, metamorphosis is more than a wicked or an empty condition of false love: it is an essential condition of all love; and it forges a link among all the types of love. The central drama of Book III, after all, is the career of Britomart, whose immature passions are as changeable as any in the Masque of Cupid.[152] Her love also finds its source in dangerous forms of seeing. The heroine first perceives her love in an enchanted mirror—a "world of glas" comparable to tapestries or, indeed, to the poem itself. And this sight must be confirmed with true substance. "It was not, *Britomart*, thy wandring eye, / Glauncing vnwares in charmed looking glas, / But the streight course of heauenly destiny, / . . . that has /

Guided thy glaunce" (3.3.24), Merlin tells her, and all her heroic activities that follow attempt to turn image to substance.

If Britomart's career bonds the changeable to the substantial, then the central link in that chain is to be found in the Garden of Adonis, the essential home of love and a place of transformation that moves beyond love. Spenser takes the world of twelfth-century nature poetry, associated with love, fecundity, and diversity, and makes explicit its connections with Plato's theory of forms and cosmology.[153] The multiplicity of forms sent forth into the "chaungefull world" is set in peaceful array within the Garden. The threat of instability is harmonized by perfect love, while the even greater threat of decay is answered by a vision of cyclical change within a larger order:

> All be he [Adonis] subiect to mortalitie,
> Yet is eterne in mutabilitie,
> And by succession made perpetuall,
> Transformed oft, and chaunged diuerslie. [3.6.47]

Transforming the principle of transformation, Spenser shows us a garden that is a place of change—of growth, development, differentiation—which is itself set against the decaying, mutable transformations of the world beyond the walls of the Garden.

Yet the Garden of Adonis, even if it is a haven for orderly change, may well seem far too rarefied and protected to be found within our world. After all, Venus cannot deny the ravages of time any more than she can deny the death of Adonis and his transformation into a flower—except within the limits of an imaginary world set apart. The problem of mutability as metamorphosis is not laid to rest in the third book of the poem, despite the suggestion (appropriate to the concerns of that book) that love will conquer mutability in the long run. For the resolution of all the metamorphic issues we must turn to the *Cantos of Mutabilitie*, which were published posthumously as a possible "Parcell of some following booke" of the unfinished poem but which may well have been intended as the conclusion of the work.[154] The *Cantos* are in the form of a debate: the Titaness Mutabilitie, a Spenserian invention, having (as she sees it) already gained control of the earth, seeks mastery over the moon and then over the gods, and she expects to win her case by appealing to the goddess Natura.

As the figure of Natura suggests, the *Cantos* are set in the world of medieval nature poetry, though with a much more explicit understanding of the relevance of Ovidian cosmologies. The milieu may be Alain's or Bernard's, but the central issue is Ovidian: the different ways of understanding the power of change in the universe. So long as the power of change is understood as earthly decay, the poet cannot really question Mutabilitie's claim.[155] But the action of the *Cantos* concerns Mutabilitie's attempt to extend her sway, to make war, like her Titan ancestors, on the benevolent rule of the Olympians. Such aspiration is to be understood allegorically in the fear lest the whole divine order be subject to decay. The first step in the Titaness's war on heaven is her struggle to overpower Cynthia, the moon. It is logical for Mutabilitie to begin there, for the moon is the boundary between earth and heaven. More important yet, in our earthly world the moon is an emblem of change and as such a fitting object for Mutabilitie's designs. Her great speech, in which she presents the elements, the seasons, the months, and so on as witnesses for her power, is deeply indebted to Ovid's Pythagoras. Such a debt reflects back on the whole relation between *The Faerie Queene* and the *Metamorphoses*. The Renaissance poet is quite consciously composing a new epic of changes; and like Ovid, he concludes his epic with a poem-within-a-poem exploring the nature of change.

By placing the Pythagorean credo within the mouth of the Titaness, Spenser makes her case for disordering change out of one of the most famous assertions of orderly change in all of classical literature. Thus, even before Nature has delivered her verdict, we are aware by historical reference, both to Ovid and to medieval descriptions of cosmic harmony, that Mutabilitie's pageant of elements, months, and seasons amounts to a series of witnesses against her and in favor of a divine order that contains and harmonizes change.[156] That is why the changes of the moon are the point of entry for the subject: cyclical and orderly, these changes, far from signaling instability or decay, instead turn transformation into order. Nature herself confirms this kind of order:

> They are not changed from their first estate;
> But by their change their being doe dilate:
> And turning to themselues at length againe,
> Doe worke their owne perfection so by fate:
> Then ouer them Change doth not rule and raigne;
> But they raigne ouer change, and doe their states maintaine.
>
> [7.58]

Spenser again echoes Pythagoras (*Metamorphoses*, 15.252–58); but he also combines the Christian with the Platonic by suggesting that the constant change is a movement toward perfection, as though the metamorphoses of nature—analogies *in bono* to the amorous transformations of the gods—are a means of shedding the taint of earthliness. Once the notion of change as decay has been replaced in this way by change as order and as Platonic cycle, it is not so large a step to a yet more sublime image of change, when the great change happens and "all shall rest eternally" (8.2).

The Faerie Queene may well be the fullest poetic exploration of metamorphosis since Ovid's time, for in it Spenser builds a hierarchy of types of transformation. Though he classifies amorous self-metamorphoses as quintessentially empty and immoral, he places them among other types of transformation in such a way as to suggest the shifting nature of the moral categories themselves. Immoral love and immature love; immature love and the process of growth; growth and fruition through love; fruition through love and a cosmos ordered by love; a cosmos ordered by love and a divine harmony expressing itself through nature; the changes of nature ultimately transcended by a great change beyond which there is no change: all are expressible through the image of metamorphosis. The system manages to contain all the contradictions of paganism and its history, and the true connective tissue within this hierarchy of transformations is the poetic technique itself. The whole poem is a sequence of images, tapestries, pageants, triumphs, masques, changing aesthetic shapes. The narrative motion is not linear but metamorphic, each subject flowing into the next with its own internal logic. Spenser has with his whole poem fulfilled the terms of Arachne's web; and the ultimate chain of changes is that which takes us from the literal Arachne's web of Busyrane's house, at the moral nadir of transformation, to the larger web of *The Faerie Queene*, which attempts to contain the cosmos of metamorphosis.

The Spenserian tapestry reminds us that the most important characteristic of Renaissance metamorphism is not focused on the history of ideas, or on essential mythic structures, or even on verbal and visual genres; what most essentially characterizes the Renaissance is a metamorphic aesthetics. *The Faerie Queene* is a gigantic tapestry ruled by poetic and imagistic transformation. Correggio, quite apart from his ideas and his iconography, paints in a soft, deliquescent, melting style. Genres like triumph and masque (not to mention Elizabethan drama) depend on sudden and extreme changes. In fact, Renaissance artists applied the doctrine of metamorphosis to the very materials from which they learned about metamorphosis: the myths themselves. Spenser invents a pagan goddess who is herself the principle of change. Ronsard elides myth and reality even as he elides the sounds and meanings of homophonic words. Titian gives us a Europa who is more transformed than the bull. Petrarch filters the Ovidian material in *Rime* 23 through a profoundly wavering psyche and retransforms the myths; then in *Rime* 323, with the further disordering spirit inspired by Laura's death, he retransforms the metamorphic myths of the earlier poem into apocalyptic visions. For Renaissance artists, as for some of the more advanced medieval intellectuals, *sic verum Proteus*.

CHAPTER SIX

Shakespeare & the Metamorphoses of Art and Life

1. Reading the Book of Ovid

Shakespeare's characters do not read many books. Romeo can help out a poor analphabetic servant with what turns out to be a fatal list of names; Polonius forces Ophelia to pretend to read a prayer-book, and he gets rewarded later with an account from Hamlet of the cynical volume the young prince is (supposedly?) reading; young Simple in *Merry Wives* wishes he had his copy of Tottel's *Miscellany*; and, of course, dozens of characters read letters, poems written by or to themselves, proclamations, and so on. Very few read a book which is clearly identifiable. Of these few readings, two are from the same book (in fact, the same passage of the same book). Either Shakespeare's Latin was even smaller than Ben Jonson thought it was, or else he liked that book (and that passage) very much indeed. The astute reader will have guessed that the book is Ovid's *Metamorphoses*. The passage is more surprising. The fact that it is not one of the Renaissance Ovidian clichés (e.g., Narcissus, Phaethon, Venus and Adonis) will be the first signal that Shakespeare knew his Ovid at first hand and that he read the *Metamorphoses* with a deliberate and original purpose. The story of Tereus, Procne, and Philomela and the manner of its appearance in the book of Ovid on Shakespeare's stage will serve as a point of entry to the powerful relation between those two geniuses.[1]

Considering the salient features of the Tereus story—rape, mutilation, cannibalism, and so on—it is not surprising that the first play in which it is read is *Titus Andronicus*.[2] At the most basic level, the Tereus story is important in *Titus* because both the atmosphere and the narrative of that play parallel the Ovidian tale. The hero's daughter is raped by a pair of brothers, savage and vengeful Goths, who mutilate their victim by cutting

243

out her tongue *and* chopping off her hands. She can only express what happened by inducing her nephew to pull down from the shelf a copy of Ovid's *Metamorphoses*. With her stumps she manages to get through the pages to Book VI, where she identifies the means of her undoing by pointing to the fate of Philomela. From this point, and with many digressions involving other mutilations, the plot pursues the classic path toward a cannibal banquet of the familiar parental kind, as Titus serves the rapists to their mother, Tamora, the barbarous queen of the Goths.

More is at work here than mirroring parallels between the stories of Tereus and Titus. In a very real sense, the presence of the book of Ovid generates the events of *Titus*. Even before the prop itself is introduced, it is clear that the characters have read the *Metamorphoses*. There is no doubt why the rapists Chiron and Demetrius cut off Lavinia's hands: they know how Philomela communicated after her mutilation, and they want to improve upon Tereus's crime. A woman without hands cannot sew a tapestry. The victims have a similar consciousness of Ovid, as Lavinia's uncle reveals:

> Fair Philomel, why, she but lost her tongue,
> And in a tedious sampler sew'd her mind:
> But, lovely niece, that mean is cut from thee;
> A craftier Tereus, cousin, hast thou met,
> And he hath cut those pretty fingers off,
> That could have better sew'd than Philomel. [2.4.38–43][3]

If the crime is worse, so must the vengeance be: "Far worse than Philomel you us'd my daughter, / And worse than Procne I will be reveng'd" (5.2.194–95), says Titus just before he cuts the rapists' throats. *Craftier* than Tereus, *worse* than Philomel, *better* than Philomel, *worse* than Procne: this is mythology viewed in the competitive mode. And the author is the most avid competitor. What is horrible in Ovid's Tereus story Shakespeare makes twice as horrible in *Titus Andronicus*. Not one rapist but two, not one murdered child but five, not one or two mutilated organs but six, not a one-course meal but a two. Just as Shakespeare reads Plautus's *Menaechmi* and twins the twins in his *Comedy of Errors*, so here he approaches a myth of competitive mutilation and adds another element of competition.

The object of all this competition is far more than the production of gore, as the taunts of the rapists suggest:

> DEMETRIUS.   So, now go tell, and if thy tongue can speak,
>   Who 'twas that cut thy tongue and ravish'd thee.
> CHIRON.   Write down thy mind, bewray thy meaning so,
>   And if thy stumps will let thee play the scribe. . . .
> DEMETRIUS.   See how with signs and tokens she can scrowl.

CHIRON.   Go home, call for sweet water, wash thy hands.
DEMETRIUS.   She hath no tongue to call, nor hands to wash.

[2.4.1–7]

These are escalating efforts to stifle communication. The Tereus story attracts Shakespeare because it is centrally concerned with communication. Ovid's Philomela engages in a lengthy tirade after she has been assaulted. Tereus mutilates her to shut her up. She must then convey her message in a tapestry. At the end of her life she is transformed into a nightingale, the very exemplar of beautiful, sad music. So it is not only a myth about communication; it is also a myth about the competition amongst media of communication as Philomela becomes a walking representative of them. Shakespeare for his part exploits the chance to compete in his own field. He deprives Lavinia of Philomela's options, first speech, then tapestry-sewing. But to this process Shakespeare adds more stages. First, Lavinia can point to the book, a compendium of words and pictures already made; second, she makes signs in the earth; finally, Shakespeare can embody the whole fable in a drama: words, pictures, book, signs, and more. Just as the characters try to outdo the myth, as the Renaissance tries to outdo antiquity, so Shakespeare struggles to find a medium by expanding and exploding other media.

Now many details in the play fall into place. Self-conscious references to the arts abound. Lavinia's mutilation not only disables her tapestry-weaving, but also, as we are told on several occasions, her music-making. A gruesomely perfect symmetry exists between digital musicianship (her hands used to "tremble like aspen leaves upon a lute"; 2.4.45) and vocal (Lavinia's tongue "Is torn from forth that pretty hollow cage, / Where like a sweet melodious bird it sung"; 3.1.84–85). More noticeable still are the dramatic references. Titus offers to lament with the suggestion that he cut off his own hands, "Or shall we bite our tongues, and in dumb shows / Pass the remainder of our hateful days?" (3.1.131–32): he is, in fact, taking part in an aesthetic redefinition of the dumb show.

Yet it is not the play's words so much as its actions that testify to Shakespeare's efforts at defining his medium. The drama abounds with strange attempts to communicate. Most of them fail. Titus sends letters on projectile weapons. To the rapists he shoots Horace's "Integer vitae," but they appreciate neither its virtuous message (Chiron vaguely remembers reading it in school) nor its witty reference to the Moor who is their henchman. To the emperor he shoots complaints that are ignored and derided. To the gods he shoots petitions for justice, but the only response comes from a clown, who confuses *Jupiter* with *gibbet-maker*. So much for satire. Another failed medium of communication is the masque. Tamora and her two sons attempt to impersonate Revenge, Rape, and Murder in a pageant, but Titus sees through the mask/masque.

Some media *do* communicate in the play, however. Ovid's book communicates very well indeed. When Lavinia first mutely indicates her interest in books, Titus is delighted to indulge her, but only because books will help her take her mind off her troubles:

> Come, and take choice of all my library,
> And so beguile thy sorrow, till the heavens
> Reveal the damn'd contriver of this deed. [4.1.34–36]

Titus is typically unaware of the irony. No communications flow to or from heaven; it is the book, rather, that tells all. Yet the book has to be translated. The name Tereus, for instance, has to be translated into Demetrius and Chiron. How can that be done by a heroine who cannot speak, write, draw, or sing? She must struggle for a new medium of communication, one that marries the book and the picture. So her uncle teaches her to write with a stick in the sand. In fact, that system of communicating comes from the same book. That is how Ovid's Io, transformed by the gods into a heifer, managed to identify herself, by scratching a line and a circle in the earth.

But the real translation of the book is the girl who acts it out. Ovid's words require Shakespeare's wordless image of the heroine reenacting them with a difference. So at the very climactic moment of the book-reading, as Lavinia finds the Philomela passage in the *Metamorphoses*, her uncle watches the spectacle and comments, "See, brother, see! note how she quotes the leaves" (4.1.50): to quote is to examine, at least in Elizabethan English, but it is also our *quote*, to reproduce—here, however, not verbatim, not using *verbum* at all, but as a dramatic image. Finally, the book must have a reader, the image an interpreter. And indeed the play is full of *reading*, not only the central event, but also the *deciphering* (that is the word the play uses) of the wrongdoers and, above all, the activity of reading that characters, author, and audience all share: the putting of words to the mute performance of Lavinia. Titus expresses this in terms that remind us how all these translations speak to Shakespeare's search for a medium:

> Hark, Marcus, what she says;
> I can interpret all her martyr'd signs.
>
> . . . .
>
> Speechless complainer, I will learn thy thought;
> In thy dumb action will I be as perfect
> As begging hermits in their holy prayers:
> Thou shalt not sigh, nor hold thy stumps to heaven,
> Nor wink, nor nod, nor kneel, nor make a sign,
> But I of these will wrest an alphabet,
> And by still practice learn to know thy meaning. [3.2.35–45]

That alphabet represents the beginnings of a definition of Shakespeare's medium and his art: part picture, part word, part sound; part ancient book, part modern dumb show; part mute actor, part vocal interpreter.

Why does Ovid's *Metamorphoses* play such a special role in this artistic investigation? The question returns us to nearly all we have observed throughout the present volume. *Titus* takes us back to the darkest side of Ovid's poem, that realm where metamorphosis is fused with the perversions of love and family relations as well as with abominations that range from exogamy to cannibalism. Yet it is not lessons in perversity that Ovid offers Shakespeare—there are many other classical sources for that—but a series of paradigms for the act of communication. Many of the great figures of Ovid's poem define themselves by their struggle to invent new languages. That is clearest in the case of metamorphic victims like Actaeon or Io, who must labor to use human language fitting their consciousness once their shape has turned beastly. But it is equally clear of other sorts of victims, like Narcissus, who must discover a language of paradox that suits his situation. Philomela's is merely the most extended of all these struggles. Her mutilation is another language-denying metamorphosis, but it is of special interest to Shakespeare because it requires her to create a new medium, a composite of words and pictures. In that respect she becomes a metonym for the whole history of the book in which Shakespeare found her story.

After all, the history of the survival of pagan myths in the Middle Ages and the Renaissance is, as we have seen, a history of competitive relations between the visual and the verbal.[4] Shakespeare need not have been aware of the jagged stepwise development of Ovidian text and picture from the end of the Middle Ages to see in his own time the *Metamorphoses* as a compendium of word and image. That is why Shakespeare can have Lavinia substitute Ovid's book for what was Philomela's tapestry. The *Metamorphoses*, especially in its Renaissance illustrated form, *is* a tapestry. That framed tapestry, with its inset perspective illustration and its Ovidian caption underneath, is also a model and a competitor for the problems of dramatic representation, a kind of blueprint for theater more apposite than words or pictures by themselves. *Titus Andronicus*, with all the dramaturgical gaucherie that hindsight has allowed us to see in it, offers a unique opportunity to observe Shakespeare in the midst of his struggle with his source and competitor. It may be the last time that he takes so little trouble to cover his tracks.

Shakespare returns, twenty years later, to the reading of the same book. *Cymbeline*'s heroine, Imogen, even if she is not so badly treated as Lavinia, suffers all sorts of victimization. Her husband ill-advisedly bets on her chastity. The villainous Iachimo can win the wager only by having himself delivered to her bedchamber in a trunk, whence he observes her intimately while she is asleep. Just before she goes to bed on that fateful night, Imogen spends, as she tells her waiting-woman, three hours reading. It is Iachimo who identifies the volume just as he is about to return to his hiding place:

> She hath been reading late
> The tale of Tereus, here the leaf's turned down
> Where Philomel gave up. [2.2.44–46]⁵

The parallels to the Ovidian story in the present situation are insignificant without the introduction of an additional myth that mediates between Philomela and Imogen. Another rape story, more historical than mythical, appears prominently in Shakespeare's works every time the Tereus story is told. At the first mention by the rapists in *Titus* of their interest in Lavinia, the Moor warns them, "Lucrece was not more chaste / Than this Lavinia" (2.1.108–09); later, when Titus suspects the Emperor of the crime, he asks, "Slunk not Saturnine, as Tarquin erst, / That left the camp to sin in Lucrece' bed" (4.1.63–64). And in *Cymbeline*, Iachimo will exit from the trunk comparing himself to Tarquin just as he reenters it with reference to Imogen's reading "the tale of Tereus." The connections between the two rape stories are ancient: in the *Fasti*, Ovid's poetical Roman calendar and an important source for Shakespeare, the Lucretia story is celebrated on the twenty-fourth of February and the Philomela story on the twenty-fifth.⁶ And there is, of course, the intermediary text of *The Rape of Lucrece*, which not only abounds in references to the Philomela story but also relates to the same moral and aesthetic issues.

Quite apart from narrative parallels, *Cymbeline* and *Lucrece* turn on issues of image and word similar to those in *Titus Andronicus*. Both contain important pictures. Imogen's bedroom is decorated with a wide range of amorous materials from antiquity. Lucrece's chamber contains a painting illustrating the entire Trojan War. The reading of these paintings figures prominently in both cases. Iachimo recounts the contents of the decoration as part of his "proof" that he has possessed Imogen, while Lucrece arrives at a decision to commit suicide by a lengthy observation of the painted figures. In this latter case particularly, Shakespeare's terms show his persistent interest in the conflicting claims of the various artistic media. Lucrece sees the painted Hecuba and swears the painter

> did her wrong,
> To give her so much grief, and not a tongue.
> "Poor instrument," quoth she, "without a sound,
> I'll tune thy woes with my lamenting tongue."
>
> . . . .
>
> Here feelingly she weeps Troy's painted woes,
>
> . . . .
>
> So Lucrece, set a-work, sad tales doth tell

To pencill'd pensiveness and colour'd sorrow:
She lends them words, and she their looks doth borrow.

[ll. 1462–98]⁷

Shakespeare appears to be still struggling with the problems of Philomela, the juxtaposition of mutilation and communication, of image,
word, and sound. The matter of ancient history and mythology appears to
Lucrece as a set of visual images to which she, like Shakespeare, can furnish words. And again, in both these works, there are letters, communications, and all sorts of reading, including in *Cymbeline* dramatic experiments with dream, masque, and book-reading in the fulfilling of
Posthumus's destiny.

But in the stories of Lucretia and Imogen there is more to reading than
the interpretation of words and pictures. For Titus and his daughter reading was a kind of cure for or solution to rape: the book solved the who-
dunit and provided both a precedent and a system for revenge. In *The
Rape of Lucrece* and *Cymbeline*, reading and raping are much more
nearly the same thing. Tarquin scrutinizes Lucrece and must possess her.
Iachimo reenacts the same scene symbolically. But what is a symbolic
rape? Here is Iachimo's definition:

> Cytherea,
> How bravely thou becomes thy bed! fresh lily!
> And whiter than the sheets! That I might touch!
> But kiss, one kiss! . . .
>
> . . . .
>   But my design.
> To note the chamber: I will write all down:
> Such, and such pictures: there the window, such
> Th' adornment of her bed; the arras, figures,
> Why, such, and such; and the contents o' th' story.
> Ah, but some natural notes about her body
> Above ten thousand meaner moveables
> Would testify, t' enrich mine inventory.
>
> . . . .
>   On her left breast
> A mole cinque-spotted: like the crimson drops
> I' th' bottom of a cowslip. . . .
>
> . . . .
>   No more: to what end?
> Why should I write this down, that's riveted,
> Screw'd to my memory? She hath been reading late
> The tale of Tereus . . .

[2.2.14–45]

A symbolic rape is a reading. Iachimo turns away from real contact with
Imogen to a reading of the architecture, of the pictures in the room, and,

climactically, of the nude and unconscious body of the woman in the center of the room. In the process he writes his own book, which the timing of the speech explicitly compares with the book on her bedside table. She went to bed reading of ancient rapes, and she becomes the book penetrated by the eyes of the modern rapist.

The act of reading has moved from words to pictures to the thing itself. Iachimo's interest in the pictures is minimal—he does not even name them until it is time to make his report to Posthumus; he is, however, a passionate reader of Imogen's body. The reading of a beautiful woman's sleeping body turns the act of reading at once into voyeurism and into rape. The voyeurism of reading is established by the scene of the husbands' wager that *Cymbeline* shares with *Lucrece*. For Posthumus to expose the perfections of his wife to the other men in Rome is the opening of a book that should remain closed to all but himself. The precisely parallel situation in *Lucrece* Shakespeare turns into a lament against the husband:

> Why is Collatine the publisher
> Of that rich jewel he should keep unknown
> From thievish ears, because it is his own?   [ll. 33–35]

The word *publisher* is not chosen at random.[8] The husband who brags about his wife to other men is minting copies of her in words. There is always the possibility that one of his readers/listeners will not be satisfied with words alone and will demand a picture.

In fact, a picture is all Iachimo gets. Voyeurism as a type of rape turns out, despite its immorality, to be peculiarly ineffectual. Iachimo has penetrated Imogen's room but not her body. The limits of his success are parodied by the immediately following scene in which Cloten, who has not even succeeded in getting into her room, stands outside attempting ineptly to *penetrate* (he uses the word three times) with music—once again Shakespeare contrasting the various artistic media. For Iachimo's part, his relation to rape is precisely that of images to reality. He passes for a man who has possessed the heroine, but he has only experienced the picture. His claim on Imogen's body is in the end no different from his mastery of the decorations in her room—Antony and Cleopatra, Diana, winking Cupids. The later scene, in which Imogen embraces the headless body of Cloten thinking it to be that of her husband, offers a complementary set of reading problems, not of voyeurism but of misreading. Because Cloten is wearing Posthumus's clothes, Imogen "recognizes" his body:

> The garments of Posthumus?
> I know the shape of 's leg: this is his hand:
> His foot Mercurial: his Martial thigh:
> The brawns of Hercules: but his Jovial face—   [4.2.308–11]

Earlier she had told Cloten that her husband's "meanest garment" was better in her eyes than Cloten's whole body. That comment persuaded Cloten to taunt Imogen by wearing Posthumus's garments. Clearly, however, the heroine does not read as well as she thinks she does. Nor do the ancient gods assist her. Imogen places her (supposed) husband's body in the Olympian pantheon of planetary forces, much as Cleopatra deifies Antony after his death, but this particular cosmic man is nothing more than a headless dolt. Faced with the (misread) body of Cloten, Imogen curses all the systems of communication: "To write, and read / Be henceforth treacherous!" (4.2.316–17).

When reading turns to voyeurism and to misreading, the ancient book becomes subject to dangers that did not emerge even in the perverse world of *Titus Andronicus*. The voyeurism in *Cymbeline* reflects at once upon pagan traditions and upon the contemporary pursuit of them. Erotic myths like those of Actaeon or Lucretia demonstrate the perils of lascivious eyesight, and the visual world in which those and other stories are depicted in the Renaissance makes voyeurism their very medium. After all, even without Iachimo's malign presence, Imogen's bedroom is decorated with erotic pagan subjects, and the innocent girl spends her time reading Ovid's book of rapes. The play itself may be just such a medium of voyeurism as are the books and pictures inside it.

As for the problems of misreading, they testify in part to a kind of hermeneutic fatigue characteristic of the late Renaissance: an overextension of all the systems of allegory, moralization, Platonization, etc. In part they are simply the obverse of the limitless aesthetic possibilities that Shakespeare perceived earlier in his career. *Cymbeline* is certainly a play in which he tries everything—which may be the signal, or the cause, of frustration. But the changes in the reading of the pagan book may in the end be less important than the continuities, the close ties between the words and pictures of antiquity and the medium that Shakespeare himself is forging. In the course of his career Shakespeare will write a new version of the book himself; that is, he will translate the pagan world of myth and metamorphosis into a dramatic language of his own. To the expressions of that language we shall now turn, first to Shakespeare's fullest and most independent response to the Ovidian tradition and then to its wider influence on his imagination. At the very end we may see the return of the book, but by that time it will have become less an artistic model than a mystic symbol.

2. Ovid "Translated"

When Theseus looks back on the action of *A Midsummer Night's Dream* as it has been narrated to him by the young lovers, he speaks dismissively and incredulously of "these antique fables," which he consigns to the realm of fantasy and wish-fulfillment. *Antique*, with its double meanings of ancient and antic, is a pun we have already observed in *The Faerie Queene*, but the significances run even deeper here. Theseus means that the lovers are telling silly old stories, familiar, grotesque, and untrue. But once we read *antique* as referring to the ancient world, we are reminded that the whole body of classical myth consists of precisely such stories, dismissed by some for the same reasons Theseus dismisses them, while being celebrated by others because of the very imaginative power that the Duke of Athens seems to hold in contempt. The joke is finally upon Theseus, of course: he is himself both ancient (as a figure of classical myth) and antic (as a player); he is also a creature of someone else's imagination. What concerns us here more than Theseus's opinions, however, is the self-conscious retrospective offered by his comments at the beginning of the fifth act. As Theseus and Shakespeare embark upon a debate concerning the uses of the imagination, they define the entire previous action of the play as "antique fables," that is, classical myth.[9]

In some ways, though it is removed from *Titus Andronicus* by only a few years, *A Midsummer Night's Dream* is the very opposite sort of exercise in reviving the classical tradition. The events of *Titus* are overdetermined by their sources—not so much the history of Rome as all the mythic traditions of savagery that are typified by the Tereus story—and the characters are burdened by their historical and mythical past. Shakespeare's relation to his text is similar: that is, he is obsessed by confronting and measuring up to the book in which the story is found. *A Midsummer Night's Dream* is one of the very few of Shakespeare's plays for which there is nothing like a general overall source. Like *Love's Labour's Lost* and *The Tempest*—which share a similar distinction—the *Dream* reveals a playwright exceptionally conscious of himself and his freedom as he sets himself in the context of his origins. That freedom makes for neither a combative nor an obsequious relation to sources (both of which are visible in *Titus*); rather, it is a relationship of equals. Ovid is not the only example—the *Dream* stands in a similarly three-dimensional relationship to *The Knight's Tale*, *The Golden Ass*, and perhaps even Shakespeare's own *Romeo and Juliet*.[10] Yet the world of the *Metamorphoses* is primary in the genesis of this play, Shakespeare's fullest attempt to respond to the inspirations afforded by Ovidian materials and to translate them into his own mythic language.

There are, of course, pieces of direct imitation. The play is crowded with explicitly named figures of myth; it reenacts (in "antic," but fundamentally faithful, fashion) a famous episode from the *Metamorphoses*; it takes place in some kind of classical Athens; its action is both explicitly and implicitly based on Ovidian metamorphosis. Let us begin with the simplest of translations: two important characters called Theseus and

Hippolyta. The dramatist either avoids the considerable body of negative associations surrounding both these figures—the husband notorious for seducing and abandoning, the wife for being a man-hating Amazon—or else he presents his characters as having been educated out of such adolescent attitudes toward love. With the help of *The Knight's Tale* and Plutarch's *Lives*, Shakespeare can with a very few strokes make of Theseus a heroic bringer of order, a firm but merciful judge, and a normative political leader in the grown-up world. Of Hippolyta (painted with even fewer strokes) he can with the help of romantic epic traditions concerning female warriors make a noble lady knight with an exotic past now brought into the fold of heroic love.[11] Such changes are well within the classical range of these myths; Shakespeare's own mythic language emerges only when we see Theseus and Hippolyta in the light of their doppelgängers in the play:

> TITANIA.   Why art thou here,
>   Come from the farthest steep of India,
>   But that, forsooth, the bouncing Amazon,
>   Your buskin'd mistress and your warrior love,
>   To Theseus must be wedded, and you come
>   To give their bed joy and prosperity?
> OBERON.   How canst thou thus, for shame, Titania,
>   Glance at my credit with Hippolyta,
>   Knowing I know thy love to Theseus?
>   Didst thou not lead him through the glimmering night
>   From Perigouna, whom he ravished;
>   And make him with fair Aegles break his faith,
>   With Ariadne and Antiopa?   [2.1.68–80][12]

Whatever the literary background of Oberon and Titania—a mixture of Celtic fairy lore, Homeric deities, and Chaucerian planetary influences —they are introduced here as variations on the theme of Theseus and Hippolyta. In the process Shakespeare creates a new mythology that bridges the domestic and the pagan. According to the Chaucerian model, pagan heroes and divinities exist on parallel planes in an abstract and allegorical set of power relations. Shakespeare unites his mythic characters not with their planetary protectors but with their own doppelgängers, who are portrayed as familiar local spirits of nature. The effect is to recreate a cosmic role for pagan gods who are assimilated into the most immediate and unexotic kind of folk-myth.

But Shakespeare's two couples are not only parallel in the way that, say, Spenser's Amoret and Belphoebe parallel Venus and Diana. They are interconnected by their mutual and illicit sexual relations. Once Oberon and Titania identify their own past involvements with Theseus and Hippolyta, the fairy couple become, as it were, the skeletons in the closet of the Athenian pair. The play opens with a grand assertion of orderly love and sovereignty; and, so far as Theseus and Hippolyta are concerned, the action never questions that order. But the comic trials of the other mythic couple expose the secret truths that lie behind mature love and power while sketching in a past that the Athenian pair barely admits to. By the end the couples are united both within and between themselves. The marital dispute is settled, and Oberon and Titania can resolve themselves into precisely such protecting deities over the other couple as those Chaucer's characters had enjoyed. The mythic parallels thus serve a double function: they may help to resolve disorder in a cosmic plan of correspondences, but they also stand as a disquieting arena of doubleness, a secret or nether side that lurks under the show of harmony, in just the way that "deeper" meanings lurk under the integumentum of pagan fable.

Another double bridges the gap between ancient and contemporary mythological creeds in A *Midsummer Night's Dream*, in this case not separate parallel characters but separate aspects of a single character. Robin Goodfellow, whom Shakespeare knows familiarly as Puck, was a well-known country spirit, particularly associated with mischievous illusion and transformation. But, as Shakespeare makes Puck the springboard to much of the play's action, the little fairy becomes a translation of Cupid. Early in the play—before there are any amorous accidents and before we have met the fairies—Helena characterizes Cupid as winged, blind, hasty, lacking in judgment, and juvenile. It is a veritable program for the actions of Puck once he is at the center of the plot. While he is not the origin of the love-juice, he is certainly its disseminator. He flies about the world like Cupid, he inspires love more or less at random, and he delights in his errors. He mistakes Lysander and Hermia for a feuding couple because he sees them sleeping separately rather than together, and he cannot construe this choice as virtue but only as "lack-love" and "kill-courtesy." So the country sprite of randomness, who is invoked upon his first appearance as a figure responsible for all sorts of otherwise inexplicable bucolic accidents, is joined by the action of the play with the great pagan figure of accidental and unexpected passion.[13]

Now the mythic world of faery, whether represented by the regal figure of Oberon or by a folk-sprite like Robin Goodfellow, exists in an atmosphere of magical transformation. In fact, Shakespeare's principal source for Puck, as well as an important source for Bottom's transformation, Reginald Scot's *Discoverie of Witchcraft* (1584), rehearses all the patristic conflicts concerning the possibility of metamorphosis. The most absolute of these is orthodox denial:

> Whosoever beleeveth, that anie creature can be made or changed into better or woorsse, or transformed into anie other shape, or into anie other similitude, by anie other than by God himselfe the cre-

ator of all things, without all doubt is an infidell, and woorsse than a
pagan. [bk. 5, chap. 3; p. 55][14]

But the text also offers various detailed descriptions of historical metamorphoses that had taken place (notably of a man into a jackass), and even
a recipe that explains how "with certeine charmes and popish praiers I can
set an horsse or an asses head upon a mans shoulders" (13.19; pp. 178
−79). Scot revives the arguments of Augustine (whom he mentions frequently) so as to mount an attack upon Catholics parallel to the Saint's attack upon pagans: that is, to declare metamorphosis a lie, but, should it be
proven to have taken place, to consign it to the impieties practiced by a
false religion. Like Augustine, Scot must postulate the existence of a demonic realm in which such transformations can at least appear to take
place.[15] Shakespeare, with no anti-Catholic axe to grind, seems rather to
have been inspired by all of Scot's questions surrounding demons and
transformations: do metamorphoses transform the body or the mind; are
they real or illusory; what divine power enables them to take place; do demons, witches, and spirits like Robin Goodfellow actually exist; are they
capable of sexuality and procreation?

We have only to look at the introduction to another of Shakespeare's
sources, Ovid's account of the Minyades narrating Pyramus and Thisbe,
to see a different form of metamorphic lore:

illa, quid e multis referat (nam plurima norat),
cogitat et dubia est, de te, Babylonia, narret,
Derceti, quam versa squamis velantibus artus
stagna Palaestini credunt motasse figura,
an magis, ut sumptis illius filia pennis
extremos albis in turribus egerit annos,
nais an ut cantu nimiumque potentibus herbis
verterit in tacitos iuvenalia corpora pisces,
donec idem passa est, an, quae poma alba ferebat
ut nunc nigra ferat contactu sanguinis arbor:
hoc placet. [4.43−53]

(She mused awhile which she should tell of many tales, for very
many she knew. She was in doubt whether to tell of thee, Dercetis
of Babylon, who, as the Syrians believe, changed to a fish, all covered with scales, and swims in a pool; or how her daughter, changed
to a pure white dove, spent her last years perched on high battle-
ments; or how a certain nymph, by incantation and herbs too potent, changed the bodies of some boys into mute fishes, and at last
herself became a fish; or how the mulberry-tree, which once had
borne white fruit, now has fruit dark red, from the blood stain. The
last seems best.)

The Minyades are as hostile to the metamorphic world of passionate love as Reginald Scot is to the "popish" world of demonic transformations. Their stories exemplify the dangers of blind passion. The illicit love of Pyramus and Thisbe gives them special sight—it is they who discover the chink in the wall that nobody else had ever noticed—but it is a murky and deceptive kind of vision. They cannot see each other properly through the chink in the wall; they escape only to meet in a darkness which is similarly unrevealing; and they are undone by the young man's failure to identify his beloved properly when he mistakes the covering (her bloody mantle) for the thing itself. In the conjunction of Scot and the Minyades we have Shakespeare's two mythologies, the fairy and the pagan, rendered *sub specie metamorphosis*. Rising to the challenge of Scot's skepticism and the Minyades' distrust of the powers of passion, Shakespeare creates a world of metamorphic love that translates Augustine's imaginative demonology to domestic fairy lore and fuses that with the great pagan anthology of transformation.

Metamorphoses are the order of business in every aspect of *A Midsummer Night's Dream*, but the epicenter of the phenomenon is the love-juice:

OBERON.   Thou rememb'rest
    Since once I sat upon a promontory,
    And heard a mermaid on a dolphin's back
    Uttering such dulcet and harmonious breath
    That the rude sea grew civil at her song
    And certain stars shot madly from their spheres,
    To hear the sea maid's music?
PUCK.   I remember.
OBERON.   That very time I saw (but thou couldst not),
    Flying between the cold moon and the earth,
    Cupid all arm'd: a certain aim he took
    At a fair vestal, throned by the west,
    And loos'd his love shaft smartly from his bow
    As it should pierce a hundred thousand hearts.
    But I might see young Cupid's fiery shaft
    Quench'd in the chaste beams of the watery moon,
    And the imperial votress passed on,
    In maiden meditation, fancy-free.
    Yet mark'd I where the bolt of Cupid fell:
    It fell upon a little western flower,
    Before milk-white, now purple with love's wound,
    And maidens call it "love-in-idleness." . . .
    The juice of it, on sleeping eyelids laid

> Will make or man or woman madly dote
> Upon the next live creature that it sees.   [2.1.148–72]

This is one of the great examples of Ovid reborn in Renaissance garb. Shakespeare's myth corresponds to no particular classical example; rather it produces an original etiology in the Ovidian mode.[16] Oberon creates a picture of sublime cosmic harmony with the familiar Ovidian layers of land, sea, and sky. Within that order Cupid is a disquieting element, and yet his irresistible force is balanced by the immovable object of the cold moon. The drama of the "imperial votress" does more than compliment Queen Elizabeth. It sets her in the great chain of powers that rule over human beings. The quarrel of Titania and Oberon, according to the play's erotic cosmology, disturbs earthly nature. In a similar but contrasting way, the unassailable virginity of the queen generates passion in "a hundred thousand hearts" as a complementary reaction. Such is the significance of the arrow's ricocheting motion: Cupid could have inspired royal passion; failing that, he produced an aphrodisiac for the masses.

But the tale of love-in-idleness goes far beyond the queen. It is a myth of transformations via love. Cupid's essence (especially at the high concentration needed to go after Elizabeth) is diverted to a tiny white flower, which is then transformed to the purple of passion. The source of that image is the etiology of the mulberry, which begins white but ripens red because of the spent blood of two young lovers, none other than Pyramus and Thisbe. It is a curious fact that Shakespeare omits all reference (apart from one brief and unmetamorphic mention of "mulberry shade") to the natural transformation in the Ovidian story that the mechanicals dramatize. The myth of love-in-idleness explains the omission. Like many Renaissance Ovidians, Shakespeare is more interested in transformation as a cause than in transformation as an effect. So he transfers the metamorphosis from the end of the story to the beginning: instead of a memorial via the oozing blood of the dead lovers, he offers a cause for the passionate blood of the living lovers. The now-purple flower is itself an emblem of metamorphosis by love and, more important, it becomes the inspiration for the metamorphoses of passion.

The career of love in the play seethes with these transformations, whether caused by the magic flower or not. In proper Ovidian fashion love is defined as metamorphosis in the world of *A Midsummer Night's Dream*. Before any anointment takes place, Hermia is declaring (in a tone that suggests she is unaware of the negative implications) that love of Lysander "hath turn'd a heaven into a hell" (1.1.207), while Helena shortly thereafter announces that her love for Demetrius turns night into day. Animals lurk on the fringes of the young lovers' experiences: Helena wishes she were Demetrius's dog and then decides she is as ugly as a bear; Hermia dreams of a serpent and is later compared to a whole gazeteer of unfortunate forms when the two young men have turned against her. The real purpose of the magic flower is to create an external drama to mirror the psychological world of adolescent changes that define young love. Lysander, upon being inspired with love for Helena, speaks in images of the most glorious forms of transformation: the victory of reason over irrational passion, of maturity over wayward youth, of true religion over heresy. The fact that we know the cause of these changes to be the love-juice turns these heroic assertions into parodies of such metamorphosis; and Demetrius's equivalent assertion when he is anointed that his heart is "home returned" to his original love Helena raises similar parodic possibilities even though his amatory transformation moves in the "right" direction.

The great central scene of the play, when the four young lovers engage in a kind of war of all against all, stages the drama of transformed identity most fully. Demetrius's hate of Helena has turned to love; Lysander's love of Hermia has turned to hate. Helena's nurturing, childlike relationship with her pretend twin sister has been exploded by the individuation of maturity. The scene is, in fact, designed so that all four characters who have deliberately been made interchangeable up to this point (and perhaps afterwards as well) are forcibly separated. Above all it is Hermia whom the scene metamorphoses. Faced with all the changes that surround her, she questions her identity in true Ovidian fashion: "Am not I Hermia? Are not you Lysander?" (3.2.273). At the same time, the "hatred" of her erstwhile lovers transforms her outward appearance, especially to Lysander, who sees her as "you Ethiope," "thou cat, thou burr! Vile thing . . . like a serpent," "tawny Tartar," "loathed medicine," "hated potion." In this context, the comic crisis concerning the relative heights of Hermia and Helena becomes a metamorphic parody of the individuation taking place among the characters. When Helena refers to her friend as a "puppet," she intends to slander not Hermia's size but her veracity. Hermia's imagination turns the accusation corporeal, however, and from that moment all are engaged in a kind of conspiracy to shrink the poor girl, until she is finally silenced by Lysander's progressive miniaturization: "Get you gone, you dwarf; / You minimus, of hindering knot-grass made; / You bead, you acorn!" (3.2.328–30). The characters are caught in the transformations of love and hate, which in turn produce metamorphoses of shape and consciousness.

Meanwhile the background for the stories of love offers more signs of metamorphosis. The woods are, after all, a world upside-down and in constant change. The aegis of the moon, under which so much of the action explicitly takes place, in itself signifies change, not only because of alternating lunar phases but also because of the moon's more radically shifting significations, from the cold and barren to the passionate and lunatic.

The similar, and metaphorically related, fluctuations of love and hate between Titania and Oberon transform the order of nature into chaos, with changes in geography and seasonal patterns that remind one of the disorders described in the first two books of the *Metamorphoses*. The cause of the fairy monarchs' contention, it should be remembered, is a dispute over the so-called changeling child, an offspring of the Indian king and queen, now part of Titania's retinue and desired by Oberon. This pretext for so much of the dramatic action stands as one of the play's most powerful enigmas. Like the magic herb, it seems to support more plot than its own significance would justify. Also like love-in-idleness, the changeling child encapsulates a whole metamorphic drama. According to traditional fairy lore, which Shakespeare would have found in Spenser and in Scot's *Discoverie of Witchcraft*, fairies were in the habit of exchanging their own (often monstrous) babies for particularly beautiful human infants; this practice could leave parents in doubt about the identity of their own children, especially when these acted wickedly or rebelliously.[17] The use of the term "changeling" between Titania and Oberon is unusual in that it applies to the human rather than the fairy infant—indeed, the play never directly asserts that any child was substituted for the Indian prince. And the accounts of the "changeling" process vary between traditional fairy abduction ("A lovely boy, stol'n from an Indian king," says Puck [2.1.22]) and Titania's story, which suggests that she is raising the boy in homage to her dear (but unfortunately mortal) friend, the Indian queen.

The verbal and narrative complications surrounding the abducted child serve to emphasize the sense of change in the story: the mortality of the mother, the abduction of the infant, Oberon's desire to abduct the child once more, the implicit sense of exchange in the fairy lore surrounding such cases. The example of the changeling child—and the alliterative phrase echoes powerfully through the Titania and Oberon plot—underlines metamorphic questions of identity in the other plots, notably the exchange of the monster Bottom for a love-object properly suitable to Titania (a changeling punishment for a changeling crime) and the destabilizing of such parent-child relationships as that of Egeus and Hermia. And the final blessings offered by Titania and Oberon to the marriage unions and their offspring tend to resolve the fairy crime of changeling children by insuring that these babies shall be free of monstrosity.

It is, finally, difficult to pinpoint single elements of the metamorphic world of *A Midsummer Night's Dream*: all the qualities of the woods—love, wish-fulfillment, dream, imagination, mystery, magic, alternations of all kinds—are closely tied to that cluster of associations inspired by the world of pagan transformations. In addition, the method of the play is metamorphic: the parallel and competing mythologies which exist in a partly harmonious and partly dissonant relationship join with all the other shifts in perception and perspective that both characters and audience experience. When—to return to where we began—Theseus sums it up in his triad of "lunatics, lovers, and poets," he offers a very accurate retrospective on the principal concerns of the Ovidian tradition, of "antique fables." It turns out that he speaks with the voice of the Minyades or Reginald Scot or a host of Christian commentators on paganism: that is, he dismisses it all as fantasy suitable for adolescents. Hippolyta offers a different valuation of the fables:

> But all the story of the night told over,
> And all their minds transfigur'd so together,
> More witnesseth than fancy's images,
> And grows to something of great constancy;
> But, howsoever strange and admirable. [5.1.23–27]

Transfiguration and the metamorphosis of changeable images into "great constancy": this is the voice with which the deepest Renaissance appreciation of paganism speaks. To understand how the truth of Hippolyta overcomes the truth of Theseus, we must turn to the one remaining transformation of pagan myth in the play, the most debasing and most profound of all the metamorphoses.

Only one character in the comedy undergoes literal Ovidian transformation: Bottom the weaver, whom Puck finds suitable for the role of Titania's monster-beloved. Like everything in *A Midsummer Night's Dream*, the Bottom subplot is Shakespeare's own mythic invention deriving from no single source. Yet it clearly owes much to Ovid's treatment of the foolish Midas, whose head is implanted with ass's ears in recognition of his boorish and blasphemous musical preference for Pan over Apollo.[18] Bottom, too, is an incongruous oaf who finds himself accidentally in the arena where the gods do combat; he also, as it happens, vaunts his sophistication in music and (more importantly) other arts. The other half of Shakespeare's obvious debt is to be paid to Apuleius, whose hero is neither a fool nor an oaf but an excessively curious, libidinous, and occult-minded foreigner punished by accidental self-transformation into a jackass.[19] He must endure a year's beastly existence before he can be rehumanized and united with the goddess who has become the object of both his religious and his sexual cravings. Though the shape of the narrative is topsy-turvy, Bottom's experience also juxtaposes the gross, the amorous, and the ethereal.[20]

Bottom's transformation underlines metamorphic issues that emerge in the rest of the narrative. From Helena's monologue at the end of the first scene, which acts as a kind of argument to the action of the whole play, we have already learned that "Things base and vile, holding no quantity, / Love can transpose to form and dignity" (1.1.232–33). She is reflecting upon the psychological metamorphoses induced by passion. When in retrospect the statement is applied to Bottom (whom it fits so well), it points to the interconnections of physical and psychological trans-

formation, for Bottom undergoes two quite different Ovidian metamorphoses: first, becoming a jackass, which alters him physically but confirms
his "base and vile" nature, and, second, ascending to the highest realm of
"form and dignity"—appropriate to neither the human nor the asinine
Bottom—in which he becomes the consort to the Fairy Queen.

Such metamorphoses conflate not only body and spirit but also subject
and object. Different responses to Bottom's transformation depend upon
different consciousnesses. His companions see him as a jackass, and they
run away in terror. We see him as such, and we laugh. For his own part
Bottom does not see himself as a jackass at all. Only his head is transformed: that may suggest a changed consciousness (e.g., wanting to eat
hay), but it also means that the victim cannot see his own metamorphosis.
He is quite surprised, in fact, when feels his head and discovers that he is
"marvelous hairy about the face" (4.1.24–25). If this represents an objective transformation of Bottom's head, then his other metamorphosis, the
assumption into "form and dignity," represents a subjective transformation of Titania's head—or, to use the idiom of the play, her eyesight. That
the Fairy Queen sees Bottom as the incarnation of beauty transforms him
upwards just as surely as the physical change imposed by Puck transforms
him downwards. And all these changes upon changes reflect upon the
metamorphic world of the young lovers, who are not literally subject to
animal transformation but must constantly take the shape into which they
are forced by others' eyesight and consciousness. The Bottom and Titania
scenes act out literally and theatrically what is for the two young couples a
psychological drama.

Bottom acts out other metamorphic dramas that are implicit elsewhere
in the play. The deliquescent sense of nature, which emerges in the play's
shifting imagery and in the experience of the Athenians who are lost in
the forest's natural labyrinth, is fulfilled in the theatrical picture of Bottom held captive by Titania's flowery decorations. In addition, the metamorphic atmosphere associated in the play with fairy lore—especially the
changes wrought by Puck's elfin abilities—impinge most literally upon
Bottom as he is attended by Peaseblossom, Cobweb, and the rest. Indeed
the world of the forest is in many ways defined by these two metamorphic
principles of naturization and miniaturization, and it is Bottom who experiences them literally and at first hand. Just as the opposition between
Bottom and Titania is overturned by a kind of elective affinity, so Bottom's qualities unite with the forest world because they stand in diametric
opposition to it: the urban mechanical meets the triumph of lush nature,
and the earthbound corporeal meets the exquisitely elfin. The opposing
principles in the play define themselves through Bottom and, especially,
through the metamorphoses that unite the oppositions.

Yet Bottom's metamorphosis is most important not in the ways that it
mirrors the changes of other characters but in the ways that it stands apart
from them. When the various sleepers arise in the fourth act, they are

neatly divided into two groups: the lovers, who awaken in public face to face with their duke and father figure, and Bottom, who awakens in one of the play's rare soliloquies. The young people complete their education as they reintegrate themselves into the good graces of their elders and into the whole society to which marriage entitles them. Bottom's alternative depends upon the quite different path that his love and his metamorphosis have allowed him to travel. When Bottom is singled out from his companions in the woods, transformed, and confronted with the Fairy Queen, he is vouchsafed a visionary experience, indeed, that special sort of sacred vision that is granted only to the (apparently) undeserving. Titania, it should be remembered, has been sleeping onstage throughout the last two scenes. The four young Athenians have come and gone and the mechanicals have held their rehearsal without seeing her. (In fact, apart from Bottom no mortal in the play ever sees any of the fairies.) The meeting of the ill-matched lovers involves mutually bewitched eyesight: not only Titania's love-under-the-influence but also Bottom's ability to see—indeed to have intimate relations with—the goddess.

The model for this meeting is that whole sequence of Ovidian tales in which metamorphosis is linked with the unsettling confrontations of mortals and gods, especially the story of dangerous eye contact between Diana and Actaeon. Shakespeare's name for the Queen of Fairy is borrowed directly from Ovid's sobriquet for Diana in this very story.[21] Titania, too, is the victim of a mortal intrusion upon her private amusements; and she, too, is identified with the moon from the first moment that we meet her. She is also a Diana in respect to chastity, criticizing Oberon's sexual escapades and banishing adult males from her company in favor of sexually naive characters like miniaturized fairies and changeling boys. Bottom, for his part, is a jackass-Actaeon whose experience depends on both the voyeuristic and the visionary traditions of that myth. The translations of Actaeon's experience into Bottom's render explicit what had been implied in some Renaissance versions of the Ovidian myth. That the animal transformation precedes the visionary experience tends to fuse metamorphic exaltation and degradation into a single, causally connected act; that the animal is not a stag but a jackass tends to polarize the opposing elements and, in proper Apuleian fashion, to identify the most earthly with the most sublime. Such an identification points toward a Platonic account of visionary experience, as Titania herself suggests in her love-making:

> I pray thee, gentle mortal, sing again:
> Mine ear is much enamour'd of thy note;
> So is mine eye enthralled to thy shape;
> And thy fair virtue's force perforce doth move me
> On the first view to say, to swear, I love thee.
>
> . . . .
>
> I'll give thee fairies to attend on thee;

And they shall fetch thee jewels from the deep,
And sing, while thou on pressed flowers dost sleep:
And I will purge thy mortal grossness so,
That thou shalt like an airy spirit go.   [3.1.132–36; 150–54]

Both characters, according to this account, are playing roles in a traditional Platonic love story. Titania moves from the enchantment of her
senses (the sound of Bottom's song; the sight of his body) to a state of rapture in recognition of his virtue. Bottom meanwhile is to attain a sublime
state pulled upward by his love of the divine.

It is the wakings up, the returns from a metamorphic condition, that
really define the nature of the experience. The four lovers, awakened by
the Duke, dimly recognize that they have undergone a doppelgänger experience in which the doubles of metamorphosis, of dream and reality, of
sleep and waking, and of their own shifting pairings have taken them beyond normal life. But they decide rather firmly to put the experience behind them. By following their elders back to Athens and joining them in
the marriage ceremony, they turn the inchoate doubleness into sharp focus and come down on the side of waking, reality, and integration into
grown-up society. Demetrius's exit-line as they head for the temple, "By
the way let us recount our dreams" (4.1.198), serves to bracket the dream
as suitable for casual amusement on the way to a more important ceremony. This is just the sort of amusement the young people seem to have
been providing in the moments preceding the opening of the fifth act,
to which Theseus responds with his famous strictures concerning the
imagination.

Bottom, who awakens moments after the young lovers, defines his experience differently:

I have had a most rare vision. I have had a dream, past the wit of
man to say what dream it was. Man is but an ass if he go about to expound this dream. Methought I was—there is no man can tell
what. Methought I was—and methought I had—but man is but a
patched fool if he will offer to say what methought I had. The eye of
man hath not heard, the ear of man hath not seen, man's hand is not
able to taste, his tongue to conceive, nor his heart to report, what
my dream was.   [4.1.203–12]

Bottom understands that the experience was a vision. He never denies its
reality, but he greets it with the wordless wonderment appropriate to
mystic rites of initiation. This particular variation on asininity, while reminding us of the fusion between beastly metamorphosis and religious vision, also suggests that only "asses" (i.e., those who are stupid) *expound*,
that is, verbalize or analyze, such events. Bottom, in a perfect complement to Titania's rapture, experiences the memory through the senses,

but so much does his ecstasy transcend them that they are all confused in his recollection. It is no accident that Bottom's mishmash of the senses is a misquotation from the ecstatic language of St. Paul, who is speaking precisely of divine mysteries at this point in I Corinthians:

> We speake the wisdome of God in a mysterie, even the hid wisdome, which God had determined before the world unto our glorie.

> Which none of the princes of this worlde hath knowen: for had thei knowe it, thei would not have crucified ye Lord of glorie. But as it is written, The things which eye hathe not sene, nether eare hathe heard, nether came into mans heart, are, which God hathe prepared for them that love him.[22]

Bottom is the antithesis of the "princes of this world"; by placing him in the path of mystery and vision, Shakespeare makes of him the complete comic hero, the holy fool, the exemplar of *docta ignorantia*. Only through multiple metamorphoses can these paradoxes come to life. In a few minutes—taken up with a mock lamentation and resurrection (even transfiguration) scene for Bottom, in which he appears to his disciples but like a true Platonic initiate refuses to tell the visionary secrets—one of the "princes of this world" will take center stage. Theseus, as we have seen, disparages the mystery; but the memory of Bottom's extraordinary (and real) transformations gives the lie to the "prince" and points instead toward Hippolyta's account involving not delusion and wish-fulfillment but transfiguration and "great constancy." In fact, the half-man, half-beast Bottom, whose secrets lie at the center of the play's physical and philosophical labyrinth, is one Minotaur whom this Theseus cannot slay.[23]

If the vile and the sublime are fused in the transformations of Bottom, then the play offers a mediation between the two that is not borrowed from Ovid or Apuleius—though its origins can be seen in Shakespeare's self-conscious reading of the book of Ovid in *Titus Andronicus*. Bottom undergoes transformation because he is an actor. Our very first impression of him is of a man who wants to play all the parts: not only is he lover, tyrant, and Hercules, but as the scene continues he wishes to usurp the roles of Thisbe and of the lion (not to mention the overarching usurpation of Peter Quince's role as stage manager). It is an anthology of classic metamorphoses, including apotheosis, sex change, and animal transformation. With the last, in fact, Bottom introduces the principle of (dare one coin the term?) meta-metamorphosis, since he offers in the person of the lion to "aggravate my voice so, that I will roar you as gently as any sucking dove; I will roar you and 'twere any nightingale" (1.2.76–78). Indeed the activity of the whole scene—the assignment of roles to those who knowingly or unknowingly are ill-suited to them—stands in telling juxtaposition to the first scene, in which the young people begin trying out their roles. And the two scenes together establish a decidedly metamorphic relationship between identity and role, whether in life or in theater.

That sense of role-playing as transformation lies at the heart of the rehearsal scene, in which the mechanicals thrash out the problems of dramatic representation. Bottom takes the lead by declaring that Pyramus's suicide onstage will be intolerable. In the same vein he enthusiastically supports Snout's objection that the representation of a lion will frighten the ladies. These problems, later joined by anxieties over the authentic presentation of moonlight and wall, result from what we might call an overliteral sense of identity, that is, that a thing cannot be anything but itself. In searching for solutions, Bottom and his colleagues discover metamorphosis as they investigate mimesis. The first problem is solved by a recognition that the actor is simultaneously himself and not himself ("I, Pyramus, am not Pyramus, but Bottom the weaver"; 3.1.19–20). Bottom's approach to the problem of Snug as lion yet more explicitly probes the question of theatrical identity in the context of animal transformation:

> Nay, you must name his name, and half his face must be seen through the lion's neck; and he himself must speak through, saying thus, or to the same defect: "Ladies," or "Fair ladies, I would wish you," or "I would request you," or "I would entreat you, not to fear, not to tremble: my life for yours! If you think I come hither as a lion, it were pity of my life. No, I am no such thing; I am a man, as other men are": and there, indeed, let him name his name, and tell them plainly he is Snug the joiner.   [3.1.35–44]

Bottom's notion of the stage lion is borrowed from the images of characters in the midst of Ovidian transformation as rendered in those picture-books that, as we saw above, had a strong influence on Shakespeare. Bottom's lion exists in just such a relation between actor and role as the mythological characters experience between essential identity and metamorphic form. (The solutions to the later mimetic problems—the moon and the wall—will also involve demi-metamorphoses with the real identity showing through all too clearly.) The climax of Bottom's impromptu speech for the lion, "I am a man, as other men are," is the great Ovidian cry of the victim of metamorphosis (notably Actaeon) attempting to assert his true self—which, in the Ovidian or the Shakespearean model, can only be discovered while in the midst of divine or theatrical transformation.

Bottom soon has the chance to make the same discovery and to bridge the gap between mimesis and metamorphosis. Some thirty lines later the stage directions have Puck enter and eavesdrop; the Folio and Quarto texts are, however, unreliable in fixing the exact moment of an actor's entrance.[24] Though it cannot be proven, it is nice to imagine Puck overhearing Bottom's performance as the lion. Whether or not that takes place, the metamorphosis imposed by Puck fits remarkably well with Bottom's impersonation of Snug: Bottom as jackass is a figure half human and half in animal costume; and he, too, devotes himself to asserting his humanity and his identity. In fact, Puck's words, both in this scene and the next (when he reports his success to Oberon), suggest that it is the *actor-liness* of Bottom which inspires the particular nature of the sprite's mischief. Oberon, it should be remembered, assumes that Titania's monster-beloved will be a real creature; and indeed there are many verbal indications that the forest abounds in such fauna as the "ounce, or cat, or bear," and so on that the Fairy King wishes upon his wife. Instead of searching out real wildlife, however, Puck comes upon theatrical wildlife: "What, a play toward? I'll be an auditor; / An actor too perhaps, if I see cause" (3.1.75–76).

Puck's treatment of Bottom amounts to a war of competing thespians. Bottom dares to attempt self-transformation. Puck contemptuously refers to him as "my mimic," suggesting at once that Bottom is an actor and that Bottom is playing the role of Puck; and he punishes Bottom with Ovidian metamorphosis. At the same time, the little sprite overwhelms and torments his victim with a virtuoso display of transformations far beyond anything a rude mechanical can attempt:

> Sometime a horse I'll be, sometime a hound,
> A hog, a headless bear, sometime a fire;
> And neigh, and bark, and grunt, and roar, and burn,
> Like horse, hound, hog, bear, fire, at every turn.   [3.1.103–06]

The metamorphoses of Cupid, of Proteus, and of the whole Ovidian cast of characters are combined in this figure of Puck;[25] all that Bottom has to say for his type of transformation is the speech he puts into the mouth of the actor/lion: "I am a man, as other men are." That is one thing Robin Goodfellow cannot say.

So the metamorphic drama of Bottom as jackass is not only moralized, amorous, and visionary; it also helps to define the art of theater. Bottom is "punished" for being an actor, and his resurrection becomes the triumph of the actor as metamorphic hero. That is the final level to be observed in his soliloquy. When Bottom draws the verbal parallel between "man is but an ass" and "man is but a patched fool," he means more than a slander upon those who verbalize visions, as was suggested above. The "patched fool" is a licensed actor, who was often represented with precisely those asses' ears that are imposed on Bottom in his "real life."[26] He thus wears proudly, as a professional artist/clown/protean, that badge of asininity with which Puck attempted to humiliate him. In other words, Bottom recognizes (dimly, to be sure) precisely what Theseus will shortly fail to recognize: that he is an actor. This recognition even takes him beyond the Pauline visionary experience into theatrical creation: "I will get Peter Quince to write a ballad of this dream: it shall be called 'Bottom's Dream,' because it hath no bottom; and I will sing it in the latter end of a play, before the Duke. Peradventure, to make it the more gracious, I shall sing it at her death" (4.1.213–17). Which play is *a* play, and whose death shall be the occasion for his song? "Pyramus and Thisbe" does not provide a sufficient answer. We must add "Bottom and Titania," *A Midsummer Night's Dream*, and even plays beyond that, for surely "Bottom's Dream [which] hath no bottom" is a kind of *impresa* for the playwright, who creates a world in which he is not, under his own name, permitted to appear. In a wonderful paradox, Shakespeare signs his name as playwright by denying the playwright's presence in the dream. That Bottom is the true figure of the author is evident from his profession: Peter Quince may be the linear carpenter who tries to hammer together the play, but Bottom is the weaver of a seamless fabric of reality and dream, of art and life, the incarnation of Arachne.

The actual performance of the mechanicals makes it clear that this equation of Bottom and dramatic art is no rhapsodic affirmation. The actors may be sublimely sincere, but the performance is terrible and the audience reaction at best contemptuously patronizing. Yet as the performers play their roles, they turn out to be walking embodiments of the metamorphic principles that Bottom has been enunciating and experiencing throughout the drama. All, in the end, are versions of Bottom's stagelion: composite creatures, partly themselves and partly their (half-assed?) roles. The doubleness is ludicrously visible; yet at the same time we can hear each of them, willingly or unwillingly, declare that, underneath it all, "I am a man, as other men are." The watching of the play becomes a metamorphic activity as well. Theseus, having just asserted that the imagination creates an illusory something out of nothing, declares that he and the rest of the audience will transform the "nothing" of the mechanicals' ability into a recognition of their real intention, characterized in such terms as "the modesty of fearful duty," "love," and "tongue-tied simplicity." To the extent that this attitude characterizes the actual reception of the play—which is problematic—it suggests that Theseus hears the actors loud and clear when they declare, "I am a man, as other men are," since that is the truth under their impersonations.

Yet if there are dueling versions of metamorphosis going on here between performers and audience, there is also persistent recourse on both sides to another system of joining one thing to another, that ancient double of metamorphosis—metaphor. The script of "Pyramus and Thisbe" is itself a tissue of figurative language, including apostrophe, hyperbole, simile, and synecdoche. Indeed, the essential absurdity of the text is its misuse of figura. Lips are not lilies, eyes are not leeks; the moon's "sunny" beams stretch the metaphoric relation to the breaking point, while "O night, which ever art when day is not" contracts it to absolute zero. The inappropriateness of all this metaphor stands in obvious parallel to the overblown nature of the whole performance; more significantly it parallels the *mal à propos* metamorphoses between the actors and their roles. The whole edifice of theater comes to be understood as the transformation of one thing into another; and that transformation, as Shakespeare understands it, seems designed to be only partial. That is why "Pyramus and Thisbe" is advertised as oxymoronic ("tedious brief," "tragical mirth"; 5.1.56–57): all the theatrical metamorphoses, like those of the lion and the jackass, maintain both identities simultaneously, just as the dizzy Petrarchan metaphorics of the young Athenian lovers or of their play-within-a-play doubles juxtapose girls and ravens or noses and cherries without fusing them. Oxymoron, after all, is a type of metamorphosis *manqué*.

Meanwhile the onstage audience is also engaged in the transforming activity of metaphor. Theseus, as we have seen, intends to treat the whole performance as an *integumentum* under which he will see the real (but unexpressed) truth. The young men do not seem to understand this doctrine; instead they attempt to score points off the performers with a series of puns, similes, and animal metaphors. In the most interesting case Theseus begins the confusion by introducing Lion and Moonshine, "Here come two noble beasts in, a man and a lion" (5.1.212–13). Is he speaking of two characters or one? We know from Bottom's impromptu prologue that Snug is both a man and a lion; Moonshine is neither a man nor a "noble beast," and if Starveling is being counted as such by Theseus, then the Duke is indeed hearing the message, "I am a man, as other men are." Snug himself complicates these multiple identities by asserting *"that I as Snug the joiner am / A lion fell, nor else no lion's dam"* (5.1.218–19). At least as the Quarto reading would have it,[27] he is a lion only insofar as he is Snug the joiner, a performer who fuses—*joins*—two identities.

These complications inspire a paroxysm of multiple animal metaphors among the viewers:

THESEUS.   A very gentle beast, and of a good conscience.
DEMETRIUS.   The very best at a beast, my lord, that e'er I saw.
LYSANDER.   This lion is a very fox for his valour.
THESEUS.   True; and a goose for his discretion.
DEMETRIUS.   Not so, my lord, for his valour cannot carry his discretion; and the fox carries the goose.
THESEUS.   His discretion, I am sure, cannot carry his valour; for the goose carries not the fox.   [5.1.222–29]

Perhaps the tedium which this sort of word-play inspires in a modern audience would be completely alien to Shakespeare's own theater—one thinks of the mental health that Romeo exudes when he returns to similar bantering with his friends after the agonized postures of his love for Rosaline. Yet it is difficult to avoid the feeling that the conversation quoted above, with its learned allusions, tortured logic, and can-you-top-this strategy, stands in pejorative contrast to the humble impersonations of Snug and Starveling, which surround it. The witticisms of the Athenians are based upon the whole tradition of beast fable and animal metaphor: monarchs should combine the strength of the lion and the cunning of the fox; geese are proverbially timorous, alarmist, and inanely noisy.[28] As handled by the young men, these equivalences become as multiple and metamorphic as Bottom's much earlier boast that he will impersonate a lion in the style of a dove—a combination just as incongruous as that between the lion and the fox, if a bit less traditional. But much has happened to metaphor and metamorphosis since the first act. The young sojourners in the forest have lived out their metaphors in real-life transformations (now put largely behind them), and Bottom has moved from the lion and the dove to the lion and the man, then the jackass-man-visionary, then the recognition of his dream, and finally the performance. In the process of those changes, expository metaphor of the kind we still see in the onstage audience has been superceded by actual performance, which is not metaphor but metamorphosis.

The distinction of metaphor and metamorphosis is clearest in a much lamer figura that emerges twice in the course of the audience repartee:

THESEUS. I wonder if the lion be to speak?
DEMETRIUS. No wonder, my lord; one lion may when many asses
do. [5.1.151–52]

BOTTOM. *Now die, die, die, die, die.*
DEMETRIUS. No die, but an ace for him; for he is but one.
LYSANDER. Less than an ace, man; for he is dead, he is nothing.
THESEUS. With the help of a surgeon he might yet recover, and
prove an ass. [5.1.295–99]

Ass is such a familiar term for a fool that one almost forgets it is a metaphor. Yet the whole action of the play—not only Bottom's asininity but the entire career of transformation in life and drama—has served to bring new life to such metaphors by translating them into metamorphosis and theater.

Yet it may in the end be wrong to give the last word to the subversive voice of learned ignorance and saintly folly in a play whose overriding purpose is to celebrate marriage. From the play's opening lines ("Our nuptial hour . . .") through the narrative complications for three couples in the woods to the penultimate speech in which Oberon blesses all new-lyweds, *A Midsummer Night's Dream* shows overwhelming evidence of having been originally composed for the occasion of a noble wedding.[29] The history of metamorphosis in the play—both the changes of adolescent love and the terrors of magic and sprites—forms part of the preparation for marriage. The union of Theseus and Hippolyta is the climax of a tale of abduction, and it is mirrored very early in the play by the abduction of Hermia, which sets in motion a whole sequence of crossings into unfamiliar territory. The psychological anxieties, with all their emotional and metaphorical changes, that focus especially upon the two young girls, are responses to the fear of leaving behind the virginal security of childhood. The terrors of the woods—which range from the "spotted snakes" that threaten Titania to Hermia's serpent dream to the "vile thing" which Oberon wishes to unleash upon his wife to the sudden inexplicable passions of the young men to the accidents of Puck to the metamorphosis of Bottom—all in some sense represent sexuality figured forth as the unfamiliar. The explicit resolution of these terrors is the wedding masque which may have concluded the original production, or else the blessings of the fairies along with the masquelike turning on the audience in Puck's final speech. The most potent resolution, however, is "Pyramus and Thisbe" itself, for the bathetic performance of that myth, in which the lovers were the fatal victims of liminality, sexuality, and metamorphosis, purges that threat for the Athenian (not to say Elizabethan) viewers in a triumphant, but properly apotropaic, wedding ceremony.[30] The pattern ought to be familiar, for it is precisely that of the Rape of Europa with all its nuptial equivalences between metamorphosis as fearful sexuality on the one hand and as triumphant marriage on the other.[31] *A Midsummer Night's Dream* may well be the greatest wedding cassone of all time.

3. Antiquity, Metamorphosis, and Shakespeare's Imagination

What pervades every moment of *A Midsummer Night's Dream* is visible—often in lesser strength, to be sure—throughout the length and breadth of Shakespeare's works: Ovid, metamorphosis, paganism, and antiquity come as close as anything does to occupying the heart of Shakespeare's imagination. Ovid, in the first place, signifies a special set of lenses with which to view antiquity. The Athenian setting of the *Dream* has nothing to do with Pericles or the Peloponnesian Wars; it has little to do with Aristophanes and not a great deal to do with Socrates. If it is anyone's Athens, it is Ovid's, a smoothly shifting set of environments in which gods, mortals, and heroes live in democratic proximity intermingling via the perils and delights of love. For the most part it is antiquity viewed as a garden of amorous excess (precisely the excesses that the action of the play will correct): the past relationship of Theseus and Hippolyta ("I woo'd thee with my sword, / And won thy love doing thee injuries"; 1.1.16–17); the amorous accidents of Pyramus and Thisbe; the literary passions of the immature lovers ("I swear to thee by Cupid's strongest bow, / . . . / By the simplicity of Venus' doves"; 1.1.169–71).

The purest view of this Ovidian antiquity is (not surprisingly) to be seen in *Venus and Adonis*. Like the past of *A Midsummer Night's Dream* —but more so—the world of Shakespeare's epyllion is that of the libertine Ovid: sensuality and sly humor wrapped in literary self-consciousness.[32] It offers a paean to the natural urges but also a powerful sense of how easily they can become entangled with perversity and violence. Animals, though not explicitly metamorphic, turn out to be figures who mediate between sex and mutilation. So Venus uses the stallion as an exemplum of proper lust, and so she—almost repellently—intermingles murderous and libidinous penetration in her account of Adonis's fatal goring by the boar, who

> "But by a kiss thought to persuade [Adonis] there;
> And nuzzling in his flank, the loving swine
> Sheath'd unaware the tusk in his soft groin.
>
> "Had I been tooth'd like him, I must confess,
> With kissing him I should have kill'd him first."   [ll. 1114–18]

In true Ovidian fashion Venus erases distinctions not only between human and animal and between love and death but also between male and female—which has been Shakespeare's strategy for the characters through the poem. And he ends this super-Ovidian exercise with an *hommage* to its originator. Venus's final angry response to her loss, a vow that from this moment love will be fickle, fraudulent, brief, stinging, transformative, overpowering, perverse, bellicose, and so on is an Ovidian-style etiology. The history of origins which it supplies happens to be that of Ovid's own world of passionate and excessive love.[33]

Yet *Venus and Adonis* does not represent the only Ovidian landscape upon which Shakespeare can open a casement. Lysander and Hermia swear amorous fidelity by Venus and Cupid. Lorenzo and Jessica in *The Merchant of Venice* take oaths that seem at first to have equally unstable Ovidian foundations:

LORENZO.   The moon shines bright. In such a night as this,
    When the sweet wind did gently kiss the trees,
    And they did make no noise, in such a night
    Troilus methinks mounted the Trojan walls,
    And sigh'd his soul toward the Grecian tents,
    Where Cressid lay that night.
JESSICA   In such a night,
    Did Thisbe fearfully o'ertrip the dew,
    And saw the lion's shadow ere himself,
    And ran dismayed away.
LORENZO.   In such a night,

> Stood Dido with a willow in her hand
> Upon the wild sea banks, and waft her love
> To come again to Carthage.
> JESSICA.   In such a night
> Medea gathered the enchanted herbs
> That did renew old Aeson.   [5.1.1–14][34]

The references are only fifty percent Ovid, to be sure, but the Trojans and the Carthaginians are clearly enveloped in an Ovidian atmosphere such as that of *Venus and Adonis*: the sensualities, the changes, the accidents of love. Yet here the myths stand as part of a larger design. The moon on "such a night" is more than an aphrodisiac; it puts Lorenzo in mind of the whole cosmic order expressed in the visual beauty of the heavens and in the harmonious music of the spheres:

> There's not the smallest orb which thou behold'st
> But in his motion like an angel sings,
> Still quiring to the young-ey'd cherubins;
> Such harmony is in immortal souls,
> But whilst this muddy vesture of decay
> Doth grossly close it in, we cannot hear it.   [5.1.60–65]

Does this universalizing turn Lorenzo away from Ovidian myth? On the contrary:

> Therefore the poet
> Did feign that Orpheus drew trees, stones, and floods,
> Since naught so stockish, hard, and full of rage,
> But music for the time doth change his nature.   [5.1.79–81]

Ovid does not need to be named because he is The Poet, just as Aristotle is The Philosopher. His presence, however, is signaled by the word *change*; and in that change the matter of Ovid has been transformed into a complete world-picture, from the sensual accidents of individual loves to the universals of cosmic harmony. That is, of course, the range of the *Metamorphoses* itself. But it is viewed through a special Renaissance rose-colored glass, like that of Titian's *Bacchanale of the Andrians*. Antiquity is seen as a golden world, in which beauty and sensuality are not subject to accident but contribute to a universal harmony. That explains the extraordinary beauty of the speeches Shakespeare gives Lorenzo and Jessica— hardly in keeping with their somewhat unsavory characters and deliberately incompatible with the financial and social tensions of the rest of the play.

The opposition between the poet of *Venus and Adonis* and The Poet of Orpheus's cosmic harmony is in many ways parallel to the twin retrospectives of Theseus and Hippolyta at the beginning of the fifth act of the

Dream. "Antique fables" are balanced with "something of great constancy." In fact, Hippolyta has herself recently sounded the note of cosmic Ovidianism:

> I was with Hercules and Cadmus once,
> When in a wood of Crete they bay'd the bear
> With hounds of Sparta; never did I hear
> Such gallant chiding; for, besides the groves,
> The skies, the fountains, every region near
> Seem'd all one mutual cry; I never heard
> So musical a disord, such sweet thunder.   [4.1.111–17]

It is no concidence that the metaphor is of the hunt.[35] At the end of *Venus and Adonis* and in the middle acts of the *Dream* the hunt is associated with the most unruly aspects of passion and violence. Here, however, the music of the dogs becomes the sound of universal harmony. Such, too, are the appearances of the ancient gods in the Masque of Jupiter in *Cymbeline* and Prospero's masque of Juno and Ceres in *The Tempest*. In every case, the violence, passion, and accident that characterize the Ovidian world of *Venus and Adonis* are transcended by the grander harmonies of an antique golden age. Like Shakespeare's various green worlds, with which they have much in common, these pagan utopias are not built to last; but that does not diminish their power as images.

More than antiquity, however, Ovid means metamorphosis. So long as Shakespeare opens lyrical windows upon the world of the pagan gods, whether that world is libidinous or celestial, he is operating within some of the narrower confines of Renaissance Ovidianism. When he takes his inspiration from Ovidian metamorphosis, on the other hand, he is touching upon the very heart of his own imagination. *A Midsummer Night's Dream*, for all its explicit Ovidianism, is not unique. Beneath its surface, and emerging in many other works, are the quintessentially metamorphic qualities of Shakespearean comedy. Some of these qualities find their origins in a set of myths of transformation. Salmacis and Hermaphroditus, the two lovers who are fused into one being, are balanced by the inevitable Ovidian parallel of Narcissus, one being who becomes two lovers and must torture himself with the paradoxes of individuality. The power of these myths owes something to Aristophanes' myth in Plato's *Symposium*, which traces human origins to twin eggs that have been split apart and are yearning to be reunited in love.[36] The two great non-Ovidian myths of transformation—Proteus and Circe—also play an important role, the first in imaging forth the varieties of human form and emotion, the second in sketching the dark possibility of a descent from the human to the animal if characters fall victim to the comic dangers that beset them. Further below the surface are all those Ovidian myths from Tereus to Myrrha which stretch the bounds of the roles people play and dangerously blur the distinctions among them. Taken together these myths inspire reflections on selfhood and love. They also provide a set of motifs that become the metamorphic matter of Shakespearean romantic comedy.[37] Two early examples set the elements in sharpest (and simplest) clarity.

The ruling metaphor of twinning in *The Comedy of Errors* sets the action of the play in a constant flow back and forth between individuation and amalgamation.[38] Before the play, the nuclear family (the adjective was never more apposite) was split into symmetrical doubles by the shipwreck that separated father, one Antipholus, and one Dromio from mother, second Antipholus, and second Dromio. At the other end of the action, all will be reunited. Yet for most of the action of the play the goal is not union but separation, as each twin must find himself by distinguishing himself from the other. The Antipholuses themselves divide the material in two: the Ephesian (on the whole) experiences the drama on the plane of society, the Syracusan on the deeper levels of spiritual uncertainty. What is at stake is, above all, individual identity, as Antipholus of Syracuse announces when first we see him:

> He that commends me to mine own content
> Commends me to the thing I cannot get.
> I to the world am like a drop of water
> That in the ocean seeks another drop,
> Who, falling there to find his fellow forth
> (Unseen, inquisitive) confounds himself.
> So I, to find a mother and a brother,
> In quest of them, unhappy, lose myself. [1.2.33–40][39]

Paradoxes and double meanings abound. "Content" is a pun, less contentment than containment, and the twinning of the term complicates the definition of identity. What does Antipholus contain? That is the question of the whole play. The water imagery has a similarly double valence, for it is the narrative medium of both separation and union just as it is an image for both the impossibility of union and the ease of flowing together. The speech ends with the more conventional paradox—so brilliantly acted out in the play—that one must lose oneself to find oneself.

All bonds between pairs of people become forms of twinning. The marriage bond is explicitly defined in terms that parallel Antipholus of Syracuse's search for his own identity. His (unbeknownst to him) sister-in-law, who thinks she is his wife, berates him:

> How comes it now, my husband, O, how comes it,
> That thou art then estranged from thyself?—
> Thyself I call it, being strange to me,
> That, undividable, incorporate,
> Am better than thy dear self's better part. [2.2.119–23]

She goes on to repeat the "drop of water" imagery. As at many other points, Shakespeare takes subtle advantage of the Pauline associations of Ephesus, where he (and not Plautus) has set the play. Here he translates the biblical definition of man and wife as one body into a metamorphic ebb and flow of union and separation between identities.[40] If man and wife are a species of twins subject to a comedy of errors, so are friend and friend, for the bond of Antipholus/Dromio operates in a similar and contrapuntal way to the bond of Antipholus/Antipholus. Shakespeare doubles Plautus's twins not only to complicate the plot but also to introduce a second kind of mirror, not of physical shape but of consciousness. Immediately after his "content" soliloquy Antipholus of Syracuse sees the entering Dromio and refers to him as "the almanach of my true date." Antipholus can look upon Dromio as his "almanach" because he can see in the servant the complete record of his own past. That shared experience makes the Dromio into an alter ego. For the Syracusan Antipholus, at least, this mirroring consciousness represents childhood security and familiarity in the midst of terrible changes; and it is only once he cannot depend on Dromio to mirror his consciousness—once the Dromios start switching at random from their appropriate masters—that Antipholus begins his descent into madness. That process begins very early, of course: the Dromio whom Antipholus of Syracuse refers to as his "almanach" is the wrong Dromio. In addition, then, to the twinning of man and wife as one flesh, the action of the play revolves around two kinds of twin for each Antipholus, one twin of consciousness and the other of shape.

That separation of consciousness and shape, as we have seen so often, is at the heart of magical transformation. In a sense the amalgamation of a single individual into half of a twin is the inverse of metamorphosis: not a multiplication but a division of physical form.[41] Yet, inverted or not, metamorphosis dominates the consciousnesses of all who participate in the action. The Ephesians (both twins and observers) see the familiar world transformed in all but physical shape, and they search for a new vocabulary to describe the change. All the familiar doubles of metamorphosis appear: madness, metaphorical transformation, verbal paradox. The two Syracusans are not in a familiar world. They can therefore see Ephesus as a place of real metamorphoses, as they are prepared to do even before the errors begin. Antipholus warns Dromio in their first scene together against "Dark-working sorcerers that change the mind, / Soul-killing witches that deform the body" (1.2.99–100). The changes within mind and body, indeed the uncertainty as to which kind of metamorphosis is operating, permeate the consciousness of the visitors:

S. DRO.   I am transformed, master, am I not?
S. ANT.   I think thou art in mind, and so am I.
S. DRO.   Nay, master, both in mind and in my shape.

S. ANT.   Thou hast thine own form.

S. DRO.   No, I am an ape.

S. ANT.   If thou art chang'd to aught, 'tis to an ass.   [2.2.195–99]

Ape and *ass* are more than casual animal metaphors. They are the beasts who parody human beings.[42] While the Ephesians can only resort to madness to explain the "changes" they observe, the Syracusans fluctuate between madness and real Circean witchcraft. The kitchen wench who claims Dromio as her husband—especially once her enormous body has been transformed into the body of the world ("She is spherical, like a globe; I could find out countries in her"; 3.2.112–13)—seems a good candidate for local Circe.

In the end it is the variety of perspectives upon the action that may be the most powerful metamorphosis of all: not only Syracusans vs. Ephesians and twins vs. observers but also the exponential confusions that arise from the different stories that can be told by four separate but interrelated twins and twice that number of observers. The comic drama of transformation eventually leads to the individuations of sanity, selfhood, and humanity, thus skirting the dangers of madness, of the infantile fusion of identities, and of degradation to the level of the animals. But that happy end can only be reached, it seems, once the characters have passed through the massive fragmentation of individual points of view. The dark center of the comedy, where madness and beastliness lurk, is a place where every individual has his own private reality. Such separation of realities stands in paradoxical relationship to the fusion of shapes and identities that characterizes the same dark period in the lives of the comic characters.

The Two Gentlemen of Verona turns on issues of identity and twinning that are at base similar to those in *The Comedy of Errors*. As in many of the comedies, the action centers on two pairs of lovers who are subject to a variety of chiastic interrelations. The title itself announces a kind of twinning, but in this case it is a relationship of mirror-opposites, the virtuous and maligned Valentine vs. the evil but successful Proteus. What sets the mirrorings and transformations in motion is a force much more central to this play than to the *Comedy*: romantic love. The name and nature of Proteus is the focal point for some of these metamorphoses. By alluding to that myth—and there can be few Shakespearean characters whose names are more often repeated in the text—the dramatist fuses two separate traditions of transforming love. The first is essentially Petrarchan Proteanism: passion produces a constant set of changes in the character and emotions of the lover. So Proteus himself muses:

Thou, Julia, thou hast metamorphos'd me;
Made me neglect my studies, lose my time,

War with good counsel, set the world at nought;
Made wit with musing weak, heart sick with thought.

[1.1.66–69]⁴³

And Valentine, for his part, acts out the changes when he is transformed in true Petrarchan fashion from a scorner to a servant of love. The second tradition, Proteus *moralisé*, focuses upon inconstancy, that is, the changes from one love object to another, such as Proteus undergoes as soon as he hears of Valentine's love for Silvia. Where the first type of Proteanism is concerned with the metamorphoses of adolescent emotion, the second is concerned with the changes involved in betrayal and faithlessness. They need not be part of the same fable of metamorphic love; yet in Shakespearean comedy they very often are.

Proteus may provide the impetus, but the real operation of metamorphic love requires all four of the young people. The two couples provide a closed system of mutual reflections in which individual identity and love must be hammered out. The transformations of the plot—Proteus's switch from Julia to Silvia, his obligation to woo Silvia for the sake of Thurio, Valentine's banishment, Julia's appearance in disguise—are only the surface level of entanglement among the four identities. In fact, the lovers are caught in a matrix of interrelations like those in Ovid's erotic tragedies. Shakespeare's men play the roles that Ovid assigns to his women. Both seem to discover introspection as they attempt to unravel the interrelations of passion and identity. This is not so surprising in the case of Valentine:

And why not death, rather than living torment?
To die is to be banish'd from myself,
And Silvia is myself: banish'd from her
Is self from self. A deadly banishment. [3.1.170–73]

Proteus, however, delves deeper into the tangle:

I cannot leave to love; and yet I do;
But there I leave to love, where I should love.
Julia I lose, and Valentine I lose;
If I keep them, I needs must lose myself;
If I lose them, thus find I by their loss;
For Valentine, myself; for Julia, Silvia.
I to myself am dearer than a friend,
For love is still most precious in itself,
And Silvia (witness heaven that made her fair)
Shows Julia but a swarthy Ethiope. [2.6.17–26]

We are witnessing the creation of a narcissistic identity. The rhetoric itself is mirrorlike in the style of Ovid's Narcissus. Proteus weaves his way tortuously through every link among the four individuals, and he pulls his own self out of the tangle only by opting for self-love as superior to any other kind. The value of that conclusion is at once ironically undercut: if Proteus can use this "logic" to metamorphose Julia into a "swarthy Ethiope," he can hardly be considered to have arrived at a set of clear perceptions about selfhood or love. This is not the way out of the tangle.

The women will provide a different set of reflections—not so much mirror words as mirror images. Principal among them is that most characteristically Shakespearean form of twinning and metamorphosis: the girl who transforms herself into a boy. Much has been written about this device.[44] For our purposes it should be emphasized that this transformation can produce, depending on the individual play, a whole new set of identity-doubles: the male and female heroine, the "boy" and "his" master-beloved, the transvestite girl and her sister-rival. *Two Gentlemen* does not probe the questions of gender as later comedies will, but it does explore the formation of identity by means of new pairings. As if to complicate Proteus's morbid catalogue of the interrelations among the lovers, the page boy enters into a companionable, even Dromio-like relationship with her former lover. She sees it as a new form of tangle: "I am my master's true confirmed love, / But cannot be true servant to my master, / Unless I prove false traitor to myself" (4.4.103–05). Proteanism, if not narcissism, seems to be contagious: words like *love, master,* and *servant* develop double meanings to fit the multiple forms of the characters.

Julia and Proteus are an old pair who appear in a new form. Julia and Silvia are a new pair, presented quite explicitly in mirroring terms. Proteus sends Sebastian (the disguised Julia) not only to woo Silvia but more specifically to fetch a picture of the new beloved. That errand becomes the occasion for a whole set of speculations concerning mirrors and images. Sebastian compares "himself" to Julia and compares Julia to Silvia, to the picture of Silvia, and to his/her own reflection in the mirror. In true Shakespearean form Sebastian moves from images to stage-images when "he" equates "himself" with Julia by recounting (inventing?) an episode in which "he" was able to wear Julia's gown as a theatrical costume:

> For I did play a lamentable part.
> Madam, 'twas Ariadne passioning
> For Theseus' perjury and unjust flight;
> Which I so lively acted with my tears,
> That my poor mistress, moved therewithal,
> Wept bitterly.   [4.4.164–69]

The current performance as Sebastian and the fictive performance of Ariadne stand in mirroring complementarity: transsexual in both directions but identical in that they capture the truth of Julia's victimization. The matter of Ovid fits this context perfectly: its associations with libertinism, with shape-change, with images, and with a text to be performed.

Once again, the search for identity leads through many protean changes. For the most part these changes lead away from mature love and selfhood. Mirrors, pictures, and performances all inhabit a metamorphic shadow-world. Even Proteus's request for a picture tips us off to the superficiality of his love, and Silvia properly links that request with his inconstancy: "Tell him from me," she announces to the all-too-appropriate messenger, "One Julia, that his changing thoughts forget, / Would better fit his chamber than this shadow" (4.4.116–18). At the end of the scene Julia draws the connection between images and immature love. Having herself engaged in a rather adolescent wish to resemble more closely the painted Silvia, she resolves herself:

> What should it be that he respects in her,
> But I can make respective in myself,
> If this fond Love were not a blinded god?
> Come, shadow, come, and take this shadow up,
> For 'tis thy rival. O thou senseless form,
> Thou shalt be worshipp'd, kiss'd, lov'd, and ador'd;
> And were there sense in his idolatry,
> My substance should be statue in thy stead.   [4.4.192–99]

The terms are profoundly Ovidian. The "statue" is the substantial fulfill-ment in true love (i.e., in three dimensions) of all the shadowy, change-able, and impercipient loves associated with the "blinded god." These "shadow" loves include not only Proteus but also the conventionalized love-by-a-picture and Julia's self-defeating performance of the messenger Sebastian.

But the determination that "I can make respective in myself" points beyond the labyrinth of shadowy proteanism toward a conclusion in which love does not merely entangle the self but also helps to define it with sharp individuality. As in the Ovidian myth which begins with Tire-sias' prophecy that the boy will live a happy life "si se non noverit,"[45] the great task in these Shakespearean comedies is to disentangle narcissism from self-knowledge. The actual denouement of the play shows, to be sure, that Shakespeare is not yet master of the craft. But beyond the hasty conversion of Proteus, the excessive nobility of Valentine's gesture to give up Silvia, and Julia's rather sententious "It is the lesser blot modesty finds, / Women to change their shapes, than men their minds" (5.4.108–09), we can still see the pattern toward which the author is striving. The comic structure begins with "two"; transformations both multiply and fuse those "twos." It ends with "one":

Come, Proteus, 'tis your penance but to hear
The story of your loves discovered.
That done, our day of marriage shall be yours,
One feast, one house, one mutual happiness.   [5.4.168–71]

"One," which can only be achieved through the experience of multiplicity, is both the mature union of lovers and an adult sense of separate individual identity.

For three other Shakespearean comedies—*A Midsummer Night's Dream*, *As You Like It*, and *Twelfth Night*—it can hardly be necessary to point out all the ways in which these metamorphic paradigms of selfhood and love operate. The *Dream* we have already discussed at length: the emphasis there is on maturation, that is, the movement from the kind of infantile fusion that Helena describes in her memories of twin sisterhood with Hermia through the terrors of shifting doubles and of madness and beastliness in the adolescent period when all identity and love is up for grabs. The effect of the paradigms in *As You Like It* is above all to define identity via the mysteries of gender. Rosalind, renamed Ganymede for the associations with metamorphosis and sexual inversion, herself displays an endless mirroring regress of transformations between male and female: she is a girl who dresses up as a boy so that she can woo her beloved by antagonizing him with her performance as an anti-feminist's version of a girl—and then, after the play is over, she reminds us that she is no girl but a boy actor. *Twelfth Night* unfolds all the twinning so that, even more than in *The Comedy of Errors*, all human relations are seen in terms of parallel or contrasting pairs, not only Viola/Sebastian and Viola/Cesario and the two eventual couples but also Viola/Olivia, Orsino/Olivia, Toby/Andrew, Sebastian/Antonio, Malvolio/Feste, and so on. The issue once again is the extraction of self-knowledge from narcissism. More sharply than anywhere else the context of all these doubles and transformations is mystical, as if there is a kind of enigma of coalescing identity that hangs over the apparent frivolities of the play, signaled, for instance, in the anagrammatic interrelations of Viola, Olivia, and Mal-volio ("MOAI doth sway my life") and in the references to Pythagoras and metempsychosis.[46]

Without letting one's critical ingenuity stretch the paradigms out of shape, it is worth pointing out that other comedies partake of them. The masks of the women, along with the intentional and unintentional disguises of the men, in *Love's Labour's Lost* set the four pairs in a set of blurring interrelations. *Much Ado about Nothing* includes a quite similar set of masks and doublings. *The Merchant of Venice* not only turns on the female in male disguise but also ends in the ring test, which both complicates and resolves the problems of identity that exist among the two couples. *The Taming of the Shrew* operates by a more independent version of

the pattern.[47] Its subject is love transforming: set in a context of the metamorphic images of love among the minor characters, the relationship of
Petruchio and Kate details the struggle, through tests of will and perception, to hammer out individual identity within the warring pair.

One quite separate metamorphic paradigm appears more rarely in
Shakespearean comedy. We have already seen it in *A Midsummer Night's
Dream*, where balanced against the twinning story of the four lovers is the
more explicitly metamorphic experience of Bottom. Its premises are entirely different. Though it depends in part on the transforming power of
love, it sets the individual not in a pair but alone, not on the path toward a
mature, socially defined identity but on the path toward vision and self-
exposure. Only once more does Shakespeare explore this type of comic
metamorphosis, with Falstaff in *The Merry Wives of Windsor*.[48] The
sheer grandeur and metaphoric potential of Falstaff's body (realized even
more brilliantly in the *Henry IV* plays) have made him a suitable figure for
literal transformation. The shapes he ends up taking—a piece of laundry
in a basket, the transsexual Wise Woman of Brainford, Herne the Hunter
"with huge horns on his head"—represent not fusions with the beloved
but, on the contrary, perversions of love and increasingly exposed versions of his basically unchanged self. His sexuality is as degraded by these
effeminizing transformations as is Bottom's intelligence by his metamorphosis into a jackass.

Yet in the final metamorphosis Falstaff pulls from the jaws of degradation something of Bottom's visionary glory. The presence of the grossly
corporeal Falstaff metamorphosed in the fairy world of Windsor Forest
speaks to the same elective affinity that joined the transformed Bottom to
Titania's elfin entourage. And Falstaff's appearance in horns itself forms a
mythic picture: they are the horns of the satyr, who will soon couple with
a pair of nymphs in the forest; they are the horns of the cuckold, for
Falstaff will be publicly emasculated in just the way he hopes to serve
Ford; they are also the horns of the stag Actaeon, who is punished for visionary and sexual presumption. Falstaff, however, sees himself only as
the multisexual, amorous Jupiter:

Remember, Jove, thou wast a bull for thy Europa; love set on thy
horns. O powerful love, that in some respects makes a beast a man;
in some other, a man a beast. You were also, Jupiter, a swan for the
love of Leda. O omnipotent love, how near the god drew to the
complexion of a goose! A fault done first in the form of a beast: O
Jove, a beastly fault! And then another fault in the semblance of a
fowl: think on't, Jove, a foul fault! When gods have hot backs, what
shall poor men do? For me, I am here a Windsor stag, and the
fattest, I think, i'th' forest. [5.5.3–13][49]

Falstaff is a subtle mythographer, another Arachne who can perceive both the glory and the degradation of amorous metamorphosis. The punishment Falstaff is about to experience—pinching and burning by mock-fairies—parodies the punishment of Actaeon (there is even a "noise of hunting" to accompany the comic dismemberment). In the end it is, as in other comedies, a mirror experience: the resulting vision, in this very down-to-earth play, is not of the gods but of one's own self and its limitations:

> MRS. FORD.   Sir John, we have had ill luck: we could never meet. I
> will never take you for my love again, but I will always count you
> my deer.
> FALSTAFF.   I do begin to perceive that I am made an ass.
> FORD.   Ay, and an ox too: both the proofs are extant.
>
> [5.5.117–19]

Deer (as well as *dear*), *ass*, *ox*: all are true forms of Falstaff, and all are exposed to the world and to him by the public performance of metamorphosis on the stage of Windsor Forest and of the theater in which the play is performed.[50]

Transformations like those of Bottom and Falstaff, or of actors performing roles and investigating the problems of illusion, stand as a reminder that metamorphosis offers a special key to dramatic technique. At the time when Shakespeare was beginning his career, metamorphosis was a literal and obvious element in Elizabethan dramaturgy. In *Gallathea* and *Love's Metamorphosis*, for instance, John Lyly translates Renaissance Ovidianism quite directly to the stage. He takes the world of amorous disguise and Petrarchan posturing, full of figurative transformations, and he gradually literalizes them as mythological stage-metamorphoses wrought by pagan love-gods.[51] Lyly's practice is, not surprisingly, in keeping with traditions of courtly pageantry, which adapted Petrarch's *Trionfi* into a metamorphic mode of spectacular shows. Such events represent, as we saw in chapter 5, one time-honored Renaissance sense in which theater is metamorphosis; that is, the transformation of quotidian reality into something rich and strange by means of a grand illusion. At the same time as Lyly is celebrating *Love's Metamorphosis*, and so on, Shakespeare is reading the book of Ovid into *Titus Andronicus* but decidedly omitting magical transformation as stage-business—just as he does in the contemporaneous *Comedy of Errors*, where metamorphosis is figurative and illusory. Yet, as it turns out, Shakespeare also defines theater as the transformation of one thing into another: of men into lions (Bottom and co.), of chairs into thrones, daggers into scepters, cushions into crowns (Falstaff and co.), of a whole set of accoutrements into a family romance (Lance and co.):

This shoe is my father; no, this left shoe is my father; no, no, this left shoe is my mother; nay, that cannot be so neither; yes, it is so, it is so—it hath the worser sole. This shoe with the hole in it is my mother, and this my father—a vengeance on't! there 'tis. Now, sir, this staff is my sister, for, look you, she is as white as a lily and as small as a wand. This hat is Nan, our maid.

[*Two Gentlemen*, 2.3.14–21]

Shakespeare has, in other words, brought metamorphosis down from Olympus (and its courtly equivalent in contemporary theater) to the level of the Globe groundlings. But it is not merely democracy at work. In the process he has recognized that transformation is a universal feature of his own art, restricting itself neither to monarchs nor to clowns, neither to amateur theatricals nor to kings who see themselves as players—though it is likely to be the clowns who keep us aware that the illusion of metamorphosis is an illusion.

At the end of Shakespeare's career he becomes interested in practicing the grand illusion of metamorphosis that he seems to have turned his back on earlier. We have already spoken of *The Tempest* in the context of royal pageants in which spectacular displays are created and uncreated before our very eyes.[52] Shakespeare has reverted to something like Lyly's Ovidian theatricalism, creating a world of the exotic, the mythic, and the magical—all in transformation. Banquets disappearing with "a quaint device" and an airy spirit who can transform himself and others at will: these *coups de théâtre* are recuperated into Shakespearean reality not because they are done by rude mechanicals whose incompetence reminds us of their mundane origins but because the whole world of grand metamorphic illusions will be so firmly laid to rest at the end of the play. Yet *The Tempest* is so concentrated, so sui generis, and so personal that we run a great risk by explaining it and subordinating it to a pattern. Let us rather consider the illusions and transformations of the other great Shakespearean romance. At the end of *The Winter's Tale*, when a woman is restored to life, a family is remade, and a statue is transformed into a living person, Shakespeare fuses the metamorphoses of art with the metamorphoses of life.[53] In the process he returns to consider the self-consciousness about art that lies so near the surface of *Titus Andronicus*; now, however, he translates questions to triumphs.

All the loose ends of the plot seem to have been resolved—mostly offstage—when Paulina takes Leontes on a tour of her gallery to see the statue of his late wife, whom his jealousy has killed. Admiration for the artistic verisimilitude of the statue gives way to wonderment as the statue moves and ultimately takes on the living, loving personality of Hermione. Perhaps nowhere else outside of Ovid does metamorphosis enjoy such a breadth of significances. To begin with, the story of Hermione embodies the transformations of love. Her real-life change, her sickening unto death in the third act, consists in the draining away of life precisely as Leontes' love leaves her. She becomes, as in the familiar Renaissance version of the Pygmalion story, a stony lady, a *donna petrosa*[54]—not quite in the Dantesque and Petrarchan sense but with a more mutual, indeed more marital, definition of love. Leontes and Hermione are not independent organisms but a pair of Shakespearean twins, two halves of a single system. The husband treats the wife lovelessly, and she becomes a stony lady. With penance, the passage of time, and the fulfillment of the mystic oracle, that hardness can melt in a newly purified love.

If Pygmalion is one model of transformations, another is offered by Deucalion and Pyrrha and all those Ovidian myths in which nature and human life are defined in a continuum between stone and flesh. The resolution of *The Winter's Tale* suggests elemental tensions throughout the play between death and life, expressed as between hardness and softness. There is more than a chance connection between a sixteen-year dormancy and Hermione's appearance in stone, for both are images of suspended life. Indeed, with the conjunction of the two, Shakespeare partly tricks us into imagining that his heroine has actually stood still for sixteen years; and, preposterous as such an image may be, it amounts to the truth, for what is a person deprived of love, family, and society but a block of stone? Hermione's life as a sixteen-year marble image is her own winter's tale, but the whole world of Sicilia has in fact been similarly hardened. Only with the discovery of Perdita does the softening begin to take place. Of the recognition scene the Third Gentleman tells us, "Who was most marble, there changed colour" (5.2.89),[55] and in Leontes' first responses to his wife it is he who is hard: "I am asham'd: does not the stone rebuke me / For being more stone than it?" (5.3.37–38). Once the transformation comes, it is for the whole world of the play a triumph of life over death, as Paulina describes it:

> Come!
> I'll fill your grave up: stir, nay come away:
> Bequeath to death your numbness; for from him
> Dear life redeems you.   [5.3.100–03]

The transformations of love and nature are only part of the story. Pygmalion, after all, was a great sculptor as well as a faithful servant of Venus; and Hermione is not just a block of stone—she is a work of art:

> The princess hearing of her mother's statue, which is in the keeping
> of Paulina,—a piece many years in doing and now newly performed
> by that rare Italian master Julio Romano, who, had he himself eternity and could put breath into his work, would beguile Nature of her

custom, so perfectly is he her ape: he so near to Hermione hath done Hermione, that they say one would speak to her and stand in hope of answer. [5.2.93–101]

Even before the statue has any chance to be transformed, it has passed that ancient metamorphic test for the mimetic power of art: it appears to be on the verge of coming to life.[56] As a result it is locked in combat with the creations of nature.

The very strangeness of citing Giulio Romano—it is a virtual *Verfremdungseffekt* taking us outside the dramatic framework, the experience of the speakers, and the chronology of the action—signals the extent of Shakespeare's aesthetic self-consciousness.[57] Among the least improbable sources for this unique example of Shakespearean art history is the first edition of Vasari's *Lives*, published in 1550. The *Life* of Giulio begins with extravagant praise—which was cut in subsequent editions—and it ends with an epitaph on the artist's (now lost) tomb:

Videbat Jupiter corpora sculpta pictaque
Spirare aedes mortalium aequarier coelo
Julii virtute Romani. Tunc iratus
Concilio divorum omnium vocato
Illum e terris sustulit; quod pati nequiret
Vinci aut aequari ab homine terrigena.[58]

(Jupiter saw sculpted and painted bodies breathe and the homes of mortals made equal to those in heaven through the skill of Giulio Romano. Thus angered he then summoned a council of all the gods, and he removed that man from the earth, lest he be exposed, conquered, or equaled by an earth-born man.)

The conceit is Ovidian: man against the gods, sculpted bodies coming to life, a council such as Jupiter convened against Lycaon. Once again, the test of art is metamorphic, and the terms of praise are competitive. Vasari's lines present his subject as multitalented and suggest that with each of his talents the artist is waging war on the creations of the gods. Earlier in the *Life* Vasari had expressed such judgments in his own words: Giulio has created buildings "le quali non abitazioni di uomini, ma case degli Dei," and of the artist's *invenzione* he says, "ne tacer voglio . . . che nessuno l'abbia paragonato" (5.523n). The *paragone* is the battle among the arts.[59] To a reader of Vasari—especially one who had never seen any of the artist's work—Giulio Romano would appear as a great and godlike creator, master of many arts and worthy opponent of Nature herself.

As we have seen before, Shakespeare rises to the challenge of such competitive language. Both Ovid and Giulio were responsible for statues coming to life, but only in myth or metaphor. Shakespeare's medium, with its three (we would say four) dimensions, has not only gone beyond transforming the pictures in the illustrated Ovid. It now can metamorphose sculpture. That aesthetic self-consciousness retrospectively explains the non-dramatic quality of the scene in which the Gentlemen first praise the statue:

> THIRD GENT.   Did you see the meeting of the two kings?
> SECOND GENT.   No.
> THIRD GENT.   Then you have lost a sight which was to be seen,
> cannot be spoken of.   [5.2.40–44]

And he goes on to speak of it for about sixty lines. The lack of dramatic three-dimensionality here sets the stage for the scene in which the three-dimensional medium of sculpture becomes that of drama by means of metamorphosis. The speech-without-drama of this scene is contrasted with the statue-with-silence of the following scene. The verbal without the visual is empty, while the visual without the verbal is frozen. Only Shakespeare's medium can effect the marriage.

Seen as a riposte to the rehearsal problems of the mechanicals in *A Midsummer Night's Dream*, the dramatic self-consciousness of the statue episode provides a concluding term in the history of Shakespeare's equation between metamorphosis and theatrical impersonation. The completeness of the equation between Snug and the Lion, the extent of Snout's or Starveling's metamorphosis into Wall and Moon: these are vital dubieties, and they have their equivalents in all the *Dream*'s analogous transformations, amorous, theatrical, and Ovidian. The same kind of anxiety—the need, however unsatisfiable, to define the "from" and "to" of metamorphosis—characterizes the sex changes and identity shifts of the romantic comedies. And the same need expresses itself in all the questions concerning actors and roles in literal and figurative plays-within-plays. The metamorphosis at the end of *The Winter's Tale* asks the same kind of question. Is Hermione a statue or not? Are we witnessing a performance of Hermione herself performing a charade, or a performance of a statue who comes to life?[60] Yet here we are not left with Snug who joins half-man to half-lion: Hermione is wholly a person and wholly a statue. In the midst of the confusions between mimesis and metamorphosis life turns to art and art turns to life.

The balance may tip to life over art, as is suggested by Leontes' sole criticism of the statue: "But yet, Paulina, / Hermione was not so much wrinkled, nothing / So aged as this seems" (5.3.27–29). Art, even when perfectly mimetic, idealizes, while the transformations of nature are the real miracles of metamorphosis. Wrinkles may be aesthetic (or mimetic) imperfections, but the time in which nature has produced them has been the necessary condition for all the happy resolutions of the play.[61] Yet it is wise to remember the play's other famous *querelle*. Perdita objects to the intrusion upon nature of the art of grafting, while Polixenes undertakes to resolve the argument. What is true for plant husbandry is also true for the statue/Hermione: "The art itself is nature" (4.4.97). Less a logical than a mystical conclusion, it is fulfilled by the whole atmosphere of the final scene. Paulina's gallery is a temple of art, in which madness and faith triumph over reason and logic. When the music sounds, those who have faith (some even kneeling) witness miraculous magic, which is purged of all "superstition" and "unlawful business." Like the offstage visit to the oracle, also described in golden, otherworldly language, the transformation of Hermione is designed as a pagan mystery. It is Shakespeare's last *hommage* to the world in which metamorphosis was born.

Actually, it is not quite the last *hommage*:

Ye elves of hills, brooks, standing lakes, and groves,
And yet that on the sands with printless foot
Do chase the ebbing Neptune, and do fly him
When he comes back; you demi-puppets that
By moonshine do the green sour ringlets make,
Whereof the ewe not bites; and you whose pastime
Is to make midnight mushrumps, that rejoice
To hear the solemn curfew: by whose aid
(Weak masters though ye be) I have bedimm'd
The noontide sun, call'd forth the mutinous winds,
And 'twixt the green sea and the asur'd vault
Set roaring war; to the dread rattling thunder
Have I given fire, and rifted Jove's stout oak
With his own bolt; the strong bas'd promontory
Have I made shake, and by the spurs pluck'd up
The pine and cedar. Graves at my command
Have wak'd their sleepers, op'd, and let 'em forth
By my so potent art. But this rough magic
I here abjure; and when I have requir'd
Some heavenly music (which even now I do)
To work mine end upon their senses that
This airy charm is for, I'll break my staff,
Bury it certain fadoms in the earth,
And deeper than did ever plummet sound
I'll drown my book.[62]

So Prospero enters upon his final celebration of magic, a retrospective upon all the metamorphoses of art and life: protean powers, the changes of nature, miraculous transformations, and by extension the arts of the theater. It is also the closest Shakespeare ever comes to an extended quotation from Ovid. The source is Medea's speech as she prepares the cauldron in which her father-in-law's youth will be restored.[63] As so often, Shakespeare plays with reversal: Prospero is a white magician and not an evil sorcerer like Medea; he is a father renewing the lives of his children rather than a child rejuvenating the father. What matters more than the changes, however, is the persistent power of antiquity and metamorphosis. Prospero enacts the pagan mystery of universal change in art and nature for the last time and closes the book. His text for that ritual, which is also Shakespeare's text, is Ovid. As he buries his mystic volume, Prospero magisterially closes the book that Lavinia so clumsily opened.

Notes

PREFACE

1. The record of large-scale approaches to the subject of metamorphosis demonstrates the difficulties of achieving any simple and clear organization. Clemens Heselhaus, "Metamorphose-Dichtungen und Metamorphose-Anschauungen," *Euphorion* 47 (1952): 121–46, is a clear introduction, but it moves rather swiftly over two thousand years with a largely taxonomical intention. Irving Massey's *The Gaping Pig* (Berkeley, 1976) takes an interesting, rather idiosyncratic approach to the topic, seeing it above all as a crisis of language. His study is framed in acknowledgments of the subject's difficulty, and the reader is not given much historical sense. Still, Professor Massey does provocative analyses of (mostly) modern texts. Harold Skulsky, in *Metamorphosis: The Mind in Exile* (Cambridge, Mass., 1981), introduces theories about consciousness and alienation but follows with readings of a wide variety of authors (from Homer to Virginia Woolf) which are not always directly consequent upon the theories. Most useful among modern treatments (and, surprisingly, not cited by Massey or Skulsky) is Pierre Brunel, *Le Mythe de la métamorphose* (Paris, 1975). Brunel's structural understanding of metamorphosis as myth situates the subject synchronically but with close relevances to many texts ancient and modern, sophisticated and primitive. His approach includes metaphorics, etiology, anthropology, biology, ethics, and religion. My book on the human body mentioned at the outset is *Nature's Work of Art: The Human Body as Image of the World* (New Haven, 1975).

CHAPTER ONE. *Tapestry Figures*

1. Ovid invented neither metamorphosis nor the anthologizing of metamorphoses. The myths, of course, existed long before his time, though he often intensifies the metamorphic elements or conflates different myths to achieve that

end. The Alexandrian collection of tales by Nicander (*Eteroiumena*), extant only in tiny fragments, seems to be one of several predecessors. The standard works on the pre-Ovidian material are Georges Lafaye, *Les Métamorphoses d'Ovide et leurs modèles grecs* (Paris, 1904); and L. Castiglioni, *Studio intorno alla composizione ed alle fonti delle Metamorfosi di Ovidio* (Pisa, 1906). For a full list of sources on sources see Michael von Albrecht's introduction to the reprint of Lafaye (Hildesheim, 1971). On origins, see below, chapter two, n. 5.

2. Citations are to Ovid, *Metamorphoses*, trans. F. J. Miller, Loeb Classical Library (Cambridge, Mass., 1966). Translations are taken from that edition except when otherwise noted. For particularly eloquent treatments of the Arachne-Minerva episode, see W. S. Anderson's review of Brooks Otis, *Ovid as an Epic Poet*, *American Journal of Philology* 89 (1968): 93–104; and Eleanor W. Leach, "Ekphrasis and the Theme of Artistic Failure in Ovid's *Metamorphoses*," *Ramus* 3 (1974): 102–42.

3. But see chapter 5 for a treatment of Spenser and Correggio in relation to Arachne's web and the loves of Jupiter.

4. The traditional title, meaning "Maids of Honor," does not do justice to the complicated subject, which comprises various court figures, the king and queen, dwarves, a dog, and numerous visual *jeux d'esprit* including the palace marshal in a doorway, the royal figures in a mirror, and facing us Velázquez himself painting on an enormous canvas which we see from the back. See Madlyn Kahr, *Velázquez: The Art of Painting* (New York, 1976), pp. 128–202, as well as the deTolnay article cited in n. 6. A lively contemporary debate among philosophers was initiated by Michel Foucault with the opening chapter of *The Order of Things* (New York, 1970), pp. 3–16. Notable in the chain of response are John R. Searle, "*Las Meninas* and the Paradoxes of Pictorial Representation," *Critical Inquiry* 6 (1980): 477–88; and Joel Snyder and Ted Cohen, "Reflexions on *Las Meninas*: Paradox Lost," *Critical Inquiry* 7 (1981): 429–47.

5. There seems to be almost universal agreement on the dating of *Las Hilanderas* around 1657. The evidence, though stylistic rather than documentary, appears convincing; still, Lopez Rey (see below) declares, without references, that "most scholars have convincingly held that" it was painted around 1644–48. The principal sources on the picture are Angulo Iniguez, "*Las Hilanderas*," *Archivo español de arte* 21 (1948): 1–19, and "*Las Hilanderas*, sobre la iconografia de Aracne," *Archivio español de arte* 25 (1952): 67–84; Carl Justi, *Diego Velázquez and His Times* (London, 1889), pp. 427–33; Kahr, *Velázquez*, pp. 203–11; Jose Lopez Rey, *Velázquez' Work and World* (London, 1968), pp. 105–09; María Luisa Caturla, "El Coleccionista madrileño Don Pedro de Arce, que poseyó 'Las Hilanderas' de Velázquez," *Archivio español de arte* 21 (1948): 292–304; and Charles deTolnay, "Velázquez' *Las Hilanderas* and *Las Meninas*," *Gazette des beaux-arts* 25 (1949): 21–38. Kahr has recently published a revisionist piece, "Velázquez's *Las Hilanderas*: A New Interpretation," *Art Bulletin* 62 (1980): 376–85, suggesting, not too convincingly, that the subject is *The Virtuous Lucretia*.

6. Multiple scholarly deductions are at work here. Enriqueta Harris, *The Prado* (London, 1940), p. 85, identified the helmeted figure as Minerva, while Iniguez (see n. 6) developed the associations more fully. Caturla, "El Coleccion-

ista," discovered the inventory reference, which applies almost exactly to the (presumed) original dimensions of *Las Hilanderas*.

7.   Velázquez waged a lifelong battle (largely, it seems, for reasons of social ambition) to dignify the status of artist and in the process gain himself a knighthood. When he finally achieved his goal, in 1658 (almost exactly contemporaneous with *Las Hilanderas*), it was—ironically, perhaps—at the cost of swearing that he had never engaged in any menial aspect of his art. So the upward motion in *Las Hilanderas* from craft to essential art may represent an unconscious purification.

8.   See the interesting analysis by deTolnay, "Velázquez' *Las Hilanderas* and *Las Meninas*," pp. 28–32.

9.   Lopez Rey (*Velázquez' Work*, p. 108) points out that the commentary on Sanchez de Viana's Spanish translation of Ovid (published in 1589) interprets the Arachne story as signifying the bitterness of an artist whose work is unfairly criticized. Such an association would certainly recommend the myth to Velázquez.

10.   I am thinking particularly of the theory of the *affetti* associated with Poussin and connected with Descartes' *Traité des passions*, published in 1649. According to this theory, different emotions have different physical attitudes associated with them, and these may be visually conventionalized. See Walter Friedlaender, *Nicolas Poussin* (New York, n.d.), pp. 35–37.

11.   The gesture is quite enigmatic. Minerva may be threatening the girl, or she may be commencing the metamorphosis. See Iniguez, who changed his mind in the 1952 article ("*Las Hilanderas*, sobre la iconografia de Aracne"). At the same time, the gesture may have the effect of hailing the girl.

12.   The painting is now in the Isabella Stuart Gardner Museum in Boston. It is among the last and greatest of Titian's *poesie*, or Mythologies. For more see chapter 5.

13.   In the present version the picture has been extended on all sides by anywhere from one inch (lower right) to a foot and a half (top all the way across). The unextended (original) picture has no archway above the tapestry. The effect in the unextended version is a much more startling source of light and a more unrealistic juxtaposition of planes.

14.   Compare the obsessive interest in frames apparent in *Las Meninas*, where Velázquez includes countless pictures on the wall, a character sharply framed in a doorway, and the king and queen reflected in a framed mirror placed in more or less the same position as Titian's *Europa* in *Las Hilanderas*.

15.   Stanzas 105–06. See *The Stanze of Angelo Poliziano*, tr. David Quint (Amherst, 1979).

16.   "Muiopotmos," ll. 277–96.

17.   See Kahr, *Velázquez*, pp. 141–63.

18.   See n. 28 and accompanying text.

19.   For the sources and the various scholarly opinions see Harold Wethey, *Titian: The Mythological and Historical Paintings* (London, 1975), 3:173.

20.   The picture of the girl on the bull is one of the commonest of all pagan images. According to E. C. Harlan, "The Description of Paintings as a Literary Device and Its Application in Achilles Tatius" Ph.D. (diss., Columbia University, 1965), it was the most frequently represented mythological theme in ancient graphic art, though she gives no statistics. Pompeiian wall decoration might tend

to confirm that estimate, and if we turn to the sixteenth and seventeenth centuries, we find an impressively long list of instances in Pigler's *Barockthemen* (Budapest, 1956), 2:78–83. For treatments of the myth in antique art see Otto Jahn, *Die Entführung der Europa auf antiken Kunstwerken* (Vienna, 1870); and Winfried Buehler, *Europa, ein Uberblick über die Zeugnisse des Mythos in der antiken Literatur und Kunst* (Munich, 1968). Europa is also one of the most uniformly reproduced of all pagan images. There is not a great deal separating, say, the girl and bull on an archaic Greek vase from the representation of the subject in Bernard Salomon's influential volume of sixteenth-century woodcuts or even from the commemoration of the transatlantic cable painted for the U.S. Capitol in 1876.

21. See Otto Keller, *Die antike Tierwelt* (rpt. Hildesheim, 1963), 1:329-72. Also see Francis Klingender, *Animals in Art and Thought* (Cambridge, Mass., 1971); and Beryl Rowland, *Animals with Human Faces* (Knoxville, 1975), pp. 43–48. It is interesting—though its meaning is ultimately enigmatic—that bulls appear in almost every story in the *Metamorphoses* which is concerned with protean self-transformation. These thoughts about the power of the image per se have been influenced by Fritz Saxl's essay, "Continuity and Variation in the Meaning of Images," reprinted in his *The Heritage of Images* (Harmondsworth, 1970), pp. 13–26; and by Erwin Panofsky's "Iconography and Iconology: An Introduction to Renaissance Art," in his *Meaning in the Visual Arts* (New York, 1955), pp. 26–54.

22. Percy Gardner finds Phoenician coins of the first two centuries B.C. on which "the mantle of Europa floats free and she seems at her ease, resembling indeed far more nearly that moon-goddess of whom she is supposed to be a variant form, and who is closely associated with the bull"; *Archaeology and the Types of Greek Coins* (rpt. Chicago, 1965), p. 95. The representation of Europa "at her ease" suggests that from early times there was a triumphal sense to the icon, probably associated with the moon-goddess riding triumphantly over the bull of the sun. Such a meaning may well connect with the insistently "female" aspect of the myth, as well as with its sense of a world-upside-down.

23. References and citations are to Philostratus, *Imagines*, and Callistratus, *Descriptions*, tr. Arthur Fairbanks, Loeb Classical Library (London, 1931). The works grouped together in that valuable collection (actually including two Philostrati, the Elder and the Younger) are part of a sophist tradition of the second and third centuries A.D. which uses description of visual works as the raw material for grand rhetorical exercises.

24. See Jean H. Hagstrum, *The Sister Arts* (Chicago, 1958), pp. 49–53.

25. References are to *The Adventures of Leucippe and Clitophon*, tr. S. Gaselee, Loeb Classical Library (London, 1969).

26. References are to *The Iliad* (18.518–22), tr. Richmond Lattimore (New York, 1969). Whenever the description on the shield includes the materials from which things are made ("benches of polished stone," "golden knives that hung from sword-belts of silver") there is a kind of deliberate *Verfremdungseffekt*: in most cases we do not know whether Homer means the shield or the reality. Perhaps the most intense "pun" of this kind appears when the living and dead on the battlefield are all described as being "like living men."

27. The story, concerning Zeuxis and Parrhasios, is to be found in Pliny's *Natural History* 25.65–66.

28. Citation is to *Dionysiaca*, tr. A. T. Murray, Loeb Classical Library (Cambridge, Mass., 1940), 1.93–97.

29. Moschus's idyll is not the first time the Europa story was told at length: there seem to have been Europa poems by Stesichoros, Simonides, and Bacchylides, and even a tragedy by Aeschylus. My translations are from the Greek text of *Die Europa des Moschos*, ed. Winfried Buehler (Wiesbaden, 1960).

30. A good introduction is Robin Fox, *Kinship and Marriage: An Anthropological Perspective* (Harmondsworth, 1967). See also Raoul and Laura Makarius, *L'origine de l'exogamie et du totémisme* (Paris, 1961), and—especially—Claude Lévi-Strauss, *The Elementary Structures of Kinship* (Boston, 1969), pp. 29–69, 233–309. From the other end of the historical spectrum, it is worth pointing out that even in antiquity there was a euhemeristic reading of the myth reducing it to an episode in which not the king of the gods but the (foreign) king of Crete arrived at the Phoenician shore in a ship decorated with a bull's head and stole away the young princess as his bride. See Palaephatus, *Peri Apiston* 15, in *Mythographi Graeci* 3.2, ed. N. Festa (Leipzig, 1902).

31. Aspects of female experience in antiquity are the subject of much interesting scholarship at the present time. Let me single out Mary R. Lefkowitz's splendid book *Heroines and Hysterics* (New York, 1981). Discussing the appearance of the transformed Io in *Prometheus Bound*, she writes,

> Union with Zeus has dire consequences for the female. The chorus has just seen Io on the stage, crazed, exhausted from wandering, deformed, physically as well as mentally: "and straightway my shape and mind were turned through (*diastrophoi/esan*) and horned, as you see, rubbed by the gadfly in maddened leaping . . ." (673–5). Io's twisted form, mind, and horns are the consequences of a god's passion and inescapable eye. [The chorus's] question follows logically: "I do not have who I might become." *Gignomai*, "am born," is the standard term for what was later called *metamorphosis* or *transformatio*, a change of shape. Who will the chorus become? A horned girl? A cow? Marriage even to a mortal with its usual consequence of pregnancy, inevitably involves physical transformation [p. 87].

Also relevant is Page duBois, *Centaurs and Amazons: Women and the Pre-History of the Great Chain of Being* (Ann Arbor, 1982), which makes a strong case for doubles and oppositions in Greek thought of the classical age. Such oppositions, among which are male/female and human/animal, are closely bound up with the subject of sexual myths of metamorphosis. See also John Onians, *Art and Thought in the Hellenistic Age* (London, 1979), p. 64, apropos of an Alexandrian goblet depicting Ganymede and Europa.

32. A particularly powerful example of this passionate emotion is to be found in Horace's Europa ode (*Carmina* 3:27).

33. Especially lines 135–52. Compare also Lucian, *Dialogues of the Sea Gods*, 15, in *Lucian*, tr. M. D. Macleod, Loeb Classical Library (Cambridge, Mass., 1961), 7:235. Also compare Nonnos, 1.128–36.

34. The clearest account is in *Der kleine Pauly* (Stuttgart, 1967), 2:446–49, s.v. "Europe."

35. "But as for Europe, no men have any knowledge whether it be surrounded or not by seas, nor whence it took its name, nor is it clear who gave the

name, unless we are to say that the land took its name from the Tyrian Europa, having been (as it would seem) till then nameless like the others. But it is plain that this woman was of Asiatic birth, and never came to this land which the Greeks now call Europe, but only from Phoenice to Crete and from Crete to Lycia" (*Histories* 4.45, tr. A. D. Godley, Loeb Classical Library, London, 1921). As always, the names of girl and continent are irresistibly drawn to threshold journeys.

36. See *The Homeric Hymns,* "Hymn to Demeter," e.g., Persephone's speech:

> We were all playing there in the lovely green meadow
> . . . .
> Playing, and with our hands picking beautiful flowers:
> Modest crocuses mingled with iris and hyacinth,
> Rosebuds and lilies and, wondrous to see, a narcissus
> That broad earth made to grow, just like a crocus.
> In delight I picked the bright blossom, but earth underneath
> Gave way, and the mighty lord, the receiver of many, rushed forth
> And carried me off all unwilling deep underground
> In his chariot of gold.

Tr. Thelma Sargent (New York, 1973), pp. 12–13.

37. See *The Suppliants* in *Aeschylus,* tr. Herbert Weir Smith, Loeb Classical Library (Cambridge, Mass., 1963), especially ll. 1–176, 525–99, 625–709, 776–835. Quite helpful in this connection is Robert D. Murray, Jr., *The Motif of Io in Aeschylus'* Suppliants (Princeton, 1958).

38. All these stories may be seen as emanations from the primitive practice of bride capture, a ritualized form of abduction that exists as part of exogamic social rules. The classic work—one of the foundation stones of anthropology—is John F. McLennan's *Primitive Marriage,* recently reissued with a valuable introduction by Peter Riviere (Chicago, 1970). For a particularly interesting application of several of these motifs—rape, flower-picking, marriage—to a variety of classical abductions, see "Kore" in C. G. Jung and C. Kerenyi, *Essays on a Science of Mythology* (New York, 1949), pp. 139–214. The relevances of bride capture need not be entirely remote in space and time. Even our own culture retains such habits as the shivaree (a kind of noisy land-triumph on the wedding night) and that ultimate liminal step of violation, carrying the bride across the threshold. Europa experiences just such a rite of passage.

39. These speculations owe a great deal to the structural study of myths. The classic work is, of course, Claude Lévi-Strauss, *Structural Anthropology* (New York, 1963), esp. pt. 3, chap. 11, "The Structural Study of Myth." Lévi-Strauss attempts to break myths down into their smallest meaningful constituent parts and then to put the system back together so as to construct the *parole,* accounting for the whole language of mythology. Pierre Brunel, *Le Mythe de la métamorphose* (see n. 1) applies this lore to metamorphosis: "A nos yeux, en effet, les histoires sacrées de métamorphoses, singulières selon les peuples et les religions, se composent en un mythe central, en un ensemble. . . . Un ensemble qui est moins une somme, comme le souhaite Claude Lévi-Strauss, qu'une organisation —répétons-le necessairement approximative—de cette somme" (p. 11). See also Gilbert Durand, *Les Structures anthropologiques de l'imaginaire* (Paris, 1969).

Lévi-Strauss himself changed his approach in his later *Mythologiques*; and it is from the first volume of that work that I find the most instructive *aperçu*. Early in *Le Cru et le cuit* (p. 20), he tells us "les mythes se pensent dans les hommes, et à leur insu." I think that proves to be as true of the literate European tradition as it is of the islanders studied by anthropologists.

CHAPTER TWO. *Ovid and Metamorphosis*

1. Citations are to Ovid, *Metamorphoses*, tr. F. J. Miller, Loeb Classical Library (Cambridge, Mass., 1956). Translations are quoted from that edition.

2. The subject of metamorphosis has not played so central a role in the critical approaches to the poem of that name as one might expect. E. K. Rand's essay, "Ovid and the Spirit of Metamorphosis," *Harvard Essays on Classical Subjects* (Boston, 1912), pp. 207–38, reviews the shifting moods of Ovid's poetry before the *Metamorphoses*. Simone Viarre's *L'Image et la pensée dans les Métamorphoses d'Ovide* (Paris, 1964) draws some interesting connections between metamorphosis and the realms of vision, magic, and mystery, even if her terms are a bit vague. Among those who deny the centrality of metamorphosis in the poem are E. J. Kenney, in a rather intemperate review of Viarre's book, in *Classical Review* n.s. 17 (1967): 51–53; and G. Karl Galinsky, in *Ovid's Metamorphoses: An Introduction to the Basic Aspects* (Berkeley, 1975), who does nonetheless offer perceptive comments connecting metamorphosis with definitions of identity. Galinsky is most influenced by Hermann Fraenkel's *Ovid: A Poet Between Two Worlds* (Berkeley, 1945), which does not take metamorphosis in itself very seriously but responds interestingly to the moods of transformation, the avoidance of tragedy, and "the phenomena of insecure and fleeting identity, of a self divided in itself or spilling over into another self" (p. 99). The principal work of the present generation is Brooks Otis, *Ovid as an Epic Poet* (Cambridge, 1966; 2d ed., 1970), a superb book with a problematic thesis. Otis does not really approach the subject of metamorphosis itself very directly: though he has interesting notions about the role it plays in expanding epic possibilities, magical transformation does not seem for him the center of the poem at all. Leo C. Curran, in "Transformation and Anti-Augustanism in Ovid's *Metamorphoses*," *Arethusa* 5 (1972): 71–91, asks all the right questions and connects the subject very interestingly with the rest of Ovid's oeuvre. He analyzes the stories well (I am indebted to his discussion of Arachne), and he joins metamorphosis with the Augustan problem in useful ways. The very best reading of the metamorphosis problem in the poem (surprisingly rarely cited) is W. S. Anderson, "Multiple Change in the *Metamorphoses*," *Transactions of the American Philological Association* 94 (1963): 1–27. Anderson begins with the words for change and for reactions to change, and from there he weaves a considerable tapestry of definitions and metaphoric extensions of the concept of metamorphic identity.

3. Not a point much noted in the treatments of the subject I have seen. Philomela, for instance, who will eventually become a nightingale, trembles "velut agna pavens" and then two lines later "utque columba suo madefactis sanguine plumis" (6.527–29). On the Ovidian simile in general, see E. G. Wilkins, "A Classification of the Similes of Ovid," *Classical Weekly* 25 (1932): 73–78, 81–86; and T. F. Brunner, "The Function of the Simile in Ovid's *Metamorphoses*," *Clas-*

sical Journal 61 (1966): 354–63, and "Deinon vs. Eleeinon: Heinze Revisited," *American Journal of Philology* 92 (1971): 275–84.

4. Ovid is clearly alluding to a Lucretian description of the atomistic origins of precipitation. See *De Rerum Natura* 6.495–526.

5. Ovid combined two related traditions, one represented by the *Aitia* of Callimachus, a poetic history of origins, and the other represented by Nicander's *Heteroiumena,* a didactic collection of natural metamorphoses. Callimachus, whose work survives in considerable fragments, explicitly rejects grand continuity: "the Telchines, who are ignorant and no friends of the Muse, grumble at my poetry, because I did not accomplish one continuous poem of many thousands of lines on . . . kings or . . . heroes, but like a child I roll forth a short tale." (Citation is to *Callimachus*, ed. and tr. C. A. Trypanis, Loeb Classical Library, Cambridge, Mass., 1958, p. 5.) It appears as though the whole plan for Ovid's poem may have been a mixture of agreement with and defiance of this opening declaration of Callimachus. Apart from structural questions, Ovid travels very far from his predecessors in connecting the metamorphoses with the history and nature of those individuals, places, and institutions which are being chronicled. See Georges Lafaye, *Les Métamorphoses d'Ovide et leurs modèles grecs* (rpt. Hildesheim, 1971), pp. 24–45.

6. Hecuba's story is closely linked to the more fully developed tale of Niobe in Book VI, which I discuss in section 5 of this chapter.

7. A multiple monster-creature like the centaur has much in common with those who undergo metamorphosis, particularly given Ovid's habit of characterizing the victims of transformation as composites of the human and the beastly. See his plays on the multiple nature of centaurs in describing the battle with the Lapiths (12.499–503). Though she does not mention Ovid or metamorphosis, Page duBois's *Centaurs and Amazons: Women and the Pre-History of the Great Chain of Being* (Ann Arbor, 1982) makes interesting arguments about the relation of centaurs to all the crucial boundaries out of which orderly Greek thought of the classical period was made.

8. As Ovid manipulates Ocyrhoe's various forms, he makes it clear that prophecy is tantamount to tiresome loquacity. That connection is confirmed by the placement of the story as the culminating member of a sequence of tales about unfeeling, garrulous truthtellers. First Juno complains to Tethys about the honors Jove has showered upon Callisto. Following upon that vignette are the beast-fables of the raven and the crow, who have told unpleasant truths to Apollo and Minerva.

9. In the *Ars Amatoria* (1.507) Mother Cybele is *exululata* in Phrygian mode, and in the *Tristia* (4.1.42) it is the Bacchant who howls, this time in the Idaean mode.

10. See Apollodorus, *The Library*, 3.8., along with the excellent note in the Loeb edition, ed. J. G. Frazer (London, 1921), 1:390–93; and Pausanias, *Description of Greece*, 8.2. The myth has complicated origins and purposes, at once justifying and setting the limits of human vs. animal sacrifice in religious ritual. For an interesting modern treatment, see Giulia Piccaluga, *Lykaon: Un tema mitico* (Rome, 1968). A more traditional approach to the rites of Zeus Lycaeus is A. B. Cook, *Zeus* (Cambridge, 1914), 1:63–99. The worship of Zeus Lycaeus in Arcadia may have been one of the latest survivals of human sacrifice; quite probably,

though, it was merely an example to the rest of the ancient world of the abominable practices of far-off foreigners, related to other mythic abnormalities—all equally interesting to Ovid—like cannibalism, incest, and homosexuality. In any event, there is a close connection not only between human sacrifice and the wolvish form but also between the problematic of piety/sacrifice and the myths of werewolfism among the priesthood.

11. See Pliny, *Natural History*, 8.34.

12. Preller, *Griechische Mythologie* (Berlin, Zurich, 1964), 1:128.

13. Ovid uses the word *canities* for Lycaon's whitish-grey color. It is a standard term with wide usage, but in this context it clearly reminds one of its *canine* etymology.

14. This panel in the poem finds its origins in many of the most ambitious cosmological works of earlier antiquity, including notably Hesiod and Lucretius. But particularly relevant is a passage in the sixth eclogue of Virgil, where a continuous poem from chaos through creation is outlined. Silenus sings

> uti magnum per inane coacta
> semina terrarumque animaeque marisque fuissent
> et liquidi simul ignis; ut his exordia primis,
> omnia et ipse tener mundi concreverit orbis;
> tum durare solum et discludere Nerea ponto
> coeperit et rerum paulatim sumere formas.

Citation is to *Virgil*, ed. and tr. H. R. Fairclough, Loeb Classical Library (Cambridge, Mass., 1965), Eclogue 6, ll. 31–36. Silenus goes on to include "lapides Pyrrhae iactos," Pasiphae, the Propoetides, the sisters of Phaethon (whom he "circumdat amarae / corticis atque solo proceras erigit alnos," as though the song itself were their transformed shape), Scylla, and "mutatos Terei . . . artus."

15. For a good introduction to the lore of the golden age (and by extension the decadence of the other ages) see Harry Levin, *The Myth of the Golden Age in the Renaissance* (Bloomington, Ind., 1969), pp. 3–31. (See p. 19 for a paean to Ovid's account of the "vitalizing and transforming power of nature itself.") A. O. Lovejoy and George Boas, in *Primitivism and Related Ideas in Classical Antiquity* (Baltimore, 1935), point out that "the Ovidian story of the ages was probably more potent than any other in its historic influence; the echoes of it in later literature are innumerable. The Greek poets were largely forgotten in medieval Europe. It was chiefly through the *Metamorphoses* that the Hesiodic tradition was kept alive" (p. 49).

16. See other examples at 11.628, 14.359, and 14.685. In each case *fingere* suggests the fashioning of a new form based on some external idea of the shape which that form should take. Like many metamorphic terms, *fingere* joins transformation with imagination. I discuss medieval plays on the word in chapter 3, section 3.

17. Ovid offers a strikingly chemical description to ground the creation in its basic elements:

> quippe ubi temperiem sumpsere umorque calorque,
> concipiunt, et ab his oriuntur cuncta duobus,

cumque sit ignis aquae pugnax, vapor umidis omnes
res creat, et discors concordia fetibus apta est.   [1.430–33]

So, as in the *Timaeus, discors concordia* is built into the very physical nature of the universe.

18.   For Hesiod, see *Works and Days*, ll. 42–105; and *Theogony*, ll. 507–616. The relevance of the *Timaeus* has to be construed in its totality, but see especially 29D–30C, 41A–D, 52D–63E.

19.   See the study of the sources in Otis, *Ovid*, pp. 389–95, by far the best (and probably the shortest) treatment of the material. Ovid seems to have joined the paternity question and Phoebus's rash promise, coming from one set of sources, with the cosmologically disastrous ride, coming from another set of sources. What is truly original in Ovid (not exactly confronted by Otis) is the sense that Phaethon is alone in the face of his desires and not acting out a family drama. For a particularly good account of this episode, see Valerie Wise, "Flight Myths in Ovid's *Metamorphoses,*" *Ramus* 6 (1977): 44–59.

20.   See chapter 1. It is a (perhaps) self-evident paradox that while ekphrasis is closely connected with the multiplicity and simultaneity of different elements in the human condition, it can also stand, especially in the midst of a poem of changes, as having quite the opposite signification, i.e., as an excessively frozen ideal.

21.   We may take as a confirmation of the tragic possibilities in the Phaethon story that it was the subject of a tragedy (preserved only in fragments) by Euripides. Yet, judging from what we have, it seems that Ovid's account is more "tragic," at least in the sense of inward, personal experience, than that of Euripides. The Euripidean hero is a young man who needs to prove his paternity not for his own sake but to forestall an unwanted marriage. See U. von Wilamowitz, "Phaethon," *Hermes* 18 (1883): 396–434; and James Diggle, *Euripides: Phaethon* (Cambridge, 1970).

22.   I shy away in this book from the risky business of attempting to posit a logical order for the whole of the *Metamorphoses*. Among the most effective of those attempts—in its larger outline, at least—is that of Otis (*Ovid as an Epic Poet*), whose basic division is as follows: Books I and II, "The Divine Comedy"; Book III to Book VI, line 400, "The Avenging Gods"; Book VI, line 401, through Book XI, "The Pathos of Love"; Books XII to XV, "Rome and the Deified Ruler." Other attempts to order the poem have been less successful. The fact is that Ovid, faced with such predecessors as Hesiod, Lucretius, and Virgil, and intending to write a poem about changes, may have deliberately chosen to create a casual chain rather than a monumental construction. The Arachne episode, as I suggested in chapter 1, along with the interaction between *carmen perpetuum* and *mutatas formas* of the opening lines, should discourage us from seeking too rigid a coherence.

23.   A particularly good summary of material concerning Bacchus is to be found in W. K. C. Guthrie, *The Greeks and Their Gods* (Boston, 1967), pp. 145–82. A. Bruhl, *Liber Pater* (Paris, 1953), covers the Roman aspects. More fanciful approaches include W. F. Otto, *Dionysus: Myth and Cult* (Bloomington, Ind., 1965); and H. Jeanmaire, *Dionysus* (Paris, 1970).

24.   Drunkenness, for all its bathos, is not insignificant as an analogue to ecstatic forms of transformation. Like the meteorological references that lie behind the petrification of Lichas, the metamorphoses of inebriation are familiar and nat-

ural. They depend on interaction between the individual and the physical world as do many Ovidian changes. Just as Ovid (along with many classical writers) will use *Ceres* when the English translator is prone to use *food* (see 3.437) or *Phoebus* when the translator speaks of *sun* (see 4.715), so there inheres in the very name Bacchus a similar natural metonymy that should make the reader think of wine and drunkenness even when the principal concern is a much more elevated form of self-alienation.

25.   Notable is his manifestation as a bull (see Euripides, *Bacchae*, ll. 1017–18). As always, it is interesting to note the occasions when Ovid avoids a metamorphic story in his source materials. Here it is clear that he wishes to place all the emphasis on Bacchus's metamorphic *effects*.

26.   Closing the catalogue of Bacchus's names with the direct address to the god as Liber is a nice, and typical, piece of Ovidian bathos. Liber was the local Italian divinity who was assimilated to the Greek Dionysus; and by citing the other names in an exotic catalogue and returning to the familiar name so directly, Ovid domesticates Bacchus even as he creates a kind of I-thou relationship with the god.

27.   Semele's fate is closely paralleled with Cadmus and others of his descendants who are destroyed by the terror of divine visions some of which they have brought upon themselves. I discuss this further later in this section.

28.   The myth is strikingly etiological in its origins: Cadmus founds Thebes, while his brothers (also sent to search out Europa, herself a figure of origins) give their names to Phoenicia and Cilicia. Cadmus himself was understood in antiquity to have introduced writing into Greece—a liminal movement from Asia Minor like that of Europa's ride. The sources make it clear that Cadmus is an appropriate figure to place at the start of a universal human history. See F. Vian, *Les Origines de Thèbes* (Paris, 1963).

29.   The heritage of Actaeon is a particularly complicated mixture involving a variety of different motivations for the young man, including lustful voyeurism and even prideful (Arachne-like) striving against Diana as hunter. In his account Ovid chooses to emphasize the hero's innocence (perhaps Ovid's invention) and to produce a grand drama of introspection. See Otis, *Ovid as an Epic Poet*, pp. 396–400, and my "Diana and Actaeon: The Myth as Synthesis," *English Literary Renaissance* 10 (1980): 317–59.

30.   There is, of course, an aspect of comic bathos that may get lost in the present analysis. To disturb Diana at her bath may be a reductio ad absurdum of the visionary experience as well as a culmination of it.

31.   It is almost too obvious to point out that Pentheus, in denying the divinity of Bacchus and then being torn apart by his own mother in her Maenadic frenzy, is another of these Thebans transformed by their encounter with mysterious divinity. This, too, happens in a sacred place; and it also involves mirroring, since Pentheus is destroyed by the woman who gave him birth. The parallels are self-consciously developed. Moments before the end Pentheus begs his aunt Autonoe to desist by reminding her of Actaeon's fate. But "illa, quis Actaeon, nescit dextramque precantis / abstulit" (3.721–22). Neither the Maenad nor Pentheus has, in fact, learned the lesson of Actaeon.

32.   Ovid seems to have been the first to join the story of the youth who refuses to love until he sees his own reflection with that of the nymph whose experience is an etiology for the echo; he was also the first to introduce Tiresias' oracle

into this blend. The story has always had associations with magic (catoptromancy, or mirror-magic; see J. G. Frazer, *The Golden Bough*, London, 1911, 3:94), with psychology, with the lore of love, and with death. Artemidorus interprets the dream of seeing one's reflection in the water as portending death for the sick (*The Interpretation of Dreams* 2.7). This tradition helps explain the narcissus flower as a death symbol as well as the ending of Ovid's account, in which the boy is frozen eternally looking at his reflected image among the dead. For a good collection of data, see Louise Vinge, *The Narcissus Theme in Western European Literature up to the Early Nineteenth Century* (Lund, 1967).

33.   Such terms in contemporary psychology appear in a number of modern approaches to metamorphosis. Curran ("Transformation," pp. 80–82) relates transformations to R. D. Laing's *Divided Self*. Galinsky (*Ovid's Metamorphoses*, pp. 45–52) wavers among different psychological approaches, cautioning against anachronisms but speaking of Phaethon's "infantile ego-ideal" (p. 50). Still, he is very wise to analyze that myth by pointing out that "the question of identity is integral to metamorphosis."

34.   The image of melting wax is a favorite of Ovid, another of the natural analogues for magical transformation. Notable uses of the image come in connection with Pygmalion and Daedalus, for which see section 5 of this chapter. Here the image serves to remind us (especially retrospectively) that Narcissus' dissolution is a proper metamorphosis.

35.   For an excellent essay on the background and meanings of the Perseus-Medusa material, see Carl Robert, *Die Griechische Heldensage*, vol. 2 of L. Preller, *Griechische Mythologie* (Berlin, rpt., 1966), pp. 222–45. See also J. M. Woodward, *Perseus* (Cambridge, 1937); and K. Schnauenburg, *Perseus in der Kunst des Altertums* (Munich, 1960).

36.   Perseus is introduced as an almost explicit parallel to Bacchus. Ovid tells us in one breath that Perseus's grandfather Acrisius denied the divinity of Bacchus and the divine parentage of his own grandson. Indeed, by leaving out the traditional explanation, the oracle that foretold Acrisius' death at the hands of his grandson, Ovid strengthens the sense of parallel between the two denials. The effect of this parallel, which continues explicitly for some lines (4.604–16), is to help set Perseus up as a different sort of hero from those of pure brawn. He is in some respects a Bacchic as well as a metamorphic hero.

37.   There seems to have been a tradition of representing Andromeda in ekphrasis which stressed the relations among life, stone, and frozen fear. So Achilles Tatius (unlikely to have been directly influenced by Ovid): "In the picture of Andromeda, there was a hollow in the rock. . . . She rested within its embrace, and while, if one gazed upon her beauty, one would compare her to a newly carven statue, anybody seeing the chains and the approaching beast would think the rock a hastily contrived tomb. (Citation is to *Achilles Tatius*, tr. S. Gaselee, Loeb Classical Library, Cambridge, Mass., 1969). Also see chapter 1, my discussion of ekphrasis and metamorphosis.

38.   The most extensive (and rather speculative) treatment of the source material is Ignazio Cazzaniga, *La Saga di Itis nella tradizione letteraria e mitografica Greco-Romana* (Varese, 1950–51). But see Otis, *Ovid as an Epic Poet*, pp. 406–10. Sophocles wrote a *Tereus* which became very popular in Rome in the Latin version of Accius. The motifs of Ovid's treatment extend beyond this particular

myth's literary history to other tragic materials concerning Medea and the House of Atreus, along with erotic traditions of unlawful love such as those concerning Myrrha and Scylla—again a cluster of Ovidian favorites. See n. 42 for more on this cluster of relations.

39. On the power of this omen compare Pliny, *Natural History*, 8.16.

40. The phrase will be used verbatim in regard to Hecuba, as we have already seen. W. S. Anderson ("Multiple Change," p. 19) is particularly incisive in seeing this condition as a metamorphosis: "she is utterly in the form (or likeness) of her vengeance. . . . Her imagination, we might say, is her real 'form.'"

41. The process of Scylla's transformation is particularly interesting: "illa metu puppim dimisit, et aura cadentem / sustinuisse levis, ne tangeret aequora, visa est. / pluma fuit: plumis in avem mutata" (8.148–50). In human form she seems (*visa est*) to be falling. Then as she falls she becomes a metaphor (*pluma est*); finally she passes from metaphor to metamorphosis when the feathers are attached to an authentic bird.

42. Ovid's account here defines itself as distinct from the *Ciris*, a nearly 550-line poem often attributed to Virgil, which tells Scylla's story in fulsome detail. Here the transformation has no organic relation to the issues of unnatural love, nor to the curse by Minos; rather it is a poetic end in itself. It is particularly interesting that Ovid ignores the extended metamorphic material in the *Ciris*, at least in his Scylla story. On the other hand, the poem is a storehouse of materials he uses elsewhere, e.g., the discussion with the nurse in the Myrrha story (in general indebted to the *Ciris*: see Otis, *Ovid as an Epic Poet*, pp. 420–21) and the motif of eternal enmity among different species of birds as in the Tereus, Procne, Philomela conclusion. Some have attributed the *Ciris* to Ovid himself. See R. F. Thomason, "The *Ciris* and Ovid," *Classical Philology* 18 (1923): 239–62, 334–44; 19 (1924): 147–56.

43. Scylla is as trapped by her rhetoric as she is by her physical position:

"laeter," ait "doleamne geri lacrimabile bellum,
in dubio est; doleo, quod Minos hostis amanti est.
sed nisi bella forent, numquam mihi cognitus esset!
me tamen accepta porterat deponere bellum
obside: me comitem, me pacis pignus haberet."   [8.44–48]

Her reasoning ends up in a series of well-traveled ruts that do not arrive anywhere. It is the same state of frozen paradox in which Ovid places all his most nearly tragic figures, including Narcissus, Medea, and Byblis. The rhetoric of paradox points to the same impasse as their lives, which in turn is met by the inescapable double nature of their metamorphosed condition.

44. Daedalus will be trapped in precisely the same elemental grid, and he, too, will react by taking to the air. For his (only somewhat figurative) metamorphosis into a bird, see section 5 of this chapter.

45. The changes of words are an important part of Galanthis's metamorphosis. "Strenuitas antiqua manet," the poet tells us of the weasel, using an extremely rare word that seems to apply to the fussy, brisk, officious motion of the rodent. But, applied back to the human story, it becomes a caricature. Alcmena has already in telling the tale described the girl's loyal service as "faciendis strenua iussis, / officiis dilecta suis" (9.307–08). Juno is effecting thus a transformation

from *strenua* to *strenuitas*, so turning a virtue into its caricatured form at the same time as she turns a human being into an animal.

46.   For an excellent treatment of Ovid's sources, see Ludwig Voit, "Die Niobe des Ovid," *Gymnasium* 64 (1957): 135–49. The tale of Niobe has important relations to two episodes that surround it in Book VI: the stories of Arachne and of Tereus, for it combines the dangerous rivalry with a god—a world in which values are quite clearly drawn—with the obscure and shifting world of the Tereus story.

47.   Otis (*Ovid as an Epic Poet*, pp. 186–89) is right to point out the importance to the action of the goddess Isis, who appears to Iphis's mother before the birth, sanctioning the deception of the father, and then effects the transformation when the mother prays to her on the night before the wedding. In concentrating on the importance of Isis, however, we may forget that the girl herself never knows of the goddess's involvement. In fact, she achieves her own worthiness independently. In many ways, as we shall see, the story parallels Pygmalion's. There, too, a goddess (Venus) surrounded by mystic invocations plays an important role in the metamorphosis, but only via the independent power, the worthiness in metamorphic skill, of the central mortal figure.

48.   To refer to Proteus in the midst of a discussion of metamorphosis in Ovid's poem is to incur an obligation to say something of the fact that Proteus plays such a minor role. As Ovid approached his subject of metamorphosis in myths, two great stories of transformation would have immediately struck home as most famous and most sanctioned by previous literary example. Both Proteus and Circe had the honor of appearing in the Homeric and the Virgilian canon; neither plays an important role in the *Metamorphoses*. I would say that the avoidance of these subjects is part of Ovid's whole attitude toward the remaking of epic materials. There is nothing intrinsically un-Ovidian about the Proteus myth (quite the contrary, as this section tries to show); it is merely that Ovid deliberately stakes out new territory. (The same is true, I think, of Circe.) Proteus forms an important episode in Menelaus's narrative of his travels in Book IV of *The Odyssey* (ll. 385–550), and Virgil recreates the figure of a metamorphic Old Man of the Sea in the *Georgics*, Book IV (ll. 387–414). In both cases Proteus not only assumes many shapes but, more importantly, acts as a seer ("novit namque omnia vates"). Ovid does not ignore these associations of the sea-god, but he plays them down because he does not wish to associate visionary capacities with constant shape-changing. Ovid's real Proteus-figure is Tiresias, not a random shape-changer but a master of change and of his own identity—furthermore, a mortal who dares to come face to face with the lords of Olympus. The Proteus we meet in Book XI is demoted to being an instrument not of his own shape-changing but introducing that of Thetis, who becomes a bird, a tree, and a tigress, all to avoid the advances of Peleus. Significantly, it is Proteus himself, abnegating his time-honored mythological role, who not only describes these changes as "centum mentita figuras" (11.253) but also directs Peleus to hold her tight so that she can be protean no longer. Ovid could hardly have undone Proteus in his own person more thoroughly than by making him inform against proteanism.

49.   Ovid's Medea also helps establish the negative associations that cling to those who can make protean use of shifting forms. The sorceress graciously offers to rejuvenate her father-in-law Aeson by means of her magic herbs and incantations. To this episode Ovid offers a direct parallel in her deliberate (and unmoti-

vated) nonrejuvenation of Jason's uncle Pelias. The ritual, which follows precisely the pattern of Aeson's metamorphosis, includes the emptying of the old man's blood. When the old man's daughters shrink from the task, Medea commits what is essentially a murder herself, and she places inoperative herbs in the brew that is supposed to rejuvenate Pelias. The juxtaposition of the two episodes, the one emphasizing the power of Medea's arts, the other the enormity of her deceptiveness, links these traits within her.

50.   Daedalus has very early associations with cleverness at handwork, connecting with the Homeric adjective *daedala*; he is also mentioned in the *Iliad* (18.590) as having constructed a *choros* (a statue of dancers or a place for dancing) for the queen Ariadne in Crete. The other motifs—the labyrinth, the flight, the nephew—have all been connected well before Ovid's time. See, for instance, Xenophon, *Memorabilia* 4, 2, 33, for the motif of Daedalus's imprisonment on Crete. An interesting, heavily linguistic modern treatment of the subject is Françoise Frontisi-Ducroux, *Dédale* (Paris, 1975).

51.   The story of Daedalus's nephew Perdix acts as a kind of mirroring subplot. The boy observes a fish's backbone and cleverly invents the saw on the same principle. Like his uncle's work, this represents an imitation of nature, but it is not a deceptive imitation. Daedalus envies his nephew's talents and hurls him down to his death in a kind of reenactment of Icarus's fall. But Perdix, with the same flexibility he showed in life, saves himself through transformation into a partridge, a notably adaptable species.

52.   An excellent discussion of this episode is to be found in Fraenkel, *Ovid*, pp. 93–97. Ovid's refashioning of the source stories is most interesting. His source (apparently to be found in Philostephanos' *Kypriaka*, not preserved) is a fundamentally obscene myth about a Cypriot king who falls in love with a statue of Aphrodite—not of his own making—and proceeds to have sexual relations with the statue. In origin, then, the story is of a piece with such other unnatural loves as fill the middle books of the poem. But Ovid radically alters the material by introducing the related issues of metamorphosis and art. As the sculptor himself, Pygmalion can inspire the life in the statue that makes his love plausible and natural. The effect of that love is in turn a metamorphosis which justifies and purifies his love.

53.   The account in the *Fasti* (5.121–28) traces the cornucopia back to the she-goat Amalthea, Jupiter's nurse and protector on Crete. The goat breaks her beautiful horn, but in recompense Jupiter fills it with fruit and plants both Amalthea and the cornucopia in the heavens.

54.   For the *Adonia* see Theocritus, *Idyl* 15. Judging from that lovely poem, the *Adonia* was a strikingly feminine expression of sexuality, with husbands excluded and mocked. As such it fits in well with the feminine world-upside-down atmosphere of metamorphosis. For a rather different view (where Theocritus is not cited), see Marcel Detienne, *Les Jardins d'Adonis* (Paris, 1972), pp. 125–28, 153–57. The Garden of Adonis is, of course, the nursery, or seedbed of young plants, again dramatizing the fertility that arises out of the young Adonis's sacrifice.

55.   The question of Ovid's orthodoxy as a citizen under the Augustan empire has been much discussed. On the one hand, there is the explicit and climactic praise of Augustus—and of Roman destiny—in the poem; on the other, there is

the naturally distanced Ovidian voice and the fact of his banishment by Augustus. Otis changed his mind between an early article, "Ovid and the Augustans," *Transactions of the American Philological Association* 69 (1938): 188–229, in which he posits that the *Metamorphoses* was a serious attempt to win back Augustus's favor, and his book (*Ovid as an Epic Poet,* 1966), in which he sees Ovid in turmoil between a desire to please the emperor and his own natural anti-Augustanism; then, once again (1970, the second edition of the book), Otis changed his mind and came to see Ovid as fully and intentionally anti-Augustan. In these changes we can read the range of current opinion. Few stand up for a pro-Augustan Ovid. See Curran, "Transformation"; Charles Segal, "Myth and Philosophy in the *Metamorphoses*: Ovid's Augustanism and the Augustan Conclusion of Book XV," *American Journal of Philology* 90 (1967): 257–92; and Douglas Little, "The Non-Augustanism of Ovid's *Metamorphoses,*" *Mnemosyne* 25 (1972): 389–401.

56. Vertumnus's origins are in the shadowy mists of the Etruscans. Though he is mentioned by Varro, Propertius, Horace, and others, the connection with Pomona appears nowhere but in Ovid. See L. Preller, *Römische Mythologie* (Berlin, 1858), pp. 397–400.

57. See *Elegies* 4.2. Most of the poem consists of plays on the etymology of the name: either from the turnings of the Tiber, or from the first fruits of the *vertentis anni,* or the turning of fruits to ripeness, or the beauty of his own shape-changing, including the forms of girl, man, reaper, warrior, lawyer, Bacchant, Phoebus, hunter, and charioteer. The poem is a perfect example of the light-hearted free sensuality of metamorphosis which is so un-Ovidian that by negation it gives the lie to those who view Ovidian transformation as a frivolity.

58. The notion of deification of human beings, almost invariably kings, goes back to Middle Eastern forms of worship and is revived in the Hellenistic period, especially in regard to Alexander the Great. But it is particularly significant in the post-Julian period in Rome. Thus it may form one of the more orthodox bases for Ovid's choice of subject in the Augustan period, since apotheosis is clearly a type, even a climactic type, of metamorphosis. See L. R. Taylor, *The Divinity of the Roman Emperor* (Middletown, Conn., 1931); F. Cumont, *Les Religions orientales dans le paganisme romain* (Paris, 1931); and A. R. Anderson, "Heracles and His Successors," *Harvard Studies in Classical Philology* 39 (1928): 7–58.

59. Ovid treats the same material without any vagueness about the equivalence of Romulus and Quirinus in the *Fasti,* 2.475–512. Even in the *Metamorphoses,* Ovid removes the doubt when Romulus's widow is told that she "dignissima tanti / ante fuisse viri coniunx, nunc esse Quirini" (14.833–34). Not surprisingly, in the *Fasti* Ovid makes less of the apotheosis and more of the orderly progression of ruling generations.

60. Much has been said about the connections between Virgil and Ovid. Galinsky, *Ovid's Metamorphoses,* pp 217–51; E. J. Bernbeck, "Beobachtungen zur Darstellungsart in Ovids Metamorphosen," *Zetemata* 43 (1967): 117–22; and R. Lamacchia, "Preciazioni su alcuni aspetti dell'epica ovidiana," *Atene e Roma,* n.s. 14, no. 2 (1969): 1–20: all offer comparative analyses of what has come to be called Ovid's *Aeneid,* i.e., the Roman material in the last three books or so of the *Metamorphoses.* Less has been said about the influence of Virgil on the whole Ovidian project. It seems to me that the *Metamorphoses* is particularly suited to an approach that studies the importance of reactions to great literary predecessors

and influences, since Ovid lived in the twilight of a time dominated not only by Augustanism but by its great poetic voice in the *Aeneid*. The choice of Ovid's subject as well as his form—that is, Arachne's web rather than Minerva's—may well represent a very conscious alternative to Virgil's epic. For comparisons broader than the last three books, see E. J. Kenney, "The Style of the *Metamorphoses*," in J. W. Binns, *Ovid* (London, 1973), pp. 116–53; and S. Doepp, *Virgilischer Einfluss im Werk Ovids* (Munich, 1968), pp. 104–40.

61. Compare Ovid's treatment of the ages of man. In the golden age, "nondum caesa suis, peregrinum ut viseret orbem, / montibus in liquidas pinus descenderat undas, / nullaque mortales praeter sua litora norant" (1.94–96); and in the iron age "quaeque prius steterant in montibus altis, / fluctibus ignotis exsultavere carinae" (1.133–34).

62. A lively debate rages about the seriousness of Ovid's connection with real Pythagoreanism. The bridge connecting the sixth-century sage of liberty, vegetarianism, mathematics, music, and metempsychosis to Ovid's consciousness would be Varro and Posidonius (see Lafaye, *Les Métamorphoses*, pp. 191–223), well known to any educated Augustan but not necessarily proving Ovid to be a committed Pythagorean. The most eloquent voice in favor of the serious connection is Viarre, *L'Image et la pensée*, pp. 211–88, where the case is based not so much on Ovid's deep familiarity with Pythagoras and his orthodoxy as upon a sense that Pythagoreanism—rather broadly defined—radiates through the poem. With this conclusion I agree; but what is really being proved here is the profound coherence of Ovid's work rather than his adherence to Pythagorean philosophy.

63. See, for instance, Fragments 8(17), 16 (26), 30 (54), 31 (37), 32 (52), 33 (39) in M. R. Wright, *Empedocles: The Extant Fragments* (New Haven, 1981). Also see Wright's introduction, pp. 22–48.

64. This collection was published several times in Lyons, first in the 1550s and again in the 1580s, with texts variously in Italian, French, and Flemish. For more on their iconographic history, see M. D. Henkel, "Illustrierte Ausgaben von Ovids *Metamorphosen*," in *Vorträge der Bibliothek Warburg* (1926–27), pp. 58–144. Also see chapter 5, section 2.

65. Structuralist approaches to ancient myth, as in the work of Jean-Pierre Vernant and Marcel Detienne, offer some remarkable adumbrations of the connections among such forces as cannibalism and the other marginalities that characterize metamorphosis. In *Dionysus Slain*, tr. M. and L. Muellner (Baltimore, 1979), Detienne's remarks about cannibalism are extraordinarily apt to Ovid's metamorphic world: "In fact, anthropophagy, which the Greeks took as a modality of *allelophagia* ('eating one another'), is an essential term in the food code that represents a privileged plane of significance in their social and religious thought for defining the whole set of relations between man, nature, and the superhuman. There is no choice, then, but to deploy this whole system with the goal of enticing cannibalism from the marginal position explicitly imposed on it by a society that categorically refuses to practice it but, by virtue of precisely the things it can say about it, forces protesting groups or individuals to express their protest by adopting the very eating behavior it refuses. . . . Whether they considered themselves an antisystem or a protest against the city-state, these four movements—Pythagoreanism, Orphism, the Dionysiac religion, and Cynicism—constitute a four-

termed ensemble each of which reflects a mirror image of the politicoreligious system in which cannibalism is marked positively in some cases, negatively in others" (pp. 55–56). The applications to metamorphosis and the poem are almost too numerous and too obvious to recount. The margins of experience, the recurrent sense of primitivism, the layers of human, beastly, and divine, the questioning of state and civilization, the interest in Bacchus, Orpheus, and Pythagoras: all these viewed together make of Ovid and the tradition a sustained meditation on the contagions implicit in cannibalism. For approaches further afield, see the *Nouvelle revue de psychanalyse* 6 (1972), an issue entirely devoted to cannibalism; Detienne, *Les Jardins*, pp. 71–113, and Jean-Pierre Vernant's introduction, pp. vii–ix, xl–xliii.

CHAPTER THREE. *Metamorphosis in the Middle Ages: Figura and Cosmos*

1. On late and Christian antiquity, see especially Peter Brown's *The World of Late Antiquity* (London, 1971), a good introduction with excellent bibliography. See also the same author's *Religion and Society in the Age of St. Augustine* (London, 1972); E. R. Dodds, *Pagan and Christian in an Age of Anxiety* (Cambridge, 1965); and Arnaldo Momigliano, ed., *The Conflict between Paganism and Christianity in the Fourth Century* (Oxford, 1963), especially the introduction (pp. 1–16) and the essays by P. Courcelle (pp. 151–92) and H. Bloch (pp. 193–218).

2. The great work on the relations between antiquity and medieval culture, E. R. Curtius, *European Literature and the Latin Middle Ages*, tr. W. R. Trask (New York, 1963), remains an inspiration. The title essay of R. W. Southern's *Medieval Humanism and Other Studies* (Oxford, 1970) distinguishes "scientific" from "literary" humanism, while Jean Seznec, *Survival of the Pagan Gods*, tr. B. F. Sessions (New York, 1953), in its medieval references, and Erwin Panofsky and Fritz Saxl, "Classical Mythology in Medieval Art," *Metropolitan Museum Studies* 4 (1932–33): 228–80, pay more attention to the learned, classicizing aspects of medieval humanism. Ludwig Traube, *Vorlesungen und Abhandlungen*, vol. 2: *Einleitung in die lateinische Philologie des Mittelalters* (Munich, 1911), conducted some crucial early research in the medieval study of ancient texts. On Ovid in particular there is no equivalent to Domenico Comparetti, *Vergil in the Middle Ages;* the most prominent general works, none of them definitive, are E. K. Rand, *Ovid and His Influence* (London, 1926); F. Munari, *Ovid im Mittelalter* (Zurich, 1960); and G. Pansa, *Ovidio nel medio evo e nella tradizione popolare* (Sulmona, 1924). Further specific references follow in subsequent notes.

3. Augustine, *Concerning the City of God against the Pagans*, tr. H. Bettenson (Harmondsworth, 1972), 7:9; p. 266. My citations to Augustine are drawn almost entirely from the *City of God* because that work deals far more fully with pagan myth and religion than anything else in the corpus, as is demonstrated (rather plaintively) by Sr. M. D. Madden in *Pagan Divinities and Their Worship as Depicted in the Works of St. Augustine Exclusive of the* City of God (Washington, 1930). The fullest approach to the pagan question in earlier Augustine (ca. 400) is to be found in *De Consensu Evangelistarum*, Book I. See *PL* 34, esp. cols. 1056–58. For discussions of Augustine's relation to pagan antiquity, see H. Marrou, *Augustin et la fin de la culture antique* (Paris, 1938); F. G. Maier, *Augustin*

und das antike Rom (Stuttgart, 1955); and H. Hagendahl, *Augustine and the Latin Classics* (Göteborg, 1967).

4.   "De Fide Resurrectionis," tr. Sullivan and McGuire, in L. P. McCauley et al., eds., *Funeral Orations by Saint Gregory Nazianzen and Saint Ambrose* (New York, 1953), p. 256.

5.   There is a complicated relation between the doctrine of *imago dei* and the fact of metamorphosis. Among early church fathers already it was not uncommon to use the term *metamorphosis* in the definition of man's divine and/or corrupted relationship to the image of God. See, for instance, Gregory of Nyssa ("In Canticum canticorum," *Patrologia Graeca* 44, col. 868), who describes the fall in terms of the divine image metamorphosed into a serpent. See also Origen, *Homilies on St. Luke* 8.2–3, (*Homélies sur S. Luc*, ed. H. Crouzel et al., Paris, 1962, pp. 164–69), in which the damned are thought to be the victims of metamorphosis. The magisterial work on this subject is Robert Javelet, *Image et ressemblance au douzième siècle* (Paris, 1967). See also nn. 72, 73, 75, 76 and accompanying text.

6.   Augustine makes this point in a work devoted to the enthusiastic support of figures and their imaginative interpretation. The passage reads as follows: "Just as the Egyptians had not only idols and grave burdens which the people of Israel detested and avoided, so also they had vases and ornaments of gold and silver and clothing which the Israelites took with them secretly when they fled, as if to put them to a better use. . . . In the same way all the teachings of the pagans contain not only simulated and superstitious imaginings and grave burdens of unnecessary labor, which each one of us leaving the society of pagans under the leadership of Christ ought to abominate and avoid, but also liberal disciplines more suited to the uses of truth, and some most useful precepts concerning morals. Even some truths concerning the worship of one God are discovered among them. These are, as it were, their gold and silver, which they did not institute themselves but dug up from certain mines of divine Providence, which is everywhere infused, and perversely and injuriously abused in the worship of demons." *On Christian Doctrine*, 2. 40. 60., tr. D. W. Robertson, Jr. (Indianapolis, 1958), p. 75.

7.   See Varro, *De Lingua Latina*, 9.21.

8.   "Figura" appears in *Scenes from the Drama of European Literature* (New York, 1959), pp. 11–76. D. C. Allen's chapter introduces *Mysteriously Meant: The Rediscovery of Pagan Symbolism and Allegorical Interpretation in the Renaissance* (Baltimore, 1970), pp. 1–20.

9.   Explicit parallels between metamorphosis and the mystery of the eucharist are, so far as I can tell, nonexistent in patristic writings—unlike the parallels between metempsychosis and Christian redemption. Still, the imagery of transubstantiation seems to borrow something from pagan transformation. So Cyril of Jerusalem speaks of change in the substances of the elements (*metaballesthai*) at the Lord's Supper, and Augustine goes to considerable lengths in his Letter to Boniface (no. 98) to elaborate the concept of *similitudo* in explaining the sacrament. It should be remembered that the same early Christian centuries which illegitimized pagan metamorphosis were also the period when the complex doctrine of transubstantiation was being forged. See Johannes Quaster, *Patrology*

(Utrecht, 1960), 3:375–77, 420–22, 479–81; Gillian Feeley-Harnik, *The Lord's Table* (Philadelphia, 1981); H. Lietzmann, *Mass and the Lord's Supper* (Leiden, 1953).

10. "De Fide," tr. Sullivan and McGuire, p. 256.

11. Augustine himself is in large part responsible for the exegetical tradition surrounding Psalm 96, where the "gods of the nations" are described (in the Greek version familiar to Augustine) as "daimonion eidola." The passage is cited numerous times, often with detailed linguistic analysis, in the *City of God* as part of a complex series of definitions encompassing demons, gentile idols, and pagan gods. See esp. 8:24, 9:23, and 19:23.

12. The "Clementine Homilies," wrongly attributed to an early Bishop of Rome, seem to date from the fourth century. They were published in French translation by Abbé Joseph Turmel (under the pseudonym A. Siouville) as *Introduction aux homélies clémentines* (Paris, 1930).

13. Arnobius, *Adversus Nationes,* ed. F. Oehler (Leipzig, 1846).

14. Isidore of Seville, *Etymologiae,* 8. 11, ed. W. M. Lindsay (Oxford, 1911).

15. Lactantius, *The Divine Institutes,* tr. Sr. M. F. McDonald (Washington, 1964), p. 48.

16. The text has been translated and well introduced by L. G. Whitbread as *Fulgentius the Mythographer* (Columbus, 1971). See especially the prologue to Book I of the *Mythologies,* pp. 40–48.

17. The bibliography of published texts is relatively brief. Between the time of Fulgentius and the twelfth century little was written, apart from the so-called First and Second Vatican Mythographers (eighth to ninth centuries), who, along with a later—and more important—source, were edited by G. H. Bode as *Scriptores rerum mythologicarum Latini tres* (Celle, 1834). In the High Middle Ages the principal figures are Arnulf of Orleans, edited by F. Ghisalberti in "Arnolfo d'Orleans, un cultore di Ovidio nel sec. XII," *Memorie del Reale instituto lombardo di scienze e lettere* 24, no. 4 (1932): 157–234. The thirteenth century sees the *Integumenta Ovidii* of John of Garland, ed. F. Ghisalberti (Milan, 1933); and the commentary by Dante's friend Giovanni del Virgilio, ed. F. Ghisalberti as "Giovanni del Virgilio espositore delle *Metamorfosi,*" in *Giornale dantesco* 34, n.s. 4 (1931): 3–110. For the later Middle Ages, the major works are John Ridewall's *Fulgentius metaforalis,* ed. H. Liebeschütz (Berlin, 1926); Boccaccio, *Genealogie deorum gentilium libri,* ed. V. Romano (Bari, 1951); and the anonymous *Ovide moralisé,* ed. C. deBoer in *Verhandelingen der Koninklijke Akademie van Wetenschappen: Afdeeling Letterkunde,* vols. 15 (1915), 21 (1920), 30 (1931), 37 (1936), and 43 (1938). Contemporary with that poetic work is the prose *Ovidius moralizatus* of Pierre Bersuire, ed. J. Engels (Utrecht, 1962). Finally there is the *De Archana Deorum* of Thomas Walsingham, ed. R. A. van Kluyve (Durham, N.C., 1968). There remain many unpublished fragments of medieval Ovidian mythography. For some valuable references, see F. Ghisalberti, "Medieval Biographies of Ovid," *Journal of the Warburg and Courtauld Institutes* 9 (1946): 10–59.

18. The reader is in particular referred to Paule Demats, *Fabula: Trois études de mythographie antique et médiévale* (Geneva, 1973); and Rosemund

Tuve, *Allegorical Imagery: Some Medieval Books and Their Posterity* (Princeton, 1966), esp. chap. 1.

19. *De Incredibilibus,* ed. N. Festa (Leipzig, 1901). Palaephatus claimed to have visited the site of each myth he analyzed and to have interviewed local folklorists. Such empiricism is somewhat belied by the ingenuity of his demetaphorizings of myths.

20. See J. D. Cooke, "Euhemerism: A Medieval Interpretation of Classical Paganism," *Speculum* 2 (1927): 396–410; and Paul Alphandéry, "L'Evhémérisme et les débuts de l'histoire des religions au Moyen Age," *Revue de l'histoire des religions* 109 (1934): 5–27.

21. See *De Natura Deorum* 1.42. Cicero elsewhere in the same volume (2.24) admits that Hercules, Castor and Pollux, Aesculapius, Liber (who more or less equals Bacchus), and Romulus were deified heroes.

22. "For a father, consumed with grief at an untimely bereavement, made an image of his child, who had been suddenly taken from him; and he now honored as a god what was once a dead human being, and handed on to his dependents secret rites and initiations. Then the ungodly custom, grown strong with time, was kept as a law, and at the command of monarchs graven images were worshiped" (*The Oxford Annotated Apocrypha,* ed. B. M. Metzger, New York, 1965, p. 119). It is worth noting that this passage furnished another close connection between idol-worship and pagan religion or mythology at the same time as it set the gods in a decidedly metamorphic context: mortals become statues who become gods.

23. Fulgentius, *Mythologies,* 1. 18–20, tr. Whitbread, pp. 60–61.

24. Arnulf, 6:9, ed. Ghisalberti, p. 216.

25. One brief example chosen from many is the exposition of Hero and Leander: "Love is often close to danger; and when it has eyes only for what it prizes, it never sees what is expedient. In Greek *eros* is the word for love, while Leander could be said as *lisiandron,* that is, the freeing of men: for release produces love in a man" (Fulgentius, *Mythologies,* 3.4, tr. Whitbread, p. 85).

26. For Semele, see Boccaccio, *Genealogie,* 2. 64, ed. Romano, 1:111. For the euhemeristic Jupiter see 2.62, 1:107–08. In demonstrating the continuities of medieval mythography, it is worth pointing out that Boccaccio, who is often seen as an innovative proto-Renaissance mythographer because of his excellent scholarship and his heroic attempt to structure the whole corpus of myth, is relatively conservative—i.e., Fulgentian—in his actual interpretations. See also his cautious statements about the propriety of pagan learning—including the question whether pagan myths count as theology ("rather physiology or ethology")—in 15:8–11 (*Boccaccio on Poetry,* tr. C. G. Osgood, Indianapolis, 1956, pp. 121–35).

27. Giovanni del Virgilio, ed. Ghisalberti, p. 100.

28. *Ovide moralisé,* ed. deBoer, 43:367. "The poets pretended that Caesar was deified and so became a star; and Ovid did the same, wanting to prove falsely by fables and by fictions the various transformations that are discussed in this book. For he hoped by doing this that he would win favor with Augustus."

29. Among the best of these works are Tuve, *Allegorical Imagery;* C. S. Lewis, *The Allegory of Love* (London, 1938); Adolf Katzenellenbogen, *Allegories of the Virtues and Vices in Medieval Art* (London, 1939); Jules Pépin, *Mythe et*

allegorie (Paris, 1958); Angus Fletcher, *Allegory: The Theory of a Symbolic Mode* (Ithaca, 1964). On the uses of allegory in scriptural interpretation, see G. R. Owst, *Literature and Pulpit in Medieval England* (Cambridge, 1937); Beryl Smalley, *The Study of the Bible in the Middle Ages* (Oxford, 1952); Jean Daniélou, *From Shadows to Reality: Studies in the Biblical Typology of the Fathers*, tr. W. Hibbard (Westminster, Md., 1960); Henri de Lubac, *Exégèse médiévale: Les quatre sens de l'ecriture* (Paris, 1959–64). On a more specific topic, see Lester K. Born, "Ovid and Allegory," *Speculum* 9 (1934): 362–79.

30. Boethius, *The Consolation of Philosophy*, tr. R. Green (Indianapolis, 1962), 4. Poem 3.

31. The distinctions within the world of beast-fable among animal simile, animal allegory, parable, exemplary tale, etc. are very interestingly developed by Klaus Grabmüller in *Meister Esopus: Untersuchungen zur Geschichte und Funktion der Fabel im Mittelalter* (Zurich, 1977), esp. pp. 9–47. Grabmüller does not draw parallels directly to the non-beast-fable literature of allegorized animals, but his analysis of the rhetorical uses of the animal image bears comparison to the Boethian tradition and that of the moralized Circe. See also n. 32, for more materials and sources on rhetoric. For other approaches to the beast-fable tradition, see Francis Klingender, *Animals in Art and Thought* (Cambridge, Mass., 1971), pp. 339–81; and H. R. Jauss, *Untersuchungen zur Mittelalterlichen Tierdichtung* (Tübingen, 1959).

32. Such distinctions go back to Aristotle's *Poetics*, where both metaphor and simile are discussed in terms that involve the shift from human to animal (or vice versa). So Aristotle quotes Gorgias addressing a swallow who has left droppings upon him: "'Nay, shame, O Philomela.' Considering her as a bird, you could not call her act shameful; considering her as a girl you could" (3.4.1406b). The basis for the metaphor is the myth of metamorphosis, and when Aristotle goes on to distinguish metaphor and simile, his quasi-metamorphic example is Achilles "leapt on the foe as a lion" as distinct from Achilles "the lion leapt." See the excellent discussion in W. B. Stanford, *Greek Metaphor* (Oxford, 1936), pp. 25–30. Medieval distinctions are not always as tight or clear as those of Aristotle; still, they continue to emphasize the *translatio* between human and animal (or animate and inanimate) and the distinction between *metaphora* and *similitudo*. Among medieval rhetoricians (e.g., Geoffrey of Vinsauf, Boncompagno, Gervasius of Melkley) the difference between simile and metaphor is often characterized as between *manifesta* and *occulta similitudo*. See references in Werner Ziltener, *Studien zur bildungsgeschichtlichen Eigenart der höfischen Dichtung* (Bern, 1972), pp. 60–65. See also Bede, *De schematibus et tropis*, tr. in *Readings in Medieval Rhetoric*, ed. J. M. Miller et al. (Bloomington, Ind., 1973), esp. pp. 106–22.

33. Lactantius, *Divine Institutes*, tr. McDonald, pp. 40–41.

34. John of Garland, *Integumenta Ovidii*, ed. Ghisalberti, ll. 85–86. "If Lycaon is a wolf, he is a wolf by reason of his wolvish ferocity. For you can be a wolf by having the qualities of a wolf."

35. The translation is taken from W. D. Reynolds, "The *Ovidius Moralizatus* of Pierre Bersuire: An Introduction and Translation," Ph.D. diss., University of Illinois at Urbana-Champaign, 1971, pp. 253–54.

36. The term is often identified (sometimes contrasted) with *involucrum*. For excellent treatments of the concept, see M. D. Chénu, "Involucrum: Le Mythe selon les theologiens médiévaux," *Archives d'histoire doctrinale et littéraire du moyen âge* 30 (1955): 75–79; E. Jeauneau, "L'Usage de la notion d'integumentum à travers les gloses de Guillaume de Conches," *Archives d'histoire . . .* 32 (1957): 35–100; H. Brinkmann, "Verhüllung ('Integumentum') als literarische Darstellungsform im Mittelalter," in. A. Zimmermann, ed., *Miscellanea Medievalia*, vol. 8 (Berlin, 1971); Winthrop Wetherbee, *Platonism and Poetry in the Twelfth Century* (Princeton, 1972), pp. 36–48; Brian Stock, *Myth and Science in the Twelfth Century* (Princeton, 1972), pp. 49–62. Also see Peter Dronke, *Fabula: Explorations into the Uses of Myth in Medieval Platonism* (Leiden, 1974), pp. 48–49n2, for an excellent review of ancient sources for *integumentum*. In the whole of my discussion of medieval humanism I am especially indebted to the works of Wetherbee, Stock, and Dronke.

37. See F. Wehrlie, *Zur Geschichte der allegorischen Deutung Homers in Altertum* (Leipzig, 1928); Allen, *Mysteriously Meant*, pp. 83–94; F. Buffière, *Les Mythes d'Homère et la pensée grecque* (Paris, 1956); and Jean Daniélou, *Message evangélique et culture hellenique au IIe et IIIe siècles* (Tournai, 1961), pp. 73–101.

38. The locus classicus in the *Republic* is Book X. On myths in Plato the best source remains J. A. Stewart, *The Myths of Plato* (rpt. Hertford, 1970), which includes texts and commentaries.

39. Dionysius the Areopagite, *De Caeli Hierarchis* 2, ed. R. Roques et al. (Paris, 1970), p. 74, cited in translation in Dronke, *Fabula*, p. 44.

40. This statement appears in a commentary on Martianus Capella discovered by E. Jeauneau and printed in "Notes sur l'école de Chartres," *Studi medievali* 5 (1964): 821–65, which see for arguments about its authorship.

41. Printed as an excursus in Dronke, *Fabula*, p. 71. See also section 3 of this chapter.

42. Theodulf, *Carmina* 4:1, *PL* 105, cols. 331–32. "I used to read sometimes Virgil, sometimes you, prating Ovid, in whose writings though there be many frivolous things, yet still more truths are hiding under the covering of falsehood. The style conveys the lies of the poets but the truths of philosophers; such falsehoods can often be turned to truth. So Proteus depicts the true, so Astraea the just, Hercules the virtuous, and poor Cacus the deceitful. In order that the truth be hidden, a thousand lies are open to view. Constrained in this way, the truth returns in its original form."

43. See Demats, *Fabula*, p. 101 and Tuve, *Allegorical Imagery*, esp. pp. 284–314.

44. Bersuire, *Ovidius moralizatus*, ed. Engels, p. 40; tr. Reynolds, pp. 139–41.

45.   Who clearly signifies humility,
       So sweet was he, so pitiable,
       So humble and loving
       And, for the sake of human kind,
       Was willing to accept shame and dishonor

And to give over his body to torment.
As he offered himself joyously
To submit to deadly pain,
So like a swan who feels
Great joy and experiences so much pleasure and sings
When he sees his death come upon him.

46. Wants to come down and abase himself
Without losing his divinity
So he goes toward Sidon in Tyre
That is: in this world we say honestly,
In order to ransom the race of man
And to deliver us from hellish servitude
He covered himself in human form.

47. Drank from the holy fountain
The water of living wisdom,
Who had such high knowledge
And was so wise and perceptive
That he knew the divine secrets
Just as God wished to reveal to him.

48. The son of God was a golden rain
When into the honored virgin
He entered without violating her
And to hide this mystery
Lest the enemy pierce through
He wished that the virgin have a husband.

49. St. Ambrose, "De Fide," in *Funeral Orations,* pp. 256–57. It is worth pointing out how familiar St. Ambrose appears to be with several Ovidian stories of metamorphosis.

50. Arnulf, 1, ed. Ghisalberti, p. 201.

51. Isidore of Seville, *Etymologiae,* 11:4.

52. See *City of God* 18:16–17. Augustine himself cites Varro. Isidore, in true medieval fashion, copies Augustine verbatim but, by omitting various passages, he leaves a considerably more positive impression of the plausibility of the transformations.

53. The classic work on the subject is C. H. Haskins, *The Renaissance of the Twelfth Century* (Cambridge, Mass., 1927); there is an excellent response in W. K. Ferguson, *The Renaissance in Historical Thought* (Cambridge, Mass., 1948), pp. 329–85. See also M. D. Chénu, *La Théologie au douzième siècle* (Paris, 1957), translated in part as *Nature, Man, and Society in the Twelfth Century* (Chicago, 1968); Richard McKeon, "Poetry and Philosophy in the Twelfth Century: The Renaissance of Rhetoric," *Modern Philology* 43 (1945–46): 217–34; and Erwin Panofsky, *Renaissance and Renascences in Western Art* (New York, 1972).

54. For a good summary of these background materials, see George D. Economou, *The Goddess Natura in Medieval Literature* (Cambridge, Mass., 1972), pp. 1–52. Also see Wetherbee, *Platonism and Poetry.*

55.   See Stock, *Myth and Science*, chap. 1, sec. 1, "Myth, Model, and Science," esp. pp. 17–20, for a good discussion of "the myth and the demythologization" offered to medieval thinkers by Plato and Chalcidius.

56.   Macrobius, *Commentary on the Dream of Scipio*, tr. W. H. Stahl (New York, 1952), p. 85.

57.   Reprinted in Dronke, *Fabula*, p. 71; tr. p. 27, 29.

58.   Herewith a selection of the encyclopedias in more or less chronological order: Honorius of Autun, *De Imagine Mundi* (early twelfth century); William of Conches, *De Philosophiae Mundi, Dragmaticon* (mid-twelfth); *De Bestiis et Aliis Rebus*, probably by Hugh of St. Victor (mid-twelfth); John of Salisbury, *Policraticus* (mid-twelfth); Alexander Neckam, *De Naturis Rerum* (late twelfth); Gervasius of Tilbury, *Otia Imperialia* (early thirteenth); Bartholomaeus Anglicus, *De Rerum Proprietatibus* (mid-thirteenth); Vincent of Beauvais, *Speculum Naturale* (mid-thirteenth).

59.   William of Conches, *Dragmaticon*, ed. G. Gratarolus (Strasbourg, 1567; rpt. Frankfurt, 1967), p. 295.

60.   This discussion is indebted to the researches of Simone Viarre in *La Survie d'Ovide dans la littérature scientifique des 12e et 13e siècles* (Poitiers, 1966). What Mme Viarre does not mention, presumably because it is a fourteenth-century development, is that Ovid's very name was construed as cosmologically significant, as it was felt to be derived from *ovum dividens*. The egg is a microcosmic figure for the universe, and in dividing the cosmic egg Ovid proves his profound understanding of it, as himself the penetrator of an integumentum. See, for instance, Cod. Ambrosius. N. 254. sup., cited in Ghisalberti, "Medieval Biographies," p. 53.

61.   Baudri, Poem 196, ll. 169–98; Alain, *Anticlaudianus*, 5, 17ff.; Albertus Magnus, *Mineralia*, 1.2.8.

62.   Gervasius of Tilbury, *Otia Imperialia*, 4; for Bernard, see *Megacosmus*, 2–3; William uses the term *metamorphoseos* in his glosses on the *Timaeus*, 162 (*Glosae super Platonem*, ed. E. Jeauneau, Paris, 1965, p. 270).

63.   Simone Viarre, for instance, cites on one observation of Pythagoras (15:389–90: the transformation of human spinal marrow into snakes) repetition and embellishment by Rabanus Maurus, Isidore of Seville, Bartholomaeus Anglicus, and Vincent of Beauvais. See *La Survie*, pp. 146–52. For Albertus Magnus, see *Mineralia*, 1.2.8.

64.   For a brilliant discussion of the metaphor of nature as a book, see Curtius, *European Literature*, pp. 319–26.

65.   Citations are to *De Naturis Rerum et De Laudibus Divinae Sapientiae*, ed. T. Wright (London, 1863). Little has been written on Neckam. See U. T. Holmes, Jr., *Daily Living in the Twelfth Century* (Madison, 1952); and Max Manitius, *Geschichte der lateinischen Literatur des Mittelalters* (Munich, 1931), 3:784–94. See also C. E. Raven, *English Naturalists from Neckam to Ray* (London, 1947). For an argument to the effect that Neckam, "Albericus Londoniensis" (author of the *Liber imaginum deorum*), and the Third Vatican Mythographer are one and the same person, see Seznec, *Survival*, pp. 170–72.

66.   One final example of the metamorphic union between nature and myth is to be found in Neckam's discussion of the spider. He begins with a purely empirical description of self-transformation: "Seipsam eviscerat aranea, ut materia

non desit cassibus contextendis" (chap. 113; p. 193). He has for the moment leapt over the mythic metamorphosis (girl into spider) toward a metamorphic vision of the spinning of webs. *Eviscerat* immediately conveys both physical and spiritual connotations, and the moral allegory is soon drawn: "Sic sic multi seipsos eviscerant, in quaestu rerum inutilium" (ibid.). He sees human futility as a self-transformation (cf. Dante, *Inferno*, 13), and he develops it along with more conventional allegories about the intricacies of spider webs. Only at the end of the chapter does he turn to the metamorphic myth of Arachne itself, which he moralizes so that her transformation is a sign not just of her being a weaver but also of the dangerous self-squandering implied by her presumption. And this allegorization is not merely rhetorical: closely watched spiders in real life continue to enact this moralized metamorphosis.

67. M.-M. Davy, "Notion de l'homme et de l'univers au XIIe siècle," *Les Etudes philosophiques* 16 (1961): 38.

68. See Ghisalberti, "Medieval Biographies," pp. 20, 52–55. "I am what you will be. I have been what you are. Or, what you are now I was before. So metamorphosis [or such metamorphosis] forbids our subjection to earthly things."

69. Arnulf, ed. Ghisalberti, p. 181.

70. Walsingham, *De Archana deorum,* ed. van Kluyve, 1.36.

71. Third Vatican Mythographer, 11.25, ed. Bode, p. 242.

72. Arnulf, 14:3, ed. Ghisalberti, p. 227.

73. See my discussion of *Inferno* 25 in chapter 4, section 2.

74. John of Salisbury *Policraticus*, ed. C. Webb (Oxford, 1909), p. 19. Thomas of Citeaux, *In Canticum* 4, *PL* 206, col. 249.

75. Arnulf, ed. Ghisalberti, p. 181.

76. *Timaeus*, 42b–c, tr. B. Jowett in *The Collected Dialogues of Plato*, ed. E. Hamilton and H. Cairns (New York, 1961).

77. Alain de Lille, *Theologicae Regulae,* 99, *PL* 210, cols. 673–74.

78. Cf. Javelet (*Image et ressemblance*, p. 266) on the interrelations of the myth of Circe with the parable of the prodigal son: "La métamorphose extérieure est le signe de la transformation intérieure; elle offre une image d'un realisme saisissant: l'ange et l'homme déchus font la bête et cette bête est l'immonde pourceau. Mais l'explication la plus propre à nos spirituels, c'est une certaine phénoménologie. Le terme ou la fin d'un être en est la réalité intentionelle. *On est ce qu'on choisit d'être."*

79. For Tiresias, see Fulgentius, *Mythologies*, 2.5 (tr. Whitbread, p. 70). Myrrha appears as *amaritudo* in Bersuire 10.10 (ed. Engels, p. 153). For Leda see Arnulf 6.8 (ed. Ghisalberti, p. 216). For Medusa see Giovanni del Virgilio 4.26 (ed. Ghisalberti, p. 60).

80. See especially Arnulf 1.10, 11 (ed. Ghisalberti, p. 203).

81. Seznec, *Survival*, p. 5.

82. The first lyric appears as "De vestium transformatione," in A. Boemer, "Eine Vagantenliedersammlung des 14. Jahrhunderts," *Zeitschrift für deutsches Altertum* 49 (1908): 178–85. The second poem is 220a in *Carmina Burana*, ed. A. Hilka and O. Schumann (Heidelberg, 1930), 1:643–47. For a discussion of the relation between the two poems, see Paul Lehmann, *Die Parodie im Mittelalter* (Stuttgart, 1963), pp. 154–58.

83. "So in the style of Proteus clothing is transformed; nor was the meta-morphic law recently invented. As the princes of the church change their sex in outward appearance, so secretly they patch up torn garments. Nor are these given away, you can be sure, without first going through the experience of Tiresias. For indeed the cape is determined to be of the feminine gender, while the mantle is of the masculine. God makes a cape out of a mantle, and therefore it can be guilty of both sides of love." It is worth remarking how frequent are the associations in me-dieval writings between metamorphosis and homosexuality. Tiresias appears in such a context not only in the Goliardic poems but also among the mythographers and natural historians. Ovidian tag lines about both Tiresias ("utriusque veneris") and Orpheus ("primos carpere flores") appear in direct quotation. It is clear that unconventional sexuality is a vivid example within real experience for medieval learned men of both the passionate and the transforming impulses behind myths and metamorphoses.

84. The lines in this lyric resist translation. The German translations in the Hilka and Schumann edition are charming, but their connection to the original is tenuous. My translation follows: "When time after time he refaced this worn out thing and once refaced time after time defaced it, he did not wish to throw it away even yet; nor did he throw it away, but to save his mantle, he made himself a tunic to cover it. So after the fashion of the Gorgon, he transformed the form; or rather the remarkable artificer changed their sex. He masculined the feminine, he femi-nined the masculine; and going Tiresias one better, he trifurcated sex. It was not enough for him to have cloaked a mantle and contrariwise successively to have mantled a cloak, not enough that the recloaked mantle has changed to a tunic, but by the end the tunic has been turned to shoes."

85. "The form, when rich clothing is transformed into new forms, is varied in succession. I would say 'In nova fert animus' [the opening lines of the *Metamor-phoses*: 'my spirit moves me to speak of new . . . ']. The old ones are changed to new, or rather to a different form of old."

86. For Tiresias, see Fulgentius (as in n. 77) as well as many others, e.g., Second Vatican Mythographer, no. 84 (ed. Bode, p. 104); on Myrrha's "gum" see Fulgentius 3.8 (tr. Whitbread, pp. 92–93), along with Third Vatican Myth-ographer 11.17 (ed. Bode, p. 239). For Medusa see Fulgentius 1.21 (pp. 61–62); and Giovanni 4.26 (ed. Ghisalberti, p. 60).

87. The relations between Venus and Natura are complex, and they do not seem to have been investigated by scholars concerned with classical origins of the medieval Natura. Alain in the *De Planctu Naturae* introduces a double Venus: she is partly God's subvicar (Natura herself being the vicar) and partly a representa-tive of vice. But Natura herself—without explicit reference to the classical love goddess—often owes something to the *Venus genetrix* of the Platonists, and im-agery such as the cloak of Natura (e.g., in *De Planctu*, Prose One) goes back to a similar garment of Venus that contains earthly creation. In that case, the descrip-tion of the cloak occasions a lengthy disquisition on the varieties of animals, but the beginning of the description is decidedly metamorphic, quite possibly with a debt to Ovidian ekphrases: "Her dress, woven from silk-smooth wool, kaleido-scopic in its various colours, served the purpose of a robe of office for the maiden. Changing circumstances, which substituted one hue for another, altered the gar-

ment with a varied display of colour" (*The Plaint of Nature*, tr. J. J. Sheridan, Toronto, 1980, p. 85).

88.   *Fulgentius metaforalis*, ed. Liebeschütz, pp. 78–79.

89.   Published with translation in Peter Dronke, *Medieval Latin and the Rise of the European Love Lyric* (Oxford, 1966), pp. 452–63. Translations are quoted from that edition. One should, by the way, be careful not to overstate the uniqueness of "Profuit ignaris." There are medieval traditions of learned, classicizing, unorthodox, and erotic poetry. The heroine of the eleventh-century "Semiramis" defends pagan love via the myth of Jupiter's transformation into a bull. The *Carmina Burana* (in more than one lyric) are filled with Ovidian materials and a highly physicalized view of life and love. The twelfth-century Regensburg manuscript is a celebration of Petrarchism *avant la lettre* with rather more obvious (in effect, pedantic) learning than Petrarch's. See Dronke, *Medieval Latin*, pp. 163–263, 422–47, and *Poetic Individuality in the Middle Ages* (Oxford, 1970), esp. pp. 33–113.

90.   "We are told that Juno united with her brother Jove, that the highest of the gods loved a mistress, and that to thwart his mother he cut off his father's organs."

91.   "Juno, Venus, Amor strike the high hearts of great men—here we see matter of the gods transform the forms and bodies of created things. Jupiter is said to have been transformed into a bull, and into gold—Amor, we are told, brought his transformations about. . . . When the poet contemplates these things under the metaphor of transformations, a great theme and work are at hand."

92.   "I wonder why the poet about to tell of so many monstrous and shameful things wished first to relate the beginnings of heaven and earth. Like Plato he gives a cosmology, and then explains the things that were changed, the varied species, the flaw in what is mutable, the unholy lewdness of the gods. Why does he do this? He wants to show us how much Natura, once guiltlessly pure, has been dragged down, seduced and defiled. When we contemplate heaven, when we philosophize about the planets' courses (believing) that the dwelling of souls is in the stars, that they must proceed from there into whatever is born, submitting to their destiny, descending into a body and inhabiting it; when we discuss how blessed souls seek their first resting place again, or else, departing in death, atone for their deeds in the just suffering of flames, by which you become pure again, destined to enjoy heaven for ever—when we expound such things about virtue and true salvation, in spirit we are flying to the stars. Then do we (truly) seek heaven—this is not to pile Ossa on Olympus! Then again you feel this state of mind changing, turning to impiety, wantonness, and luxury. Jove, drawn deep down, fills human action, the mind sins, overcome by vice, casting virtue aside."

93.   "Yet there is something you can learn from the nature of these gods: it is not without significance that they are said to make their way to the depths. . . . Whatever comes to pass in this world under a cruel or a kindly star, whatever has influence on these, from which we see every created form established, whatever you know and feel, whatever is begotten and exists by virtue of these elements —all this men saw in the sexual unions of these gods!"

94.   It is the final survey of the natural world subsumed under a single force that suggests the poet's indebtedness to the opening of Lucretius's *De Rerum Natura*, an invocation to Venus which places in her power all the natural impulses

of earthly life. Lucretius's work was certainly not well known in any complete form to the Middle Ages, but there seems to have been enough citation of important passages (including the opening) to have made them accessible. See G. D. Hadzsits, *Lucretius and His Influence* (New York, 1963), pp. 198–247. The Lucretian connection links together the concept of nature with the sexual impulse implicit in the whole Chartrain tradition. Furthermore, the switch from Lucretius's nature or Venus to the twelfth-century poet's "coitum deorum" as the cause of all things represents a considerable paganizing of what was already a departure from orthodox Christian cosmology.

CHAPTER FOUR. *Taccia Ovidio:* Metamorphosis,
Poetics, and Meaning in Dante's *Inferno*

1.　*European Literature and the Latin Middle Ages,* tr. W. R. Trask (New York, 1963), p. 350.

2.　Citations are to *The Divine Comedy,* tr. Charles S. Singleton (Princeton, 1970), and translations are taken from that edition. A special debt for the formation of my ideas is owed to the brilliant Dante commentary of Hermann Gmelin (*Die Göttliche Komödie,* Stuttgart, 1954). Amongst materials on the whole question of Dante and antiquity (in addition to Curtius) I would especially single out Augustin Renaudet, *Dante humaniste* (Paris, 1952); Hermann Gmelin, "Dante und die römischen Dichter," *Deutsches Dante Jahrbuch* 31–32 (1953): 42–65; Paul Renucci, *Dante disciple et juge du monde gréco-latin* (Paris, 1954); and Alessandro Ronconi, "Per Dante, interprete dei poeti latini," *Studi danteschi* 41 (1964): 5–44.

3.　See the influential commentary of Isidoro del Lungo, *Prolusioni alle tre cantiche e commento all' "Inferno"* (Florence, 1921), p. 15, for an eloquent expression of this psychological allegory. Virgil's *lungo silenzio* has been read in other ways as well. Interesting connections with the "vox clamantis in deserto" of Matthew 3:5 and Isaiah 40:3 are developed by André Pézard, *Dante sous la pluie du feu* (Paris, 1950), pp. 339–45; and Bruno Porcelli, "'Chi per lungo silenzio parea fioco' e il valore della parola nella Commedia," *Ausonia* 19 (1964) 5:32–38. Others have pointed out that *fioco* suggests visual as well as auditory obscurity. See Roger Dragonetti, "Chi per lungo silenzio parea fioco," *Studi danteschi* 38 (1961): 47–74. For the best reading of the *lungo silenzio* as a piece of cultural history, see Robert Fitzgerald, "The Style that Does Honor," *Kenyon Review* 14 (1952): 278–85.

4.　In spite of his medievalizing arguments, Curtius sees the meeting with Virgil in terms that transcend Dante's own temporal surroundings: "The conception of the *Commedia* is based upon a spiritual meeting with Virgil. In the realm of European literature there is little which may be compared with this phenomenon. . . . The awakening of Virgil by Dante is an arc of flame which leaps from one great soul to another. The tradition of the European spirit knows no situation of such affecting loftiness, tenderness, fruitfulness. It is the meeting of the two greatest Latins. Historically, it is the sealing of the bond which the Latin Middle Ages made between the antique and the modern world" (*European Literature,* p. 358). For somewhat more sober and historicist views see Rocco Montano, "Dante and Virgil," *Yale Review* 60 (1971): 550–61; and Erich Auerbach, "Dante und Virgil," in *Gesammelte Aufsätze zur romanischen Philologie* (Bern and Munich, 1967), pp. 115–22. See also the excellent summary of Virgil's roles in the *Divine Comedy* offered by G. B. Townend in "Changing Views of Vergil's Greatness," *Classical Journal* 56 (1960): 67–77.

5. This continuity is not limited to the poetic; it may even be theological. Capaneus is one of the Seven Against Thebes, a giant who climbed the wall of the city and hurled defiance to Jupiter. His place in the *Inferno* is among the blasphemers, and after the giant has uttered a ferocious pronouncement, Virgil explains, "ebbe e par ch'elli abbia / Dio in disdegno" (14.69–70). The god whom Capaneus blasphemed, and whom he continues to blaspheme, translates almost without mediation *(e par che)* into the God who controls Dante's own universe. And not only is Virgil, prophet of the Christian age, a fitting interpreter between these two gods, but he is also drawing directly on the account of the Theban story written by Statius, the putatively Christian classical poet who will receive the baton of continuity from Virgil at the earthly paradise in the *Purgatorio*.

6. Considering the volume of commentary on the role of Virgil in the *Divine Comedy*, there has been remarkably little interest in the poetic relations between the texts of the two authors. Edward Moore, in *Studies in Dante*, 1st ser. (Oxford, 1896), pp. 166–97, gives a sampling of borrowings, some obvious, others more subtle and suggestive. For an exhaustive list of parallels, see *Enciclopedia dantesca* (Rome, 1976) 5:1044–49. See also Alessandro Ronconi, "Virgilianismi danteschi," in *Interpretazioni grammaticali* (Rome, 1971), pp. 95–105; and Robert Hollander, "Dante's Use of *Aeneid* I in *Inferno* I and II," *Comparative Literature* 20 (1968): 142–56.

7. These were collected by Petrarch in Book XXIV of the *Familiares*. See *Petrarch's Letters to Classical Authors*, tr. M. E. Cosenza (Chicago, 1910). For an account of Petrarch in this connection see Thomas M. Greene, *The Light in Troy* (New Haven, 1982), esp. pp. 81–103.

8. The presence of Statius in purgatory and his relations with Virgil account for perhaps the most sweeping Christian tributes from Dante to Virgil. By explicitly using the medieval tradition that the Fourth Eclogue foresaw the coming of Christ, Dante makes its author into a prophet who converts his poetic follower Statius to Christianity, even though the prophet himself was not a Christian. The meeting of the two classical poets in *Purgatorio* XXI and XXII, one of the poem's most moving episodes, climaxes with Statius's account of his conversion: "Per te poeta fui, per te cristiano" (22.73). That combination of gifts from one soul to another—not only poetry but also salvation—almost makes Virgil a Christian saint.

9. The limbo of virtuous pagans appears to be a Dantesque invention based upon limbos envisioned by Peter Lombard and Thomas Aquinas but limited by them to unbaptized children and Old Testament patriarchs. Just how far Dante meant to go in honoring the virtuous pagans within Christian eschatology is a matter of interest and controversy. On the cautious side, see Mario Frezza, *Il Problema della salvezza dei pagani* (Naples, 1962); and Fiorenzo Forti, "Il Limbo dantesco e i megalopsichoi dell' etica nicomachea," *Giornale storico della letteratura italiana* 138 (1961): 329–64. For somewhat more radical views, see Amerindo Camilli, "La Teologia del limbo dantesco," *Studi danteschi* 30 (1951): 209–

14; David Thompson, "Dante's Virtuous Romans," *Dante Studies* 86 (1978): 145–62; and Gino Rizzo, "Dante and the Virtuous Pagans," in W. J. DeSua and G. Rizzo, eds., *A Dante Symposium in Commemoration of the 700th Anniversary of the Poet's Birth* (Chapel Hill, 1965), pp. 115–39. What underlies (or should underlie) these debates is the question of Dante's attitude toward antiquity. Exactly how he could succeed in manipulating received theological opinion on the subject is less important than the obvious fact that the invention of a pagan limbo, the figure of a theologically sophisticated Virgil in close touch with heaven, and the Christianizing of Statius all represent bold steps in translating intellectual or aesthetic respect for the ancients into a reified theological system. For a particularly measured and subtle analysis of these underlying questions as they apply to historical categories like "medieval" and "humanist," see Giorgio Padoan, "Dante di fronte all' umanesimo letterario," in *Atti del congresso internazionale di studi danteschi* (Florence, 1966), 2:377–400.

10. Curtius, *European Literature*, p. 366. It is interesting in this regard that Curtius, discussing what he calls the "personnel" of the *Commedia*, declares that of all classical or medieval poems only Ovid's *Metamorphoses* can compare in number and variety of characters.

11. The seminal treatment of Virgil's medieval fortunes is Domenico Comparetti, *Vergil in the Middle Ages*, tr. E. F. M. Benecke (London, 1895), as superlative in its learning as it is literal-minded in approaching Dante. On Virgil as magus, see esp. pp. 239–324, and on *The Divine Comedy*, pp. 210–31. See also Rudolf Palgen, "La légende virgilienne dans la *Divine Comédie*," *Romania* 73 (1952): 332–90, which argues for the placement of Virgil well within the medieval traditions of magic and demonology.

12. In refuting Manichaeanism, Augustine explained the presence of evil in a universe ruled by an all-powerful good deity with the assertion that evil "was not a substance but a swerving of the will" away from God. See *Confessions*, 7.16.

13. Perhaps the best introduction to the subject of Dante and Ovid is Ettore Paratore's article s.v. "Ovidio" in the *Enciclopedia dantesca* 4:225–37, which supercedes the pioneering work of Edward Moore, *Studies*, 1st ser. pp. 206–28. For a well-documented treatment of Dante in relation to the medieval Ovid, see C. A. Robson, "Dante's Use in the *Divine Comedy* of the Medieval Allegories on Ovid," in *Centenary Essays on Dante* (Oxford, 1965), pp. 1–38. The most eloquent assertion about the relations between Ovidian and Dantesque metamorphosis, with which I am in very little agreement, is that of Leo Spitzer, "Speech and Language in *Inferno* XIII," in *Dante: A Collection of Critical Essays*, ed. John Freccero (Englewood Cliffs, N.J., 1965), pp. 78–101: "Thus the whole spirit of the Dantean metamorphosis is opposed to that of Ovid: the pagan poet with his pantheistic love for nature (of which man is a part), who could discover a nymph in every fountain, a dryad in every tree, was able to see in metamorphosis only the principle of the eternal change of forms in nature. . . . It could be said that in Ovid the (gradual) transformation of a human into a vegetal being seems to take place almost *naturally*; but with Dante the link between nature and man has been broken by a tragic-minded Christianity; where Ovid offers to our view the richness of organic nature, Dante shows the inorganic, the hybrid, the perverted, the sinful, the damned" (p. 82). The argument about the *Inferno* is valid up to a point, but

the distinction between Dante and Ovid rests on a simplistic view of the Latin poet's range, as well as of the varieties of medieval Ovidianism. For other Ovidian approaches to Dante, see n. 60.

14. For a particularly well-documented discussion, see Robert Javelet, *Image et ressemblance au douzième siècle* (Paris, 1967), esp. pp. 246–97. Also see above, chapter 3, section 4.

15. Origen, *Homélies sur S. Luc* 8, ed. H. Crouzel et al. (Paris, 1962), pp. 166–68.

16. Thomas of Cîteaux, *Commentum in Cantica Canticorum* 4; *PL* 206:249a.

17. See above, chapter 3, section 4.

18. The origins go back to "an eye for an eye" in Exodus 21:23–25. Compare also Leviticus 24:17–22 and Deuteronomy 19:21. The idea is replicated and balanced by Christ's golden rule in Matthew 7:2. The term *contrapassum*, referring to reciprocation for wrongs, appears in the medieval Latin translation of Aristotle's *Nichomachean Ethics*, 5,5,1132b, where it is upheld neither as a principle of justice nor as a good civil practice. Aquinas comments upon *contrapassum* (*Summa Theologica* 2,2,61,4), understanding it less as a principle than as revenge or retribution in the civil sense, and he views it as a crime in itself equal to that which provoked it. The background for Dante's term, then, is the very reverse of a proper Christian principle, and the poet uses that reversal to create a special hellish justice. Apart from Ovid, the poetic sources of the *contrapasso* may well include the fitting punishments of the damned in Virgil's netherworld (*Aeneid* 6.735–51). The seminal discussion of the *contrapasso* is by Francesco d'Ovidio, "Sette chiose alla Commedia," *Studi danteschi* 7 (1923): 27–44. See also F. von Falkenhausen, "Dantes Vergeltungsidee," *Deutsches Dante Jahrbuch* 14 (1932): 61–81; and Steno Vazzana, *Il Contrapasso nella Divina Commedia: Studio sulla unità del poema* (Rome, 1959). See also the interesting distinction made by the Anonimo Fiorentino between *contrapasso* and justice in *Commento alla Divina Commedia*, ed. Pietro Fanfani (Bologna, 1866), p. 612.

19. The avaricious and the prodigal, for instance, have not only lost all distinction from each other but have also one by one lost their physical shape and hence their individuality; much the same is true for the wrathful, who are hidden in wet mud and whose hymn is barely audible for being gurgled under water. Having a body at all is in some important ways a property of living. Thus on at least four occasions (8.27; 12.80; 17.99; 24.30), we—or the damned—are reminded that the living Dante is unique in hell because his corporeality has actual weight and mass and therefore has a material effect on the environment. See Romano Guardini, "Corpo e corporeità nella *Commedia*," in his *Studi su Dante* (Brescia, 1967), pp. 221–45. The question of having a body is also conjoined with that of the ultimate fate of bodies and souls at the Last Judgment. Each of the gluttons, Virgil tells Dante, "ripiglierà sua carne" (6.98) at the final trumpet, a phrase which in this case has grotesque connotations mirroring the sin and suggesting a kind of cannibalism. I discuss the suicides at the Last Judgment in section 2 of this chapter.

20. See chapter 2, section 4.

21. Leo Spitzer makes a cogent argument for the significance of the anonymous suicide ("Speech and Language," pp. 96–105) largely on account of his Florentine origins and consequent personal relevance for Dante. Spitzer sees the *case*

as metonymic for the whole of Florence, with all its riches and self-destructive qualities.

22. It should be noted that the rigorous account of the types and causes of sin in Canto XI rests heavily upon distinctions in principle between man and beast such as those we have seen (and shall see) in composite mythological figures and in metamorphosis. So in upper hell, Virgil explains, the sins of *frode* are more severely punished than those of *forza* because the former is a peculiarly human ability; conversely, in the lower circles "la matta / bestialitade" (11. 82–83) seems to characterize the worst sins, perhaps even below the punishments of *incontinenza* and *malizia*. See Alfred A. Triolo, "'Matta Bestialità' in Dante's 'Inferno,'" *Traditio* 24 (1968): 247–92.

23. See Gmelin, *Göttliche Komödie*, Kommentar, 1:293.

24. A particularly lucid treatment of the attacks on simony by means of inversion and parody is Ronald B. Herzman and William A. Stephany, "'O miseri seguaci': Sacramental Inversion in *Inferno* XIX," *Dante Studies* 96 (1978): 39–65. Charles Singleton, "*Inferno* XIX: O Simon Mago!," *Modern Language Notes* 80 (1965): 92–99, offers a suggestive iconographic background to the upside-down nature of Simon himself. On the autobiographical parenthesis and its enigmatic final line, see Mark Musa, "*E questo sia suggel ch' ogn' uomo sganni*," *Italica* 41 (1964): 134–38; Antonino Pagliaro, "Una nota al canto XIX dell' *Inferno*," in *Studi di varia umanità in onore di Francesco Flora* (Milan, 1963), pp. 289–301; and John A. Scott, "The Rock of Peter and *Inferno* XIX," *Romance Philology* 23 (1970): 462–79.

25. The instances of a close mirroring relationship between Dante and certain of the sinners can add up to a kind of negative self-portrait of the poet—a motif which, by the way, continues into the purgation of the sins in the next *cantica*. Notable examples in the *Inferno* include Dante's swoon "com' io morisse" in the presence of the fainting lovers Paolo and Francesca (5.141); the extensive face-to-face exchange (unusually free of Virgil's mediation) with Farinata and Cavalcanti, which turns upon the poet's own concerns, notably friendship, exile, and the dangers of public life; and the contrasting concealment of Dante before those guilty of barratry (Canto XXI), a sin of which Dante himself had been accused. I discuss Dante's relation to suicide in section 2 of this chapter.

26. The brilliant essay of John Freccero, "Bestial Sign and Bread of Angels (*Inferno* 32–33)," *Yale Italian Studies* 1 (1977): 53–66, goes far beyond previous criticism in understanding the christological levels that, for instance, distinguish between the sacramental/sacrificial offer of the children and the bestial interpretation to which the father puts that offer. So Ugolino's crime becomes a *misreading* (as he misreads his dream and his children's offer), a mistaking—quite literally—of flesh and word. The *mythic* reverberations of cannibalism add an Ovidian sense of the collapse of orderly creation to these sacramental inversions. See also Ronald B. Herzman, "Cannibalism and Communion in *Inferno* 33," *Dante Studies* 98 (1980): 53–78.

27. Ovid is not the only mythic source for the cannibalism of the Ugolino episode. The whole destiny of Thebes, with its origins in the Thyestean banquet, hangs over these cantos, expressly at 33.89 with the comparison of Pisa to Thebes. In a more particular sense, the punishment that unites Ugolino and Ruggieri is set up with explicit reminiscences of the episode in Statius's *Thebaid* where Tydeus,

dying from wounds he has received at the hands of Melanippus, bites through his enemy's skull and gnaws on his brains. See *Thebaid* 8.750–66, 9.1–31, and *Inferno* 33.130, along with various verbal parallels at 33.57 and 33.76.

28. On Ovid's Lycaon, see chapter 2, section 1.

29. The final line in Ugolino's account ("Poscia, più che 'l dolor, poté 'l digiuno," 33.75) is one of the most troubling cruxes in Dante, if not in all literature. The literal meaning is quite clear—"afterwards fasting had more power than grieving." But the perfect balance of the sentence infolds two almost opposite significations: Ugolino's starvation terminated his life and hence his sorrowing, or his hunger overcame his grief at the death of his children and thus induced him to satisfy it in the only means at his disposal. This second reading might be far-fetched were it not for the fact that Anselmuccio has already offered himself for cannibalistic sacrifice, the fact that Ugolino presents the story as though it has a more terrible climax than mere death, and the fact of his anthropophagic punishment in hell. Given these facts, Charles Singleton's gloss (*Divine Comedy*, 2:617), "Some commentators have held the curious view [that Ugolino tried to feed on his sons' bodies]. . . . But such a view of the meaning here is hardly worth a serious rebuttal," seems like a strangely ingenuous attempt to protect Ugolino's reputation. For other readers it seems too late for that. A less squeamish account is offered by Giovanni Pasoli, *Minerva oscura* (Leghorn, 1898), pp. 160–76.

30. The doubleness of man-and-beast is wittily emphasized by a simile comparing the Minotaur to "quel toro che si slaccia in quella / c'ha ricevuto già 'l colpo mortale" (12.22–23). A simile is meant to compare things that are not identical; the juxtaposition of Minotaur and bull reminds us that they are and are not the same thing. The procedure reminds us of the connections between simile and metamorphosis. See chap. 3, n. 33 and accompanying text.

31. Much the same image, as we have seen, is suggested by the placement of Ugolino upon Archbishop Ruggieri, gnawing him "là 've 'l cervel s'aggiugne con la nuca" (32.129), again suggesting the different layers of the body and soul.

32. This canto has received much critical attention. The fullest treatment is that of Francesco d'Ovidio, "Il Canto di Pier della Vigna," *Nuovi studi danteschi* (Milan, 1907), pp. 143–333. See also Renato Serra, "Su la pena dei dissipatori," *Giornale storico della letteratura italiana* 43 (1904): 278–98. Leo Spitzer's extremely suggestive work ("Speech and Language") has already been considered in nn. 13 and 21. I dispute Spitzer's view of the Ovidian connection, but I am very much in agreement with his analysis of the nature and function of language in the canto—not merely a rhetorical exercise to pay homage to Pier but as a vital medium of expressing the tortures of self-destruction. Thus "parole e sangue," which the metamorphosed trees put forth, are inextricably bound together.

33. On this perplexing episode, see John Freccero, "Medusa: The Letter and the Spirit," *Yearbook of Italian Studies* 2 (1972): 1–18. The essay's intricate argument reads the Medusa allegorically (as the poet warns the reader to do) in terms of a *stony* Letter and an *unveiled* (i.e., like Dante's eyes) Spirit. Most appropriate to our present concern is the metamorphic background of Medusa in medieval mythography, which joins petrification with the power of sexual attraction. The terms are closely connected to those of Dante's *Rime petrose*. For the links to Petrarch, see chapter 5, section 3, and Robert M. Durling, "'Io son venuto': Seneca, Plato, and the Microcosm," *Dante Studies* 93 (1975): 95–129.

34.   In Aeneas's confrontation with Polydorus-become-bleeding tree (*Aeneid*, 3.19–68), Virgil's emphasis is upon the young man's wrongful death—not a heroic end on the plains of Troy but the result of a betrayal by a former ally of the Trojans who has no further cause to keep his bargain with Priam once the city has fallen. The arborified spirit of Polydorus haunts the spot where he was murdered (indeed, his vegetable form imitates the collection of spears that murdered him), and Aeneas, like Dante-the-pilgrim theoretically innocent, is somehow implicated in the wrongful death by his accidental breaking of the branch. Like Ovid's Cadmus (whose story may be in part an imitation of this episode), Aeneas calls up dangerous spirits in the attempt to make a holy sacrifice. He can only proceed on his journey by quieting the spirits with a proper funeral. For Daphne and Myrrha, see chapter 2, sections 4 and 5.

35.   The Sibyl directs Aeneas (*Aeneid* 6.135–48) to find and snatch the golden branch sacred to Proserpina, since only that achievement can demonstrate fate's willingness to have Aeneas enter the underworld. The connection with Dante's suicides is made stronger by the fact that the Sibyl presents the golden bough as one of two prerequisites for the hero's underworld journey. The other task is the proper burial of Palinurus, who is, like Dante's suicides, a figure hovering between life and death. The Sibyl even suggests a (proto-Dantesque?) mirroring of Palinurus in Aeneas, himself at this point awaiting waftage to the nether world.

36.   For Ovid's Actaeon, see chapter 2, section 3. Also see my "Diana and Actaeon: The Myth as Synthesis," *English Literary Renaissance* 10 (1980): 227–80, and my discussion below, chapter 5.

37.   Out of the considerable bibliography on the events of these cantos, I would signal especially Attilio Momigliano, "Il canto XXV dell' *Inferno*," *Giornale storico della letteratura italiana* 68 (1916): 43–81; and Piero Floriani, "Mutare e trasmutare: Alcune osservazioni sul canto XXV dell' *Inferno*," *Giornale storico della letteratura italiana* 149 (1972): 324–32. See also Daniele Mattalia, *Il canto xxv dell'* Inferno (Florence, 1962); and Aleardo Sacchetto, "Il canto delle allucinanti trasmutazioni," *Due letture dantesche* (Rome, 1953).

38.   The history is quite garbled. For summaries, see Singleton, *Divine Comedy* 2.420–21, and Giovanni Fallani, *Poesia e teologia nella Divina Commedia* (Milan, 1961), pp. 126–28.

39.   See *Aeneid* 8.193–275, where Evander tells the story of the violent thief Cacus and his fight with Hercules. Cacus is not only *semihomo* but also a *monstrum* with *dira facies*. Yet there is no indication that Virgil means these terms in a literal corporeal sense.

40.   See the extremely suggestive essay of D. L. Derby Chapin, "io and the Negative Apotheosis of Vanni Fucci," *Dante Studies* 89 (1971): 19–31. The author gives a selective survey of medieval metamorphic lore but is particularly revealing in discussing the mark of io in the sand that Ovid's transformed girl/heifer uses to identify herself. If that mark in the sand is actually a cloven hoofprint (and Chapin does not mention the fact that Ovid never suggests this directly), then it is a particularly appropriate image for the speed of writing io and for its associations with animal transformation and identity.

41.   The legendary death and rebirth of the Phoenix makes it one of the earliest pieces of Christian iconography, dating from the first century writings of St.

Clement of Rome. See Lactantius, *Carmen de ave Phoenice;* and R. van den Broek, *The Myth of the Phoenix,* tr. I. Seeger (Leiden, 1972). For Pythagoras, see *Metamorphoses* 15.392–402.

42. See *Metamorphoses* 4.373–79, esp. "nec duo sunt et forma duplex, nec femina dici / nec puer ut possit, neutrumque et utrumque videntur." For my discussion of that episode, see chapter 2. Also relevant (once again) is Ovid's treatment of Actaeon, in which the reaction of former companions to the metamorphosed shape plays a significant role in the plot of transformed identity.

43. Dante's similes for metamorphosis are notably Ovidian. "Ellera abbarbicata mai non fue / ad alber sì, come l'orribil fiera / per l'altrui membra avviticchiò le sue" (25.58–60) is taken from the Salmacis and Hermaphroditus episode (*Metamorphoses* 4.365: "Utve solent hederae longos intexere truncos"), though at the turning point of the comparison *(come)* Dante deliberately transforms an equivocal image of powerful love into one of beastly strangulation. The following simile ("Poi s'appiccar, come di calda cera / fossero stati, e mischiar lor colore, / né l'un né l'altro già parea quel ch'era"; 25.61–63) is one of Ovid's favorites, appearing in both the Pygmalion and the Daedalus stories and, even more notably, in Pythagoras's metamorphic account of the origins of the universe: "utque novis facilis signatur cera figuris / nec manet ut fuerat nec formas servat easdem, / sed tamen ipsa eadem est" (15.169–71).

44. See chapter 3, section 3.

45. See chapter 2, section 3.

46. See *The Divine Institutes,* 2.11. For text and discussion, see chapter 3, section 1.

47. So much for the orthodox account. In fact, however, Ovidian metamorphosis is one of the crucial sources for a Christian understanding of the wavering *imago dei*. The transformations of Jupiter and the other deities, though they do not presume (and may even affront) the idea that man is in the image of God, nonetheless offer a fascinating source of lore to suggest that God is in the image of man. That in turn creates a medium of travel ranging from the beastly to the divine.

48. The terms *moral, allegorical,* and *anagogical* derive from the medieval tradition of interpreting scripture. They have their origins in Augustine (*De genesi ad litteram* 2.5) and Aquinas (*Summa Theologica* 1, 1, 10); and Dante defines them himself in the *Convivio* (2.1). No very consistent set of definitions for the terms emerges in the period, and there has been much dispute whether a system of theological allegory can be applied to poetry—a dispute encouraged by Dante's own distinctions between "allegory of theologians" and "allegory of poets." See Robert Hollander, *Allegory in Dante's* Commedia (Princeton, 1969), esp. pp. 28–56. The seminal work on the whole subject is Henri de Lubac, *Exégèse médiévale: Les quatre sens de l'Ecriture* (Paris, 1959–64).

49. Dante's interest in the various mutilated sinners is so intense that it accounts for the two rebukes that Virgil administers. After seeing the mutilated schismatics, the poet is gently reproved for staring intently "là giù tra l'ombre triste smozzicate" (29.6), while his interest in the fight between the feverish Sinon and the dropsical Master Adam occasions a sterner chiding. It is not that Dante pities the sufferers but that he remains curious about their distorted condition.

50. For a suggestive set of arguments about Canto XX and especially about Dante's deliberate misreading of Ovid's Tiresias, see Robert Hollander, "The

Tragedy of Divination in *Inferno* XX," *Studies in Dante* (Ravenna, 1980), esp. pp. 173–84.

51.   An interesting figure indeed, not the least because of his name. His crime of coinage is implicitly metamorphic, and it finds close relations with alchemy, which is explicitly metamorphic. The name conjures up visions of cosmic order undone. See Gianfranco Contini, "Sul XXX dell' *Inferno*," *Paragone* 4 (1953): 3–13; and Sally A. Mussetter, "*Inferno* XXX: Dante's Counterfeit Adam" in *Traditio* 34 (1978): 427–35.

52.   See the intricate discussion of narcissism and false images of reality inspired by Master Adam's comment that Sinon should "leccar lo specchio di Narciso," in Roger Dragonetti, "Dante et Narcisse ou les faux-monnayeurs de l'image," *Revue des études italiennes*, n.s. 11 (1965): 85–146.

53.   A closely related corporeal image of disorder is to be found in the possibility of a warped anthropomorphism to the whole physical fabric of hell. This notion has been most interestingly pursued by Robert M. Durling in "Farinata and the Body of Christ," *Stanford Italian Review* 2 (1981): 5–35, and "Deceit and Digestion in the Belly of Hell," in *Allegory and Representation*, ed. S. J. Greenblatt (Baltimore, 1981), pp. 61–93. The corporeal grotesque also exists on the individual level in the *Inferno*. When Mahomet, who is punished by ceaselessly splitting open his own torso, begins to speak, "con le man s'aperse il petto" (28.29); Piero da Medecina, who is mutilated about the head, also about to address the travelers, "aprì la canna" (28.68). Only on second glance do we realize that both these figurative descriptions—opening one's heart and clearing one's throat—are here actual physical activities. The corporeal metaphors have been rendered horridly literal.

54.   The simile is doubtless influenced by the visual tradition, especially strong in cathedral sculpture, illustrating the cycle of the peasant's year, month by month or season by season. The theme of these representations has always been closely connected with the orderly analogies of microcosm and macrocosm. See James Carson Webster, *The Labors of the Months in Antique and Medieval Art* (Evanston, 1938). For the larger cosmic significances of such icons, mostly after Dante's time, see Samuel C. Chew, *The Pilgrimage of Life* (New Haven, 1962). See also G. D. Economou, "The Pastoral Simile of *Inferno* XXIV," *Speculum* 51 (1976): 637–46.

55.   The *Inferno* contains other large-scale images of the cosmos, also characterized by natural metamorphoses. In the fable of the Old Man of Crete (Canto XIV), the poet depicts decay from the time of the golden age with an image of the endless flow of earthly tears generating the rivers of hell. A similar aqueous cosmology characterizes the motion of the prophetess Manto through the world (Canto XX) and thereby provides an etiology for Virgil's home territory. These are not such positive pictures as that beginning Canto XXIV, but they reinforce the sense of a natural order of changes. See D. J. Donno, "Moral Hydrography: Dante's Rivers," in *Modern Language Notes* 92 (1977): 130–39.

56.   The principal relevant passage is *The City of God*, 18:18. For a discussion of the relations between Augustine's demonology and metamorphosis, see chapter 3, section 1.

57.   Another of the most important arenas of transformation in the *Inferno* is the person of Dante the pilgrim himself. From the perplexities of the opening cantos ("E qual è quei che disvuol ciò che volle . . . "; 2.37) to the doubts of "io

rimango in forse, / che sì e no nel capo mi tenciona" (8.110–11) to the reflective assertion "Io non mori' e non rimasi vivo" (34.25), the persona is one of wavering complexities. And the character constantly reflects his milieux, including hell, our world, and the guiding spirit of Virgil. The metamorphoses of hell are mirrored in the self-transforming personality of the voyager.

58. See Singleton, *Divine Comedy*, 2:430, for an interesting note on this reading of *acerbo*.

59. For an excellent history of these notions of development, see Umberto Forti, "L'embriologia fino all' età di Dante," *Cultura e scuola* 15 (1976): 209–21.

60. Since defining the heritage of Ovidian metamorphosis largely in relation to the *Inferno*, I have been quite impressed by arguments that see its mark strongly on the two later *cantiche*. Rudolf Palgen, in a very suggestive article, "Dante e Ovidio," *Convivium*, n.s. 27 (1959): 277–87, sees Ovidian metamorphosis understood in a Platonic sense as a generating principle in the turning of the human soul toward God. Kevin Brownlee, "Dante and Narcissus (*Purg.* XXX, 76–99)," *Dante Studies* 96 (1978): 201–06, describes Dante on his whole pilgrimage as a "corrected Narcissus," and he says of the Narcissus material in general that it "should be seen as an important example of the continuing valorization of the pagan poetry of antiquity within the Christian poetic context of the *Commedia*" (p. 203). Without wishing to dispute the validity of these claims, I defend my emphasis on the grounds that the tradition of metamorphosis traced in this book shows a persistent preference for the earthly over the divine. Compare the treatment of *The Faerie Queene* below (chap. 5, sec. 5), in which Busyrane counts for a great deal more than Spenser's "great Sabaoth sight."

61. The closest thing to a full-scale treatment of Dantean commentary is B. Sandkühler, *Die frühen Dantekommentare und ihr Verhältnis zur mittelalterlichen Kommentartradition* (Munich, 1967). Useful material is also to be found in Guido Biagi, *La Divina Commedia nella figurazione artistica e nel secolare commento* (Turin, 1924), which, as its title suggests, draws interesting connections between the two traditions we are considering here. For editions of individual commentaries, see below.

62. The magisterial work of Peter Brieger, Millard Meiss, and Charles Singleton, *Illuminated Manuscripts of the Divine Comedy* (Princeton, 1969), makes the study of this tradition possible. I am much indebted to the three introductory essays and, of course, to the catalogue and reproductions.

63. The fourteenth-century classicist Giovanni del Virgilio, author of a set of allegorical treatises on Ovid (cited chap. 3, n. 17), was in close correspondence with Dante toward the end of the poet's life. Whether Giovanni's work on mythography was known to Dante or influenced him is uncertain; but it is clear that Giovanni tried to press his classical learning on the poet. See P. H. Wicksteed and E. G. Gardner, *Dante and Giovanni del Virgilio* (London, 1902), for their correspondence.

64. See, for instance, the discussion of the categories of transformation in Arnulf of Orleans, cited in chapter 3, section 4.

65. See *Expositiones et Glose super Comediam Dantis*, ed. Vincenzo Cioffari (Albany, 1974), pp. 222–23.

66. Citation is to *Comedia di Dante degli Allagherii col commento di Jacopo della Lana*, ed. Luciano Scarabelli (Bologna, 1866), 1:191.

67.   See, for instance, Jacopo della Lana, *Comedia*, p. 250. The Anonimo Fiorentino (cited above, n. 18), p. 315, turns the question into a whole developmental embryology that demonstrates the physical and spiritual growth of man from the vegetative upwards.

68.   The tensions of such a suspension bridge are increased when the commentators must respond to a Dantesque transformation that is not theologically orthodox. In the tale of the suicides not returning to their bodies at the Last Judgment, virtually all the commentators recognize a theological problem. Absolving Dante of heresy, they must look behind the apparent impossibility, as commentators on pagan literature did. Several point out (quite sensibly) that the information is given by one of the damned themselves and therefore may be in error. Benvenuto da Imola, *Commento latino sulla Divina Commedia di Dante Allighieri*, tr. G. Tamburini (Imola, 1855), p. 336, sees the error as a sign of suicide itself, that is, a disbelief in the immortality of the soul. None of the commentators can successfully reconcile Dante's fiction with Christian faith, but they must apply considerable imaginative effort on behalf of his scriptural authority.

69.   See Brieger et al., *Illuminated Manuscripts*, pp. 88–89.

70.   For a fuller discussion, see chapter 5, in connection with early Renaissance images of pagan material.

71.   See chapter 1.

72.   Respectively, in Brieger et al., *Illuminated Manuscripts*, Florence, B. N. Palat. 313, 37v; pl. 188a; London, B. M. Egerton 943, 28v; pl. 189b; and Modena, Estense α R.4.8, 22v, Paris, B. N. it. 74, 47v, and Florence, Laur. Plut. 40.1, 52v; pls. 192b, 193a, b.

73.   Vatican, lat. 4776, 22v, 23r; pls. 112a, b; Chantilly, Musée Condé 597, 129r; pl. 207c, in Brieger et al., *Illuminated Manuscripts*.

74.   The suicides-become-trees in manuscript illustration, unlike the thieves, retain no real sense of metamorphosis or double identity. The artists have read the texts carefully, no doubt, and recall that the transformation is complete and natural. They do, however, tend to depict the Harpies in the trees, so that they create a composite set of creatures made up of human, animal, and vegetable parts. The Harpies stand in relation to the tree-metamorphoses much as the centaurs will stand in relation to the serpent-metamorphoses.

75.   See Florence, Laur. Strozz. 152, 20v, and Florence, B. N. Palat. 313, 59r; pls. 254a, 260a, in Brieger et al., *Illuminated Manuscripts*.

76.   Holkham Hall 514, pp. 38–39. See *Illuminated Manuscripts*, 1:252–57.

77.   Modena Estense α R.4.8., 34v.

78.   See Brieger et al., *Illuminated Manuscripts*, 1:52–64, 94–96, 216–19.

79.   For connections between commentary and iconography, see Brieger et al., *Illuminated Manuscripts*, p. 85, and Biagi, *La Divina Commedia nella figurazione*, p. 201.

CHAPTER FIVE. *Metamorphosis, Paganism, and the Renaissance Imagination*

1.   Questions about the originality of the Renaissance in regard to pagan myth should not be confused with the argument that there was no Renaissance or that the period is too confusing and heterogeneous to be set apart from the late Middle Ages. One should not be dazzled by periodization in general or by Burck-

hardt in particular; still it is ultimately reductive and misleading to deny the special qualities of life and art between 1450 and 1600 in Western Europe. On the particular question of relations between the concept of Renaissance and antiquity, see Erwin Panofsky, *Renaissance and Renascences in Western Art* (Stockholm, 1960), esp. pp. 162–210; Paul Oskar Kristeller, *The Classics and Renaissance Thought* (Cambridge, Mass., 1935); and Fritz Saxl, "*Rinascimento dell' antichità,*" *Repertorium für Kunstwissenschaft* 43 (1922): 408–37. For an especially persuasive treatment of one Renaissance survival of antiquity closely related to questions of metamorphosis, see A. Bartlett Giamatti, "Proteus Unbound: Some Versions of the Sea God in the Renaissance," in *The Disciplines of Criticism: Essays in Literary Theory, Interpretation, and History* (New Haven, 1968), pp. 437–75. In a sense the most fundamental innovation of the period, more basic than its view of antiquity itself, is the development of a concept of history, and in that area the great "Renaissance" innovator is a man who died in 1374: Francesco Petrarca. "To say that Petrarch 'discovered' history," writes Thomas Greene, "means, in effect, that he was the first to notice that classical antiquity was very different from his own medieval world, and the first to consider antiquity more admirable. . . . Thus Petrarch took more or less alone the step an archaic society must take to reach maturity: he recognized *the possibility of a cultural alternative*" (*The Light in Troy: Imitation and Discovery in Renaissance Poetry*, New Haven, 1982, p. 90). For other approaches to the subject of Petrarch and history, see Theodor Mommsen, "Petrarch's Concept of the Dark Ages," *Speculum* 17 (1942): 226–42; and Peter Burke, *The Renaissance Sense of the Past* (London, 1969), pp. 21–49. Finally, on the particular question of the Renaissance and classical mythology, the standard work is Jean Seznec, *The Survival of the Pagan Gods*, tr. B. F. Sessions (New York, 1961). Seznec argues persuasively for the continuities of medievalism in the Renaissance approach to the pagan pantheon, suggesting not only the limits of Renaissance originality but also the extent of the medieval search for an authentic antiquity. See, for instance, pp. 211–13.

2. For Petrarch's sestina, see below, n. 97. Titian's version of Venus and Adonis is discussed in section 2 of this chapter; Shakespeare's in chapter 6, section 3. Milton's version of Narcissus as applied to Eve appears in *Paradise Lost* at 4.449–91.

3. Lorenzo died in 1492, Pico in 1494, Ficino in 1499, and Botticelli in 1510. The Sistine Chapel ceiling was finished in 1513, and Pope Julius died the same year. Bellini died in 1516 and Raphael in 1520. Ariosto first published the *Orlando Furioso* in 1516; editions revised by the author appeared in 1521 and 1532.

4. Editions of Ovid's complete works appear in both Bologna and Rome in 1471, edited by Franciscus Puteolanus and Joannes Andreae respectively. The *Metamorphoses* by itself first appears around 1472 in Venice. Bono Accursio edited a 1475 edition published in Milan, and in the same year the first edition appears north of the Alps, in Louvain. Leonardo's work on Leda, including several important extant sketches, begins around 1508 and reaches its culmination around 1516. Michelangelo's dates from around 1530. I discuss the *Ledas*, and the wedding chests, in sections 2 and 4 of this chapter.

5. See, for instance, the facsimile reproduction of geometric diagrams in R. Salomon, *Opicinus de Canistris* (London, 1936); compare S. K. Heninger, *The*

Cosmographical Glass (San Marino, Calif., 1977), for later developments in this charting. For general comments, see Jean Seznec, *Survival*, pp. 124–25, and my *Nature's Work of Art: The Human Body as Image of the World* (New Haven, 1975), pp. 38–42.

6. Fritz Saxl and Aby Warburg both studied this phenomenon extensively. See "The Revival of Late Antique Astrology," and "The Belief in Stars in the Twelfth Century," in Saxl, *Lectures*, pp. 73–95; also see his "Probleme der Planetenkinderbilder," in *Kunstchronik*, n.s. 30 (1919): 1013–21. For Warburg, see "Italienische Kunst und internationale Astrologie im Palazzo Schifanoia zu Ferrara," in *Gesammelte Schriften* (Leipzig and Berlin, 1932), pp. 459–81, 627–44. See also Anton Hauber, *Planetenkinderbilder und Sternbilder: Zur Geschichte der menschlichen Glaubens und Irrens* (Strasbourg, 1916).

7. For more discussion, see Fritz Saxl, *La Fede astrologica di Agostino Chigi* (Rome, 1934), and "The Villa Farnesina" in *Lectures*, pp. 189–99. Excellent reproductions and a general description of the paintings throughout the building can be found in Paolo d'Ancona, *The Farnesina Frescoes at Rome* (Milan, 1955).

8. See *The Romance of the Rose*, ll. 20817–21175. The story is further "medievalized" by being presented in some respects as a dream of Pygmalion. See notes to the translation by Charles Dahlberg (Princeton, 1971), p. 422, including an illustration from B. N. fr. 1565, in which Pygmalion is depicted as a dreamer, parallel to the poem's central dreamer. Jean de Meun suggests some subtle thinking about the nature of images by introducing the Pygmalion story with reference to the beautiful image of a girl in the tower; and an interpolated passage published by Ernest Langlois, *Le Roman de la Rose*, in *Société des anciens textes français*, vol. 120 (Paris, 1924), pp. 107–09, adds the comparison of Medusa's death-dealing image with those images, presumably like Pygmalion's, that pertain to love.

9. See, for instance, the Orpheus and Eurydice of B. M. Harley MS. 4431, 126v, or the Minos of Oxford MS. Laud Misc. 570, 32r., both illustrations for Christine de Pisan's *Epître d'Othéa*. Both are reproduced in F. Saxl and H. Maier, *Catalogue of Astrological and Mythological Illuminated Manuscripts of the Latin Middle Ages* (London, 1953), vol. 3: *Manuscripts in English Libraries*, pls. 105, 117, dated 1410–15 and 1454 respectively.

10. In addition to the Aby Warburg essay cited in n. 6, see Paolo d'Ancona, *The Schifanoia Months at Ferrara* (Milan, 1954); and Seznec, *Survival*, pp. 74–76, 203–09.

11. See section 5 of this chapter.

12. Edgar Wind's influential work is devoted to the proposition that some strands of Neoplatonism, at least, include the carnal in the realm of the transcendent, rather than bypassing it. See *Pagan Mysteries in the Renaissance* (New York, 1968), e.g., pp. 53–96.

13. Apart from discussions of particular works in the profane tradition, Correggio's general relations to antiquity have not been extensively considered. By far the most valuable treatments are those in Cecil Gould, *The Paintings of Correggio* (Ithaca, 1976). Titian is another matter. My thinking has been most influenced by the work of three scholars, each masterful in its own way: Harold E. Wethey, *The Paintings of Titian*, vol. 3: *The Mythological and Historical Paintings* (London, 1975); several essays by Philipp Fehl, esp. "Ovidian Delight and Studies in Iconology: Notes on Titian's *Rape of Europa*," *Storia dell'arte* 26

(1976): 23–30, *"The Rape of Europa* and Related Ovidian Pictures by Titian," *Fenway Court,* Isabella Stuart Gardner Museum (Boston, 1979, 1980), pt. 1, pp. 2–23, pt. 2, pp. 2–19, and "Titian and the Olympian Gods: The Camerino for Philip II," *Tiziano e Venezia: Convegno internazionale di studi* (Venice, 1980), pp. 139–47; and, finally, Erwin Panofsky, *Problems in Titian, Mostly Iconographic* (New York, 1969).

14.   Vasari establishes at the outset of his *Life of Correggio* the terms of naiveté and refinement in which we still see that painter's work: "What is more, seeing what he produced without ever having set eyes on any antiques or good modern work, it inevitably follows that if he had done so his style would have gained immeasurably and he would eventually have reached absolute perfection. Certainly, as it is no one ever handled colours better than Correggio or produced paintings of greater delicacy and relief, such was the softness of the figures he painted and the grace with which he imbued his finished works" (*Lives of the Artists,* tr. George Bull, Harmondsworth, 1965, pp. 278–79).

15.   See, for instance, the range of analyses of *Sacred and Profane Love* represented by Erwin Panofsky, *Studies in Iconology* (New York, 1939), pp. 150–60; Edgar Wind, *Pagan Mysteries,* pp. 142–51; and Charles Hope, *Titian* (London, 1980), pp. 34–37.

16.   For a particularly persuasive analysis of the *poesie,* especially in terms of the name Titian gave them, see David Rosand, "Ut Pictor Poeta: Meaning in Titian's Poesie," *New Literary History* 3 (1971–72): 527–46.

17.   The first (and still valuable) essay on the Camera, published shortly after the room's rediscovery, is Ireneo Affò, *Raggionamento sopra una stanza dipinta dal celeberrimo Antonio Allegri da Correggio* (Parma, 1794). The other principal treatment is Erwin Panofsky, *The Iconography of Correggio's Camera di S. Paolo* (London, 1961). See also Gould, *Correggio,* pp. 51–59, 242–45. Good reproductions can be found in Roberto Longhi, *Il Correggio nella Camera di San Paolo* (Milan, n.d.).

18.   For background on Gioanna, see Panofsky, *Iconography,* pp. 1–14; and Affò, *Raggionamento,* pp. 23–55.

19.   The warning theory was initiated by Affò (*Raggionamento,* p. 47) and developed by Seznec (*Survival,* pp. 117–19). Panofsky (*Iconography,* passim) argues for the Platonic program, seeing the room as an initiation via the four elements on the east wall into a universe that transcends the natural, concentrating on invisible forces and on the extent and limits of the power of pagan gods. Panofsky's argument does not place much emphasis on the putti. Arnaldo Barilli, *L'Allegoria della vita umana nel dipinto corregesco della Camera di S. Paolo in Parma* (Parma, 1934), pp. 23–61, divides the ovals into phases of hunting, agriculture, civilization, and war, thus recreating the Ovidian ages of man; and in the lunettes he traces the events of human history.

20.   The plaything of the figures in the second vault of the east wall is not a hunting implement but the head of Medusa. In the process of their play, the putti seem to be defusing the very instrument of petrification. The tradition of playful putti cavorting in a pagan landscape does not begin with Correggio. From at least the time of Botticelli (e.g., *Venus and Mars*), such figures had acted as gentle parodists of more heroic goings-on. The immediate source for Correggio may have been the Sala di Psiche, designed by Raphael, in the Villa Farnesina (1517), in

which *amorini* are seen toying with the solemn emblems of the Olympian gods: thunderbolt, trident, forge, etc. In the *amor vincit omnia* context of an Olympian banquet celebrating the marriage of Cupid and Psyche, these images of the *amorini* suggest the victory of love over the powers of the gods. See Elsa Gerlini, *La Villa Farnesina in Roma* (Rome, 1981), p. 29.

21. For Michelangelo's influence see Gould (*Correggio*, p. 53), who refers to the Camera putti as "a set of variations on Michelangelo's theme" in the putti of the Sistine Chapel ceiling. As for Raphael, S. J. Freedberg, *Painting in Italy, 1500–1600* (London, 1970), p. 180, makes a case for the influence of the Psyche chamber in the Villa Farnesina. Also see above, n. 20.

22. The range and importance of Este patronage—from the time of Borso and the Schifanoia in the mid-fifteenth century to the time of Tasso near the end of the sixteenth, including literature, music, and the visual arts—is unparalleled in the Renaissance. It may be argued that much of this production reflects the most "progressive" view of the integration of pagan with Christian culture. For a more Burckhardtian view—integrating art and politics, especially in the earlier period—see the fine work of Werner L. Gundersheimer, *Ferrara: The Style of a Renaissance Despotism* (Princeton, 1973), esp. pp. 229–71. See also the invaluable assemblage of letters between artists and Isabella d'Este collected by D. S. Chambers in *Patrons and Artists in the Italian Renaissance* (Columbia, S.C., 1971), pp. 126–50. On the more literary side, see Giacomo Grillo, *Poets at the Court of Ferrara* (Boston, 1943); and Antonio Piromalli, *La Cultura a Ferrara al tempo di Ludovico Ariosto* (Rome, 1975).

23. For the fullest treatment of the sources, see Charles Yriarte, "Isabella d'Este et les artistes de son temps," *Gazette des beaux-arts* 13 (1895): 13–32, 189–206, 382–98; 14 (1895): 123–38; 15 (1896): 215–28, 330–46.

24. Letter of 19 January 1503, reprinted in Fiorenzo Canuti, *Il Perugino* (Siena, 1931), p. 212.

25. But see the fascinating essay, "The Sources and Meaning of Mantegna's *Parnassus*," by Phyllis Williams Lehmann, in *Samothracian Reflections* (Princeton, 1973), pp. 57–178.

26. The argument in favor of *The Feast of the Gods* as originally intended for Isabella was put most persuasively by Edgar Wind in *Bellini's Feast of the Gods* (Cambridge, Mass., 1948), esp. pp. 4–5, 21–26. The hypothesis rests on somewhat inferential reasoning; and subsequent scholars have tended to accept it cautiously or else point to its flaws without being able to disprove it. See, for instance, John Walker, *Bellini and Titian at Ferrara* (New York, 1956), pp. 17–19; and Giles Robertson, *Giovanni Bellini* (Oxford, 1968), pp. 134–44.

27. *Fasti* 1.391–440.

28. The Sala di Psiche is decorated with the banquet of the gods honoring the marriage of Cupid and Psyche; the frieze is inscribed with Francesco's name and titles and the legend "Honesto ocio post labores ad reparandam virt. quieti. construi mandavit," equating the Olympian festivities with the pleasures of the room's real-life occupants. See Frederick Hartt, *Giulio Romano* (New Haven, 1958), pp. 126–40.

29. See Walker, *Bellini and Titian*, esp. pp. 48–74.

30. The loci in Philostratus are *Imagines* 1.6 (*Worship of Venus*) and 1.25 (*The Andrians*). The ekphrasis in Catullus appears in *Carmina* 64.50–266; the

narrative sources of the *Bacchus and Ariadne* are Ovidian, including the *Fasti* 3.459–516 and the *Ars Amatoria* 1.525–64. See also n. 31.

31.   See Panofsky's excellent analysis of "a tergo forte secutus" (*Fasti*, 3.508) and "Dixit et e curru, ne tigres illa timeret / Desilit" (*Ars Amatoria*, 1.559–60), in *Problems*, pp. 142–43. The Ovidian phrases help to account for the extraordinary positions of the two principal characters—which, down to Keats's "swift bound of Bacchus from his chariot," have captivated viewers.

32.   In addition to Panofsky's account cited above in n. 31, see Wind, *Bellini's Feast*, pp. 56–58; and Wethey's survey of opinions in *Titian*, 3:148–49.

33.   The lyrics—visible in the picture—are "Qui boyt et ne reboyt / Il ne scet que boyre soit." They derive from a real canon composed by Adrian Willaert, a Flemish musician in residence at the Este court. For a fascinating account of musical/artistic relations, see the (interrelated) work of Panofsky, *Problems*, pp. 100–01; and Edward E. Lowinsky, "Music in Titian's *Bacchanale of the Andrians*: Origin and History of the *Canon per tonos*," in David Rosand, ed., *Titian: His World and His Legacy* (New York, 1982), pp. 191–282.

34.   The classic work, albeit from a rather specialized ideological perspective, is Arnold Hauser, *Mannerism: The Crisis of the Renaissance and the Origin of Modern Art* (New York, 1965). A superb (and more reliable) introduction to the subject is John Shearman, *Mannerism* (Harmondsworth, 1967). See also Walter Friedlaender, *Mannerism and Antimannerism in Italian Painting* (New York, 1965); along with the remarks by E. R. Curtius in *European Literature and the Latin Middle Ages* (New York, 1953), pp. 273–301.

35.   See, for instance, Howard Hibbard, *Michelangelo* (New York, 1974), pp. 122–23: "All of the *ignudi* are in a sense ideal restorations of the famous *Belvedere Torso*, which of the surviving antique statues was perhaps the most evocative for Michelangelo's muscular art." See also Arnold von Salis, *Antike und Renaissance* (Zurich, 1947), pp. 182–85.

36.   Roberto Weiss's *The Renaissance Discovery of Antiquity* (Oxford, 1969), esp. pp. 59–89, 105–15, demonstrates the academicism of what we might call intellectual archaeology in the early Renaissance. From Poggio Bracciolini's *De varietate fortunae* (ca. 1435) to the work of Pomponio Leto (1425–1497) and Andrea Fulvio (ca. 1470–1527), the study of ancient remains in Rome is largely technical, determined by the objects themselves rather than by the contexts of ancient history. The historicism of the archaeological movement is more pedantic and philological than actually historical.

37.   In Fulgentius see, for instance, Mercury (*Mythologies* 1.18, in L. G. Whitbread, *Fulgentius the Mythographer*, Columbus, Ohio, 1971, p. 59): "His heels are feathered because the feet of businessmen are everywhere in a rush as if winged. . . . He is depicted with his head covered by a cap because any commerce is always concealed." On Albericus, see the extensive treatment in Seznec, *Survival*, pp. 170–72, 193–95.

38.   Citation is to *Petrarch's Africa*, ed. and tr. T. G. Bergin and A. S. Wilson (New Haven, 1977). Petrarch was very much at the center of late medieval mythography. He possessed manuscripts of Fulgentius and Albericus, and—possibly with this passage—he seems to have influenced Bersuire, as the commentator directly asserts: "Because I was nowhere able to find either written accounts or pictorial representations of the images of the gods set forth in an orderly

manner, I had to consult that eminent teacher Francis Petrarch ["Franciscum de Petato" in the original], famous orator and poet, skilled in all moral philosophy and likewise in every historical and poetic discipline, who describes these images in an elegant poetic work" (W. D. Reynolds, "The *Ovidius Moralizatus* of Pierre Bersuire: An Introduction and Translation," Ph.D. diss., University of Illinois at Urbana-Champaign, 1971, pp. 35–36). See Pierre de Nolhac, *Pétrarque et l'humanisme* (Paris, 1907), 1:204–06; and Seznec, *Survival*, pp. 173–75.

39. The Ovidian material comprises the fifteenth book of Bersuire's *Reductorium Morale*, an encyclopedia in the tradition of Bartholomaeus Anglicus, proceeding from man and the natural world (first fourteen books) to a moralization of the Bible (Book 16). The intervening section is divided in two: the first chapter, "De Formis Figurisque Deorum," which moralizes the images of the gods, and the next fifteen chapters, which proceed through the books of the *Metamorphoses*.

40. Pictor's most "pictorial" work, the *Apotheosos tam exterarum gentium quam Romanorum deorum,* published in 1558, is in dialogue form. Though the attributes of the gods are extensively moralized, it is the images of the gods that particularly engage the questioner, Evander. He persistently demands both description and exegesis of these images. Cartari's *Le Imagini degli dei degli antichi* went through something like twenty editions within a century of its first publication (1556), exercising an enormous influence on literature, art, and public ceremonials. The volume represents an important departure in the application of learned Renaissance mythography to a specifically pictorial tradition; the first edition even includes a preface suggesting the usefulness of the book to artists and writers.

41. The *Hieroglyphica* of Horapollo, a text of the Hellenistic period, was discovered in 1419, and it exercised wide influence even before its first publication in 1505. This set of "explanations" for the Egyptian hieroglyphs not only disseminated Neoplatonic mystery learning but also associated mysteries specifically with enigmatic ancient *images*, more than with words. So Ficino, in his annotation of *Ennead* 5, describes these hieroglyphs as pictorial renderings of Platonic ideas, a claim Horapollo himself does not make. See *The Hieroglyphics*, tr. G. Boas (New York, 1950), including the good introduction. Piero Valeriano Bolzani's *Hieroglyphica*, first published in 1556, extends the symbolic language to a universe of animals, vegetables, and minerals, with a rather less pictorial focus than that of Horapollo. For a comprehensive discussion of the hieroglyphic tradition, see D. C. Allen, *Mysteriously Meant: The Rediscovery of Pagan Symbolism and Allegorical Interpretation in the Renaissance* (Baltimore, 1970), pp. 107–19.

42. The first edition of Alciati was published in 1521, and the text was reprinted many times in the succeeding century. While not all the images are of ancient gods, the majority are inspired by antiquity. See Mario Praz, *Studies in Seventeenth-Century Imagery*, 2d ed. (Rome, 1964), on the origins and destination of the emblematic tradition.

43. See Erwin Panofsky and Fritz Saxl, "Classical Mythology in Medieval Art," *Metropolitan Museum Studies* 4 (1932–33): 228–80. For Seznec, see *Survival*, pp. 166–83, 189–99. My example of the cleric-Apollo comes from a Christine de Pisan illumination of the very early fifteenth century (B. M. Harley 4431), reproduced in Wolfgang Stechow, *Apollo und Daphne* (Leipzig, 1932), fig. 5.

44. See Fritz Saxl, "Continuity and Variation in the Meaning of Images," in *A Heritage of Images* (Harmondsworth, 1970), pp. 13–26.

45. But see Seznec, *Survival*, esp. pp. 219–24, who argues that the men of the Renaissance were often content with second-hand images of antiquity, especially in the literary sources they consulted and composed.

46. The fullest treatment of the subject remains M. D. Henkel, "Illustrierte Ausgaben von Ovids Metamorphosen im XV., XVI., und XVII. Jahrhundert," in *Vorträge der Bibliothek Warburg* (1926–27), pp. 58–144.

47. See chapter 3, sections 2 and 3.

48. See chapter 1 and chapter 3, section 1.

49. Panofsky (*Problems*, p. 15) characterizes Titian in all his work as having "an almost claustrophobic dislike of boxed interiors closed on all sides" and as a result producing settings in which "the indoors osmotically penetrates with the outdoors." He cites the *Portrait of Charles V* (Munich) as well as the various reclining Venuses. But it should be noted that only in the Venus and Danae canvases does the mixture of indoor and outdoor begin to transcend the earlier Venetian conventions of distant landscapes visible beyond a closed interior space.

50. For an account of the *Danaes* and their various pedigrees, see Wethey, *Titian*, vol. 3, catalogue nos. 5, 6, 7, X–10, X–11, X–12, X–13; pp. 132–36, 209–11.

51. See Panofsky, *Problems*, p. 25–26, 147, and Wethey, *Titian*, 3:57. Titian possessed a plaster cast of the Michelangelo statue (see his letter to his son Orazio of 17 June 1557, quoted in E. Tietze-Conrat, "Titian as a Letter Writer," *Art Bulletin* 26 [1944]: 117–23, esp. 120–21). On the Michelangelo statue as an *hommage* to the ancient, see, e.g., Herbert von Einem, *Michelangelo* (London, 1973), p. 127.

52. See chapter 3, section 2.

53. For the *Ovide moralisé* (6.867–72), see chapter 3. The De Retza text is a strange attempt to justify belief in the Virgin by reference to pagan beliefs (as though the latter were widely accepted and the former needed to be proved). See the facsimile reprint (Leipzig, 1925), p. 10.

54. It is difficult to assess the chances of Titian's exposure to earlier *Danaes*. His familiarity with the *Hypnerotomachia* is reasonably well documented in connection with the Ferrara Bacchanals and *Sacred and Profane Love*. Correggio is a more vexed subject, but both artists were certainly in the Este/Gonzaga orbit ca. 1529–32; whether or not they met, Titian did visit Federico Gonzaga in Mantua during that time, when the *Amori di Giove* were there awaiting presentation to the emperor. The Primaticcio *Danae* was painted in the 1540s and engraved by Léonard Thiry. There was also a representation of Danae in the little Ovidian frieze by Baldassare Peruzzi in the Farnesina, which Titian might well have seen during his one stay in Rome.

55. On Leonardo's *Leda*, see the excellent treatment in Martin Kemp, *Leonardo da Vinci: The Marvelous Works of Nature and Man* (Cambridge, Mass., 1981), pp. 270–77. For the Michelangelo, see Johannes Wilde, "Notes on the Genesis of Michelangelo's Leda," in *Fritz Saxl: Memorial Essays*, ed. D. J. Gordon (London, 1957), pp. 270–80. See Wethey (*Titian*, 3:57) on the specific relations of Titian to the Michelangelo *Leda*.

56. See, Wind, *Pagan Mysteries*, esp. pp. 164–70.

57. The Cupid does not conform to any of the literary sources for the Danae story; Wethey's assertion that his presence "is justified by his association in amo-

rous affairs" (*Titian*, 3:57) is not quite sufficient to explain his massive weight in this picture. There are precedents in the visual tradition, including Primaticcio and Correggio—both of whom may have been unknown to Titian.

58.   The nursemaid has almost as little literary authority as the Cupid of the first *Danae*. Sources offered by Wethey (*Titian*, 3:134) in Apollonius Rhodius and Horace mention the nursemaid so offhandedly that they are hardly necessary or sufficient to account for the importance Titian assigns her. Precisely as with the Cupid, prior representations in word or image may have given Titian an idea; but the conception in both cases is fundamentally his own. The meager history of these figures in past versions of the story serves to demonstrate how much they express Titian's own signature.

59.   Panofsky, *Problems*, p. 20.

60.   In fact, the Vienna *Danae* was probably not the first to include a figure in the clouds. Wethey (*Titian*, 3:134) cites a 1626 description of the Madrid picture by Cassiano dal Pozzo which includes a reference to Jupiter's face in the sky; there is also an inventory of 1636 in which the eagle of Jupiter, but not the face, is said to be visible in the clouds of the same picture. The canvas would seem to have been cut down since that time. The Chicago *Danae* (Wethey, no. X–10), a workshop piece which alone of all the versions contains no second figure at all, does nonetheless include a sharply visible Jupiter in the clouds.

61.   The standard treatment of the whole series, a bit enslaved to a thesis about their placement in the Palazzo del Te, is Egon Verheyen, "Correggio's *Amori di Giove*," *Journal of the Warburg and Courtauld Institutes* 29 (1966): 160–92. For other approaches, see E. R. Knauer, "Leda," *Jahrbuch der Berliner Museen* 2 (1969): 5–55, and "Zu Correggios *Io* und *Ganymed*," *Zeitschrift für Kunstgeschichte* 33 (1970): 61–67; and the particularly valuable discussion in Gould, *Correggio*, pp. 130–35.

62.   Such speculation rests on a letter from Federico Gonzaga to the Governor of Parma in which he complains that the painter owes him fifty ducats, and he hopes that he can at least retrieve "miei cartoni nelli quali sono designati li amori di Jove et quelli pezzi cominciati . . ." (*Giornale di erudizione artistica* 1 [1872]: 329). The "pezzi cominciati" need not, of course, be more Loves of Jupiter, though Verheyen's speculations about the placement of the series in the Sala di Ovidio of the Palazzo del Te require a larger number than four. See Verheyen, "Correggio's *Amori*," pp. 164–65, 185; also see n. 66. For another set of conjectures about an additional series of Jupiter's loves, see A. E. Popham, *Correggio's Drawings* (London, 1957), pp. 95–96.

63.   Correggio's (few) earlier profane works, apart from the Camera, appear to come in pairs, like the *Amori*. One pairing is conjectural—the London *School of Love* and the Louvre *Venus and a Satyr*, often called the *Dream of Antiope*—and the other indisputable: the Louvre *Allegories of Virtue and Vice*. The allegories clearly show the painter's penchant for emblematic representations in a binary system. On the first pair as a heavenly vs. earthly Venus, see L. Soth, "Two Paintings by Correggio," *Art Bulletin* 46 (1964): 539–44; and Egon Verheyen, "Eros et Antéros: L'Education de Cupidon et la prétendu Antiope du Corrège," *Gazette des beaux-arts* 65 (1965): 321–40.

64.   See the speculations of Verheyen, *The Palazzo del Te in Mantua* (Baltimore, 1977), pp. 19–21.

65. Verheyen cites an Italian translation by Betussi (incorrectly named "Bernussi") of Boccaccio's *Genealogia Deorum*, in which "orantemque [Io] tenebris superinductis detinuit et oppressit" (7.22) becomes "quella che fuggiva con una nube la ricoperse et la impregno" (*La Genealogia de gli dei de Gentili*, Venice, 1574, fol. 124r). But this falls rather short of metamorphosis, and in any case the translation was not published until 1547. More apposite is the commentary by Bernardo Lapini (also known as "Illicino") on Petrarch's *Trionfi* (cited simply as "Bernardo" by Verheyen), in which Jupiter's attachment to the Chariot of Cupid is glossed with a list of the god's particular amours. Io is placed first: "Unde in prima se innamorò di Io figliola di Inaco e lei comprese in forma di nebula" (*Li Sonetti Canzone Triumphi del Petrarcha con li suoi commenti* . . . , Venice, 1519, fol. 15r).

66. As our discussion of Arachne's web in chapter 1 may have suggested, the Lives of Jupiter have a special historical significance as an artistic series—that is, as a large-scale construction built out of individual transformations. From Ovid's Arachne to Nonnos, who creates a canonical series of twelve loves ritually inscribed on Cupid's quiver (*Dionysiaca*, 7.117–28), to the commentary by Lapini on Petrarch's *Trionfi* mentioned in n. 65, to the various Renaissance versions of Arachne's web, these loves represent a kind of archetypal grouping. Given this unbroken literary tradition, it is somewhat surprising that there was no real pictorial tradition of this composite subject. Verheyen finds the beginnings of a series in Peruzzi's Sala del Fregio in the Villa Farnesina, and yet Peruzzi's Loves of Jupiter are mixed in with other Ovidian material involving Hercules, Midas, Bacchus, Actaeon, and so on. It seems reasonable, then, to argue that even if Peruzzi helped inspire Correggio, we can still ascribe to the latter an original determination to build a pictorial grouping where only words had formed a series hitherto.

67. In fact, the Ganymede is in his position (though not in his person) a precise copy of an upward-floating angel whom Correggio earlier painted in one of the squinches under the cupola of the Parma cathedral. The descending angel of the Duomo, whose garments are naturally buoyed upwards, explains the anomalous position of the ascending Ganymede's garments.

68. Compare Antony's metamorphic observations on clouds and his own shape-changing (Shakespeare, *Antony and Cleopatra*, 4.14.2–14), which includes the painterly term *dislimn*, as well as the famous cloud lines of Hamlet to Polonius (also involving animal transformations), 3.2.367–73.

69. The attribution of the sketch was made by A. E. Popham (*Correggio's Drawings*, pp. 94–96). For a discussion of the probabilities of influence on both the *Leda* and the *Danae*, see Gould, *Correggio*, pp. 134–35.

70. The dog finds its origin in Virgil and Statius, both of whom refer to the boy's dogs left barking savagely while their master is carried aloft. The animal's presence reminds us both conceptually and compositionally of the distance between earth and heaven, for both classical poets make that very point. In the *Aeneid*, the barking of the dogs rises "in auras" (5.257), while in the *Thebaid* the dogs "umbram . . . petunt et nubila latrant" (1.551), terms that could well have interested a painter so concerned with clouds and shadows. If Ganymede's dog points upward pushing us from earth to heaven, it is no surprise that Io's stag is at the bottom of her picture and facing downwards. Guy de Tervarent makes refer-

ence to a fifteenth-century manuscript and works of Correggio's contemporaries Giulio Romano and Pinturicchio, all suggesting that the stag is a figure of sexual ardor, as he is for Valeriano several decades after Correggio's time. See *Attributs et symboles dans l'art profane* (Geneva, 1955), cols. 66–67. For a different reading of the stag, based on post-Correggian texts and (in my opinion) forced into a predetermined argument, see Verheyen, "Correggio's *Amori*," pp. 186–87.

71.   Vasari cites Giulio Romano's description: "There were also several Cupids, depicted with superb craftsmanship, who were shooting their arrows, some of gold and some of lead, at a stone" (*Lives*, p. 280). The account is a bit garbled, the more so since it is credited to a *Venus* rather than a *Danae*.

72.   See the interesting speculations on the significance of music in the *Leda* in Verheyen, "Correggio's *Amori*," pp. 189–90. For traditional connections between the Leda myth and music, not mentioned by Verheyen, see, e.g., *Ovide moralisé*, 6.842–44.

73.   For an interesting discussion, see Wethey, *Titian*, 3:76–77, 172–75, who—unaccountably, to my way of thinking—characterizes Titian's version of the myth as "high comedy." See also Arthur Pope, *Titian's Rape of Europa* (Cambridge, 1960); Panofsky, *Problems*, pp. 163–66; and M. L. Shapiro, "Titian's *Rape of Europa*," *Gazette des beaux-arts* 77 (1971): 109–16. Paul Watson's "Titian's *Rape of Europa*: A Bride Stripped Bare," *Storia dell'arte* 28 (1976): 249–58, is particularly appropriate to the nuptial traditions in which we have placed the myth. Richard B. Carpenter, "Woman, Landscape, and Myth," *College Art Journal* 21 (1962): 246–49, discusses the picture in terms that link it closely with the whole "female" tradition we explored in chapter 1. Philipp Fehl, especially in the first of his *Fenway Court* articles, offers a brilliant analysis of *Europa* in terms of a *paragone*, or competition, with the verbal representations of Poliziano and Lodovico Dolce and with the visual example of Raphael's *Galatea*.

74.   The late Actaeon picture contrasts sharply with the *poesie*. As narrative, the representation of Actaeon being mortally menaced both by his pack of dogs and by the goddess's threatening gesture with her bow makes little sense—and even less when we remind ourselves that the bow has neither string nor arrow. In that context the shadowy representation of a semi-metamorphosed Actaeon returning to the earth and to nature seems more allegorical than narrative.

75.   See the perceptive discussion of this work (to which I am much indebted) by Ellis Waterhouse, *Titian's Diana and Actaeon* (Oxford, 1952). For more speculative approaches, see Lars Skarsgard, *Titian's Diana and Actaeon: A Study in Artistic Innovation* (Goteborg, 1968); and Marie Tanner, "Chance and Coincidence in Titian's *Diana and Actaeon*," *Art Bulletin* 56 (1974): 535–50.

76.   Early woodcuts, particularly the first illustrated edition (Venice, 1497), had offered individual representations of an untransformed Actaeon as part of a sequence of images, and Titian may well have drawn inspiration from them. It should also be pointed out that there is one rather emblematic (even Correggioesque) bit of prolepsis: a theatrically placed animal (stag?) skull atop the pillar which is surrounded by the naked nymphs.

77.   The planned *Actaeon Torn by His Own Hounds*, mentioned in a letter from Titian to Philip II on 19 June 1559, opens up the much vexed question of the plans for the whole series of *poesie*. Whether the late *Death of Actaeon* is the same as the picture mentioned in that letter is moot; whether the canvases exe-

cuted for Philip are the original versions of the *poesie* and which of the individual works or pairs were first painted for Cardinal Farnese are also open to question. The whole conception of a series must be approached cautiously, for Titian's letters to Philip, which proclaim a number of pictures that were never executed or never sent, must be taken with a grain of salt. On the other hand, there is considerable evidence, both historical and conceptual, for the pairings of the pictures. See Wethey, *Titian*, 3:56–60, 71–84; Harald Keller, *Tizians Poesie für König Philipp von Spanien* (Wiesbaden, 1969); and especially Fehl, "*Europa* and Related Ovidian Pictures," pt. 2. It should be noted that the first *Danae*, of which we spoke earlier, was twinned with *Venus and Adonis* before the time of the Philip II *poesie*. That pairing, very interestingly discussed in the Fehl article (pt. 2, pp. 4–10), appears more compositional than iconographic, especially since Titian enclosed with the *Venus and Adonis* a letter claiming that the new picture would show the female body from the back in contrast to the frontal view in the *Danae*. Yet there is still a stimulus and response in this pair (not discussed by Fehl), particularly if we consider the Philip II version of the *Venus*, in which Venus is visible in her heavenly chariot after Adonis's death. Given that composition—with *Danae* on the left—the narrative begins with a god emerging from the sky and ends with a goddess returning there. See below for the similar sequencing of the *Europa* and the *Perseus*.

78.   On this detail see Augusto Gentili, *Da Tiziano a Tiziano* (Milan, 1980), pp. 138–39; and Shapiro, "Titian's *Rape*," pp. 111–12.

79.   Both Europa and Andromeda are treated to extensive ekphrases in Achilles Tatius's *Clitophon and Leucippe*, in Books 1 and 3 respectively. Given the terms of the description and the close interest in painterly effects, it is very tempting to believe that Titian was familiar with that text, especially since Dolce published a translation of part of it in 1544 (not, in fact, including Books 1 and 3). But see Fehl, "Ovidian Delight," pp. 24–28.

80.   A number of conjectures are involved in this pairing. Considerations of date are complicated and controversial (see Wethey, *Titian*, 3:169–70; and Panofsky, *Problems*, p. 167), as are the interpretations of various letters from Titian and of assertions by Lodovico Dolce. Documentary evidence for the pairing is lacking, but conceptual and compositional links are strong. See, for instance, Gentili, *Da Tiziano*, pp. 141–43; Panofsky, *Problems*, p. 165; Cecil Gould, The *Perseus and Andromeda* and Titian's *Poesie*," *Burlington Magazine* 105 (1963): 112–17; and M. L. Shapiro, "Titian's *Rape*," pp. 109–10. The question of left-right positioning is also conjectural. For this viewer, however, aesthetic considerations, with the girl on the bull pointing upward as a kind of grace note toward the erect Andromeda, suggest that *Europa* belongs on the left.

81.   X-rays taken in 1962 suggest that in an earlier version of the composition Perseus arrived on foot rather than in the air. If that is the case, then it may be that the picture was recomposed after the completion of the *Europa* and that Perseus's position was altered so as to balance the putti of the pendant canvas. See Panofsky, *Problems*, pp. 166–67, on these changes, which Wethey disputes (*Titian*, 3:170).

82.   No. 216 in Terisio Pignatti, *Veronese* (Venice, 1976), 1:90, 142–43, who dates it between 1570 and 1580.

83. Citation is to *Evvres en Rime de Ian Antoine de Baif*, ed. C. Marty-Laveaux (Paris, 1881), 10:421–31.

84. Citations are to *Spenser's Minor Poems*, ed. Ernest de Sélincourt (Oxford, 1960).

85. Plato refused to "Platonize" the myth (see *Laws* 1.636c–d), but Xenophon's Socrates (*Symposium*, 8:30) declares that it was not the boy's beauty but his spirit that inspired Zeus to carry him to heaven.

86. For Dante, see *Purgatorio* 9.13–33. Alciati's emblem picturing Ganymede is entitled "In deo laetandum" ("Consilium mens atque Dei cui gaudia praestant, / Creditur is summo raptus adesse Iovi"). The numbering of the emblems is not consistent among the myriad editions of Alciati. In the Paris, 1542, edition, Ganymede is no. 32. Mignault's commentary appears in Alciati, *Emblemata* (Paris, 1608).

87. For Pignorius, see Alciati, *Emblemata* (Padua, 1621). For Bocchi, see *Symbolicarum quaestionum* (Bologna, 1574), p. clxvi.

88. Comes, *Mythologiae* (Frankfurt, 1596), 9.13.

89. See the brilliant analysis by Erwin Panofsky in "The Neoplatonic Movement and Michelangelo," in *Studies in Iconology*, esp. pp. 213–23.

90. See *Aeneid* 6.595–600. From antiquity Tityus had been seen as a figure for the pains of the libido. See Lucretius, *De Rerum Natura* 3.983–84; and Servius's commentary on the Virgilian reference.

91. The subject of metamorphosis in the *Rime sparse* has been most illuminatingly discussed by Robert M. Durling in his Introduction to *Petrarch's Lyric Poems* (Cambridge, Mass., 1976), pp. 26–33, an essay to which I am much indebted. Among other relevant treatments, see Pierre de Nolhac, *Pétrarque*, especially the list of references to the *Metamorphoses* in the *Rime* on 1:157; Ugo Dotti, "Petrarca: il mito dafneo," *Convivium* 37 (1969): 9–23; and Robert M. Durling, "Petrarch's 'Giovene donna sotto un verde lauro,'" *Modern Language Notes* 86 (1971): 1–20.

92. Citations are to Durling, *Petrarch's Lyric Poems*, and translations are taken from that edition.

93. See *Metamorphoses* 7.694–865. Cephalus, though married, has been forcibly seduced by Aurora (Dawn), and, ascribing his own guilt to his wife, he transforms himself to test her fidelity. She wavers momentarily, mirroring him, and so both are, in effect, guilty. In the second phase of the story Cephalus playfully woos the disembodied *Aura*, but Procris takes her to be a flesh-and-blood rival. *Aura* and *Aurora* not only have similar names; they are also both impalpable forces in nature, and both blend into each other and into nothingness. The whole story has depended on insubstantiality and mirror images, and when Cephalus fails to recognize his wife and kills her accidentally through the agency of the magic javelin she has herself given him, the tale of shifting identities and perceptions is complete.

94. Amongst mythographic works (all cited above in chapter 3, esp. section 2), see especially Arnulf of Orleans, *Allegoriae*, 1.9; Alexander Neckam, *De Naturis Rerum* (ed. Wright), p. 116; and the *Ovide moralisé*, 1.3245–50. Compare Petrarch's own words in the Coronation Oration, discussing Ovid's Daphne story: "Nor is this poetic fiction without a basis, for though every tree is dear to the

sun, from which all life and growth descend, the one tree that is adorned with an eternal verdure most worthily holds the title of the loved one." Cited in Aldo S. Bernardo, *Petrarch, Laura, and the* Triumphs (Albany, 1974), p. 77. For a translation of the complete text, see E. H. Wilkins, *Studies in the Life and Works of Petrarch* (Cambridge, Mass., 1955), pp. 300–13.

95.   For the *Rime petrose*, as well as their connection to Petrarch's poems, see Durling, *Petrarch's Lyric*, pp. 29–33, his "'Io son venuto': Seneca, Plato, and the Microcosm," *Dante Studies* 93 (1975): 95–129; and John Freccero, "Medusa: The Letter and the Spirit," in *Yearbook of Italian Studies* 1972, pp. 1–18.

96.   Compare the fourth stanza of Canzone 129, which begins with the poet imagining his beloved "ne l'acqua chiara et sopra l'erba verde . . . viva" (ll. 41–42) and ends, once the vision has passed, with the poet "freddo, pietra morta in pietra viva, / in guisa d'uom che pensi et pianga et scriva" (ll. 51–52).

97.   The sestina "Giovene donna sotto un verde lauro" (Poem 30) offers another complicated set of changes, concentrating on the Daphne myth. The metamorphosis of Daphne into a laurel, the transformations of age, and the great cyclical flow of time are all captured in the continuities of sound and the changes in meaning of the repeated words *lauro, neve, anni, chiome, occhi,* and *riva.* See Durling, "Petrarch's 'Giovene.'" On Poem 23, see Dennis Dutschke, "The Textual Situation and Chronological Assessment of Petrarch's Canzone XXIII," *Italian Quarterly* 18 (1974): 37–69; John Brenkman, "Writing, Desire, Dialectic in Petrarch's '*Rime 23*,'" *Pacific Coast Philology* 9 (1974): 12–19; and Marguerite Waller, *Petrarch's Poetics and Literary History* (Amherst, 1980), pp. 84–104. Particularly apposite to the present discussion is the analysis of the poem in Greene, *Light in Troy,* pp. 127–31, in which a subtext consisting of "metamorphoses of the *Metamorphoses*" is illuminated, along with a most revealing allusion to concepts of spiritual transformation in Augustine's *Confessions.*

98.   In addition to Poem 30, compare Poem 122, in which the speaker reflects on the seventeen years of his attachment to Laura, repeating the proverb "ch'altri cangia il pelo / anzi che 'l vezzo" (ll. 5–6), or Poem 195, in which he contrasts his own changes ("Di dì in dì vo cangiando il viso e 'l pelo") with the unchanging nature of the evergreen laurel, "l'arbor che né sol cura né gelo" (ll. 1, 4).

99.   See, for instance, the *blazon* in Poem 213, which lists the perfections of his beloved—*grazie, vertù, leggiadria, andar celeste, spirto ardente, belli occhi,* etc.—and concludes by declaring "da questi magi transformato fui."

100.   Compare the characterization of age in 195: "Non spero del mio affanno aver mai posa / infin ch' i' mi disosso et snervo et spolpo" (ll. 9–10), and the word play in 15: "come posson queste *membra* / da lo spirito lor viver lontane? / Ma rispondemi Amor: 'Non ti *rimembra* / che questo è privilegio degli amanti, / sciolti da tutte qualitate umane?'" (ll. 10–14).

101.   Consider not only Ovid's account, discussed in chapter 2, section 3, but also Nonnos's self-conscious Actaeon (*Dionysiaca,* 5.415–532) and especially the Actaeon allusions in *Inferno* 13, in which two profligates are attacked by dogs who themselves come to represent the ravenous desires of their victims (see chapter 4, section 2). Appropriate glosses on Actaeon by Giordano Bruno are discussed below in section 5 of this chapter.

102.   Much valuable work has been done on Ronsard and his relations to my-

thology and metamorphosis. I am indebted to the essays in *Ronsard the Poet*, ed. Terence Cave (London, 1973), especially I. D. McFarlane, "Aspects of Ronsard's Poetic Vision," pp. 13–78; and Terence Cave, "Ronsard's Mythological Universe," pp. 159–208. Equally important has been the magisterial work of Guy Demerson, *La Mythologie classique dans l'oeuvre lyrique de la "Pléiade"* (Geneva, 1972). For a more radical approach to Ronsard's relation to Ovidian and Petrarchan originals, especially interesting in regard to "Je vouldroy bien richement jaunissant," see Greene, *Light in Troy*, pp. 197–219.

103.　See the introduction to Pierre de Ronsard, *Les Amours*, ed. Henri Weber and Catherine Weber (Paris, 1963). All citations in the text are taken from that edition. The texts of Ronsard's poems are almost as fluid as the contents, since he revised them constantly in the preparation of new editions. On the rationale for their own textual decisions, see the Webers' edition, pp. xli–lix. On one particular set of textual alternatives in a poem significant to my argument here, see Grahame Castor, "Ronsard's Variants: 'Je vouldray bien richement jaunissant,'" *Modern Language Review* 59 (1964): 387–90.

104.　The AI is both an expression of grief and the first two letters of Ajax's name. In the *Metamorphoses* (10.205–16; 13.394–98), the myth is conflated with that of Hyacinthus, so that the flower commemorates both a hero and a boy.

105.　An important element in the heritage of Ronsard's mythology as distinct from, say, Petrarch's is the rediscovery and imitation of Alexandrian poetry. We have already seen how Ronsard's friend Antoine de Baif translated Moschus's Europa poem. Ronsard himself wrote a number of mythological poems in the same tradition, including "Le Ravissement de Céphale" and "La Défloration de Lède"; and imitations of Theocritus and the writers of the Greek Anthology, as well as their Latin imitators, appear everywhere in his work. See James Hutton, *The Greek Anthology in France and in the Latin Writers of the Netherlands* (Ithaca, 1946).

106.　The wish to become a flea is a cliché of neo-Latin and vernacular love poetry in the sixteenth century. Donne's "The Flea" is, of course, the most famous to speakers of English, but the tradition begins with the medieval *Carmen de Pulice* ascribed to Ovid. It continues through a large number of (mostly neo-Latin) encomia in the sixteenth century, culminating in a collection of poems by various hands in various languages published in 1582 on the subject of *La Puce de Madame des Roches*. See Marcel Françon, "Un Motif de la poésie amoureuse au XVIème siècle," in *PMLA* 56 (1941): 307–36. Note that in the 1578 edition of his collected *Oeuvres* Ronsard replaced the flea metamorphosis with a continuation of the Europa material.

107.　Much interesting work has been done on the close connections between Ronsard and contemporary artistic developments like mannerism and the School of Fontainebleau. See especially Marcel Raymond, *La Poésie française et le maniérisme* (Geneva, 1971): Jean Adhémar, "Ronsard et l'école de Fontainebleau," *Bibliothèque d'Humanisme et Renaissance* 20 (1958): 344–48; and R. A. Sayce, "Ronsard and Mannerism: the *Elegie à Janet*," *L'Esprit créateur* 6 (1966): 234–47. Also see below, n. 112.

108.　Ronsard clearly found this sonnet a bit risky (as well as risqué). In the 1578 edition it is excluded from the "Amours pour Cassandre," and it disappears altogether from the 1584 edition. See the excellent analysis by Grahame Castor, "Petrarchism and the Quest for Beauty in the *Amours* of Cassandre and the *Sonets pour Helene*," in *Ronsard*, ed. Cave, pp. 92–95.

109.   Terence Cave is especially eloquent: "The would-be metamorphoses of the lover mirror the function of the poem itself, which is to compensate for the intractability of reality by transforming it into fable" ("Ronsard's Mythological Universe," p. 180).

110.   See Ovid, *Metamorphoses*, 2.852–53: "quippe color nivis est, quam nec vestigia duri / calcavere pedis nec solvit aquaticus auster."

111.   See chapter 1.

112.   A quite different aspect of Ronsard's career must be mentioned in connection with Renaissance developments in myth and metamorphosis. Especially in his later years, the poet worked in the preparation of court entertainments at Fontainebleau, thus confirming his links with mannerist movements and the visual arts. Though the subject of Catherine de Medici's festival of 1564 has much more to do with the glories of royal order than with the fragmentations of passion, it still operates by the medium of transposition to the golden world of classical myth just as Ronsard's love poetry does. Marcel Raymond, speaking especially of the 1571 entry of Charles IX, makes explicit the connections between metamorphosis and translation into the mythic realm: "Quand au lieu de la fête, c'est *le lieu quotidien de la ville*, mais cette ville se métamorphose. . . . Toutes ces créations . . . étaient l'ornement de la vie quotidienne, qu'elles métamorphosaient pour un temps très bref, aux yeux des hommes du XVIᵉ siècle" ("La Pléiade et le maniérisme," in *Lumières de la Pléiade*, Paris, 1966, p. 401). For more on the relation between court festivals and metamorphosis, see below.

113.   See Lauro Martines, *Power and Imagination* (New York, 1979), esp. pp. 241–76; Martin Wackernagel, *The World of the Florentine Renaissance Artist*, tr. A. Luchs (Princeton, 1981), esp. pp. 193–295; and Peter Burke, *Tradition and Innovation in Renaissance Italy* (London, 1972), esp. pp. 97–151.

114.   See Thomas M. Greene, "Spenser and the Epithalamic Convention," *Comparative Literature* 9 (1957): 215–28. For a general survey, see Virginia Tufte, *The Poetry of Marriage* (Los Angeles, 1970).

115.   The standard work, still not superceded despite its limitations, is Paul Schubring, *Cassoni* (Leipzig, 1923). For a list of the myths most commonly depicted and an interesting argument about the relevance of ancient carnal legends to the occasion of a wedding, see pp. 178–92. Among more recent treatments are Ernst Gombrich, "Apollonio di Giovanni: A Florentine Cassone Workshop Seen through the Eyes of a Humanist Poet," in *Norm and Form* (London, 1966), pp. 11–28; G. L. McCann, "Florentine Cassoni of the Fifteenth Century," *Bulletin of the Cincinnati Art Museum* 3 (1932): 85–97; and Ellen Callmann, *Apollonio di Giovanni* (Oxford, 1974).

116.   "Vita di Dello," in *Vite*, ed. Gaetano Milanesi (Florence, 1906), 2:148.

117.   *Prediche di F. Girolamo Savonarola*, ed. G. Baccini (Florence, 1899), p. 401. The reference to Mars and Venus comes from his sermon on the Book of Ruth.

118.   Cited in Schubring, *Cassoni*, p. 183, without specific reference to the works of Burckhardt.

119. Alatiel (Day 2, Story 7) has her virginity restored after a long sequence of lusty travels; Nastagio (Day 5, Story 8) convinces his beloved to cease her refusals to love by exposing her to a hellish pageant in which a *donna crudele* is punished for her militant chastity. For Boccaccian representations on wedding chests, see Schubring, *Cassoni*, pp. 196–99.

120. Attributed by Berenson to Francesco di Giorgio Martini (1439–1502), the work is catalogued as no. 466 in Schubring, *Cassoni*.

121. The structures of narrative art have been far too little studied. For related discussions, see Otto Pächt, *The Rise of Pictorial Narrative in Twelfth-Century England* (Oxford, 1962), pp. 1–32; Kurt Weizmann, *Studies in Roll and Codex* (Princeton, 1970), pp. 12–46; Peter Parshall, "Lucas van Leyden's Narrative Style," in *Lucas van Leyden: Studies, Netherlands Yearbook for History of Art* (Haarlem, 1979), pp. 185–237; and Nelson Goodman, "Twisted Tales; or Story, Study, and Symphony," *Critical Inquiry* 7 (1980): 103–19.

122. The classic statement remains Jacob Burckhardt, *The Civilization of the Renaissance in Italy*, pt. 5, "Society and Festivals" (London, 1921), pp. 359–428. The best general treatment in recent years is Roy Strong, *Splendour at Court* (London, 1973). Most influential is the theoretical approach in Stephen Orgel, *The Illusion of Power* (Berkeley, 1975), and the excellent collection of essays in the various volumes of *Les Fêtes de la Renaissance*, ed. Jean Jacquot (Paris, 1956, 1960). For specific countries and courts, the bibliography is enormous: see Strong, *Splendour*, pp. 252–62, for an excellent sampling, along with vols. 1 and 11 (n.s.) of *Renaissance Drama*.

123. See the fine treatment in Andrew Martindale, *The Triumphs of Caesar by Andrea Mantegna* (London, 1979), esp. pp. 47–55, 97–102.

124. For Charles V see Jacquot, ed., *Fêtes*, vol. 2, *Fêtes et cérémonies au temps de Charles Quint*. On the French court, see Frances Yates, *The Valois Tapestries* (London, 1959), esp. pp. 51–72.

125. See Burckhardt, *Civilization*, pp. 417–18.

126. See the account in Vasari, *Vite*, 8:567–614; and Jean Seznec, "La Mascarade des dieux à Florence en 1565," *Mélanges d'archéologie et d'histoire* (1935), p. 224.

127. See Strong, *Splendour*, pp. 56–65; Seznec, *Survival*, pp. 279–85; and Walter J. Ong, "From Allegory to Diagram in the Renaissance Mind: A Study of the Significance of the Allegorical Tableau," *Journal of Aesthetics and Art Criticism* 17 (1959): 423–40.

128. See Frances Yates, "Poètes et artistes dans les entrées de Charles IX et de sa reine à Paris en 1571," in Jacquot, *Fêtes*, 1:61–91.

129. On the subject of triumphs in general, see W. Weisbach, *Trionfi* (Berlin, 1919); G. Carandente, *I Trionfi del primo rinascimento* (Turin, 1963); and Martindale, *Triumphs*, pp. 47–55. For Petrarch himself, see Bernardo, *Petrarch*, pp. 102–14, 163–92, the latter relating the *Trionfi* to issues we have considered in the *Rime*. The Triumph, it should be noted, bears the closest possible relation with both cassoni and public ceremony. The importance of Roman triumphs for royal processions has already been discussed. In addition, the Petrarchan *Trionfi* are second only to Ovidian materials in the frequency of their representation on wedding chests. See Schubring, *Cassoni*, pp. 21–22, 58–60.

130. The pattern owes a great deal to Dante's strategy in the *Inferno,* with its contrasts between grand constructions and the insubstantialities both of evil and of the dream-world of the poet. See chapter 4, section 1.

131. The best modern edition is that of G. Pozzi and A. Ciapponi (Padua, 1968; rev. ed., 1980), which includes excellent notes and bibliography. Citations below are to that edition. The standard work on the author is M. T. Casella and G. Pozzi, *Francesco Colonna: Biographia e opere* (Padua, 1959). See also Peter Dronke's Introduction to the facsimile of the 1499 edition published in the *Colecciòn Mnemòsine* (Zaragoza, 1981).

132. The rear panels of the chariots cover the individual psyche of love. Each is a scene of judgment, and in each case the power of love supercedes the rationality associated with judgment. In one panel Jupiter rejects Mars's plea that the war-god, as Cupid's father, should be immune from his son's power; in another Jupiter admits the boy's power over himself by falling in love with Venus; and in the final panel Cupid is his own victim as he falls in love with Psyche. The Judgment of Paris confirms the same theme, as Paris is said to make his choice "dal'operoso Cupidine seducto" (1:157).

133. "A celebratory choir of seven nymphs clad in white addressing themselves to sacred singing with solemn reverence. Afterwards these same nymphs were transformed into verdant trees of brilliant emerald covered with shimmering sea-blue flowerets; and they were bowing most reverently to the high godhead. Nor were all the nymphs being metamorphosed into leaves: the nearest was entirely transformed into a tree, the next all but her feet, the third from her waist upwards including the beginning of her arms, and each one afterwards in a similar fashion. But at the top of the virgin head was visible the metamorphosis which was to follow for each of the nymphs successively."

134. Citation is to *Antony and Cleopatra,* ed. M. R. Ridley (London, 1954), 2.2.191–213.

135. Compare, for instance, the conceptual transformations based on the Circe myth in La Chesnaye's *Balet comique de la reine.* See Frances Yates, *The French Academies of the Sixteenth Century* (London, 1947), pp. 238–51.

136. These are arguably the best documented and certainly the most adroitly studied of all the Renaissance festivals. The standard work is Stephen Orgel and Roy Strong, *Inigo Jones: The Theatre of the Stuart Court* (London, 1973); along with Stephen Orgel, *The Jonsonian Masque* (Cambridge, Mass., 1965); and D. J. Gordon's important essay, "Poet and Architect: The Intellectual Setting of the Quarrel between Ben Jonson and Inigo Jones," *Journal of the Warburg and Courtauld Institutes* 12 (1949): 152–78.

137. Citation is to Ben Jonson, *The Complete Masques,* ed. Stephen Orgel (New Haven, 1969).

138. Citation is to *The Tempest,* ed. Frank Kermode (London, 1954), 4.1.148–56.

139. The subject of Platonism among Renaissance artists and thinkers has been extremely well studied by many scholars. My own partiality to Edgar Wind's *Pagan Mysteries* has doubtless already revealed itself. But see also Ernst Cassirer, *Individual and Cosmos in Renaissance Philosophy* (Philadelphia, 1972); Ernst Gombrich, "Icones Symbolicae: The Visual Image in Neoplatonic Thought," *Journal of the Warburg and Courtauld Institutes* 11 (1948): 163–92; Paul Oskar

Kristeller, *The Philosophy of Marsilio Ficino* (New York, 1943); and Erwin Panofsky, *Studies in Iconology* (New York, 1962), pp. 129–230. Also see the recent work of M. J. B. Allen, *Marsilio Ficino and the Phaedran Charioteer* (Berkeley, 1981), and his edition, *Marsilio Ficino: The Philebus Commentary* (Berkeley, 1975).

140. For somewhat differing views see Ernst Gombrich, "Botticelli's Mythologies: A Study in the Neo-Platonic Symbolism of his Circle," *Journal of the Warburg and Courtauld Institutes* 8 (1945): 7–60; and Wind, *Pagan Mysteries*, pp. 113–40.

141. On the Graces, see Wind, *Pagan Mysteries*, esp. pp. 26–52, 83–86, 117–21. The standard work on Hercules is Erwin Panofsky, *Herkules am Scheidewege* (Leipzig 1930). For the Judgment of Paris see Ficino's letter to Lorenzo de' Medici (cited by Wind, *Pagan Mysteries*, p. 82): "Our Lorenzo, however, instructed by the oracle of Apollo [Ficino himself?], has neglected none of the gods. He saw the three [that is, the three goddesses who had appeared to Paris] and all three he adored according to their merits; whence he received wisdom from Pallas, power from Juno, and from Venus grace and poetry and music" (the first interpolation is mine, the second Wind's). Notice that in the mode of compliment the Platonic union is more poetical than seriously philosophical.

142. The famous passage occurs in secs. 3-4 of the Oration. See P. O. Kristeller et al., *The Renaissance Philosophy of Man* (Chicago, 1965), pp. 224–25.

143. See Wind, *Pagan Mysteries*, pp. 199–200.

144. Citation is to *Giordano Bruno's* The Heroic Frenzies, tr. Paul E. Memmo, Jr. (Chapel Hill, 1964), p. 225.

145. On the Renaissance Apuleius, see Elizabeth Haight, *Apuleius and His Influence* (New York, 1927), pp. 111–27; P. G. Walsh, *The Roman Novel* (Cambridge, 1970), pp. 232–41; and Wind, *Pagan Mysteries*, pp. 58–59, 236–37. Among primary texts, see especially the commentary by Beroaldus (Venice, 1516; Lyons, 1587); and the second dialogue of Bruno's *Cabala del cavallo pegaseo* (*Opere*, ed. A. Wagner, Leipzig, 1830, pp. 275–89.)

146. Amidst the enormous Spenser bibliography a few works stand out as especially relevant. William V. Nestrick, "Spenser and the Mythology of Love," *Literary Monographs* 5 (Madison, 1975): 37–70; and David W. Burchmore, "The Unfolding of Britomart: Mythic Iconography in *The Faerie Queene*," *Renaissance Papers* 1977, pp. 11–28, are both concerned with classical topoi in the central books of the poem. The classic essay on one important mythic structure is Kathleen Williams, "Venus and Diana: Some Uses of Myth in *The Faerie Queene*," *ELH* 28 (1961): 101–20; and the best treatment of the Busyrane episode is Harry Berger, Jr., "Busirane and the War between the Sexes," *English Literary Renaissance* 1 (1971): 99–121. Among the many volumes treating the whole poem, I was particularly influenced by C. S. Lewis, *Spenser's Images of Life*; William Nelson, *The Poetry of Edmund Spenser* (New York, 1963), esp. pp. 229–35; and Kathleen Williams, *Spenser's World of Glass* (Berkeley, 1966), esp. pp. 107–11.

147. Citations are to *The Faerie Queene*, ed. Thomas P. Roche, Jr. (Harmondsworth, 1978).

148. See the excellent treatment of the Domus Aurea and its influence on Renaissance art in von Salis, *Antike*, pp. 35–55. Also see J. Schulz, "Pinturicchio and the Revival of Antiquity," in *Journal of the Warburg and Courtauld Institutes*

25 (1962): 47–51. The standard work on the Domus Aurea paintings themselves is Fritz Weege, *Das goldene Haus des Nero* (Berlin, 1913).

149.　Citation is to *The Collected Dialogues of Plato*, ed. Edith Hamilton and Huntington Cairns (New York, 1961), p. 1165.

150.　Spenser, Protestant (perhaps even Puritan) though he was, is in part influenced by a Counter-Reformation attitude toward pagan images. Attacks against the revival of mythology, like those of Cardinal Paleotto (*Discorso intorno alle imagini sacre e profane*, Bologna, 1584), not only revive medieval arguments about the immorality and insubstantiality of the pagan pantheon, but they also drive artists further into allegory and the doctrine of integumentum. See Seznec, *Survival*, pp. 263–69.

151.　For instance, "So that when I now asked what is iniquity, I realized that it was not a substance but a swerving of the will which is turned toward lower things and away from You, O God, who are the supreme substance." *Confessions*, 7.16, tr. F. J. Sheed (New York, 1943), p. 149.

152.　Britomart has been subject to particularly changeable emotions herself in regard to love. Her reaction to the sight in Merlin's mirror ("Sad, solemne, sowre, and full of fancies fraile / She woxe"; 3.2.27) is a piece of psychological instability that could be applied almost verbatim to Malecasta, Hellenore, and others with serious moral shortcomings in the book.

153.　See chapter 3, esp. n. 87 and accompanying text.

154.　In addition to those works cited in n. 146, see Harry Berger, Jr., "The *Mutabilitie Cantos*: Archaism and Evolution in Retrospect," in *Spenser: A Collection of Critical Essays*, ed. Berger (Englewood Cliffs, N.J., 1968), pp. 146–76; and Michael Holahan, "*Iamque opus exegi*: Ovid's Changes and Spenser's Brief Epic of Mutability," in *English Literary Renaissance* 6 (1976): 244–70.

155.　The expression of this mutability (see 7.6.5: "she the face of earthly things so changed, / . . . And all the worlds faire frame . . . / She alter'd quite") makes implicit reference to Phaethon's ride in the *Metamorphoses*, an important allusion because Spenser is attempting to recapitulate the cosmological Ovid and thus to fit the changes of mutability into an ultimate pattern of order despite the immediate sense of decay.

156.　A significant intermediary between Ovid's Pythagoras and the *Cantos* is provided by the speech of Theseus in Chaucer's *Knight's Tale*, especially I(A) 3017–40, which mingles Boethian consolations of cosmic harmony with the Ovidian imagery of orderly change.

CHAPTER SIX. *Shakespeare and the Metamorphoses of Art and Life*

1.　Shakespeare's relation to Ovid, beyond the question of indebtednesses in individual plays, for which see notes below, has not attracted the attention it deserves. Most of the work consists in (often useful) catalogues of references, analogies, and echoes. See Robert K. Root, *Classical Mythology in Shakespeare* (New York, 1903); J. A. K. Thompson, *Shakespeare and the Classics* (London, 1952); and Dietrich Klose, "Shakespeare und Ovid," *Deutsche Shakespeare Gesellschaft West Jahrbuch 1968*, pp. 72–93. T. W. Baldwin, *William Shakespeare's Small Latine and Lesse Greeke* (Urbana, 1944), 2:417–55 provides the most useful of these accounts, setting Ovid at the top of all those classical models used principally for verse-making. Hence Holofernes' comment that "Ovidius Naso was the man: and why indeed Naso, but for smelling out the odoriferous flowers of fancy, the jerks of invention" (*Love's Labour's Lost*, 4.2.127–29) and Touchstone's self-comparison to Ovid at just the moment when he is seeking to explain "poetical" to Audrey (*As You Like It*, 3.3.6–26). In a less directly Ovidian vein is William C. Carroll, *The Metamorphoses of Shakespearean Comedy* (Princeton, 1985), a volume that appeared during the final stages of this work. This is not the place for a review of Professor Carroll's book: suffice it to say that it contains many excellent readings of the plays, some of which correspond to views I have long held, some of which influenced me in the revisions of this chapter, and some of which I can agree to disagree with. Not solely concerned with Ovid, but full of learning and wisdom in regard to all classical origins and their interplay with Shakespeare's originality, is Leo Salingar's *Shakespeare and the Traditions of Comedy* (Cambridge, 1974).

2. Eugene Waith's "The Metamorphosis of Violence in *Titus Andronicus*," *Shakespeare Survey* 10 (1957): 39–49, is the classic treatment that rehabilitated the play while setting it in its Ovidian context. Waith is one of the few critics of English literature who reads more of the *Metamorphoses* than the narrow purpose of source-hunting requires him to do, and the results are a revelation. One of Waith's concluding statements is of particular interest (perhaps by way of challenge) to my account of the play: "In taking over certain Ovidian forms, Shakespeare takes over part of an Ovidian conception which cannot be fully realized by the techniques of drama" (p. 48).

3. Citation is to *Titus Andronicus*, ed. J. C. Maxwell, New Arden Edition (London, 1961).

4. See chapter 5, section 2.

5. Citation is to *Cymbeline*, ed. J. M. Nosworthy, New Arden Edition (London, 1966).

6. See *Fasti* 2.685–856.

7. Citations of *Lucrece* and of *Venus and Adonis* (below) are to *The Poems*, ed. F. T. Prince, New Arden Edition (London, 1960). See the excellent discussion of Lucrece's tapestry-reading and Renaissance theories of art in Clark Hulse, *Metamorphic Verse: The Elizabethan Minor Epic* (Princeton, 1981), pp. 175–94. Hulse demonstrates Shakespeare's relation to the ancient and contemporary literature of the *paragone*, or competition among the arts. See section 3 of this chapter for a discussion of these ideas in *The Winter's Tale*.

8. The word *publish* in Shakespeare's time was finely poised between the pre-Gutenbergian general meaning of "make public" and our more limited sense of issuing a printed book. The earliest OED listing for *publisher* in the sense of "one who publishes a book" is 1654. But there are many Renaissance usages of the verb in the sense of book-making, including (from the 1611 introduction to the King James Bible) "He could no sooner write any thing, but presently it was caught from him and published, and he could not haue leaue to end it."

9. My study of *A Midsummer Night's Dream* is much indebted to two contemporary classics of criticism: C. L. Barber's *Shakespeare's Festive Comedy* (Princeton, 1959), esp. "May Games and Metamorphoses on a Midsummer Night," pp. 119–62, whose discussion of metamorphosis in the play far transcends the book's general thesis concerning folk-ritual; and David Young's *Something of*

Great Constancy (New Haven, 1966), a lens through which a whole generation of readers, including this one, have seen the play. Deserving of similar status is Marjorie Garber's *Dream in Shakespeare: From Metaphor to Metamorphosis* (New Haven, 1974), pp. 59–87. The distinction drawn in the title has influenced my thinking about Ovidian matters well beyond the case of this one play or this one author. For a useful grounding in Shakespeare's use of sources, see Walter F. Staton, Jr., "Ovidian Elements in *A Midsummer Night's Dream*," *Huntington Library Quarterly* 26 (1963): 165–78. At the opposite end of the critical imagination is René Girard, "Myth and Ritual in Shakespeare: *A Midsummer Night's Dream*," in *Textual Strategies: Perspectives in Post-Structuralist Criticism*, ed. Josué V. Harari (Ithaca, 1979), pp. 189–212.

10.   Shakespeare demands a study of *imitatio* and intertextuality whose assumptions lie somewhere between those applicable to Dante and Petrarch—supremely conscious as they were of literary history—and those applicable to such innocent soakers-up of the past as Homer or the poet of the *Chanson de Roland*. (The terms and examples, but not the reference to Shakespeare, come from Thomas Greene's lucid discussion in *The Light in Troy*, New Haven, 1982, pp. 16–19). Shakespeare's response to *The Knight's Tale* reveals both what we might call an unconscious desire to mine the original for its motifs with all their literary effects and a deliberate wish to rewrite the source in a pattern such that the original shines through in a persistent dialogue with the new work. In effect, the Chaucerian text becomes one of the imaginative structures upon which Shakespeare builds his inventions—not only in the case of the *Dream* but throughout the writing of the comedies and the romances. See E. Talbot Donaldson, *The Swan at the Well: Shakespeare Reading Chaucer* (New Haven, 1985), for a perceptive reading of the two poets' interconnections. The intertextualities of the *Dream* and *Romeo and Juliet* are naturally of a different order. Chronological questions must be put to the side since there is no consensus on which play came first. The real confluence is between *Romeo* and "Pyramus and Thisbe." The fact that the latter is so clearly part of a self-conscious aesthetic examination (see below) makes it clear that Shakespeare was searching for both an emotional tone and an aesthetic medium appropriate to the common subject.

11.   See Geoffrey Bullough, *Narrative and Dramatic Sources of Shakespeare* (London, 1957), 1:368–69, 377–89. For more speculative source-study in this area, see the works cited in n. 23 and the excellent interpretive essay of D'Orsay W. Pearson, "Vnkinde Theseus: A Study in Renaissance Mythography," *English Literary Renaissance* 4 (1974): 276–98.

12.   Citations are to *A Midsummer Night's Dream*, ed. Harold F. Brooks, New Arden Edition (London, 1979).

13.   There are other mythological doubles in the play, some more and some less obvious. The performance of Pyramus and Thisbe doubles that myth with the actors who perform it and with the young Athenians whose lives are parallel to those of Ovid's lovers. For Bottom's mythological doubles, see below and n. 23.

14.   Citations are to *The Discoverie of Witchcraft*, intr. M. Summers (London, 1930).

15.   See chapter 3, section 1.

16.   Most of the attention paid to these lines has been devoted to elucidating the topical reference (if such there is). H. H. Furness, *A New Variorum Edition of*

Shakespeare, vol. 10 (Philadelphia, 1895), p. 75, declares, "This speech of Oberson has been the subject of more voluminous speculation than any other twenty-five lines in Shakespeare," and he proceeds to document that speculation in the next fifteen pages. More revealing than the (supposed) references to Elizabeth's marriage prospects are the references to courtly masques that may have taken a form similar to Oberon's description of the mermaid, if not of Cupid's arrow as well. See the pithy account in Brooks's introduction to the New Arden Edition, pp. lxvii–lxix, along with the suggestion of a source in Seneca's *Hippolytus* (p. lxiii). The important point, as suggested by Brooks and by Barber (*Festive Comedy,* p. 122), is that the composite image of mermaid, vestal, moon, and Cupid partakes of the nexus that joins the Ovidian landscape with its three-dimensional realization in courtly pageants and learned comedy of the earlier Elizabethan period. (See section 3 of this chapter for more on Shakespeare's relation to that tradition.) Beyond those pageants, the fugitive Eros appears everywhere from Hellenistic poetry to *The Faerie Queene;* he is, as I have suggested, directly represented in the play by the traveling and self-transforming Puck.

17. Spenser discusses the changeling in the House of Holiness when the hermit Contemplation identifies Redcrosse and his destiny (*Faerie Queene* 1.10.65). Reginald Scot mentions changelings in his catalogue of spirits invoked to frighten children (7.15). The context of the term in *The Faerie Queene* may well have influenced the *Dream:* Spenser's woods, like Shakespeare's, are a place of shifting identities, and one of the most basic shifts has to do with indigenous creatures of "faery" and heroic figures like Redcrosse (or Arthur) who must nonetheless prove themselves in fairyland. Shakespeare's use of "changeling" to refer to the stolen rather than the substituted child may not be an error, as some have thought it, but quite purposeful in adding to the interplay of doubles. See K. M. Briggs, *The Anatomy of Puck* (London, 1959), esp. pp. 44–47, for a convincing argument about the "active kindness" of Shakespeare's fairies even in this theft, especially in comparison with the Childe Roland story, which Shakespeare cited in *King Lear.* For a fuller treatment of the changeling, see Briggs's *The Fairies in English Tradition and Literature* (Chicago, 1967), pp. 115–20.

18. See the *Metamorphoses* 11.92–193. Bullough also cites Thomas Cooper's *Thesaurus Linguae Romanae et Britannicae,* published in 1565 (*Sources,* 1:397).

19. There is some controversy over the question of Shakespeare's first-hand knowledge of Apuleius, since he could have found the essential information in Scot's *Discoverie.* But it seems perverse to claim that such a voracious reader would be unfamiliar with William Adlington's great translation of *The Golden Ass,* published in 1566. See Bullough, *Sources,* 1:372, Sr. M. Generosa, "Apuleius and *A Midsummer Night's Dream,* Analogue or Source, Which?" *Studies in Philology* 42 (1945): 198–204, and D. T. Starnes, "Shakespeare and Apuleius," *PMLA* 60 (1945): 1021–50.

20. For some well-researched background materials relevant to many of the metamorphic issues and some slightly overenthusiastic application of them, see Deborah Baker Wyrick, "The Ass Motif in *The Comedy of Errors* and *A Midsummer Night's Dream,*" *Shakespeare Quarterly* 33 (1982): 432–38.

21. Such is Bullough's conclusion (*Sources,* 1:371). The name essentially signifies "daughter of a Titan," and Ovid also uses it to refer to Circe (*Metamor-*

phoses 14.382, 438), which would insure further metamorphic associations. The fact that Golding does not use the name at all represents one of the indications that Shakespeare consulted Ovid at first hand.

22.   Citation is to the *Geneva Bible: A Facsimile of the 1560 Edition* (Madison, 1969). See the subtle and suggestive analysis of Bottom's speech, his name, and his dream by Ronald F. Miller, "*A Midsummer Night's Dream*: The Faeries, Bottom, and the Mystery of Things," *Shakespeare Quarterly* 26 (1975): 254–68. Miller points out that in the Tyndale version St. Paul goes on to say, "the sprete [spirit] searcheth all things, ye the *bottome* of Goddes secrets" (p. 265). See also Thomas B. Stroup, "Bottom's Name and His Epiphany," *Shakespeare Quarterly* 29 (1978): 79–82; and Robert F. Wilson, Jr., "God's Secrets and Bottom's Name: A Reply," *Shakespeare Quarterly* 30 (1979): 407–08. For other treatments of Bottom's Dream in the same rhapsodic vein as my own, see Andrew D. Weiner, "'Multiformitie Uniforme': *A Midsummer Night's Dream*," *ELH* 38 (1971): 329–49, esp. pp. 343–49; and J. Dennis Huston, "Bottom Waking: Shakespeare's 'Most Rare Vision,'" *Studies in English Literature* 13 (1973): 208–22.

23.   I do not mean to slight the importance of this myth in the genesis of *A Midsummer Night's Dream*: like Actaeon and Apuleius's hero Lucius, the Minotaur is clearly one of the inspirations for Shakespeare's own myth-making. The labyrinth of the woods, the thread of Bottom the weaver's skein, Puck's delight in the fact that "my mistress with a monster is in love": all testify to the significance of the Minotaur. See David Ormerod, "*A Midsummer Night's Dream*: The Monster in the Labyrinth," *Shakespeare Studies* 11 (1978): 39–52; and M. E. Lamb, "*A Midsummer Night's Dream*: The Myth of Theseus and the Minotaur," *Texas Studies in Language and Literature* 21 (1979): 478–91. Most important to me in the parallels (and not stressed by Ormerod or Lamb) is the additional level of identity that the Minotaur gives to Bottom—not just as a temporary victim of metamorphosis but also as a permanent double creature. The Cretan monster also suggests an underlying but hidden battle between two powerful figures (Theseus and Bottom) who meet only in the closing moments of the play. In that sense the Minotaur provides a doppelgänger for Bottom analogous to the pairings between the fairy monarchs and the Duke and Duchess of Athens.

24.   The F and Q texts of *A Midsummer Night's Dream* in particular reveal confusions about the timing of entrances. In the present case F calls for Puck's entrance at l. 50 (Bottom: "Find out moonshine!") rather than at the moment when he speaks. Modern editions tend to treat this as a mistake and introduce Puck when he speaks—even though Puck's speech indicates clearly that he has been listening to the actors. It is clear that the F and Q texts do not make sharp distinctions between "enter" and "come forward," as is suggested by W. W. Greg, *The Shakespeare First Folio* (Oxford, 1955), pp. 244–45.

25.   Puck's metamorphoses, his ubiquity, and his mockery of the self-important world around him all suggest a relation to the visual traditions of playful Cupids deriding the emblems of human or divine solemnity, as in Correggio's Camera di S. Paolo or the Raphael-designed Loggia in the Villa Farnesina. See chapter 5, section 2.

26.   The association of fools with asses' ears goes at least as far back as Martial (indeed Ovid's Midas story may be a kind of etiology of the practice). But so far as the costume of the professional fool is concerned, the asses' ears are well en-

trenched in Northern Europe beginning in the later Middle Ages. See, for instance, Quinten Massys's *Allegory of Folly*, catalogued as no. 44 in Larry Silver, *The Paintings of Quinten Massys* (Montclair, N. J., 1984), along with Silver's fine discussion of the iconography of the Fool, pp. 145–52. See also Enid Welsford, *The Fool* (London, 1935), pp. 121–24; and E. Tietze-Conrat, *Dwarfs and Jesters in Art* (New York, 1957), pp. 7, 94.

27.   The Folio reads, "Then know that I, one Snug the Ioyner am / A Lion fell . . ." The Folio is, however, of lesser textual authority than *Q1*, and in this case the reading seems to be an ex post facto attempt to smooth over a designedly difficult original line. On the merit of *Q* and *F*, see Brooks's edition, pp. xxii–xxxiv.

28.   The animal associations partake of popular proverb lore. R. A. Foakes in his New Cambridge edition (Chicago, 1984) cites Tilley, *A Dictionary of the Proverbs in England in the Sixteenth and Seventeenth Centuries* (Ann Arbor, 1950), L308 ("As fierce [valiant] as a lion"), F645, 647, 659, which all speak of the wiliness of the Fox, G346 ("as dizzy as a goose"), and G348 ("as wise as a goose [gander]"), apparently ironic. But see also F656 ("When the Fox preaches, beware the geese"). The "discretion" of the goose may be an allusion to the geese on the Roman capitol who sounded the warning against barbarian invaders—in this case not a stupid noise but a (justifiably) alarmist one. The lion and the fox certainly allude to Machiavelli's metaphor for the qualities of the perfect ruler, which is quite apposite to the courtier-like (even sycophantic) roles that the young men are playing with Theseus. See *The Prince*, chaps. 18–19, and E. M. W. Tillyard, *Shakespeare's History Plays* (London, 1951), pp. 186, 227, 317, who sees this animal dyad—with the crucial addition of the pelican—as a principle of rulership in *Henry VI, Part Two*, *King John*, and *Macbeth*.

29.   See the excellent summary of the historical research in Brooks's New Arden edition, pp. liii–lvii. But see Stanley Wells's dissent in the New Penguin edition (London, 1967), pp. 13–14. Paul A. Olson, "*A Midsummer Night's Dream* and the Meaning of Court Marriage," *ELH* 24 (1957): 95–119, sets the specifics of the historical occasion aside and analyzes the issues of marriage and harmony in the play, including some excellent mythographic interpretations.

30.   Carroll (*Metamorphoses*, esp. pp. 141–48, 154) is especially persuasive in conjoining the monstrous, the erotic, and the nuptial in the play. The argument goes back to Barber's thesis of ritual exorcism (*Festive Comedy*, p. 139).

31.   For the full discussion of this nexus, see chapter 1.

32.   See Hulse's good analysis of the three Venuses, "comic, sensual, and violent" (*Metamorphic Verse*, p. 157); one should not forget, however, how inextricable the categories are. Douglas Bush, *Mythology and the Renaissance Tradition* (Minneapolis, 1932), pp. 139–49, gives a detailed account of the poem's Ovidianism.

33.   Perhaps it is not too obvious to point out that the medium of *Venus and Adonis* is intensely Ovidian, and not just in the sense that it is an erotic pagan tale. I would single out especially Shakespeare's play on the ekphrastic tradition: the perfection of Adonis's stallion owes a great deal to Ovid's description of Europa's bull, while the characterization of Adonis as "Lifeless picture, cold and senseless stone, / Well-painted idol" (ll. 211–12, Venus speaking) reverts to a similar description of Narcissus. The goddess's direct reference to Narcissus—"Narcissus so himself himself forsook, / And died to kiss his shadow in the brook" (ll. 161–

62)—depends on a witty and very Ovidian piece of linguistic mirroring, even if the mythology is oversimplified, as Venus's arguments tend to be. Shakespeare's great change in Ovid's story—turning Adonis into an unwilling participant in Venus's embraces—in fact out-Ovids Ovid, since the boy's fatal choice gains significance immeasurably by arising out of a stern virginity and not just from a masculine preference for hunting.

34.   Citation is to *The Merchant of Venice*, ed. John Russell Brown, New Arden Edition (London, 1959).

35.   See the subtle and learned treatment of these questions by Michael J. B. Allen in "The Chase: The Development of a Renaissance Theme," *Comparative Literature* 20 (1968): 301–12.

36.   *Symposium* 189b–193e. In this connection see Northrop Frye's analysis of marriage and the hermaphrodite in Shakespearean comedy, *A Natural Perspective* (New York, 1965), pp. 82–87.

37.   For interesting reflections on these problems of identity see Marjorie Garber's *Coming of Age in Shakespeare* (London, 1981), esp. pp. 30–51; and Thomas Greene's brilliant essay, "The Flexibility of the Self in Renaissance Literature," in *The Disciplines of Criticism*, ed. Peter Demetz et al. (New Haven, 1968), pp. 241–64, the influence of which permeates the present volume. See also Joel Fineman, "Fratricide and Cuckoldry: Shakespeare's Doubles," in *Representing Shakespeare*, ed. Murray M. Schwartz and Coppelia Kahn (Baltimore, 1980), pp. 70–109. For a more down-to-earth view of the same issues, see Thomas F. Van Laan, *Role-Playing in Shakespeare* (Toronto, 1978), esp. pp. 21–42.

38.   My thinking about the play has been influenced by R. A. Foakes's excellent introduction to his edition (see n. 39), esp. pp. xliii–xlix; and Harold Brooks, "Themes and Structures in *The Comedy of Errors*," in *Early Shakespeare*, ed. J. R. Brown and B. Harris, *Stratford-upon-Avon Studies* (London, 1961). See also Carroll, *Metamorphoses*, pp. 63–80.

39.   Citations are to *The Comedy of Errors*, ed. R. A. Foakes, New Arden Edition (London, 1969).

40.   See Bullough (*Sources*, 1:9–10) for an excellent discussion of the Ephesus question in the play, including St. Paul's homilies on the subject of orderly family relations (Ephesians 5:22–33, 6:5–17). Foakes (New Arden Edition, pp. xxix, 113–15) adds interesting material from Acts 1:1–29 in regard to the sorcery practiced in Ephesus—precisely the reason why St. Paul worked so hard to bring the Ephesians the Christian religion.

41.   The intricacies of this proposition may be clarified (or complicated) by reference to the metamorphoses of fusion and separation in *Inferno* 25 and 26 (see chapter 4, section 2). Direct connections between Dante and Shakespeare are very conjectural. See Eric R. Vincent's summary of the problem, s.v. "Shakespeare" in the *Enciclopedia dantesca* (Rome, 1976), 5:209–10.

42.   The ape's very name was used to signify a deformed type of imitation. Guy de Tervarent, *Attributs et symboles dans l'art profane* (Geneva, 1958, 1964), cols. 354, 439, speaks of the ape at the mirror as well as the ape as a figure of artistic imitation. The ass is a somewhat more complicated case. He does not in himself represent the imitation of a man, but one whole line of ass iconography is concerned with dressing up the animal in human clothes—usually he is playing a

musical instrument—so as to demonstrate the deformation of knowledge. See Tervarent, *Attributs*, cols. 29, 30, 415; also see Tilley A366, who cites Thomas Cooper's *Bibliotheca Eliotae*: "An asse at a harpe. A proverbe applied vnto theym, whyche haue no iudgement in wysedome and learnyng" (*Proverbs*, p. 21). The same sort of mock-human (in both senses of the term) treatment is repeatedly accorded to Lucius in *The Golden Ass*.

43.   Citations are to *The Two Gentlemen of Verona*, ed. Clifford Leech, New Arden Edition (London, 1969).

44.   The fullest modern treatment is Juliet Dusinberre, *Shakespeare and the Nature of Women* (London, 1975), esp. pp. 231–71. See also Paula S. Berggren, "The Woman's Part: Female Sexuality as Power in Shakespeare's Plays," in *The Woman's Part: Feminist Criticism of Shakespeare*, ed. C. R. S. Lenz et al. (Urbana, Ill., 1980). A less gender-oriented view is offered by F. H. Mares in "Viola and Other Transvestist Heroines in Shakespeare's Comedies," *Stratford Papers 1965–1967*, ed. B. A. W. Jackson (Shannon, 1969), pp. 96–109. My own thoughts were shaped especially by Nancy K. Hayles, "Sexual Disguise in 'As You Like It' and 'Twelfth Night,'" *Shakespeare Survey* 32 (1979): 63–73, in which notions of gender and notions of identity are brought into subtle interplay.

45.   *Metamorphoses* 3.348; see chapter 2, section 3.

46.   A number of interesting essays have set *Twelfth Night* in the Ovidian tradition. See D. J. Palmer, "Art and Nature in *Twelfth Night*," *Critical Quarterly* 9 (1967): 201–12; as well as William C. Carroll, "The Ending of *Twelfth Night* and the Tradition of Metamorphosis" (reprinted in his *Metamorphoses of Shakespearean Comedy*), and M. E. Lamb, "Ovid's *Metamorphoses* and Shakespeare's *Twelfth Night*," both in *Shakespearean Comedy*, ed. Maurice Charney (New York, 1980), pp. 49–61, 63–77. Carroll concerns himself more with the fusions of pairs, while Lamb ranges quite widely among mythic equivalences, paying special attention to the significances of names (e.g., Orsino as bear/Callisto, Olivia as tree), without discussing the metamorphic interrelation of the names.

47.   J. A. Roberts, in "Horses and Hermaphrodites: Metamorphosis in *The Taming of the Shrew*," *Shakespeare Quarterly* 34 (1983): 159–71, is particularly subtle in treating the beastly and metamorphic atmosphere of the play. See also Carroll, *Metamorphoses*, pp. 41–59; and Garber, *Dream*, pp. 26–34.

48.   On Falstaff's transformation, see John Steadman's exemplary essay in dramatic iconography, "Falstaff as Actaeon: A Dramatic Emblem," *Shakespeare Quarterly* 14 (1963): 230–44. Jeanne Addison Roberts, "Falstaff in Windsor Forest: Villain or Victim?" *Shakespeare Quarterly* 26 (1975): 8–15, offers some interesting pieces of deer lore that take Falstaff's experience in a number of contrasting directions, the most interesting of which is that of the scapegoat. Her later treatment of the subject, "Animals as Agents of Revelation: The Horizontalizing of the Chain of Being in Shakespeare's Comedies," in *Shakespearean Comedy*, ed. Charney, pp. 79–96, equates the metamorphoses of Bottom and Falstaff, ironically, with stasis. This somewhat limiting view is offered as part of a larger thesis about the development of Shakespeare's thinking in regard to animals. Barbara Freedman, in "Falstaff's Punishment: Buffoonery as Defensive Posture in *The Merry Wives of Windsor*," *Shakespeare Studies* 14 (1981): 163–74, perceptively delineates the play's psychological darkness and its relation to the tragedies of the middle period. In regard to our present concerns, such an approach suggests that the

solo metamorphosis of the Bottom and Falstaff type may have disappeared from Shakespeare's comic repertory because that sort of action was itself being transformed into a tragic paradigm such as is visible in Lear's journey of visions and changes.

49.　Citations are to *The Merry Wives of Windsor*, ed. H. J. Oliver, New Arden Edition (London, 1971).

50.　For those who know Verdi and Boito's *Falstaff* it is difficult to view the *Merry Wives* without the feeling that Shakespeare was attempting to write the work that the two Italians finally realized in the 1890s. My sense, for instance, of the self-realizations that emerge in the concluding dialogue between Falstaff and Ford is very much influenced by Boito's decision to make Nanetta (i.e., Anne) into Ford's, and not Page's, daughter. As a consequence the public humiliation of Falstaff, in which Ford takes such a delighted role, is directly balanced by the public exposure and failure of Ford's plan for his daughter's marriage to Dr. Caius. The collective humiliation of the men is the more pointed since the Mrs. Ford of the opera is from the start favorable to Nanetta's love for Fenton. Ford's taunts of Falstaff can thus be returned (with a marvelous medley of repeated tunes from earlier moments in the opera) and finally turned into a universal "Tutto nel mondo è burla." The result is, at least in this case, more Shakespearean than Shakespeare.

51.　My account has paid less attention than is perhaps deserved to early Elizabethan traditions of comic stage metamorphosis. Such a set of backgrounds was first sketched by M. C. Bradbrook in *The Growth and Structure of Elizabethan Comedy* (London, 1955), pp. 61–93. G. K. Hunter's magisterial treatment, *John Lyly: The Humanist as Courtier* (London, 1962), esp. pp. 194–212, 298–349, makes the fullest case for Shakespeare's indebtedness to and independence from Lyly. But see also Leah Scragg, *The Metamorphosis of Gallathea* (Washington, D.C., 1982), where more sweeping claims are made. Carroll, *Metamorphoses,* esp. pp. 40, 166–67, develops a contrast between "conventional transformations" in Lyly's works and a more universal and internalized metamorphosis in Shakespeare.

52.　See chapter 5, section 4.

53.　Among the more interesting treatments of the statue scene, and those which have influenced my thinking, are Adrien Bonjour, "The Final Scene of *The Winter's Tale*," *English Studies* 33 (1952): 193–208; Nevill Coghill, "Six Points of Stagecraft in *The Winter's Tale*," *Shakespeare Survey* 11 (1958): 31–41; and Rosalie Colie, *Shakespeare's Living Art* (Princeton, 1974), pp. 278–83. My discussion here is based in part on my "'Living Sculptures': Ovid, Michelangelo, and *The Winter's Tale*," *ELH* 48 (81): 639–67, which details the history and aesthetics of statues more fully than the present version. Contemporaneous with that article was an interesting essay with some of the same conclusions (and a quite relevant treatment of *A Midsummer Night's Dream* as well), Garrett Stewart, "Shakespearean Dreamplay," *English Literary Renaissance* 11 (1981): 44–69. For a very thought-provoking argument that connects the statue scene with Alcestis rather than Pygmalion, see Martin Mueller, "Hermione's Wrinkles, or, Ovid Transformed: An Essay on *The Winter's Tale*," *Comparative Drama* 5 (1971): 226–39.

54.　For more on this figure, see chapter 5, section 3.

55. Citatitions are to *The Winter's Tale*, ed. J. H. P. Pafford, New Arden Edition (London, 1963).

56. See chapter 1.

57. Giulio Romano has caused a lot of trouble for Shakespeareans. How did Shakespeare know of him, and in what connection? Could Shakespeare have seen any of his works? Why, if Shakespeare knew anything at all about the artist, did he choose a man renowned for painting and architecture to be the exemplary sculptor? For some conjectures, see H. R. Fairchild, *Shakespeare and the Arts of Design*, University of Missouri Studies 12 (1937): 71–78, 145–47; Ernst Künstler, "Julio Romano im Wintermärchen," *Shakespeare Jahrbuch* (Weimar) 92 (1956): 291–98; and D. E. Baughan, "Shakespeare's Confusion of the Two Romanos," *Journal of English and Germanic Philology* 36 (1937): 35–39; as well as my "'Living Sculptures,'" pp. 655–58.

58. *Le Vite de' più eccellenti pittori scultori ed architettori*, ed. G. Milanesi (Florence, 1906), 5:557 and *n*.

59. See my "'Living Sculptures,'" pp. 652–55.

60. Given the fanciful nature of the play and the doubtless nonrealistic style of the original performance, an audience new to the text might simply not know what the actor was trying to make them believe.

61. Nature has her own mimetic system, just as art does. The infant Perdita's physical resemblance to her father is just as important as the statue's resemblance to the mother, as Paulina makes clear when she is attempting to establish the baby's paternity:

> Although the print be little, the whole matter
> And copy of the father: eye, nose, lip;
> The trick of 's frown; his forehead; nay, the valley,
> The pretty dimples of his chin and cheek; his smiles;
> The very mould and frame of hand, nail, finger.   [2.3.97–102]

The terms are similar to those in which the work of art is praised, but the triumph of verisimilitude is that of "good goddess Nature."

62. Citation is to *The Tempest*, ed. Frank Kermode, New Arden Edition (London, 1966), 5.1.33–57.

63. *Metamorphoses*, 7.192–219.

Illustrations

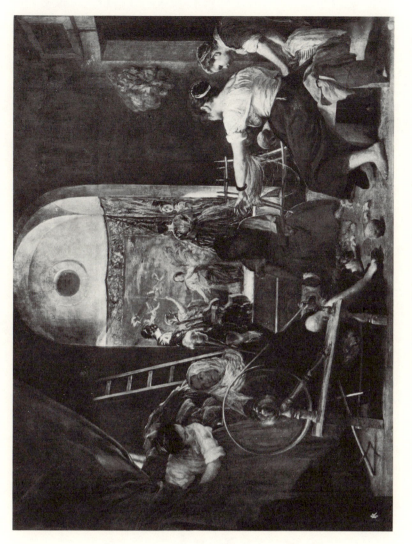

FIGURE 1. Diego Velázquez, *Las Hilanderas*.

FIGURE 2. Italian MS, third quarter of fourteenth century, Dante and Virgil; Cacus, Agnello, two thieves. Bodleian Library MS Holkham Hall Misc. 48, p. 38.

FIGURE 3. Italian MS, third quarter of fourteenth century, Metamorphosis of Buoso and Cavalcanti. Bodleian Library MS Holkham Hall Misc. 48, p. 39.

FIGURE 4. Italian MS, early fifteenth century, Dante and Virgil; Agnello and Cianfa. Modena, Biblioteca Estense, MS α R.4.8.

FIGURE 5. Italian MS, mid-fourteenth century, Dante and Virgil; Vanni Fucci; Cacus. Chantilly, Musée Condé, MS 597.

FIGURE 6. Italian MS, mid-fourteenth century, Dante and Virgil; serpent and Agnello. Chantilly, Musée Condé, MS 597.

FIGURE 7. Italian MS, mid-fourteenth century, Dante and Virgil; Cavalcanti and Buoso. Chantilly, Musée Condé, MS 597.

FIGURE 8. Correggio, Vault of Camera di S. Paolo, Parma. North Wall.

FIGURE 9. Correggio, Vault of Camera di S. Paolo, Parma. East Wall.

FIGURE 10. Correggio, Vault of Camera di S. Paolo, Parma. South Wall.

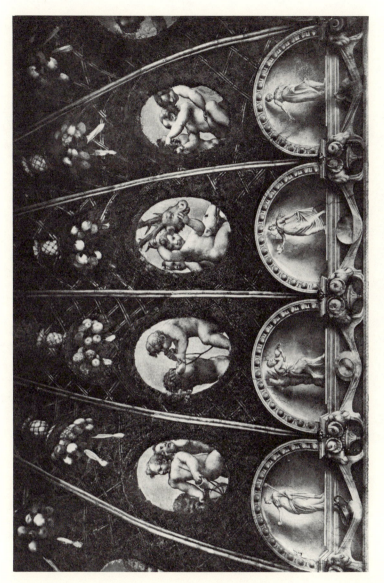

FIGURE 11. Correggio, Vault of Camera di S. Paolo, Parma. West Wall.

FIGURE 12. Giovanni Bellini and Titian, *Feast of the Gods*. Washington, National Gallery of Art (Widener Collection).

FIGURE 13. Titian, *The Worship of Venus*. Madrid, Prado Museum.

FIGURE 14. Titian, *Bacchus and Ariadne*. London, National Gallery. *(Reproduced by courtesy of the Trustees, The National Gallery, London)*

FIGURE 15. Titian, *Bacchanale of the Andrians*. Madrid, Prado Museum.

FIGURE 16. Deucalion and Pyrrha. From *La Bible des poètes,* Paris, 1493.

FIGURE 17. Tiresias. From Lodovico Dolce, *Le trasformazioni,*
Venice, 1553.

FIGURE 18. Bernard Salomon, *Actaeon Transformed into a Stag by Diana*.
From *La vita e metamorfoseo d'Ovidio*, Lyons, 1557.

FIGURE 19. Bernard Salomon, *Ants Transformed into Human Beings*. From
La vita e metamorfoseo d'Ovidio, Lyons, 1557.

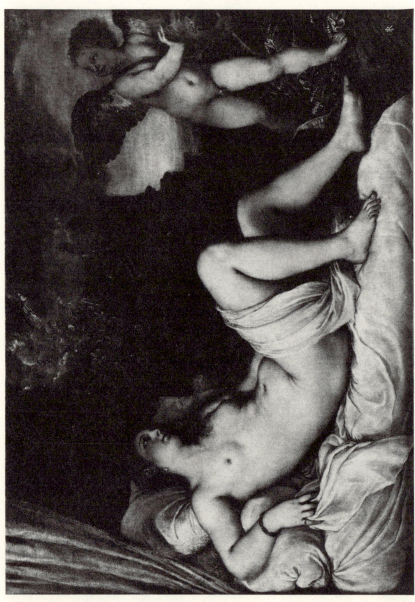

FIGURE 20. Titian, *Danae*, ca. 1545–46. Naples, Galleria Nazionale di Capodimonte.

FIGURE 21. Titian, *Danae*, ca. 1553–54. Madrid, Prado Museum.

FIGURE 22. After Leonardo da Vinci, *Leda and the Swan*. Rome, Galleria Borghese.

FIGURE 23. After Michelangelo, *Leda and the Swan*. London,
National Gallery.

FIGURE 24. Titian and Workshop, *Danaę*, ca. 1555–60. Vienna,
Kunsthistorisches Museum.

FIGURE 25. Correggio, *Io*. Vienna, Kunsthistorisches Museum.

FIGURE 26. Correggio, *Ganymede*. Vienna, Kunsthistorisches Museum.

FIGURE 27. Correggio, *Leda*. Vienna, Kunsthistorisches Museum.

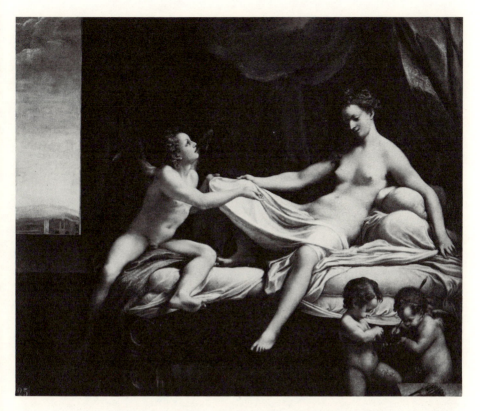

FIGURE 28. Correggio, *Danae*. Rome, Galleria Borghese.

FIGURE 29. Titian, *The Rape of Europa*. Isabella Stuart Gardner
Museum, Boston.

FIGURE 32. Titian, *Perseus and Andromeda*. London, Wallace Collection.

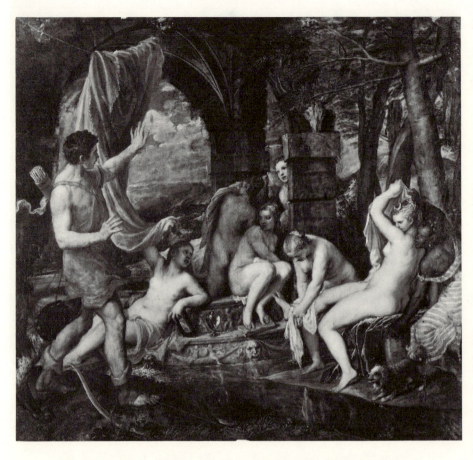

FIGURE 30. Titian, *Diana and Actaeon*. Edinburgh, National Gallery.

FIGURE 31. Titian, *Diana and Callisto*. Edinburgh, National Gallery.

FIGURE 33. Veronese, *Rape of Europa*. Venice, Palazzo Ducale.

FIGURE 34. After Michelangelo, *Ganymede*. Windsor Castle.

FIGURE 35. Michelangelo, *Tityus*. Windsor Castle.

FIGURE 36. Francesco di Giorgio Martini, attrib., *Rape of Europa*. Paris, Musée du Louvre.

FIGURE 37. Cupid in the Heavens. From Francesco Colonna, *Hypneroto-machia Polifili*, Venice, 1499.

FIGURE 38. Nymphs Transformed into Trees. From Francesco Colonna, *Hypnerotomachia Polifili*, Venice, 1499.

Index